THE LEGACY OF ISLAM

THE LEGACY OF
ISLAM

SECOND EDITION

EDITED BY THE LATE
JOSEPH SCHACHT
WITH
C. E. BOSWORTH

OXFORD NEW YORK TORONTO MELBOURNE
OXFORD UNIVERSITY PRESS
1979

Oxford University Press, Walton Street, Oxford OX2 6DP

OXFORD LONDON GLASGOW
NEW YORK TORONTO MELBOURNE WELLINGTON
KUALA LUMPUR SINGAPORE JAKARTA HONG KONG TOKYO
DELHI BOMBAY CALCUTTA MADRAS KARACHI
NAIROBI DAR ES SALAAM CAPE TOWN

ISBN 0 19 285081 4

First published 1974
First issued as an Oxford University Press paperback 1979

Printed in Great Britain by
Lowe and Brydone Printers Limited
Thetford, Norfolk

FOREWORD

THE production of this new *Legacy of Islam* has had a not dissimilar course from that of the original 1931 version. The principal editor of the first *Legacy of Islam*, Sir Thomas Arnold, died before the book appeared, and it was Professor Alfred Guillaume who finally brought it out. In the present case, the late Professor Joseph Schacht began the project as sole editor. But he died on 1 August 1969, leaving a gap amongst senior Islamic scholars, he being *facile princeps* in regard to Islamic legal studies; his own chapter in this present book, 'Islamic religious law', terse but full of insights, shows his mastery of this complex aspect of our studies.

Schacht chose all the contributors, and when he died the typescripts of almost all the contributions had come in, whilst those submitted in foreign languages were being translated into English. It was at this point that the Delegates of the Oxford University Press invited me to take over the editorship, involving completion of the editing of contributions and the supervision of the book through the press. Schacht had not had the opportunity of getting a conspectus of the chapters contributed when they were in their final edited form, and I found that there was some inevitable overlapping and variation in emphasis. It seemed to me that the differing viewpoints of the contributors, each an expert in his or her own particular field, had to be allowed to stand, if only as a testimony to those many problems in our studies which are capable of more than one type of treatment or interpretation. I have nevertheless endeavoured to draw the chapters together by judicious cross-referencing; and use of the index should further help the reader where a particular topic spans more than one chapter. A consequence of the original editor's death and the ensuing hiatus has been an unavoidable delay in publication, so that some chapters reflect the state of knowledge in their subject as it was some years ago. In many cases bibliographies have been revised at the proof stage, but it has not been possible to make any major alterations to the text itself.

The reader who compares the new *Legacy of Islam* with the original one of forty-two years ago will note that some chapters are roughly common to both volumes, such as the chapters on art and architecture, on literature, on law and theology, and on the natural sciences and music, even though the exact titles may differ. In the other chapters, however, there have been made major changes of scope and emphasis. The chapters in the original *Legacy of Islam* on specific topics like 'Spain and Portugal' and 'The Crusades' have been replaced by chapters on the general course of cultural, ideological, and economic interaction between Islam and the outside world, above all, between Islam and the western Christian world as mediated through the Mediterranean basin. Political and military challenge and response have further been included, as has a consideration of the impact of Islam on such non-Christian regions of the Old World as sub-Saharan Africa, Inner Asia, the Indo-Pakistan subcontinent, and South-East Asia. In many of this second group of chapters the reader will discern an emphasis on newer approaches to the study of the phenomenon of Islam and its manifestations, notably those drawing upon the historical and social sciences. It is accordingly hoped that the new *Legacy of Islam* will reflect the progress and broadening-out of Islamic studies during the last half-century.

When he wrote the Preface to this book, Schacht noted that, of the contributors to the original *Legacy of Islam*, only Sir Hamilton Gibb remained, but since then, Sir Hamilton has died.

In conclusion, may I personally express my thanks to the staff of the Clarendon Press, who did so much to help me pick up the editorial threads, and were ever-helpful guides and collaborators in the work of actual production?

C. E. BOSWORTH

Manchester, 1973

PREFACE

In this book, the word legacy is used in its two senses, to mean the contribution of Islam to the achievements of mankind in all their aspects, and the contacts of Islam with and its influences on the surrounding non-Islamic world. It is not concerned with the influences which the surrounding religions and civilizations may have exercised on Islam, nor with the different shades which Islamic civilization acquired in the several countries within its orbit, from Morocco to Afghanistan, from Turkey to the East Indies, however attractive such a comparative study might be. Neither does it aim at adding to the long list of general accounts of Islam as a religion or as a civilization, although there are still important gaps to be filled in here. The formula of this book is thus the same as that of its predecessor with the same title, edited by the late Professor Sir Thomas Arnold and the late Professor A. Guillaume in 1931, which this new edition is intended to replace, not merely by bringing it up to date but by reformulating the problems and reconsidering the answers in the light of modern scholarship. That is why most of the chapters do not correspond with those of the first edition, and even those which do correspond are radically different.

The *Legacy of Islam* takes Islam in the sense of a civilization, not merely a religion (although the distinction itself needs qualification, as will appear from the Introduction). Thus in addition to chapters on Islamic theology, philosophy, and mysticism, and on Islamic religious law and constitutional theory, it contains others —and they are the majority—on aspects of Islamic political, economic, and cultural history, on Islamic art and architecture, and on Islamic medicine, science, and music. Although it was the responsibility of the editor to assemble a harmonious team of contributors, no rigid uniformity of opinion, or agreement with the opinion of the editor, have been imposed, and each author is responsible for his or her contribution exclusively. The same persons and the same subjects are occasionally discussed in more than one chapter; this follows from the fact that they are of importance to more than one aspect of the *Legacy of Islam*.

In theory, the number of subjects to be included in an account of the contributions of Islam to the achievements of mankind is almost limitless; in practice, the size of this book had to be kept within manageable limits. I hope, however, that a comparison of its contents with that of its predecessor will show that all essential areas have been adequately covered. There are two more limitations which apply to the present volume. It is concerned with Sunnī Islam only, and has had perforce to leave aside the highly original manifestations of Islam in the several Shīʿī and in the Ibāḍī communities. It is also, in principle, restricted to 'classical' or medieval Islam—and the 'Middle Ages' in the history of Islam extend, generally speaking, to the time of the Napoleonic expedition to Egypt, or about 1800; it would be impossible to include in a work of this scope the very lively but, as yet, indecisive movements of recent and contemporary Islam. However, this time limit, in the nature of things, does not apply to Chapter I, and has occasionally been exceeded in other chapters, whenever the subject-matter seemed to call for it. I am convinced, however, that a solid understanding of the part played by Islam in the past is a necessary foundation for a correct assessment of its present tendencies.

The one surviving contributor to the first edition of the *Legacy of Islam* is Sir Hamilton Gibb. The chapter on Literature was again offered to him as a matter of course, but he asked to be excused for reasons of health. For the rest, let the names of the present contributors speak for themselves.

J. S.

CONTENTS

LIST OF ILLUSTRATIONS

INTRODUCTION

THE Legacy of Islam, in whichever sense we take the word, is not uniform in its several fields, either as regards its character or its chronological limits. Perhaps it is not out of place to try to trace in this Introduction some of the great unifying lines which run through the manifestations of Islam as a religion and a civilization. There is, to begin with, the thinking of the Arabs which manifests itself in the Arabic language, a thinking which is essentially analogical and not analytical. This shows itself in the casuistical method of religious law, in the atomist theory of theology, in the structure of Arabic lexicography, in the contents of the works of *adab*, that is, the Arabic belles-lettres, and even in the nature of Arabic decorative arts.

At the same time, there exists a conflict between the values of Arab Bedouin society and the values of Islam. This conflict is already clearly stated in the Koran (ix. 90, 97–102, 120; xxxiii. 20; xlviii. 11–13, 16; xlix. 14–17), and the second half of the first century of Islam (*c.* A.D. 670–720) saw a resurgence of ancient Arab beliefs and practices from which neither Islamic theology nor Islamic religious law were ever able completely to free themselves. The search for a balance between the two elements remained a feature of the whole intellectual life of the Muslims for a long time. In the modern period, this has been replaced by the search for a balance between the values of nationalism (or any other political ideology) and the values of Islam.

Generally speaking, the same great problems confront the Islamic thinkers in the modern period as confronted them in the first and second century of Islam (seventh and eighth centuries A.D.). This book, however, is essentially concerned with the Islamic 'Middle Ages' which for most of the world of Islam continued until about the year 1800, and to which most manifestations of a Legacy of Islam belong.

There are many unresolved tensions all through the history of Islam, mostly arising from the fact that the religious ideal cannot be realized in the world as it is. The most important of these tensions is between piety and correctness, or in institutional terms, between mysticism and religious law. I said mysticism and not theology, because theology is not identical with religion or faith, just as formal correctness or religious legality is not identical with piety. But if we look at two great representatives of Islam towards the end of its first century, Ḥasan of Baṣra (d. 728) and Ibrāhīm al-Nakhaʿī of Kūfa (d. 713 or 715), we find that Ḥasan's concern with theology was religiously motivated, just as Ibrāhīm's concern with questions of religious practice was. This pious, religious spirit in Islamic law was kept alive by Mālik of Medina (d. 795) and by Dāwūd al-Ẓāhirī (d. 884), and in theology, too, it remained well in evidence until the ninth century, being revived, about 1100, by al-Ghazālī. Later, both Islamic law and Islamic theology tended to become technical exercises, and the same fate finally overcame Islamic mysticism too. A similar tension, arising from the impossibility of realizing the religious ideal in this world, is that between theory and practice in Islamic law, their discordance and their mutual interference, a tension which dominated the history of the legal institutions of the Muslims during the whole of the Islamic Middle Ages and, in some countries, well into the present century.

From its very beginnings, Islam was a religion of action rather than of belief. The first half of the Islamic profession of faith, 'There is no god but God, and Muḥammad is the messenger of God', posed no problem for Muḥammad's pagan contemporaries in Arabia, and even less for the adherents of the revealed religions in the surrounding territories when, having been conquered by the Arabs, they came to adopt the religion of the ruling class. And the acknowledgement that Muḥammad was the messenger of God amounted for all practical purposes to unquestioning obedience to the Prophet; this is why the Koran is full of injunctions to 'obey God and His messenger', who is the exclusive transmitter of God's commands. For the same reason, Islamic religious law and not Islamic theology has always been at the centre of Islamic religious learning, and even the great al-Ghazālī, that champion of mystical piety in Islam, while putting religious law firmly in its place as a science of this world and not of the world to come, nevertheless continued to regard it as a religious and not a secular science. Also the modernist legislators, who ride roughshod over practically the whole of traditional Islamic law (except only the religious duties in the narrow meaning of the term), cannot get away from the postulate that law is not a secular institution but must be ruled by religion. The late rector of al-Azhar University, Shaykh Maḥmūd Shaltūt, who by virtue of his office was one of the most authoritative spokesmen of orthodox Islam, in 1959 published a book, reprinted several times since, with the title *Islam, a Faith and a Law* (*Islām ʿaqida wa-sharīʿa*). In this volume of 582 pages (in the second printing) the exposé of the faith of Islam occupies 69 pages, one-eighth of the whole, whereas all the rest is devoted to an account of the institutions of traditional Islamic law. This shows how much in the view of this high Muslim authority Islam is not merely a religion in the Western meaning of the term, but a form of society, albeit an ideal one, an ideal which has survived the disappearance of 'medieval' Islamic society in the greater part of the world of Islam.

The bearers of this Islamic civilization were not exclusively Muslims; Christians and Jews, too, made notable contributions to it at the higher intellectual level, particularly in the fields of medicine and science, but they did not remain encapsulated in these fields. So the great renovator of spiritual and religious values in Islam, al-Ghazālī, justified the systematic arrangement of his work on *The Revival of Religious Sciences* (*Iḥyāʾ ʿulūm al-dīn*) by the example of the arrangement he had found in a medical work by the Christian physician and theologian Ibn Buṭlān

(d. 1066). It is common to find scholars who made their name in more than one field of knowledge; medicine, science, and philosophy regularly went together, theology and religious law formed a similar close group, and persons who combined all these branches are not unknown, such as Ibn al-Nafīs (d. 1288), the discoverer, by theoretical reasoning, of the lesser circulation of the blood (between heart and lung), 300 years before William Harvey discovered the greater circulation by experiment. Lawyers were not rarely also men of letters and poets, certain forms of mysticism and gnostic philosophy went hand in hand, and there are numerous encyclopedic and all-round scholars in the records of Arabic literature.

Whereas we are fully entitled to speak of Islamic art and architecture, we speak of Arab medicine and science because of the important participation of non-Muslims in those fields, and the element that connects their work with that of their Muslim contemporaries is the Arabic language. Arabic, too, is the general language of Muslim civilization, overlaying the literatures in other languages of Muslim peoples which, notwithstanding the beauty and importance of their productions, remained of local influence only in the world of Islam.

A typical feature which spread over the whole of Islamic learning and which was connected with the development of Islamic religious law, theology, and literature, is the rigid distinction between the *khāṣṣa* and the *ʿāmma*, the specialists and the common people; it is only the opinion of the specialists which is taken into account in any way, and that of the non-specialists, which we would call public opinion, is completely disregarded. This accounts for the aristocratic or exclusive character of much if not all of Islamic literature and learning, and also, more even than the existence of the language of the Koran as the perfect norm of literary expression, for the distinction between the literary language and the colloquial. It is no doubt this exclusive character of Islamic learning which in due course led to an excessive veneration of authorities in all branches of learning and to the concept of a defined amount of things which can be known, which in its turn brought with it an almost complete ossification of traditional Islamic learning. This accounted, for instance, for the fact that the important discovery of the lesser circulation of the blood by Ibn al-Nafīs remained practically without effect on his contemporaries and successors, and that the highly original ideas of Ibn Khaldūn were praised more for the allegedly elegant language in which they were expressed than for their content.

It remains to trace, as a background for the chapters which follow, the great periods of the development of Islam. It proceeded in a curious series of progress and regress, with some notable disparities in the advancement of the several elements which make up Islamic civilization. As we have seen, the lifetime of the Prophet set the tension between the old Arab and the new Islamic values. The period of the Caliphs of Medina (632–61) represented a turbulent interval which culminated in the first civil war and in the great political schism which has divided Islam until the present into Sunnīs, who form the great majority, Shī'īs, and Khārijīs, whose only surviving branch, the Ibāḍīs, form a small minority only. The Caliphate of Medina was followed by the rule of the Umayyads (661–750) which in many respects represented the consummation of tendencies inherent in the nature of the community of Muslims under the Prophet. Under the Umayyads there emerged the beginnings of Islamic theological thought and, somewhat later, Islamic religious law. This is really not in conflict with the superiority of action over belief in the structure of Islam which has been mentioned before, because the earliest theological problems were exactly problems of political choice. But the first century of Islam also witnessed relapses into the spirit of Arab paganism; examples are extreme predeterminist doctrines and the exacerbation of tribal attitudes in marriage and other social relationships.

The Umayyads were overthrown by the 'Abbāsids and these last, in somewhat exaggerated opposition to the ruling house which they had superseded, recognized the religious law of Islam as the only legitimate norm of the state, and extended their positive favour to one particular school of theology, the Muʿtazila, which had identified itself with their political propaganda. The second half of the first century of Islam (*c.* 670–720) had already seen the beginning of Iranian and Hellenistic influences, and this process reached its zenith in the second century. Its effects showed themselves first in the field of law. A few decades later, there appeared an Arabic literary prose, adapted, as Islamic law was, to the intellectual and spiritual needs of a new, urban society. Concepts of popular Hellenistic philosophy finally appear in Islamic theology. During the second century of Islam, religious law, theology, and literature developed each in their own, though subtly parallel, ways.

But this is not the whole of the story, because in theology we find also the diametrically opposite movement of the Traditionists (or ultra-conservatives) which gained the upper hand in reaction against the excesses of the Muʿtazila without, however, eradicating the search for compromises between reason and belief—another area of permanent tension in Islam. This reaction was supported by the second massive interference of a government in the field of theology, but religious law was spared both. Islamic law reached its full development as early as about A.D. 800, the following century saw the working out of details, and by the beginning of the tenth century a point had been reached when the scholars of all schools felt that all essential questions had been thoroughly discussed and finally settled. This is the so-called 'closing of the gate of independent reasoning' which has as its corollary the duty to follow the recognized authorities of each school. It ushered in a long period of doctrinal near-immutability which lasted until the present century when modern legislators took over. But it was not the cause but a symptom of a state of mind which had been induced by fear of doctrinal disintegration, a fear which was not far-fetched at a time when Sunnī Islam was threatened by the extreme Shīʿī movement of the Ismāʿīlis and their esoteric propaganda.

Again we notice a time-lag between religious law and theology, because the great systems of classical Islamic theology were formulated only at the beginning of the tenth century, and even then theology did not allow reliance on the doctrine of a recognized authority as a sufficient basis of belief but insisted on personal conviction. But what is more important than all this, from the beginning of the eleventh century onwards we notice that general stagnation in the intellectual life of the Muslims which I discussed before, and this extended to their literary life as well, so that it would be meaningless for us to look for any particular reason for this in any branch of their religious sciences. There were, of course, numerous individual writers and poets of merit, but creative invention was lacking, the great classical models were imitated again and again, and the accepted judgements of value were not called into question.

A further turning-point, not for theology but for Islamic law and for Arabic literature, came in 1517, with the conquest of Egypt by the Ottomans, which made Constantinople or Istanbul the new centre of the eastern-central part of the Islamic world and brought about a real Renaissance in those two fields. But this, too, gradually came to an end, until a new start was made in Arabic literature during the last century, and in Islamic law by modern legislation from the second decade of the present century onwards. However, these are developments which fall outside the purview of the present volume, and Islamic theology has not taken part in this revival so far.

JOSEPH SCHACHT

I

THE WESTERN IMAGE AND WESTERN STUDIES OF ISLAM

1. *The Middle Ages: the struggle between two worlds*

THE Muslims were a threat to Western Christendom long before they became a problem. There had been a shift of power in the remoter parts of the East, and a turbulent and pillaging people—a non-Christian one to boot—had overrun and ravaged vast territories and snatched them from the grasp of Christianity (for a more detailed discussion of the political and military aspects of this historical process, see below, Chapter IV, pp. 174 ff.). The scourge ultimately reached Spain, the Italian seaboard, and Gaul, and it was always the same wave of marauding barbarians which was responsible. When the venerable Bede revised his ecclesiastical history of the Angles shortly before his death in 735, he summarized the most recent events in these words: 'At that season, that most grievous pest, the Saracens, wasted and destroyed the realm of Gaul with grievous and miserable carnage; but they soon after received and suffered the due punishment of their perfidy.'[1]

It seems that few questions were asked about this people. In the eyes of the Christian countries of the West they were merely a scourge like so many other barbarian populations. The alternately successful and disastrous campaigns on the borders of Spain, including even alliances with dissident Umayyads who occasionally came to Aix-la-Chapelle for help; the fight against raiders in Gaul and against pirates off the coasts of Provence,

[1] *The Old English Version of Bede's Ecclesiastical History of the English People*, edited with a translation and an introduction by T. Miller, Part 1, section 2 (London, 1891), p. 477.

Corsica, Sardinia, and Italy; such operations as the landing by Boniface of Lucca in the Tunisia of the Aghlabids in 828: all these things had little effect upon the basic attitude of the Franks. Christians had known about the Saracens long before Islam, and at first the Saracens' change of religion was hardly noticed. An account of the world dating from the fourth century, for instance, stated that the Saracens obtained 'by the bow and by plunder all they need to live'.[1] There was no need to know any more. Scholars alone argued about their name, which was derived from Sarah, Abraham's wife, although they were descended, as their other name *Agareni* showed, from Hagar, the servant who was driven into the desert with her son Ishmael; this discrepancy was a problem.

The only people to look further than this were, for obvious reasons, the Christians in Moorish Spain, the Mozarabs. The Muslim political dominance under which they lived gave free rein to an Arab cultural influence damaging to the Christian faith, and they therefore needed to form a clearer, though perhaps not more exact, image of their masters and of their masters' ideas. As in all the conquered lands of the East, depreciatory and insulting legends were current among the Christian and Jewish masses, mixed with more accurate impressions arising from daily contacts. Again, as was the aim of Eastern Christian apologists like John of Damascus, the goal of scholars in the West was to extend their analysis of Islam, thereby combating any influence it might have. But the militant ardour of Eulogius, Alvarus, and their followers in the short period between 850 and 859, their unavailing attempts to convince the Christian hierarchy and the Christian masses, and their thirst for martyrdom were little conducive to the serious intellectual effort necessary for knowing and understanding their opponents.[2]

In the eleventh century, the image of the Muslim world be-

[1] *Expositio totius mundi et gentium*, xx, ed. J. Rougé (Paris, 1960).

[2] Cf. summary of events in E. Lévi-Provençal, *Histoire de l'Espagne musulmane* (2nd edn., Paris–Leiden, 1950), i. 225 ff.

comes a little more precise, for fairly obvious reasons. The Normans, the Hungarians, and some of the Slavs had been converted. The Muslim world remained the chief enemy. The battles waged against it in Spain, in southern Italy, and in Sicily were no longer purely defensive. The Christian advance, slow and fluctuating as it was, was beginning to entail more frequent political, and even cultural relations with the conquered peoples. Gone were the days of local wars: all Europe was mobilizing to fight side by side with the Spaniards in the *Reconquista*. The Christian unity extolled by the Popes needed consolidating by grandiose schemes pursued in concert under papal guidance. What common task could be more stimulating than the *Reconquista*, if it could be spread over the whole Mediterranean world, a world in which the Italian trading cities were operating with such increasing success in the economic field?

The image of Islam arose, not so much as some have said from the Crusades, as from the slowly welded ideological unity of the Latin Christian world which led both to a clearer view of the enemy's features and also to a channelling of effort towards the Crusades. In the eleventh century, the example set by the increasingly numerous and well-organized pilgrimages to the Holy Land that had already turned into armed attacks against the pillaging Bedouins, the eschatological value of Jerusalem and the Holy Sepulchre defiled by the presence of infidels, the cleansing value of pilgrimage, the notion that help was due to the humbled eastern Christians, all made of the expedition to the Holy Land a holy task to put before the faithful.

The fight having thus become more concentrated and better focused, the enemy must of necessity be given sharper, more specific features and his image must be simplified and stereotyped. To the pilgrims, the Saracens are little more than faceless supernumeraries and uninteresting infidels, *de facto* rulers among whom one moves unheeding, and the fabulous and satirical *Charlemagne's Pilgrimage* in the eleventh century or at the beginning of the twelfth still shows the Emperor moving about Jerusalem without making contact with the inhabitants. Yet the *Chanson de Roland* at about the same time and in the same fabulous vein, reveals an Islam that is powerful and rich, whose potentates come to one another's help, admittedly with their numerous pagan bands of mercenaries, Nubians, Slavonians, Armenians, Negroes, Avars, Prussians, Huns, and Hungarians (*Roland*, 3220 ff.), but nevertheless an Islam united in the worship of Mahomet, Tervagant, and Apollo.

Roger of Hauteville set about the recovery of Sicily in 1060, Alfonso VI entered Toledo in 1085, and Geoffrey of Bouillon entered Jerusalem in 1099. These three fronts brought close contact with the Muslims. An image of Islam was in the making and was becoming gradually clearer and more precise. But for many centuries that image was to be affected by the inevitable distortions of ideological rivalry.

In fact, Christian Europe did not have one single image of the hostile world with which it clashed, but several. So far, scholars had dealt mainly with the Europeans' concepts of the Muslim religion, but now it was the whole Muslim world that rose before them, to their bewilderment and shock. Roughly, three aspects of their reaction to it can be discerned. The Islamic world was above all a hostile politico-ideological structure. But it was also a different civilization, and an alien economic region. These various aspects often evoked varying interest and different reactions, even in the same people.

The political divisions of the Muslims were known, often at first hand. But it was also realized that behind these divisions there was basically an underlying solidarity, that unity could at any time be resumed against Christendom, and that a common outlook and faith were the core of this brotherhood. The Muslim states formed a hostile complex of powers. Their rivalries could occasionally be turned to political advantage; a temporary alliance could be made with one of them, and Christians might at times enter the service of Muslim rulers, as related in the *Chanson de Roland*, where the young Charlemagne faithfully serves Galafre, the Saracen king of Toledo, and marries his daughter (who, of course, becomes a convert). Such things frequently happened in Spain and in the East, but enmity was latent and could always be reawakened.

Statesmen, their officials, their informers, and their spies, must have had a view of the Muslim world that we know little about. It must have been more delicately shaded than that of the religious polemicists or of the masses. Their nearest neighbours, the lords of the Holy Land, must have known a great deal about the internal divisions of the Muslim states. But this treasury of knowledge that the Christian soldiers and statesmen in the East had acquired remained very little diffused outside their own circle. Western chancelleries dipped into it only for the minimum needs of their eastern policy. There was no demand in the West for a detailed account of the political history of Islam, nor was there any wide interest in the political quarrels among the 'infidels'. On the other hand the Crusades created a vast and eager demand for a full, entertaining, and satisfying image of the opponents' ideology. The man in the street desired an image that would both show the hateful character of Islam by presenting it in crude terms and would also be such as to satisfy the literary taste for the wonderful which strikes one so strongly in all the works of that time; the average person wanted a picture of the most outstanding of the exotic traits that had struck the Crusaders in their dealings with the Muslims.

Thus it happened that the Latin authors who, between 1100 and 1140, undertook to meet this need of the common man, directed their attention to Muḥammad's life, with little regard for accuracy and, in R. W. Southern's words, gave free rein to 'the ignorance of triumphant imagination'. Muḥammad was a magician who had destroyed the Church in Africa and in the East by magic and deceit, and had made his success doubly sure by allowing sexual promiscuity. Legends from world folklore, from classical literature, from Byzantine stories of Islam, and even from Muslim sources (after vicious distortion by Eastern Christians), all these were made to adorn the image. Southern tells us that Guibert de Nogent acknowledged that he had no written sources and gave only the *plebeia opinio*, having no means of telling the false from the true. And, naïvely laying bare the true basis of all ideologists' criticism, he said in conclusion: 'It is safe to speak evil of one whose malignity exceeds whatever ill can be spoken.'[1]

As is always the case, the vision shown in works of popular appeal must have contributed more to the image retained by posterity than that shown in more scholarly and more conscientious works. That image was to be embellished further by many literary works. Pure fiction, whose only object was to spur the reader's interest, was mixed in varying proportions with misrepresentations of belief which inflamed hatred of the foe. The epics reached the greatest heights of fabulous invention. The Muslims were charged with idolatrous worship, even as they themselves accused the Christians of polytheism and associationism (*shirk*). Their chief idol was Muḥammad, whom, with few exceptions, the troubadours thought to be the Saracens' chief god. His statues were of rich substances and of enormous size. Varying numbers of acolytes went with him, the figure reaching 700 in a German author of the thirteenth century, Der Stricker.[2] Probably on the Christian pattern, these acolytes were at times headed by a trinity in which Tervagant and Apollo joined Muḥammad, to be worshipped in synagogues (thereby bringing Islam closer to the equally unacceptable Jewish belief) or in 'mahomeries'.[3]

An objective attitude was alone met with in a quite different sphere, which was only loosely connected with the Islamic religion. I am referring to science in the widest sense of the word. From the very beginning of the tenth century, small groups of men had attempted to increase the store of theoretical knowledge about

[1] R. W. Southern, *Western Views of Islam in the Middle Ages* (Cambridge, Mass., 1962), pp. 28 ff.

[2] *Karl der Grosse*, l. 4,205 ed. K. Bartsch (Quedlinburg and Leipzig, 1857), p. 111; cf. H. Adolf, 'Christendom and Islam in the Middle Ages: New Light on "Grail Stone" and "Hidden Host"', *Speculum*, xxxii (1957), 103–15, at p. 105.

[3] Cf. Y. and Ch. Pellat, 'L'Idée de Dieu chez les "Sarrasins" des Chansons de geste', *Studia Islamica*, xxii (1965), 5–42.

the world and man that was contained in the few Latin books that had been salvaged from the wreck of ancient civilization. Men in those few groups had learnt that the Muslims possessed Arabic translations of the basic works of the Ancient World, and had access to complete manuals of the sciences that were considered essential.

Gradually, Latin translations of these works appeared, and the wealth of Arab science spread to England, to Lorraine, to Salerno, and above all to Spain, where contact was more easily made. The work of translation grew and became organized in that country after the fall in 1085 of the great city of Toledo, one of several centres of intellectual activity there.[1] Of course, what was being sought in the Arab manuscripts was in no way an image of Islam or of the Muslim world, but the objective knowledge of nature. All the same, something inevitably became known about the Muslim providers of this knowledge; and there was also established a close contact with the translators whose services were used, and who were Mozarabs or Jews or in some cases Muslims with a wide, first-hand knowledge of the Muslim world.

It was inevitable that a more accurate knowledge of this world should be diffused by means of this channel. Therein must be found the explanation of the occurrence in the first half of the thirteenth century of some observations which, by their objective accuracy, stand out from the flood of the fabulous literature of entertainment. The proof is to be found in Pedro de Alfonso, a Spanish Jew, who was baptized at Huesca in 1106 and became physician to Henry I of England. He translated works on astronomy, and he also wrote the first book containing information of some objective value about Muḥammad and Islam.

At the meeting-place of this stream of intellectual interest in the Muslim scientific inheritance with the stream of popular curiosity about Islam, we find the outstanding effort made by Peter the Venerable, Abbot of Cluny (*c.* 1094–1156), to gain and

[1] Cf. U. Monneret de Villard, *Lo studio dell'Islām in Europa nel XII e nel XIII seculo*, Studi e Testi, cx (Vatican, 1944), pp. 2 ff.

to transmit an objectively based scientific knowledge of the Islamic religion. We can discern several reasons for his astonishing enterprise. There was the knowledge which he had gained, indirectly at least, during his visits to the houses of his order in Spain, of Muslim questions and of the activity of translators. There was his concern to fight the heresies, Judaism and Islam, with valid intellectual arguments, albeit earnestly and charitably towards 'erring' individuals, as befitted the Abbot of Cluny's personal character and as he himself showed on many other occasions. He was also acutely conscious of the dangers which the Church was facing in an age of intellectual turmoil, of threatening schisms, and of spreading unrest. Both from personal conviction and as head of an order that was pledged to this aim, he wished to arm the Church against such perils. Because of his own nature and also perhaps because of the faint light shed by the still very narrow yet new attitudes of mind, he wanted the weapons to be strong, but he did not want a breach of the charity that every ideal Christian owes to all men of good faith. It may also be that unconsciously he was moved by a disinterested curiosity, of which he was ashamed and which he concealed even from himself.

He knew that his initiative would be little understood, and the reception it met, notably from his friend and occasional opponent, Bernard of Clairvaux, confirmed him in that opinion. In his apology, he uses the very arguments that have always been used against the attacks of the pure 'militants' by the intellectual theorists who stand, or seem to stand, aloof from contemporary strife, or at least, consider it with some detachment:

> If my work seems pointless because the enemy remains invulnerable to such weapons, I answer that in the land of a great king some things are done for protection, others for adornment, others again for both. Solomon the Peaceful forged weapons for protection which were not needed in his day. David prepared ornaments for the Temple, although they could not be used in his day . . . This work, as I see it, cannot be called useless. If the erring Muslims cannot be converted by it, scholars who are zealous in the cause of justice must nevertheless not fail to forewarn those weak

members of the Church who are easily scandalized and unwittingly moved by insignificant causes.[1]

Hence in Spain Peter the Venerable financed a company of translators working as a team. An Englishman, Robert of Ketton, completed his translation of the Koran in 1143. The team translated a series of Arabic texts and produced compilations of their own. They are known as the Cluniac Corpus, and include a synthesis by Peter the Venerable himself. The corpus had a fairly large circulation, but it was not used to the extent to which it could have been; only those parts which were of direct and immediate polemical use were drawn upon and quoted without comment. The material contained in the collection was unfortunately not used as a basis for further study in depth of Islam. No one was interested in such a study. It did not seem to be of any use in the current struggles, all the more so because religious polemic was aimed at fictitious Muslims who were easily annihilated on paper. As a matter of fact, the aim seems rather to have been to provide Christians with sound arguments to shore up their own faith. Furthermore, the Latin West's state of mind was little conducive to an interest in religious systems in themselves, such as existed in the Muslim East.[2]

There was another field where several streams of interest converged, and where the Latins discovered yet another image of Islam which was strikingly at variance with their religious preconceptions, that is, philosophy. At first philosophy and the natural sciences were hardly differentiated. The approved manuals of the natural sciences were in need of supplementation from works of what we would call scientific methodology, works on logic and on the theory of Man and Cosmos. The same encyclopedic writers had dealt with these last, above all Aristotle and

[1] Migne, *Patrologia Latina*, clxxxix. 651–2. Cf. Southern, op. cit., pp. 38 ff., and Dom J. Leclercq, *Pierre le Vénérable* (Abbaye St. Wandrille, 1946), pp. 242 f.

[2] Cf. especially, M.-Th. d'Alverny, 'Deux traductions latines du Coran au Moyen Age', *Archives d'histoire doctrinale et littéraire du Moyen Age*, xxii–xxiii (1947–8), 69–131, and J. Kritzeck, *Peter the Venerable and Islam* (Princeton, 1964).

then Avicenna. The Latin West only gradually became aware of Aristotle. In the twelfth century, his brief *Categories* and his *De Interpretatione* were already known through old Latin translations by Boethius, while the rest of the Aristotelian corpus was slowly becoming known, but only to a handful of people, through new translations made directly from the original Greek. Gerard of Cremona (*c.* 1114–87) went to Toledo in search of Arabic versions of Greek texts which he would translate and thereby add to the store of Western philosophy.[1] At about the same time a start was made with the translation of the *Kitāb al-shifā'* ('Book of the Cure'), Avicenna's great philosophical encyclopedia. About 1180 a first corpus of Avicenna's philosophical works was completed and began to circulate in Europe.[2] Its influence was immense, and translations of other philosophers followed in quick succession.

There was thus an image of the Muslim world as the cradle of philosophers of great stature forming in the minds of western thinkers. This was in violent contrast to its image as a political structure dominated by a hostile and erroneous faith, the image which ridiculous and odious fables had created in the minds of people, and it was difficult to reconcile the two images. Philosopher-theologians managed to transfer to Christianity Avicenna's references to Muslim civilization; for instance, Roger Bacon (*c.* 1214–92) applied to the exalting of the Pope's office what Avicenna had said of the Muslim Imām.[3] In some respects, the Saracens appeared

[1] Cf. L. Minio-Paluello, 'Aristotele dal mondo arabo a quello latino', *L'Occidente e l'Islam nell'alto Medioevo* (Settimane di studio del Centro italiano sull'alto Medioevo XII, 2–8 Apr. 1964; Spoleto, 1965), ii. 603–37.

[2] Cf. among others M.-Th. d'Alverny, 'L'introduction d'Avicenne en Occident', *Millénaire d'Avicenne*, *Revue du Caire*, no. 141 (June 1951), 130–9; idem, 'Notes sur les traductions médiévales d'Avicenne', *Archives d'histoire doctrinale et littéraire du Moyen Age*, xix (1952), 337–58; M. Steinschneider, *Die europäischen Übersetzungen aus dem Arabischen bis Mitte des 17. Jahrhunderts* (Leipzig, 1904–5, reprinted Graz, 1956), pp. 16–32.

[3] *Opus majus*, ed. Bridges, ii. 227 f. quoted by R. de Vaux, *Notes et textes sur l'Avicennisme latin aux confins des XII ième–XIII ième siècles* (Paris, 1934; Bibliothèque thomiste, XX), p. 58, n. 9.

to be a philosophical nation. At times, as with Abelard (who died in 1142 and, it should be noted, was a friend of Peter the Venerable) 'philosopher' seems virtually to mean 'Muslim';[1] a century later, it was in practice to the Saracens that Thomas Aquinas addressed the *Summa contra Gentiles*, a treatise in which it is intended to prove Christian theses by the sole light of reason 'because some [of the gentiles], such as the Muslims and Pagans, do not agree with us concerning the authority of any Scripture' (i. 2). We know that the work was written round about 1261–4 at the request of St. Raymond of Peñafort, 'a zealot for spreading the faith among the Saracens',[2] for use in his evangelizing missions in Spain.

The Muslim world was of interest not only on political or military grounds, or from a religious or scholarly point of view. It also awoke various interests in minds that hungered for strange and exotic tales. Here again, the proliferation of contacts that followed the reconquest of Spain, the conquest of Muslim Sicily, and the setting up of Latin states in the East, necessitated more detailed and more discriminating knowledge; this knowledge did not, however, obliterate simplistic views of Islam as a religion nor the widely diffused fantastic stories of literary entertainment. All the same much information, largely accurate, was gained concerning the geography of the Muslim world, its climate, its towns, its government, its flora and fauna, and its agricultural and industrial production. Much became known also about the ways of the Saracens and the Bedouins, and later of the Tartars, meaning the Mongols.

The same motives actuated the first significant attempts at

[1] Cf. J. Jolivet, 'Abélard et le philosophe (Occident et Islam au XIIième siècle)', *Revue de l'histoire des religions*, clxiv (1963), 181–9. It is a striking fact that Abelard, exasperated by his difficulties with the theologians of his country, was thinking of settling on Muslim soil, where he could earn his living and enjoy a legal status, even though he would be living among enemies of Christ. (Abelard, *Historia calamitatum*, ed. J. Monfrin (Paris, 1959), pp. 97f.; cf. R. Roques, *Structures théologiques de la gnose à Richard de Saint-Victor* (Paris, 1962), p. 261.)

[2] Monneret de Villard, op. cit., p. 36, cf. p. 37, n. 5.

historical investigation. In the twelfth century, Godfrey of Viterbo, secretary to the German Emperors, included a well-informed sketch of Muḥammad's life in his Universal Chronicle.[1] At the beginning of the following century, Cardinal Rodrigo Ximenes, Archbishop of Toledo, wrote the first History of the Arabs composed in the West, beginning with Muḥammad and the first Caliphs but centred primarily upon the Arabs' activities in Spain.[2]

Yet another impulse led to an increased knowledge of the Muslim world; that is, the economic motive, the pursuit of commercial profit, for the Muslim world was an economic area of primary importance to a large number of European merchants.

At first, western merchants traded with the Muslim East through foreign intermediaries, Greeks and Syrians, or semi-foreign ones like the Jews. But as early as the ninth-century, this trade was partly taken over by Italian cities under Byzantine rule, Venice, Naples, Gaeta, and Amalfi, which gradually became independent (see below, pp. 227 ff.). The Scandinavians also began to play an important role, and their conversion was to bring them into the orbit of Western Christendom. Finally, the other peoples of the Christian world joined the group. This entailed a small number of common practices which brought the two worlds closer; Moorish money or copies of it circulated in the West, and oriental types of commercial contracts were adopted. Among the Saracens, western merchants first met and feared the Muslim pirates. But the Italians, in the first place, soon became powerful enough to avoid and then to withstand them, later going over to the attack themselves. But much more often, on the strength of guarantees of safe conduct (*amān*; see on this institution, below, Chapter IV, p. 177), they got into direct touch with their opposite numbers, whether Muslims or eastern Christians. This entailed contacts with customs officers and other petty civil servants,

[1] Cf. E. Cerulli, *Il 'Libro della Scala' e la questione delle fonti arabo-spagnole della Divina Commedia* (Vatican, 1949), pp. 417 ff.

[2] Ed. Thomas Erpenius, *Historia saracenica* (Leiden, 1625), following al-Makīn's *Chronicle*.

until officials of ever higher standing were reached as the exchanges grew in importance and the power of the western world increased. Very soon trade demanded contacts at government level. It was at such a level that, inevitably, alliances between the cities of the Campagna, notably Amalfi, and the Saracens were concluded in the ninth century, despite the Pope's threats and counter-offers and despite the lamentations of the Emperor Louis II, in whose eyes Naples had become another Palermo or another Mahdiyya.[1] At the beginning of the eleventh century, the Amalfitans must have had such contacts in Palestine for them to restore the church of Santa Maria de Latina in Jerusalem, which the Fāṭimid caliph al-Ḥākim had destroyed, and to hold an annual market there on 14 September at which anyone could display his wares on payment of two gold pieces.[2] It is probable that they already occupied a quarter in Antioch before the first Crusade. Of course, these few contacts became more numerous and more important after the Crusades. We know how these Italian trading stations multiplied and came to play an increasingly important role. It is obvious that, whatever their attachment to their Christian faith, the European merchants who had business relations with the Muslim world could not share the sketchy notions of that world current among other European communities. We have sporadic but significant testimony to the existence of friendly relations between Christian and Muslim traders.[3]

This esteem also sprang up in a very different context, in the fighting itself between Crusaders and Saracens in the East. Despite all the hatred, there were occasions when it was acknowledged that the foe himself recognized the values which medieval chivalry had taught men to hold in high regard. An unnamed Italian Crusader who, at the time, set down his impressions of

[1] A. Schaube, *Handelsgeschichte der römischen Völker des Mittelmeergebiets bis zum Ende der Kreuzzüge* (Munich-Berlin, 1906), pp. 30f.

[2] Ibid., p. 36.

[3] Ibid., pp. 33, 296f.; cf. J. Le Goff, *Marchands et banquiers du Moyen Âge* (Paris, 1956), p. 75, and R. S. Lopez, 'L'importanza del mondo islamico nella vita economica europea', *L'Occidente e l'Islam nell'alto Medioevo*, i. 433–60, at p. 460.

the first Crusade, greatly admired the courage, sagacity, and soldierly qualities of the Turks at the battle of Dorylaeum, in which he had fought in 1097. According to him the esteem was mutual and the Turks 'say they belong to the Frankish race and assert that no one, they and the Franks excepted, has the right to call himself a Knight'. Realizing how much audacity was needed to write such words (*veritatem dicam quam nemo audebit prohibere*) he stated that if only they had held fast to the faith of Christ 'none could be found to equal them in strength, in courage or in the science of war'.[1]

A century later, the arch-foe Saladin (on whom see below, p. 196) aroused widespread admiration among the people of the West. He had waged the war humanely and chivalrously, albeit with scant reciprocation by the Crusaders, notably by Richard Cœur-de-Lion. During the breaks in fighting at the siege of Acre (1189–91), the opposing forces were seen fraternizing, all dancing, singing, and playing together, not to mention the fact that the loose women of Europe who had come to comfort the Crusaders bestowed their favours equally readily upon some of the Muslims.[2]

It was in this ambience that tales sprang up, and, after an interval when the Ayyūbid Sultan was regarded rather unfavourably (due to tales which undoubtedly originated among the Levantine Christians, who possessed a sound knowledge of the country), redounded to his glory.[3] It came to the point that in the fourteenth century a vast poem, conventionally called *Saladin*, was written in which all the episodes of the former legends about

[1] *Histoire anonyme de la première Croisade*, ed. and tr. Louis Bréhier (Les Classiques de l'histoire de France au Moyen Age, Paris, 1924), pp. 50–3.

[2] Cf. R. Grousset, *Histoire des Croisades* (Paris, 1936), iii. 28 f.

[3] As early as the second half of the thirteenth century the *Novellino* put forward as a paragon 'Saladino . . . soldano, nobilissimo signore, prode e largo' who, during a truce, admonished the Christians, and, sickened by their disdain of the poor and by their irreverence towards their own religion, took up arms again, whereas in other circumstances he would have become a Christian (§XXV, ed. E. Sicardi, Strasbourg, n.d., pp. 52 f.). It should be noted that the story had been told earlier.

Saladin were rehearsed.[1] So perfect a knight must of necessity be brought within the Christian fold. Hence his mother is said to be one Countess of Ponthieu who had been shipwrecked on the Egyptian coast, and he himself is said to have been converted on his death-bed.[2]

In the same way, great Muslims like Zangī and Qilij Arslān were assumed to be of Christian origin, and later Thomas à Becket was credited with a Saracen mother;[3] it was indeed true that marriages had been mooted between European and Muslim monarchs.

2. *The growth and decline of a less polemical image*

The accumulation of accurate information about Islam and its origins as well as about the Muslim peoples, the increasing contacts in the political as well as in the commercial sphere, the mutual esteem which in certain cases sprang from them, the deep appreciation of scientific and philosophical doctrines originating in Islamic lands, all these things added to the slow internal evolution of the Western mind and brought about a change in the angle from which the alien world was seen. But the essential factor in this evolution was the transformation of the Latin world and the Western trend towards the secularization of ideologies.

From the brutally polemical image of a diabolical foe there was a gradual change to a more finely shaded concept, at least in some circles; for the image that had been implanted in men's minds during the earlier Middle Ages and cultivated through popular literature, was still influencing the minds of the masses. The concept of the relativity of ideologies was of course still

[1] This poem, the work of an anonymous Flemish author, survives only in substantial fragments. See Gaston Paris, 'La Légende de Saladin', extract from *Journal des Savants* (Paris, May–Aug. 1893); S. Duparc-Quioc, *Le Cycle de la Croisade* (Paris, 1955), pp. 128–30; and N. Daniel, *Islam and the West, the Making of an Image* (Edinburgh, 1960), pp. 199–200.

[2] Duparc-Quioc, op. cit., pp. 128–30; cf. Daniel, op. cit., p. 199.

[3] Cf. D. C. Munro, 'The Western Attitude toward Islam during the Period of the Crusades', *Speculum*, vi (1931), 329–43, at p. 339.

unknown, except in isolated cases like that of the Islamophile Arabist, the Emperor Frederick II of Hohenstaufen, who discussed philosophy, logic, medicine, and mathematics with Muslims, was influenced by their Islamic ways and established at Lucera a colony of Saracens in his service, with its own mosque and all the amenities of eastern life.[1]

When Pope Gregory IX excommunicated Frederick II in 1239 he charged him, among other misdeeds and displays of friendliness towards Islam, with having asserted that the world had been deceived by three impostors, Moses, Jesus, and Muḥammad. The charge may have been unfounded, as the emperor claimed, but the fact that it was levelled at all shows at least that the topic, which seems to have originated in the Muslim world, was current at the time in Christian Europe. Moreover, it appears that, shortly before Frederick II, a canon of Tournai was charged with uttering the same blasphemy.[2] That Muslims were held up to Christians as examples for their piety of worship and their everyday virtues, as happened repeatedly,[3] may have come from moralists' guile or have been a barb protruding from the well-known current of medieval anti-clericalism; in either case, it strengthened the tendency to see in Muslims men very much like others, who worshipped God in their own way, even if it were an erroneous one.

At the time of Frederick II, this attitude is best exemplified in the works of the Bavarian minstrel Wolfram von Eschenbach. In his *Willehalm*, he borrows freely from the early twelfth-century French epic, *La Prise d'Orange*, about the siege of Orange, but the fighting between Saracens and Franks, all equally endowed with chivalric virtues, is characterized by an attempt at understanding. The Muslim beauty Arabele, now a Christian by the

[1] Cf. E. Kantorowicz, *Kaiser Friedrich de Zweite* (Berlin, 1927–31, reprinted Düsseldorf-Munich, 1963), i. 122, 170f., 321ff., etc.

[2] Ibid. 455; L. Massignon, 'La légende *de tribus impostoribus* et les origines islamiques', *Revue de l'histoire des religions*, lxxxii (1920), 74–8, reprinted in idem, *Opera Minora* (Beirut, 1963), i. 82–5; Southern, op. cit., p. 75, n. 16.

[3] Cf. Daniel, op. cit., pp. 195ff. *et passim*.

name of Gyburg, launches an appeal for toleration. The poet comments: 'Is it not a sin to slaughter like cattle people who have never heard of Christianity? I would even say it was a grievous sin, for all the men who speak the seventy-two tongues are God's creatures.' Wolfram's *Parzival* changes in like manner the atmosphere of his model, Chrétien de Troyes. Here we see Parzival's father, Gahmuret, setting out for the East, but in no way within the framework of the Crusades. On the contrary he enlists in the service of the 'Baruc', (*mubārak*, 'blessed one' ?) of Baghdad (Baldag) who was, as Wolfram knew, the spiritual leader, the Pope of the Muslims: 'He received life in Anjou, he lost it before Baghdad for the Baruc' (stanza 108). He is buried in the Islamic capital at the Baruc's expense in a sumptuous grave, at which the Saracens venerate and mourn him. The chivalrous Saracen Feirefitz is, as a result of Gahmuret's amorous successes, Parzival's half-brother. Scholars have hazarded many theories, some very daring, concerning Wolfram's eastern sources (see further on this question below, Chapter VII, p. 338). Whatever the verdict on these theories may be, it must be pointed out that our author transcribes fairly correctly the Arabic names of the planets (stanza 782), that he professes that his main source was a Muslim manuscript that the enigmatic Kyôt discovered at Toledo and which goes back to the magician and astrologer Flegetanis (*al-falak ath-thānī*, 'the second heavenly sphere' ?), half-Jewish, half-Muslim in origin. It is striking to notice that the acme of the medieval legend of the Grail, one of the highest points reached in the literary expression of the medieval Christian mind, with its well-known Celtic sources, is an epic that is imbued with Muslim elements and is full of gnostic and Manichean tendencies originating in the Eastern world. Wolfram, who seems to have been a good Christian, nevertheless preaches absence of hatred towards pagans (Muslims) who are as they are only because they have not had a chance of hearing Christ's message.[1]

[1] Cf. now H. Goetz, 'Der Orient der Kreuzzüge in Wolframs *Parzival*', *Archiv für Kulturgeschichte*, xlix (1967), 1–42; M. Plessner, 'Orientalistische Bemerkungen

Progress in that direction was hastened on the one hand by the realization of the Mongol peril and the discovery of a pagan world beyond Islam; and on the other hand by the unleashing on the Christian world of divisions at a spiritual level, in the universalist ideology of Christianity itself, a more serious matter than the former conflicts between political bodies and national and ethnic ideologies. The feeling that Islam had the same basic conception, religious monotheism, which had occasionally made fleeting appearances before, now grew in strength. In 1254 William of Ruysbroeck, Saint Louis's envoy, took part in a controversy before the Great Khan between Nestorians, Muslims, and Buddhists, siding with the first two against the last.[1]

This trend towards a deeper understanding of Muslim thought, which sprang from these conditions, was to be short lived. Roger Bacon and after him Raymond Lull (*c.* 1235–1316) talked of replacing military endeavour by missionary efforts, based upon the profound study of Muslim doctrine and of the Islamic languages. Bacon took account of Islam's positive contribution to the divine scheme of revelation, just as has recently been done by the more advanced Catholics on the road to ecumenism. Islam must still be fought, of course, but a more profound knowledge of it could only lead to greater objectivity and, in the long run, to greater relativism. At the beginning of the fourteenth century, Dante excused from Hell and placed in Limbo Avicenna, Averroes, and Saladin, the only moderns to join the sages and heroes of the Ancient World.[2] The council of Vienne in 1312 ratified Bacon's and Lull's ideas concerning the learning of languages, particularly Arabic.

But this was too late. The fall of Acre in 1291 put a decisive end to all the hopes which the Crusades had sustained. For a

zu religionshistorischen Deutungen von Wolframs *Parzival*', *Medium Aevum*, xxxvi (1967), 253–66.

[1] *The Journey of William of Rubruck*, tr. from the Latin by W. W. Rockhill (London, Hakluyt Society, 1900).

[2] *Inferno*, iv. 129, 143 f.

long time, the fight against the infidels in the East had failed to rouse the West to arms any more. The political schemes of individual nations had completely replaced the plan for the expansion of a united Christian Europe. Only in Spain did the *Reconquista* continue, but there also it was made to fit into schemes of this kind.

Latin Europe, intent upon its internal struggles, and advancing on the cultural plane, no longer regarded the ideological conflict with Islam as of prime importance. She was losing interest in it. It was internal ideological strife which was becoming of capital importance. For John Wycliffe (*c.* 1320–84) the reform of the Church was the first consideration, and the return to the fountainhead of Christendom would suffice to bring about the withering away of Islam. The vices of which Islam was accused were found to be equally rife in Latin Christendom. The Church is Muslim; Greeks, Jews, Muslims are no further from salvation than many Christians.[1] This latter opinion spread just as the witticism about the three impostors had spread.[2]

From the intellectual point of view, the great Muslim authors whose discovery had been an innovating force were now gradually being assimilated and merged into the common culture. For centuries Avicenna, Averroes, and Algazel in philosophy, Avicenna, Haly (ʿAlī b. ʿAbbās), and Rhazes in medicine, other writers in other sciences, were all to be copied, reprinted, commented upon, and studied. It was indeed a typical physician whom Chaucer (who also compiled a *Treatise on the Astrolabe* after the Latin translation from the Arab Māshā' Allāh) must have met at the Tabard Inn at Canterbury about 1390. He knew little of the Bible but

> Wel knew he the olde Esculapius,
> And Deyscorides, and eek Rufus
> Olde Ypocras, Haly and Galyen,
> Serapion, Razis and Avycen,

[1] Cf. Southern, op. cit., pp. 77ff.

[2] Ibid., pp. 75f.

Averrois, Damascien and Constantyn
Bernard and Gatesden and Gilbertyn.
(*Canterbury Tales*, Prologue, 429–34.)

Thus in the Middle Ages, the Arabs enjoyed great prestige, but with Aristotle as the dominating figure. This prime emphasis on the Greek classics continued at the Renaissance, and the Renaissance humanists attacked all the medieval translations, whether from Greek or from Arabic, as barbarous medieval Latin versions of the originals; in this blanket condemnation, the Arabic translations of Greek texts came to be regarded as part of this falsification of Antiquity by the 'gothic' spirit of medieval scholars. The new approach was to consist in going back to the original sources; the term 'Arabism' was to become pejorative.[1] The contempt for the barbarian age was now extended to include everything Arabic. Already in the fourteenth century, Petrarch had vigorously expressed his distaste for the Arab poets' style, though he certainly had not read them.[2]

It was not that this in any way prevented the cultural borrowings from the Muslim East from becoming more numerous than ever, nor the literary borrowings from increasing, no doubt thanks to trade relations which were becoming closer and more regular. But so far as theory is concerned, the earlier eagerness to know and understand Muslim thought was, in certain circles at least, giving way to indifference.

3. *Coexistence and rapprochement: the enemy becomes a partner*

From the end of the fourteenth century, the growth of the Ottoman Empire at the expense of the Christian Balkans reawakened for a brief while among theologians an interest in the Muslim religion. While the crusading spirit proved difficult to

[1] Cf. H. Schipperges, *Ideologie und Historiographie des Arabismus* (Wiesbaden, 1961).

[2] Petrarch, *Senila*, XII, Ep. 2; *Opera* (Basel, 1581), p. 913. Cf. E. Cerulli, 'Petrarca e gli Arabi', in *Studi in onore di A. Schiaffini = Rivista di cultura classica e mediovale*, vii (1965), 331–6.

rekindle in the decaying state of the Christian concept itself, some theologians were driven to consider whether the resort to arms could really produce results, whether peaceful missionary endeavour was enough in itself, or even useful in its usual form, or whether the bearers of a common message in substantially identical terms could not be brought closer together. This was the 'moment of vision' mentioned by R. W. Southern which significantly occurred at about the time of the fall of Constantinople, i.e. between 1450 and 1460. In 1454 Juan of Segovia (*c*. 1400–58) proposed a series of conferences with the Muslim *fuqahā*ʾ. That method would be useful, he asserted, even if it did not result in the conversion of the disputants. He undertook a translation (now lost) of the Koran which would avoid the error made in the Cluniac translations of changing the original meaning by adapting it to Latin concepts. Juan of Segovia incurred the disapproval of Jean Germain (*c*. 1400–61), the bishop of Chalon-sur-Saône, who believed in military action and the revival of the crusading spirit. But he had the approval of Nicholas of Cusa who considered the practical means of carrying out his plans and who attempted in his *Cribratio Alchoran* (1460) an exact philological and historical study of the Koran. Juan of Segovia was also partly responsible for Pius II's letter to Muḥammad II (1460), a masterpiece of skilful dialectic aiming at intellectual persuasion, but the work of a politician and, at bottom, a contrivance completely devoid of sincerity.[1]

The Ottoman Turks were a considerable danger, but in the new climate of the fifteenth century they were seen as a political or cultural, rather than as an ideological danger. From then onwards the Ottoman Empire became in the eyes of realists a power like any other, and by virtue of its conquests, even a European power, much less remote than any other Muslim power had been for a long time and with which it was therefore imperative to have political contacts. Alliances, neutrality, war would henceforth depend upon political considerations unrelated to religious ideology. Though this ideology remained a faith staunchly en-

[1] Concerning all this, cf. Southern, op. cit., pp. 86ff.

shrined in men's hearts, it was believed that it could be suspended (temporarily as it was thought) in view of 'momentous' political moves.

Ottoman envoys began to spend long turns of duty in Europe, for instance in Venice. There were negotiations with the Turks. While the fanciful Charles VIII thought he would overrun Italy as a base from which to launch a crusade, the Papacy, from 1490 to 1494, was receiving an annual payment from Bayezid II for keeping his rival brother Jem in prison. In 1493 at Rome, the Grand Turk's ambassador was received with great solemnity at a Secret Consistory by Pope Alexander VI, the meeting being attended by cardinals, bishops, and European envoys. Indeed, the Pope had sent to the Sultan a letter in which he warned him of Charles VIII's projected crusade and asked him to get the Venetians to intervene against the French king, warning him only to abstain 'for a time' from attacking Hungary or other Christian countries, since such an attack might place him in a delicate position. In return, Bayezid urged him to raise Nicholas Cibo to the cardinalate, but first and foremost to put Jem to death in return for the payment of 300,000 ducats and a promise on the Koran not to do anything to harm the Christians.[1] Two years later Milan, Ferrara, Mantua, and Florence agreed to pay the Turks to attack Venice.[2] Two years later again, with Venice and France preparing to attack Milan, Ludovico il Moro, Duke of Milan, and other Italian princes warned Bayezid that the taking of Milan would be the first step towards the crusade, whereupon the Sultan declared war on Venice.[3] A few decades later when Sulaymān the Magnificent was conquering Hungary and was about to turn the Mediterranean into a Turkish lake, Francis I made an alliance with him and joined him in military operations against Charles V (1535). But he took precautions on the ideological plane

[1] J. Burchard, *Liber notarum*, ed. E. Celani (Città di Castello, 1907–13), i. 547 f., French translation by J. Turmel (Paris, 1932), pp. 175 ff.

[2] J. R. Hale in *The Cambridge Modern History*, i. *The Renaissance* (Cambridge, 1957), 265.

[3] V. J. Parry, in *The Cambridge Modern History*, i. 403.

to defend himself. In 1580 Elizabeth of England denounced the King of Spain to the Sultan as a leader of idolaters. On this occasion, an alliance was proposed on purely ideological grounds.[1]

Bargains of the same kind as those of the fifteenth and sixteenth centuries had been brought about in the East in the days of the Crusader states. But these came under the heading of colonial policy. That such things should happen in the very heart of Europe was quite a different matter. In Italy whole regions made it known to their oppressive governments that they would heartily welcome an eventual Turkish invasion, as some Balkan Christians had done (see further on this point below, pp. 199–201).[2]

The Turks were thus, at the political level, integrated into the concert of Europe. That is not to say that they were integrated in all respects. However, the bitterness of religious hatred within Christendom itself made Islam look less extraordinary and less repugnant. It had already been looked upon in the Middle Ages as a schism, a heresy within Christianity. It was thus that Dante saw it.

Islam was practically identical with the Turks and 'Turk' was becoming synonymous with 'Muslim'. People were beginning to know the Persians, whose hostility to the Ottoman Empire opened the way for devious and involved political bargainings. Further away, contact was made with the Muslims of India and their splendid rulers the Great Moguls. As for the Arabs, they had practically no influence politically and were of minor significance in the picture people had of the East. They had once again come to be little more than pilfering Bedouins as had been the picture at least from the time of Joinville. The word 'Saracen' gradually dropped out of current speech.

Although pedants had traced their origins back to the Scythian barbarians,[3] the Muslim Turks nevertheless remained in control

[1] Cf. Daniel, *Islam, Europe and Empire* (Edinburgh, 1966), pp. 12f.

[2] J. Burckhardt, *Die Kultur der Renaissance in Italien* (Basle, 1860), English translation (London, 1944), p. 60.

[3] Cf. R. Schwoebel, *The Shadow of the Crescent, the Renaissance Image of the Turk (1453–1517)* (Nieuwkoop, 1967), pp. 148, 189, etc.

of the most powerful empire in Europe, and remained in possession of Constantinople and all its wonders, now made more accessible through improved means of communication. The pomp of the Sublime Porte much impressed the Europeans, and its power was imposing. It has been remarked that Louis XIV risked excommunication when he sent a delegation to Rome in 1687 because the Pope dared to ask him to waive the privileges of his embassy, which had been extended to cover a whole district where evildoers sought refuge, yet allowed his ambassadors at Constantinople to be imprisoned, humiliated, and taxed, and their staffs to be subjected to endless vexation.[1]

4. *From coexistence to objectivity*

An objective study of the Muslim East was being made easier by proximity, by close political contacts, by increased economic relations, by the large number of travellers and missionaries who visited the East, and by the decline of the ideological dominance of Christianity in Europe. For statesmen and traders, this 'objective' study was becoming an even more imperious need than formerly. Detailed, precise, sober, and as far as possible objective descriptions proliferated after Arnold von Harff's of 1496.[2] The way of life was no longer examined from the standpoint of its wider or narrower divergence from Christian morality. The Ottoman Empire's political, administrative, and military system was the object of thoughtful studies which were often critical but equally often praised its efficiency in many respects.[3] Considered as a whole, the Muslim East was a rich and prosperous land, with a high degree of civilization, magnificent architecture, and marvellous princely courts of unequalled splendour.

[1] Cf. Voltaire, *Siècle de Louis XIV*, ch. XIV; F. Grenard, *Grandeur et décadence de l'Asie* (Paris, 1939), p. 130.

[2] Schwoebel, op. cit., p. 188, cf. p. 180.

[3] Cf., for example, Machiavelli, *The Prince*, ch. XIX, for a comparison between the Ottoman form of government and that of the Mamelukes, the latter being compared with the Papacy as an instance of elective monarchy. Cf. also ch. IV and *Discorsi sulla prima Deca di Tito Livio*, bk. II, foreword.

The cosmopolitanism and the encyclopedism of the Renaissance, the mannerisms of its cultural expression, had allowed their share to the Muslim East and to Near Eastern studies. But keen interest in the East had not yet become exoticism, that taste for *dépaysement* artificially created in one's own environment either by art or by one's mode of life. Only the first signs of it were discernible, as in the isolated cases of the travellers who, having returned to Europe, wore Turkish dress.[1] But the Eastern world was more often given a Western guise than vice versa, even if it was heightened by magic and marvels as in Ariosto or Tasso, even if some episodes or themes were genuinely of Eastern origin,[2] and even if the subject-matter came wholly from Eastern history, as in Marlowe's *Tamburlaine*. Though readers and audiences were enthralled by these fabulous tales, no one looked to them for information about the history or manners of the Muslim East.

But the pressure of the accurate reports that travellers and diplomats brought back gradually made itself felt, and local colour gradually imposed itself. For a long time, in paintings of the lives of Jesus and the martyrs, members of the Sanhedrin and Eastern potentates had been decked out in turbans. Othello retained from his Moorish background only the fatal magic handkerchief that an Egyptian witch had given to his father (Othello, III. iv. 53 ff.). But in 1670 Molière took the trouble to insert real Turkish sentences into the burlesque scene of his *Bourgeois gentilhomme*, and in 1672 Racine, in his preface to his *Bajazet*, dwelt upon the care he had taken to inform himself on Turkish history. Corneille and others blamed him for not having put on the stage a single character 'who has the feelings that he ought to have, that people have at Constantinople; they all, though wearing Turkish dress, express the feelings common in France'.[3] In later prefaces, Racine thought

[1] Schwoebel, op. cit., p. 178.

[2] Cf., for example, G. Levi della Vida, 'Fonti orientali dell'Isabella ariostesca', in his *Anedotti e svaghi arabi e non arabi* (Milan-Naples, 1959), pp. 170-90.

[3] *Segraisiana*, quoted by G. Lanson in *Théâtre choisi de Racine* (7th edn. Paris, 1910), p. 437.

it necessary to retort: 'I have made a point, in my play, of stating accurately what we know of the manners and sayings of the Turks.'

Since the Middle Ages there has been no break in the use of exotic subjects in literature. Some effort to enrich such literary works with accurate details is noticeable in many authors; exoticism broke into art in the seventeenth century and swamped it in the eighteenth. Yet it took a long time to advance from the abstract notion of the relativity of civilizations which was clearly formulated in the eighteenth century to the integration of exotic facts into wholes that were free of all ethnocentrism; perhaps the process is not complete even now.

5. *The birth of Orientalism*

People began to study the languages and to gather materials for purely ideological purposes. In the Middle Ages in Spain, Arabic studies had started in response to the needs of missionary work. These studies lost all their interest with the fall of Granada in 1492, and the survival only of the Romance-speaking Morisco minority. They were resumed, as part of Semitic studies in general, in Rome, where the Curia was interested in the union of the Eastern churches. Humanism, in its search for a world-wide culture, as well as political and commercial interests, widened them into a body of Muslim studies. Guillaume Postel (1510–81) a committed scholar if ever there was one, despite his mysticism, his ardent devotion to the service of the faith, his French patriotism, and even his insanity, contributed richly to the progress of the study of the languages and even of the peoples, at the same time assembling in the East an important collection of manuscripts.[1] His pupil, Joseph Scaliger (1540–1609), a man of encyclopedic learning, pursued Orientalism and gave up his missionary

[1] Cf. J. Fück, *Die arabischen Studien in Europa bis in den Anfang des 20. Jahrhunderts* (Leipzig, 1955), pp. 36ff. Concerning G. Postel, see also more particularly F. Secret, *Les Kabbalistes chrétiens de la Renaissance* (Paris, 1964), pp. 171ff. *et passim*.

zeal. In 1586 Arabic typography in Europe was to have the use of the printing-works established by the Cardinal Grand Duke of Tuscany, Ferdinand de' Medici. Of course, the avowed aim was to help the missionary effort, but from the very first it printed the medical and philosophical works of Avicenna, and grammatical, geographical, and mathematical books. The attempt was to be repeated at the end of the sixteenth and the beginning of the seventeenth century in Paris, Holland, and Germany, particularly with a view to a better knowledge of Avicennan medicine.

The Papacy and a great many Christians took an interest in the union of the churches and sought an agreement with the Eastern Christians, which meant studying their language and their texts. England, France, and the United Provinces were more concerned with trade and with their political schemes in the East. The increased ease of travel brought learned Maronites to Europe and even Erpenius met a Moroccan Muslim trader at Conflans in 1611. Biblical exegesis, which was one of the chief subjects for discussion between Protestants and Catholics, also led to the study of the philology of Eastern languages. Physicians still kept up an interest in Avicenna, despite the 'anti-Arabist' reaction. The Turkish menace led to a closer study of the Ottoman Empire and of Islam. As it declined the study could be pursued more serenely. The growth of European power and culture caused the Eastern courts to show an interest in the ever more numerous European travellers who brought useful practical information and formulas dealing with a number of activities which were still limited, but which included in particular military science.

Such closer ties and concerns of the time, and the general trend towards the organization of scientific research, account for the appearance of a fine-meshed Orientalist network. The first chair of Arabic was founded in 1539 at the newly established Collège de France for Guillaume Postel, an enlightened, highly typical scholar of the Renaissance, as we have seen, but one who published pioneer manuals and, above all, trained disciples like Scaliger whose grounding in Oriental scholarship was already of no mean order. Collections of manuscripts in the libraries provided scholars with the materials necessary for serious study. Printing—and particularly printing in Arabic characters, whose beginnings we have noted—began to make each scholar's work available to all others. One specialist after another made it his business to supply such indispensable tools as grammars, dictionaries, and editions of texts. In the very forefront there stand two Dutchmen: Thomas van Erpe or Erpenius (1584–1624) who published the first Arabic grammar and the first edition of a text based on sound philological principles; and his disciple Jacob Golius (1596–1667). In Austria in 1680 a Lorrainer, Franz Meninski, brought out his massive Turkish dictionary. Chairs of Oriental studies became numerous. Paris no longer stood alone. Francis van Ravelingen or Raphelengius (1539–97) was teaching Arabic at Leyden as early as 1593. Urban VIII in 1627 founded at Rome the College of the Propaganda, a lively centre of studies. Edward Pocock was the first holder of a chair of Arabic at Oxford in 1638.

Relativism in belief affected the intellectuals and the cultivated public before the scholars. But the atmosphere which it created opened the way for them. Those whom a very keen personal inclination attracted to the Muslim East could work unhampered. B. d'Herbelot (1625–95), making use of an already fairly rich accumulation of material, wrote his *Bibliothèque orientale* (which was published posthumously by Galland in 1697), the first attempt at an *Encyclopaedia of Islam*.

A. Galland helped decisively to foster the taste for things oriental when, at the beginning of the eighteenth century, he published his translation of the *Arabian Nights* (1704–17), the influence of which was to be enormous.[1] Thenceforward Islam was no longer seen as the land of Antichrist but essentially that of an exotic, picturesque civilization, existing in a fabulous atmosphere peopled by good or evil, wayward genies—all this for the

[1] See M. Abdel-Halim, *Antoine Galland, sa vie et son œuvre* (Paris, 1964).

delight of an audience that had already shown so much taste for European fairy tales.[1]

6. *The age of reason*

People could now view the religious faith which competed with Christianity in an impartial light and even with some sympathy, unconsciously seeking (and obviously finding) in it the very values of the new rationalist trend of thought that was opposed to Christianity. In the seventeenth century many authors took up the defence of Islam against medieval prejudices and polemical detractors, and demonstrated the worth and sincerity of Muslim piety. One such author was Richard Simon. He was a sincere Catholic but the soundness of his scholarship made him fight against the dogmatic perversion of objective facts, both in the reading of the Bible and the study of Eastern Christendom. In his *Histoire critique des créances et des coutumes des nations du Levant* (1684) he dealt first with the beliefs and rites of the Eastern Christians, then with those of the Muslims which he expounded clearly and soberly on the basis of a work by a Muslim theologian, without vituperation or disparagement and occasionally with real appreciation and even admiration. When Arnauld accused him of having been too objective towards Islam, he advised him to ponder the 'excellent teachings' of Muslim moralists.[2] A Dutch Arabist, A. Reland, who had a more specialized knowledge of things Islamic than Simon, was to write, in 1705, an objective view of the Muslim religion based exclusively on Muslim sources.[3] The philosopher Pierre Bayle, an admirer of Muslim tolerance, gave in the first edition of his *Dictionnaire critique* (1697) an objective account of Muḥammad's life which was

[1] See M.-L. Dufrenoy, *L'Orient romanesque en France, 1704–1789* (Montreal, 1946–7), 2 vols.

[2] *Histoire critique des créances et des coutumes des nations du Levant*, par le sieur de Moni (Frankfort, 1684), ch. XV; cf. Simon's *Lettres choisies* (Amsterdam, 1730), iii. 245 f., 258 f., and J. Steinmann, *Richard Simon et les origines de l'exégèse biblique* (Paris, 1960), pp. 157 f.

[3] *De religione mahommedica libri duo* (1st edn., Utrecht, 1705; 2nd edn. 1717).

revised in later editions in the light of subsequent scholarly work.

The next generation was to go on from objectivity to admiration. The Ottoman Empire's toleration of all sorts of religious minorities was given as an example to Christians by Bayle and many others: that was the time when, following the example set by the Spanish Jews two centuries earlier, the Calvinists of Hungary and Transylvania, the Protestants of Silesia, and the Cossack Old Believers of Russia sought refuge in Turkey or looked to the Porte in their flight from Catholic or Orthodox persecution.[1] Islam was looked upon as a rational religion, far removed from the Christian dogmas which were so strongly opposed to reason, and containing a minimum of mythical concepts and mystical rites (the minimum, it was thought, necessary to secure the adherence of the masses). Further, it reconciled the call to a moral life with a reasonable regard for the needs of the body, of the senses, and of life in society. In brief, as a religion it came very close to the Deism that most of the 'Men of Enlightenment' professed. On the historical level, the civilizing role played by Islam was highlighted: civilization had not emerged from the monasteries, but had had its origins among the pagan Greeks and Romans and had been brought from Europe by the Arabs who were (and so much the better to the mind of the time!) non-Christian.[2]

Leibniz (1646–1716) was already thinking along these lines. Then came the anonymous author of a pamphlet challengly entitled *Mahomet no impostor!* (1720);[3] Henri de Boulainvilliers whose apologetic *Vie de Mahomet* was published in 1730; and Voltaire, an admirer of Muslim civilization. This last, however,

[1] Cf. T. W. Arnold, article 'Toleration (Muhammadan)', in J. Hastings, *Encyclopaedia of Religion and Ethics*, xii (Edinburgh, 1921), 365–9.

[2] See Voltaire, Robertson, Herder. Cf. Schipperges, *Ideologie und Historiographie des Arabismus*, pp. 29, 34. The subject was dealt with to the fullest possible extent by the Spanish Jesuit Juan Andrès (1740–1817) in his book *Origen, progresos y estado actual de toda la literatura* (Italian edn., Parma, 1782–98; Spanish tr. 1784–1806).

[3] Daniel, *Islam and the West*, p. 288.

wavered between putting forward an apologia for the profound-thinking *politique*, founder of a rational religion, and on the other hand taking advantage of the official faith of his country to denounce this selfsame Muḥammad as the prototype of all the impostors who had enslaved people's souls by religious fables.[1]

The spirit of the age eventually affected even the specialists, more particularly of course those who were outside the universities and the academic tradition. One of them was the lawyer and Arabist George Sale (*c.* 1697–1736), an enlightened Christian who, in 1734, published a remarkable translation of the Koran with a *Preliminary Discourse*, accompanied by terse, balanced, and well-informed notes, of which many later writers have made use. Another person in the front rank was the brilliant self-taught German scholar J. J. Reiske (1716–74). He was a dedicated student—incomparably the best in his day—of Arabic literature and history, an indefatigable scholar who was persecuted by Professors Schultens and Michaelis because they wanted to keep Arabic studies within the ambit of 'sacred philology' and biblical exegesis. This great scholar too saw something divine in the founding of Islam.[2] The Oxford professor Simon Ockley, when writing his *History of the Saracens* (1708–18), the first attempt at making the results of Orientalist research available to the general reader, exalted the Muslim East above the West.[3] Erudite facts and new ideas were put into circulation by these scholars and synthesized by such writers as Voltaire, to whom we have already referred, and Edward Gibbon (1737–94), whose balanced assessments award a high place to the Muslim world in the cultural and intellectual history of mankind. A myth was building up: that of Muḥammad as a tolerant and wise ruler and law-giver.[4]

[1] An oscillation in his point of view, of which Muslims and Orientalists alike have seldom been aware. Compare, for instance, the tragedy of *Mahomet* with chapters VI, XXVII, and XLIV of *Essai sur les Mœurs*.

[2] Fück, op. cit., pp. 108–24.

[3] Cf. P. Hazard, *La Crise de la conscience européenne (1680–1715)* (Paris, 1935), i. 22.

[4] M. Petrocchi, 'Il mitto di Maometto in Boulainvilliers', *Rivista storica italiana*, lx (1948), 367–77.

The eighteenth century really looked upon the Muslim East through fraternal and understanding eyes. The idea of the equality of natural gifts in all men, which a lively optimism, the true religion of the age, had helped to spread, now enabled men to examine critically the charges which earlier ages had levelled at the Muslim world. Cruelty and savagery were rampant in the East, it was true, but was the West above reproach? It was pointed out that slavery was gentler in Turkey than elsewhere, and that piracy was practised also by Christians.[1] Despotism was a deplorable political system, but appropriate to be studied and, like any other system, to be explained by reference to ecological and social causes; the geographical conditions of the East might well have been favourable to it, but it had on occasion developed elsewhere. Montesquieu, who held strong beliefs about the importance of geographical factors, mentions Domitian as the forerunner of the Sophy of Persia.[2] The comparative broad-mindedness of the Muslims in sexual matters, which had horrified (or else ambivalently or unconsciously attracted) people in the Middle Ages, was becoming highly attractive to a society which assiduously cultivated eroticism. In the Age of Enlightenment, the Muslims were looked upon as men just like other men, with many of them indeed superior to the Europeans. 'The Turk, when he is not under the influence of fanaticism, is as charitable as he is trustful', wrote Thomas Hope, who stayed in the East on various occasions towards the end of the century.[3]

At the end of *Candide* the heroes, now wiser, find peace near Constantinople, after following the advice of a 'very famous dervish who was reputed to be the best Turkish philosopher' and of an aged Muslim, who was industrious, sober, and indifferent to politics. There were many travellers through Eastern lands, and while some were narrow in vision, as were the missionaries

[1] Daniel, *Islam, Europe and Empire*, pp. 14f.

[2] *Esprit de lois*, iii. 9.

[3] *Anastasius or Memoirs of a Modern Greek* (London, 1819), ch. XXXII, French translation by J. A. Buchon (Paris, 1844), p. 419.

who whilst in the East lived in a self-enclosed world, a few, such as James Bruce, Carsten Niebuhr, H. Maundrell, R. Pocock, J. de la Roque, N. Savary, and Thomas Shaw, returned with intriguing pieces of information which were added to the perennially read accounts of such men as Chardin and Tavernier from the preceding century.

Lady Mary Wortley Montagu penetrated into the women's world of Constantinople, and gave an account of it that was free from mysteries and myths.[1] Contrariwise, some Easterners, mostly Christians, visited Europe. The youthful J.-J. Rousseau, son of a clock-maker at the Imperial Palace in Constantinople and relative of a consul in Persia and of the latter's son, who held consulates at Basra, Aleppo, Baghdad, and Syrian Tripoli, evinced no surprise when he met near Neufchâtel a bogus Archimandrite of Jerusalem, who was doubtless a Greek adventurer and a subject of the Grand Signior.[2] The theme of the Turkish spy who gives a critical account of European manners and customs, a theme which was launched upon its prodigiously successful career in 1684 by a Genoese adventurer called G. P. Marana, who had long been resident in Egypt, was to lead to Montesquieu's *Lettres Persanes* of 1721.[3]

On the other hand the pre-romantic tendency, revelling in the exotic and enchanting vision of the Muslim East that A. Galland had launched, was still strong and produced a masterpiece in William Beckford's *Vathek* (1781), whose author was in 1788 to become in Madrid the lover of a Muslim youth named Muḥammad. *Vathek* is enlivened by the strong tendency towards esoterism that characterizes the end of the century of which the symbol is Cagliostro, the 'great Copt', who boasted of prolonged journeys in the East. A somewhat less fantastical aestheticism drove William Jones towards the study of Eastern literatures but,

[1] Cf. B. Lewis, 'Some English Travellers in the East', *Middle Eastern Studies*, iv (1968), 296–315, and Daniel, op. cit., pp. 13, 20ff.

[2] *Confessions*, Bk. IV.

[3] Hazard, op. cit., i. 20, 23f.

like Voltaire and so many others, he was to constrain both form and content into European canons and categories as much as possible, transposing Arabic verse, for instance, into the classical Greco-Latin metres. Yet, the realistic, positivist, and universalist tendency, which was in the line of the Encyclopedists, was still very strong and shaped such a mind as Volney's, whose *Voyage en Syrie et en Egypte* (1787) is a masterpiece of careful analysis, remarkably sagacious in political and social matters, distrustful of the picturesque and dedicated to the observation of realities. Volney knew the Eastern languages, his scholarship was imposing, but his interest lay in contemporary affairs. He was to take an important part in the planning of the Egyptian expedition that led to the admirable *Description de l'Egypte* (1809–22), an unequalled collection of penetrating and exact archaeological, geographical, demographic, medical, technological, and (anticipating the term) sociological studies. Volney was well acquainted with Eastern history, but he held that the best way of getting to understand it was to start from observation of the contemporary East. He tried to further the practical study of spoken Arabic and criticized the scholars who knew a great deal about medieval Arab grammarians but could not make themselves understood by a living Arab.

The preoccupation with the present, and the passion for understanding the true mechanics of things, are little conducive to purely philological studies, and these wilted during the whole of the eighteenth century. Maronites like the Assemanis in Italy and Casiri in Spain catalogued collections of manuscripts. Louis XIV in 1700 and Maria Theresa in 1754 founded schools for the essentially practical purpose of training interpreters. In India in 1784, William Jones founded the first learned Orientalist society, the Asiatic Society of Bengal. There was there, in Muslim territory, a body of Britons who were equally interested in Muslim and in classical Indian languages and literatures. In 1800 the East India Company, for practical ends, founded Fort William College in Calcutta, under whose auspices there were published and translated, often by native writers, many of the Persian and Arabic classics, as well as manuals and other works of a practical nature. Out in India, they still thought that a knowledge of the East was a basic necessity. But around the 1820s a westernizing attitude was beginning to predominate, and the older attitude was now adjudged unnecessary; in 1835 Lord Macaulay anglicized the whole of the Indian school system.[1]

7. *The nineteenth century: exoticism, imperialism, specialization*

In the nineteenth century three tendencies are apparent: a utilitarian and imperialistic sense of Western superiority, full of contempt for other civilizations; a romantic exoticism, with its delight in a magical East whose increasing poverty spiced its charm; and a specialized scholarship whose main concern lay with past ages. Despite appearances, the three tendencies are more complementary than opposed.

Romantic exoticism did not spring from a change in the relations between East and West, but from an internal transformation of Western sensibilities now craving for the bizarre. What was foreign had always appeared at the same time strange, but there was now a delight found in the most *outré*. It is from this that English pre-romanticism derived, with its love for so-called primitive poetry, the atmosphere of which must have given the direction to William Jones's interests. So also the German *Sturm und Drang* to which Herder (1744–1803) belongs with his deep interest in Eastern literatures among others, and whose studies in historical synthesis place the Muslim contribution in the first rank, the Arabs having been 'Europe's teachers'. But the desire to know and understand exotic worlds was for a long time linked to the classical, universalist approach of men who were searching first and foremost in the East, as elsewhere, for the man of all times and of all places. Goethe's poems to the glory of Muḥammad, and in particular his *Mahomets Gesang* of 1774, are incomparably more poetical

[1] Cf. Fück, op. cit., pp. 135–40; R. Schwab, *La Renaissance orientale* (Paris, 1950), pp. 208f.

than Voltaire's *Mahomet* (1742), but have even less of local colour. More than forty years later, in 1819, Goethe wrote his *West-östlicher Divan* with its twelve *nāmehs*, its opening call to a 'Hegira' towards the East where the poet will recover his youth in the spring of Khiḍr (Chiser) and its learned notes and appended comments full of Oriental erudition. Lucid as he always was, Goethe felt impelled to apologize for having allowed his irrepressible European origin to show through, as well as his specific accent that marked him as a foreigner.[1] The Orientalist Merx went too far when he declared Goethe's East to be a 'wholly invented phantasmagoria', for, as H. Lichtenberger has said, 'he did not intend to depict either the East or the West, but man as intuitively he found him, in one as much as in the other'.[2] (See also on Goethe as a figure in the growing understanding of the East by the West in the Romantic period, below, Chapter VII, pp. 342–3.)

The renewed vogue of Oriental studies, which indeed looked like a Renaissance, supplied the Romantics with a wealth of material. Nevertheless, scholarly Orientalism was rooted in the preoccupations of the Enlightenment. Anyone in Europe who wanted a worthwhile introduction to the languages and civilizations of the Near East turned to the École de Langues Orientales Vivantes in Paris which had been set up by the Convention in March 1795 at the instigation of Langlès. The latter laid very special stress upon practical usefulness, but not before he emphasized the contribution which Eastern languages could make to the progress of literature and science.[3] Paradoxically, the great pioneer here was Silvestre de Sacy, a Legitimist, a Jansenist, and a positivist, who clung to the values of the past and who, for example, envisaged linguistics within the framework of an abstract universalism, as defined by the 'grammaire générale' in the spirit of Port Royal. Sacy became the master of all European Orientalists and Paris the Mecca of all who wished to specialize in the study of

[1] See his *West-östlicher Divan*. Noten und Abhandlungen, Einleitung.

[2] Lichtenberger, Introduction to the edition with French translation of the *Divan* (Paris, 1940); cf. Schwab, op. cit., p. 386.

[3] Fück, op. cit., p. 141.

the Near East.[1] He was a scrupulous and meticulous philologist, extremely cautious in reaching conclusions and anxious not to put forward anything which the texts did not clearly exemplify. He was a positivist before the word was coined, and imposed upon the European world of specialists the rigorous purism to which his Jansenism had predisposed him. His style of work has remained to this day that of a large number of Orientalists. The criticisms that are now levelled at this attitude were discernible in his own day. The narrowness of mind which it fostered (but which is not in the least an inevitable consequence of it, since many of its ablest and most gifted exponents have escaped it) irritated Volney and later Renan. Scholarly purism tended to keep the problems of the past separate from those of the present world, to the occasional impairment of understanding of the former. It also often led to the unconscious acceptance of the opinions that were common in its own environment. Rejection of rash conclusions in the work of synthesis could lead to a rather barren agnosticism or to an uncritical promulgation of implicit ideologies, underwritten, as it were, by the prestige of impressive scholarship. But this was only the reverse side of exceptional qualities and advantages indispensable to scientific progress. The mistrust by Sacy and his disciples of brilliant and facile syntheses, however unjust it may sometimes have been to certain valid and important theories, was a necessary condition for building new superstructures on a secure foundation.

Another condition was the final severance of all ties with theology that had been achieved in England and in France in the eighteenth century. The training of dragomans in Paris and in Vienna had led to the liberation of teaching from theological fetters, and resulted in the founding of the Paris School of Oriental Languages, which, created in the fervour of revolutionary France, provided under the devout Silvestre de Sacy the model of an Orientalist institution both scholarly and secular. In German-speaking

[1] Fück, op. cit., pp. 140–58; H. Dehérain, *Silvestre de Sacy, ses contemporains et ses disciples* (Paris, 1938).

countries, the universities were still controlled by the theologians, and secular Orientalism had at first to be practised by amateurs, with the prolific Josef von Hammer-Purgstall (1774–1856) in the forefront. He was a pupil of the Vienna Oriental Academy and a professional dragoman. He lacked philological precision but was an unequalled popularizer of knowledge of the East, founding the first specialist Orientalist review in Europe, the *Fundgruben des Orients* (1809–18), to which all European Orientalists contributed as well as some Eastern scholars. Von Hammer divided his interests equally between the past and the present.

The recourse to objectivity, to arduous specialized work, was in line with the deeper trends of an age when scientific research in depth was being organized, and of a society in which capitalism was inspiring an unprecedented industrial development. The success of Silvestre de Sacy's teaching throughout Europe is a reflection of this, as is the flowering of specialist institutions. The Paris Asiatic Society was founded in 1821, and in 1823 it launched its own periodical, the *Journal Asiatique*. In 1834 there appeared the *Journal of the Royal Asiatic Society of Great Britain and Ireland*, the Society dating itself from 1823. In 1839 a regularly produced journal, the *Journal of the Asiatic Society of Bengal*, took the place in India of the *Asiatick Researches* of William Jones's group. In 1841, the Bombay branch issued its own journal. The year 1842 saw the founding of the American Oriental Society which also had its own periodical. In 1849 the *Zeitschrift der deutschen morgenländischen Gesellschaft* was launched in Leipzig. It was published by the German Oriental Society which had been formed two years earlier. The westernizing of Russia had, from the second half of the eighteenth century, brought forth a certain flowering of Orientalist works. From 1804 the teaching of oriental languages at university level was extended at Kharkov and, above all, to Kazan, which lay in Muslim territory. The internal Muslim policy of the Russian state stimulated the rapid growth in importance of this centre at Kazan.[1]

[1] Cf. V. V. Barthold, *La Découverte de l'Asie*, French translation (Paris, 1947).

Such was the origin of Orientalism. The term 'Orientalist' occurred in England towards 1779, and 'orientaliste' in France in 1799. 'Orientalisme' finds a place in the *Dictionnaire de l'Académie Française* of 1838. The idea of a special discipline devoted to the study of the East was gathering support. There were not yet enough specialists to justify the establishment of journals or societies dealing exclusively with one country or one people or one region of the East. Instead, the ambit of the journals and societies extends over several domains, not all receiving the same depth of treatment. A scholar was therefore an 'orientalist'. The concept of 'orientalism' betokens a greater depth of study, but also a withdrawal and a retrenchment. In the eighteenth-century works of synthesis, the East and the West stood side by side as aspects of a universalist view. It had now been realized that there could be no serious discussion of the East without a preliminary study of the original texts, which in turn involved a profound knowledge of the native languages. With the materials that had become available this preliminary work was seen to be immense, involving the editing and translating of texts, the compilation of scientifically planned dictionaries and grammars, the exposition of narrative history, and so on. Specialists might well hold general ideas, but they should as far as possible keep them out of their scientific work. They were left with too little time to keep informed of scientific trends outside their own special field.

Literary and artistic Orientalism was of course fostered by all the events concerning the Muslim East, particularly the 'Eastern Question' which was one of the great problems of European politics in the nineteenth century. Significantly, Romantic exoticism has its origin in the Greek War of Independence that attracted Byron (and in which he died in 1824) and was the subject of the

pp. 264ff.; J. Fück, op. cit., pp. 155, 195ff.; B. M. Dancig, 'Iz istorii izučeniya Bliznegio Vostoka v Rossii', *Očerki po istorii russkogo vostokovedeniya*, iv (Moscow, 1959), 3–38; I. Yu Kračkovski, *Očerki po istorii russkoy arabistiki* (Moscow-Leningrad, 1950), pp. 73ff., German translation by O. Mehlitz, *Die russische Arabistik, Umrisse ihrer Entwicklung* (Leipzig, 1957), pp. 69ff.

first Orientalist painting (*Le Massacre de Scio* by Delacroix, which was exhibited in the same year). In that picture and in Victor Hugo's collection of lyrics *Les Orientales* (in which the first poem is dated 1825) is present in all its essentials the Romantic's image of the East, which flourished and persisted for so long in the public imagination: a riot of colour; sumptuousness and savage ferocity; harems and seraglios; heads chopped off and women thrown in sacks into the Bosphorus; feluccas and brigantines flying the Crescent banner; roundness of azure domes and soaring whiteness of minarets; viziers, odalisques, and eunuchs; cooling springs beneath the palms; *giaours* with their throats slit; captive women subjected to the victor's ravenous lust. Such highly coloured pictures provide inexpensive satisfaction to the deeper instincts, the murky sensualism, the unconscious masochism and sadism of the peaceful Western bourgeoisie, as Heine had already discovered. Even when Westerners actually went to the East, this was the image they sought out, ruthlessly selecting what they saw and ignoring what did not fit in with their preconceived picture.

This image, tinged with European sensibility at its own stage of evolution, also reflected a real situation. In the nineteenth century the Muslim East was still an enemy, but an enemy doomed to defeat. Eastern lands were like decaying witnesses of a great past; one could enjoy the luxury of praising them at the same time as the politicians and businessmen were doing all they could to hasten their decay. The possibility of their recovery or modernization aroused no enthusiasm. They might, in the process of modernization, lose the whiff of exoticism which lent them their charm. In the Middle Ages, the Oriental had been regarded as a fierce enemy, but nevertheless on the same level as Western man; in the eighteenth-century enlightenment and the resulting ideology of the French Revolution the Oriental was, underneath his disguise, essentially a human being; now he became a creature apart, imprisoned in his specificity, an object of condescending praise. Thus the concept of *homo islamicus* was born, and is still far from being overthrown.

The theory that there are different civilizations each evolving in its allotted sphere was becoming universally accepted. Each civilization had been endowed with a particular essential nature. The search for this essential nature accounted for the increasing tendency of scholars to forsake the study of recent periods and to specialize in the 'classical' ages when civilizations were deemed to have shown their 'purest' characteristics. This tendency was intensified by the two humanist sciences that were favourite pursuits in the nineteenth century: the history of religions, and historical and comparative linguistics. The history of religions, born of the struggle between secular relativist pluralism and the Christian monopoly of ideas, stimulated great interest in the study of Eastern religions as alternatives to Christianity, both in the past and in the present.

The discoveries of historical and comparative linguistics gave to language, indeed to each specific language, a key role. A nation was considered to be identified with its language and to be defined by the characteristics of that language. Biological evolutionism and the creation of the science of physical anthropology focused attention upon the classification of races. Races themselves were looked upon as essential forces endowed with a particularly high efficiency quotient. Increasingly narrow specialization could only hinder the correct appreciation of the contributions made by these sciences. They reached specialists in other fields only in their most vulgarized, mechanistic forms.

Despite the enormous mass of documents and precise pieces of information assembled together by the specialists, there was an ever-widening divergence between two streams of knowledge. On the one hand, the specialists' knowledge was deep but focused upon a view of a cultural whole that had now disappeared as such but to which there was attributed an immutable, underlying influence. This influence derived its direction from the most general ideas of the time, which transmitted the findings of the history of religions, of historical linguistics, and of physical anthropology, in the popularized form of a boundless magnification of the power of religion, language, and race. On the other hand, the problems of actual contemporary life in those societies were considered an ignoble subject better left to the practical observation of traders, travellers, diplomats, and economists. While theoretical knowledge in the eighteenth century attempted to help the practical man in understanding the present, it can be said, in a very general sort of way, that in the nineteenth century and at the beginning of the twentieth, on the rare occasions when scholars interfered in this field, they did more harm than good, influenced as they were by current prejudices rather than by science.

Less schematic views of the countries of the Muslim East as evolving societies capable of progress, given favourable conditions, are found principally among statesmen, technicians, and economists when the circumstances were more or less favourable. So it was with Muḥammad ʿAlī's Egypt, which aroused some enthusiasm in France within the framework of its anti-British policy. Aesthetic exoticism, while it plunged most of its followers into nostalgia of the past and fear of Europeanizing modernization, paradoxically led others, through their sincere and passionate interest in the countries concerned, to opt for progress and therefore to pay more attention to the movements that were taking place there. Here again there was a parting of the ways, and several courses were open, from the envisaging of the desired evolution as taking place under the aegis of the European homeland of this exoticism (Lyautey, L. Massignon, T. E. Lawrence at first), to a stand in opposition to that country (W. S. Blunt), through all possible intermediate positions and with changes of position in the course of one man's life. The influence of the generally accepted opinions of the time gave a different twist to ideas. In his schemes for the regeneration of Islam and the Arab world by a partial and modified return to medieval forms, W. S. Blunt provided very important material that was later to be appropriated, assimilated, and made their own by the early theorists of Muslim and Arab nationalism.

The phenomenon that had most to do with the conditioning of the European view of the East, particularly after the middle of the nineteenth century, was imperialism (for the earlier background of this historical trend see below, Chapter IV, pp. 200 ff.). The economic, technical, military, political, and cultural superiority of Europe was becoming overwhelming, while the East was sinking into under-development. For all practical purposes, Iran and the Ottoman Empire were becoming European protectorates, while the field of direct colonization was spreading into Central Asia to the benefit of the Russians; into the Maghrib and the Ottoman East to the benefit of the British, French, and Italians, particularly after 1881 when Egypt and Tunisia were occupied. All this, inevitably, could only encourage a natural European self-centredness, which had always existed, but which now took on a very markedly contemptuous tinge. The unconscious eighteenth-century view of things from a European standpoint, guided by the universalist ideology of the age, respected non-European peoples and cultures and rightly found in their historical evolution or their contemporary structures of society universal human characteristics, with pre-critical *naïveté* crediting them with the same underlying bases as European civilization, with only very superficial specific differences. The conscious, theoretical European self-centredness of the nineteenth century made the opposite mistake. Irreducible specificity was assumed at all levels and universal traits or motives were ignored or denied. Moreover, Easterners themselves began in some cases to adopt the European model, starting with its most superficial aspects, and in other cases rejecting totally this model whilst clinging to the most archaic values of their culture, although these had often been renewed from within. Scholars made ever more numerous and more profound specialized studies of the classical ages and of the things that were most closely connected with the culture of those ages. They noted with understandable relish all the signs of their enduring influence at the present time, and consciously or unconsciously they often lent the guarantee of their scientific authority to such a presentation of things.[1]

The humiliating situation in which the Muslim world found itself encouraged Christian missionaries and opened new ways for them. Within the framework of normal human inclinations and even in accordance with the general ideas of contemporary science, they attributed the successes of European nations to the Christian religion, just as they attributed the failures of the Muslim world to Islam. Christianity was made out to be by its very nature favourable to progress, and Islam to mean cultural stagnation and backwardness. The attack upon Islam became as fierce as it could be and the arguments of the Middle Ages were revived with up-to-date embellishments. The Islamic religious orders (on whose origins see below, Chapter VIII, pp. 378–9), in particular, were presented as a network of dangerous organizations animated by a barbarous hatred of civilization.[2] Paradoxically and significantly, similar conclusions were reached by anti-clericals in the line of Voltaire, who extolled the virtues of Hellenism, a civilization based upon the freedom of the spirit, the worship of reason and beauty, the spring of European greatness, as opposed to the Semitic spirit that made for intolerant rigidity, scholastic dogmatism, fundamentalism, enervating fatalism, and contempt for the plastic arts; to this latter spirit were attributed all the associated misdeeds of Judaism, of Christianity, and of Islam.[3]

Pan-Islamism was a fashionable bogy in the same way and at

[1] Daniel in his *Islam, Europe and Empire* gives more precise information and quotations than anyone else. With regard to explanations, however, his work needs emending in accordance with A. Hourani's suggestions in his review in *Middle Eastern Studies*, iv (1968), 325f.

[2] Of outstanding significance is *Les Sociétés secrètes chez les Musulmans* (Paris–Lyons, 1899) by Father Rouquette of the Lyons Society of African Missions.

[3] With some hesitancy, Renan tends towards this view. See especially the famous lecture he gave at the Sorbonne on 29 Mar. 1883, *L'Islamisme et la science* (Paris, 1883). This tendency is taken to its extreme in a book eloquently entitled *La Pathologie de l'Islam et les moyens de le détruire* (Paris, 1897) by a militant anti-semitic Greek who called himself D. Kimon and who was also the author of an anti-Jewish book, *La Politique israelite, étude psychologique* (Paris, 1889).

the same time as the Yellow Peril was. Any anti-imperialistic demonstration, even when it sprang from purely local feelings, was attributed to pan-Islamism. The very word suggested an attempt at domination, an ideology of aggression, a conspiracy on a world-wide scale. Thanks to the popular press, to popular literature, and to children's books, this view was penetrating the great mass of European minds, and it was not without influence among the scholars themselves, particularly when they took it upon themselves to offer supposedly competent advice to those directing the colonial policies of governments. Those scholars who took the greatest interest in contemporary studies, like Snouck Hurgronje or C. H. Becker, and who were more or less obsessed by pan-Islamism, analysing it with a greater or lesser degree of subtlety, tended to see it, however, as a reactionary movement.[1] Without subscribing to all the commonly held myths, they were nevertheless inclined to see more unity and organization than there really was in what were in reality loose and widely divergent tendencies.

The majority of specialists, however, took no interest in these problems and were content to adopt the current views of their time whenever they had to deal with matters outside their own branch of knowledge. These specializations of theirs evolved only slowly in their spirit and methods. The philological bias retained its undisputed hold upon Oriental studies. Material for investigation accumulated. Methods of study became increasingly rigorous. Relations between scholars became more numerous and better organized, particularly on the international scale, thanks to such contacts as international conferences of Orientalists, of which the first was held in Paris in 1873. Yet, the analysis of societies, of cultures, of ideas progressed only as a result of the understanding of a few outstanding scholars.

The slow emergence of the social sciences brought little change into this picture. Sociology, psychology, demography, and political

[1] Cf. J.-J. Waardenburg, *L'Islam dans le miroir de l'Occident* (Paris-The Hague, 1963), pp. 102-6.

economy were unknown to most specialists of the Muslim East, who did not realize their usefulness for their studies. It is true that the early sociologists looked upon the Muslim world as coming, among other worlds, within their sphere of interest. But they meant either the classical Muslim world or the archaic manners and traditions of the modern Muslim world. General sociologists derived their knowledge from Islamists and, with commendable caution, refrained from venturing too far into a field about which they knew little. The ethnography of the Muslim peoples was the field in which the influence of the new and energetic disciplines was most marked, and yielded such remarkable works as those of E. Doutté (e.g. his *Magie et religion dans l'Afrique du Nord*, 1908) and E. Westermarck (e.g. his *Marriage ceremonies in Morocco*, 1914).

The lack of a detailed theoretical model of social structures and their evolution kept history, in the Oriental field as elsewhere, at the level of a purely descriptive discipline. It had, however, been given fresh life by the critical vigour that B. G. Niebuhr (the son of Carsten Niebuhr, the traveller in Arabia) and Leopold von Ranke introduced into source analysis. Such Orientalist historians as G. Weil, A. Sprenger, R. Dozy, and M. Amari followed the same pattern; they were rigorous in the establishment of facts, open-minded in principle about the nature of the historical factors involved, but in fact influenced by the ideas generally current in their time regarding the understanding of the development of events. Thus Sprenger (who by his critical approach in *Das Leben und die Lehre des Moḥammed*, 1861–5, revised the history of the Prophet) was influenced by the Hegelian conception of the *Zeitgeist*. Alfred von Kremer (1828–89) was doubtless the first specialist to see the history of Islam as an integral whole. His presentation of this was built round the doctrine of the influence of the ideas dominating each age that would supply 'the key to the understanding of the religious and social system of Islam'.[1] Most

[1] *Geschichte der herrschenden Ideen des Islams* (Leipzig, 1868, reprinted Hildesheim, 1961), p. xvii.

specialists remained attached to the general idea—often implicit—of the predominance of the religious and ideational factor. The school of French historians in the years 1820–50, who based their historical analysis upon the internal dynamics of the conflicts between social groups, had had no influence on the Oriental field where the conflicts that were outlined were those between 'races' and those between religions. Thus Shīʿism was usually explained as a reaction of the Aryan Persian spirit against Semitic Islam.

However, under the influence of the social conflicts of his time, the philologist H. Grimme was the first to investigate in his *Mohammed* (1892–5)—much too summarily of course—the influence of social factors in Muḥammad's life. A theologian, J. Wellhausen, who had achieved fame through his theses concerning Biblical criticism and the history of Ancient Israel, showed in his *Die religiös-politischen Oppositionsparteien im alten Islam* (1901) that the appearance of religious schisms in the early days of Islam evinced the dynamism of political and social conflicts. C. H. Becker was to proceed along the same road in his *Islamstudien* (1924–32) and L. Caetani was to go even further in the evocation of economic factors (e.g. in his *Studia di storia orientale*, 1914). And so at the beginning of the twentieth century, under the influence of the current concerns of the time, there was some tendency to question the eclectic positivism of the time, not replacing it by a general theoretical analysis of social structure and social dynamics, but simply transposing and emphasizing the predominant factors of the contemporary European world. Most of the specialists reacted rather sceptically to these attempts, some of which were indeed excessive and open to criticism; they remained cautiously agnostic.

8. *European ethnocentrism is shaken*

In this field as in others, the war of 1914–18 shook the self-confidence of European civilization, with its belief in indefinite progress on the same lines, and thereby shook European ethnocentrism. The Arab revolt in the East, the Kemalist movement in

Turkey, the shaking up of the diverse nations of the old Russian empire, the revolts in India, Indonesia, and elsewhere, all of them in line with the Young Turk and Iranian revolutions of the 1908–14 period, showed that European hegemony could be called in question. On the morrow of the war, O. Spengler's dazzling work *Der Untergang des Abendlandes* (1918–22) was published. On a more specific subject, the American Lothrop Stoddard brought out *The Rising Tide of Color against White World-Supremacy* (1920). The same author produced a book significantly entitled *The New World of Islam* (1921). This publicist, a non-specialist, was well informed, and without denying his racist viewpoint he showed that profound changes were creating a 'strange new East', in large measure the result of Western influences. The new image that he propounded was basically that of a world revolving round a mysterious, fundamentally different, hostile, and slightly repugnant nucleus made up of an ignorance and savagery barely restrained by religion, custom, and a small enlightened élite. But he made room too for universal factors like the struggle against foreign intrusion. Such a view of things remained roughly that of the great European and American public, except that the emphasis was laid rather on the first factor, the latent and inadequately restrained savagery, the fanaticism that had been unleashed to meet the civilizing thrust from the West.

This undermining could not fail to have its effect. The figure and work of T. E. Lawrence are a dramatic example of the collision between romantic exoticism and a reality apprehended empirically in its universal aspects but still infused with the magic delusions of local colour. Exoticism at times led to a deeper understanding of native aspirations, as in the case of the Turcophile disciples of Pierre Loti. More often, however, the anti-colonialists were universalists with little interest in the past or in the specific characteristics of the present, which they regarded as the vestigial traces of a barbarous past that had better be destroyed. Exoticism tended rather to lead colonial statesmen to try to preserve the older forms and seek allies among the indigenous conservatives, to denounce the nationalist intellectuals—whether reformists or revolutionaries, socialists or not—as pale imitators of Europe, and driven by abstract, ill-digested ideas to destroy their own inheritance. Generally speaking that was also the verdict of the public at large. Modernization was looked upon as a spurious element, a betrayal of individuality.

Under the same heading we may perhaps range the view of the esoterists who sought in the Muslim East, as well as e.g. in the Buddhist East, a pattern of the wise life, a contact with supra-sensory realities and with the ancestral secrets that a long line of initiates had handed down. Far from seeing in the Muslim Ṣūfī brotherhoods the inspiration of the Devil, they saw in them rather cells through which the ancestral theosophical tradition was transmitted. Some, like René Guénon (1886–1951), were converts to Islam and died on Muslim soil. In Europe and America this spiritual tendency, this fabulous vision of an esoteric Islam made possible the success of numerous sects which in varying degrees derived from Islam and, allowing for all kinds of misconceptions, even from Orthodox Islam and from such a religion as Baha'ism.

The irresistible tide of anti-colonialism caused in narrow but influential sectors of Western society a change in the image of the Muslim world. The movement towards independence, which on its purely nationalistic side was represented by the upper-class Muslims who wished to adapt themselves to the West in order to acquire the dynamic and dominating virtues of private enterprise, evoked much sympathy in Western governmental and business circles. In 1945 an Englishwoman, Freya Stark, wrote a book with the significant title *East is West* which she dedicated to 'her brothers the young effendis' and in which she stood in opposition to Kipling's imperialistic and exoticizing attitude. Islam was considered to be a religion like any other which, while supplying its followers with spiritual reasons for living, must not hinder their economic activities, and which could be used as a bulwark against the ravages of atheistic Communist ideology.

. he anti-colonialist ideology of the left took an altogether different course. Conversely, the universalism which it had derived from its liberal or socialist roots tended to change into recognition or even exaltation of individuality. Thenceforward the values appertaining to the former colonized peoples were to receive their meed of admiring praise, even when the very normal misunderstandings tended towards the discovery in them, albeit in specific forms, of the very values that animated the European communities concerned. To some of those who were most deeply committed in this direction, Islam appeared intrinsically to be a naturally 'progressive' factor. There were even conversions to Islam.

This tendency was particularly striking in a group of left-wing Catholics at the head of which stood a very learned French specialist, Louis Massignon. Imbued with a mystical view of history and rooted in the secular Christian tradition of devotion to the poor and humble, he carried to the utmost limit the latent tendency of the Christianity of recent times which had found its most forceful and perspicuous exponents in the Roman Catholic Church. The menace of atheism, the revision of traditional standpoints whose responsibility for the dechristianization of the Western masses seems obvious, the return to the fundamental and original values of the Christian faith, have all brought about a feeling of oneness with, rather than hostility towards, other religions. The ecumenical movement, though it has not given up its claim to be in possession of the whole truth and must gradually bring the wayward to it, has nevertheless renounced extra-spiritual pressure and recognized that the upholders of other beliefs are partners in debate and eventual allies, men of good faith attached to values worthy of respect, no longer enemy forces to be crushed. In October 1965 the Vatican Ecumenical Council paid homage to the 'truths' that Islam had handed down concerning God and His power, Jesus, Mary, the Prophets, and the Apostles. While in the Middle Ages it was thought that such 'truths' were masks under whose guise the fundamental Islamic imposture gained admission, people are now coming round to the view that Muslim 'errors' are of doubtful importance in the face of the basically important monotheistic message which Islam bears.

This revolution in thinking has made a Christian appraisal of Muḥammad a matter of some delicacy. It is no longer possible to see him as nothing but a sheer devilish impostor, as in the Middle Ages. While the greater number of the Christian thinkers who give some attention to the problem cautiously suspend judgement, some Roman Catholic specialists in Islam see him as a 'religious genius'. Others go even further and have come to ask whether, in a way, he was not a true prophet, seeing that St. Thomas Aquinas speaks of directive prophecy not necessarily implying unerringness and impeccability.[1] In line with Massignon, some Christians have been struck by the spiritual value of Muslim religious experiences and disturbed by the historic injustices of their own people towards Islam, both as a religion and as a group of peoples quite recently reduced to submission and despised. They have accordingly been led to formulate opinions which might justify the charge of syncretism and 'islamizing heresy' that indignant supporters of the integrity of the Church have levelled at them.

In this way the anti-colonialist left, whether Christian or not, often goes so far as to sanctify Islam and the contemporary ideologies of the Muslim world, thereby going from one extreme to the other. An historian like Norman Daniel has gone so far as to number among the conceptions permeated with medievalism or imperialism, any criticisms of the Prophet's moral attitudes, and to accuse of like tendencies any exposition of Islam and its characteristics by means of the normal mechanisms of human history. Understanding has given way to apologetics pure and simple. As for specialist scholars, they are split between indifference on the one hand and the various shades of opinion on the other.

The influence of the new problems posed by the social sciences now extends to Oriental studies. In ever greater numbers specialists, whether concerned with the medieval Muslim world or with

[1] Already typical of this view is the book *Mahomet, Israël et le Christ* (Paris, 1956) by the theologian Ch.-J. Ledit.

later periods, approach the problem from the sociological angle.[1] Economic history and social history, which were so long ignored, have at last been taken up by a fairly large number of scholars.[2] Over the whole field of Islamic studies an effort is being made to go beyond purely philological work and reach, at least in part, syntheses which are no longer based on simple common-sense or philosophical generalities, but on the results achieved by scholars working in a chosen field of social phenomena: historians who study such and such a coherent group of phenomena, demographers, economists, sociologists, etc.

At the same time contacts with indigenous scholars have multiplied. The main obstacle was for a long time the small number of specialists who had freed themselves from the medieval modes of study and thought. Collaborators in these fields were in the past often merely informants, whose contribution had to be totally thought out afresh by the European scholar. The social obstacles to the setting up of really specialized teams came partly from the colonial status of the Muslim East and partly from social and cultural traditions.[3] These difficulties have been overcome in part only. Others have sprung up, arising mainly from the trenchancy of ideological options open to the Muslim world at a time of bitter struggle against the traces and after-effects of European domination. Such times are eminently favourable to ideological extremism which itself makes objective study difficult. European scholars

Moslim Scholars

[1] The first congress of Islamic studies with a sociological trend was held at Brussels in 1961 (*Colloque sur la sociologie musulmane, 11–14 septembre, 1961, Actes*, Brussels, n.d.).

[2] Cf. Cl. Cahen's 'Histoire économique et sociale de l'Orient musulman médiéval', *Studia Islamica*, iii (1955), 93–115, in which he lays down a programme for future studies. The first symposium specifically devoted to the medieval, modern, and contemporary economic history of the Muslim world was held in London in 1967. Some of the pioneers, whose viewpoints are largely at variance, have been Jean Sauvaget, Bernard Lewis, and Claude Cahen.

[3] Particularly enlightening is Bichr Farès's article, 'Des difficultés d'ordre linguistique, culturel et social que rencontre un écrivain arabe moderne, spécialement en Egypte', *Revue des études islamiques*, x (1936), 221–42. The difficulties which literary men face are equally valid for research workers in the social sciences.

are often put off by this extremism, whose motives they do not always understand, just as they also overlook the ideological components of their own judgements. But the obstacle is serious, even though it may be easily overcome in the case of research bearing on narrow and well-defined points.[1]

Another very marked general trend consists in taking more interest than formerly in what used contemptuously to be called the 'low periods'. A cultural essentialism stressing the paramountcy of religion and 'race' and acknowledging the existence and perdurability of a 'pure' type for each civilization, had led to the dominance of the study of the Muslim Middle Ages. Under the influence of economic and social research, of the new sociological direction, of contacts with economists, demographers, and anthropologists, as great an interest is now taken in the study of more recent periods, a situation encouraged by much more plentiful documentation. It has been pointed out that, for instance, the Ottoman Empire, Ṣafavid Persia and the Great Mogul Empire, represent Islam at the height of its powers.[2] Even the period of close contacts with the West and that of the birth of modern ideologies present problems which, though more or less modern, are not on that account unimportant or contemptible.

As in the other social sciences, the accepted view now is that problems must be defined, debated, and illuminated in every possible way. This entails inter-disciplinary co-ordination and excludes any factitious hierarchy of noble and ignoble disciplines. The trend towards the accumulation, collation, and indexing of material prepared and presented as well as possible, a trend which

[1] This was not given its due weight by the Egyptian sociologist A. Abdel-Malek in his criticism of European orientalism where, however, there are many things of value ('L'Orientalisme en crise', *Diogenes*, xliv (1964), 103–40); cf. the rejoinders by Cahen in a letter to *Diogenes*, xlix (1965), 135–8, and F. Gabrieli, 'Apology for Orientalism', *Diogenes*, l (1965), 128–36.

[2] Confirmation is already to be found in a book by an enlightened non-professional scholar, F. Grenard, *Grandeur et décadence de l'Asie* (Paris, 1939). The same trend is apparent in B. Lewis's 'The Mongols, the Turks and the Muslim Polity', *Transactions of the Royal Historical Society*, 5th series, xviii (1968), 49–68.

was moreover never exclusive, is giving way to a tendency towards rational discussion of the problems. Both have their good and bad points. The ascetic pursuit of perfection which occasionally led to an undue narrowing of outlook has been replaced by panoramic views that may lead to futile platitudinizing. Such a course may endanger in a deplorable way the indispensable task of publishing basic documents that, in overwhelming numbers, are awaiting editing, collating, and indexing. It is true, however, that modern techniques afford the hope that, within limits, such material may be dealt with more speedily.

Taking an extreme view, some have spoken of the end of Orientalism. The question must, however, be examined very delicately. What is at stake is the end of the dominance of philology. There are signs of the abandonment of the view held implicitly for over a century that a philological training is adequate to the solving of all the problems arising within a linguistically defined field. This idea, which cannot be maintained on rational grounds, sprang from the pressing necessity of a philological training for the serious study of the problems raised within that field. The vast increase in available material, together with the tools of research and the progress of methods of study, now enables one, if not to by-pass the philological stage, at least to devote less time to it. Progress in the social sciences has also shown the complexity of problems that could not be solved with the sole help of common sense, a profound knowledge of the language and, possibly, the inspiration of broad philosophical principles. The pursuit of oriental studies, and particularly of Islamic Studies, has therefore become more arduous and less specific. Contact with other disciplines, once a luxury, is now an inescapable need. The progress which lies before us is impressive; the price that will have to be paid for it is not too high.

MAXIME RODINSON

II

ISLAM IN THE MEDITERRANEAN WORLD

BORN in one of the most primitive and backward regions of the ancient world, Islam soon overstepped its frontiers, developing from a local phenomenon and an internal factor in Arabian life into a universalist religion and a world force, in a process about which historians still dispute. For those who study the obscure dynamism of this process, it is neither Oriental nor Occidental, nor can it be given any other geographic or cultural specification; it is only the mysterious force radiating from the new faith, and of the state founded by it, which developed in every direction and produced a surprisingly united civilization despite the very diverse environments and cultural levels upon which it flourished. But the aim of this book and of this chapter is not to follow and characterize Muslim civilization in its full extent, but to consider its influence and its 'legacy' to the Western world, and in this chapter more especially, to the Mediterranean West, the lands around that sea over which at one time the Roman Empire extended and which, when Islam made its appearance, were still in part subject to the 'second Rome', Byzantium, and in part liberated from it by the profound disturbances of the barbarian invasions and migrations. Some of these lands were then to become lasting Muslim territory (*Dār al-Islām*) and are still so today; others were so in the Middle Ages and in modern times for a longer or shorter period and have later ceased to be so, and these first come to mind when one speaks of an inheritance or a legacy left to their subsequent history and culture from the Muslim period. Still others were never to know a permanent settlement of Islam within their confines but experienced, by their contiguity to Islamized lands or at any rate by spiritual and material contact with them, the more or less profound influence of Muslim civilization. In this chapter we shall refer mainly to the second and third of these categories of the Mediterranean lands, those transiently Islamized and those which were in frequent even if indirect, contact with the world of Islam. Translated into geographical terms this means, above all, the Iberian Peninsula, Sicily, Crete, and, later, a large part of Greek and Balkan territory; and of those lands influenced but never dominated by Islam, it means a great part of what is, or was, the geo-political and cultural area of Europe—France, the Italian peninsula, 'Mitteleuropa', and all the Balkans.

The contacts of conquest and penetration which all these European lands had with Islam are divided chronologically into two main periods and aspects. The first of these is the more important from our point of view: its 'legacy' covers both the earlier and later Middle Ages and essentially concerns Islam in its origins, ethnically Arab with a strong Berber infiltration. The second, which concerns eastern Europe almost exclusively, falls within modern times, and the Islam which is the protagonist is that of the Ottoman Turks, representing the last wave of conquest under the symbol of the faith of Muḥammad in the Mediterranean world. These two periods are, despite the identity of faith, profoundly different. In the first, Islamic civilization is still itself in the course of formation, absorbing elements of pre-existing Oriental cultures, of Hellenism and, generally speaking, the late classical period, and handing them on, after having assimilated and elaborated them to the countries and peoples with whom it came in contact. This is the most fruitful and glorious phase of the 'legacy', in which as well as raids and invasions, the medieval West received from Muslim civilization the full benefit of its cultural inheritance, which was decisive for its own further development. Rather different are the characteristics of the second and later period, contemporaneous with, or later than, our Renaissance. At that time the West had attained full consciousness of itself and was following, with vital energy, the path of modern civilization, whereas the Muslim East, which opposed it and in part also threatened it, had not progressed equally. A new power, that of the Ottoman Turks, conquered the less advanced parts of south-eastern Europe, but when it tried to penetrate into the European heartlands, it was repulsed. Turkish Islam brought with it a culture based largely on the older Arabo-Persian foundations, although it would be untrue to say that no individual and original cultural traits developed in the Ottoman Empire. Nevertheless, this second 'legacy', even though like the first it lasted for centuries, was a poorer, less easily definable one. This qualitative difference between the two periods will justify, we believe, the different scale with which they are treated here and the different methods of treatment. We intend to devote most of our space to the first and more significant period, the medieval 'legacy' of Arab Islam to the West, divided into the three geographical zones of the eastern Mediterranean (Byzantium and Greece), the central Mediterranean (Sicily and Italy and, indirectly, France and the Germanic world), and the western Mediterranean (the Iberian Peninsula), and to reserve for a single and more summary exposition an appraisal of 'Turkocratia' over eastern Europe in modern times. We do not forget that the rest of the present volume will treat analytically individual fields of contact and influence, from the military to the economic, to the historical and artistic, to literature and culture, and that this treatment, even when extended to zones outside Europe, will have to pivot on Europe for more than one phenomenon of transmission and influence. Here, at the beginning, we consider it our task to give a general panorama of what the irruption of Islam into Mediterranean Europe meant and to anticipate its principal results in the various fields in which this contact took place.

From what has been said in Chapter I we have seen how the Western Middle Ages regarded the rise and diffusion of Islam: a diabolical laceration in the breast of the Christian Church, scarcely three centuries victor over paganism, a perverse schism perpetrated by a barbarous people. The central feature of the message of Muḥammad, the strict affirmation of monotheism as opposed to traditional polytheism, was clouded in the sentiment and judgement of Christendom by the anti-Trinitarian polemic and above all by the declared prophetic and messianic identity of the founder of the new faith. Therefore the appearance of the Arabs in the Mediterranean basin, the mutilation of the Byzantine Empire, the rapid obliteration of the Latinity of northern Africa, were regarded above all by contemporaries and also by the men of the Middle Ages as a religious catastrophe, a judgement fully justified for those who conceived the religious conflict in dogmatic and sectarian terms, but which did not take into account the historic significance of the great event. Looking at it from a wider and more detached viewpoint, modern historiography has tended to emphasize the ethnic, political, economic, and social aspects of the event, in addition to its obvious religious importance. In the explosion and propagation of Islam, historians like Wellhausen, Becker, and Caetani have concentrated on the emergence of the Arabs, for the first and so far the only time, as the leading factor in world history: the triumph of Islam in this, its original phase, was *das arabische Reich*, the expansion over two continents, with unheard-of energy and fortune, of a people till then confined in their desert patrimony. This interpretation tends to overlook the brevity of the initial and purely Arab moment of such a diaspora, the germs of universalism within Islam which were rapidly to get the better of the self-centred nationalism of the leading race, and the capacity of the new faith to win over and assimilate ethnic elements of the most diverse origins, fusing them into a single cultural and religious community. Such religious-cultural unity survived far longer than the brief Arab political hegemony and constitutes the essential factor of the millenary Muslim civilization. But, on the other hand, it must certainly not be forgotten that the Arabs gave to this millenary civilization their language, and elements of their national traditions were enshrined in the Revelation; even after the dissolution of the united Caliphate they left an ethnic and cultural foundation which still allows us to call 'Arab' the great states of the Islamic Middle Ages, like those of the Fāṭimids of Egypt and the Umayyads of Spain, and later (though in their case with a strong Berber admixture) the Almoravids and the Almohads. All these examples come to us from the shores of the Mediterranean and that is sufficient to show that Arabism, through the varied directions of its diffusion, found a particularly favourable terrain in the area of the ancient *mare nostrum* and, born in the sun-scorched peninsula of Arabia, was later able to acclimatize itself to the milder breezes of Syria, the long African coast, Sicily, and Spain.

But more or less purely Arab as may have been that Islam which spread so victoriously along the eastern and southern coasts of the Mediterranean in the seventh and eighth centuries, our task requires us to assess the consequences of its intrusion in the changed balance in the Mediterranean itself. To this argument Henri Pirenne in the thirties devoted a celebrated book, setting out a thesis which has since been vigorously debated and, although finally rejected, has proved fruitful and stimulating. According to the Belgian historian, the seventh century, with the sudden appearance of Islam in the Mediterranean, marks the real end of the ancient epoch, even more than the preceding invasions and the dichotomy between the Byzantine world and the Latin West. From the economic standpoint (and on economic history Pirenne's thesis mainly rests) this dichotomy, previously non-existent, came about only after the Arabs destroyed the safety of communications in the Mediterranean and created a final break between East and West. The latter, cut off from regular contact with Byzantium and the Byzantine Empire, retreated into itself, substituting for the maritime economy of the Merovingians the essentially land-locked and continental Carolingian economy, and, in the final analysis, became poor and barbarian, thanks to the ancient robbers of the desert now turned pirates and corsairs in the Mediterranean. 'Sans Mahomet, pas de Charlemagne' runs the Pirenne formula, in which the restorer of the Western Empire appears not so much as a symbol of renewed greatness as of renunciation, signifying a change of direction in the destinies of the Latin West.

This thesis, as we have said, is today substantially rejected both by 'Western' and 'Eastern' medievalists alike.[1] Even its point of departure, the asserted closure of the Mediterranean as a result of the Arab invasion, has not been proved. That this invasion should have, at certain times and in certain sectors, made communications more difficult and less frequent can certainly be admitted, but to suggest that it led to a paralysis of seaborne trade is a false generalization, contradicted by the facts. As we shall show later, the Arabs never achieved an uncontested rule over the seas, not even over the eastern Mediterranean which with much exaggeration has been called 'an Arab lake'. The long rivalry with Byzantium never went so far, even in times of war, as to cause an interruption of economic relations between the two Empires. As for the trade between the two parts of the Mediterranean across the Italy–Sicily hinge, it was never for long interrupted, as is proved by reports from Arab, Byzantine, and Western sources concerning voyages, pilgrimages, and trade; for trade the testimony of the geographer Ibn Khurdādbih (ninth century) is important. He speaks of the Jewish 'Radanite' merchants who came from southern France to Egypt by sea and thence continued their voyage by land to the East. Whatever may be the answers to the various questions that this passage provokes,[2] his documentary evidence remains sound concerning the existence of such trade (which is not referred to in that source as anything exceptional or abnormal) and therefore the whole edifice founded on the supposition of its interruption is radically weakened. Pirenne's error, in our opinion, was to have considered the state of war (endemic

[1] A considerable bibliography already exists on the work of Pirenne and the discussions aroused by it; cf. A. F. Havigurst, *The Pirenne Thesis. Analysis, Criticism and Revision* (Boston, 1958). See also F. Gabrieli, 'Greeks and Arabs in the Central Mediterranean', *Dumbarton Oaks Papers*, xviii (1964), 59–66, and in the book by Eickhoff mentioned in the bibliography.

[2] Cl. Cahen, 'Y a-t-il eu des Rahdānites?', *Revue des Études Juives*, 4th series, iii (1964), 499–505.

and recrudescent at stated periods) in the society of the early Middle Ages as automatically paralysing international social and economic relations, in the way of modern totalitarian wars (he had had recent experience of the First World War); on the evidence of medieval texts such a comparison seems false. During the long duel between Islam and Christendom that was fought in the Mediterranean, we find that economic and cultural relations continued to spread in spite of it, and that they did so consistently over a long period. The exchanges between Arabic Spain and the East, not only Muslim but also Byzantine, are extensively documented as well as those along the supposed line of fracture, between the Italian maritime republics and Fāṭimid Egypt. The stories of Western pilgrimages to the Holy Land before the Crusades and for the most part by sea are sufficient to prove that the threads between the shores of the ancient *mare nostrum*, though certainly entangled and at times worn thin by the *jihād* and piracy on both sides, were never completely broken.

Contrary to the rigid dichotomy of Pirenne's thesis, contacts between Christendom, mutilated and restricted, and Islam, the invader in the Mediterranean area, appear to have been frequent and fruitful. They developed in a triangular relation, both from the point of view of geography and of civilization; opposed to the new Muslim power established in Syria, in Africa, and in Spain, there was on the one hand ancient Byzantium, with its Greco-Roman and Christian heritage, and on the other the Latin West, with the Italian peninsula and its islands, and France, now become a frontier facing Andalusian Islam. It was by these three routes that the 'legacy' of medieval Islamic civilization filtered into and penetrated the West.

The Byzantine power, by land and sea, was the greatest force with which the Arabs had to contend on the shores of the Mediterranean, and Byzantium itself, in the first, purely Arab phase of Islamic expansion, was its most cherished goal, the principal adversary and at the same time the model more or less consciously imitated by the young Muslim state. Here perhaps, rather than the legacy transmitted by Islam, we should speak of the legacy received by it, by contact with this Empire which to us is a part of the East but which for the East was rather the advance-point and guardian of the West. Rapidly despoiled of its provinces of Palestine, Syria, and Egypt and then, bit by bit, of northern Africa, Byzantium succeeded in halting the Arab advance at the Amanus Mountain and the Taurus ridge, and for several centuries kept Asia Minor within the boundaries of Christendom, although the Arabs were raiding it as far as the Sea of Marmara and the capital itself. The attempted siege and capture of Constantinople by the Arabs failed on three occasions, and after the last effort at the end of the eighth century it was no longer a question of a direct Arab danger to the capital itself but of frontier wars between Asia Minor, Mesopotamia, and Syria, and of naval strife for the supremacy in the Mediterranean. The former dragged on throughout the ninth and tenth centuries and for a time led to a partial and transient Byzantine reconquest of Syria, but in practice left the adversaries in their original positions until the Arabs, exhausted as a political force, were replaced by the Seljuq Turks who resumed the Muslim advance in Asia Minor. At sea also, from the Arab victory of Phoenix (655) until the total elimination of Byzantium from the central Mediterranean in the eleventh century, the struggle continued with supremacy alternating between Arabs and Byzantines without either side ever achieving a definite superiority. In the eastern Mediterranean, then, a part of its coasts became permanently Muslim whereas another part remained Greek and Christian for several centuries; but, as we have said, the presence of Byzantium did not make itself felt by arms alone. A feeling of inferiority, of admiration, and a desire to emulate the Byzantine empire in the administrative and social field, in ceremonial and in art, had been apparent from the start; despite the arrogance of the new faith, the Muslim Arabs of Syria, the Caliphs included, looked on Byzantium somewhat as their co-nationals, the Ghassānids, the *phylarch*s in Byzantine pay on the boundaries of the Empire in the fifth and sixth centuries, had done. Only towards the close of the Umayyad dynasty, according to a recent appraisal, did this attraction begin to diminish, and the Caliphate shift its centre of gravity eastward, anticipating that change of political orientation which the ʿAbbāsid revolution was to sanction a little later. Before then, in addition to the frontier wars, there were embassies and trade missions between the Muslim and Byzantine states, with all their correlative artistic and cultural influences, which ran from the Bosphorus to Syria and vice versa.[1] The Arab administration in Syria was at first only a continuation, and then an imitation, of the Byzantine one, arabizing the language, the currency, and the protocol. Even when the Empire of the Caliphs disintegrated and was succeeded by minor states and dynasties, the Byzantine model continued to exercise its fascination on them, as on the Fāṭimid Empire of Egypt. The distant inheritance of Rome and the Christian-Oriental majesty of the capital on the Bosphorus imposed itself upon their greatest adversaries with an influence which one can trace more and more tenuously until after the year 1000.

What could Muslim civilization, once formed, hand on to that part of the Eastern Empire which had remained non-Muslim? Contacts between Byzantine and Islamic theological thinking were many times indicated, but the direction which these influences took is often problematic, as in the controversy over images where it is doubtful whether iconoclasm re-echoed and accentuated the well-known Semitic aversion to figural representations of living beings. In the field of literature also, the border wars between the eighth and tenth centuries undoubtedly provided for both sides the occasion and the historical basis for the 'Akritic' poems and songs among the Byzantines, and the celebratory poems of court poets and the popular romances of al-Baṭṭāl and ʿUmar al-Nuʿmān among the Arabs; yet one perceives clearly an osmosis of motives and a historical interlocking

[1] H. A. R. Gibb, 'Arab-Byzantine Relations under the Umayyad Caliphate', *Dumbarton Oaks Papers*, xii (1958), 219–33.

between these two forms, the epic lyric and narrative, without being able decisively and unambiguously to affirm the direction.[1] Mythical and gnomic material of ancient Oriental origin certainly passed from the Arabs to the Byzantines, as proved by the fortunes of the *Kalīla wa-Dimna* and the *Sindibād*, where the direction from East to West is beyond doubt; but as regards refined literature, courtly and religious art, and science, the debt of Islam to Byzantium or, if you prefer, to the Greek influence through the mediation of Greeks and Syrians, former Byzantine citizens, is greater than anything Islam could offer in exchange.

Traces of the Arab diaspora in a Greek land which was only transiently in the power of the Arabs, or was never so, have been revealed by recent researches in what had been the heartland of ancient Hellenic civilization, which had declined under the Eastern Empire to a miserable provincial existence. The patient investigations of Miles have discovered these traces of former Arab dominion or influence in the Aegean basin and in Greece proper; in Crete, which was for almost a century and a half (827–961) the seat of an emirate; in the movement back across the Mediterranean of Arabs from Spain; in Attica and Euboea, at Corinth and even at Athens, where numismatic and to a lesser extent epigraphic finds testify to the presence or the passage of the Arabs in the early Middle Ages.[2] As an Arab mosque rose for a time on the shores of the Bosphorus in a suburb of Constantinople—allegedly a record of the unsuccessful siege by Maslama in 717–18—and another for some time at Reggio on the contested Italian mainland, so also it seems that in Athens itself, at the foot of the Acropolis, the Semitic Allah was adored for a time, as may be inferred from a Kufic inscription found during excavations of the Agora.[3]

[1] H. Grégoire and R. Goossens, 'Byzantinisches Epos und arabischer Ritterroman', *Zeitschrift der deutschen Morgenländischen Gesellschaft*, N.F. xiii (1934), 213–32.

[2] G. C. Miles, 'The Circulation of Islamic Coinage of the 8th–12th Centuries in Greece', *Atti del Congresso Internazionale di Numismatica* (Rome, 1961), ii. 485–98.

[3] Idem, 'The Arab Mosque in Athens', *Hesperis*, xxv (1956), 329–44.

If no epigraphic or architectural traces of Arab dominion seem till now to have been found in Crete, Islamic ornamental motifs, authentic or imitative and counterfeit, flourished in many parts of Greece and, as Miles points out, are more abundant in the period after the Arab rule in Crete; at Athens and in Attica, at Corinth, in Phocis, and in Laconia, remains—sometimes minimal—of archaic Muslim art have been found by the sagacious eye of the modern scholar; not to speak of the considerable numismatic harvest, which, naturally, besides lasting settlements, as with the currency of the emirs of Crete, is to be explained by trade relations, and sometimes also by chance visits, especially in the times of the Crusades.

For this eastern part of the Mediterranean, the relations between Islam and the West may, therefore, be thus summarized: the violent conquest and fairly rapid assimilation of some lands, not without very many cultural elements of the conquered becoming part of the intellectual patrimony of the conquerors. A direct centuries-long contact along a shifting frontier, crossed in both directions by wars and forays, and therefore fruitful in meetings which are reflected on both sides in popular literature. Elastic resistance and invincible survival in the heart of the Eastern Empire, which the Arab assault, with all its initial impetus, did not succeed in eliminating, showing the balance of the two opposing forces, neither of which ever succeeded in paralysing or eliminating its adversary. Meanwhile, notwithstanding the wars by land and sea, instead of the paralysis which Pirenne discerned, an intense interchange of trade and in a lesser degree of cultural benefits, which have left to us tenuous but still distinguishable traces. Such traces are of quite different degree and importance when we pass to the central Mediterranean, to Sicily and Italy.

In the central Mediterranean the settlement of Islam during the early Middle Ages was partial, and shorter than in the Iberian Peninsula, but longer and more fruitful than in isolated points in Greece and the Aegean. It is, however, necessary to make a distinction between the Italian mainland, where (with the exception of two ephemeral Arab emirates at Bari and Taranto in the second half of the ninth century) there was never stable Muslim rule, and Sicily, where political and religious domination lasted more than two centuries or three centuries if you add (and culturally it must be added) the Norman period. The Arabs took more than seventy years (827–902) to make themselves complete masters of Sicily and about thirty years (1060–1090) to lose it. In the 150 years of uncontested rule, and also naturally in the two long periods of conquest and retreat, they had time to make the island entirely a *Dār al-Islām*, a territory entirely Muslim, which does not mean entirely inhabited by Muslims. Christianity was never totally extinguished in Sicily but was considered a tolerated cult of the *Dhimmī*s, according to the classic conception of Muslim law. The Muslims were the dominant class, the warriors and landowners, merchants and artisans. Even though the internal history of the island under Muslim rule is, save for Palermo, little known, we can follow in the main the varied intensity of Islamization, almost total in the western zone and lessening little by little in the eastern zone, where the Greco-Christian element maintained itself more tenaciously. By an analogous process, after the Norman conquest Islam was more rapidly extinguished in the eastern regions of the island but held out in the west for the whole of the twelfth century, disappearing only in the first decades of the thirteenth with the final revolts and deportations under Frederick II.

The ethnic element which came with the expedition of Asad b. al-Furāt and that which followed, little by little, in its wake was of western Arabs, mainly from present-day Tunisia but, as is the regular phenomenon in all islamized North Africa, with a strong admixture of Berbers. The ethnic basis of the conquerors was therefore Arabo-Berber, as was their contribution to the preceding strata of the Sicilian population, indigenous, Punic, Greek, and Latin. This ethnic component is clearly recognizable today, a thousand years later, though thinned and modified by successive contributions and crosses. As to the characteristics of Arabo-Islamic rule in Sicily and the traces of it left to us, we note above all that it was a marginal, we could even say provincial, form of Maghribī Arabism and was regarded with a certain disdain by travellers like Ibn Ḥawqal (tenth century), accustomed to the cosmopolitanism of the Muslim world.[1] Looked at, however, with Western and Italian eyes (we are thinking primarily of its greatest historian, M. Amari) it appears positive and beneficial because of the influx of new blood which suffused the depressed ethnic structure of Byzantine Sicily and above all for the changes introduced in the economic and social conditions of the island, where it broke up the latifundia, promoted small-scale holdings, and revived and enriched Sicilian agriculture with new techniques and cultures. The decisive importance of the Arab period in this field is proved by the vocabulary of economic life, preserved in Sicilian and transferred also to Italian, which in great part refers to the agricultural sphere, to irrigation, to farm and household implements, and to products of the soil.[2] Arab historians and travellers of the time describe the island as rich in waters and woods (whence was drawn the timber for the Arab navies of the central Mediterranean), blossoming with fruits and harvests. There was a shortage of olives (Sicily imported oil from Africa) and of vines, but on the other hand cotton, hemp, and vegetables were abundant. It was probably in the Muslim period that the cultivation of citrus fruits (still today a pillar of Sicilian economy), sugar-cane, palms, and mulberries was begun. As for the cultivation of cotton, it seems to have been continued as long as the influence of the material civilization of the Arabs lasted, disappearing in the fourteenth century, but surviving in Malta, Stromboli, and Pantelleria. The most famous descriptions of Arab Sicily, from which much

[1] F. Gabrieli, 'Ibn Ḥawqal e gli Arabi di Sicilia', *Rivista Studi Orientali*, xxxv (1961), 245–53.

[2] See, on this and other similar points touched on concerning linguistics in this chapter, G. B. Pellegrini, 'L'elemento arabo nelle lingue neolatine, con particolare riguardo all'Italia', in *Settimane di studio del Centro Italiano di studi sull'Alto Medioevo XII, L'Occidente e l'Islam nell'Alto Medioevo* (Spoleto, 1965), ii. 697–790.

information on such cultures may be inferred, date in fact from Norman times (Idrīsī and Ibn Jubayr) but substantially reflect the conditions of the preceding Muslim rule. On the other hand, it was just in this period that the retrograde process began of restoring the great landowning properties, with the reconstitution of the great ecclesiastical patrimonies, enriched by the piety and policy of the kings, and the appearance of feudalism which was to exercise so inauspicious an influence on the social and economic life of the succeeding periods. It is to this Arabo-Norman period that we owe our most ancient documentation of the bilingual Arabo-Greek charters, wherein we see reflected the obscure and tenacious toil of the Muslim peasants of Sicily and the retrogression, already begun, towards types of agricultural economy both socially and technically inferior. The Arab period remains in fact the highest point attained by the great Mediterranean island as regards the exploitation of its resources and the material life connected with it.

Little evidence of spiritual life, culture, and art during the period of purely Arab rule in Sicily, and that indirect only, has been preserved; almost all contemporary monuments and documents have perished and almost all the documents which we still have date back to the splendid Norman period. It is certain, however, that Muslim Sicily took part—we do not know with what local characteristics—in the general intellectual life of Islam and, in particular, of Maghribī Islam. The study of law, theology, philology, and grammar flourished there; poetry blossomed at the Kalbī court of Palermo and around the small local emirs, as we know in general and would know better if there had been preserved for us the relevant anthology of the Sicilian philologist Ibn al-Qaṭṭāʿ, who later emigrated and died in Egypt.[1] Judging from what has survived from the eleventh century, this poetry was classical in language, metre, and form, and no trace remains of popular linguistic forms and metres similar to those which were

[1] U. Rizzitano, 'Notizie biobibliografiche su Ibn al-Qaṭṭāʿ "il siciliano"', *Rendiconti Lincei*, ser. 8, ix (1954), 260–94.

at the same time developing in Muslim Spain; this does not necessarily mean that they did not also exist in Sicily. The greatest Arabo-Sicilian poet, Ibn Ḥamdīs (d. 1133), linked in his wandering life his homeland with Andalusia, the greatest centre of Arab poetry in the West, to whose literary fashions Sicily appears to have been tributary. But the last efflorescence of Arab poetry and of the Arab language itself, of which some brilliant essays remain, took place in the island under the Norman kings, whose enlightened policy of tolerance and cultural syncretism is well known. Later, with the coming of the German dynasty, Sicilian Arabism collapsed rapidly, to be followed shortly afterwards by the *Contrasto* of Celo d'Alcamo and the school of poetry which took its name from regal Sicily, the first voices of Italian poetry in the vulgar tongue. It has been suggested, but not so far proved, that there might be some subterranean link between the last manifestations of Arabo-Islamic spiritual life on the island with these first fruits of lyrical romance on Italian soil. Whether these traces of the civilization of Islam have been entirely erased or live again concealed in new forms, is still a subject of discussion among scholars.

Glorious and evident, however, are the remains of Muslim figurative art in the island, even if, as we have said, they belong to a period and an environment no longer purely Islamic. From the wholly Islamic period there survive only the half-destroyed baths of Cefalà near Palermo and a few coins and inscriptions; but the Arabo-Norman monuments of world fame (the Cappella Palatina with its ceiling entirely decorated by Muslim artists, perhaps from Egypt; the palaces of Zisa and Cuba; and the remaining architecture of this period in Palermo and elsewhere) unmistakably preserve, as will be shown more fully later, the record of their association with the Arab art of the West. To conclude these brief comments on the 'legacy' of Islam in Sicily, over and above every romantic idealization, we cannot fail to note its multiple presence (especially noticeable today in personal and geographic names) and the comprehensiveness of its influence. A dispassionate analysis of the customs and of the individual and collective psychology of Sicilian people today could lead us back to the Arab inheritance, even in some less positive aspects. But the balance of the economic, social, and cultural history of the Muslim period is largely to its credit.

A different argument must be put forward for mainland Italy, which in varying degree also experienced the diffusion of Islam in the Mediterranean. Here it never succeeded in establishing permanent settlements, save for the two small and short-lived Arab emirates in Apulia to which we have already referred. The Straits of Messina were, however, several times crossed by the Arabs of Sicily and all the Italian coasts were exposed, in the ninth and tenth centuries, to the attacks of the corsairs (it is enough to recall the sack of the basilicas of St. Peter and St. Paul in Rome in 846 and the battle of Ostia in 849); but as in France, the Muslim forays never managed to transform themselves into a stable rule. Therefore southern Italy knew the 'Saracens' only as a permanent source of disorders, raids, and incursions for the whole of these two centuries and a disturbing factor in the internal struggles of the south. Longobards, Byzantines, and the maritime republics allied alternately with each other and with the Muslims, squeezing profit and booty from one and all. The harmful influence of the Saracens in southern Italy has already been several times underlined in Italian historiography, from Amari to Schipa, and only recently has a scholar tried to revise the traditional judgement, dropping its 'risorgimento' outlook and seeking some positive factor of the Arab presence among the contending forces.[1] Even admitting such a reassessment, the fruitfulness of the effects of Arab penetration on the Italian mainland is considerably less than that of Arab rule in Sicily. In Italy, the Arabs never had time to organize a more stable and well-ordered life than that of war and plunder (bands in the service of the Longobard princes, the colony of the Garigliano) and therefore the early Middle Ages in Italy suffered only the destructive influences of the *jihād*. Culture, science, and art did not come with these barbarian raiders, who remained a foreign body in the social structure of the Italian south,

[1] G. Musca, *L'Emirato di Bari (847–871)* (2nd edn., Bari, 1964).

to be expelled from it as quickly as possible. Nor was any benefit of civilization brought to Italy by that other wave of Arabo-Islamic invaders which, especially in the ninth century, descending from the Alps devastated Piedmont and Liguria many times, sometimes penetrating as far as the Po valley.

None the less, elements of Muslim material culture, science, and art were to reach medieval Italy, especially southern Italy, by other routes. Rather than through destructive forays, these elements came through commerce (the coexistence of both these aspects, contrary to the Pirenne thesis, is certain, although it cannot be sufficiently attested for this period), by the enterprise of individual travellers and learned men, and a little later through the great cultural transmigration from Muslim Spain. Travellers like Ibn Ḥawqal speak of trade exchanges in the early Middle Ages with the maritime republics of Campania and we have reports on Italian commercial depots in the East, for example the Amalfitans in Fāṭimid Egypt.[1] Well-known examples of 'Arab elements' in the art of southern Italy are the monuments of Salerno, Amalfi, Canosa di Puglia, and the presence of numerous works of the minor Muslim arts in the church treasuries not only of the south but also of central Italy (Lazio, the Marches, Tuscany). Finally the work of the translators, amongst whom stands out the mysterious figure of Constantinus Africanus,[2] began to reveal to Latin culture in Italy the fruits of Arab medical science and pharmacology up to the second half of the eleventh century, that is before the flow of Islamic science to Europe through Spain. Once this last route was opened, Arab science and philosophy (and also, as has recently been proved, notions of popular Muslim eschatology and piety) crossed the Pyrenees into France and Italy, and perhaps also began to exert an influence even on masterpieces of Western thought and art. But let it be clear: the best and greatest part of all that

[1] Cl. Cahen, 'Un texte peu connu relatif au commerce oriental d'Amalfi au X siècle', *Archivio Storico per le Province Napoletane*, N.S. xxxiv (1954).

[2] F. Gabrieli, 'La Cultura araba e la scuola medica salernitana', *Rivista di studi Salernitani*, i (1968), 7–21.

reached Italy after the year 1000 came not directly from the East, but from its cultural bridgehead in the Iberian Peninsula, and is thus a radiation of its legacy by that route.

A summary of Arab influences on the Italian civilization of the Middle Ages through all these channels is provided by the Arab linguistic material which has penetrated into Italian. This has often been treated in a dilettante manner, and only recently with scientific rigour. The systematic survey of this linguistic element now being made is, according to the most qualified student of it today, G. B. Pellegrini, 'centred on trade exchanges, the vocabulary of the customs-house, and of the products imported from the Maghrib and the East'. Terms like *dogana* (customs, customs-house) and *magazzino*, *maona* (a trade society), and *moatra* (a kind of loan with interest), names of coins (*tari*), measures (*rubbio*), receptacles (*caraffa*, *giara*, *ziro*), materials and articles of clothing (*giubba*, *caffettano*, *borzacchino*, and the like) are among the most quoted examples in this field. But to this nucleus, which represents preponderantly business and trade, must be added terms referring to quite other interests: the sciences (astronomy, astrology, mathematics), chemistry, pharmacology, and medicine, the techniques of art, and philosophy. The variety and abundance of such loan-words, which cover so large a part of the material and intellectual life of the Mediterranean, certainly cannot be linked with the activities of the Arab raiders and plunderers in the Mezzogiorno, who were not always of Sicilian origin, so that a great part of these loans cannot be considered of specific Arabo-Sicilian origin. In their twofold current of learned terms and words relating to trade and everyday life, they correspond well to the two main currents of Italian contacts with the world of Mediterranean Islam: scientific study and book-learning, and the lively world of practical activities, both rich in results even if not comparable either in extent or in quality with the fruits of the Andalusian encounter.

It was in the Iberian Peninsula that the most brilliant and fruitful contact between Islam and nascent European civilization developed over the course of seven centuries. Here, more than in any other Mediterranean land, the Arab settlement and the dominance of their faith had time and means to infiltrate the pre-existent ethnic, social, and cultural structure and, on their eventual withdrawal, to leave it greatly modified. Whereas in the Aegean the passage of the Arabs was only an episode, and in Sicily a parenthesis in the course of its Greco-Latin history, in Spain the Arab component remained a basic element in the appearance and destiny of the country, far beyond the material presence of the Arabs and of Islam on its soil. The awareness and assessment of this component in themselves form a chapter of modern Spanish historiography, and if the two greatest present-day investigators in this field, A. Castro and Cl. Sánchez Albornoz, seem to reflect two opposing theses (the former positive, albeit with considerable reservations, and the latter, all things considered, negative) concerning the role of the Arab period in the history of Spain, the two positions converge on the capital importance of this period in the subsequent events in the country. According to Castro, who considers the Visigothic era as alien and intrusive to the authentic Iberian tradition, the Spanish nation was born of the crossing of the Arabs (and Jews) with the indigenous element, and the history, the customs, the psychology, and the faith of the future Spain were totally conditioned, as effect or reaction, by such a crossing and development. Sánchez Albornoz, however, considers the Arabs and Islam as a disturbing and on the whole inauspicious factor, which deflected Spain from the evolution of the Roman heritage known to the other Latin nations and which imprinted on the Spanish character certain negative characteristics (religious fanaticism and intolerance, supreme ecclesiastical power, regal absolutism, and isolation from the rest of Europe), the effects of which are felt even today. But whether this Arabo-Islamic influence on Spain be considered as positive or negative, fundamental or intrusive, the opposing theses agree in recognizing its scale and decisive importance for the destinies of Spain, as also for the whole of Western Europe.

Spanish Arabism itself in its great days was aware of the nature and the price of its presence on Andalusian soil, and attempted an evaluation of it. Naturally, this had for background and comparison the other regions of Muslim civilization and not, as often happens with us, the rest of Christian Europe. The 'Praise of Spanish Islam', as García Gómez has entitled the *risāla* of al-Shaqundī in praise of Andalusia (thirteenth century),[1] contains, however, elements valid also for such a comparison, elements which stand out clearly from the polemico-rhetorical content of this pleasant little work: the former power of the Umayyad Caliphate, and the holy war indefatigably pursued by it against the infidels; the splendid cultural Maecenism of the Reyes de Taifas, the prodigious flowering of literature, and the refined social life of their courts; the economic wealth of the country and the skilful exploitation of its agricultural resources, which was one of the greatest titles to the glory of Arab rule in Spain; and finally its imposing scientific production, of which the Arab author forgets what, to our eyes, forms its greatest merit, namely the continuance and propagation of ancient science, but rightly stresses the greatness of individual representatives such as Ibn Ḥazm, Ibn Zuhr, Averroes, and others. The shining picture of al-Shaqundī was, in fact, composed at a time when the destinies of Arab Islam in Spain were already waning, at first under Berber patronage and later under the Christian *Reconquista* (the author died in Seville in 1232, fifteen years before Ferdinand III wrenched it from Islam). In the light of subsequent history it reads, therefore, like a commemoration of what was already ending rather than a presage of the future. But before concerning ourselves with that future, with the *Ausklang* or *Auswirkung* of the Arab legacy in Spain when the political, religious, and cultural presence of the Arabs had declined, we should recall what that presence meant in fact: the extreme diffusion of Arabism in the West, grafted in a climate of

[1] The text in the seventeenth-century North African historian al-Maqqarī, *Nafḥ al-ṭīb* (new edition, Damascus, 1968), ii. 126–50, tr. E. García Gómez, *Elogio del Islam español* (Madrid–Granada, 1934).

relative tolerance and cultural osmosis on to the remains of Iberian Latinity, scarcely grazed by Visigothic rule, and Western Christendom. There were two centuries of rising political fortunes culminating in the great era of ʿAbd al-Raḥmān III, of al-Ḥakam II, and of Almanzor; a century of political crumbling and of wonderful literary and artistic exuberance; a final century of Berber supremacy (Almoravids and Almohads) and of fervid scientific mediation with Christian Europe. Then, after the thirteenth century, which saw the decline of Islam over a great part of the Peninsula, there was the long epilogue in its last bastion of Granada. And, finally, the 'Moor's Lament', the cross on the Alhambra and the age-long agony of the Moriscos until their final expulsion in 1609. Taking for granted here the general lines of the *histoire événementielle* of all this period, we must stress two or three points fundamental for the assessment of the Arabo-Islamic achievement in this part of the Mediterranean and in Europe as a whole. First of all there was the speed and completeness of the conquest of al-Andalus, where the first invaders, under Tāriq and Mūsā, reached the extreme northern limits at which stable Arab settlement stopped in barely three years, though they even passed these limits later in a thrust beyond the Cantabrian mountains. But these areas of the extreme north were only touched, never firmly held, and the frontier between Muslims and Christians was farther to the south, between the Douro and the Ebro until, in the eleventh century, it was gradually overrun by the *Reconquista*. Was it intention, necessity, or chance that halted the Arabs at these precarious frontiers and prevented them assuming total dominion over the peninsula? The same question arises for the prosecution of the Arab offensive in Europe, beyond the chain of the Pyrenees, in France (Roussillon and Septimania, Provence and Dauphiné), and beyond the Alps in Switzerland and northern Italy. The reason seems to be that the military and demographic power of the Arabs to transform these raids into stable conquests was insufficient, and the dangerous extension of their lines of communication by land from their Iberian and African bases prevented any organic plan for eventual expansion. This was left to the individual initiative of predatory groups which lacked the reinforcements and supplies to hold permanently the plundered lands. Covadonga and Poitiers are, in this context, just the undertow of the wave which, in the opening years of the ninth century, caused the abandonment to the Christian kingdoms of the lands beyond the Douro and the Ebro (Asturias and Leon, Navarre and Catalonia), so many times penetrated by raids but never again held under stable rule.

Within these confines, in the ninth and tenth centuries, arose the great Umayyad state, the greatest political formation for that epoch of the western Arabs and, at the same time, a decisive factor in the balance of the western Mediterranean.[1] Renouncing more or less consciously any final thrust beyond the Cantabrian mountains and the Pyrenees, the Umayyads of Spain centred their foreign policy on supremacy over the African coasts and the command of the seas; that is to say, they limited their task as an advance-guard against Christendom to the periodic guerrilla warfare of the *jihād* and limited their imperialism to lands already permanently won for Islam. Their long maritime duel with the rival Fāṭimids of Egypt was a salient feature, and the Umayyads preferred to seek agreements and alliances with the maritime power of the eastern Mediterranean, Byzantium, partly because of the struggle against their common enemy, the ʿAbbāsids. All these great plans collapsed after the internal crisis of the Caliphate of Cordova, which came soon after the period of its greatest splendour in the first years of the eleventh century. Thenceforward, the axis of Islamic power in the West shifted from Spain to Africa, and the empires which arose there occupied and took under their control as a dependent state the Andalus that had for a time dreamed of subjugating the African coast. Once the ephemeral Umayyad

[1] E. García Gómez, *La trayectoria omeya y la civilización de Córdoba*, as an introduction to the Spanish version (Madrid, 1950) of the *Histoire de l'Espagne musulmane* of Lévi-Provençal (see bibliography), the most acute and brilliant synthesis of the historical role of the Umayyads of Spain.

thalassocracy had disappeared, nothing remained to Islamic Andalus save the more modest task of maintaining a holy corsair war in the western Mediterranean (the expeditions of Mugetto against the Balearic islands and Sardinia), against which the Italian maritime republics were able to hold their own. Looking forward to the later Middle Ages, the political and military relations between Islam and Christendom in this part of the Mediterranean were restricted to local actions between these Tyrrhenian merchant republics (to which was added in the twelfth century the Norman kingdom of Sicily) and the Muslim coastal dynasties of north Africa (Zīrids, Almohads, and their successors); while in the Iberian Peninsula the impetus of Islam little by little slowed down and diminished under the increasing Christian pressure. From the thirteenth to the fifteenth century the long survival of the kingdom of Granada had become an internal affair of Spain and what remained of Islam in Europe fought without hope its last defensive battle.

Over so long a period and over a territory covering three-quarters of the Iberian Peninsula, it is no cause for wonder that Islam and Arabism established firm and deep roots; but, as in the more restricted field of Sicily, neither the faith nor the race nor the language of the conquerors entirely supplanted those of the conquered, and it was just from this coexistence and mingling that the composite and extraordinarily fecund character of Arabo-Spanish civilization was born. Ethnically, many waves of Arabs and Berbers poured into al-Andalus in the eighth century, but they were not isolated there and very soon mingled with the indigenous population, Visigothic and Ibero-Latin. Their racial purity (they belonged in any case to two very distinct races) was rapidly lost, as appears from the physical appearance, in the descriptions of the chroniclers, of certain princes of the Umayyad dynasty itself, far from pure Arab types; Latin blood, and also Germanic and Nordic, was quickly crossed with Arab and African in the society of Arab Spain, producing a mixed type with Oriental, African, and European traits. The religion of Arabia, which the invaders brought with them into the Peninsula, was rapidly diffused as in every other land of the diaspora, and quickly became dominant but not exclusive. Alongside the Islam of the foreign conquerors and of the natives won over to it (the *muwalladūn*), the Christian religion, which in Spain had already developed its own religious and cultural festivals, its special rites, its writers, and its saints, was tolerated, in a position of inferiority but with full legal status. This Christianity, it is true, was very rapidly arabized linguistically and culturally, and an Arabic word (*mustaʿriba*, *mozarabes*), designated those natives who had remained faithful to the religion of their fathers under Muslim rule, but who became arabophone or at least bilingual.[1] This linguistic duplication, even multiplication, is another of the characteristic aspects of Arab Spain. It has now been confirmed that the Arabic of the rulers, in the purity of the classical and learned language and in the spoken dialect, always coexisted with the Latin, more or less barbarized, of the Church and of official documents among the Christians, and the new-born Romance languages. Of this variety there is abundant evidence from the early centuries of Arab rule and these documents gradually increase in number becoming important also, as we shall see, for their literary value. Culturally, the superiority of the foreign rulers rapidly asserted itself and the impoverished Latinity of the Peninsula bowed in admiration to their science, literature, and poetry; in the ninth century the testimony of Alvarus of Cordova is well known. In this, he laments the 'arabizing' fashion of the Christian intellectuals of his time, the passion with which Arab letters were studied and imitated to the detriment of the Holy Scriptures and the Latin authors. This Arabic culture came to al-Andalus in great part from the Orient, because of the efflorescence in the ninth and tenth centuries of the great ʿAbbāsid culture in Iraq, of which Spain, politically the rival, was culturally the tributary; but it was not long before specifically Maghribī and Andalusian seeds began to sprout and it was just

[1] G. Levi Della Vida, 'I Mozarabi tra Occidente e Islam', *Settimane di studio del Centro Italiano* . . . (1965), ii. 667–95.

these which were to be congenially gathered and transplanted in Romance surroundings.

A deep linguistic imprint, above all in the vocabulary, is even today the most conspicuous trace of these seven centuries of the Arab presence in the Peninsula. It covers the most varied aspects of life, from agriculture to the arts and crafts, from trade to administration, from war to science. From the spheres of religion, administration, and crafts come words like: *mezquita*, *almirante*, *alcalde*, *alguacil*, *almojarife*, *zalmedina*, *zabazoque*, *almotacén*, *alfaquí* (Arabic: *al-faqīh*), *alfaquim* (Arabic: *al-ḥakīm*), *alhagib*, *alatat*, *alcahuete*, etc. Examples of military terms, widely diffused considering the endemic state of war with the Christians, include: *aceifa*, *algarada*, *adalid*, *arraez*, *alcaide*, *rehen*, *atalaya*, *alarde*, *rebate*, *alcázar*, *alcazaba*, *añafil*, *arriaz*, *alfaraz*, *jinete*, *almofre*, *adarga*, and very many others, some of them archaic and out of use, others still very much alive. Commercial terminology provides: *aduana*, *almacén*, *tarifa*, *zoco*, *almoneda*, *atijara*; weights, measures, and currency: *arroba*, *cahiz*, *fanega*, *almud*, *adarme*, *arrelde*, *ceca*, *maravedí*, *metical*, and so forth. Names of minerals and products of Arab origin are also frequent, such as: *azogue*, *albayalde*, *marfil*, *alcanfor*, *alkohol*, *annofaz*, *rejalgar*, *algalia*, *almizque*, *aceche*; names of garments and stuffs of eastern provenance, such as: *aljuba*, *albornoz*, *zaraguelles*, *alquinal*, and the word for the tailor himself, *alfayate*; but rich above all is the Arab element in the vocabulary of agriculture and irrigation (*acequia*, *noria*, *azud*, *arcaduz*, *aljibe*, *alberca*, *acena*, *tahona*, *almazara*, *almunia*), in part also common to Sicily, a living testimony to the high technical level reached by the Arabs, and of the great importance of agriculture in the economy and social life of these lands. There are also in Spanish very many names of plants, fruits, and vegetables which are Arabic in origin, such as: *alcachofa*, *arroz*, *naranja*, *limón*, *azafrán*, *azucar*, *aciete*, *toronja*, *berengena*, *albericoque*, *arrayán*, *azucena*, *alhucema*, *adelfa*, and many others. Among animals we find the *adive*, the *alcotán*, the *alforre*, and the *alacrán*. Among domestic terms are: *jarra*, *taza*, *alcuza*, *alcolla*, *alfombra*, *alifafe*, *almadraque*, *azote*, *alhaja*, etc. Particularly rich is the terminology referring to housing in general and the technique of architecture: *aldea*, *arrabal*, *barrio*, *albañil*, *alarife*, *alfoz*, *azotea*, *alcoba*, *zaguán*, *azulejo*, *abode*, and many other similar terms, while names of games (*aljedrez*) and of musical instruments (*laúd*, *atabal*, *adufe*) afford a glimpse of joyous court life.[1]

Another, and considerable, linguistic thread flourishes in Spanish place-names, even today very frequently compounded with Arabic elements; often it is a question of compounds with current common terms: *qalʿa*, *wādī*, *manzil*, *qaṣr*, *rabaḍ*, *rābiṭa*, easily recognizable even to the layman in place-names like Alcalá, Alcolea, Calatayud, Calatrava, Guadalquivir, Guadarrama, Alcázar, Arrabal, Rabida, and so on. In other cases the phonetic and semantic transformation is less immediately discernible to one who has not a wide familiarity with the Arabic vocabulary and with the rules of Ibero-Arabic phonetics, laid down scientifically by Lopes and by Steiger;[2] it is enough to say here that in addition to the classic work of Dozy-Engelmann on Arab vocables which have entered the Iberian languages, Asín has been able to devote an entire volume to Arabo-Spanish place-names, including more than 1,000 which have been explained and several hundreds which are uncertain.[3] Nor, alongside the direct linguistic transformations, should the semantic and phraseological models (*calques*) be forgotten, in which Arab morphology appears materially transposed into Romance, retracing the mental process or the image which governs it; a typical but by no means certain example would be the famous *hidalgo*, which, according to such Arab derivation, would have to be retraced to the Arabic *ibn* (that is *ṣāḥib*) *māl* in the sense of 'a man endowed with goods, i.e. a rich man'. Castro

[1] Dozy-Engelmann, *Glossaire des mots espagnols et portugais dérivés de l'arabe* (Leiden-Paris, 1869); Pellegrini, 'L'Elemento arabo . . .', pp. 705-19.

[2] D. Lopes, 'Toponimia arabe de Portugal', *Revue Hispanique*, ix (1902); A. Steiger, *Contribución a la fonética del hispano-árabe y de los arabismos en el ibero-románico y el siciliano* (Madrid, 1932).

[3] M. Asín Palacios, *Contribución a la Toponimia árabe de España* (Madrid-Granada, 1940).

has suggested other examples, such as *poridad* retraceable semantically to the Arabic *ikhlāṣ* in the sense of 'secret, confidence, integrity', or *vergüenza* reproducing a semantic nuance of the Arabic *ʿār*. This is a particularly delicate and conjectural field, about which it is difficult to reach conclusions of absolute certainty.

The same Castro, the Spanish historian who, without himself being an Arabist, has most perseveringly followed up and perhaps even exaggerated every trace of Arab influence in his country, has dwelt on a whole series of phenomena, of material and spiritual life, of customs and of religion, where the heritage of Islam is shown more or less clearly: from the public baths, still widely diffused in Christian Spain in the thirteenth century and then banished for moral and religious reasons, to the ritual washing of the dead; from the covering of the face by women to the habit of sitting on the floor on carpets and cushions; from formulas of knightly courtesy and hospitality which today are regarded as typically Spanish (the placing of his house 'at the disposition of the guest', the offer to others of food that a man is eating, the custom of kissing the hand), to welcomes and good wishes involving the name of God, the formulas for asking alms and for excusing a refusal, up to the predilection for Moorish dress, especially feminine, attested in the highest social circles right into the fifteenth century, that is to say when the *Reconquista* was almost totally achieved. All these factors are so many tesserae of a mosaic in which the arabization of Spanish customs appears to have been tenaciously preserved a considerable time after the decline and fall of Islamic dominion. Of the strictly literary influences we shall have more to say later, but from the external aspects of social life and customs we are recalled to the depths of the individual and collective soul by the problem of the influence of Islam on what was, and is, Christianity, its antagonist in the Iberian Peninsula: at first conquered and submissive, then starting on the long duel for recovery, and finally victorious, but marked in its turn by the rival faith with indelible stigmata.

That Spanish Catholicism represents a form of Western

Christianity *sui generis* is a fact admitted even independently of the role ascribed to it in its struggle with Islam; on the other hand, if one agrees with Castro that 'the history of Spain is essentially the history of a faith and a religious sensibility, and at the same time of the grandeur, the misery, and the paralysis aroused by it', we cannot but consider the centuries-long *Auseinandersetzung* of this faith with another rival as a fundamental element of its evolution, even of its own formation. The central position which faith has in the soul of the Spaniard, individually and socially considered, is only comparable with that of Islam in the Muslim individual and in his society; and from this central position arise analogous consequences for both of these religious confessions. The vision of *homo islamicus* has been described as theocentric and that of *homo hispanicus* is also theocentric (we are speaking, naturally, of traditional Islam and Spain, before the modern revolutions), and if it is admitted that the latter was born out of contact with, and in contrast to, the former, one cannot but agree once more with Castro that 'from the ninth century to the seventeenth, the axis of Hispanic history, of what there was in it of the affirmative, the original, and the grandiose, was an ultra-mundane belief that emerged as a heroic reply to another, hostile belief . . .'.[1] In this bond of cause and effect between Islam and subsequent Spanish history, even those who assess it differently, such as Sanchez Albornoz, agree. It is now a question of referring to some of its main manifestations.

The Apostle James and his shrine in Galicia glitter at the head of Spanish Christianity in the Middle Ages. We do not know if there are any traces of such a cult previous to the Muslim invasion, but it was certainly the Muslim invasion which gave it vitality and gave it the aspect of a palladium and shield of the Christian faith in the Iberian Peninsula. As at one time the Dioscuri were seen in ancient Rome, the companion of the Lord was seen leading the faithful to victory on his white horse, and his temple in that corner of the Peninsula appeared even to the Muslims as the symbol of

[1] A. Castro, *The Structure of Spanish History* (Princeton, 1954), p. 128.

Christian resistance. Perhaps Castro pushes his intuition too far when he considers that this figure and the function which it undoubtedly had in moulding Spanish medieval religiosity may have been an unconscious counterpart of what the Prophet was to the Muslims, but to anybody who knows the need of individuals and of 'imaginative' peoples to give themselves a concrete object of veneration and cult, closer to them than any theological abstraction, the parallel, and perhaps the interdependence, of the two phenomena appears suggestive and probable. Still more probable, and even in our opinion certain, was the influence of the Islamic idea and practice of the *jihād*, or holy war, and the correlative organization of fighting piety, with which is associated the institution of *ribāṭ* and, later, the name and movement of the Almoravids, on certain aspects of the Christian 'holy war' and the rise of the Knightly Orders of Santiago, of Calatrava, and of Alcantara, so famous in the annals of the *Reconquista*. Passing from the clash of arms to mystic contemplation, the influence of Islamic Ṣūfism (on which see below, Chapter VIII, pp. 366 ff.) on the illustrious tradition of Spanish Catholic mysticism is no longer a bold hypothesis of the dilettantes, but a phenomenon illuminated with scientific rigour by a specialist like Asín;[1] Asín's work here is considered further, below, Chapter VIII, pp. 387–8. Spanish Christianity, in fact, absorbed from the enemy faith ideas, institutions, and states of mind. Its own intrinsic impulses towards intolerance and the relentless pursuit of integralism may have been strengthened through absorption of some of these currents within Islam, although one must always remember that Islam assigned to the 'Religions of the Book', Christianity and Judaism, a definite and legally protected, if subordinate, place in the state, and only at times of stress and insecurity were there prolonged periods of rigorism and persecution. The law of Christianity, on the other hand, had no place at all for toleration of another faith; hence it passed, when victorious over Islam, very rapidly and with logical

[1] M. Asín Palacios, *Huellas del Islam* (Madrid, 1941) (Averroes and Saint Thomas, Ibn ʿAbbād of Ronda and Saint John of the Cross, etc.)

development, to intolerance and persecution; that was the lamentable religious history of Spain from the seventeenth to the nineteenth century and even beyond.

But if Islam as a religion exercised on the destinies of Spain an influence that it is hard to regard as positive, quite another judgement is needed when it comes to the cultural, literary, and artistic influences that penetrated Spanish civilization from medieval to modern times. Many of these will be considered in other chapters, but it is essential to refer to them now, above all as a part of the Mediterranean 'legacy' of Arabism, for what the Arabo-Islamic civilization bequeathed to Spain in these spheres it also bequeathed to the whole of Europe as a fruitful component of Western civilization. Spanish literature, and indeed all the literatures of the Iberian Romance tongues, was born in the centuries of the Arab presence in the Peninsula and received from it ideas, points of departure, form, and artistry about which there have been lively disputes in the past which have continued up to the present day. The epic with which Castilian literature opens, *Poema de mio Cid*, sings of an episode and an illustrious figure in the duel between Christianity and Islam, whereas among the Arabs themselves the epic, by common consent, is non-existent; however, Ribera and Menéndez Pidal have also examined this field in the Arab period and have found there traces of very ancient epic material (for example, in the story about Count Artobas) preserved in Arab historical sources, though these are probably of Romance origin. If in this case the Arabs received from the Romance source-material which they limited themselves to elaborating into a story, an influence in the opposite direction runs between the two literatures and cultures in every other field of contact, in lyrics, gnomics, apologetics, and narrative. In the lyric field, postponing for a moment the problem of eventual formal dependence, a continuity of elaborate and baroque taste seems undeniable between the court poetry of the Reyes de Taifas, descriptive and artificial, and the Castilian lyrics of the sixteenth and seventeenth centuries, of Góngora and his school. In the romances, the flower of Castilian lyrics in the fifteenth century, the Arabo-Islamic element is predominant in the double form of the *romance fronterizo*, celebrating in a series of episodes the culminating events of the *Reconquista* (*Abenámar*, *Pérdita de Antequera*, *Conquista de Alhama*, etc.), and in the *romance morisco* (the *Mora Moraima*, the famous *Tres morillas*) which introduces Muslim characters who played no part in the historical events of the time. The rival world is here more an object for representation, since we do not know of any analogous epic-lyric poetry on the Arab side, except for the isolated case of the Arab elegy for Valencia (known to us only in a Castilian version or paraphrase), a sample of what may have been the Muslim poetry concerning the struggle. But Spanish narrative, the fabulous and gnomic literature from the thirteenth century until Renaissance times and even later, is mainly of Arab origin, or at least derived through Arab sources, even if these cannot be documented by preserved texts. This can be seen from the *Conde Lucanor* of Don Juan Manuel to the *Libro de buen amor* of the Archpriest of Hita, from the apologetic works of Ramond Lull to those of the renegade Anselmo de Turmeda, from the *Historia del Caballero Cifar* to the *Criticón* of Gracián, which show the presence of Oriental sources (the *Thousand and One Nights*, *Sindibād*, the *Ḥayy ibn Yaqẓān* of Ibn Ṭufayl, on which see below, Chapter VIII, pp. 386–7, or more likely a common popular Arabic source, the *Ṭawq al-ḥamāma* of Ibn Ḥazm, and so forth). And the last echo of the Moorish tradition still vibrates in the golden century of Spanish literature in the *Cidi Hamet ben Engeli*, the alleged Muslim source of Cervantes, and in the Moorish songs of Calderón's dramas.

This great Arab literary tradition, at first based on a direct familiarity with the language, and then little by little on translations, had its greatest centre of elaboration in the reign and at the court of Alfonso the Wise (1252–84) whose noble and brilliant work was decisive for the cultural acclimatization of so great a part of the eastern patrimony in the West. The sovereign, who by his own *Cantigas* gave Iberian religious lyrics one of their most ancient monuments and by sponsoring the *Primera Crónica*

General gave so exalted an increment to Castilian historiography, also encouraged with indefatigable cultural curiosity the popularization, derived from their Arab editions, of works like the *Kalila wa-Dimna* and the *Sindibad*, which proved so fecund for subsequent Spanish narrative and gnomics. He translated, or had translated, works of science, entertainment, apologetics, and religious edification, and, among these last, that *Escala de Mahoma*, a popular sample of an Arabo-Spanish *Miʿrāj* which, in the French and Latin versions of Bonaventura of Siena, crossed the Pyrenees and introduced into France and Italy notions of Arab eschatology, which perhaps were not unknown to Dante and contributed to the structure of the *Divina Commedia* (the discovery of this translated popular source definitely belies the earlier hypothesis of Asín about Dante's contact with learned Arab sources, such as the *Risālat al-Ghufrān* of al-Maʿarrī or the mystical and theosophical works of Ibn al-ʿArabī, see a more detailed consideration of this whole topic below, Chapter VII, pp. 344–5).[1]

The attested diffusion of Islamic eschatological ideas in the Latin West in the thirteenth and fourteenth centuries (apart from the knowledge which Dante may have had of them and of which he could have made use) is one of the salient points that modern inquiries have revealed in that 'legacy' of Islam to Europe by way of Spain. Another, still greater and much discussed, is the formal and substantial influence of the Arabo-Spanish strophic poetry on the emerging Romance lyrics. This point, already hinted at in the sixteenth century by Barbieri and in the eighteenth century by Andrés, has been the centre of discussion between Arabists and Romance philologists since 1912, when Ribera, in his study of the songbook of Ibn Quzmān, drew attention to the bilingualism of Muslim Spain and to the *zajal*, that is to say a strophic poetry in popular Arabic of which Ibn Quzmān was the greatest master.[2]

[1] E. Cerulli, *Il 'Libro della Scala' e la questione delle fonti arabo-spagnole della Divinia Commedia* (Vatican, 1949), with an extensive bibliography.

[2] J. Ribera y Tarragó, *El Cancionero de Abencuzmán*, now in *Disertaciones y Opúsculos* (Madrid, 1928), i. 3–92.

His *zajal*s (then the only known instance of this style, which was later to spread both in the West and in the East) were sprinkled with Romance words, and their strophic structure, a rich combination of verse forms and rhymes, revealed surprising analogies with certain metrical schemes of the first Provençal troubadours, specifically William of Poitiers, Cercamon, and Marcabru. Ribera's thesis, of a passage 'across the Pyrenees' of such strophic schemes and of their essential element, rhyme, confirmed and historically developed the intuition of Andrés and received in its turn confirmation in the researches of the prominent Spanish Romance philologist, R. Menéndez Pidal. In his studies on *Poesía árabe y poesía europea* (in the *Bulletin Hispanique*, 1938, and in a separate volume in 1942) he extended the comparison between such a type of Arab poetry and Provençal lyrics to the whole Romance area and showed the *zajal*'s metrical scheme to be present in Gallego-Portuguese lyrics (*Cantigas de amigo*, Alfonso's *Cantigas* for the Virgin), in Castilian through the successive developments of the *villancico* and the *copla*, in ancient Italian (the Franciscan *lauda*), and in the *langue d'oil*. The 'Arab thesis' on the origins of rhyme and the early Romance metres was thus strongly established, supported by the greatest authorities of the early twentieth century in the Arabo-Andalusian and Hispanic fields; it was upheld and corroborated by Arabists like Nykl (editor of the *Dīwān* of Ibn Quzmān, and author of a popular book on Arabo-Spanish poetry and the first troubadours),[1] García Gómez, Lévi-Provençal, as well as Romance scholars like Tallgren-Tuulio and, with many nuances of reserve, Damaso Alonso, Monteverdi, and Roncaglia.[2] But from the start a more or less rigid opposition to the Arab thesis has not been absent. In the

[1] A. R. Nykl, *Hispano-Arabic Poetry and its relations with the old Provençal Troubadours* (Baltimore, 1946).

[2] E. Li Gotti, *La tesi araba sulle origini della lirica romanza* (Florence, 1955); *Oriente e Occidente nel Medio Evo* (Atti del Convegno Volta della Accademia dei Lincei, May-June 1956, Rome, 1957), pp. 294-359 (papers by García Gómez and Roncaglia on 'The Hispano-Arabic Lyrics and the emergence of Romance Lyricism', and discussions).

Romance sector Spanke, Le Gentil, and Errante have in particular opposed the arguments in favour of the Arab origin of rhyme, reaffirming the autonomous late-Latin precedents. And finally the Arabist S. M. Stern has taken a stand against the affirmed relationship of cause and effect between the popular Andalusian metrics and the lyrics of the whole Romance area, on either side of the Pyrenees.[1]

The scepticism of Stern (which in the opinion of this writer does not quite rule out the conclusions of Ribera and Menéndez Pidal, but suggests rather that they should be reconsidered) acquires greater weight as we are largely indebted to him for a discovery which has considerably advanced the study of the subject and opened up fresh perspectives on the whole literary relationship between the Arab and Romance worlds in Andalusia; we allude here to the *kharaja*s, the final strophes in a language wholly or partially Romance, tagged on to lyrical compositions in Arabic (classical or dialect) and Hebrew, these last in imitation of Arab models in the multilingual society of Muslim Spain. With the discovery of these new texts[2] this proto-Iberian Romance language which at first appeared only in isolated words in the *zajal*s of Ibn Quzmān is now found to have been more widely and organically exploited in the final verses of the *muwashshaḥāt* (strophic poetry in the classical tongue), which are themselves concentrated lyrical compositions (*cantigas de amigo* in miniature), included in the far wider structure of either Arab or Hebrew song. Are they fragments of proto-Romance lyrics in an Arab setting, picked up and inserted by the Arab or Hebrew poets in their own compositions? Or are they themselves inventions, a product of the well-known bilingualism, but always in imitation of something already pre-existent and coexistent with the Hebrew-Muslim lyrical production

[1] S. Stern, 'Esistono dei rapporti letterari tra il mondo islamico e l'Europa occidentale nell'Alto Medioevo?', *Settimane di studio del Centro Italiano* . . . (1965), ii. 639–66.

[2] Later studied mainly by García Gómez: see *Las jarchas romances de la serie árabe en su marco* (Madrid, 1965).

of Andalusia? Whatever the answer, these *kharja*s or strophic verses in Semitic tongues (the most ancient date from the tenth century) oblige one to postulate at least a coeval, germinal production in Romance, earlier than any written source previously known, among the population of Muslim Spain, which would threaten to invert once more the direction of the influence; the Arabs of Spain instead of being the inventors there of strophic and rhymed poetry would themselves have culled such forms from their Romance surroundings (there exist, moreover, precedents in the Arab East itself). That explains the general scepticism of Stern about the passage from the Arab to the Romance world of the metrical principle and of rhyme, for its appearance in an Andalusian environment can be explained as a spontaneous germination there of a general European phenomenon.

These problems are still, however, *sub judice*, and it is doubtful if it will ever be possible to reach a conclusion universally acceptable. There remains the fact that this Arab poetry of Spain, strophic and popular in appeal (different from the rigidly classical poetry of the language and metres current among the learned) offers us a clue to a linguistic and literary proto-history of Spain itself and of the whole Romance world. The Arabs either transmitted to the West this creation of theirs, or else gathered, developed, and preserved in their own local production metrical and thematic novelties which had budded in the West itself. An associated topic is the question of Arabic influences in Spanish music, and these are discussed in Chapter X (c) below, pp. 497, 504.

Also outstandingly to the credit of Arabism in Spain and its cultural diffusion throughout Europe is the transmission of Arab science and philosophy, that is to say a great part of the science and philosophy of Antiquity as inherited and elaborated by Islam. Even if it is something of an exaggeration to attribute to this Arab route the exclusive transmission of the ancient patrimony of the Latin West (there was also a direct route, by way of Byzantium, which in some cases came before and not, as has often been said, after the Arabo-Spanish transmission), it is certain that as the political power of the Arabs in Spain declined their scientific legacy to the West assumed imposing proportions. In the twelfth and thirteenth centuries, Barcelona, Toledo, and Seville, all of them then lost to Islam, became the centres of intense activity by translators, Jews, Spaniards, and Christians of other European countries. They aimed to unearth the treasures of arabized Greek knowledge, that is of the great cultural movement which took place in the ninth and tenth centuries when the ʿAbbāsid culture had appropriated, mainly through the mediation of the Syrians, a notable part of Hellenistic science and philosophy. This period of transmission of Greek culture to Islam in the early Middle Ages corresponded to an analogous transmission of culture from the Islamic to the Christian civilizations through the labours of translators on Spanish soil. It was often the fruit of a united labour, of a Jew or a Muslim convert who translated the Arab text into Romance, and of a learned Christian, Spaniard or not, who put that first literal interpretation into Latin, though it is possible that the linguistic experience thus acquired sometimes permitted the Christian translator to work directly from the Arabic version. From this activity emerged, half-way through the twelfth century, a group of translators at Toledo under the patronage, if not in a real collegiate organization, of the Archbishop Don Raimundo (1130–50);[1] apart from the Toledan Marco, this noble band counted among its leaders the famous Spanish pair Domenico Gundisalvi and John of Seville, a typical example of the collaboration referred to, and among the foreigners Robert of Retines, Adelard of Bath, Albert and Daniel Morlay, Michael Scotus, Hermann of Dalmatia, and Gerard of Cremona. Through the work of these men, and a century later of another group working at Seville around Alfonso X, the scientific works of Hippocrates, Euclid, Ptolemy, Galen, and other Greek scientists, in the Arabic translations and revisions of al-Khwārizmī, al-Battānī, al-Farghānī, Avicenna, al-Rāzī, al-Biṭrūjī, and al-Zarqālī, were made acces-

[1] A. González Palencia, *Noticias sobre don Raimundo, arzobispo de Toledo*, now in the volume *Moros y Christianos en la España medieval* (Madrid, 1945), pp. 101–76.

sible to the West. (For further details on this process of the communication of scientific knowledge see below, Chapter X (b), pp. 425–60.)[1] 'Arab science', its dependence on late-Classical and Classical science more or less clearly understood, flooded and fecundated Europe. All the centuries of the later Middle Ages were impregnated by it, even if in the fourteenth century we notice in Petrarch a reaction to the authority of the 'Arabs' in medicine and in other sciences like astrology and astronomy, in which until then they had been considered absolute masters.[2] With these vicissitudes of ancient science, transmitted to the West through Muslim Spain, were interwoven those of philosophy in that close medieval symbiosis of the two terms. The Arab–Jewish–Christian translators played some role, albeit a subordinate one, in the transmission of certain works of Aristotle's *Organon* to the West, and also in the transmission of Neo-Platonic works, the names of al-Kindī, al-Fārābī, Avicenna, and al-Ghazālī being of significance in this process. In its sunset period, Muslim Spain gave to Islamic Aristotelianism its last illustrious representative, Averroes (1126–98) (on Averroism and its influence in the West see below, Chapter VIII, pp. 357–9, 383–6). The already mentioned al-Shaqundī, referring to the works of the great Cordovan philosopher, says that Averroes disowned his own books on philosophy when he saw this science 'hated in al-Andalus' and unwelcome to his Almohad masters. In this phrasing, certainly not to be taken literally, is reflected the fate of this extreme effort of Arab speculative thought to reconcile philosophical rationalism with orthodoxy, and its defeat in the Islamic field where the achievement of Averroes remained to all intents and purposes a dead letter. His later eminence was due mainly to the labour of translators in the Christian

[1] General recapitulations are in F. Wüstenfeld, 'Die Übersetzungen arabischer Werke in das Lateinische', *Abhandl. Göttinger Gesellschaft der Wissenschaften*, xxii (1877); R. Lemay, 'Dans l'Espagne du XII siècle: les traductions de l'arabe au latin', *Annales: Economies, Sociétés, Civilisations*, xviii (1963), pp. 639–65. Individual studies exist on almost all the translators.

[2] F. Gabrieli, 'Il Petrarca e gli Arabi', *Rivista di cultura classica e mediovale*, vii (1965), 487–94.

West and the consequent spread of Averroism, the relationship of which to the original thought of Averroes, though not without some bold and indeed logical connections with the founder's authentic doctrines, was often tenuous or false. Certainly Averroes was not an impious denier of the faith, as the tradition of Averroism and even more of Latin anti-Averroism represents him; a sincere Muslim (without, in historical fact, any special anti-Christian bias) he believed that a reconciliation was possible on two distinct levels (whence the theory attributed to him of the double truth) between the sacred revelation and rational speculation, the dignity of which he felt strongly, and which he defended against the attacks of al-Ghazālī. He was the last voice of Islamic thought in the West, where it received its deepest, even if deformed, response.

With a simple reference to the artistic legacy, which is treated in detail in Chapter VI below, let us close this magnificent balance sheet of the legacy of Arabo-Spanish Islam and of its most fruitful presence on European soil. It is quite obvious that such exceptional fecundity owed much to the soil upon which the encounter took place, and to the multiplicity of the elements that existed there and which influenced one another. There was enough time for the Arabo-Berber wave to follow conquest and destruction with a stable religious, social, and cultural establishment; it absorbed and gradually amalgamated various elements of race, language, and indigenous culture, Iberian, Latin, Visigothic, and Jewish. Thence arose the fascinating syncretism of the Arabo-Hispanic civilization, which enchanted Romanticism and which cannot fail to impose itself upon the most sober modern assessment.

The presence of Islam in the Mediterranean for almost the whole of the Middle Ages was due to the Arab element, its oldest and most dynamic component. The Berbers, who were also ethnically to have great weight in the Muslim history of the Maghrib and of Spain itself, were culturally assimilated to Arabism, and after fierce initial resistance accepted and propagated the Arabic-Islamic civilization. This primacy of the first-born people began to decline in the East about the year 1000, supplanted by the Turkish element; the Crusaders no longer had to face a mainly Arab military force, but Turkish and Kurdish, and the political advancement and diffusion of Turkish power continued in the centuries after the year 1000 from the Seljuqs to the Atabegs and finally to the Ottomans. With these last began the second phase of the Islamic offensive and of Islamic imperialism in the Mediterranean.

A last Arab state, Arab if not in the blood of its sovereigns then in the language and culture of its subjects, was created in the eastern Mediterranean between the thirteenth and sixteenth centuries, the Syro-Egyptian Sultanate of the Mamlūks; while further to the west flourished the Arab-Berber states sprung from the disintegration of the Almohad Empire, Ḥafṣid in Tunis and Marīnid in Morocco, at the time when Andalusian Arabism was fighting its last hopeless defensive action. This approximate balance between Christian and Muslim states on the shores of the Mediterranean was to be broken in the fifteenth century by the Ottomans who, bursting out of Anatolia, swept away the last traces of Byzantium, dismantled the Latin outposts in the Aegean set up at the beginning of the thirteenth century, and finally permanently occupied Greece. In the early sixteenth century the Ottoman Empire took over the Mamlūk state, intensified its naval struggle against Venice, and set out to achieve if not the conquest then at least the leadership of the Maghrib. There only Morocco succeeded in preserving its original Arabo-Berber form; from Libya to present-day Algeria the Barbary States became an ethnic mixture of Arabs and Turks, with a formal dependence on Constantinople and with a strong Turkish linguistic influence. It was, in fact, the second Islamic wave under Turkish hegemony that beat upon the coasts of the Mediterranean. From its zenith in the sixteenth and seventeenth centuries, it later declined in the eighteenth and nineteenth centuries, finally to exhaust itself in the agony of 'the sick man of Europe' and the resurgence of the national states of our century.

Was there a 'legacy' of Islam from this second period and if so of what did it consist? European historiography on the Ottoman Empire has tended to reply in the negative, inspired as it has been by the principle of nationality (of which this last supranational Islamic formation was the negation), and by the corresponding principles of the modern state; only in a period very near to our own have there been the beginnings of a more balanced consideration of this phenomenon and of the positive aspects which undoubtedly exist alongside the negative ones, as is pointed out in Chapter I above, p. 61. But since this consideration is only in its infancy, and a vast amount of research remains to be done even in providing the basic corpus of information from which general conclusions may be drawn, this is hardly the time for an evaluation of this 'second legacy'. Suffice it to note that whereas in the Middle Ages Arab expansion in the Mediterranean had either confronted an empire already old, as Byzantium was, or had faced fresh forces emerging from the barbarian invasions of Europe and at a low social and cultural level, the emergence of the Ottoman Empire coincided, on the other hand, with the birth of modern Europe, the appearance of the nation state and of modern philosophical and scientific thought. What superiority the Ottoman state possessed was in the field of military organization and, initially at least, of political organization.

In the face of this new Europe, Islam in the Mamlūk and Ottoman periods was inevitably on the defensive, and Islamic modernism, the attempt to bring Islamic political and religious theory into line with modern conditions, appears only towards the end of the nineteenth century, and then in the Arab lands rather than the ethnically Turkish ones. As explained above, we simply do not have the requisite knowledge for pronouncing an informed judgement on the cultural achievements of the Islamic world in the Mamlūk and Ottoman periods. Undeniably, fields such as architecture, painting, ceramics, book-production, and carpet-making display a distinctive stylistic form and have considerable aesthetic value, as is expounded in detail in Chapter VI (c) below, where, for instance, it is noted that the late fifteenth and sixteenth centuries form a second period (the first being the eleventh to the thirteenth centuries) for cultural borrowings by the West in the sphere of the decorative arts (see pp. 301 ff.). The Arabic literature of the period has so far been little explored, but it would be strange if amongst such a vast literary production there were not some authors of lasting merit. The achievements of Persian literature at this time are better known, and a marvellously flexible and rich Ottoman language and literature emerged from the interpenetration of the native Turkish with Arabic and Persian linguistic elements. There is, indeed, much to make one suspect that the simplistic view of the period between the Mongol invasions and modern times, that of the Mamlūks and Ottomans in the Near East and that of the Ṣafavids and Moguls further east, as one of intellectual stagnation and cultural negligibleness, may no longer be tenable in the future. However, it must be conceded that the actual legacy of Islam to Europe in this second period cannot be compared with that of the first period, the essential subject of this book. It was at this later time that Renaissance and Reformation Europe was acquiring a self-awareness and an intellectual curiosity quite alien to the world of traditional Islam, itself increasingly menaced by the political and economic expansionism of the Europeans; the consequences of this for East-West relations are discussed in Chapter I above, pp. 29 ff., but the question of the cultural interaction in this period must be deferred for some future synthesis.

FRANCESCO GABRIELI

BIBLIOGRAPHY

Only works of a general nature are given here, whereas items on particular problems are mentioned in the preceding notes. On the Mediterranean in general: H. Pirenne, *Mahomet et Charlemagne* (Paris-Brussels, 1937); A. Lewis, *Naval Power and Trade in the Mediterranean, 500–1100* (Princeton, 1951); E. Eickhoff, *Seekrieg und Seepolitik zwischen Islam und Abendland* (Berlin, 1966). On Islam and Byzantium: A. Vasiliev, *Byzance et les Arabes* (French version of the Russian original) (Brussels,

1935–68). On Islam, Sicily and Italy: M. Amari, *Storia dei Musulmani di Sicilia* (2nd edn., Catania, 1933–8); U. Rizzitano, 'Gli Arabi in Italia', *Settimane di studio del Centro Italiano di studi sull'Alto Medioevo XII, L'Occidente e l'Islam nell'Alto Medioevo* (Spoleto, 1965), i. 93–114. On Islam in Spain: E. Lévi-Provençal, *Histoire de l'Espagne musulmane* (2nd edn., Paris, 1950–3) (three volumes, covering the whole of the Umayyad period); A. Castro, *La realidad histórica de España* (Mexico City, 1954; Italian version, Florence, 1955); Cl. Sánchez Albornoz, *España. Un enigma histórico*, 2nd edn. (Buenos Aires, 1962); idem, 'España y el Islam', *Rivista de Occidente*, xix (1929), and idem, 'El Iṣlam de España y el Occidente', *Settimane di studio del Centro Italiano . . . XII* (1965), i. 149–308. On the linguistic legacy of Arabic in the West, G. B. Pellegrini, *Gli arabismi nelle lingue neolatine* (Brescia, 1972). On Turkish Islam in Europe see the general histories of the Ottoman Empire; for Greece in particular the classic, although now outdated, general study by K. Sathas, *Tourkokratoumene Hellas* (Athens, 1869).

III

ISLAMIC FRONTIERS IN AFRICA AND ASIA

(*A*) AFRICA SOUTH OF THE SAHARA

SOUTH of the Sahara, in the vast expanse of territory stretching from Senegal in the west to Somalia in the east, Islam today claims some fifty million adherents and thus commands a following equivalent in strength to that in North Africa. In distinction to the latter, however, and consonant with its ethnic complexity and discontinuities in geographical distribution, this sub-Saharan Muslim population exhibits a much wider range of variation in the character of local Islam. In many places it is interrupted by large Christian communities and by major tribal groupings whose main attachment is still to traditional African religions. Frequently Muslims form small minority enclaves; and even where they are numerically dominant few of the countries in which they live are today officially Islamic states. In much of the region Islam is thus in dynamic contact and competition with long-established traditional cults as well as with Christianity. But, though it now lacks generally the special appeal which it formerly enjoyed through the association of Christianity with colonization, there is no doubt that it is still on the march and making steady progress. This is particularly true of the situation in West Africa, and in Ethiopia where Islamization is encouraged by the fact that the politically dominant Amhara rulers have been Christians for centuries.

In some places, elements of Islamic culture such as circumcision, or astrological and divinatory techniques, have been adopted by peoples who are not Muslim and have been incorporated within their traditional cultural systems. Everywhere Islam has been accommodated to the local cultural and social setting, and in some cases this has led to the development of such unique new syntheses as that of Swahili culture. Only in the northern Sudan where, alone of the countries with which we are concerned here, Arabic has become fully adopted as the local language, is the association between Arabization and Islamization complete. Elsewhere, although some degree of Arab identity is sometimes asserted, Islam is not viewed as an exclusive property of the Arabs, and Islamic and Arab loyalties are not synonymous.

Some two-thirds of the total sub-Saharan Muslim population live in West Africa, where Nigeria claims the largest Islamic community, while Senegal, Guinea, Mali, and Niger are mainly though not exclusively Muslim. Smaller communities are found in Liberia, Ghana, and Togo. In central, eastern and north-eastern Africa, Muslims are in the majority in the northern Sudan, and have virtually no rivals in Zanzibar and the Somali Republic. The Islamic component is also strong in Ethiopia (especially in Eritrea) and in Tanzania, too, accounting for perhaps a third of the total population in each of these states. Smaller Muslim communities live in Kenya, Uganda, Malawi, Zambia, and the Congo. Despite the former congruence of Islamic and political frontiers in the old Muslim empires of the pre-colonial history of the region, today only the Somali Republic and Mauritania are formally constituted as Islamic states, but neither is a member of the Arab League. Paradoxically the Sudan Republic, which is a member of the League, has not yet decided to adopt an Islamic constitution and may not do so in view of the interests of its large non-Muslim southern population.

Outside these states Islam plays a highly significant role in the internal politics of many countries, notably in Senegal, Mali, Niger, and Nigeria, in Ethiopia, and to a lesser extent in Tanzania. It also offers important inter-state links with a political potential which future generations may build upon; and less formally, a badge of identity and bond of mutual interest on the basis of which Muslims of different ethnic origin and political affiliation readily associate in the heterogeneous conditions of town life. This recognition of a wider Muslim solidarity which, of course, is very flexible and relative to particular circumstances, is most vividly expressed in the large-scale African participation in pilgrimages to Mecca as well as to a host of lesser local shrines.

As well as affecting habits of dress and other aspects of material culture, most notably architecture, the adoption of Islam has strongly coloured the character of all the life-crisis rituals which mark the passage of the individual from the cradle to the grave. Notwithstanding local embellishments reflecting pre-Islamic elements, these rituals have a remarkable uniformity throughout sub-Saharan Islam. In the same way, the Muslim calendar with its public rituals, particularly Ramaḍān, the month of fasting, gives a uniformity to the regulation of life where traditionally great differences occurred from one group to another. Similar regularities bridging the great ethnic and cultural diversities of this vast region are evident in the traditional pattern of Islamic instruction with, however, interesting differences in the extent to which local schools of higher learning, such as those of Timbuctu and Jenne in West Africa, or Harar in the north-east, have grown up to produce religious and historical literature in Arabic.

As far as social life is concerned, the greatest uniformities are evident in family life where Islamic law[1] has unquestionably had its greatest social impact. Although naturally overlaid with pre-Islamic practices, such as bride-wealth, marriage shows basically the same features from Senegal to Somalia: husbands may marry up to four wives concurrently; divorce is easy for men but difficult for women; the *ʿidda* or waiting period before remarriage is observed after divorce and the husband's death; and children belong to the husband or his heir. In inheritance the *Sharīʿa*, applied by the ubiquitous courts of the qāḍīs or judges, is normally followed only as far as it does not conflict with deeply entrenched traditional patterns of property rights. In much the same fashion, the *Sharīʿa* rules regarding the *diya* or payment of compensation

[1] See J. N. D. Anderson, *Islamic Law in Africa* (London, 1954).

for homicide and other injuries are applied, but often modified in the light of pre-Islamic social institutions. Thus, for instance, among the Somali, a wide range of patrilineal kin accept responsibility for the *diya* in cases of deliberate murder where, according to Islamic law, the killer alone should bear responsibility. Finally, in politics, Islamic principles of government and political institutions have in various degrees been grafted on to the political structures of those traditional African kingdoms which adopted Islam, the best surviving examples being the Hausa states of northern Nigeria. Today, as in other formally Islamic countries, the sphere of effective Islamic law is shrinking and it is increasingly applied only in matters of family and personal status, this being often a reversion to the position in pre-colonial times and circumstances.

Little can be said here of the long history of Islam in this sub-Saharan region. We must note, however, that both the eastern Sudan and parts of North-East Africa were already open to Islamic influence in the seventh century, whereas the implanting of Islam in East and West Africa cannot be traced back securely beyond the tenth century. By this time, virtually the whole of sub-Saharan Africa lay exposed to the new religion by the wide-ranging network of caravan routes which led across the Sahara to the north, and in the east to the ports of the Red Sea coast and Indian Ocean.[1] It was in fact principally through the association of Islam with trade that so many of the peoples of this part of the continent were won for Islam, despite the fact that for centuries over vast areas slaves constituted one of the major resources sought by the Muslim merchants. External conquest by Muslim invaders played a negligible role except in the eastern Sudan, the only part of the region where extensive Arab settlement played a crucial part in the dissemination of Islam.[2] Conquest of pagan societies by local Islamized states was a significant factor in the western Sudan, and to some extent in Ethiopia, though there, paradoxically, the

[1] See E. W. Bovill, *Caravans of the Old Sahara* (London, 1933).

[2] See Yusuf Fadl Hasan, *The Arabs and the Sudan* (Edinburgh, 1967).

final extension of the Christian Amhara empire in the nineteenth century had a far more profound and permanent effect on the promotion of Islam.

Elsewhere and more generally, it was the Muslim trading factor which exerted the paramount influence, and here those who played this crucial role in the implanting of Islam were often not themselves Arabs. In the early period of the introduction of Islam into the western Sudan, pride of place must be assigned to the camel-owning Berbers whose great trade caravans plied along the Saharan routes. In the north-east, the nomadic Somali played a similar part both as caravan traders and through their western and southern migrations from their earlier homelands in the north-east corner of the Horn. There were also, of course, other local groups such as the West African Hausa and Dyula who, converted to Islam, similarly extended the faith through their wide-ranging trading connections. In East Africa, by contrast, although gold, ivory, and slaves and the other readily exploitable resources of the interior found their way to the coastal Muslim merchants, these latter did not themselves penetrate the hinterland in any substantial numbers until the late eighteenth century.

Whether these early Muslim traders were themselves Arabs, or non-Arabs fired by the zeal of the converted, they exerted a powerful effect in the initially pagan societies through which they travelled and in which they often settled. Although they were normally not primarily active proselytizers, their esoteric religious devotions attracted wide attention and their involvement in the literate culture of Islam and their far-flung trading connections gave them and the holy men who travelled with them a special lustre in local eyes. In the great pagan kingdoms in which they settled as small minority communities under the king's protection they were soon found to possess special attributes which could be usefully employed to advantage. Here, like the early colonial administrators who succeeded them, pagan kings and their officials found it convenient to apply the services of such a Muslim trading diaspora to a variety of tasks. These ranged from employment in tax-collecting, accounting, and diplomatic service, to recruitment to palace bodyguards where their lack of local attachments, and often superior military equipment and expertise, made them uniquely valuable. At the very least, it often became the fashion for a pagan monarch to adorn his court with the possession of a few Muslim courtiers, and more significantly to flirt with the new religion, seeking, like Mansa Mūsā of Mali (1312–37) or Askia Muḥammad of Songhay (d. 1528), reinforcement for the traditional ritual power of the kingship, sometimes with disastrous results. Once adopted as a new royal prerogative, Islam of course afforded the ambitious ruler, as Gouilly[1] has put it, 'a doctrine, a flag, and an arm', and could provide a powerful justification for the conquest of surrounding pagan kingdoms, and aid to their subsequent political incorporation. Equally, those warrior leaders and merchant adventurers who, in circumstances of economic and social change, have often come to the fore, and who sought to establish and consolidate new kingdoms and dynasties where none had previously existed, frequently turned to Islam as a convenient rationale for the novelty of the positions which they had established. In Ethiopia, such ambitious petty chiefs and war leaders as economic change encouraged amongst the traditionally republican Galla in the eighteenth and nineteenth centuries were equally prone to adopt either Islam or Christianity as a basis for their new and traditionally unconstitutional authority.

Utilitarian considerations of this kind which facilitated the extension of the faith were of course reinforced by Islam's limited doctrinal requirements and its ready tolerance of traditional religious beliefs and of custom which was recognized with the *Sharīʿa* as a parallel source of practical law. And it was by no means only to traditional rulers or upstart leaders that these aspects appealed. More generally, the new religion was also particularly attractive as a source of novel ritual techniques to people who, lacking any substantial scientific control of their environment or fortunes, were constantly on the look-out for powerful super-

[1] *L'Islam dans l'Afrique occidentale française* (Paris, 1952).

natural remedies. This aspect was again all the more significant where new circumstances created new possibilities for social advancement and new tensions within society.

Although detailed evidence regarding the interplay of such factors as these in the early Islamization of sub-Saharan Africa is generally lacking, their involvement can be seen in some areas in which Islam is today spreading. Thus, for example, amongst the Giriama people of Kenya economic changes in this century have led to the emergence of a new class of cash-crop farmers. These successful entrepreneurs have naturally attracted the jealousy and envy of their less progressive neighbours still engaged in subsistence cultivation and have thus become a major target of sorcery and witchcraft. As a protection such men have turned to Islam and are known locally as 'therapeutic Muslims'. This both safeguards them against the spite and malice which their success attracts and enables them to dispense with traditional obligations in sharing food on the grounds that as Muslims they have to observe orthodox dietary restrictions which at once isolates and insulates them from their jealous neighbours. Although we cannot be certain, there is every reason to assume that motives of this kind have played a crucial role in the gradual dissemination of Islam in periods and places for which we lack such detailed information.[1]

But if considerations of this kind have greatly encouraged Africans to turn to Islam as a remedy for the afflictions of this life, treating the new religion in effect as a new source of supernatural power for dealing with the difficulties and disasters of everyday life in the manner of traditional African religion, we must not forget that the wider eschatological doctrines which the faith enshrines represent a radically new departure. The belief in an afterlife in which the rewards and punishments for man's conduct in this life are experienced is generally foreign to traditional African religions, and its introduction with Islam offers a new basis for evaluating morality and a source both of quietist acquiescence and of militant messianism. These contrary interpretations have both

[1] See I. M. Lewis (ed.), *Islam in Tropical Africa* (London, 1966).

found ready advocates in the past history of sub-Saharan Islam and will no doubt also in the future.

Finally, as far as its actual implanting is concerned, we must record the important effect exerted by the locally prevailing currents of population movement and migration. Where, as generally in West Africa, the over-all flow of tribal migrations coincided with that followed in the spread of Islam through trade, this conjunction reinforced the latter. Much the same applies in the history of the eastern Sudan and also in North-East Africa. In East Africa, however, the tides of migratory movement tended to run from the hinterland towards the coast thus running counter to the spread of Islam and reinforcing its restriction to that region. Here in fact coastal Islam, symbolized in the very word Swahili, acted as a magnet drawing tribal elements from the interior into its ambit on the coast where it became a town religion, not restricted to any one tribal group, and led to the development of the unique cultural and linguistic synthesis of Bantu, Arabic, and Persian elements which Swahili represents today.

In conformity with their various sources of Islamic influence different parts of sub-Sahara follow different schools of the *Sharīʿa*. In West Africa, the Mālikī school, given currency initially by the Almoravid movement in the eleventh century, is dominant and is also the principal rite in the northern Sudan where, however, the Ḥanafī school was introduced during the Turco-Egyptian period (1830–96) as the official code of the courts. In North-East and East Africa, where Ḥaḍramī influence was paramount, the Shāfiʿi school holds sway although minority communities adhere to other rites.

The religious orders or *ṭarīqa*s (on whose beginnings see below, Chapter VIII, pp. 378–9) are similarly widely represented with the Qādiriyya universally the earliest introduced and probably possessing the widest following. In the sixteenth century this order was introduced in the western Sudan through the great Niger seat of learning at Timbuctu, and in the same period was brought to Harar which occupied a comparable position in North-East Africa. In West Africa the order achieved its most dramatic realization in the nineteenth century Hausa *jihād*s inspired by ʿUthmān dan Fodio (1754–1817). In the first decades of the present century its followers were similarly active in organizing resistance to the German colonizers in Tanganyika under the inspired leadership of the Somali Shaykh Uways b. Muḥammad al-Barāwī (1846–1909) whose teaching and voluminous writings have given rise to the Uwaysiyya branch of the order which is today very popular in southern Somalia and parts of the East African coast. The latter-day proto-nationalist *jihād* (1900–20) led by Shaykh Muḥammad ʿAbdallāh Ḥasan (1864–1920) against the British, Ethiopian, and Italian colonizers of Somaliland was associated not with the Qādiriyya, to which it was in fact bitterly opposed, but with the Ṣāliḥiyya, a derivative of Sayyid Aḥmad b. Idrīs al-Fāsī's Meccan order, the Aḥmadiyya. Further north again, the Mahdiyya of Muḥammad Aḥmad (1843–85) in the Sudan was not based on any single order but rather designed to cut across such denominational barriers and to appeal to all Muslims in their resistance to external domination. Yet despite these differences in the *ṭarīqa* affiliation of the *jihād* leaders, and the contrasting positions assumed by the same orders in different colonial territories, the available documentary evidence shows that these movements were in fact linked, and that those in the western Sudan helped to inspire the eastern Sudanese Mahdī just as he in turn served as a shining example for the Somali Shaykh Muḥammad ʿAbdallāh Ḥasan.

Throughout sub-Saharan Africa it is to the local leaders of the orders that we owe much of the religious and historical literature in Arabic and in local vernaculars which has survived to the present day. Today the orders remain important as a denominational basis for worship, and in the Sudan particularly, where over twenty separate organizations have been described by Trimingham,[1] as significant factors in politics. More recently the Tījāniyya order,[2]

[1] *Islam in the Sudan* (London, 1949).

[2] J. M. Abun-Nasr, *The Tijāniyya. A Sufi Order in the Modern World* (London, 1965).

founded by Aḥmad al-Tījānī of Fez (d. 1815), and the Murīdiyya order of Shaykh Aḥmad Bamba (d. 1927), whose tomb at Touba in Senegal attracts flocks of pilgrims from West Africa, have become important rivals of the older *ṭarīqa*s in the western Sudan. In this region also the Indian Aḥmadiyya movement has introduced a further element of controversy, while in East Africa recent Indian and Pakistani immigrants provide the only Shīʿī community in sub-Saharan Africa.

Frequently, but not always closely associated with the *ṭarīqa*s, strong emphasis is placed on the cult of saints as mediators who are invoked to bridge the wide gulf which is felt to separate man from God and the grace of the Prophet. This is particularly the case in the eastern Sudan and North-East Africa where to a significant extent the saint cult conforms well with the traditional emphasis placed on lineage ancestors, although by no means all those so venerated are merely canonized ancestors. Cults such as that of Sayyid Barkhadle in northern Somalia, to visit whose tomb three times is considered of religious merit equal to going once to Mecca, and that of Shaykh Ḥusayn Baliale in south-east Ethiopia provide primary local foci for the practice of the faith. These cults both represent all that is conserved in popular Islam today of the memory of the Sultanates of Ifat and Bali which, in medieval times confronted the expanding Christian Amhara kingdom and for a brief period in the sixteenth century almost overthrew it completely.

For men and women alike such cults as well as the magical apparatus of Islam provide for those recurrent needs which are not adequately met in the lofty eschatological doctrines of Islam. In the same vein, the regular exclusion of women from the main cult of official Islam leaves a gap which is filled by local spirit-possession cults such as those of the Hausa *bori* spirits, the *zār* spirits in Ethiopia, the Sudan, and Somalia, and the *pepo* spirits of the Swahili coast. These cults involve a galaxy of intruding familiar spirits which faithfully mirror the changing circumstances of society. Thus during General Abud's military regime, soldier spirits were popular in the Sudan while when the first Sudanese national football team was formed footballer spirits became fashionable. Such spirits are identified as the source of affliction and illness, and the treatment of these conditions, which invariably involves the possessed woman's husband in unwelcome expense, leads eventually to induction into a woman's spirit-possession coterie. These societies provide an outlet for the expression of women's interests and often perform a therapeutic function, while the periodical relapse into a state of possession enables the hard-pressed segregated wife to put pressure on her husband when other methods fail. The opinion of orthodox ulema tends to condemn these practices as uncanonical, yet since the Koran offers scriptural warrant for the existence of evil *jinn*, with which they are usually identified, it is difficult to find any watertight doctrinal basis on which they can be forbidden.

Here, indeed, we see a further indication of the generous phenomenological resources of Islam and of the possibilities which the Muslim religion offers for the tolerance of traditional cults as long as these can be fitted within some Koranically justified framework. It is this elasticity and lack of narrow exclusiveness which above all else explains the popularity of Islam for Africans and allows the rich cultural resources of sub-Saharan Africa to colour the variegated patterns of Islam in this region.

I. M. LEWIS

BIBLIOGRAPHY

In addition to the works referred to in the footnotes to this chapter there are recommended for further reading: I. Cunnison, *Baggara Arabs* (Oxford, 1967); M. Dupire, *Peuples nomades* (Paris, 1962); H. J. Fisher, *Aḥmadiyyah: a Study in Contemporary Islam on the West African Coast* (London, 1963); G. S. P. Freeman-Grenville, *The Medieval History of the Tanganyika Coast* (Oxford, 1962); P. M. Holt, *The Mahdist State in the Sudan 1881–1898* (Oxford, 1958); M. Last, *The Sokoto Caliphate* (London, 1968); I. M. Lewis, *The Modern History of Somaliland* (London, 1965);

V. Monteil, *L' Islam noir* (Paris, 1964); J. Rouch, *La Religion et la magie soghay* (Paris, 1960); M. G. Smith, *Government in Zazzau* (London, 1960); J. S. Trimingham, *Islam in Ethiopia* (London, 1952); idem, *Islam in West Africa* (London, 1959); idem, *Islam in East Africa* (London, 1964); idem, *The Influence of Islam upon Africa* (London, 1968).

(*B*) CENTRAL ASIA

THE northern horizons of the first Muslims, those of the generation contemporary with Muḥammad, were bounded by the two great empires of the Byzantines and the Sāsānids. Of the regions beyond, the steppes across which a man could travel from the Carpathians to the shores of Lake Baikal and the fringes of the Chinese world without meeting any obstacles except for the great rivers, virtually nothing was known. Traditions about the Turks were attributed to the Prophet, such as 'Don't disturb the Turks as long as they leave you alone', and a saying attributed to God Himself announced in a minatory fashion that 'I have an army in the East which I call the Turks; I set them against any people that kindle my wrath.'[1] These aphorisms are not authentic and were put into circulation later, when the Turks had come into contact with the Islamic world; they are included in collections of traditions made in the ninth century. If Muḥammad and his contemporaries had any knowledge of the regions beyond Khurāsān or eastern Persia, it must have come from the legends and popular romances which were circulating all over the Near East at that time. Thus the Koran, xviii. 93–6, mentions the giants Gog and Magog as the tribes Ya'jūj and Ma'jūj, and records how Dhu'l-Qarnayn or Alexander the Great had built in the east a wall of iron and brass against these barbarians.[2]

[1] See I. Goldziher, *Muhammedanische Studien* (Halle, 1889–90), i. 270–1, Excursus VI, 'Traditionen über Türken'; English translation by S. M. Stern, *Muslim Studies*, i (London, 1967), 245–6.

[2] See *Encyclopaedia of Islam*, 1st edn., article 'Yād̲j̲ūd̲j̲ wa Mād̲j̲ūd̲j̲' (by A. J. Wensinck).

However, Inner Asia was by no means unknown to the Byzantines and Sāsānids, for there had been diplomatic, military, and commercial contacts between these two great empires of the Near East and the peoples of Central Asia well before the rise of Islam. Both the Persians and the Greeks endeavoured to secure the alliance of the powerful kingdom of the Western Turks (or T'ü-kiu, as they appear in Chinese sources), whose centre of power lay north of Qarashahr in the modern region of Dzungaria in eastern Turkestan. After failing to secure trading concessions from the Persians, the Turkish Yabghu or tribal ruler Éshtemi negotiated with the Byzantine Emperor Justin II (565–78), and diplomatic missions arrived in the Yabghu's camp; much of our knowledge of these early Turks comes from the accounts of the Greek envoys.[1] The facilitating of trade was, indeed, always one of the prime goals of the Near-Eastern powers in their dealings with successive steppe empires. The enterprising Soghdians, the Iranian inhabitants of the Zarafshan valley towns of Transoxania, traded extensively with the steppe peoples and established contacts with China. Soghdian commercial colonies were planted as far east as the Lop Nor region to the east of the Tarim basin, and it was in the Soghdians' wake that the culture and beliefs of the Iranian world—Sāsānid ceremonial and regal practices, and religions like Manicheism and Nestorian Christianity—came to the peoples of Central Asia. It was also through the intermediacy of the Soghdians that the Uyghur Turks acquired their alphabet; the Uyghur script was to be one of the principal media for the spread of culture within Central Asia (see further below, p. 128). From the time of the Soghdians onwards, the merchant and the missionary become typical figures of the Inner Asian scene, and through them, this somewhat closed and introspective region becomes linked with the higher cultures of the adjoining Near Eastern, Indian, and Chinese worlds.

The Arabs first crossed the Oxus in 654, but the conquest of Transoxania was arduous and protracted, for the local Iranian

[1] R. Grousset, *L'Empire des steppes*, 4th edn. (Paris, 1952), pp. 128–30.

princes resisted strongly, and at various times called in Turkish and even Chinese help against the invaders. Thus in the years after 730, Ghūrak, prince of Soghdia, allied himself with the Qaghan of the Western Turks or Türgesh, Su-lu (the name is only known from Chinese sources), against the Arabs; it was only Su-lu's murder and the consequent break-up of the Türgesh empire that enabled the Arabs to reassert their dominion over Transoxania. Not until the early ʿAbbāsid period, i.e. the second half of the eighth century, was the position there of Islam at all firm. The adjacent province of Khwārazm, on the lower reaches of the Oxus, was invaded by the Arab general Qutayba b. Muslim in 712, the indigenous ruling family of Khwārazm-Shāhs made tributary, and Islam introduced. The Arab advance eastwards was at last halted against the mountain barriers of the Pamirs and T'ien-Shan; a report in the historical sources that the Arabs penetrated to Kāshghar in eastern Turkestan is probably to be rejected.[1]

Whilst the Arab soldiers of Baṣra and Khurāsān were struggling in the inhospitable terrain and extreme climate of Central Asia, troops from Kūfa were raiding across the Caucasus towards the steppes of South Russia. They reached Darband or Bāb al-Abwāb in Daghestan as early as 643, and a few years later came up against the Turkish Khazars, who had just established a powerful kingdom in the basins of the lower Don and lower Volga, with their capital at Atil or Itil. The Khazar state endured down to the end of the tenth century, when it seems to have been destroyed by the Scandinavian Rūs; during this period, Muslim arms achieved no lasting success north of the Caucasus, although the faith did spread peacefully, together with Christianity and Judaism, amongst the Khazars.[2] To the north of the Khazars, on the middle

[1] See on this general topic, H. A. R. Gibb, *The Arab Conquests in Central Asia* (London, 1923), and idem, 'The Arab Invasion of Kāshghar in A.D. 715', *Bulletin of the School of Oriental Studies*, ii (1923), 467–74.

[2] See D. M. Dunlop, *The History of the Jewish Khazars* (Princeton, 1954), pp. 46 ff.

Volga and around its confluence with the Kama, lived another Turkish people, the Bulghārs. The Bulghārs were already partly Muslim at the opening of the tenth century, but had apparently received the faith not via the Khazars—whom they regarded with hostility—but from Khwārazm and Central Asia. The Bulghārs were by far the northernmost Islamic people, and the high latitude of their country, with short days and long nights in winter and the reverse in summer, posed problems for the performance at correct times of the five daily prayers and the observation of the fasting month of Ramaḍān. Arab travellers such as Ibn Faḍlān and Ibn Baṭṭūṭa (see below) advert to these difficulties, and as late as the nineteenth century treatises on the legal and ritual questions involved were still being composed by the Tatar Muslim scholars of Kazan.[1]

The prime commodity which the Eurasian steppes offered to the Arabs was, of course, slaves. From the earliest years of Islam, there was a demand for domestic slaves, and during the ninth century a requirement arose for military slaves (*ghilmān*, *mamālīk*, sing. *ghulām*, *mamlūk*), who now replaced what remained of the old free Arab cavalry and the Khurasanian guards of the first ʿAbbāsids. Men from all races were pressed into service, but the Turks were supremely favoured. In the manuals of war and the 'Mirrors for princes' of Muslim writers, the Turks are regarded as the military race *par excellence*: excellent horsemen and archers, brave and loyal, and through their hardy steppe background inured to hardship. These writers credit them with some of the attributes of the noble savage. Thus al-Jāḥiẓ of Baṣra (d. 869) in his *Epistle on the outstanding qualities of the Turks* says that they are strangers to flattery, deceit, and hypocrisy, and have a strong sense of solidarity and faithfulness.[2]

The acquisition of slaves was thus an impelling motive behind almost all Arab raids into the steppes. In the western steppes, the

[1] See *Encyclopaedia of Islam*, 2nd edn., article 'Bulg͟hār' (by I. Hrbek).

[2] Cited in the chapter of C. E. Bosworth, 'The Turks in the Islamic World before the Selǧuqs', *Fundamenta Turcicae Philologiae*, iii (Wiesbaden, 1970).

Khazars acted as entrepreneurs in the slave trade, and the markets of Atil sent slaves across the Caucasus and to Khwārazm; these must have included Turks from several different tribes, as well as Slavs and Ugrian peoples like the Burṭās, if these last are to be identified with the later Mordvins. In the eastern steppes, the powers controlling Transoxania and Khwārazm flourished on the trade, and Turkish slaves were always an important part of the tribute forwarded by these powers to the ʿAbbāsid Caliphs in Iraq. The frontiers facing the steppes were dotted with fortified points, *ribāṭ*s, manned by ghāzīs or volunteer fighters for the faith. These *ribāṭ*s were not only defensive positions against nomad incursions, but were also the starting-points for raids into the steppes, and it was to them and to frontier towns like Isfījāb and Shāsh that large numbers of slaves were brought. Under the Sāmānid dynasty of Bukhārā (819–1005), the slave trade reached a peak of organization; the Sāmānid government controlled the export of slaves, levying a toll at the Oxus crossing of from 70 to 100 dirhams for each Turkish slave, and requiring in addition to this a licence for the transit of each slave boy across their territories.[1] Once assigned a place within the Islamic military system, a slave might rise to the highest commands or even become ruler of an independent principality. Sebüktigin, founder of the Ghaznavid Sultanate in Afghanistan and northern India (977–1186), was originally a pagan Turk from Barskhān (in what is now Soviet Kirghizia), captured in tribal warfare and sold as a slave in the Sāmānid lands.[2] The slave traffic continued at a high level till the Mongol invasions and after. Out of the slave guard of the Ayyūbid Sultans (whose founder was the famous Saladin) sprang the dynasty of the Mamlūks, a military slave aristocracy whose leaders reigned as independent Sultans in Egypt and Syria from 1250 till the Ottoman conquest of 1517, and thereafter as the ruling caste in Egypt till the beginning of the nineteenth century and their destruction by Muḥammad ʿAlī. Since the central and eastern Islamic lands were

[1] Idem, *The Ghaznavids, their Empire in Afghanistan and Eastern Iran 994–1040* (Edinburgh, 1963), pp. 208–9

[2] Ibid., pp. 39–41.

controlled first by the Mongol Great Khans and then by their epigoni the Il-Khāns, both hostile to the Mamlūks, the Mamlūks' main source of slaves had to be the western steppes, utilizing trade routes across Anatolia or through the Straits. The first generations of Mamlūks were mainly Türkmen and Qipchaq Turks from the South Russian steppes, but from the later fourteenth century onwards, the region of Circassia in the Caucasus became the enduring source for replenishing the Mamlūk ranks.[1]

Yet warfare and slave-raiding were by no means the sole activity along the Islamic frontiers with Central Asia; for long periods there was much peaceful intercourse. The agricultural economies of the Khurasanian and Transoxanian oases complemented the pastoralist economy of the steppelands. Camels and sheep were reared on the steppe fringes by such Turkish tribes as the Oghuz and Qarluq, and this livestock, together with hides and dairy produce, was exchanged for agricultural and manufactured products. According to the tenth-century geographer Ibn Ḥawqal, the town of Sarakhs in northern Khurāsān was 'the entrepôt for pack animals, supplying both Transoxania and the Khurasanian towns', and an early nineteenth-century British traveller, J. B. Fraser, found that it was still a great mart for horses and cattle from the steppes.[2] Products came into the Islamic world not only from the steppes but from regions beyond: from the deciduous woodlands of central Russia, from the forests of Siberia and even from the Far East. This is clearly shown by the list of imports given by the geographer al-Maqdisī (*c.* 985). There were brought from Bulghār, he says, furs of the sable, grey squirrel, ermine, mink, weasel, and fox, together with hides of the beaver, mottle-coloured hare, and wild goat. Also imported from there were iron, arrows, birch bark, fur caps, fish glue, fish (? walrus) teeth, castoreum, amber, tanned horse hides, honey, hazel nuts, falcons, swords and cuirasses, maple wood, Ṣaqlabī (Slav) slaves, sheep,

[1] See D. Ayalon, 'The Circassians in the Mamluk Army', *Journal of the American Oriental Society*, lxix (1949), 135–47.

[2] Cited in Bosworth, *The Ghaznavids*, pp. 154–5.

and cattle. In return, Khwārazm exported agricultural and manufactured products, including grapes, raisins, confectionery, sesame, cloaks, carpets, coarse cloth, satin brocades of a quality fit for giving as presents, coverings of cloth woven with a silk warp, locks, coloured garments, bows which only the strongest could bend, cheese, yeast, fish, and boats.[1] It was such trade as this which caused Islamic coins to be carried via the riverways of Russia to northern Europe. These coins, comprising above all Sāmānid silver dirhams struck in the ninth and tenth centuries, have been found in tens of thousands throughout Russia and the Scandinavian coastlands, and two specimens have even been found as far afield as Iceland; moreover, the English king Offa of Mercia (757–96) minted his famous gold coin on the pattern of the Islamic dīnār.[2]

The steppe dwellers acted as entrepreneurs for the trade with the northern regions, and no Muslim travellers or merchants are known to have journeyed thither. The sparse information given in Muslim sources seems to have been gathered by visitors to the intermediate regions, such as Tamīm b. Baḥr in the Uyghur lands of Outer Mongolia and by Ibn Faḍlān in Bulghār (see further below), or else obtained from envoys and travellers coming from remote parts of the world of Islam, such as the delegates from the K'i-tan of northern China and from the Uyghurs who came to Maḥmūd of Ghazna *c.* 1027. To the Muslims, the lands which lay towards the *Baḥr al-Ẓulumāt*, 'the Sea of Darkness', i.e. the Arctic, were remote and frightening. They knew that north of Bulghār lived such peoples as the Wīsū and the Yūra, who travelled across the snows on skates or snow-shoes and whose trade with the Bulghārs (at least in the case of the Yūra) was conducted by dumb bartering; the Wīsū are generally identified with the Finnish Ves,

[1] W. Barthold, *Turkestan Down to the Mongol Invasion*, 3rd edn. by C. E. Bosworth (London, 1968), pp. 235–6.

[2] See R. Hennig, 'Der mittelalterliche arabische Handelsverkehr in Osteuropa', *Der Islam*, xxii (1935), 247–8; C. E. Blunt, 'The Coinage of Offa', in *Anglo-Saxon Coins, Studies presented to F. M. Stenton* (London, 1961), pp. 45, 50–1.

and the Yūra or Yugra with Ugrian peoples such as the Ostiaks and Voguls who lived between the Pechora river and the Urals.[1] The Muslims distinguished the Rūs or Varangians (i.e. the Scandinavian adventurers who explored the river systems of Russia and who launched their ships on the Caspian, sacking the Islamic town of Bardhaʿa in Arrān in 943) from the western Slavs of Central Europe (the name of the Moravian king Svetopluk I, who reigned from 870 to 894, was known to the historian al-Masʿūdī only a few decades later), but they tended to confuse the eastern Slavs of Russia with the Rūs. Amongst peoples of northern Siberia, Muslim accounts like those of the anonymous *Ḥudūd al-ʿālam* (written after 982) and of al-Marvazī (end of the eleventh or beginning of the twelfth century) mention the Fūrī or Qūrī, apparently to be localized beyond Lake Baikal in the Khingan Mountains region and accordingly of possible Mongol or Tungusic stock; these people are described as brutal cannibals, as having a language unintelligible to any but themselves and as copulating with their wives *more animalium*.[2] From these north-eastern regions came the highly prized medicament and anti-toxic *khutuww*, a term which was in China applied to walrus and narwhal ivory, but which may have meant to the Muslims rhinocerus horn or even fossilized mammoth ivory.[3]

The connections of Transoxania with the Chinese world were, as we have noted above, of long standing, for across the heart of Asia ran the historic 'Silk Road'. The Muslims regarded China as the home of finely wrought luxury articles. The eleventh-century writer al-Thaʿālibī of Nīshāpūr comments that 'the Arabs used

[1] See the information collected by J. Marquart in his article, 'Ein arabischer Bericht über den arktischen (uralischen) Länder aus dem 10. Jahrhundert', *Ungarische Jahrbücher*, iv (1924), 261–334.

[2] *Ḥudūd al-ʿālam*, translated by V. Minorsky, 2nd edn. by C. E. Bosworth (London, 1970, pp. 97, 283–4; V. Minorsky, *Sharaf al-Zamān Ṭāhir Marvazi on China, the Turks and India* (London, 1942), pp. 26, 105–6, 161. The Qūrī are perhaps to be identified with the modern Buryat Khori tribe living to the east and south of Lake Baikal.

[3] See on *khutuww*, A. Z. V. Togan, *Ibn Faḍlāns Reisebericht* (Leipzig, 1939), pp. 216–17, Excursus §74b.

to call every delicately or curiously made vessel and such-like, whatever its real origin, "Chinese", because finely made things are a speciality of China'. He goes on to mention their fine, translucent porcelain, their particoloured and shot silks, their gold brocades, their coats proofed with wax against the rain, their asbestos table napkins, and their steel mirrors.[1] Some of these products certainly came to the Muslims by means of the sea-route round the South-East Asian and Indian coasts. There was already in the eighth century a flourishing colony of foreign merchants at Canton, amongst whom are mentioned the *Ta-shi* (Arabs) and *Po-se* (? Persians from Sīrāf); these two groups were powerful enough to revolt in 758 against the Chinese authorities. It is probable that the bulk of the T'ang dynasty porcelain which has been found in the excavated ruins of ʿAbbāsid palaces at Sāmarrā (this town being the seat of the Caliphate from 836 to 889) came to Iraq through the Indian Ocean and up the Persian Gulf.[2] Yet it seems also likely that some Chinese goods made the incredibly long and hazardous land journey across Central Asia, as did certain Tibetan specialities such as musk, yaks' tails, and gold; Chinese porcelain (*chīnī faghfūrī*, 'Imperial china') was amongst presents forwarded to Hārūn al-Rashīd by his governor in Khurāsān ʿAlī b. ʿĪsā b. Māhān.[3]

During the period when the Caliphate was still expanding, and later when powerful states like the Sāmānid and Ghaznavid empires were constituted in the eastern Islamic world (ninth to twelfth centuries), there must have been a fair number of Muslim travellers and envoys who penetrated Inner Asia. On a humble level, traders and also dervishes and other Muslim evangelists voyaged in the steppes. We have very little specific knowledge about the latter groups, but accounts of some political and diplomatic mis-

[1] al-Thaʿālibī, *Laṭā'if al-maʿārif*, translated by C. E. Bosworth, *The Book of Curious and Entertaining Information* (Edinburgh, 1968), p. 141.

[2] See P. Kahle, 'Chinese Porcelain in the Lands of Islam', *Opera Minora* (Leiden, 1956), pp. 326–61.

[3] Abu'l-Faḍl Bayhaqī, *Ta'rīkh-i Masʿūdī*, ed. Q. Ghanī and A. A. Fayyāḍ (Tehran 1324/1945), p. 417.

sions have survived, usually enshrined in fragmentary form within larger geographical works. A mission to the Turks in the reign of the Caliph Hishām (724–43) is mentioned, and under al-Wāthiq (842–7) Sallām al-Tarjumān ('the Interpreter'; he is said to have known thirty languages) was sent to the wall of Gog and Magog to investigate a report that the barrier had been breached; not surprisingly, his account is simply a traveller's tall tale. Of hardly greater historical value is the account of the littérateur and traveller Abū Dulaf Misʿar b. Muhalhil. This purports to describe his trip through Central Asia with a Chinese embassy returning from the Sāmānid court of Bukhārā *c.* 940. He describes the various Turkish tribes through whose lands he passed, including the Pechenegs, Kimek, Oghuz, Kirghiz, Qarluq, etc., and his details include the familiar story of the Turks' 'rainstone' (*yada-tash*, bezoar), by means of which their shamans induced rain. But although much of his material is clearly genuine, it is impossible to form a logically connected itinerary from it.[1]

On the other hand, the account of Tamīm b. Baḥr al-Muṭṭawwiʿ ('the Volunteer fighter for the faith') and his journey to the Uyghurs—unfortunately surviving only in abridged form—has yielded important evidence on certain obscure Central Asian problems, notably on the connection of the Uyghurs with another frequently mentioned Turkish people, the Toquz-Oghuz. Tamīm's account is a sober one, unembellished by reports of marvels. It seems likely that his journey was made in the early ninth century and that he penetrated to the Uyghur capital of Qara Balghasun on the Orkhon river in Outer Mongolia. Amongst other points, he mentions the Uyghurs' enthusiastic adoption of Manicheism and their close relations with the Chinese Emperors.[2] Of

[1] Abū Dulaf's *First Epistle*, on his Central Asian travels, is translated into French by G. Ferrand in his *Relations de voyages et textes géographiques arabes, persans et turcs relatifs a l'Extrême-Orient des VIIIe au XVIIIe siècles*, i (Paris, 1913), and into German by A. von Rohr-Sauer, *Des Abû Dulaf Bericht über seine Reise nach Turkestan, China und Indien* (Bonn, 1939).

[2] See V. Minorsky, 'Tamīm ibn Baḥr's Journey to the Uighurs', *Bulletin of the School of Oriental and African Studies*, xii (1948), 275–305.

outstanding value for our knowledge of the more westerly steppe peoples in the tenth century is the account of Aḥmad b. Faḍlān's trip from Khwārazm across the steppes to Bulghār in 921; the recently converted kings of Bulghār were at this time aiming to strengthen links with the ʿAbbāsid Caliphate and to secure, if possible, help against the Bulghārs' Khazar suzerains. The journey had to be made in spring and summer, but even so, Ibn Faḍlān's caravan started off in intensely cold and snowy weather. On the Üst Urt plateau between the Aral and Caspian Seas, they met a group of Oghuz Turks, who were wandering 'like wild asses'. These nomads were totally irreligious, except that they venerated running water, and the Muslim merchants in the caravan had to perform their ritual ablutions late at night out of the Turks' sight; a similar reverence for water was later enshrined in the *Yasa* or tribal law of the Mongols. They also had the custom of erecting on the tomb of a great man wooden statues of slain warriors who might attend him in the next life, corresponding to the stone pillars or *balbals* of the Orkhon Turks. Ibn Faḍlān thought that the Oghuz were total barbarians, though he commented favourably on their abhorrence of adultery and pederasty. His evidence is almost our only material on the pre-history of the Seljuq Turks, who sprang from the Oghuz and who in the eleventh century overran the greater part of the Middle East, setting up their own Sultanate. In Bulghār, Ibn Faḍlān marvelled at the short summer nights and at such phenomena as the northern lights. The Bulghārs were half-nomadic and half-sedentary, but Islam was not yet general amongst them; he says that the pagan Bulghārs sacrificed outstandingly clever men to the gods, and the shamans' influence was still great.[1] He also noted the importance of trade amongst the Bulghārs, and commercial contacts with the Islamic heartlands grew over the next century. In the early eleventh century, a Nīshāpūr merchant could have a business partner in Bulghār, and in 1024 we find the Bulghār king sending money for

[1] See the edition of Ibn Faḍlān's *Riḥla* cited at p. 123 n. 3 above, with very copious notes and commentary.

the repair of mosques in the Khurasanian oasis of Bayhaq or Sabzavār.[1]

It has been observed above that we know little about the process whereby the steppe Turks were converted to Islam. By the sixteenth century, virtually all the Turkic peoples of Eurasia, with the exception of some of the Chuvash and the still animist Yakuts and Altai Tatars, were Muslim, and the other faiths which had competed for the allegiance of the Turks—Christianity, Manicheism, Buddhism—had given place to it. The work of evangelism was done not by representatives of the official religious institution but by dervishes and other enthusiasts, who preached a simple, hell-fire gospel which the steppe-dwellers could understand. The eastern group of the Qarluq Turks (from whom the Qarakhanid dynasty, heirs to the Sāmānids in Transoxania, very probably sprang) became Muslim in the middle decades of the tenth century; here, the name of one of those who worked amongst them, Abu'l-Ḥasan Kalimātī, is known.[2] In the early eleventh century, the south-western Turks of the Oghuz group, including the Seljuq family, adopted the new faith. But the spread of Islam into what became known in the course of that century as the Qipchaq steppe, was slow. Even at the end of the twelfth century, the Qipchaq of the lower Syr Darya region were largely pagan; the Khwārazm-Shāhs recruited them into their armies, and their savagery made the Khwārazmian troops hated in Persia.[3]

Because the conversion of the steppes was undertaken mainly by Ṣūfī mystics and holy men, and not by the rigorists of the ulema, Islam there has always shown a considerable elasticity in both belief and practice. In general, the Turks adopted the comparatively liberal Ḥanafī law school; the Shāfiʿī Ibn Faḍlān comments unfavourably on the Bulghārs' addiction to *būza*, a drink fermented from honey and wheat, and four centuries later, the Mālikī Ibn Baṭṭūṭa noted the popularity in the steppes of *nabīdh*,

[1] Bosworth, *The Ghaznavids*, p. 149.

[2] Barthold, *Turkestan*, p. 255.

[3] See idem, *Histoire des Turcs d'Asie Centrale* (Paris, 1945), pp. 109 ff.

here a liquor fermented from millet. Nor were the animistic beliefs of the Turks immediately overlaid by the new faith. There was, rather, a process of adaptation and assimilation on these margins of the Islamic world, just as there was in India, Indonesia, and Black Africa. A Ṣūfī saint like Aḥmad Yasawī (d. 1166), whose tomb on the lower Syr Darya was for long highly venerated by the Turks, was regarded with much the same sort of respect as had been given to the Turks' shamans; indeed, the modern Turkish scholar Fuad Köprülü detected more than one element of the shamanistic past in the practices of the Yasawiyya order which Aḥmad founded.[1]

In the twelfth century, the Buddhist K'i-tan or Qara Khitay (the latter name being the one by which they became known in the Islamic world) migrated westwards from northern China and conquered Transoxania; their defeat of the Seljuq Sultan Sanjar favoured the growth in Christian Europe of the belief that there ruled beyond the Islamic lands a powerful monarch, anti-Muslim and therefore presumably Christian, the famous Prester John. In the next century, the Mongols constituted a vast empire right across Asia, and a fresh wave of influences, political, ethnic, and cultural, reached the Islamic world from the Inner Asian steppes and the Far East. The Mongols' Uyghur secretaries, the *bitikchi*s, made the Uyghur script familiar in the Near East as far west as Mamlūk Egypt; the Ottomans occasionally used it down to the end of the fifteenth century. Chinese practices appeared in the west; in 1294 the Mongol Il-Khān Gaykhatu introduced into Persia a paper currency on the Chinese model, with disastrous economic consequences.[2] In the artistic field, indigenous traditions benefited from an admixture of Chinese influences, seen in painting styles and in ceramics. The Mongols in the west were comparatively few in number, but vast numbers of Turks poured

[1] *L'Influence du chamanisme turco-mongole sur les ordres mystiques musulmans* (Istanbul, 1929).

[2] See K. Jahn, 'Das iranische Papiergeld', *Archiv Orientální*, x (1938), 308–40, and idem, 'Paper Currency in Iran', *Journal of Asian History*, iv (1970), 101–35.

in from Central Asia, accelerating the Turkicization of large stretches of the Middle East, such as Anatolia, Transoxania, and parts of Persia. Within the steppe itself, the descendants of Chingiz Khan's son Jochi headed two great Turco-Mongol nomadic confederations, the Golden Horde in South Russia and the White Horde in western Siberia. The former endured for more than two centuries, and through its commercial links with Anatolia and the Mamlūk dominions, became to some extent integrated with the Levantine Islamic world.[1]

An important source for the history of the Golden Horde and the sister-dynasty of the Chaghatayids of Transoxania is the narrative of the most-travelled and most intrepid of all medieval Muslim figures, the Moroccan Ibn Baṭṭūṭa, whose peregrinations ranged from West Africa to China. In 1332–3 he crossed South Russia to the Golden Horde's capital of Saray on the Volga, travelling in one of the large carts with a tented superstructure (*ʿaraba*s) which have been a characteristic mode of conveyance through the steppes since the time of the Scythians. Ibn Baṭṭūṭa asserts that he visited Bulghār, inquisitive to see whether the summer nights there were as short as they were said to be, but it is generally agreed that his account is a fabrication, doubtless made up from reports of Bulghār which he heard in Saray. He later journeyed from the Volga to Khwārazm by camel-drawn wagon, and found it as dangerous and arduous a trip as his predecessor Ibn Faḍlān had done.[2]

The penetration of the Eurasian steppes by Islamic religion and culture continued till Russian expansionism checked it and forced Islam on to the defensive in such regions as the Volga basin, the Caucasus, and Siberia. During the preceding centuries, Islam had successfully overlaid such rival faiths as Latin and Nestorian Christianity and Manicheism, and only the Lamaist Buddhism

[1] See the standard work of B. Spuler, *Die Goldene Horde, die Mongolen im Russland 1223–1502* (Leipzig, 1943).

[2] See the translation of H. A. R. Gibb, *The Travels of Ibn Baṭṭūṭa A.D. 1325–54*, ii (Cambridge, 1959), pp. 469 ff.

adopted by the Mongols had withstood its dynamic; the civilizing influence of Islam has thus been a leading factor in the historical development of Inner Asia.

C. E. BOSWORTH

BIBLIOGRAPHY

There is no single work specifically devoted to the Islamic frontiers in Central Asia, but much useful background information can be derived from W. Barthold, *Turkestan Down to the Mongol Invasion* (3rd edn., London, 1968); idem, *Histoire des Turcs d'Asie Centrale* (Paris, 1945); R. Grousset, *L'Empire des steppes* (4th edn., Paris, 1952); and G. Hambly (ed.), *Zentralasien* (Fischer Weltgeschichte, Band 16) (Frankfurt, 1966).

On Islamic trade connections with eastern Europe, see the outdated but still useful book of G. Jacob, *Der nordisch-baltisch Handel der Araber im Mittelalter* (Leipzig, 1887, reprinted Amsterdam, 1966), and R. Hennig, 'Der mittelalterliche arabische Handelsverkehr in Osteuropa', *Der Islam*, xxii (1935), 239-64. Amongst the accounts left by Muslim travellers, for Ibn Faḍlān, see A. Z. V. Togan, *Ibn Faḍlāns Reisebericht* (Abh. für die Kunde des Morgenlandes, xxiv/3) (Leipzig, 1939), or M. Canard, 'La Relation de voyage d'Ibn Fadlân chez les Bulgares de la Volga', *Annales de l'Institut d'Études Orientales d'Alger*, xvi (1958), 41-146; for Abū Dulaf, see G. Ferrand, *Relations de voyages et textes géographiques arabes, persans et turcs relatifs a l'Extrême-Orient des VIIIe au XVIIIe siècles*, i (Paris, 1913), 89-90, 208-31; and for Ibn Baṭṭūṭa, see H. A. R. Gibb's abridged translation, *Travels in Asia and Africa 1325-54* (London, 1929), and his full translation, *The Travels of Ibn Baṭṭūṭa A.D. 1325-54*, ii (Hakluyt Society, 2nd series, vol. cxvii) (Cambridge, 1959).

(*C*) INDIA

THE Islamic frontier in India is in itself a significant factor in the political, social, and to some extent the religious history of Islam. In India Islam came face to face with one of the oldest religions and civilizations of the world, the Hindu; there in its own right it established great sub-continental empires, it preserved, as in Egypt and in North Africa, the heritage of Islamic orthodoxy when the heartlands of Islam were overwhelmed by the Mongols; and finally India was one of the places where Islam first felt the political, intellectual, and institutional impact of the West.

Muslims arrived in India in three distinct waves. Muslim Arabs arrived on the coasts of southern India as missionaries and merchants as their pagan ancestors had arrived before them, and though this arrival was a mere trickle it continued well into the fifteenth century. Colonies of these immigrant Muslims, such as the Moplas, still survive on the Malabar coast. An account by two Arab merchants, Sulaymān (*c.* 851) and Abū Zayd Ḥasan al-Sīrāfī (*c.* 916), represents the Muslim intellectual reaction to certain aspects of Hindu life and manners at that time.[1]

Conquest of the part of India now known as Sind (on the lower Indus) was planned by ʿUmar I's generals but discouraged by him; later under the Umayyads a successful expedition was organized by Ḥajjāj b. Yūsuf and led by Muḥammad b. Qāsim in 711. This expedition annexed Sind (with part of the lower Punjab) to the Umayyad Caliphate. The province eventually passed into the hands of the Ismāʿīlis who held it until their overthrow by Muḥammad b. Sām Ghūrī in 1175, after which it became part of the Delhi Sultanate and so joined the mainstream of Muslim power in India.

Sind was the only province directly ruled by Arabs or which came in direct contact with them. Though an outlying province of the Caliphate it was the main channel through which ancient Indian sciences passed to Baghdad. Arab Sind was visited by the Muslim geographers al-Masʿūdī (d. 956), Ibn Ḥawqal, and al-Iṣṭakhrī who left interesting accounts of it.[2]

The third, final, and continuous wave of the Muslim conquest of and immigration into India was through the north-east passes of Afghanistan. It began with the invasions of Maḥmūd of Ghazna (998–1030) and the establishment of Ghaznavid power in the Punjab. Under the Ghaznavids Lahore became a significant

[1] Sulaymān and Abū Zayd Ḥasan al-Sīrāfī, *Akhbār al-Ṣīn waʾl-Hind*, French translation by G. Ferrand, *Voyage du marchand arabe Sulayman* (Paris, 1922).

[2] Majoudi, *Les Prairies d'or*, ed. with French translation by C. Barbier de Meynard and Pavet de Courteille, 9 vols. (Paris, 1861–77); revised French translation by Ch. Pellat, 3 vols. (Paris, 1962–).

outpost of Islamic culture in India. The Ghaznavid Muslims of the Punjab began to speak a language akin to modern Punjabi, enriching it with a strong mixture of Persian loan-words; this language later developed into Urdu, which after Arabic, Persian, and Turkish became the fourth major language of the Muslim world.

The Ghaznavids were followed by the Ghūrids. Muḥammad b. Sām Ghūrī (d. 1206) put an end to the rule of the Ghaznavids in the Punjab in 1186; and in a series of invasions he and his generals conquered the greater part of northern India, establishing a Muslim state there, the Delhi Sultanate (1206–1555).

Quṭb al-Dīn Aybak (1206–10), a slave of Muḥammad b. Sām, was the first ruler in the dynasty of the 'Slave Kings', Turkish in origin, Persian by culture. Iltutmish (1211–36) established the Sultanate more firmly, and his court in Delhi became a flourishing centre of Islamic culture. Iltutmish had strong religious and mystic inclinations, and under his encouragement Ṣūfism established itself as an outstanding spiritual force in medieval India where it was represented by two orders, the Suhrawardiyya and the Chishtiyya, whose thought came to dominate the systems of belief in Indian Islam. The last outstanding ruler among the Slave Sultans was Balban (1266–87), who kept the Mongols at bay on the Indian frontiers after they had sacked Baghdad in 1258; and though his dynasty did not long survive him, at his death the Sultanate itself was firmly established on Indian soil.

The next dynasty, that of the Khaljīs (1290–1320), was of Afghan origin; its most powerful ruler, ʿAlā' al-Dīn (1296–1316), converted the Sultanate into an empire by conquering almost the whole sub-continent; and though illiterate he enforced Ḥanafī religious conformity on his Muslim subjects. It was about this time that the influence of Ibn al-ʿArabī's theistic mysticism reached India and made compromises with certain indigenous elements of Hindu origin. Indo-Persian poetry reached its highest mark in the work of Amīr Khusraw, with whom also begins a synthesis of Muslim and Indian music.

The dynasty of the Tughluqs was Turkish, but partly Indianized. Muḥammad b. Tughluq sought and obtained investiture from the Cairene ʿAbbāsid al-Mustakfī in 1343 and tried to establish relations with the other rulers of the Islamic world; but he lost the greater part of the empire in India to feuding governors who founded regional kingdoms, and the southern part of the Deccan was lost to the Hindu kingdom of Vijyānagar. Unstable and eccentric, even cruel by nature, Muḥammad b. Tughluq was an intellectual of high calibre interested in rationalism and suspicious of mysticism. During his reign the North-African traveller Ibn Baṭṭūṭa (see above, p. 129) visited India and was given high offices in the state; he has left interesting accounts of India in that age.[1] The next ruler, Fīrūz Tughluq (1351–88), devoutly religious, ran the state as a theocracy, passed a law aimed at abolishing all corporal punishments illegal according to the *Sharīʿa*, and patronized religious studies. Two significant works of Islamic jurisprudence compiled in India, the *Fiqh-i Fīrūzshāhī* and the *Fatāwā-i Tātārkhānī*, date from the reign of his successor, Muḥammad b. Fīrūz.

Timur's invasion (1398) considerably weakened the Delhi Sultanate. Provinces had begun to break away from it and there arose in the provinces regional kingdoms, some of them with distinctive cultural features. Bengal, which was a far-off province, had become independent earlier and was ruled by several dynasties, one of them African and one Arab. Under the Sultans of Bengal indigenous Bengali literature developed, both a Hindu and a Muslim stream, both of which often met together, and an architecture arose suited to the damp and rainy climate of the region. Propagation of Islam met with greater success in Bengal than in any other part of the sub-continent except the north-west, but culturally the Bengalis remained closer to their Hindu origin.

[1] Ibn Baṭṭuṭa, *Voyages*, ed. with French translation by C. Defrémery and B. R. Sanguinetti, 4 vols. (Paris, 1853–8); *Travels in Asia and Africa*, translated and selected by H. A. R. Gibb (London, 1929); complete translation by Gibb, *The Travels of Ibn Baṭṭūṭa*, 3 vols. (The Hakluyt Society, 2nd series, vols. cx, cxvii, cxli (Cambridge, 1958–71, in progress).

In the extreme north-west the establishment of a Muslim state in 1346 by Shāh Mīrzā Swātī and the gradual conversion of most of the people of Kashmir to Islam was brought about by efforts unconnected with the Delhi Sultanate. Among the Sultans of Kashmir, Sikandar the Iconoclast is known for his intolerance but his son Zayn al-ʿĀbidīn (1420–70) is remembered not only for his tolerance but for his patronage of letters and for the first attempts to bring about an intellectual understanding between Muslim and Hindu civilizations. Under its Sultans, Kashmir developed refined handicraft techniques particularly the weaving of shawls and carpets, woodwork, and embroidery.

The maritime state of Gujarāt lasted from 1391 to 1583 and had closer commercial and ethnic relations with the rest of the Islamic world than any other regional state in India. When challenged by the Portuguese it was prepared to fight them at sea in co-operation with naval detachments of the Mamlūk al-Ashraf Qānṣūh al-Ghawrī (1501–17) and later the Ottoman Sultan, Sulaymān the Magnificent (1520–66). To the commander of the last Ottoman naval expedition is due the only Ottoman Turkish account of contemporary events and the Muslim social milieu in India.[1] Gujarāt carried on a flourishing trade with the Islamic maritime countries until the Portuguese won control of the Indian Ocean.

The Sharqī dynasty ruled Jawnpūr in the valley of the Ganges from 1394 to 1479 when it was reabsorbed into the Delhi Sultanate. Its rulers were patrons of art, especially of music, while its mosque architecture developed an individuality of its own by giving predominance to the *maqṣūra* (see below, p. 253). The Sultanate of Mālwa (1401–1531) in central India, ruled by two successive dynasties, also created some remarkable architectural monuments.

A distinctive variety of Indo-Muslim culture developed in southern India, known as the Deccan, under the Bahmanids (1347–1527), and in their five successor states, Golconda, Bijāpūr, Aḥmadnagar, Berar, and Bīdar. The first three of these, as well

[1] Sīdī ʿAlī Re'īs Efendī (Kātib-i Rūmī), *Mir'āt al-mamālik*, ed. Ahmed Jevdet (Istanbul, 1895); English translation by A. Vambéry (London, 1899).

as some of the Bahmanid sultans, were Shīʿite though they failed to convert the bulk of their Muslim subjects to Shīʿism. The Deccani Muslim civilization, long cut off from northern India, was more tolerant of the Hindus, more responsive to indigenous linguistic and social influences, in its later stages emotionally attached to Ṣafavid Persia, perhaps less refined but mellower than the north. Its principal cultural achievement, apart from its regional architecture, was the development of the Deccani variety of Urdu which produced a rich and healthy literature in prose and verse long before northern India turned to Urdu as a literary language. Trading relations carried the influence of Bahmanid architecture to the Muslims on the coast of East Africa.

The Mogul empire, which marks the highest point of splendour, of political power, and of cultural efflorescence in Islamic India, was founded by Bābur, a Timurid Turk, in 1526. During his reign and that of his successor Humāyūn (1530–40, 1555–6) Turkish vied with Persian to become the literary language of India, but Persian emerged supreme. Bābur's Turkish memoirs constitute the finest specimen of Chaghatay Turkish prose. Humāyūn's rule in India was interrupted by a successful rebellion of the Pathāns (Afghans), and during this interregnum (1540–55) Shīr Shāh Sūrī laid the foundations of the land revenue and communications system on which the Mogul administration came to be based. Akbar (1556–1605), in many ways a unique personality in Muslim India, extended the borders of the empire to incorporate the whole of northern and central India, integrated the martial Hindu Rājpūts who had so far been hostile to Muslim rule into his army and administration, encouraged intermarriage with Hindus, and turned away from traditional Islam to a religion of his own, the *Dīn-i Ilāhī*, a kind of solar monotheism. His able Hindu minister, Rāja Todar Mal, organized an efficient land revenue system. Civil and military administration was run by a hierarchy of non-hereditary nobility called *manṣabdān*s.

His son Jahāngīr (1605–27) and his grandson Shāh Jahān (1628–58) ruled over a prosperous empire in unprecedented splendour. Jahāngīr was a *bon viveur* of very artistic tastes, and is the author of an autobiography, a landmark in the brilliant historical literature of the Mogul age, which combined the heritage of the historiography of the Delhi Sultanate with the traditions of Timurid historiography. Shāh Jahān was a master-builder, creator of some of the finest architectural monuments in the world, including the Taj Mahal.

The Moguls maintained relations with the Ṣafavids, the Ottomans, and the Uzbeks without overtones of political ambition or sectarian proclivities. There was an influx of administrative and intellectual talent from Persia and Central Asia which kept Muslim India in the mainstream of Islamic culture. Poetry, discouraged by the Ṣafavids, flourished at the Mogul court, and in this period a particular school of Indo-Persian poetry, the *sabk-i Hindī*, assumed its specific features, though its beginnings can be traced back to the Ghaznavid Punjab. In the art of epistle-writing (*inshā'*), diplomatic, administrative, or personal, the secretaries of the Mogul, the Ottoman, and the Ṣafavid courts vied with each other.

The last of the grand Moguls was Awrangzīb (1658–1707), who rose to the throne after a war of succession in which he eliminated his brothers and dethroned his father. Under him almost the entire sub-continent came under Mogul sway, but there were also the beginnings of decline as he could only temporarily check the insurgence of the predatory Marāthas. Awrangzīb, like Fīrūz Tughluq, ran the state as a theocracy, reimposed the *jizya* or poll tax on non-Muslims, which had been abolished by Akbar, provided welfare measures for the Muslim élite, and governed with exemplary personal rectitude and puritanism. The *Fatāwā-i Hindiyya*, a comprehensive work of Ḥanafī jurisprudence, was compiled under his patronage.

Two mystical orders, the Naqshbandī and the Qādirī, became popular in the time of the great Moguls. The Naqshbandī Shaykh Aḥmad Sirhindī developed a doctrine of phenomenological monism which was a reaction against the almost pantheistic doctrine of ontological monism as expounded by the Spanish Arab mystic, Ibn al-ʿArabī (d. 1240). The Naqshbandī movement emphasized the exclusiveness of the Muslim community which became a state policy under Awrangzīb. The Qādirī mysticism which flourished under Shāh Jahān was, comparatively speaking, more eclectic.

With the death of Awrangzīb in 1707 the visible decline of the Mogul empire suddenly began. Various non-Muslim militant communities rose and carved out for themselves large chunks of the empire, the Marāthas in the Deccan, the Sikhs in the Punjab, the Rājputs in their territories, and the Jāts in the valley of the Jumna. Muslim governors of other provinces became autonomous, only nominally acknowledging the authority of the emperor of Delhi whose actual jurisdiction became confined to Delhi and its environs. Early successors of Awrangzīb were puppets in the hands of Shīʿī king-makers, the Sayyids of Barha. Invasions from the north-west by the Persian Nādir Shāh in 1739 and by the Afghan Aḥmad Shāh Abdālī between 1747 and 1761 were even more disastrous for the Moguls.

During the eighteenth century, in the Mogul 'time of troubles', when the court was ineffectual and the élite on the decline, a theologian, Shāh Walī-Allāh (1703–62), emerged as a spiritual leader of great eminence. His theology was fundamentalist with a liberalism which has paved the way for modernist trends in Indian Islam. His reaction against the narrow interpretation of jurisprudence, his emphasis on the Koran and the sayings of the Prophet as the essential sources of law, his realization that the law of Islam had to be presented 'in a new dress', and his synthesis of traditionalism and mysticism, were significant landmarks in the development of religious thought in Muslim India. His son Shāh ʿAbd al-ʿAzīz continued his work and ran a religious seminary in Delhi which propagated Walī-Allāh's teaching.

In the early nineteenth century, under the influence of Walī-Allāh's ideas, a movement, that of the *mujāhidūn* (holy warriors), gathered momentum. This fundamentalist movement was closely parallel to that of Muḥammad b. ʿAbd al-Wahhāb in Nejd, by which it may have been partly influenced. The *mujāhidīn*, led by Sayyid Aḥmad Barīlwī, built up an organizational network among the Muslim masses of northern India, preaching abandonment of pseudo-religious social customs borrowed from the Hindus, denouncing the association of other persons with God (*shirk* or polytheism) in all its forms, leading and advocating a puritanical life, and finally conducting a *jihād* against the Sikhs; though they temporarily carved out a theocratic principality in the north-west, their movement was shattered when Sayyid Aḥmad was defeated by the Sikhs and died in 1831.

In the meantime, in the chaos and anarchy which prevailed in the sub-continent during the decline of Mogul power, the British East India Company gradually created an empire for itself. The three principal landmarks of the establishment of British rule in India are the Battle of Plassey (1757), when the British defeated Sirāj al-Dawla, the autonomous Mogul governor of Bengal, and established their power in that province; the grant of the *dīwānī* (land revenue collection) of the eastern provinces of north India to the East India Company by the helpless Mogul emperor, Shāh ʿĀlam II in 1763, which gave the company *de jure* authority over a wide area of the country; and the uprising or 'Sepoy Mutiny' of 1857 which put an end to the rule of the East India Company and led to its replacement by the direct rule of the British Parliament and Crown.

Muslim response to British rule and institutions was not as receptive as that of the Hindus. The government of the East India Company favoured Hindus rather than Muslims. In its first areas of expansion in Bengal and in Arcot on the south-eastern coast its adversaries had been Muslims. Its administrative policy in certain regions, especially Bengal, was detrimental to the Muslims, as in 1793 the Governor-General Cornwallis and Sir John Shore introduced a land revenue system called the Permanent Settlement which reduced Muslim farmers and peasants to the level of agricultural labourers and created a class of Hindu landlords (*zamīndārs*) who thrived at the expense of the Muslim masses. The Ḥanafī law as amended by the Moguls was the law of the land throughout India when the British took over. By incorporating tradition and elements of British common law, the Company's government formed it into Anglo-Muhammadan law, which came to be confined to personal law as applied to Muslims. In 1835 English replaced Persian as the official language. For Hindus it meant merely a change from one foreign language to another; Muslims had undergone no such experience earlier.

During the eighteenth century Urdu had replaced Persian as the language of poetry. The British helped the development of Urdu prose in the beginning of the nineteenth century by sponsoring at Fort William College, Calcutta, works written in simple, conversational, utilitarian prose.

In 1859 Sayyid Aḥmad Khān made an effort towards adjustment to British rule, which soon developed into a modernist religious, educational, and social movement. In politics he persuaded the Muslims to adopt a policy of loyalism. For the education of Muslim youth he founded a College at Aligarh which later became a university and which was to produce much of the Muslim intellectual and political leadership in the future. But Sayyid Aḥmad Khān's most dynamic contribution was religious. Of the four sources of Muslim law he relied solely on the Koran which he interpreted apologetically; he doubted the authenticity of much of the *ḥadīth* (traditions); he denied the validity of *ijmāʿ* (the consensus of the jurists); and instead of *qiyās* (analogy) he followed Walī-Allāh in his emphasis on *ijtihād* (individual reasoning) which he regarded as the birthright of every Muslim. Though much of Sayyid Aḥmad Khān's political thought was rejected in detail even by the succeeding modernists, he left an indelible impression on the religious thinking and belief of the new generations of the Westernized Muslim élite.[1]

[1] J. M. S. Baljon, *The Reforms and Religious Ideas of Sir Sayyid Aḥmad Khān* (Leiden, 1949); see Aziz Ahmad, *Islamic Modernism in India and Pakistan* (London, 1967), for the subsequent history of Islamic modernism in the sub-continent.

In politics his policy of loyalism bore fruit by 1870 when the British Indian government changed its attitude towards the Muslims. But with the introduction of Gladstonian liberalism into India and the foundation of the predominantly Hindu Indian National Congress in 1885, he sensed the economic and political threat to the Muslim minority in India from the overwhelming Hindu majority. He gave to Muslim politics in India an orientation which consisted of two components: wariness of the Hindus and loyalty to the British. In the succeeding development of Muslim politics the former came to be intensified, and the latter was discarded. When he died in 1898, Sayyid Aḥmad Khān left behind a Muslim community politically awake, educationally taking preliminary steps towards modernization, and economically with better prospects than in the preceding century.

In the triangular political manœuvres between the Hindus, Muslims, and the British, Sayyid Aḥmad Khān's political successors insisted on safeguards for their community and on separate electoral bodies for the Muslims. This was the main plank of the Muslim League, founded in 1906. At times there were tactical alliances with the Indian National Congress as during the First World War, and especially during the Khilāfat Movement (1919–24) which stood for the restoration to Turkey of its territory lost in the World War. But after 1924 the Congress-Muslim League alliance broke up, never to be formed again. Muslim nationalism took a different path from that of Hindu nationalism.

In 1930 the eminent poet and philosopher Muḥammad Iqbāl (1875–1938) presented the idea of a separate homeland for Muslims in the provinces in which they were in the majority within the sub-continent. In 1937 Muḥammad ʿAlī Jināḥ (M. A. Jinnah) revived the Muslim League, and within a decade made it overwhelmingly representative of Muslim opinion in favour of political separatism from the Hindus. In 1940 the Muslim League adopted a resolution demanding the creation of a Muslim sovereign state in the areas of Muslim majority in the north-west and in Bengal. This resolution, in fact, demanded Pakistan, a name mnemonically formed from the names of Muslim majority areas in the north-west: Punjab, Afghania, Kashmir, Sind, and Baluchistan. The concept of Pakistan was bitterly resented by the Hindus, but as the movement gathered momentum the idea gained recognition by the British government and by some Hindu politicians. After the Second World War, the British Labour government decided to hand over the reins of power to the Indians, and partition of the sub-continent took place, after much bitterness, in 1947.

Islamic identity in the sub-continent found a new lease of life with the creation of Pakistan. But the new state had to face from the outset tremendous challenges: a distance of 1,000 miles between its two wings in the west and in the east with different ethnic, linguistic, and cultural backgrounds, and united only by religion and a common fear of India; riots in India and Pakistan in 1947 which involved the transfer and resettlement of millions of individuals; the untimely death of its two founding leaders, Muḥammad ʿAlī Jināḥ in 1948 and Liyāqat ʿAlī Khān in 1951; the incompetence of the political leadership which brought the new state to the verge of chaos between 1951 and 1958; and finally, its disputes with India, the most critical of which was the question of the accession of the overwhelmingly Muslim state of Kashmir, a problem which led to two wars between India and Pakistan, in 1948 and 1965.

The country was given considerable stability by the military revolution of 1958 and by the Second Republic which came into being in 1962 under the leadership of Muḥammad Ayyūb Khān, so that by 1968 Pakistan was making the fastest progress economically of all the developing nations of the world.

In modern Islamic history the significance of Pakistan lies in its self-identification with Islam and its claim to call itself an Islamic state. The secular-minded founders of Pakistan were concerned primarily with safeguarding Muslim political and economic interests which they saw endangered in an undivided India; they paid merely lip-service to Pakistan. The *ulema* of Deoband, a conservative theological antithesis to Aligarh since the late nineteenth century, were opposed to the concept of Pakistan. But after the creation of the new state a number of conservative *ulema* made Pakistan their home, the most influential of them being the fundamentalist/externalist Abu'l-Aʿlā Mawdūdī. The *ulema* joined forces with certain politicians and formed a pressure group which struggled against the westernized ruling élite's concept of a secular democracy with a nominal Islamic veneer. This struggle between orthodoxy and modernism is reflected in the series of compromises in Pakistan's constitutional documents which on the whole proclaimed sovereignty as vested in God and exercised by the people of Pakistan 'within the limits prescribed by Him'. These documents from 1950 to 1963 accepted the principle that the law of the land should not be repugnant to Koran and *sunna*. These provisions were, however, interpreted differently by the modernists and the religious conservatives. The former regarded them essentially as theoretical formulas to be translated into practice with as much reserve and resistance as possible, while the latter, especially Mawdūdī and his party, interpreted and enlarged them with the aim of making the country a complete theocracy. The conflict between modernism and orthodoxy in Pakistan is still unresolved, and the drama of the process of modernization of an Islamic state continues to be an intriguing one.[1]

The partition of the sub-continent left the Muslim minority in the Republic of India, which forms 10 per cent of its population, in an insecure position. Politically mistrusted, economically rejected and ignored, educationally backward, their future is bleak.[2] But Islam in India has its saving graces. Mawdūdī's movement, which is a threat to modernization in Pakistan, is a source of communal stability and organization in India. The governments of the Indian National Congress, though indifferent to the particular

[1] Leonard Binder, *Religion and Politics in Pakistan* (Berkeley and Los Angeles, 1961); E. I. J. Rosenthal, *Islam in the Modern National State* (Cambridge, 1965), pp. 125–53; Ahmad, op. cit., pp. 237–53.

[2] S. Abid Husain, *The Destiny of Indian Muslims* (London, 1965).

concerns of the Muslim masses, have appointed individual Muslims to some of the highest offices of the state, including that of President of the Republic.

Islam in the Indian sub-continent has had two external challenges which could threaten its identity, the Hindu and the Western. Hindu civilization, notwithstanding its caste-structure, is more assimilative than any other civilization. Islam alone, rigidly monotheistic, communally insular, resisted Hinduism's assimilative pull. But the contact and conflict between the two religions and the two civilizations led to the rise of microscopic communities on the fringe such as Ḥusaynī Brahmans, influenced by the two principal Ismāʿīlī groups in India, the Bohras and the Khojas, and within Hinduism led to the rise of the syncretistic mystical Bhakti movement in the thirteenth century and to the formation of the Sikh religion, which later became bitterly anti-Muslim. Much of the political conflict between Hindus and Muslims in modern times is a heritage of the religious and cultural conflict of medieval and early modern history.

AZIZ AHMAD

BIBLIOGRAPHY

A. Ahmad, *Studies in Islamic Culture in the Indian Environment* (Oxford, 1966); W. Haig, and others, *Cambridge History of India*, vols. iii and iv (Cambridge, 1928–37); S. M. Ikram, *Muslim Civilization in India* (New York, 1964); A. Karim, *Social History of the Muslims in Bengal* (Dacca, 1959); R. C. Majumdar (ed.), *The Delhi Sultanate* (Bombay, 1960); M. Mujeeb, *The Indian Muslims* (London, 1967); I. H. Qureshi, *The Muslim Community of the Indo-Pakistan Sub-Continent* (The Hague, 1962); idem, *The Struggle for Pakistan* (Karachi, 1965); W. C. Smith, *Modern Islam in India* (London, 1946); M. Titus, *Islam in India and Pakistan* (Calcutta, 1959).

(*D*) INDONESIA

This section tries to outline a profile of Islam in Indonesia as a historically developed phenomenon with acute contemporary significance. The method of presentation will be a series of fairly brief statements, each of which should, ideally, emerge as the conclusion of a properly reasoned exposé for which, unfortunately, the present volume cannot offer the necessary space. But before giving these statements, it is necessary to preface them by an equally summary statement about the history of Indonesian Islam. This history, as a sequence of meaningful events and as the Indonesian Muslim's perception of it (this perception being one ingredient of the Muslim Indonesian's self-view), is an intrinsic element of the contemporary significance of Islam in Indonesia. The fact that it has been inadequately studied and is therefore somewhat unevenly known has no doubt contributed to the differences of opinion, amongst Indonesian Muslims and amongst non-Indonesian Islamic specialists alike, concerning the characteristics of Indonesian Islam.

Islam is one of three major culture waves that have reached Indonesia from the north-western direction and that have, in gradually penetrating large parts or all of the archipelago, moulded its civilization. It has followed upon, and gradually superseded, the Hindu-Buddhist wave, traces of which nevertheless remain noticeable, especially in Bali. It has been followed by, and has for quite some time now existed in concurrence with, a European wave mediated by the Dutch. Like the two other cultural waves, Islam is said to have come in the wake of trade and to have spread on its wings. This explanation accounts for part, but not necessarily all, of its success. Another part of the explanation may be the religious by-product of political and commercial competition between mainly Western powers, in so far as this affected indigenous populations. Rather than embracing Christianity, and by implication submitting to any of the foreign powers promoting its competing versions, people are said to have gone for Islam—which had no major sponsoring power—whenever they felt the time was right to substitute something new for beliefs and practices that were crumbling under the sheer weight of outside pressure. These and other explanations are gratuitous in that they are hard to substantiate with historical evidence, but they tally with the general picture of the spread of Islam so far as we know it. This is often said to resemble an oil stain: gradual yet effective. Many, too, have praised its peaceful nature. Again so far as we know, the acceptance of Islamic doctrine has been a gradual process, partly thanks to the practice of conversion prior to indoctrination. The accent has not been on critical rethinking of tenets and positions as much as on the quiet absorption of those elements of creed and practice which at a given time must have appeared compatible with the ongoing life style, including any persistent elements of earlier religious, philosophical, and legal patterns. If the basic currents of this procedure can be described as syncretic, they appear as typically Indonesian rather than strictly Islamic ones. Conversely, this may help to explain the fact that one of the signal characteristics of Indonesian Islam is a continual struggle for purity.

Islam reached the Indonesian shores towards the end of the thirteenth century A.D., in a gradual movement subsequent to its establishment as the ruling power in large parts of India. There is no doubt that its first foothold was in northern Sumatra; but there is unending dispute as to which part of India it came from. Malacca, closely related to Java, served as a major diffusion centre from the early fifteenth century onwards, and Java had Islamic pockets on its north coast from the sixteenth. From then onwards, the spread of Islam has been linked to the commercial-political power games being played throughout the archipelago, with first the Portuguese and then the Dutch as major participants from outside. In Java especially, Islamization shows political correlations at crucial moments, to the extent that its spread provides a fairly exact indication of the decay of the Hindu empire.

Conversion in the other major islands—Sumatra, Kalimantan (Borneo), and Sulawesi (Celebes)—has proceeded gradually and in a somewhat spasmodic sense; depending on circumstances, a particular region would either hold its own and stick to pagan tradition or gradually succumb to Islam or again, in rather fewer cases, embrace Christianity. The same basic pattern, with a further delay factor involved, applies to the many lesser islands and archipelagoes. Even today there remain pockets, invariably in remote parts in the interior of islands, that have not yet embraced Islam.

A few features of this ill-documented, and therefore somewhat elusive, process stand out.

In the early seventeenth century and still in northern Sumatra, we see a struggle between two conceptions of Islam which were being introduced, namely mysticism (a mixture of the philosophic and the aesthetic variants) and orthodoxy. This struggle is exceptionally well documented. The general picture shows the mystics going in first. It seems likely that the Ṣūfī brotherhoods played a role in this connection, but this role is not clear. Wherever the mystics went, the orthodox followed on their heels. In the end, orthodoxy has for all practical purposes superseded mysticism, yet without eliminating it everywhere. In certain areas (e.g. northern Sumatra, southern Sulawesi, central Java) it has lingered on. At the present time it is once more visible, but in a role that remains to be determined.

In the first half of the nineteenth century, Islam appears as part of the budding Indonesian feeling of self-identification, in the still fairly restricted sense that it helps to rationalize and indeed to galvanize forceful resistance against further Dutch penetration. The most noted case in point is the Dipo Negoro episode in Java (1825–30). In rewriting Indonesian history, modern nationalists have perhaps made more of this episode than is warranted, but it is hard to deny that there is a basis of truth to their claims.

In the second half of the nineteenth century, Indonesian Islam began to show the results of an increasingly effective communication with the rest of the Islamic world, notably with the Indian sub-continent and then also with the religious centres of Mecca and Cairo. The first symptoms appear in an Indonesian response to the budding movements towards reform and reassertion, as originating in Syria and Egypt and then carried forward in India. Gradually, this tendency has become part of the emerging national awareness, which took organizational shape in the first decade of the twentieth century.

This concludes the historical prelude, and the scene shifts to the present.

In the process of unification of the Indonesian *nation* and *polity*, Islam has been the second factor in order of importance, colonial rule with the response elicited by it being the first. In respect of the cohesion of present-day Indonesian society it is one of several factors, one of which is a keen national awareness. These are of undetermined relative significance, and mutually competitive to a certain extent. When and where their simultaneous occurrence appears as a struggle for predominance, the outcome is uncertain. There is no saying in advance that Islam must win every round. Yet its persistence appears as a basic datum.

Rather than actually representing a full way of life, in the manner it is supposed to, Islam is one, undoubtedly important, ingredient of Indonesian *culture*. Its effective significance is variable, both locally and chronologically. On the other hand, its importance for purposes of socio-cultural self-identification of the Indonesians is outstanding. Indonesian society and to a considerable extent also Indonesian culture present themselves under the imprint of Islam.

Contrariwise, Islam has not proven a major factor in moulding the patterns of *authority* and *administration* at any levels whether in pre-colonial, colonial, or post-colonial times. It has happened and does happen that honorific titles (especially of rulers) and, to a much lesser extent, legitimizing of power are nominally Islamic. It usually turns out, however, that even in such cases the effective significance of Islam is either of a short-span emotional nature or merely verbal. The supportive role that the religious institution

821913X

(scholars, judges, mosque functionaries, leaders of religious associations) may elsewhere have in respect of the ruler is barely reflected in the Indonesian setting.

In this connection, the administration of *law* constitutes a special chapter. Throughout the area the Shāfiʿī school is predominant, so far as Muslim conceptions of law are concerned. This predominance, however, does not mean much for the efficacy of Islamic law as such. From the very first moment and up to the present day, Islamic law in Indonesia has been at loggerheads with many, diverse yet related, systems of customary law that were fully operational by the time of its advent and that still are very important for many purposes in many parts of the archipelago. On top of this, it has suffered unequal and systematic competition from the increasingly effective legal and judiciary provisions of colonial rule, many of which survive even today: the spread of Islam and that of colonial rule having run roughly parallel courses for a considerable length of time. The consequence is that the application of Islamic law in Indonesia has tended to be very limited, mostly to family law.

A related matter is the *institutionalization of Islam*. Traditionally, institutionalization did not go beyond a motley array of organizational provisions, such as variously organized judgeships, the position of independent scholars in their own institutions of learning (acting, from time to time, as *muftī*s without formal investiture), of trustees of *waqf*s, and the committees and personnel of ever so many mosques and *langgar*s (places of worship not usable for the Friday service). As mentioned before, in precolonial times as well as under colonialism, local rulers acted so as to render the sanction of Islam a mere formality, if not fully supererogatory, in most cases. The only notable exception to this pattern was the role played during the earlier phases of Islamization by scholars, some of whom were rated subsequently as holy men and bringers of Islam, as the supporters of recently Islamized princes. Colonial rule was on the whole wary of Islam, a state of affairs that did not really change even when an enlightened—

yet at the same time expansive—colonial policy was guided by none other than C. Snouck Hurgronje, one of the founders of modern Islamic studies in the West. It kept a watchful eye on the Muslims. This was in due course institutionalized in a special, but quite small bureau. In the meantime, the Muslim component of the budding nationalist movement began to grope for organizational forms, as a means to become more articulate in public life and also to develop strength. The Japanese occupation brought, especially in Java, a development of the bureau for Islamic affairs of which the Indonesians were somewhat slow to detect the double face: a network of organs allegedly meant to maintain close contact with the Muslim community, and in reality a machine for propaganda and incidentally for religiously phrased political pressure. Since independence, this apparatus has been revamped to an extent, and its centrepiece has become the Ministry of Religion. This ministry is in a somewhat precarious position, being supposed on the one hand to cater for the interests of all religious groups as such, but being staffed largely by Muslims and being expected by many in the Muslim community to fill its felt organizational lacunae. Quite separately, several Islamic political parties and other organizations exist.

For a considerable period Islam has, in large parts of the archipelago, been in a position to provide most if not all of the *pattern of associations* and of the *educational system*. The educational pattern, never formalized in any systematic way until it was too late for tradition to be maintained, used to embrace the full range from elementary to college-level education. (Those seeking the top levels would go to Mecca or Cairo.) It has suffered severe setbacks under the impact of the colonial educational system which strictly paralleled that of the mother country in Europe. It appears unlikely to achieve a come-back under conditions of national independence, at least not without a major overhaul. A notable aspect of traditional Islamic education in Indonesia is that it did not rely on the mosque as its operational centre. Particularly the middle and higher levels used to have their own kind of facilities.

Notwithstanding their Arabic name, *madrasa*, these recall the Indian *ashram* or perhaps the Iranian or Turkish Ṣūfī confraternity centre rather than the Arab mosque-university. Turning now to the associational pattern, its vicissitudes are perhaps even more complex. Like everywhere else in the world of Islam, associations tend to have Islamic aspects in any kind of mixture with any other aspects. During the days of the early spread of Islam into and through Indonesia, religious brotherhoods, many of a pronouncedly mystical character, played an important, albeit unascertained, role. Some forms of organization must have supported the occasional outbursts of more or less religiously identified opposition against spreading colonial rule. A 'modern' organizational pattern took over in order to bring Islam into the framework of political nationalism, as one of its pillars. Religious, allegedly Islamic, esoterism stands at the root of some contemporary associational phenomena.

In the *arts*, Indonesia could not possibly be regarded as an offshoot of traditions established elsewhere in the Muslim world, whether in the Near East or in the Indian sub-continent. Indonesia has at least two major artistic traditions of great riches, one belonging to the old pagan stock and the other influenced by Hinduism and Buddhism. Either tradition embraces such art forms as music, sculpture, architecture, and literature (sometimes oral, sometimes written tradition). For good measure one might add historiography, whether as myth or legend or as chronicle. The impact of Islam—or to put it more correctly, of Islamization—on these traditions shows itself mostly as a subduing influence. There is relatively little effective modification and even less new impulse. Surely the shape of the tombs of Muslims conforms to the generally known Islamic pattern, also the more elaborate ones of holy men. The mosque, on the other hand, is entirely Indonesian for its architecture in the more typical cases: a high, layered roof and often no minaret. (The call for prayer is supported by the beating of a heavy drum, *bedug*.)

With Arabic the *language* of the Koran and of all the basic literature of Islam, with Islam—including the pilgrimage—as a network of communications abroad, and with the presence of colonies of Southern (Ḥaḍramī) Arabs in parts of the archipelago, it was natural for at least some of the Indonesian languages to signal the Islamization of their speakers through a degree of Arabization. Particularly some languages of Sumatra, for example Achehnese, are illustrative. In a possible shift from oral to written tradition, they adapted the Arabic alphabet. Besides, they incorporated, to some extent, Arabic vocabulary. Technical terms from theology and philosophy were natural choices for adoption; so were a good many abstract notions. For good measure, a number of common words have also crept in; some of these may well have served purposes of simple human snobbery, if one is to judge by the availability of adequate synonyms belonging to the language concerned. It so happens that one of the languages relatively most affected is Malay, the language that has in the course of time become the lingua franca in all coastal areas, first for commercial purposes and in the end even for political expression. Under the name of Indonesian, it is now the official language of the country; on the anvil of nationalism, it has been hammered into becoming an adequate tool of articulate expression for all purposes, including literature. The achievement of this status, however, has coincided with a de-emphasis of its Arabic element. The Arabic alphabet—unlike, for example, the Javanese alphabet—has been discontinued in all languages that were previously written in it in favour of the Latin alphabet.

As regards *literature*, it must be assumed that the budding Islamic literature of Indonesia to a certain extent filled a void, namely the need for information ensuing upon Islamization. To another extent, it inevitably had to make room for itself by supplanting the literary forms of older tradition in those regions where it took over as the major cultural feature. Given the tenacity of the oral tradition, it must also be assumed, and indeed it may be perceived here and there, that this was a slow process. There is little evidence of blending: it was rather a matter of the two being in mutual competition. Blending has occurred, on the other hand, in the encounter between two written traditions. Javanese literature is the outstanding example. There, the continuing tradition, deeply imbued with Indian elements, has accommodated a measure of Islamic accretion, yet without a decisive change of its character. This kind of admixture is negligible or non-existent in a case such as Batak literature, the Batak area (eastern Sumatra) having resisted Islamization to a large extent. It is rather more traceable in Buginese and Makassarian, the two leading languages of southern Celebes, where Islamization was even signalled by adoption of the Arabic script. The clearest cases of a fully Islamic literature occur in, once again, Achehnese and Malay. In all these languages a written tradition has flourished, in manuscript form, during at least three centuries, from the beginning of the seventeenth till the beginning of the twentieth century. Started by mystics, Indonesian as well as Indian, and by at least one fervent anti-mystic, of Indian extraction, this tradition found its origin in the manner in which the early scholars channelled Islam into the minds of their pupils. Their presentation, necessarily eclectic, is reflected in manuscripts full of scattered lecture notes intermingled with fragments, often beginning and ending brusquely, that must have been copied from available originals, mostly Arabic. A number of basic texts in *tafsīr*, *kalām*, and *fiqh* have found their way into Indonesian usage in basically the same manner. Often they carry interlinear translation into some Indonesian language. On the whole, this manuscript tradition cannot have left much scope to Indonesian originality in matters of religious thought. Even in the matter of apparent preferences for certain authors one should perhaps refrain from drawing conclusions as to Indonesian predilections. There is no saying how much of established preferences is conscious choice and how much goes back to random availability of sources in the early days. Towards the end of the nineteenth century, the manuscript tradition began to give way to printed books. Printing presses in Indonesia, operating in Latin script, have, since the beginning of the century, produced a constantly growing stream of tracts, pamphlets, booklets, and occasionally also sizeable books, on Islamic subjects. A major factor in this connection has been the Indonesian response to so-called modernism, of the Egyptian-Syrian and especially of the Indian type. Another contributive factor has been the emergence and growth of Muslim political parties and other organizations, each adding to the expanding market for information. Qualitatively speaking, there is perhaps not very much in this ever-increasing output that could be considered a match for the writings of leading authors of the Near East or of India and Pakistan. On the other hand, there does exist comparability if it comes to the manner in which writers will present and discuss topical issues. In order to round off this section one should perhaps mention, in passing, contemporary Indonesian literature—poetry, short stories, novels—that, even if mostly written by Muslims, is Islamic in no more than its vague general spirit and in occasional references. During the critical final years of the struggle for independence, this literature has played an important part.

The spread of Islam throughout Indonesia had a *commercial* aspect prior to acquiring—largely due to the upsurge of European colonialism—a political one. It can be argued that Islam reached Indonesia, and began spreading into Indonesia, on the wings of commerce. One must be careful in trying to draw conclusions from this circumstance. It may all have been a matter of coincidence: it need not tell anything about the intrinsic relationships, if any, between the Muslim's outlook on life and the typical mind of the businessman.

The *numbers* of Muslims in Indonesia are such that the Indonesians can rightly pride themselves on being one of the largest Muslim nations in the world. It is often maintained by Indonesian Muslims, and seldom overtly contradicted by others, that out of the total population of roughly 120 million, some 90 per cent are Muslims.[1] In the absence of relevant census data, the

[1] The remaining ten per cent are divided over mainly four categories. The oldest of these is paganism of various kinds, typical of the oldest known stages of Indonesian civilization. Then there is so-called Shiwaism-Buddhism, the Balinese

figure is hard to contradict or, for that matter, to corroborate. It is quite eloquent, however, in one particular respect. It says that it is the effective wish of many Indonesians that the Indonesian nation be identified as Islamic. It does not, and could not, say that the same number of Indonesians would with equal efficacy desire this identification to become formalized: those who would overtly wish to proclaim Indonesia as an Islamic state do not now appear as either numerous or influential. There are certain groups of Indonesians who will, by (white) dress and general conduct, appear as live specimens of Islamic piety; in central Java, they are known as *wong putihan*, white people. As a rule, however, Indonesians do not appear better or worse, in the observance of religious duties, than Muslims elsewhere, but for a marked zeal in favour of the pilgrimage to Mecca, which is perhaps to be ascribed to a feeling of distance, physical and spiritual, from the true centres of Islam. Indonesian Islam has a distinctly Indonesian flavour, but the flavour occurs to highly variable degrees and in highly variable ways according to locale. In central Java, where the influence of Hinduism and Buddhism was quite profound, Islam appears almost like a thin veneer overlying an earlier and persistent culture pattern, which will not, however, prevent individual persons from being devout Muslims. On the other hand, in the Hulu Sungai area to the north-east of Banjarmasin, south Kalimantan, no specific local culture can be traced because most of the populace are relatively recent immigrants from various parts, and Islam fills a cultural void in an apparently haphazard yet clearly not unsatisfactory manner.

Indonesia has a five-point state philosophy that dates back to

variant of Indonesian religiosity as moulded under Indian influences. Firmly entrenched culturally, socially, and to an extent even politically, this appears of lasting vitality. It shows no inclination to spread. Thirdly, there is the philosophic religiosity of Chinese tradition, restricted to the Chinese in Indonesia. Fourthly, and most vigorous among the four, Christianity in its many forms. Having successfully relinquished the stigma of being a white man's religion, Christianity nowadays is a social and political force in the country far beyond its numerical proportions, and it appears to be growing in numbers too.

the days shortly before the Japanese surrender. One of the five points is the assertion of what is called *keTuhanan Jang Maha-esa.* Untranslatable for its compactness, this sentence asserts that He Who is The absolute One is the Lord. It distinctly evokes the Islamic creed, except that the wording deviates on purpose, so that the adherents of other religions may equally well agree with the assertion. Interestingly, when the five points were first presented some of the Muslim leaders appear to have been reluctant to accept it. However, whether the matter appears as ambiguity or as vagueness, the virtually inevitable consequence is a state of confusion amongst many diverse, occasionally clashing, opinions in the Muslim camp. None the less this camp will try to hold its own as if it were one in the face of opposition from other ideological camps. Amongst these, nationalism *per se* counts for less and less. Christianity, important as a social factor effectively championing the developmental needs of the country, does not yet appear in a distinct role as an ideology on and by itself.

What stands out is that Indonesia appears in the world as an Islamic nation and that at the same time Indonesian Islam is not merely a more or less accurate copy of Islam elsewhere: whether of Islam in India, from where it first came to Indonesia, or of Islam in the heartlands, which have for such a long time been the pole of orientation for Indonesian Muslims. There have been those—non-Muslims, no doubt—who thought they saw an ambiguity here. If ambiguity it be, it could in no way be an exclusive feature of the Indonesian situation. In ever different variants, ever the same ambiguity should be traceable anywhere in the world of Islam, perhaps more manifestly in the outlying parts, but essentially everywhere, even in the original centres of Islam. What is at stake today in respect of Indonesian Islam is closely parallel to, and effectively comparable with, events and phenomena occurring in other parts of the world of Islam, including the heartlands.

C. A. O. VAN NIEUWENHUIJZE

IV

POLITICS AND WAR

MUSLIMS, like Christians, governed and made war; like them too, they managed to involve their religion in both activities. But in the manner and nature of the two involvements there were great differences. The Founder of Christianity bade his followers 'render unto Caesar the things which are Caesar's; and unto God the things which are God's'—and for three centuries Christianity grew as a religion of the oppressed, until Caesar himself became a Christian, and initiated the processes by which the Church became involved in the State, and the State in the Church. The Founder of Islam was his own Constantine. During his lifetime, the Muslims became a political as well as a religious community, with the Prophet as sovereign—governing a place and a people, dispensing justice, collecting taxes, commanding armies, conducting diplomacy, and waging war. For the early generations of Muslims, there was no long testing by persecution, no apprenticeship in resistance to an alien and hostile state power. On the contrary, the state was their own, and the divine favour manifested itself to them in this world in the form of success, victory, and empire.

For Muḥammad and his companions, therefore, the choice between God and Caesar, the snare in which not Christ but so many Christians were to be entangled, did not arise. In Islam, there was no Caesar, there was only God, and Muḥammad was His Prophet, who both taught and ruled on His behalf. The same authority, from the same source, sustained the Prophet in both tasks; the same revelation provided the content of the one, and the basis of the other. When Muḥammad died, his spiritual and prophetic function—the promulgation of God's message—was completed; his religious, and with it his political work remained. This was to spread the law of God among mankind, by extending the membership and authority of the community which recognized and upheld that law. In the leadership of this community, a deputy or successor to the Prophet was needed. The Arabic word *khalīfa*, by which that successor was known, combined the two meanings.

In its origins, the great Islamic institution of the Caliphate was an improvisation. The death of the Prophet, with no succession arranged, precipitated a crisis in the infant Muslim community. There was grave danger that the community might disintegrate into its component parts—the tribes choose new tribal chiefs and revert to tribal custom, the word of God be lost and forgotten. Thanks to the swift and resolute action of a few of the Prophet's closest associates, this danger was averted. A new leader was chosen and accepted, and under his rule and that of his successors, the community of Muḥammad grew by conquest and conversion into a world religion and a universal empire. To the early Muslims, it must have seemed that it was only a matter of time—and not a very long time—before the whole world and all mankind were brought into that community.

The Arabic word used to designate the community is *umma*, probably borrowed from the Hebrew *ummāh*, nation. In classical Arabic it is used of both ethnic and religious entities, and even of groups of men linked by some common quality or attribute. It occurs frequently in the Koran, where it is applied to the Christians, the good Christians, the Jews, the Arabs, and the virtuous, as well as to the followers of the Prophet. In a contemporary document preserved in the traditional biography of Muḥammad, the community of Medina is described as *umma dūn al-nās*—a community apart or distinct from (other) men.

From the start, the Islamic *umma* had a dual character. On the one hand it was a political society—a chieftaincy which swiftly grew into a state and then an empire; on the other it was a religious community, founded by a Prophet and ruled by his deputy. In its origins, it followed the only acceptable political model, that of the Arabian tribe or tribal confederacy. Already during the lifetime of Muḥammad, this model underwent important changes, both of content and of emphasis. Under the rule of the Caliphs these changes were vastly extended and accelerated. The Caliphate was a polity defined by Islam. Religion replaced kinship as the ultimate basis of corporate identity and loyalty; it either supplanted or sanctified custom as the law of the community. While the tribal sheikh presided by the voluntary and revocable consent of the tribe, Muḥammad came to rule by absolute spiritual prerogative, deriving his authority not from the governed but from God. The Caliphs did not claim to inherit the spiritual functions and privileges of prophethood; they were, however, the religious heirs of the Prophet, as heads of the *umma* which he had founded, with the same task of upholding the law of God and bringing it to all mankind. As formulated by the great jurists of Islam, the law itself requires and regulates the office of the Caliphate, which is necessary for the propagation of Islam and the well-being of the Muslims (see further on the *umma* below, Chapter IX (*B*), p. 405).

In recent years it has become fashionable to distinguish between the 'governing institution' and the 'religious institution' in Islam. Whatever relevance this distinction may have to the later Islamic Empires—and even this has been questioned—it has none to early Islam. In the classical Caliphate, government *is* the religious institution, and there is no other. The Germanic invaders of the West found a state and a religion, the Roman Empire and the Christian Church, which had grown along different lines from diverse origins, each retaining its own institutions, hierarchy, and law. The invaders recognized and accepted both, giving expression to their own aims and needs within the dual structure of Roman and Christian polity. The Arab invaders of the Middle East and North Africa brought their own faith and created their own polity, in which Church and State were one and the same, with the Caliph as supreme head. Such pairs of words as religious and secular, spiritual and temporal, clergy and laity, even sacred and profane, had no real equivalents in Islamic usage until much later times, when new terms were devised for new concepts; in classical Islam the dichotomy which these terms denote was unknown and therefore unexpressed. It is sometimes said that the Caliph was pope and emperor in one. The analogy is misleading. The Caliph had no pontifical or even priestly functions, and did not receive the professional training of the men of religion, the *ulema*. His duty was not to expound, still less to interpret the faith, but to uphold and protect it, and to create and maintain conditions in which men could live the good Muslim life in this world, and thus prepare themselves for the world to come. To accomplish this, he had to preserve law and order within the frontiers of Islam, and defend those frontiers against external attack. Where possible, it was his duty to extend those frontiers, until in the fullness of time the whole world was gained for Islam.

The Caliph had various titles. As head of the faith, he was the *Imām*—the leader, and therefore, *par excellence*, the leader in prayer—of the Muslims. This is the term preferred by theologians and jurists when discussing his office. As head of state, he was the *Amir al-Mu'minīn*, conventionally translated Commander of the Faithful. It was by this title, denoting political and military authority, that he was normally designated in official usage. The title *khalīfa* was also frequent in official usage, and, with its abstract equivalent *khilāfa*, caliphate, is the term most commonly used by historians.

In early usage, the Caliph was *khalīfat rasūl Allāh*, the deputy of the Prophet of God; in later times he was often known by the briefer and more powerful formula *khalīfat Allāh*, deputy of God. Despite the disapproval of the jurists, this title was widely, if informally, used. It is very striking that where Western polities speak of the city, crown, state, or people, classical Islam named God as the ultimate repository of authority. The community was God's community, *ummat Allāh*; its property was God's property, *māl Allāh*; its officials, army, even booty, were similarly ascribed. Its enemies, naturally, were God's enemies, *'aduww Allāh*.[1]

[1] D. Santillana, *Istituzioni di diritto musulmano*, i (Rome, 1925), 4, n. 23.

So central an institution as the Caliphate inevitably received a good deal of attention from Muslim scholars and thinkers. In Islam as elsewhere, there were men who sought to observe and define the nature of political authority, and to regulate its exercise. In the West, these tasks have been variously discharged by theologians, philosophers, politicians, constitutional lawyers, and social scientists. In the Islamic world, a somewhat different classification is required. By far the most important body of Muslim writers on the State is that of the Sunnī jurists whose approach, given the nature of Muslim theology and law, is theological and legal at one and the same time. Their starting-point is God's concern for man and intervention in human affairs. Though man is a political animal, he is by nature warlike and destructive, and is incapable by himself of attaining to a knowledge of the good or achieving an orderly social existence. These deficiencies are remedied by revelation and divine law. To uphold and apply the law, a supreme ruler is required, whose office is thus part of the divine plan for mankind. This is the Caliph, or, to use the term favoured in juristic and theological writings, the Imām. The appointment of such a ruler, and obedience to him once appointed, are an obligation of the Muslim community—a religious obligation, failure in which is a sin as well as a crime. As there is only one God and only one divine law, so there must be only one supreme ruler on earth, to represent God and enforce the law.

The schools differed on who should be Caliph and how he should be chosen. There was general agreement that the Caliph must be adult, male, and free, sound of mind, body, and character, wise and courageous, and that he must have a sufficient knowledge of the divine law. Sunnīs and Shīʿīs agreed that he must be of the kin of the Prophet, but differed in their definition of this requirement. For the Sunnīs, it was sufficient that he should be of Quraysh, the Arab tribe to which the Prophet had belonged; for the Shīʿīs, the definition was gradually narrowed to the clan of the Prophet, then his family, and finally his direct descendants through his daughter Fāṭima.

A more important difference arose over the manner of selection. The Shīʿīs came to adopt the doctrine that the Imām held office by divine appointment. Not only therefore could there be only one Imām in the world; there could only be one rightful candidate for the succession at any one time, who would normally be made known by his predecessor. The Sunnī jurists adopted the principle of election, in a form drawn from the procedure by which an Arabian tribe acquired a new chief. Any candidate who met the conditions of eligibility could be elected. The electors were not of course the whole body of Muslims, but those who by virtue of their position and qualities were able to perform this task—in other words, the dignitaries and notables of the community. The composition and numbers of the electorate were never authoritatively defined, nor was the procedure of the election. Some required the concurrence of all competent electors—but without defining their competence; others were content with a quorum of five, three, two, or even one elector. The one elector might be the reigning Caliph, who could thus nominate his successor. The elector or electors, on behalf of the *umma*, offer the Caliphate to the candidate, in accordance with the provisions of the law; the candidate's acceptance constitutes a binding legal contract. The contract is sealed by the *bayʿa*, the giving and taking of homage, symbolized in a handshake. The Caliph is bound to uphold the law and safeguard the *umma*; the subjects are bound to obey the Caliph, and to help him in these tasks. The contract is dissolved or suspended if the Caliph becomes physically or morally unable to carry out his obligations, or seeks to impose what is contrary to the faith and law of Islam. This last point is expressed in two well-known sayings, attributed to the Prophet: 'There is no [duty of] obedience in sin', and 'Do not obey a creature against the Creator'.

Such was the theory; the practice was lamentably different. The first four Caliphs, sanctified by Muslim tradition as the righteous rulers, did indeed emerge from the Muslim élite on a non-hereditary basis, by processes which might be described as electoral in the Sunnī legal sense; but three of the four reigns were ended by murder, the last two amid civil war. Thereafter the Caliphate in effect became hereditary in two successive dynasties, the Umayyads and the ʿAbbāsids, whose system and style of government owed rather more to the autocratic empires of antiquity than to the patriarchal community of Medina. The subject's duty of obedience remained, and was indeed reinforced; the Caliph's obligation to meet the requirements of eligibility and fulfil the conditions of incumbency was emptied of most of its content.

This disparity between theory and practice—between the noble precepts of the law and the brutal facts of government—has led some scholars to dismiss the whole political and constitutional system of the classical Muslim jurists as an abstract and artificial construction, as little related to reality as the civil liberties enshrined in the constitutions of modern dictatorships. The comparison is exaggerated and unjust. The great jurists of medieval Islam were neither stupid nor corrupt—neither ignorant of reality, nor suborned to defend it. On the contrary, they were moved by a profound religious concern, arising precisely from their awareness of the gap between the ideals of Islam and the practice of Muslim states. The problem of the juristic writers on Muslim government was deeper than that posed by the conduct of one or another individual ruler. It concerned the direction taken by Muslim society as a whole since the days of the Prophet—a direction that had led it very far from the ethical and political ideas of prophetic Islam. Yet to impugn the validity of the system of government under which the Muslims lived was to impugn the orthodoxy of the Islamic *umma*, a position unacceptable to the Sunnī *ulema*, whose very definition of orthodoxy rested on the precedent and practice of the community. The jurist was thus obliged, in some measure, to justify the existing order, so as to vindicate the Sunnī faith and system against the charge that they had gone astray and had led the Muslims into a state of sin.

But, if the Sunnī *ulema* were powerless to change the realities of politics, they were equally unable to change the basis of their political thought. For them, the origins and functioning of the state were not matters for philosophical speculation, for Utopian fantasies, nor even, primarily, for practical observation—though all these exercises had their adepts in the world of Islam; for the *ulema*, they were part of the law, that is, of the God-given holy law of Islam, which could be neither abrogated nor amended by man on earth.

It could, however, be interpreted, and in this way the jurists were able to achieve some accommodation between theory and practice. In traditional Islamic states, the men of religion still shared a common universe of discourse with rulers. While on the one hand they used what influence they had to bring the practice of rulers nearer to the ideals of Islam, on the other they sought, by interpretative ingenuity, to insert existing practice, suitably disguised, into their expositions of the law of God. The Caliphate was elective, but the Caliph could be nominated by his predecessor; the Caliph was the sole supreme sovereign of all Islam, but ministers or governors might acquire and hold office by 'seizure', and an 'established band of rebels' could exercise legally valid authority, both as rulers and as belligerents. In this way the jurists were able to admit the hard facts that the Caliphate had become a dynastic monarchy, that the Caliph was often a mere puppet, and that the political unity of Islam had given way to a multiplicity of separate, sometimes conflicting sovereign states, in which the Caliphate itself was finally submerged. Successive jurists made further accommodations with a deteriorating reality, until finally the whole system of juristic constitutional theory was tacitly abandoned, and a new approach devised, based on the principle that any effective authority, however obtained and however exercised, was better than unrestrained private violence. 'Tyranny is better than anarchy', became a favourite theme of the jurists. 'Whose power prevails, must be obeyed.' The only requirements were the possession of effective military power and, in the broadest terms, respect for Islam. By this time, the contribution of the men of religion to political thought amounts to little more than conventional piety and exhortation; the more interesting expositions came from philosophers, historians, men of letters, and men of affairs.

There was much for them to observe and discuss, for great changes had taken place in the Islamic polity. The elective Caliphate lasted for barely thirty years, from the death of the Prophet and accession of Abū Bakr in 632 to the murder of ʿAlī and recognition of Muʿāwiya in 661. To solve the obviously acute problem of succession and continuity, Muʿāwiya nominated his son Yazīd as successor-designate, and persuaded the Arab leaders to accept this nomination. In this way he initiated the process by which the Caliphate in fact, though never in theory, became hereditary in a single family. The elective principle remained strong enough to prevent the emergence of any recognized rule of dynastic succession. Instead, it remained the practice, under the ʿAbbāsids as well as the Umayyads, for the reigning Caliph to nominate one of his sons or kinsmen as successor, and obtain promises of allegiance to him. Often a Caliph would nominate two or more heirs to reign successively. Such attempts to regulate the future were rarely successful, and sometimes disastrous. In later times, when the Caliphs fell under the control of their ministers and generals, it was these who appointed and replaced their sovereigns at will, in accordance with their own purposes and rivalries.

These changes in the nature of the Caliphate and of the Islamic polity were neither unnoticed nor unresisted. The Umayyads, though generally accepted by the Muslims, had to face opposition from two important quarters, both of which challenged their title to the Caliphate. On the one hand were the Khārijīs, who rejected both the monarchical and hereditary principles. For them, the head of the *umma* should be freely chosen by the Muslims, and should remain head only for as long as they wished him to. There was to be no restriction of eligibility by descent or by status, but only by worth. To the Sunnī doctrine that the Caliph had to be a free man and an Arab of Quraysh, the Khārijīs retorted that any man, of whatever status or origin, could be Caliph, if he obtained and retained the consent of the believers.

At the opposite extreme were the Shīʿis, who agreed that the Caliph should be a free Arab of Quraysh, but insisted that he must be of the clan of the Prophet. This narrower definition excluded the Umayyads, but admitted the ʿAbbāsids, who eventually succeeded in wresting the Caliphate from them. The Shīʿī opposition to ʿAbbāsid rule thereupon defined their claims even more narrowly, and in effect restricted them to the direct descendants of the Prophet through his daughter Fāṭima and his cousin and son-in-law ʿAlī.

Despite these and other opposition movements, the principle of unity—of a single Caliphate embracing all Islam—was for long maintained intact. In patriarchal and Umayyad times, the Caliph was indeed the sole sovereign in all the lands which the Muslims had conquered, and local governors and commanders were appointed and dismissed by him. The first permanent infringement of the unity of the Caliphate came in 756, when an Umayyad prince, who had fled from the ruin of his family in the East, became ruler of Muslim Spain in defiance of the ʿAbbāsids, repelled an attack by ʿAbbāsid forces, and set up what became an independent emirate, outside the Eastern Caliphal Empire.

The process of political fragmentation continued rapidly. It began, naturally enough, at the extremities, and soon spread towards the centre. After Spain, Morocco and Tunisia fell to independent dynasties (late eighth to early ninth centuries); others appeared in eastern Iran (late ninth to early tenth centuries). Finally, Egypt, Syria, Arabia, and even parts of Iraq were by the middle of the tenth century lost to the imperial government, which retained effective control of little more than the capital and the province surrounding it. In time, even these ceased to be ruled by the Caliphs, who became the helpless puppets of their own military commanders.

These independent dynasties were of varying origins. Some—usually the smaller and weaker among them—were of local origin;

sometimes such principalities were founded by members of the landed nobility or gentry, more frequently by tribal chieftains, occasionally even by brigands and other outlaws. More commonly, the founders of dynasties were officers or soldiers of fortune, who were appointed to the governorship of a province, and in due course succeeded in making their governorship first autonomous and then hereditary. In Iran, such governors were often Iranian by origin or assimilation, and their regimes, drawing on local loyalties, were associated with a revival of Iranian political, social, and cultural traditions. Elsewhere, the dynasts were usually aliens, at first Arabs, later Turks; their regencies, even when beneficent, rested on a foreign soldiery rather than on any real local support, and were accompanied by no comparable revival.

The Umayyad emirs of Spain founded their state in defiance of the Caliphate, and remained outside it. Elsewhere, the ruling princes of the Empire were content with the reality of independence, and did not insist on the form. For the most part they were willing, even anxious, to recognize the titular supremacy of the Caliph as head of all Islam, and to obtain a diploma of appointment from him in return. In time, the Caliph came to be a sort of legitimating authority, whose recognition gave formal legal validity to sovereignties established by the less formal procedures of rebellion, usurpation, and war. The real content of Caliphal suzerainty over such rulers varied with personal and political factors; it was usually small.

Often, an independent principality might be established in direct defiance of central authority. When such a regime survived, its rulers usually managed to reach some accommodation with the Caliph and his regents. There were, however, exceptions. Rebels inspired by Shīʿī or Khārijī ideas not only rejected the authority of the Caliph in their region, but impugned his title to the Caliphate itself. For such the question of mutual formal recognition could hardly arise, though some measure of tacit mutual toleration was not unknown. With one great exception, such technically rebel regimes survived only in remote and inaccessible regions, and offered no serious threat to the nominal political unity and substantial social unity of the Islamic world under the Sunnī Caliphate.

That one exception was the Fāṭimid dynasty, whose enthronement in Tunisia in 909 marked the victory of the second great revolutionary movement in medieval Islam, after that which had brought the ʿAbbāsids to power a century and a half earlier. The Fāṭimids were something different from the local leaders, mutinous soldiers, and ambitious governors who were founding dynasties in east and west. They were the heads of a major religious schism in Islam, that of the Ismāʿīlī Shīʿa; as such, they refused to submit even to the titular suzerainty of the ʿAbbāsids, whom they denounced as usurpers. By inheritance and by God's choice, so they said, they were the Imāms—the sole rightful claimants to the universal Caliphate. It was their intention, by conquest and conversion, to win all Islam to their cause, and overthrow the ʿAbbāsids as the ʿAbbāsids had overthrown the Umayyads.

They came remarkably near to succeeding in this objective. After ruling in North Africa for half a century, they moved eastwards, and in 969 conquered Egypt, where they built a new capital, the city of Cairo. From Egypt they extended their power to Palestine, Syria, western and southern Arabia, and even, for a brief interval in 1057–9, to Mosul and to Baghdad itself. This was the high-water mark of their Empire, which thereafter dwindled and declined, until the Fāṭimid Caliphate was finally terminated in 1171 and Egypt restored by Saladin to ʿAbbāsid suzerainty and Sunnī orthodoxy.

During the tenth and eleventh centuries, the prospects of Sunnī Islam and of the ʿAbbāsid Caliphate must have seemed very insecure. The rival and schismatic Fāṭimid Caliphate ruled half the Islamic world, and offered a major threat, both religious and political, to the remainder. Even within the ʿAbbāsid domains, the Shīʿa were flourishing, with growing influence both in the world of ideas and in the seats of power. For a while, the Caliphs themselves were dominated by a dynasty of Persian Shīʿī mayors of the palace. In the far West, the Umayyad emir of Cordova, confronted with the unprecedented spectacle of two Caliphs—a schismatic one in Tunisia, and an orthodox one far away in Baghdad—sought to protect himself from Fāṭimid subversion by proclaiming his own Caliphate, in 929. Thereafter there were for a while three Caliphs in Islam. The collapse of the Cordova Caliphate in 1031 again reduced the number to two and the extinction of the Fāṭimids in 1171 to one—the ʿAbbāsid in Baghdad. The principle of unity had been restored.

In this restoration several factors were at work. One was the internal decline and disunity of the Fāṭimid state and faith; another was the emergence of a new political and military order in the East, under the aegis of the Turkish Sultans.

These represent the culmination of a new form of sovereignty in Islam. During the ninth century, the rule of the emirs—provincial governors in theory, independent dynastic rulers in effect—became an accepted part of the pattern of Islamic government. It was given formal legitimacy by the practice whereby the ruler made token submission to the Caliph, who in return gave him a diploma of appointment—in effect a licence to rule. The fee for such a licence became increasingly modest. In time the Caliph ceased to exercise any real power even in his own capital, where effective political authority passed into the hands of a succession of military commanders. In 935 the position was regularized, when the emir of the capital assumed the title *amīr al-umarāʾ* (emir of emirs), to indicate his primacy among the princes of the Empire. The same title was adopted in 946 by the Persian Būyids, the new masters of Baghdad and Iraq. In their hands, it came to be a title of imperial sovereignty, distinct from the Caliphate and in most practical respects superior to it. Significantly, the Būyids also revived the old Persian title *Shāhanshāh*, 'King of Kings', and used it together with its Arabic equivalent *malik al-mulūk*. If the masters of the provinces were kings, the master of the capital was a king of kings.

From the provinces to the centre a new system of imperial

authority was emerging, associated with that of the Caliph, but with a prior right in political and military affairs. The process was completed in the middle of the eleventh century, with the establishment of the dominion of the Seljuq Turks over most of southwestern Asia, and the creation by them of the Sultanate.

The Arabic word *sulṭān* is an abstract noun meaning authority or rule, and was used from early times to denote the government. In a society where state and ruler are more or less synonymous terms, it came to be applied to the holder, as well as to the function, of political authority, and was used, informally, of ministers, governors, and other rulers—even, on occasion, of the Caliphs themselves, Fāṭimid as well as ʿAbbāsid. By the tenth century it had become a common designation of independent rulers, which served to distinguish them from those who were still appointed and dismissed by a superior power. Its use, however, remained informal; while it occurs frequently in literary sources, in letters, for example, and poetic eulogies, it has not yet been encountered in the more formal usage of coins and inscriptions. It first became official in the eleventh century, when it was adopted by the Seljuqs as their chief regnal title. In Seljuq protocol, the word Sultan acquires a new sense, and embodies a new claim—no less than the supreme political sovereignty of all Islam, parallel and at least equal to the religious primacy of the Caliph.

On the whole, the Caliphs fared rather better under the Great Seljuq Sultans than under the Shīʿī Būyid *amīr al-umarā*ʾ. The Seljuqs were devout Sunnīs, with a sense of religious and imperial mission. They did not, like the Būyids, depose the Caliphs at will; on the contrary, they treated them and their office with respect. But they were equally firm in reserving all real power to themselves, and far more explicit in asserting their right to do so. The Seljuq point of view is clearly expressed in a letter of 1133 from Sultan Sanjar to the Caliph's vizier: 'We received from the lord of the world . . . the kingship of the world, and we received this by right and inheritance, and from the father and grandfather of the Commander of the Faithful . . . we have a standard and a covenant.'[1]

Sovereignty, in other words, belongs to the house of Seljuq. It is given by God and ratified by the Caliph as religious authority. Like the Caliphate, the Sultanate was unique and universal. As there was only one Caliph, as religious head of the Islamic community, so there could be only one Sultan, who was responsible for the order, security, and government of the Islamic Empire. This division of authority between Caliphate and Sultanate became so well established that when, during a period of Seljuq weakness, a Caliph attempted to exercise independent political power, the Sultan and his spokesman protested against what they now regarded as an infringement of Sultanic prerogatives. The Caliph, they said, should busy himself with his duties as Imām, as leader in prayer, which is the best and most glorious of tasks and the protection of the rulers of the world; he should leave the business of government to the Sultans to whom it was entrusted.[2]

The emergence of a dual sovereignty did not escape the attention of writers on politics and statecraft. The awareness of change is naturally clearest in the writings of those whose acquaintance with politics was practical, chiefly bureaucratic; it can, however, also be detected in the works of theologians and even of jurists. For Muslim thinkers, the basic division was not the familiar Western one between religious and secular. The Sultanate too was conceived as a religious institution, maintained by and maintaining the Holy Law, and the relations between the state and the professional men of religion became much closer under the Seljuq Sultans and their successors than they had ever been under the rule of the Caliphs. As expressed in Muslim, and especially Persian

[1] Cited by Ann K. S. Lambton, 'Quis custodiet custodes: Some Reflections on the Persian Theory of Government', *Studia Islamica*, v (1956), 129–30; the original of the letter was published in ʿAbbās Eghbāl, *Vizārat dar ʿahd-i salāṭin-i buzurg-i Saljūqī* (Tehran, 1959), pp. 302 ff.

[2] Ibn al-Rāwandi, *Rāḥat al-Ṣudūr*, ed. Muh. Iqbal (Leiden, 1921), p. 334; cf. W. Barthold, *Turkestan Down to the Mongol Invasion* (3rd edn., London, 1968), pp. 346–7.

writings, the real distinction is between two kinds of authority, the one prophetic, the other monarchical. 'Know', says an eleventh-century Persian author, 'that the lord most high has given one power to prophets and another to kings; and He has made it incumbent upon the people of the earth that they should submit themselves to the two powers and should acknowledge the true way laid down by God.'[1] The Prophet is chosen and sent by God, and his task is to promulgate and establish God's law. The polity which he establishes is a divine one. Human polity, however, must be ruled by a monarch, who obtains and preserves his authority by political and military means. Possession of this authority confers on him the right to give orders and to punish transgressors, independently of—though not contrary to—the law of God. If he knows the law of God and administers it justly, then his authority is sanctified by God, and he and his subjects qualify for the 'two felicities', of this world and the next. There is no need for a Prophet in every age, and there has been none since Muḥammad, but there must always be a monarch, for without a monarch order would give way to anarchy. The relationship between religious orthodoxy and political stability was well understood and frequently expressed. It is summed up in a dictum often cited by Muslim authors, sometimes as a piece of old Persian wisdom, sometimes as a saying of the Prophet: 'Islam (or religion) and government are twin brothers; one cannot thrive without the other. Islam is the foundation and government the guardian. What has no foundation, collapses; what has no guardian, perishes.'[2]

The Seljuqs and later Sultans insisted strongly on their role as the upholders of the faith and the law, and on the consequent divine sanction for their sovereign authority. Even some part of the prophetic authority, according to some authors, could thus be claimed

[1] Bayhaqi, *Tārīkh-i Bayhaqī*, edd. Qāsim Ghanī and ʿAlī Akbar Fayyāḍ (Tehran, 1324/1946), p. 99. Translation in C. E. Bosworth, *The Ghaznavids* (Edinburgh, 1963), p. 63.

[2] See, for example, I. Goldziher, *Streitschrift des Gazālī gegen die Bāṭinijja-Sekte* (Leiden, 1916), pp. 101–2.

by a righteous Sultan. In general, however, the prophetic authority resided in the Holy Law, and therefore also to some extent in the *ulema* as custodians of that law. Thus the *qāḍī*s, as judges administering the Holy Law, were designated as deputies (*nā'ib*s) of the Prophet. But there were other courts and other judges, enforcing the Sultan's orders, and punishing those who disobeyed them; and even the qāḍīs were nominated not by the Caliph, but by the Sultan, who alone, as the holder of real power, could make an effective and therefore valid appointment. In the same way and for the same reason the Sultan would choose and appoint the Caliph himself—and then swear allegiance to him as the head of the community and the embodiment of the principle of Sunnī unity. The distinction between Caliphate and Sultanate is not so much one between religious and secular, as rather, in Bagehot's terms, between the 'dignified' and the 'efficient' parts of the government—between those which 'excite and preserve the reverence of the population' and those 'by which it, in fact, works and rules'. The Caliph represented authority, the Sultan power. The Sultan empowered the Caliph, who authorized him in return. The Caliph reigned but did not rule; the Sultan did both.

For a while the Seljuq great Sultanate was respected as a single universal Sunnī institution. Other monarchs used the title Sultan informally, as in earlier times, but refrained from putting it on their coins. With the decay and break-up of the Seljuq Empire, however, 'Sultan' was more widely and more commonly used, becoming the normal Sunnī title for anyone who claimed to be the head of state and did not recognize any suzerain. As such, the title was used by rulers in North Africa, Egypt, Turkey, Persia, India, and other countries.

In 1258 the Mongol invaders of Iraq executed the last Caliph of Baghdad, and in so doing laid the ghost of an institution that was already dead. Until 1517 a line of shadow-caliphs held office—or rather title—in Cairo, as pensioners of the Mamlūk Sultans; they exercised no power, and won only limited recognition outside the Egyptian dominions. After the Ottoman conquest of Egypt, the last of them was sent to Istanbul, whence he returned as a private citizen some years later. Thereafter there were no Caliphs, and the Sultans ruled alone as the supreme sovereigns of Islam, every Sultan his own Caliph. The word Caliph became one of the many titles which the Sultans added to their titulature, and retained little or nothing of its old significance, until it was revived in the eighteenth century.

Yet, despite the extinction of the Caliphate and the dismemberment of the world of Islam into a multiplicity of separate, often warring sovereignties, the feeling of identity and cohesion, of a single *umma dūn al-nās*, a community apart from other men, remained powerful and effective. Though too weak to preserve the political unity of the world of Islam, it was strong enough to prevent, for a very long time, the emergence of permanent and stable political entities within that world, whether national, territorial, or dynastic. The titulature of Muslim monarchs offers an interesting contrast with that of the rulers of Christendom. In Christian Europe, besides a pope and two Roman emperors, there were kings of the Franks, Goths, and other peoples, later of France, England, and other lands. In Islam, ethnic titles are rare, and even where they occur are of minor importance; territorial titles of sovereignty are virtually unknown. The titles used by Muslim rulers are elaborate and significant; they do not, however, normally include any designation of the territory or people over which the sovereign claims authority. In pre-Mongol times this silence reflected the instability and variation of the political entities of that time, when it was very rare for two successive rulers—let alone successive dynasties—to rule over precisely the same territory. But it remains a feature even of the post-Mongol period, when countries came to have more permanent frontiers and more durable regimes. At the beginning of the sixteenth century, there were three large monarchies in the Middle East, governed by rulers whom modern scholars know as the Sultan of Turkey, the Sultan of Egypt, and the Shah of Persia. None of these titles was used by the rulers themselves, though all three—in slightly modified forms—were applied to them by their neighbours. For a Muslim sovereign, the only acceptable definition of the extent of his sovereignty was Islam itself—and all three claimed, in their own titulature, to be lords of Islam, of the Muslims, or of the Islamic lands. A territorial or an ethnic designation was derogatory, and was applied to a rival to show the limited and local nature of his rule. It is in this spirit that, in the correspondence between the Turkish Sultan and the Persian Shah, each refers to himself as the sovereign of Islam, and to his neighbour as the Sultan of Rūm (the Turks or Turkey) or the Shah of ʿAjam (the Persians or Persia). Territorial sovereignties did of course exist, and some of them were of very long duration. Turkey was the seat of the greatest and most lasting of all the Muslim Empires, with a strong sense of identity, loyalty, and mission—yet the name Turkey was unknown there until it was borrowed from Europe and officially adopted by the Republic in 1923. Iran and Egypt are ancient names, rich in memories and associations—the former the home of a distinctive language and culture, the latter a country vividly defined by both geography and history, and for centuries the base of an independent Muslim power. Yet neither name appears in the protocol and titles, the coins, documents, or inscriptions of its rulers. Only in the nineteenth century did Muslims, under the impact of European ideas and example, begin to think in terms of ethnic and territorial nationhood, and to redefine their sovereignties and aspirations accordingly. Even in the present-day world of nation states, there are signs of imperfect acceptance of the new classification, and of a hankering for older loyalties, larger yet more exclusive.

The sense of common identity, which inhibited the development of states and nations within Islam, also dominated the relations between the Muslim community and the outside. 'Unbelief is one nation', runs a saying attributed to the Prophet. Though the attribution is dubious, the sentiment is authentic, and finds more formal expression in the legal doctrine according to which the world is divided into the House of Islam (*Dār al-Islām*) and the

House of War (*Dār al-Ḥarb*). The former consists of the lands where the law of Islam prevails—that is, broadly, the Muslim Empire; the latter is the rest of the world. As there is only one God in heaven, so there can only be one sovereign and one law on earth. The Muslim state must tolerate and protect the unbelievers under its rule, provided that they are not polytheists and follow one of the permitted religions; it may not, however, recognize the permanent existence of another polity outside Islam. In time, all mankind must accept Islam or submit to Muslim rule. Meanwhile, it is the duty of the Muslims to struggle until this is accomplished.

The name of this duty is *jihād*, an Arabic word meaning effort or striving; one who performs it is called *mujāhid* (see above, pp. 137–8, for a use of this term in the Muslim Indian context). The word occurs in the Koran a number of times in the military sense of making war against the unbelievers. In the early centuries of Islam, during the great age of religious and imperial expansion, this came to be its normal meaning. The *jihād* was the holy war for Islam, a religious duty prescribed by the faith. It is a collective duty of the community as a whole, but becomes an individual duty of every Muslim in border areas, in battle areas, or wherever the sovereign decides that the time has come to make it so. It is also a perpetual duty, which will lapse only when all the world is won for Islam.

Between the Muslims and the rest of the world there was therefore, according to the classical jurists, a religiously and legally obligatory state of war, which could only end with the conversion or subjugation of all mankind. A treaty of peace between the Muslim state and a non-Muslim state was thus juridically impossible. The war could not be terminated; it could only be interrupted, for reasons of necessity or expediency, by a truce. Such an arrangement could, in the view of the jurists, only be provisional. It should not exceed ten years in duration, and could at any time be repudiated unilaterally by the Muslims, who were, however, required by the law to give the other side due notice before resuming hostilities. Other provisions of the law regulate the opening of hostilities, the conduct of warfare, and the treatment of prisoners and non-combatants.

The law of *jihād*, like much else in Muslim jurisprudence, received its basic shape during the first century and a half of the Islamic era, when the victorious armies of the universal Caliphate were advancing on France, China, and India, and there seemed no reason to doubt that the final triumph of Islam in all the world was not only inevitable but near. Thereafter, in international as in constitutional matters, a widening gap appeared between legal doctrine and political fact, which politicians ignored and jurists did their best to conceal. While the universal Caliphate broke up into smaller states, the irresistible and permanent *jihād* came to an end, and a relationship of mutual tolerance was established between the Muslim world and the rest. The latter remained the 'House of War', but its conquest was postponed from historic to messianic time. In the meantime, a more or less stable frontier existed between the two, on which peace rather than war was the normal condition. The peace might be infringed by raiding on land and sea; the frontier might occasionally be violently displaced, through some renewal of major conflict—but from medieval times onwards such displacements could mean the withdrawal, as well as the advance, of the boundaries of Muslim rule.

These changes, and the consequent development of political and commercial relations with the non-Muslim world, posed new problems for the jurists to solve. They responded, as in other fields, with skilful interpretations. The duty of *jihād* was qualified and attenuated.[1] The cessation of hostilities with the House of War could be effected only by a limited truce, but such a truce could be renewed as often as necessary, and thus become in fact a legally regulated state of peace. Some jurists, though not all, recognized an intermediate status, the House of Truce or House of Covenant (*Dār al-Ṣulḥ* or *Dār al-ʿAhd*), between the Houses of War and of

[1] In modern times, apologists have appeared who entirely disregard the classical juridical tradition, and interpret *jihād* as a purely defensive obligation—some of them even as a purely moral struggle.

Islam. This consisted of non-Muslim states which entered into a contractual relationship with the Muslim state, undertaking to recognize Muslim overlordship and pay tribute, but retaining their own autonomy and form of government. By choosing to regard gifts as tribute, Muslim rulers and their legal advisers could extend the range of the covenant (*ʿahd*) to cover a wide variety of political, military, and commercial agreements with non-Muslim powers. The safe-conduct given to a *ḥarbī*—i.e. a non-Muslim from the House of War, visiting the Muslim lands—was called an *amān*; its holder was a *mustaʾmin*. Any free adult Muslim could give an *amān* to one or a few persons; the head of the Muslim state could give a collective *amān* to a larger entity, such as a city, a country, or a commercial interest. The practice of *amān* greatly facilitated the growth of diplomacy and commerce between Islam and Christendom, and made possible the emergence of resident communities of European traders in Muslim cities. It provided the main legal basis, on the Muslim side, for peaceful contacts and communications with Christian states, until, from the late Crusades period onwards, these were to an increasing extent regulated by European commercial and diplomatic practice.

The Islamic Empire and community expanded principally to the west and to the east. In the north and south, the empty Eurasian plains and the deserts and jungles of Africa offered few attractions, and the advance of Islam in these regions was slow and late (see above, Chapter III (*A*) and (*B*)). The main effort of the conquerors and missionaries was directed to more populous and more rewarding countries—westwards to North Africa and Europe, eastwards across Persia to Central Asia and the approaches to India and China. On both sides there were formidable adversaries; in the West, the Empires and kingdoms of Christendom; in the East, the great Empire of Persia, and beyond that the warlike peoples of the steppes and forests.

Almost from the start there was a radical difference between the two struggles, in East and West. The Empire of Persia was wholly overwhelmed by the Muslim invaders, and all its territories and peoples brought under Muslim rule; the Byzantine barrier to Muslim advance was battered and pushed back, but remained standing. The Christian Roman Empire still lived, and a Caesar reigned in Constantinople. His fleets and armies, in defending their city, preserved not only the remnants of the Byzantine Empire, but Christian Europe from invasion and conquest.

The historical tradition of the West acclaims the Frankish victors at Poitiers in 732 as the saviours of Christendom from Islam; Muslim tradition mentions the battle, if at all, only as a minor episode, but has much to say, in history and legend, about the decisive struggle under the walls of Constantinople. There can be little doubt that the Muslim view is the truer. The Franks at Poitiers stilled the last tremor of a force that had reached its limit and was spent; the defenders of Constantinople met and halted that force when it was still fresh and strong. Through eastern Europe the way to the Rhine was shorter and easier than that which the Arabs had taken to the Oxus; it was their failure to conquer Constantinople which saved the Byzantine Empire, and with it Western Christendom, from sharing the fate of Iran and Central Asia.

The Arab conquest, and the resulting political extinction of Iran, had momentous consequences not only for the Persians but also for Islam itself. From Syria, Egypt, and North Africa, the Byzantine magnates could withdraw to Byzantium, leaving their former subjects to the care of new masters. No such escape was open to the magnates of the fallen Persian Empire. Apart from a small group who fled to India, the Persians had to remain where they were, endure the new domination, and find their place in it as best they could. It is not surprising that the Persian nobility, gentry, and priesthood, with their reserves of skill and experience and their recent memories of lost greatness, should have played so great a role in the development of Islamic society and culture, government and opposition—even of the Islamic religion, as the old Persian faiths dwindled into insignificance, and their followers took refuge in Islam from defeat and despair.

In the East, Islam had triumphed. Iran was conquered entirely; the Empire of Chosroes was dead, the faith of Zoroaster was dying. The political talents and religious fervour of the Iranians were both gained for the cause of Islam. Beyond the eastern borders of Iran there were many peoples and great kingdoms—but none that could offer any serious threat or competition to the universal message of Muḥammad and the universal law of his community. India and China, during the formative classical period of Islam, impinged only remotely on the Muslim consciousness; they were known, however, to be inhabited by polytheists and idolators, who possessed no revealed religion of their own, and were therefore ripe for conversion to Islam. The same was true of the warlike but teachable peoples of the steppes who, once converted, brought an immense accession of new strength to the Muslim cause. In the East there seemed to be no real limit to the expansion of Islam. The process was continuous and irreversible—and each new advance brought new resources, human and material, to help prepare the next.

In the West, the position was entirely different. The Christian populations of the conquered lands, sustained by their awareness of a free Christendom beyond the frontier, were better able than the Persians to survive the rigours and blandishments of conquest. The Islamization of these countries was slower, and to this day numerous Christian minorities remain. Even more important was the danger and challenge which the Christian Empire offered to Islam itself. In the West, unlike the East, Islam was compelled to recognize a rival, even a peer—another revealed religion and universal state, with a profound sense of mission and a message for all mankind. Far from being ready for conversion, they were themselves anxious to convert others to their faith, and enjoyed no small success in this enterprise.

This difference in quality between the war against Christendom and the wars on the other frontiers of Islam was soon recognized. The latter were merely stages in the progressive and inevitable Islamization of the pagan peoples; the former was a struggle against a hostile religious and political system, which denied the very basis of the Islamic world role—and did so in terms which were both familiar and intelligible. The Muslim conviction of predestined final victory did not entirely conceal the significance and uncertainty of this wide-ranging and long-drawn-out conflict between the two faiths and societies, whose successive ideological stages are described in detail in Chapter I above, pp. 9 ff. In Muslim writings, the Christian world becomes the 'House of War' *par excellence*—and the war against Christendom the very model and prototype of the *jihād*.

The struggle between Islam and Christendom, in its military aspect, may be seen in four overlapping phases—two of attack, and two of counter-attack. In each of these phases, vast and populous territories were transferred by conquest from one side to the other, with profound and far-reaching effects on both.

The clash between Islam and Christendom began during the lifetime of the Prophet. In the earlier stages of his career, when the main fight was against Arab paganism, his attitude to the Jews and the Christians was friendly and respectful. The leadership of the community brought him into contact and then conflict with both. At first the Jews, strongly represented at Medina, were the immediate enemy, while the Christians remained potential allies and converts. Later, when the expanding influence of the community of Medina brought the Muslims into collision with Christian tribes in Arabia and on the northern borders, relations with Christianity, as with Judaism, culminated in war:

Fight against those who do not believe in Allah nor in the Last Day, who do not forbid what Allah and His Apostle have forbidden, nor practise the true religion, among those who have been given the Book, until they pay the *jizya*[1] from their hand, they being humbled.[2] The Jews say:

[1] This term was later specialized to mean the poll-tax paid by the non-Muslim subjects of the Muslim state. In the Koran it probably has the more general meaning of payment or recompense.

[2] The precise meaning of this phrase has been disputed by modern scholars. In

'ʿUzayr[1] is the son of God.' The Christians say: 'Christ is the son of God.' This is what they say, with their own mouths, imitating what was said by the unbelievers before. May God fight them! How they are deceived! [Koran, ix. 29–30.]

These verses were taken as abrogating previous revelations which expressed a friendlier and more hopeful attitude to the non-Muslims; they provided the scriptural basis for the legal doctrines which required Muslims to fight and conquer the Christians and Jews, and, if they refused Islam, to impose on them fiscal and social penalties.

According to Muslim tradition, in the year 7 of the *hijra* (A.D. 628), the Prophet sent letters from Medina to Caesar and Chosroes—the Roman and Persian Emperors—informing them of his mission, and summoning them to accept Islam or suffer the penalties of unbelief. The texts of these letters, and even the story of their being sent, are now generally regarded as apocryphal, but, like so much of the Muslim tradition, they reflect an accurate, if subsequent, assessment of realities. Whether Muḥammad really contemplated the conquest and conversion of the two great Empires is a matter on which scholars have differed. There can, however,

two recent translations of the Koran, it is rendered 'jusqu'à ce qu'ils paient la *jizya*, directement(?) et alors qu'ils sont humiliés' (R. Blachère); 'bis sie kleinlaut aus der Hand Tribut entrichten' (R. Paret). Other recent renderings are: 'until they give compensation (tax) for support from solidarity (shown by us to them), while they are in a state of lowliness' (F. Rosenthal); 'until they pay the *jizya* out of ability and sufficient means, they (nevertheless) being inferior' (M. J. Kister); 'until they give the reward due for a benefaction (since their lives are spared), while they are ignominious (namely, for not having fought unto death)' (M. Bravmann). See Rosenthal in *The Joshua Starr Memorial Volume* (New York, 1953), pp. 68–72; Kister and Bravmann in *Arabica*, x (1963), 94–5; xi (1964), 272–8; xiii (1966), 307–14; xiv (1967), 90–1, 326–7. Whatever the original meaning of the text, the commentators and jurists have interpreted it as imposing a tax, and prescribing the manner in which it should be paid.

[1] The Muslim tradition identifies ʿUzayr with the Biblical Ezra. The significance of this phrase has baffled modern scholarship. The least improbable suggestion is that of Paul Casanova, 'Idris et ʿOuzair', *Journal Asiatique*, ccv (1924), 356–60, who identifies ʿUzayr with Azael—Uzael, a fallen angel in Rabbinic literature.

be no doubt that he initiated the processes by which this was in large measure accomplished.

The first Islamic conquest was Khaybar, an oasis some 100 miles north of Medina, on the road to Syria. It was inhabited by Jews, including some who had been evicted from Medina. In 628 Muḥammad led an army of about 1,600 men against Khaybar, and in six weeks was able to conquer the whole oasis. The Jews were allowed to retain their families, and practise their religion. Their lands and property were forfeit to the conquerors, but they were allowed to remain in possession of their fields and till them, in return for paying half the harvest to the new owners.

At a later date the Jews of Khaybar were expelled from their oasis by the Caliph ʿUmar, allegedly so that there should be only one religion, Islam, in the holy land of Arabia. The arrangement originally imposed on them by the Prophet, however, became, with minor variations, the pattern followed in later conquests. The expansion to the north, into Christian territory, began during Muḥammad's last years; his successors brought under Muslim rule vast regions of Christendom, including the Christian heartlands in the Near East, the whole of North Africa, Spain, parts of France and Italy, and most of the Mediterranean islands.

For the medieval Muslim, the swift and overwhelming victories won by the Arabs in the heroic age of Islam were providential—proof that their religion was the true one and that God was on their side. In an age of scepticism, historians have sought, with varying success, for more worldly and measurable explanations.

Of the military history of the Arab conquests, little is known. From that little, it would appear that, unlike some other builders of Empire, the Arabs possessed no special tactical or technical device, which could give them superiority over their opponents—nothing like the Macedonian phalanx, the Roman legion, the horses of the *conquistadores*, or the fire-power of the colonialists.[1]

[1] G.-H. Bousquet, 'Observations sur la nature et les causes de la Conquête arabe', *Studia Islamica*, vi (1956), 48.

On the contrary, as outsiders attacking the two great military Empires of the day, they suffered from a certain inferiority in skills and armaments as well as in numbers. They had no experience of fighting in large formations.[1] In the early days they had no siegecraft and no siege-weapons, and could therefore only blockade, but not besiege, fortified cities. They had no fleet, and even on land had no equivalent of the heavy armoured cavalry, the cataphracts, of Byzantium and Persia.

These disadvantages, though important, should not, however, be exaggerated. In the seventh century the technological gap between a sedentary, civilized state and the warriors from the steppe or desert was still narrow, and could be bridged. In other respects, the Arabs had much the same equipment as their enemies.

To offset their inferiority in weapons and professional skill, the Arabs had certain important advantages over their enemies. One of these was both logistic and strategic—the use of the camel and therefore of the desert. Though of little or no value for fighting, the camel was of immense importance for transport—for the movement of men, equipment, and supplies. By this means, the Arabs were able to use the desert as the modern maritime empires used the sea, as a safe line of communication beyond the reach or knowledge of the enemy. Through the desert they could achieve surprise in attack, or safety in retreat; they could advance, withdraw, or reinforce at will. In each of the conquered provinces, they established their seat of government on the edge of the desert and the sown, using an existing city like Damascus where possible, or

[1] On this point, an acute observation by Professor W. H. McNeill should be noted: 'It is worth pointing out that daily prayers must have had much the same psychological effect upon an army on campaign as does modern close-order drill. Precise gestures and recitation of prayers conducted in unison five times daily must have inculcated sentiments of solidarity within the ranks and habits of obedience to the commander, who in the early days was also prayer leader. Such exercises no doubt did much to overcome the chronic weakness of any nomad confederacy—insubordination resulting from tribal and personal rivalries. The further conviction that death fighting in Allah's cause assured immediate access to Paradise gave an additional dash of recklessness to each warrior's charge' (McNeill, *The Rise of the West* (Chicago, 1963), p. 468, n. 11).

founding a new one like Kūfa, Fusṭāṭ, or Qayrawān, where it was not. These garrison cities were the Bombays, Calcuttas, and Singapores of the Arab Empire, the ports of the desert through which the provinces were first penetrated, then conquered, and for a while governed.

A second advantage was one of morale. The Arabs were warriors in a holy war—full of faith and enthusiasm, sustained by a belief in divine favour which was reinforced by each successive victory and the rewards that it brought; their opponents were highly trained professionals, mostly mercenaries—proficient but indifferent, and discouraged by dissension within their own ranks and hostility from the civil population. The Arab fighters, less hampered by status, caste, or privilege, threw up commanders of a brilliance which the military hierarchies of Byzantium and Persia could not equal. It was in similar circumstances that the ragged conscripts of the French Revolution routed the veterans of the continental monarchies.

While retaining their own advantages, the Arabs were able in a remarkably short time to acquire and master the weapons and techniques which they had lacked. In pre-Islamic Arabia the usual method of combat was the famous *karr wa-farr*, which might be approximately translated as hit and run—a technique admirably suited to tribal warfare and raiding, but ill adapted to fighting against disciplined armies. According to the traditional biographies, the Prophet introduced the notion of an order of battle (*taʿbiya*), and at Badr arranged his few hundred followers in ranks, which he dressed himself. A Koranic verse, 'Allah loves those who fight for His cause in ranks, like a lead-sealed building' (lix. 4), has been taken as indicating divine approval for close formation warfare.[1] In the wars against the Byzantines and Persians, the Arabs soon learnt to manœuvre and fight in large regular formations, to construct and maintain an order of battle, to procure and use the most up-to-date engines of warfare known at the time. Most

[1] Ibn Khaldūn, *Muqaddima*, ed. E. Quatremère (Paris, 1858), ii. 66; English translation by F. Rosenthal (New York, 1958), ii. 75.

astonishing of all, they were able, with the help of the native Christian population of Syria, Egypt, and North Africa, to build and man war-fleets which could defeat the Byzantine and other Christian navies in the Mediterranean waters which they had so long dominated.

With the aid of their new naval power, the Arabs launched a series of land and sea attacks on Constantinople. By 674 they were able to occupy the peninsula of Cyzicus, in the sea of Marmara, and establish an operational base, from which, for several years, they attacked and blockaded the city during the spring and summer months. In 678 they were decisively defeated in a great sea-battle before the walls of the city, and compelled to withdraw—the first real defeat suffered by the Muslims in their Holy War. A period of comparative inactivity followed, during which warfare between the Muslim and Byzantine Empires was restricted to border raiding for prisoners and booty.

A new advance began in the early decades of the eighth century. In the East, Arab armies reached the Jaxartes and the Indus; in the West, with their Berber auxiliaries, they crossed the Straits of Gibraltar, and began the conquest of Spain. In the centre, the Umayyad prince Maslama took over the command of the frontiers, and launched a series of land offensives against Anatolia. These culminated in the greatest attempt by the Arabs to capture Constantinople, the combined land and sea attack in 716–17. This expedition, which also ended in defeat and withdrawal, is famous in Muslim myth and folklore, and especially in the later heroic tales and sagas of the Holy War. These stories, together with the prophecies that became current at the time, illustrate the changing Muslim attitude to the Holy War. The mighty battles against the infidel belong to a remote and heroic past, the final Muslim victory to a distant and messianic future.

After the withdrawal from Constantinople in 717, the Muslim armies continued to advance, both in the far east and the far west of their empire—but they were reaching the limits of their expansion. In the West, the conquest of Sicily in 827–902 was the only major success. In the East, Muslim power stopped at the borders of India and China. The Byzantine frontier was relatively tranquil, until in 782 another prince, this time of the ʿAbbāsid house, led an army across Anatolia to the Bosphorus, where he won a victory, exacted tribute—and then went home. The victory brought great prestige to the young prince Hārūn. It was on this occasion, a chronicler tells us, that his father the Caliph al-Mahdī appointed him second heir and conferred on him the title al-Rashīd, the Rightly Guided.

This was the last major expedition sent by the Arab Caliphate in the direction of Constantinople, the capture of which was postponed—mistakenly as it turned out—to the end of time. There were several reasons for the end of the *jihād*. The fire and passion of the early conquerors were long since spent, their hunger, whether for booty or martyrdom, satisfied; in place of the warriors in the Holy War, there were now regular, professional armies, not vastly different from those which the Arabs had defeated. The ʿAbbāsids had shifted the capital eastwards, and were transforming the Caliphate into an oriental Empire; their interest in warfare was perfunctory, their concern with their Western borders minimal. For a while new Muslim states, based on Mediterranean countries, continued the struggle, but even these came to share the general Muslim acceptance that the heroic age was over, that the boundaries between the House of Islam and the House of War were more or less permanent, and that some form of recognition of non-Muslim states was unavoidable.

In the meantime, the great Christian counter-offensive was already beginning, encouraged by the obvious weakness and disunity of the Muslim world. The first serious inroads into Muslim territory were made by heathen peoples—the Khazars in the East, the Vikings in the West. These were, however, mere episodes. Of far greater consequence was the recovery of Christian power, and the growing determination to reconquer the former Christian lands which had been lost to Islam. The reconquest began at the extremities. In Spain, the Christian principalities that had managed to survive precariously in the far north of the peninsula began to consolidate and extend their realms, helped by Frankish and later Norman attacks on the Muslim lands. In the East, the Christian peoples of the Caucasus, the Georgians and the Armenians, raised their heads again, and won a steadily increasing measure of freedom from their Muslim overlords. In the second half of the tenth century, the Byzantine Empire was able to launch a series of major offensives against the Muslims, which resulted in the recovery of Crete, Antioch, and Samosata, the annexation or subjugation of parts of northern Syria and Mesopotamia, and the advance of Byzantine raiding parties as far south as Jerusalem.

During the eleventh century, the Christian advance against Islam was in full flood. In the East, the kingdom of Georgia survived Muslim attacks, and entered on its great age of expansion, in which it dominated the whole Caucasian area from the Black Sea to the Caspian. In Spain and Portugal, the tide of reconquest reached Toledo and Coimbra; in the Mediterranean, Christian invaders recovered Sardinia and Sicily from their Muslim rulers. Finally, from 1098, Western European Christians conquered and for a while held parts of Syria and Palestine, through a series of campaigns which were known in Christendom as Crusades.

They were not so known among the Muslims. It has been remarked as odd that the Arabic historiography of the Crusades, so rich and sophisticated in other respects, shows little knowledge or even curiosity concerning the movement that had brought these invaders to the East. The words Crusade and Crusader do not appear in contemporary Muslim writings, and indeed have no equivalents in Arabic, until these appeared in Christian Arabic writings at a somewhat later date. For Muslim contemporaries, the Crusaders are simply the Franks or the infidels—one more group among the many barbarians and unbelievers who were attacking the world of Islam, distinguished only by their warlike ferocity and the success that it brought them.

Much has been written about the influence of the Crusades on Europe; and in Chapter I above, the effects of contacts in the

Crusading period on the western image of Islam are considered (see pp. 21 ff.). Rather less has been written about the effects of these and related struggles on the lands of Islam. For the first time since the beginning, the Muslims had been compelled by military defeat to cede vast areas of old Islamic territory to Christian rulers, and to leave large Muslim populations under Christian rule. Both facts were accepted with remarkable equanimity. In both West and East, Muslim rulers were willing to have dealings with their new neighbours, and even on occasion to make alliances with them against brother Muslims. The jurists, who had demonstrated the necessity—as an obligation of the Holy Law—of submitting to tyrants, had little difficulty in extending the argument to include unbelievers. 'Whose power prevails must be obeyed', provided only that he allow Muslims to practise their religion and obey the Holy Law. The realm of such a sovereign may even, according to some jurists, be considered as part of the House of Islam.

At first, the Muslim world responded to the loss of the Levant with almost total indifference. The original *jihād* had long since ended, and the spirit of the *jihād* was lost and forgotten. The age was one of violence and change, when Muslim lands were subject to a whole series of attacks and invasions, from Central Asia and Berber Africa as well as from Christendom. Even in Aleppo, Damascus, and Cairo, the loss of Palestine and of the Syrian coast evoked very little interest. Elsewhere, it passed virtually unnoticed.[1] In the fragmented Syria of the time, the new states created by the Crusaders, like those of the Turks from the East, soon found their place in the local political balance, and before long were involved in a pattern of rivalries and alliances to which religion and origin had little relevance.

[1] Ibn al-Athīr, *Kāmil*, ed. C. J. Tornberg (Leiden, 1851–76), x. 192–3, writing in the early thirteenth century, describes how the first refugees from Palestine arrived in Baghdad, told of their troubles, and appealed for help. None was forthcoming. The lack even of information is shown by an Iraqi poet who, lamenting the fall of Jerusalem and the failure of the Muslims to rally to its defence, speaks of the conquerors as Rūm-Byzantines.

In the West, the Christian reconquest achieved complete and final victory. Muslim rulers, and then even Muslim subjects, were evicted from Spain and Portugal, and before long the triumphant Spaniards and Portuguese were descending on the shores of North Africa. In the East, the Crusaders managed to maintain themselves for a while, thanks to repeated reinforcements from Europe—but their possessions were weakened and reduced by successive Muslim attacks, until the last bastion of Latin power in Palestine, the port of Acre, fell to the Mamlūks in 1291.

Only two relics of the Crusades now remained in the East—the Latin kingdom of Cyprus and the Franco-Armenian kingdom of Cilicia. Significantly, both monarchs are denoted in Muslim protocol not by the word *malik*—king—but by *mutamallik*, pseudo-king or *soi-disant* king, since both were regarded as usurpers in what was rightfully Muslim territory.[1] Both countries were in due course reconquered for Islam—Cilicia by the Mamlūks, Cyprus, rather later, by the Ottomans.

Some remnant of the Crusading spirit lingered on in Europe for a while, and inspired some rather futile expeditions against the Mamlūk Sultanate of Egypt and against the new and menacing power of the Ottoman Turks. But Europe had lost interest, and was occupied with other things. And while Christians forgot the Crusade, Muslims remembered the *jihād*, and once again launched a Holy War for the faith—first, to restore and defend what had been lost to infidel invaders, then, in triumph, to bring the message and power of Islam to new lands and peoples that had never known them before.

The influence of the Crusaders in the countries which they had ruled for up to two centuries was slight. They had never been more than a dominant minority, consisting of Catholics of West European origin—barons, clergy, and merchants, with their various retainers and subordinates. The mass of the population, including almost all the villagers, was indigenous, consisting of Muslims, eastern Christians, and some Jews. After the departure of the

[1] al-Qalqashandī, *Ṣubḥ al-Aʿshā* (Cairo, 1331-40/1913-22), viii, 51-2.

Crusaders, these lands were reincorporated into Islamic society without difficulty.

In two respects, however, the Crusades left a permanent mark,[1] One of these was the worsening of the position of the *dhimmīs*, the non-Muslim subjects of the Muslim state. In the early days of the Islamic expansion, these had been subjected to a number of restrictions, mostly precautions for the safety of Muslim garrisons in newly conquered provinces. Though some of these restrictions had found their way into the law-books, they were rarely strictly enforced,[2] and the *dhimmīs* had on the whole enjoyed a large measure of social and economic as well as religious freedom. The embitterment resulting from the long struggle with Christendom, the needs of security in areas of mixed population, at a time when religious loyalty was primary, and the example of persecution set by Christian kings and prelates, all combined to bring a harsher attitude. From Crusading times onwards, relations between Muslims and their Christian or Jewish compatriots became more distant and more difficult. The *dhimmīs* are socially isolated, subject to discrimination, and occasionally—though not often—even to persecution.

The other permanent change is in relations with Europe. Before the eleventh century, these were insignificant. The oft-cited exchange of embassies between Charlemagne and the Caliph Hārūn al-Rashīd is attested only by the Frankish chronicler Einhard. If it took place at all, it was of too little importance to attract the attention of the Muslim historians, since they made no mention of it. A later embassy, sent by Bertha of Tuscany to the Caliph al-Muktafī in 906, is recorded merely as a curiosity. Even in the far west of Islam, in North Africa and Spain, diplomatic exchanges with Europe were minimal. A single embassy, that of the

[1] See C. Cahen, 'Crusades', in *Encyclopaedia of Islam*, 2nd edn.

[2] It may be noted that one ruler who did enforce them, the ʿAbbāsid Caliph al-Mutawakkil (d. 861), was the originator of the famous yellow badge, which he required the *dhimmīs* to wear on their garments. On this point see E. Strauss, 'The Social Isolation of Ahl adh-Dhimma', in *P. Hirschler Memorial Book* (Budapest, 1949), p. 76.

Spanish Jew Ibrāhīm b. Yaʿqūb al-Ṭurṭūshī, sent by the Caliph of Cordova to the Emperor Otto in the mid tenth century, is the source of most Muslim information concerning Frankish Europe in the early Middle Ages. Ibrahim's account of his travels is lost, but is known from quotations in later Arabic geographical writings.

The reconquest and the Crusades brought new knowledge, notably through the writings of Western Muslim geographers like al-Idrīsī (d. 1169) in Sicily and the Andalusian Ibn Saʿīd (d. 1274). More important, they vastly increased the previously rather limited commercial and personal contacts between Muslims and European Christians. During the Crusades, European merchants, chiefly Italian, established themselves in the Levant ports under Latin rule, where they formed organized communities subject to their own chiefs and governed by their own laws. The Muslim recapture of these ports did not end the activities of the European merchants; on the contrary, Muslim rulers were careful not to discourage this trade, which was a source of advantage to them as well as to those engaged in it. Before long colonies of European merchants appeared even in Egypt and other places which had never been under Crusader rule.

From the point of view of the Muslim jurists, the arrangements made with the European colonies were a variant of the classical *amān*, and the resident merchants had the status of *mustaʾmin*. In fact, however, the pattern of the agreements was a European one, modelled on the treaties which the Italian merchant republics had concluded with the Byzantine Empire and the Crusader states. The concept of a bilateral contract or treaty between governments was alien to both Muslim law and Muslim political practice; its adoption was a sign of growing European influence.[1] The essence

[1] It is noteworthy that even when such treaties had become the normal pattern in relations between Muslim and Christian states, they did not occur in relations between Muslim governments. Thus, the Turkish collections of the treaties of the Ottoman government contain only treaties with Christian powers. They do not, before the nineteenth century, contain agreements with Persia, Mogul India, or other Muslim powers. Even the famous and decisive Peace of Amasya, concluded

of such a treaty was the privilege accorded by a Muslim ruler to a Christian state, authorizing the citizens of that state to trade and reside in his dominions, without becoming liable to the disabilities imposed on his own non-Muslim subjects. Numerous agreements of this kind were obtained by European states from the rulers of Turkey, Egypt, and other Muslim countries in the Mediterranean. In Ottoman times, these privileges came to be known as capitulations, from the chapter-headings—Latin *capitula*—into which they were divided.

While European commerce flourished and grew, European arms suffered a series of devastating defeats. The Crusaders were evicted from all their conquests—and vast areas of hitherto Christian territory were lost to Muslim attackers. Once again, as in the early days of Islam, a Holy War was launched against Christendom—and this time the Muslim advance reached to the very heart of Europe.

The movement which defeated the Crusaders did not arise from countries which they had occupied, nor indeed among the peoples whom they conquered or threatened. The new impetus came from further East, and from a new power in Islam, that of the Turks. Their coming preceded, and in a sense provoked, the Crusades. The Muslims first encountered the Turks on the Central Asian borders of their Empire, and from an early date began to import them as slaves, chiefly for service as soldiers. These military slaves came to be known as *mamlūk*s, an Arabic word meaning 'owned', to distinguish them from the humbler slaves, usually African, employed in the house or on the land. Though technically of servile status, the Mamlūks became a privileged military caste, wielding a great and growing power in the Muslim state. Recruited as children by capture or purchase, they received a long and rigorous professional training, and were bound by strong corporate loyalties. From the ninth century onwards, the Caliphs relied almost entirely on Turkish soldiers and commanders, who thus

in 1555 between Turkey and Persia, does not figure in the collections, and survives only in the form of an exchange of letters between the Sultan and the Shah.

gained first military and then political hegemony. Commanders became governors, and governors founded dynasties. The first Turkish rulers in Islam appeared in the ninth century; by the eleventh century there were few rulers, from Central Asia to Egypt, who were not Turks.

Most of these Turkish regimes were founded by men of Central Asian origin, who entered the Islamic world as slaves, were converted to Islam as part of their training, and in due course rose through the military hierarchy to become generals or *condottieri*. They had little or no connection with the free Turkish tribes beyond the frontier, from whom they had been taken and separated in childhood. It was the westward movement of these free Turks, at a slightly later date, that was to have momentous effects on both Islam and Christendom.

The Turks of Central Asia were never conquered by the Muslims but only by Islam. Wandering mystics and missionaries, themselves for the most part Turks, travelled among the unsubjugated tribes beyond the Jaxartes, preaching the simple and militant faith that flourished on the frontier between Islam and heathendom (see above, Chapter III (*B*), p. 127).

The westward migration of the steppe peoples reached its peak during the eleventh century. They advanced along two main routes, north of the Caspian into southern Russia and Eastern Europe, and south of the Caspian into the lands of Islam. The northern invaders are known as Qipchaqs, after the name of the dominant Turkish tribe among them; the southern as Seljuqs, after the family that ruled over them and founded a new Islamic Empire, the Great Sultanate.

The Qipchaqs, also known as Polovtsi and Cumans, for a while ranged over the whole area from the Ural river to the borders of Hungary. To some extent this was old Turkish territory, having been ruled by such Turkic peoples as the Khazars, the Pechenegs, and the Volga Bulghārs; from the mid eleventh century until the coming of the Mongols in the thirteenth, it was dominated by the Qipchaqs, who, even after the Mongol Conquest, were able to assimilate their Mongol masters and impress their own character on the Mongol Khanate formed in their country.

Before the coming of the Qipchaqs, Islam had made some headway among the Turkic peoples of the Don and Volga basins. The Bulghārs, who founded a city and state at the confluence of the Kama and Volga rivers, were predominantly Muslim by the tenth century, and were active in spreading Islam among their neighbours. In 986 they even tried, unsuccessfully, to convert Prince Vladimir of Kiev to Islam. They had greater success among the Turkic tribes.

The Qipchaqs themselves were still pagan when they migrated to Eastern Europe. Some of them became Christian and were merged with the Slavonic-speaking population; others became Muslim, and it was these who came to play a dominant role in the Mongol Khanate on the Volga.

The Mongol conquest of Eastern Europe, in the third and fourth decades of the thirteenth century, for the first time provided a political framework for the steppe peoples that had hitherto ranged over that area. The Mongols established a capital, at Saray on the lower Volga, and founded a dynasty in the line of Batu Khan, the conqueror of Russia, the grandson of Chingiz Khan. The Mongols were few in number, and relied heavily on the Qipchaqs, in time adopting their language and merging with them. Their state was known in Russian and hence in European usage as the Golden Horde. This name appears to have no equivalent in Oriental sources, which call it the Khanate of the Qipchaq steppe. With the conversion of this Khanate to Islam during the late thirteenth and early fourteenth century, a Muslim state dominated the whole of Eastern Europe, from the Baltic to the Black Sea. In the Crimea, in the great river valleys, above all along the Volga, waves of settlement and conversion produced a numerous and active Muslim population, with thriving cities, such as Kazan, Astrakhan, and Baghche Saray, which after the break-up of the Golden Horde became the capitals of independent Muslim Khanates.

The southern invaders, led by the house of Seljuq, were Muslims from the start, and as Great Sultans came to rule over the heartlands of Islam. The Seljuq Sultans did more than restore the shattered territorial and political unity of Islam. They also brought to it, from the frontier, a deep religious earnestness, which is in marked contrast with the laxness and cynicism of the preceding period. Unlike their brothers who had gone to Baghdad and elsewhere as *mamlūk*s, and had been brought up amid the sophistications of the old Islamic cities, the free Turks who came with the Seljuqs retained the fervent and militant faith of the frontier, of the warriors in the Holy War.

The advance of the Turks from Central Asia across Iran to Mesopotamia was accompanied by a great religious revival—more specifically, a revival of Sunnī orthodoxy. While the Turkish armies expelled the infidel and suppressed the heretic, Sunnī jurists and divines, brought for the first time since the beginnings of Islam into an intimate relationship with the state, began to formulate and disseminate the orthodox answer to unorthodox ideas. The sense of mission and authority of the Turks can be seen in a number of texts. One of the most striking is a passage written by a Turk of Kāshghar in about 1072, in the introduction to a book on the Turkish language: 'I have seen that God has caused the sun of Empire to rise in the mansions of the Turks and has made the circles of the heavens revolve about their kingdom. He gave them the name of Turk and conferred kingship on them and made them kings of the age and placed in their hands the reins of the people of this time and set them above mankind. . . .'[1]

During the centuries of Muslim-Christian coexistence along the Byzantine borders, the Holy War had smouldered on among the march-warriors in the remote lands beyond the Jaxartes. The coming of these frontier-peoples to the West reopened the Holy War against Christendom on a scale unknown since the early days of Islamic expansion. In Transcaucasia, the Seljuqs tried to restore Muslim authority over the Georgians and Armenians. Far more important was the Turkish conquest of eastern and central

[1] Maḥmūd Kāshgharī, *Dīwān lughāt al-Turk*, facsimile edn. (Ankara, 1941), p. 2.

Anatolia, the great bastion of the Greek Christian Empire, which had for so long stood in the way of Muslim advance.

The conquest of Anatolia was accomplished by bands of march-warriors and consolidated by migrating nomadic tribes. When the process had already begun, the Sultan sent a Seljuq prince to take charge of the new lands. While the march-warriors fought their way further westwards, officers and officials came from the East to govern and administer what they had won. Thanks to their efforts, a powerful Turkish state was established in Anatolia, with its capital at Konya, the ancient Iconium. The Seljuq dynasty who ruled there until the beginning of the fourteenth century were known as the Sultans of Rūm.[1]

During the period that followed, the Islamic lands of South-West Asia suffered two invasions, from West and East. The invasion of the Crusaders affected only the countries of the eastern Mediterranean; it was soon halted, contained, and eventually repelled, with little permanent effect. The counter-crusade began with an ambitious Turkish officer in the Seljuq service, called Zangī, who carved himself a principality in Mesopotamia and northern Syria. It was continued, with religious fervour as well as political ambition, by his son, Nūr al-Dīn, and brought to an almost successful conclusion by one of Nūr al-Dīn's officers, the famous Saladin, who founded his own dynasty in Egypt and Syria, and dealt what proved to be the decisive blow to the Latin states. Saladin was a Kurd, and relied to some extent on his kinsmen, but his regime and army were of the Turkish type, and under his successors were almost entirely Turkicized. The elimination of the last

[1] This title, one of the very few with a local connotation that have been used by Muslim rulers, requires a note of explanation. Originally, the Sultan of Konya was a regional subordinate of the Seljuq Great Sultan, and the title Sultan of Rūm is a formal recognition of that fact. The subsequent retention of the title is due in part no doubt to normal conservatism, in part to a desire to profit from the continuing power of the great name of Rome. Rūm in Islamic usage means East Rome—that is, the Byzantine Empire. In the Seljuq title it is to be understood in a territorial, not an ethnic sense, and indeed sometimes occurs in the form *Sulṭān bilād-i Rūm*—Sultan of the lands of Rūm.

remnants of Crusader power in Palestine was completed by the Qipchaq Mamlūk rulers of Egypt during the thirteenth century.

The invasion of the Mongols from the East was far more serious. For the first time since the rise of Islam, the Muslims suffered the humiliation of pagan conquest and domination in the central lands of Islam. The Baghdad Caliphate was abolished; Central Asia and Persia, Muslim Anatolia and Iraq were incorporated in a heathen Empire which had its capital in Eastern Asia, from 1267 in Peking. The damage to the Muslim lands has sometimes been exaggerated; there can, however, be no doubt of the blow to Muslim confidence, the shattering impact on Muslim government and society. For a while it seemed that the very survival of Islam was in question, as the Mongol Khans in Persia threatened the last Muslim bulwark in Egypt, and negotiated with Christian powers in Europe for an alliance against the common Islamic enemy.

The danger passed. The negotiations with Europe came to nothing, and within a century the Mongol rulers of West Asia, with their followers, had become Muslim, mostly adopting a Turkish language and character. In retrospect, the coming of the Mongols—the second great migration, after the Turks, of the steppe peoples into south-west Asia—may be seen as a strengthening, not a weakening, of the political and military power of Islam. The monarchies that arose under Turkish and Turkicized Mongol auspices had a quality of stability, steadfastness, and endurance that is lacking in earlier times. This can be seen both in their political institutions and in their military effectiveness. The fourteenth-century Arab historian Ibn Khaldūn saw in the almost universal supremacy of the Turks in Islam a proof of God's concern for the welfare of the Muslims. At a time when the Caliphate had become weak and degenerate, incapable of defending itself against attack, God in His wisdom had brought new rulers and defenders, from among the Turks, 'to revive the dying breath of Islam and restore the unity of the Muslims'.[1]

[1] Ibn Khaldūn, *Kitāb al-ʿIbar* (Būlāq, 1867), v. 371; cf. D. Ayalon, 'The Wafidia in the Mamluk Kingdom', *Islamic Culture*, xxv (1951), 90.

During the age of Turkish hegemony, the world of Islam recovered its own militancy, and embarked on a series of new *jihāds*, which brought important territorial gains, some of them permanent, to the world of Islam. In the East, the most significant advance was into India. The Arab attack on India in the eighth century was inconclusive, and did not reach beyond the Indus; the effective establishment of Islam and of Muslim power in the Indian sub-continent was the work of a succession of Turkish soldiers and rulers, from the eleventh century onwards.

In the West, there were two major advances into Europe, one by the Qipchaq-Mongol Khanate of the Golden Horde, the other by the Ottoman Turks.

The Ottoman state began as a principality of march-warriors, one of the several states that appeared in Anatolia after the break-up of the Seljuq Sultanate of Rūm. Its European name is a corruption of that of its first ruler, Osman, who is said to have reigned from 1299 to 1326. This principality was neither the biggest nor the strongest of the Anatolian states; it was, however, the westernmost, on the borders of what remained of the Byzantine Empire, and offered the greatest opportunities for Holy War, attracting volunteers from all over Anatolia. In responding to these opportunities, Ottomans created a great Empire and an imperial civilization.

Muḥammad the Conqueror (1444–6, 1451–81) achieved in 1453 the conquest of Constantinople, for so many centuries the coveted goal of Muslim arms, and by the reign of Sulaymān the Magnificent (1520–66) the Ottoman Empire was at the peak of its power. In Europe, the Ottoman armies, masters of Greece and the Balkans, advanced across Hungary, and laid siege to Vienna in 1529; in the East, an Ottoman fleet challenged the Portuguese in the Indian Ocean; in the West, the Muslim rulers of North Africa, now under Ottoman suzerainty, brought Muslim naval power to the western Mediterranean and even, on raids, into the open sea and as far as the British Isles and Iceland.[1] Once again the advance of Islam

[1] In 1627 Algerian corsairs raided Iceland, and took several hundred captives. The

offered a mortal threat to Christendom. The Crusade was over; the *jihād* had taken its place. Richard Knolles, the Elizabethan historian of the Turks, was expressing the common feeling of Europe when he spoke of the Turkish Empire as 'the present Terror of the World'.

The clash between Christian Europe and Ottoman Islam has sometimes been compared with the confrontation, in our own time, between the free world and the Soviets. The comparison is not without merit. On both occasions the West has been threatened by a militant and expanding Empire, impelled by the twin imperial attributes of appetite and a sense of mission, and exalted by a dogmatic belief in perpetual struggle ending in inevitable victory. But the comparison should not be pushed too far. There were exaltation and dogmatism on both sides—and greater tolerance on the Turkish. In the fifteenth and sixteenth centuries the movement of refugees—of those who, in Lenin's vivid phrase, voted with their feet—was from West to East and not, as in our day, from East to West. The flight of the Spanish Jews to Turkey is well known, but is by no means unique. When Ottoman rule in Europe came to an end, the Christian nations they had ruled for centuries were still there, with their languages, their cultures, their religions, even to some extent their institutions, intact, and ready to resume their separate national existence. There are no Muslims today in Spain or Sicily, and no speakers of Arabic.

Muslim and Jewish refugees, Christians with heretical religious and political views, were not the only European beneficiaries of Ottoman rule. The peasantry in the conquered provinces also found their lot much improved. Ottoman imperial government brought unity and security in place of conflict and disorder. There were also important social and economic consequences. In the course of the wars of conquest, a large part of the old hereditary landowning aristocracy was destroyed, and their ownerless estates granted as fiefs to Ottoman soldiers. In the Ottoman system,

event is commemorated in the *Tyrkjaranssaga* of the contemporary Icelandic author Björn Jonsson of Skardsa, as well as in other writings.

however, a fief was basically a grant of the right to collect revenues; it was, theoretically at least, for life or some shorter period, and was forfeit when the holder ceased to perform military service. It carried with it no hereditary rights, and no seigneurial jurisdiction. The peasants, on the other hand, usually enjoyed a form of hereditary tenure which was protected by Ottoman usage from both fragmentation and concentration of ownership. They enjoyed far greater freedom on their farms than previously; the taxes they paid were modestly assessed and humanely collected, in comparison with the practice of previous and neighbouring regimes. This security and prosperity did much to reconcile them to other less attractive aspects of Ottoman rule, and account in large measure for the long tranquillity that reigned in the Ottoman provinces until the explosive irruption of nationalist ideas from the West. As late as the nineteenth century, European visitors to the Balkans comment on the well-being and contentment of the Balkan peasantry, which they compare favourably with conditions in parts of Christian Europe.[1] The contrast was far more striking in the fifteenth and sixteenth centuries, the age of the great peasant revolts in Europe. Even the much-condemned *devshirme*, the compulsory collection of boys from the Christian peasantry for recruitment into the Ottoman army and state service, had its positive aspects. By this means, the humblest villager could rise to the highest and most powerful offices in the Empire. Many did so, and brought their families with them—a form of social mobility impossible in the aristocratic societies of contemporary Christendom.

The Ottoman Empire, besides being a dangerous enemy, also exercised a powerful fascination. The disaffected and the ambitious were attracted by Ottoman opportunity and tolerance; downtrodden peasants looked hopefully to the enemies of their masters—even Martin Luther, in his 'Admonition to prayer against the Turk', published in 1541, gives warning that the poor, oppressed

[1] For some characteristic examples, see M. Leo, *La Bulgarie et son peuple sous la domination ottomane tels que les ont vus les voyageurs anglo-saxons (1586–1878)* (Sofia, 1949), pp. 135ff.

by greedy princes, landlords, and burghers, might well prefer to live under the Turks rather than under Christians such as these.[1] The chivalry of Europe fought bravely against the Turks—but their peasants had little interest in their victory. Even the defenders of the established order were impressed by the political and military efficiency of the Turkish Empire. A large proportion of the vast literature produced in Europe on the Turkish menace is concerned with the merits of the Turkish order, and the wisdom of imitating it.

Though it was not realized at the time, the victories of Sulaymān the Magnificent were the high-water mark of the Turkish tide. The Ottoman armies withdrew from Vienna, the Ottoman fleets from the Indian Ocean. For some time the imposing façade of Ottoman military might concealed the real decline of Ottoman power; in Hungary, Turks and Christians fought a long and inconclusive war, and in 1683 the Turks could even make a second attempt to capture Vienna. But it was too late, and this time the Ottoman defeat was final and decisive. Instead of the strength, it was now the weakness of the Ottoman state that posed a problem to Europe. That problem was known as the Eastern Question.

In some parts of the world, notably in tropical Africa and South-East Asia, the power and faith of Islam continued to advance. In the West, however, they encountered a decisive reverse, which the victories of the Ottomans had for a while obscured and delayed, but not prevented.

The response of European Christendom to the first great *jihād* had been the Reconquest and the Crusades; the response to the second wave of Islamic advance culminated in the great expansion of Europe which has come to be known as imperialism (for a consideration of how this wave of imperialism coloured European attitudes towards Islam, especially in the nineteenth century, see above, Chapter I, pp. 51 ff.). It began, naturally enough, at the two

[1] *Vermanunge zum Gebet wider den Türcken*, cited by K. M. Setton, 'Lutheranism and the Turkish Peril', in *Balkan Studies*, iii (Salonica, 1962), 161; cf. Dorothy Vaughan, *Europe and the Turk; a Pattern of Alliances 1350–1700* (Liverpool, 1954), pp. 25 ff., 155 ff.

extremities of Europe, in countries which had themselves been subject to Muslim rule—in the Iberian peninsula and in Russia. It spread until it engulfed almost the whole world of Islam.

The great migrations of the Turks had only touched North Africa, and never reached Spain. The effects of Turkish hegemony in the far west of Islam were therefore small. A similar role was, however, played by another people, the Berbers. During the eleventh and twelfth centuries the Berbers of Africa, like the steppe-peoples of Asia, swept aside the faltering regimes of the established Islamic states, and set up a new political and religious order. The martial prowess and militant piety of the Berbers, like that of the Turks, made it possible for their leaders to create new and powerful states, and to resume the *jihād* with renewed fervour. Their power soon spilled over from Africa to Spain, where for a while it halted the advance of the Christian reconquest.

But only for a while. In the West there were no further infusions of strength, no renovation of political and military structures like that of the Mongol regimes. The Berbers, once settled in the cities, soon lost their ardour, and the decline of Muslim power was resumed. In 1492 the last centre of Muslim power in Spain was conquered by the armies of the Catholic monarchs. In the meantime, the European counter-stroke had already begun.

The Portuguese had completed their reconquest by 1267, almost two and a half centuries before Spain. In 1415, with the capture of Ceuta, they carried the war into the enemy camp, and during the fifteenth century made a determined effort to establish themselves in Morocco, briefly occupying Casablanca and Tangier. The Portuguese attempt at expansion on the North African mainland ended with the victory of the Moroccans at the battle of al-Qaṣr al-Kabīr, in 1578. The Spaniards, too, in the impetus of reconquest, followed their defeated Muslim enemies from Europe to Africa, and between 1497 and 1510 captured a series of towns on the North African coast, from Melilla as far east as Tripoli. This enterprise, too, came to nothing. The Spanish purpose was limited and precautionary—to discourage any attempt at a Muslim restoration, and to protect their shores and ships from Muslim corsairs. With the rise of Ottoman naval power in the Mediterranean, the Spaniards abandoned any serious attempt to invade North Africa, and like the Portuguese were content to hold a few strongpoints with small garrisons.

The real counter-blow of the West against the East came in quite another direction. When Vasco da Gama arrived in Calicut, he explained that he came in search of Christians and spices. It was a fair summary of the motives that sent the Portuguese to Asia—as indeed also, suitably adjusted, of the *jihād* to which, in a sense, their voyages were a long-delayed reply. The sentiment of religious mission was very strong among the Portuguese who went to the East. The voyages of discovery were seen as a religious struggle—a continuation of the Reconquest and the Crusades, and against the same Islamic enemy. When the Portuguese arrived in Eastern waters it was the Muslim powers of Egypt, Turkey, Persia, and India who were their opponents, and whose hegemony they overthrew. After the Portuguese came the Spaniards, the French, the English, and the Dutch, who between them established a West European supremacy in Africa and Southern Asia that lasted until the twentieth century.

The same pattern of recovery, reconquest, and counter-attack can be seen in the other European country conquered by Islam in the Middle Ages—that is, in Russia. The Muslim domination of Russia, in the time of the Golden Horde, was of briefer duration and more limited effect than Moorish rule in Spain. Nevertheless, like the *Turkokratia* in Greece and the Moorish dominion in Spain, the 'Tatar yoke' left a profound mark on the Russian memory. So too did the struggle to end it.

The Russian recovery began in the last quarter of the fourteenth century. In 1380 Dimitri Donskoy, grand-prince of Moscow, defeated the Tatars in a pitched battle at Kulikovo field. This victory, though celebrated in Russian history and legend, was not decisive, for two years later the Tatars rode north again, devastated the Russian lands, and captured Moscow, where they reimposed the tribute. A more deadly blow to the power of the Golden Horde was dealt by a new conqueror from the East, the famous Timur or Tamerlane, who attacked and defeated them in 1395. During the fifteenth century the Khanate of the Golden Horde broke up. Its dominions were split between the three rival Khanates of Kazan, Astrakhan, and the Crimea, as well as other independent groups in the steppes east of the Volga and of the Urals.

These divisions allowed Ivan the Great of Moscow to free himself, in 1480, from all tribute and dependence. Like the Spaniards and Portuguese, but with far greater success, the Russians set out to pursue their former masters. After a long and hard struggle against the Volga Tatars, the Russians finally captured Kazan in 1552. This was the decisive victory. With Kazan in their hands, it was a comparatively easy task to advance right down the Volga and seize Astrakhan in 1556. With this victory, the Russians controlled the Volga trade route, and had reached the Caspian. The stage was set for the great Russian advances in Asia.

While the maritime powers of Western Europe sailed round Africa and established themselves in Southern and South-Eastern Asia, the Russians advanced overland—to the Black Sea, the Caspian, the Pamir, and the Pacific—and incorporated the Muslim peoples of the Crimea, Daghistan, northern Azerbaijan, the Volga, Kazakhstan, and Central Asia in their far-flung domains.

The Russian and West European expansion into Asia and Africa was helped by a substantial superiority in arms. The Russians encountered no major power in their way eastwards; the maritime empires, with ships built to withstand the Atlantic gales and fight one another, had an advantage in navigational skill and naval armament which no Asian country could equal. Only in Europe did the Ottoman Empire, even in its decline still the most powerful of all the Muslim states, stubbornly resist the advance of Christian Europe towards the Balkans, the Aegean, and Constantinople.

In 1606, after an inconclusive war, the Ottomans and Austrians signed a treaty of peace at Sitvatorok, on the banks of a stream on the border between the two Empires. This treaty was a turning-point. For the first time the war was ended, not by a truce dictated in Istanbul by the victor to the vanquished, but by a treaty, negotiated between the parties, and signed between equals on the frontier. In this treaty, for the first time, the Habsburg monarch is no longer called the 'King of Vienna', as in early Turkish documents, but is graced with the imperial title.

The seventeenth century began with a concession of equality; it ended with an admission of defeat. The second failure at Vienna, and the headlong Turkish retreat that followed it, meant a clear and unmistakable victory for the Austrians and their allies. The treaty of Carlowitz, of 1699, was the first signed by Turkey as a defeated power; it was also the first in which the Turkish ministers sought the good offices of friendly governments in the West, to mitigate by diplomatic means the consequences of military failure. The Turks were forgetting the strategy of the Holy War; they were learning the politics of survival, and the new art of diplomacy.

The art of diplomacy was in itself no novelty to the Muslims. The Prophet himself had received and dispatched envoys, and the practice was followed by the Caliphs and other Muslim rulers. From Crusading times onwards, envoys from Christian Europe were frequent visitors at Muslim courts. The practice and purposes of diplomacy were, however, from the Muslim side, limited. There were no permanent, resident embassies, until European states, from the sixteenth century onwards, began to set them up in Istanbul. The Ottomans made no attempt to establish permanent embassies in Europe until the end of the eighteenth century—other Muslim states even later. Instead, they preferred to rely, for the necessary minimum dealings with infidel governments, on occasional special missions sent to one or another European country, and on the European envoys in their own capital. The main purpose of such exchanges was commercial; there was indeed little else to discuss. Political conflicts were resolved by war, and the solution determined by the victor. Other political relationships between Muslims and non-tributary Christian states were to be kept to the indispensable minimum—and even that was very largely left in the care of non-Muslim officials of Muslim states. The much-discussed 'alliance' between Francis I of France and Sulaymān the Magnificent existed largely in the European imagination. On the Turkish side, there was no more than a limited tactical co-operation, which has an appropriately limited place in Turkish historiography.

The negotiation of the treaty of Carlowitz, in which the penalties of defeat were alleviated through the diplomatic skill of the British and Dutch envoys, gave the Turkish government their first insight into the scope and possibilities of international diplomacy. Even after this lesson, however, progress was slow. Curiosity about Europe was still very limited, and dealings with European diplomats still entrusted to the chief Dragoman of the Sublime Porte, who was a Greek. Not until the end of the eighteenth century did the Ottoman Empire sign treaties of alliance with Christian powers. Turkey was at war with Russia and Austria; Sweden too was at war with Russia, joined a little later by Prussia. Treaties with the two countries were accordingly signed in 1789 and 1790. The military judge Shanizade Efendi denounced this innovation of a military alliance with a Christian country as contrary to the Holy Law, citing the Koranic verse: 'O you who believe! Do not take My enemies and your enemies as friends!' (lx. 1). He was over-ruled by the Chief Mufti, who cited the tradition that 'God will help the cause of Islam with men who are not of it'.[1]

During the eighteenth century there had been some improvement in Turkish fortunes. By the treaty of Passarovitz of 1718, Turkey was compelled to cede some further territories. Thereafter, thanks largely to the dissensions of her enemies, she was able to recover some ground. But the improvement was of brief duration. In 1768 war broke out with Russia, and after a series of military and naval defeats, Turkey was compelled to sign the treaty of Küchük Kaynarja of 1774, in which, among other provisions, the

[1] Jevdet, *Tārikh* (Istanbul, 1309/1891–2), v. 12; cf. T. Naff, 'Reform and the Conduct of Ottoman Diplomacy in the Reign of Selim III, 1789–1807', *Journal of the American Oriental Society*, lxxxiii (1963), 310.

Sultan renounced his ancient suzerainty over the Crimean Tatars, who became 'independent', and conceded to the Russian Empress a right to protect the Russian Church in Istanbul which grew into a virtual protectorate over his own orthodox Christian subjects. In compensation the Sultan was allowed to exert religious authority, as 'supreme Muhammadan Caliph', over the Crimean Muslims. This was a meaningless phrase, which was in any case forgotten when the Russians annexed the Crimea a few years later. It did, however, give rise to some rather remarkable consequences within the Islamic world.

The authentic Islamic Caliphate had been dead for many centuries. The Ottoman Sultan had indeed used the title Caliph—but so had many other Muslim sovereigns, including some very minor ones. In the usage of the time, Caliph was one of the numerous titles used by a Muslim sovereign within his own boundaries. No sovereign claimed or exercised any religious authority beyond his boundaries, and no such authority was known or recognized in the Islamic world. The claim to religious jurisdiction over the Crimean Tatars incorporated in the treaty of Küchük Kaynarja was partly a device to save the Sultan's face, partly a forlorn attempt to preserve some link with the Crimea—the first genuinely Muslim country that the Sultan had been compelled to abandon. Earlier cessions had been of Christian lands, with no more than a small ruling minority of Muslims. The Crimea was old Muslim territory, with a Muslim population. Its loss was a bitter blow.

It was also the first of a long series of similar blows, which brought vast areas of the Islamic world under Christian rule, and left only two Muslim sovereigns reigning over independent states of any size. Of these two, the Shah of Persia was a Shīʿī. It was natural that Sunnīs everywhere, deprived of their own leaders, should look towards the last great Sunnī Sultan for guidance.

The theory of the Ottoman Caliphate, first suggested in the treaty of Küchük Kaynarja, was supported a few years later with a new argument—the story that the last ʿAbbāsid Caliph in Cairo had transferred the Caliphate to the Ottoman conqueror of Egypt,

Selīm I. This, it was argued, had brought the Islamic Caliphate to the house of Osman, who had retained it ever since.

The story of the transfer is an obvious myth, and the Ottoman claim to the Caliphate received little support during the late eighteenth and early nineteenth centuries. From the mid nineteenth century onwards, however, Ottoman claims were propounded with increasing vigour, and received a growing measure of acceptance, especially in Russian Central Asia and British India. The Ottoman Caliphate, and the pan-Islamic movement associated with it, served to rally Muslim morale during this period of West and East European domination.

The Ottoman Caliphate was finally abolished by the Turkish Republic in 1924, and various attempts to create a new Caliphate have come to nothing. In the meantime, the confrontation between Islam and Christendom has taken new forms—very different in the areas of West and of East European domination. Western Europe, through a failure of will, faith, and finally power, has relinquished its hold on those parts of the Muslim world which it ruled. Some economic and cultural influences remain—though even these are dwindling; political and military influences have almost completely disappeared. Eastern Europe on the other hand has not only maintained but has strengthened its grip, and extended it to new areas; no longer Christian, it has found another creed, militant and proselytizing, with which to challenge the ideas and values and standards of Islam.

For the first time in centuries, the greater part of the Islamic world consists of independent states, whose rulers have a real chance to choose between alternatives. The future of Islam, and of much else besides, will depend on the choice that they make.

BERNARD LEWIS

BIBLIOGRAPHY

Sir T. Arnold, *The Preaching of Islam* (3rd edn., London, 1935); idem, *The Caliphate* (ed. Sylvia Haim, London, 1965); D. Ayalon, *Gunpowder and Firearms in the Mamluk Kingdom* (London, 1956); L. Beckmann, *Die muslimischen Heere der Eroberungszeit* (Hamburg, 1952); L. Caetani, *Studi di storia orientale*, iii (Milan, 1914); M. A. Cheira, *La Lutte entre Arabes et Byzantins* (Alexandria, 1947); *Encyclopaedia of Islam*, 2nd edn., articles 'D̲jaysh', 'D̲jihād', 'Ḥarb'); A. M. Fahmy, *Muslim Sea-Power in the Eastern Mediterranean from the Seventh to the Tenth Century A.D.* (Alexandria, 1950); J. N. Fries, *Das Heereswesen der Araber zur Zeit der Omayyaden näch Tabari* (Tübingen, 1921); L. Gardet, *La Cité musulmane* (Paris, 1954); H. A. R. Gibb and H. Bowen, *Islamic Society and the West* (London, 1950–7); M. Hamidullah, *Muslim Conduct of State* (2nd edn., Lahore, 1945); J. Hatschek, *Der Musta'min* (Berlin-Leipzig, 1919); W. Heffening, *Das islamische Fremdenrecht* (Hanover, 1925); P. M. Holt, A. K. S. Lambton, and B. Lewis (eds.), *Cambridge History of Islam* (Cambridge, 1970); M. Khadduri, *War and Peace in the Law of Islam* (Baltimore, 1955); W. Montgomery Watt, *Islamic Political Thought: the Basic Concepts* (Edinburgh, 1968); R. Pierre, *Russian Central Asia 1867–1917* (Berkeley-Los Angeles, 1960); E. I. J. Rosenthal, *Political Thought in Medieval Islam* (Cambridge, 1958); D. Santillana, *Istituzioni di diritto musulmano*, i (Rome, 1926); K. M. Setton (editor-in-chief), *A History of the Crusades*, i and ii (Philadelphia, 1955–62); D. Sourdel, *Le Vizirat ʿabbāside de 749 à 936* (Damascus, 1959–60); W. B. Stevenson, *The Crusaders in the East* (Cambridge, 1907); E. Tyan, *Institutions du droit public musulman* (Paris-Beirut, 1953–6); A. Vasiliev, *Byzance et les arabes* (Brussels, 1935–50); D. Vaughan, *Europe and the Turk: a Pattern of Alliances 1350–1700* (Liverpool, 1954).

V

ECONOMIC DEVELOPMENTS

THIS chapter contains three things: an account of the agricultural legacy of Islam in southern Europe; an account of trade between the Muslim lands of the Mediterranean and Latin Christendom in the Middle Ages, with some reference to the rather elusive legacy of Islam that has been claimed in this domain; and finally, an attempt to dissuade the reader from regarding the paucity of the legacy so identified as the result of some problematic backwardness in the economic life of the Islamic world.[1] Two admissions should be made at this point. In the first place the selection of topics gives the chapter a medieval and European bias.[2] For example, nothing has been said of the transfer of the technique of sugar refining from Egypt to China described by Marco Polo, or of the spread of the cultivation of coffee from the Yemen to Java in the seventeenth century; and the trades carried on across the southern and eastern frontiers of the Islamic world appear only incidentally. Secondly, the attempt to study the history of a pre-industrial economy by identifying its 'achievements', or by listing its 'influences' on other economies, tends in practice to be rather unilluminating. The reasons for this are in part stated or implied below. The point is mentioned here to account for a certain arbitrariness in the content of this chapter.

[1] I am particularly indebted to the following for criticisms of an earlier draft of this chapter: Dr. M. Brett, Prof. J. M. Cook, Dr. M. I. Finley, Mr. and Mrs. G. R. Hawting, Mrs. N. Keddie, Dr. I. M. Lapidus, Dr. H. M. Rabie, Mr. F. H. Stewart, Prof. A. Tietze, and Dr. J. Wansbrough.

[2] Even here the account is not intended to be exhaustive—I have not discussed the role of the Muslims in the introduction of paper-making to Europe, or, less securely, of the Merino sheep.

I

One reason why it is so hard to handle questions of economic influence to any purpose is simply the inadequacy of the evidence available to us. This point applies most obviously to the commercial legacy of Islam discussed later in this chapter; but it is also illustrated in the case of the agricultural legacy of Islam in southern Europe. This legacy can be identified tentatively as the arrival of a number of new plants, ultimately from further Asia, and a number of irrigation techniques from the Middle East.

The list of plants allegedly introduced to southern Europe by the early medieval Muslims is quite a long one. It is headed by rice, cotton, and sugar-cane; but it includes also such items as the orange and the lemon, several vegetables (e.g. the egg-plant), and even some varieties of grain. The basic problem is the lack of a sufficiently specific account of the actual introduction of these plants in our sources. The first Umayyad ruler of Spain is related to have brought 'strange plants and noble trees' from Syria and elsewhere; but this was a matter of homesickness rather than economics, and the only item specified in this account is a particular variety of pomegranate. In general, the arrival of the new plants has to be inferred from a combination of evidence for their cultivation in the Muslim period on the one hand, and a lack of such evidence for the pre-Muslim period on the other.

For the Muslim period there are fairly reliable sources to indicate what was cultivated. In addition to scraps of information in the works of the Muslim geographers, a number of agronomical treatises survive from Muslim Spain; these books have considerably more bearing on the realities of medieval agriculture than the literary regurgitations of the classical tradition found in the lands further east. This means that the evidence, here as in general, is much fuller for Spain than for Sicily; indeed there are cases where Sicilian evidence is available only from the Norman period, and the state of affairs in the Muslim period is itself a matter of inference. On the whole, however, it would be ungracious to complain too much of the quality of the Islamic evidence. It is sufficient for what follows that the first three items of the list given above—rice, cotton, and sugar-cane—are already firmly entrenched in the agrarian practice of Andalusia as it appears in the 'Calendar of Cordova', an almanac of the mid tenth century.

It is the pre-Islamic evidence that is problematic. It is hard to judge whether the inferior evidence from Visigothic Spain and Byzantine Sicily can legitimately bear the argument from silence on which the case for attributing the introduction of these plants to the Muslims must necessarily depend. For Roman times the evidence is better, and hence the presumption stronger. Rice then appears sporadically in the Fertile Crescent; cotton shows a similar distribution, and in any case seems to have been known primarily from imports from India; sugar-cane does not appear at all within the empire. Even here, however, the sources may seem silent only because they have not been sufficiently studied—the traditional view of the role of the Arabs in the diffusion of the citrus fruits in the Mediterranean world seems to be a case in point. Moreover, it is impossible to exclude some unrecorded transplantation in the century or two before the Arab conquests. All that one can say to this is that it does seem more likely that the Arabs were responsible. First, the Muslim conquest and its aftermath provides a more plausible context for the displacement of agricultural techniques over long distances; and secondly, for what it is worth, most of the relevant plants appear in the dialects of Spain and Sicily (and hence often in the languages of Western Europe as a whole) under names that betray immediate—though not ultimate—Arabic origin.

The second component of the agricultural legacy is irrigation techniques. Here the evidence suffers from the same defects, with the added problem that the agronomists are much less helpful. It is, however, clear that the Muslims were not responsible for the introduction to Spain of either the irrigation canal, the current-powered water-wheel, or the primitive water-raising device usually known by its Egyptian name as the *shādūf*; all three are known from archaeological or literary evidence to have existed in pre-Islamic Spain. It is only in the case of the animal-powered water-wheel that the argument from silence gives ground for attributing the introduction of a specific irrigation technique to the Muslims. This does not, of course, preclude the hypothesis that, as often stated, the Muslims greatly developed irrigation agriculture in Spain and Sicily. The irrigation canals which the Christians took over in the course of the reconquest—those in the valley of the Ebro, for example, or along the Valencian coast—may well have been constructed by the Muslims, or extended by them, or remodelled by them in a hydraulically more sophisticated form. But this is hypothesis, not established fact.

There is, however, a hydraulic technique which belongs fairly clearly to the legacy of Islam, although it appears only rarely in southern Europe, and then in a context which is more urban than agricultural. This is the *qanāt*, an underground watercourse formed by linking up a series of wells and used to tap ground-water resources at what may be very considerable distances. The distribution of *qanāt*s at the present day, combined with the literary evidence for their history, indicates an Iranian technique which has occasionally wandered. *Qanāt*s appear sporadically in Arabia, were introduced to Egypt on a small scale in Achaemenid times, and appear in many parts of North Africa in the Islamic period. In Spain, they appear mainly in the environs of Madrid; it was the creation of such a system of underground watercourses which made possible the existence of a city in so superficially arid a territory prior to the modernization of the city's water supply in the middle of the last century. That the technique was introduced by the Muslims seems highly probable. Madrid has virtually no pre-Islamic history (the name itself being perhaps of Arabic origin, and a reference to these watercourses). One should nevertheless note that the *qanāt*s of Madrid are not attested in the few references to the city found in the Islamic sources, and first appear in the documents of the Christian reconquest.

I have tried above to list tentatively the main items of the agricultural legacy of Islam to southern Europe. There is, however, little point in such an attempt unless something can be said about the historical significance of this heritage. In the case of irrigation techniques it is hard to say anything at all. Conceivably they were an important contribution to the intensification of agriculture in southern Europe, and perhaps even further afield (the irrigation techniques of Muslim Spain are said to have spread to Roussillon in the central Middle Ages, and a *qanāt* of Spanish workmanship has been reported as far away as Chile). Perhaps they were necessary adjuncts to the cultivation of rice, cotton, or sugar. But the idea that they brought Oriental despotism to southern Europe is hardly a plausible one.[1]

The botanical contribution was likewise nothing very momentous in its immediate consequences. It added some variety to the diet of southern Europe without disturbing the primacy of grain. Sicily remained one of the great granaries of the Mediterranean, as it had been in Roman times. Andalusia became an area of grain deficit, dependent on North African grain in the tenth century and Sicilian grain in the sixteenth; but this economy was based on the traditional export of oil and wine, not on new cultures brought in by the Arabs. It is true that there were at some periods significant exports of Sevillian cotton and Valencian rice. In general, however, in Spain and Sicily as in the Middle East itself,[2] these

[1] Perhaps the organizational demands of irrigation systems provide an explanation of the *origins* of Oriental despotism. They are much less helpful in explaining its geographical distribution in historical times. In the Middle East, irrigation is in general too fragmented to require such a superstructure. Even in Egypt, the irrigation system appears to have been capable of functioning in the not infrequent absence of a central government; the Iraqi system is more fragile, but historically this has led as often to the collapse of the irrigation system as it has to an effective despotism. At a local level, the organizational demands of an irrigation system can be satisfied by co-operation as well as domination; Valencia is a case in point. Cf. K. A. Wittfogel, *Oriental Despotism* (New Haven, 1957).

[2] Rice was cultivated in a small way all over the Middle East, with important concentrations only in the Kaskar district of Iraq and along the Caspian coast. Cotton cultivation was similarly dispersed, and in any case did not challenge the

crops spread in the interstices of already well-developed agricultural economies.

It is only with the subsequent diffusion of these plants outside the areas to which they were brought by the Arabs that the pattern changes significantly. Thus rice was the basis of the extension of agriculture over large parts of the Lombard plain, part of the process whereby this riverain morasse was transformed by the sixteenth century into one of the most precociously capitalistic agricultural regions of Europe. There were, however, few areas of southern Europe which possessed the combination of emptiness and fertility necessary for so uninhibited a development of a cash-crop economy; and though rice played a small part in the development of plantation agriculture in the New World, it never attained the primacy which it has traditionally had in the Far East. Cotton had the most momentous future of all the plants introduced by the Arabs: with coal it was to be one of the two basic raw materials of the Industrial Revolution. Its cultivation was developed at an early stage by the Portuguese in the plantations of the Cape Verde Islands. But the explosion of cotton cultivation in the Americas did not take place until the end of the eighteenth century; and by then the plant had been interbred with varieties indigenous to the New World to such a degree that any connection with the Muslims in Spain becomes extremely tenuous.

The significance of sugar-cane, by contrast, is simple and dramatic: in combination with black slave labour, it provided one of the foundations of the world's first colonial empires. The earliest such plantations appear in the fifteenth century in the islands of the Portuguese Atlantic, whence in the sixteenth century they spread to Brazil; the Spanish established them in the Canaries and Hispaniola. Of course, this is a story for which the Arabs in Spain provide only a starting-point; they may have brought sugar-cane to Europe, but the rest is a matter of what others did with it. The dispersed sugar production of Andalusia is a long way from

primacy of flax until modern times. Only sugar-cane showed a marked degree of concentration, with the bulk of production located in Khūzistān and parts of Egypt.

the consolidated plantation economies of Mauritius or Cuba. Nevertheless something of the modernity of sugar can be seen in retrospect long before the Portuguese made it the basis of their Atlantic empire. Because of the scale of the inputs of labour and irrigation required for its cultivation, sugar cannot be produced within the framework of peasant agriculture and cottage industry. Sugar refining is first heard of in the Middle East in Khūzistān in the eighth century. By the time the Muslim geographers begin to shed a little light on the economy of the Islamic world in the tenth century, sugar-cane was being cultivated in Khūzistān as a major cash-crop and the product exported over most of the eastern Islamic lands; at the same time it appears in Egypt, where the sheer size of the sugar refineries dominated the industrial landscape of medieval Cairo. Sugar was one of the few products of a medieval economy which could elicit the plantation and the factory. There is a real if extended sense in which the legacy of Islam lies behind the Cuba of Batista and Castro.

2

The mercantile legacy of Islam, in so far as one cares to identify one, arises out of a period of rapid change within a fairly persistent structure. After outlining the basic elements of this structure, I shall describe the radical change in its entrepreneurial aspect which took place in the central Middle Ages. Finally I shall consider whether it is in fact possible to identify any specific Islamic legacy to Western Europe arising out of this change.

In some ways resources have been distributed with remarkable evenness in the Mediterranean world of historical times. Physically, climatically, and botanically it is a region of marked homogeneity, a series of domains of rainfall agriculture broken up by numerous mountain ranges, with timber and mineral resources scattered here and there. In this narrow band, compressed between the northern and southern limits of the olive tree, there is little in the natural environment to force a sharp differentiation between the economies of Syria, Cyrenaica, North Africa and the northern agricultural peninsulas. This fact is both a disincentive to trade within the Mediterranean world and a reason for the early development of a number of external trades. The most persistent, or at least the best documented of these is of course the spice trade with the Orient. The routes followed by this trade have shown a marked degree of instability through history, culminating in the development of the Cape route in the sixteenth and seventeenth centuries; but the trade itself, and the return trade in precious metals, is a constant. Less conspicuously, the trades in Malayan and Cornish tin, in Sudanese gold, and in furs and amber from northern Europe, are attempts to remedy some of the inconveniences of Mediterranean homogeneity.[1]

This picture of a homogeneous Mediterranean needs three important qualifications. The first is an obvious geographical point. East of Tunisia, the African coast reproduces the normal pattern of the Mediterranean only in the abortive agricultural peninsula of Cyrenaica. The greater part of this coast is desert, a land whose population has been so diffuse and impoverished as to carry almost no commercial weight in the Mediterranean.

Egypt is, of course, an obvious exception to this, and forms the second qualification. The importance of Egypt lies in a unique combination of two features. First, a number of factors make it possible for Egypt to export a large and reliable agricultural surplus: an intensive irrigation economy, a harvest more dependable than any other in the Mediterranean, a tradition of centralized bureaucratic exploitation, and an unusual accessibility to river transport. The second feature is that Egypt was compelled to disgorge a part of her agricultural surplus. The compulsion lay in the

[1] An exception is the silk trade with China. The absence of the silk worm from the Mediterranean before the sixth century arose from Chinese secretiveness, not natural deficiency; thereafter this trade was replaced by numerous centres of production in Iran and within the Mediterranean world, so much so that by the eleventh century Egypt obtained silk mainly from Spain and Sicily.

poor endowment of the country in a number of key resources, most obviously timber and metals. Throughout their history the Egyptians have been forced by these deficiencies into a mixture of substitution, deprivation, and import. In the case of timber, Islamic Egypt still possessed meagre reserves of acacia which constituted a state monopoly. Everyday life tended to be so constructed as to minimize the need for wood—furnishings rather than furniture, dung rather than firewood. There remained, however, a substantial dependence on imports, above all from across the Mediterranean. In the case of iron, the Egyptians originally dealt with the problem by continuing to live in the Bronze Age until the arrival of the Ptolemies; in the Middle Ages they used leather buckets and wooden locks, but were also heavily dependent on supplies from India and Western Europe. Other metalliferous ores had existed in the mountains to the east of the Nile as late as Roman times, but the increasing cost of exploiting them in a desert without fuel or water was by the Islamic period a sufficient disincentive to the working of any but the newly discovered gold mines.

The third qualification is that even within the relatively homogeneous Mediterranean the distribution of natural resources has been sufficiently uneven to give rise to some finer lines of relative advantage. Thus Andalusia and the coast of southern Tunisia appear in ancient times and again in the Middle Ages as exporters of olive oil, Sicily is traditionally one of the granaries of the Mediterranean, North Africa is an exporter of hides and leather. Two factors in particular have tended to bring out such potential specializations. The first is the relatively low level of maritime as opposed to overland transport costs: a Mediterranean economy was a possibility in a sense in which an Anatolian economy, for example, was not. The second is the development of the human resources of the area, leading to a more intensive exploitation of its natural resources. There has been a tendency over historical times for the region to become one of dense as opposed to diffuse population, intensive as opposed to extensive agriculture, territorial states rather than tribes, where the sheer extent of mountain and desert has not precluded such a development. The process is obviously one for which the evidence is fragmentary, and it has included devolution as well as evolution; but the overall trend is not in doubt, and is aptly illustrated by the contrast between the relative ease with which the Phoenicians and Greeks brushed aside indigenous populations in founding their colonies in ancient times and the intense naval and diplomatic activity required to create the mercantile empires of Venice and Genoa in the Middle Ages.

The results of a similar demographic trend, operating unevenly in the northern hinterland of the Mediterranean through the Middle Ages, are perhaps visible in such information as is available on Islamic trade with northern Europe and Russia. In the ninth and tenth centuries this trade was not entirely homogeneous. The maritime routes, in the Atlantic and Mediterranean, could carry bulk commodities such as timber; the overland routes to Spain and Central Asia could not. More puzzling than this, the western sector of the trade is represented in the coin hoards of Europe by a mere few hundreds of Muslim coins, the eastern sector by some hundreds of thousands.[1] What is of interest in this context, however, is, the exports rather than the imports of the north. Here the primary items on all routes (leaving aside the case of timber) were iron, slaves, and furs. Iron is hardly significant in this context, since mining can take place in almost any economic environment.[2] The slave trade is, however, a pointer to the social and political organization of the north. The roots of slave trades lie in tribal backlands, in the wars which tribal societies carry on among themselves, and in the raids which others make against them. The rulers of consolidated peasant societies are not normally prepared to supply the commodity from within their own territories. Similarly the fur trade indicates the extent to which the northern lands were

[1] See Figs. 17 and 18. The circulation of Muslim coins in medieval Europe is attested in the literary and documentary sources of the eighth to eleventh centuries.

[2] Mining techniques themselves are often sophisticated, but little beyond food, water, and fuel is required from the local economy; compare the modern oil industry in Saudi Arabia.

still dominated by forest rather than farmland. What is interesting is the subsequent divergence of the eastern and western sectors of this northern trade. The eastern sector seems to have preserved the old pattern for centuries. By contrast the western sector seems to have changed in two important respects by, say, the twelfth century. In the first place, the roots of the old slave trade were cut away. Enslavement through piracy remained a hazard on the Mediterranean down to the nineteenth century; but an overland slave trade comparable to that which crossed the Sahara throughout the Middle Ages had ceased to exist in Western and Central Europe by the eleventh century. Charlemagne's raiding against the pagan Slavonic tribes was no longer feasible with the emergence of a series of Christian kingdoms in the area. By the late Middle Ages, when the Mamlūks were in the habit of replenishing their ranks in southern Russia and the Caucasus, such a trade would have been inconceivable further to the west. Secondly, the export of European textiles became a major feature of trade with the Islamic lands. Thus in the second half of the twelfth century, cloth replaced precious metals as the main commodity exported by the Genoese to Syria, while at the same time Genoa was exporting considerable quantities of cloth to North Africa; some of this cloth was local, but some significantly was Flemish or English.[1]

The structure outlined above is in many ways a remarkably stable one; indeed some of its key components are as old as Pharaonic times. There is no comparable stability in the agencies through which these potential flows of goods have been realized. It might be supposed that the various peoples of the Mediterranean would have participated in the long-distance trade of the sea on a more or less equal and stable basis. There is a plausible contrast in this respect between the Mediterranean and the other great domain of Muslim navigation, the north-western Indian Ocean,

[1] This is, however, an argument from the near-silence of earlier sources on cloth exports to the Muslim Mediterranean, and it is not altogether clear how significant this is.

where the entrepreneurial structure has been particularly unstable. The Mediterranean coastlands are on the whole well populated, adequately provided with food, water, and anchorage. Only the desert coast of Africa is comparable to the desolate north-western shores of the Indian Ocean. The Mediterranean is ideal for cabotage, the habit of pottering from port to port and island to island which contrasts so sharply with the deep sea crossing of the Indian Ocean practised since Hellenistic times. Even in its supply of timber the Mediterranean is privileged: few of its populated regions lack some small quantity of usable ship timber, whereas the Arabs of the Indian Ocean had in general to sail to India or East Africa for this commodity. For all these reasons the greater part of the Mediterranean supports at least some level of spontaneous local maritime life.

On the other hand, this background activity was not in fact as dense as one tends to imagine it, very much less dense for example than it has been along the northern coasts of Europe. The reason is that the Mediterranean lacks shallow water; hence it lacks fish on a scale comparable to the North Sea and the Baltic, and hence it lacks the enormous fishing fleets of these waters. (One of the few exceptions lies at the northern end of the Adriatic, where Venice is appropriately situated.) This means that the step from a maritime subsistence economy, as it were, to participation in the long-distance trade of the Mediterranean is a difficult and expensive one; the inventory of long-distance trade is not to any great extent provided or sustained by the background pattern of local activity. Thus at any given time relatively few of the Mediterranean peoples will actually be found making the attempt, and it is usually excessively difficult to shed any light on the reasons for their espousal or rejection of the role. The most obvious and immediate factor, the changing distribution of the timber supply, is in fact by no means so explanatory as one might suppose it to be. No doubt it favoured to some degree the emergence of Italian enterprise in the Middle Ages which will shortly concern us. It is, however, striking that the location of the timber resources of the Indian Ocean did not preclude a considerable amount of Arab navigation on that sea; and in the Mediterranean itself the Barbary corsairs throve on imported timber in a later period. Even Egypt possessed mercantile shipping.

Moreover, it is probably a mistake to think of the long-distance trading role as in itself a peculiarly desirable one, to be correlated with the general economic well-being of the people concerned. Deprivation is at least as plausible a background to the assumption of the role as prosperity. The United States at the present day does not possess her share of mercantile shipping, and the reason is that American shipping companies cannot offer both a service which is competitive in the international shipping market and a wage which is competitive in the domestic labour market. Conversely the most maritime population in modern Turkey, the Laz, is also the most land-hungry. In other words shipping is a poor man's job. Hence the reluctance of the traditional sailors of the Mediterranean to go to sea in the summer if they could find something better to do on land the previous winter. Of course what is true for seamen is not automatically true for merchants—the decline of Venetian, Genoese, and Ragusan shipping in the late sixteenth century involved no immediate decline in the trade of these cities, and the Jewish merchants of the Geniza papers[1] travelled in Muslim or Christian ships. But such a separation of the two roles was the exception rather than the norm. Moreover, just as many seamen were in a sense unsuccessful peasants, so many merchants given the opportunity preferred to be landowners. The view of Cato, that the mercantile profession was just too risky for a man to choose it willingly for his livelihood, epitomizes a great deal of Mediterranean history. Even the Venetians, once the advantages of their political and naval power had been cancelled by the arrival

[1] The (Cairo) Geniza was a sort of communal waste-paper basket of the Cairene Jews, and contains much material for the economic and social history of the eleventh to thirteenth centuries. The study in this material by Prof. Goitein cited in the bibliography is the most substantial contribution to the economic history of the medieval Muslim world that has yet appeared.

of the English and the Dutch in the late sixteenth and early seventeenth centuries, ended by retiring into the *terra firma*.

But the activities of merchants and seamen were never set in a political vacuum. Rulers acted in or upon the mercantile economy in numerous ways. They might replace it altogether, as when they produced textiles for their own use in the *ṭirāz* establishments found all over the Islamic world (and in Norman Sicily). They might participate in it by dabbling in the open market: *ṭirāz* cloths were sometimes sold to the public; Aq Qoyunlu and Ṣafavid rulers sold silk in fifteenth-century Bursa; slaves attached to the seraglio wove silks for disposal on the Istanbul market in the sixteenth century; many Muslim rulers owned and operated mercantile shipping; an Ottoman Grand Vizier dispatched his own ship with a cargo of corn for Venice in 1551. Often such economic enterprise was reinforced by political bullying: the ruler of Aleppo in the tenth century established a monopoly of the purchase and sale of all goods entering and leaving the city, the Mamlūk rulers in the fifteenth century and the Portuguese kings in the sixteenth monopolized the spice trade. Governments sought to ensure supplies of goods on which their military or naval power depended: the Fāṭimids had a government office which had a right of pre-emption on all incoming timber and iron, the Mamlūks were intensely concerned with the maintenance of the slave trade on which their recruitment depended, the rulers of the Ottoman Empire saw trade with England in the late sixteenth century primarily as an opportunity to secure their supply of Cornish tin. Rulers manipulated the economy in the course of favouring their friends, spiting their enemies, and generally playing power politics: permission to export Thracian grain was as much a political matter under the Thracian kings in the fifth century B.C. as it was under the Ottomans; the Ḥafṣids rarely allowed the export of Tunisian grain to Venice or Genoa, but when they did so they waived the customs duties to indicate that what was involved was an act of grace, not an economic transaction; Byzantium tried to prevent the export of timber to Egypt in order to undermine Muslim naval power;

Justinian in the sixth century and Sulaymān the Magnificent in the sixteenth sought to erode the revenues of the ruler of Persia by suppressing the import of Persian silk.

All this is in many ways as unstable as the mercantile economy. Thus while the great granaries of the Mediterranean—Sicily, Thrace, and Egypt—are a constant in the history of the sea, the distribution of their surplus product has changed as often as that of political power. What is stable and significant in this confusion is the political inertness of mercantile interests. That is to say, the interests represented or respected by rulers were not those of merchants. The interests which rulers represented were those of a ruling segment to which the merchants did not belong. Equally the only group outside this ruling segment which exercised any systematic constraint on the economic policies of governments was not the merchants but, curiously enough, the poor in the great cities. Most governments preferred to expend some of their resources on seeing that the populations of their capital cities were fed, rather than face the threat of riot from a hungry mob. Hence an enormous amount of coercion has been applied to the distribution of grain in the Mediterranean in the interests of the great cities of powerful states. But characteristically, this one effective constraint operated against the interests of merchants, who could have realized higher profits from the sale of grain in a market undistorted by the anxieties of governments.

The claim advanced here is not that governments were hostile to mercantile interests as such, simply that they were indifferent to them. Merchants did not directly enjoy the exercise of power, nor could they benefit from the constraints on government policy which protect the interests of many such groups in some of the more delicately constituted societies of the modern industrial world. Government policies might, of course, lend an adventitious support to the interests of merchants. In this respect the most persistent of all motives behind the economic policies of governments (or the lack of them), the desire to raise more taxes, is ambivalent. A government sufficiently hard pressed or irresponsible to push fiscal exploitation to the point of depleting the current resources of the economy without regard to future revenue may do considerable damage to the interests of merchants. On the other hand, a government able or willing to forgo some of its current revenue in favour of increased future revenue may do a lot to promote them. The Ottoman government in the fifteenth and sixteenth centuries engaged in considerable investment of this kind (either directly or by remission of current taxation) with a view to creating new market facilities. The Mamlūks began by maintaining very favourable conditions for the operation of private enterprise on the Indian Ocean, but ended with confiscations and state monopolies. Which way the fiscal interest swung—the rate at which the government discounted the future—was not a matter over which merchants exercised any control. And even when the fiscal interest pursued was a long-term one, it might be overridden by purely political considerations—as mentioned above, Sulaymān the Magnificent encouraged and protected the silk trade because, among other things, it was an attractive source of revenue; but like Justinian he was prepared to sustain the loss of this revenue in order that the ruler of Persia should suffer the same deprivation.

Did the rise of Islam result in any radical change in the entrepreneurial structure outlined above? It makes sense that it should have involved some change. I have stressed the importance of rulers in the redistribution of Mediterranean commodities, and a change in the political structure of the region is thus likely enough to have had economic consequences. The most obvious example of this is access to the Egyptian grain surplus: Constantinople lost this with the Arab conquest and did not regain it until Egypt became an Ottoman province in the sixteenth century. In the other direction, Byzantine rulers in the centuries after the Arab conquests at least attempted to prevent the export of timber to the Muslim lands. A more interesting question, however, concerns the identity of the merchants. In the fifth and sixth centuries they were easterners—Greeks, Jews, Egyptians, and above all Syrians. Their colonies appear as far afield as Paris and western Germany. By the eleventh or twelfth century they have clearly lost this position to the merchants of Latin Christendom. Did they lose it because of the Muslim conquests? There is certainly rather less evidence of their activities in the centuries following the rise of Islam; but this may reflect not a decline in their activity but merely the general paucity of evidence for Mediterranean trade in this period. All that can be said is that the theories which would explain their demise as a consequence of the rise of Islam are neither plausible as exercises of the historical imagination nor economical as constructs out of the known facts.

Equally there seems to be little reason to suppose that the rise of Islam made rulers more sensitive to the interests of merchants. It is true that the new religion had originated, according to its own tradition, in a desert city in which political power was to some extent in the hands of a mercantile oligarchy. But this memory contributed more to the religious imagery of Islam than to the power-structure of subsequent Islamic societies. The emphasis sometimes placed on the peculiarly bourgeois and mercantile character of Islamic society in its first few centuries should not be allowed to obscure this point. Muslim writers of this period do tend to be more sympathetic to mercantile activity than those of Christian Europe (not always so—the classic defence of gainful activity is known from an abridgement given in a work written to refute it). These pro-mercantile values have been seen as middle-class ideology, and this does lead to an important point: much of early Islamic literature was in fact written in a mercantile environment. This explains the disparity between the tenderness of conscience with which these writers regarded riches amassed in government service and the enthusiasm with which they commended mercantile profit; it explains why Muslim law, unlike the Canon law of the Christian clerics, took such pains to accommodate the practice of usury; and it explains why the fiscal provisions of this law at times read like the legal fantasies of men who dislike being taxed. But is it after all such a surprise to find that the literature of Muslim merchants embodies mercantile values, just as that of Christian clerics embodies clerical values? And is there any reason to suppose that the Christian merchants of early medieval Europe, had they been in the habit of writing books, would have shown themselves any less self-congratulatory than their Muslim peers? There is of course a genuine historical problem here: why should the *locus* of religious literacy have been so different in the two societies? But the existence of this problem does not justify the claim that the mercantile sector of the economy was economically more prominent, still less politically more powerful, in the Islamic case. There were of course individual merchants who rose to positions of power in the state, perhaps more often under the ʿAbbāsids than under the Umayyads. But this is a matter of social origins, not of class power. It does not mean that the ʿAbbāsid putsch was a bourgeois revolution, only that the more effectively despotic rulers of the new dynasty were under fewer constraints in picking their servants. The literature of the mercantile bourgeoisie can indeed be read as a powerful expression of the political alienation of this class: it combines a prostrate acceptance of the fact that rulers behave iniquitously with a concern to avoid at all costs the moral contamination of association with this iniquity.

It is against this background that one must see the emergence along the shores of Latin Christendom, above all in Italy, of a small number of independent or autonomous cities in which mercantile interests determined policies. The earliest evidence of their participation in the long-distance trade of the Mediterranean dates from the ninth century in the case of Venice and Amalfi and from the eleventh in the case of Genoa and Pisa (see above, p. 20). The unequivocal outcome of this development is well indicated in the fact that in the twelfth and thirteenth centuries spices reaching Muslim North Africa from the Muslim lands of the eastern Mediterranean by sea did so in large measure through such entrepôts as Genoa and Marseilles. In these cities, as in no territorial state of medieval times, naval and diplomatic resources were at the disposal of the pursuit of mercantile profit. This convergence proved so powerful that the Mediterranean rapidly became something approaching an Italian lake. The symbols—and in some ways the embodiment—of this domination were the republican constitution and the galley. On land, the early constitutional history of Venice was largely concerned with the reduction of the Doge to an elected official; the history of Amalfi begins effectively with a rising against Lombard rule and the inception of a regime of elected magistrates shortly before the middle of the ninth century; the history of Pisa and Genoa in the years before their commercial efflorescence at the end of the eleventh century is one of social revolution and the creation of communes. The emergence of such a pattern of city-state politics made possible an immediacy in the domination of policy by a class interest which is impossible in a territorial state; compare medieval Venice, where the government really was something like the executive committee of the bourgeoisie, with the ambiguity of the relationship between nineteenth-century English capitalists and the haughty aristocrats in the Foreign Office. At sea, the central point is the dual role of the galley. Again the innovation was organizational, not technological. The naval history of the Mediterranean had been dominated since ancient times by the galley with its speed, manœuvrability, and large complement of oarsmen; the economic history of the sea had by contrast been almost entirely the domain of the sailing ship. Hence the mercantile galley is a rare occurrence in the Geniza papers, for example. By contrast the Venetian or Genoese galley was a flexible instrument that could be used for warfare or high-class trade at will: the cream of the merchant marine could be transformed into a navy by administrative fiat.

The phenomenon was not new in the Mediterranean. Ancient Carthage was as good an example of merchant power as medieval Venice. Indeed the point which I have laboured at such length was succinctly put by the prophet Isaiah when he referred to Tyre as a city 'whose merchants are princes'. Nor is it unknown outside the

Mediterranean: there is an obvious parallel in the medieval Baltic, where the Hanseatic cities monopolized the trade of the Scandinavian kingdoms; and perhaps in the success of the Dutch, the first mercantile *nation*, in the Indian Ocean of the seventeenth century. There had not, however, been any instances of the phenomenon in the Mediterranean since Carthage had been destroyed by the Romans. It is therefore a very fair question why the phenomenon reappeared in the area during the period which concerns us. There is in fact no clear answer to this question, and the core of the problem is in any case the history of Europe, not the history of Islam. The brief comment offered below is intended only to place the problem in some kind of perspective before proceeding to the repercussions of the development for the Islamic Mediterranean.

The kind of politics with which we are concerned is most easily explained when it occurs in areas isolated by geography from the political and agricultural nexus of the territorial states. Hence examples in Islamic history are to be sought where international transit trades crossed the vast empty spaces that separated the domains of civilized life—Hormuz at the entrance to the Persian Gulf; Mecca in the Arabian desert; and perhaps such Saharan cities as tenth-century Wārgla, ruled by its council of notables, or later the five Ibāḍī cities of the Wādī Mzāb. At the other end of the spectrum, the last place where one would expect to find the phenomenon would be a territorial state such as the Mamlūk empire, where mercantile interests were inevitably submerged in the sheer size of the agricultural economy and the overwhelming domination of the Mamlūk military élite. All this is trivial enough. It does not fully explain the various instances—ʿAydhāb, like Hormuz, was a classic example of a town which existed solely to facilitate the operations of a long-distance transit trade through a desolate environment; but while the claims of territorial rulers over Hormuz tended to be half-hearted, ʿAydhāb was held firmly in the grip of the rulers of Egypt. But if this simple geographical axiom does not explain the particular instances of mercantile politics in the Islamic world, it does seem to account for their general location.

This point retains a certain purchase in the case of the Latin cities. To some degree Venice, founded by refugees from the mainland on the islands of the lagoon, stood clear of the agricultural economy, as did Amalfi with its hinterland of barren mountain. Again, it is clearly crucial for the emergence of the communes of southern Italy that there was a political vacuum created by the failure of any territorial authority—Lombard, Byzantine, or Arab—to establish permanent rule in the area; just as they lost their leading role in the commercial life of the Mediterranean with the consolidation of the Norman kingdom. Likewise the rise of Genoa and Pisa was possible only because of the break-up of the Lombard kingdom with its elaborate fiscal underpinning. However, the position of the cities outside the nexus of territorial authority was not something God-given, as it tended to be in the Islamic instances; and far from being situated in the desert, these cities were located in an area the economy of which was to be in all respects one of the most developed in medieval Europe. This helps to show why the phenomenon was so significant, but equally it makes it even more difficult to explain how it ever came about.

The actual application of merchant power in the Mediterranean was more straightforward, though far from unitary. Its simplest and most direct form was embodied in the domination of the sea itself. This domination is not hard to explain. The rulers and aristocracies of territorial states fight on land, not at sea: the creation of a navy requires the calculated investment of scarce resources in a form of warfare which is alien to their skills and values. Moreover just because the navy of a territorial ruler exists for almost exclusively naval purposes, the cost of maintaining it is not offset by such economies as the dual use of galleys characteristic of the merchant cities. Thus what came naturally to the merchant cities was for the territorial rulers an uphill struggle. The only exception to this was the case where warships doubled as privateers. There are several instances of this symbiosis of piracy and politics in the history of the Islamic Mediterranean—the activities of Mujāhid in Sardinia in the early eleventh century, those of Jabbāra, emir of Barqa, a few decades later, the depredations of the rulers of Tunisia which provoked the counter-attacks of the merchant cities in 1087 and 1390, the emirate of Menteshe in Asia Minor in the fourteenth century, and of course the Barbary States. However, a territorial state of any size usually has too many interests which are damaged by a systematic use of this particular way of financing a fleet, and the instances cited are all of relatively minor potentates. Moreover their activities tended to be short-lived in comparison to those of the mercantile communes.

There was of course nothing to prevent a determined ruler from challenging the cities on the high seas if he really wished to. Few in fact did so for any length of time. The Fāṭimids maintained several arsenals in Egypt, but the effort was allowed to slacken. Saladin virtually conceded the sea to the merchant republics. The Mamlūks maintained no standing fleet and their few naval actions on the Mediterranean were the work of *ad hoc* flotillas. Even Bāybars I, the sultan who showed the greatest determination in naval affairs, was not in fact very persistent. In general the Mamlūks cut their losses and destroyed the coastal settlements they were unable to defend. Only the Ottomans, with their remarkable series of expansionist rulers in the fifteenth and sixteenth centuries, made a sustained attempt to gain control of the seas. The result was very impressive: the Black Sea closed to the Italians, the maritime empires of Venice and Genoa largely liquidated, and a brief period of Ottoman rule in North Africa. But this was an extraordinarily determined effort for a territorial state to sustain over so long a period, and there was no comparable challenge to the supremacy of the merchant cities in the Middle Ages.

On land the situation was more complex. Here the basic fact was the inability of the merchant republics to compete with the territorial states in terms of brute military strength—they lacked the sheer quantity of revenue and manpower available to kings and sultans. The resulting situation is illustrated in one of the earlier applications of mercantile force in the Islamic world, the attack on the Tunisian port of Mahdiyya carried out largely by the Pisans and Genoese in 1087. The attack had been provoked by Zīrid piracy and by the maltreatment of Italian merchants in the territories of the Zīrid ruler. Mahdiyya was taken without significant resistance. What matters is the sequel. In the first place, there seems to have been no question of retaining Mahdiyya in Italian hands. Secondly, in one source there is a statement that the Italians offered the town to Roger I, the Norman ruler of Sicily; Roger, however, was preoccupied in Sicily and preferred to honour his truce with the Zīrid ruler. Thirdly, the Italians then handed back the town in exchange for a considerable indemnity and commercial privileges. The episode aptly illustrates the options available in the use of naval power to further mercantile interests on land.

The first point, the inability to digest territorial conquests, is in fact overstated in this example. Many of the islands of the Mediterranean, including such large ones as Crete and Cyprus, eventually became direct possessions of the Venetians and Genoese. On the mainland, the merchant republics were very closely involved in the attempts to take and hold the Egyptian port of Damietta in the thirteenth century. There was, however, nothing remotely parallel to the development of British India out of the activities of the East India Company. The largest territory ever held by one of the merchant republics, the Venetian Morea, was a brief episode of the late seventeenth and early eighteenth centuries. In general, to secure the most favourable conditions for their commercial activities on the mainland it was necessary for the merchant republics to secure the existence of friendly governments, or, more cynically, the existence of governments which could be blackmailed into co-operation by inexpensive applications of naval power. A Norman Tunisia, dependent on Italian sea-power, might have served this purpose excellently. The classic example of this situation is of course the Latin Kingdom of Jerusalem; the existence of this insecure and weakly constituted Frankish minority regime set against a hostile Muslim hinterland provided the best possible solution to the problem of translating naval power into influence on land, the benefits of empire without its costs. The usual price of naval support to these regimes was exemptions from customs duties and immunity from the jurisdiction of the Frankish authorities. A slight variant occurred in Cilicia, where the role of the Franks was played by the Christian Armenians. The system usually worked well: only in the case of the Lusignan kings of Cyprus were the rulers insufficiently responsive to the blackmail, with the result that the island was eventually brought under full Genoese occupation.

But there were not enough Frankish armies to go round, even had it been desirable to extend the system to cover the entire non-Latin Mediterranean. Where it was supremely desirable, in the case of Egypt, the attempts failed; and the last Syrian possessions were lost in the thirteenth century. Thus in the Muslim Mediterranean the Italian cities had for the most part to accept the existence of entrenched Muslim regimes. The Italians could still monopolize trade to and from the ports of such regions if they chose, but their power rapidly dwindled to nothing inland. Hence the comparative rarity of journeys into the interior by Christian merchants. They did occasionally go inland to Qayrawān, Damascus, and more especially Cairo; but in doing so they left the domain of merchant power. It is a significant detail that Venetian merchants doing business in the villages of Syria in the later Middle Ages had obtained the right to travel in *native* costume for safety. All that remained here were the diplomatic resources of the communes. Unlike the Geniza merchants, the communes could at least negotiate treaties to rationalize an environment which they could not significantly alter in their favour. A treaty with the ruler of Aleppo might remove causes of friction and render the behaviour of the local authorities more predictable; but it could not do much for the level of customs dues. What happened on the coast itself was more varied. Occasionally naval force could be used very crudely to bully minor local potentates, as in the case of the raid on Mahdiyya. Thus in the mid-fourteenth century the Italians defeated and killed the Turkish ruler of Izmir and imposed on his brother in nearby Ayasoluk a treaty under which piracy was to be supressed and his principality opened up to Italian merchants. At about the same time the Venetians took advantage of the weakness of the Muslim lord of Tripoli in Libya to secure the virtual cession of the salt-pans. Further west naval force was used by Genoa to open up Tunis, Bougie, and Ceuta; Venice exported lead from Ḥafṣid Tunisia free of duty, and both cities had the right to provision their fleets in Ḥafṣid ports.

It was in Egypt that the exchange rate between naval power and commercial concessions was least favourable—indeed force usually proved counter-productive. The bureaucratic defences of Egypt against the penetration of Western mercantile enterprise were not to be dismantled until the 1840s. Thus the *funduq*s of Alexandria (like the ancient Naucratis) were not foci of merchant power but obligatory residences, and it is a significant detail from the fifteenth century that they were locked at night from the *outside*. Similarly a treatise of the later twelfth century describes the regulations under which merchants sold their goods either direct to the authorities at officially arranged auctions—contrast the freedom of merchants importing goods into thirteenth-century Ceuta to dispose of them as they pleased. And of course the level of Egyptian customs duties tended to be high. This situation reflects a combination of Egyptian bureaucratic tradition, military strength (except in the later Fāṭimid period), and the importance (in Mamlūk times the monopoly) of Egypt in the supply of spices. Against this the main leverage of the Western merchants was for once not the naval power behind them but the fact that the Egyptian government was dependent on them for its supplies of essential strategic goods.

The rise of the merchant cities meant that their citizens could take over virtually any entrepreneurial role in the trade of the Mediterranean. They did not always choose to do this. We hear, for example, of the participation of two Jews and an Alexandrian

Muslim in the Ceuta trade of Marseilles in the thirteenth century. The most interesting case of this kind is the existence of a group of Eastern merchants—their origins are not always clear, but seem to be varied—in the earliest run of Genoese notarial records in the middle of the twelfth century. In the Genoese example the anomaly is perhaps to be explained in terms of the history of class struggle in the city and a tendency, probably general, to relegate the non-Latins to sectors of trade which the merchant cities did not think it worth while to capture.[1] But the over-all trend towards the monopolization of Mediterranean trade by the merchant cities seems clear and its ultimate outcome unequivocal.

The process appears most clearly in the history of the Jewish communities of the Mediterranean. Under the old dispensation, the social structures of Jewish life had constituted a very favourable basis for participation in long-distance trade. They combined international contacts with a tightly organized communal life which contrasted with the much less organized Muslim and Christian environments. The advantages of membership of such a community can be seen from the Geniza papers. The community possessed its own administration, with communally appointed officials acting on behalf of communal interests; it had the machinery for making and enforcing communal decisions, and maintained its own law-courts; it provided a number of social services, including (and this is perhaps important for the prospects of a mercantile society) much education. There were of course certain costs attached to being Jewish, even in so tolerant a state as the Fāṭimid empire. Hence a Geniza reference to flax-dealers in Tunisia who

[1] Genoa in the mid-twelfth century was dominated by a small number of aristocratic families who used their power to monopolize the lucrative Syrian trade. The African trade by contrast was a fairly open one, a small man's trade in which the aristocrats were not particularly interested. It was precisely here that the easterners were most conspicuous. Towards the end of the century the aristocratic regime was overthrown, and its more broadly based successor threw the Syrian trade open to all Genoese. It is plausible enough that this development should have 'politicized' other trades—that the middle class should have used its newly acquired power to eliminate its Oriental rivals.

behaved high-handedly to Muslims, 'let alone Jews'. Courts might be more dilatory, officials more obstructive. Perhaps the fact that the Geniza merchants traded in flax rather than grain indicates their prudence, well judged in a religious minority, in avoiding a commodity which caused riots. On the other hand, the costs of second-class citizenship are hardly very serious where the benefits of first-class citizenship scarcely exist. Their lack of influence on the political process was after all something which they shared with merchants of all religious persuasions. The limits on the purposes for which the communal organization could be used were the limits of merchant power in general. Belonging to a community which would ransom its members if they fell into the hands of the Cyrenaican pirates was a distinct advantage in the Mediterranean world in the days before the emergence of communes capable of sending punitive expeditions to destroy such pirate bases. It did not greatly matter that Jewish merchants had Christian or Muslim competitors, as long as these competitors lacked power.

The rise of the communes was the moment at which they came into the power they had lacked. A characteristic use of this power took place in 945, when Venice forbade her ships to carry Jews or their merchandise in the eastern Mediterranean. Gradually the Jews were forced by the rise of the communes to relinquish their entrepreneurial roles in the trade of the Mediterranean as a whole. The culmination of this development is of course the relegation of the Jewish communities of Christian Europe to money-lending—the one profitable activity which was too disruptive of the emerging communal society to be practised among its own citizens.

From this account it follows at once that in taking over the maritime and mercantile life of the Mediterranean, the Italians were likely to acquire also any Islamic accretions to this tradition.[1] On

[1] And any new commodities that might appear in the Islamic world. This applies particularly to styles in textiles ('Saracen' cloths were imported into Italy—and, characteristically, Italian imitations of these were later exported to the Muslim Mediterranean, where they were called *sārasīnā*).

the other hand it is a dispiriting enterprise to attempt to identify these accretions. The Mediterranean is a domain in which interaction in maritime and mercantile practices takes place easily and elusively, and the documentation, in so far as problems of origin are concerned, is usually unhelpful.[1] The question of the origin of the lateen sail may serve to illustrate this. The historical significance of this sail lies in its superiority to the traditional square rig of the Mediterranean for tacking against the wind: its hybridization with other elements of Mediterranean and, later, north-east Atlantic naval technology is considered to have been a necessary condition for the feasibility of the voyages of discovery of the late fifteenth and sixteenth centuries. It is most at home in the western Indian Ocean; its earliest accredited appearance in the Mediterranean is in two Byzantine illustrations which have been dated to the late ninth century. As a result there has been little hesitation in ascribing its introduction into the Mediterranean to the Arabs. But there are two characteristic difficulties here. First, there is an irritating lack of pre-Islamic evidence for the lateen sail on the Indian Ocean. Secondly, it has recently transpired that something very close to the lateen sail was already known in the Mediterranean in ancient times.

The issues become still more confused where commercial practice is concerned. This subject is conventionally presented in terms of a series of etymologies (French *douane* from the Arabic *dīwān*, etc.) which are interpreted to indicate substantive borrowings.[2] This mode of inference is a little strained—what exactly do we learn about the history of the egg from the fact that the English took their word for it from the Danes? There are in fact two sorts of problem to be faced in corroborating such an inference, or in establishing an Islamic influence independently of etymology. In

[1] Contrast with what follows the clear-cut evidence of the occasional numismatic influences in the lands bordering on the Dār al-Islām and even further afield—the English coin (Fig. 19) reproduces an ʿAbbāsid *dīnār* of 774.

[2] For these etymologies, and a more generous account of the mercantile legacy of Islam than has been given here, see the recent article of A. E. Lieber cited in the bibliography.

the first place, the earliest evidence of a practice does not in itself indicate the date at which the practice first arose. As with the agricultural legacy, the argument has to turn on the silence of earlier sources; and given the general paucity of material for the history of Mediterranean trade before the rise of the Italians, this silence does not mean very much. The similarities between the banking practices of the Geniza merchants and those of Latin Christendom may well point to some connection between the two, but the nature of this connection is hardly to be inferred from the accident that the evidence for banking practice is older in the Islamic world than it is in Europe. The inconclusiveness of a similar argument from silence is one of the main obstacles to a conclusive demonstration that the form of partnership known in a medieval Italian context as the *commenda* derives from the analogous Muslim *qirāḍ*. The second kind of problem can be illustrated from the same issue. The *commenda* is unknown to Roman law. It can, however, be seen as a hybridization of two arrangements which were already familiar in the Mediterranean, the bottomry loan and the ordinary partnership. The beginnings of the *commenda* as an accepted legal category in the Italian mercantile cities may have arisen from an acquaintance with the commercial practice of the Arabs; but, and this is the point, they may be more importantly related to the flexibility given to legal forms in these cities by the fact that their legal systems were communal as opposed to imperial property. In other words the Italian mercantile cities provided a peculiarly favourable environment for the spawning of innovations in commercial practice, and the problem of eliminating the possibility of parallel developments therefore arises in a particularly acute form.

3

The legacy of Islam identified in this chapter has not been a very substantial one. It consists of a number of diffusions, which might have taken place anyway, but were plausibly accelerated by the Muslim conquests and their aftermath. In no case was there a question of a Muslim invention, and the latter is a category of which there appear to be no known examples at present—none at least that belong properly to the history of the economy as opposed to that of art or fashion. What I wish to do in these final paragraphs is to dissuade the reader from jumping to the conclusion that this arises from some problematic economic backwardness of the medieval Muslims.

It is of course true that the Muslims did not anticipate the economic triumph of Western Europe—capitalism, sustained technological inventiveness, and the like. But if one wishes to call this backwardness, it is certainly not problematic. In this sense all non-Western cultures were backward, and it is the Western development that constitutes the problematic deviation. The only proper answer to the question why the Muslims failed to anticipate this development is to ask why they should be expected to have done so. There is no reason to suppose that there was some particular spanner lodged in the works of Islamic history the removal of which would have enabled it to conform to the European pattern. It is the untypical trajectory of Western Europe that needs to be elucidated, and the study of the economic history of the Islamic world is unlikely to bring to this more than occasional illumination.

The attempt to identify some specific factor behind Muslim economic backwardness in this sense has been correspondingly unsuccessful. This has recently been shown with great elegance in one particular instance by Professor Rodinson, in his critique of the idea that Islamic religious values inhibited the development of capitalism in Muslim society.[1] The central point here is the permissiveness of the relationship between a formal religious heritage and a set of concrete modes of action. This is most obvious where the values themselves are incompatible, as in the case of fatalism. The Koran indicates that all events are determined by the will of God, but also that men are responsible for what they do; Muslims, like Calvinists, have been left to make what sense they can of this.

[1] The substance of this paragraph is taken from Prof. Rodinson's book *Islam et capitalisme*; see also his remarks above, pp. 51 ff.

What sense they make of it cannot in principle be determined by the values themselves. In other cases the values themselves may be clear enough, but have simply not been applied. The Koran prohibits usury; but the outcome of this prohibition has been the development of a carefully contrived range of legal fictions under which usurious transactions can take place, rather than any reduction in the volume of credit in Islamic societies. In general, the heritage of a great religion displays enormous plasticity in application. The content of the heritage is so varied, and the rules for exploiting it so lax, that it may in practice be used to justify almost any kind of behaviour.[1] There were Christian reasons for creating the monasteries, and Christian reasons for dissolving them. Similarly Muslim writers do not seem to have experienced any great difficulty in defending the pursuit of mercantile profit in terms of the Islamic heritage when they felt disposed to do so. Whether or not they were so disposed is not readily explained by reference to the heritage.

None of this, however, implies that it would be inappropriate to compare the level of economic inventiveness of medieval Muslim society with that of other traditional cultures, and it is conceivable that a genuine problem of Muslim backwardness could emerge here. Since the issues are neither simple nor adequately studied, I shall confine my remarks at this point to a couple of caveats.

The first and most important is that the apparent lack of Muslim inventions may reflect more on the state of our knowledge than it does on the inventiveness of the Muslims. It is not wholly unlikely that we will some day be able to credit the medieval Muslims with a rate of innovation comparable to that of China or medieval Europe. The facts simply have not been established yet.

The second caveat is that one should not accept uncritically the views often advanced on other grounds for supposing the economic history of the Islamic world to have been of a particularly backward character. In the first place there is little reason to treat as estab-

[1] This of course is a point which applies much more to economic than to political life in an Islamic context.

lished fact the common picture of an initial efflorescence followed by a long and dismal decline. This view creates a neat symmetry between the economic and cultural history of Islam. But, as the historiography of the Renaissance has shown, it is often misleading to attempt to see the history of all activities in a given age in terms of the same unitary matrix. More importantly, the evidence available to support such a view of the long-term trend in the economic history of the Islamic world is not impressive. The case leans heavily on the idea that the first few centuries of Islam were distinguished by an expanding commercial economy unparalleled either in the Europe of the time or in the later history of Islam. But as I suggested above, one needs to consider very seriously the possibility that this picture is an illusion to be explained in terms of the shifting *locus* of religious literacy. The common-sense assumption is surely that the economies of the Muslim lands have expanded and contracted many times since the rise of Islam. Little that we know at present either confirms or refutes this. This is partly because secular changes of this kind have not been much studied, partly because with the kind of documentation normally available to us they are extremely difficult to study, and partly because in what has been written on the subject the relationship between the facts accumulated and the conclusions advanced is rather tenuous.

It is easy enough to notice some of the more obvious catastrophes—the impact of the Mongol invasions on parts of Central Asia, the initial incidence of the Black Death in Syria and Egypt. A case can also be made out for supposing a sustained decline in the Egyptian economy in the later Middle Ages. On the other side, the expansion of the Ottoman economy in the later fifteenth and sixteenth centuries provides one of the few cases in Islamic history where secular change can be documented from reasonably systematic archival sources. Both the Egyptian and the Ottoman examples, incidentally, run parallel to the economic history of Western Europe in the same periods. Certainly on the basis of the fragmentary information at present available the idea that the economy of the Muslim world underwent a definitive downturn around the turn of the millennium does not seem particularly plausible. There is evidence of economic disruption after the eleven century, but equally there is evidence of it before. More than this is needed to show a decisive change for the worse.[1]

Moreover if the general trend of Muslim economic history is thus in doubt, one needs to be equally careful in scrutinizing the particular instances of Muslim economic backwardness that have been put forward. The obvious example here, since it has already been raised in this chapter, is the commercial passivity of the Muslims in the Mediterranean—the fact that they made over the sea to Italian enterprise. Of course this is a perfectly genuine instance of economic decline (though the extent of its over-all effect on the economies of the Muslim Mediterranean lands is open to dispute). But does this show that there was something wrong with the structure of the Islamic mercantile economy? The fallacy here is to mistake a difference in the structure of power for a difference in economic rationality.[2] The commercial passivity of the Muslims in the Mediterranean was not a mistaken economic choice, because it was not an *economic* choice at all; it arose from the distribution of mercantile *power* in the Mediterranean, from the fact that certain groups of merchants were able to reinforce their economic activities politically. In so far as Muslim merchants failed, they failed politically; and only by pointing to contexts in which they had the same kinds of opportunity to seize power as the merchants of the Latin cities, and failed to do so, could one establish their political failure, as opposed to their acceptance of a feature of the structure of their societies over which they had no

[1] But for a different view and a more extended discussion, see Prof. Issawi's paper in the volume edited by D. S. Richards cited in the bibliography.

[2] Compare the fact that the Ottomans assimilated the use of firearms on the battlefield while the Mamlūks did not. There is no obvious reason why the Ottoman élite troops should have been less conservative in their attitude to this distasteful innovation than the Mamlūks. But there was an obvious difference in the structure of power: in the Mamlūk case it was in effect the élite troops who ruled, in the Ottoman case it was a dynasty for whom the army was an instrument of policy.

control. It is only with the post-medieval economic advances of Western Europe, and the very limited extent of their assimilation in the Muslim world, that more compelling problems of Muslim economic backwardness begin to arise, and even here they are remarkably hard to specify with any conviction.

M. A. COOK

BIBLIOGRAPHY

E. Ashtor, *Histoire des prix et des salaires dans l'Orient médiéval* (Paris, 1969); F. Braudel, *La Méditerranée et le monde méditerranéen à l'époque de Philippe II* (2nd edn., Paris, 1966); M. A. Cook (ed.), *Studies in the Economic History of the Middle East* (London, 1970); T. F. Glick, *Irrigation and Society in Medieval Valencia* (Cambridge Mass., 1970); S. D. Goitein, *A Mediterranean Society: the Jewish Communities of the Arab World as Portrayed in the Documents of the Cairo Geniza, I. Economic Foundations* (Berkeley-Los Angeles, 1967); W. Heyd, *Histoire du commerce du Levant au Moyen Âge* (Leipzig, 1885-6); A. E. Lieber, 'Eastern Business Practices and Medieval European Commerce', *The Economic History Review*, xxi (1968), pp. 230-43; D. S. Richards (ed.), *Islam and the Trade of Asia* (Oxford, 1970); M. Rodinson, *Islam et capitalisme* (Paris, 1966); A. L. Udovitch, *Partnership and Profit in Medieval Islam* (Princeton, 1970).

VI

ART AND ARCHITECTURE

(*A*) ARCHITECTURE

OF the two ways of looking at a legacy either from the point of view of its impact or that of its achievement, the first is almost meaningless in the case of Muslim architecture. There are many reasons for this, some connected with the nature of architecture itself, others more peculiar to the Muslim phenomenon. Before photography and rapid travel the contemporary impact of an architecture was limited and slow, because architecture is more strongly tied than other arts to its setting and to concrete aims and means. Exceptions are found, no doubt, as in certain frontier areas like central Spain where Muslim architecture—and not merely decorative motifs—inspired Christian and Jewish monuments during and after the times of Muslim domination.[1] In general, however, until the Renaissance the contemporary impact of a culture's architecture beyond the frontiers of the culture itself was minimal and usually the result of some unique historical circumstance.

Matters are different when a tradition is no longer alive. In Western architecture revivals occur constantly and there is an endless return to classical or medieval architectural sources. The position of Islamic architecture—or of any one of its individual phases—in a pattern of life, death, and rebirth is still almost impossible

[1] The whole problem of *mudéjar* architecture still awaits a proper historical as well as formal investigation. In the meantime see G. Marçais's chapter in *L'Architecture musulmane d'occident* (Paris, 1954), pp. 361 ff. A major controversy exists around the question of the possible impact of Islamic architecture on the Gothic and even on the Romanesque. For a recent statement with bibliography see A. U. Pope, 'Possible Contributions to the Beginning of Gothic Architecture', *Beiträge zur Kunstgeschichte Asiens. In Memoriam Ernst Diez* (Istanbul, 1963). In our judgement such an impact, if it existed, was secondary and poses many more problems than it solves. Hence we shall not deal with it here.

to establish properly. Internally, within the culture itself, revivals of earlier forms did occur in classical periods and, partly under the impact of a Western Levantinized taste; a revival of actual or presumed traditional forms took place in the garish villa architecture of Alexandria around the turn of the century or, much more successfully, in the Morocco of the thirties, or else with a sort of Muslim historical eclecticism in the concrete of the recent mosque at Kuala Lumpur. Yet none of these revivals has had the force and the importance of the continuous dialogue of Western architecture with its own past; or, if they did (as may be suggested in a number of features of Ṣafavid architecture of Iran or in Mamlūk architecture in Egypt), contemporary scholarship has not yet been able to capture them properly.

Externally, the impact of Islamic architecture occurred in several different ways. Specific themes of Islamic architecture, such as actual writing or imitations of it, are quite common all over the world, but, like certain floral or other motifs, these imitations of writing derived in all likelihood from textiles, ceramics, or metalwork, not from architecture as such. With a few possible exceptions in Byzantium or in Italy[1]—and always excepting Spain—it is not until the eighteenth century that an actual impact of Muslim architecture can be detected. It was part of the fascination with the exotic of late Classical and Romantic Europe. Its most important examples were not much more than *turqueries*, but in the peculiar palace of Brighton there appears a luxurious Islamic mood in Western architecture which continued in cinemas and restaurants called Alhambras or Taj Mahals and in occasional public buildings. At its most absurd in the unique Corn-Palace of Mitchell, South Dakota, whose Near Eastern cupolas are made of imitation corn-stalks, this tradition of exotically decorative wealth

[1] See E. Grube, 'Elementi islamici nell' architettura veneta del mediaevo', *Bolletino del Centro Internazionale di Studi d'Architettura 'A. Palladio'*, viii (1966); G. Miles, 'Byzantium and the Arabs', *Dumbarton Oaks Papers*, xviii (1964); R. A. Jairazbhoy, *Oriental Influences in Western Art* (New York, 1965), esp. pp. 49 ff. about one group of examples.

has also influenced the far more creative works of Yamasaki. But such examples are not very numerous and it would be difficult to argue that most of them are major works of non-Islamic architecture.

There is, therefore, not much point in attempting to search for a major impact of Muslim architecture—as opposed to Muslim decorative arts—on other, contemporary or later, architectural traditions. The legacy of Islamic architecture should therefore be sought in terms of achievement, and we could list those structural or aesthetic characteristics which best expressed the needs of the Muslim world and identify those monuments which are acknowledged masterpieces of the culture. Yet this sort of roster of quality might not, in the final analysis, succeed in identifying the true legacy of the culture, for it would measure the achievement in non-Islamic terms, according to some abstract criterion of value. Furthermore, there are considerable intellectual dangers in attempts to determine priorities of invention or scales of quality when comparing cultures to each other. If an architectural tradition has not had (as the classical tradition has had) a long and highly documented impact, and if we try to avoid the useless exercise of ranking according to comparative merits, what then can the legacy of an architecture be? Very much like literature, it is a unique combination, or a series of combinations, of forms which, in the time and space of a culture, succeeded in expressing something of value or necessity to that culture. Some of these combinations, a village mosque for instance, are merely folk creations and barely literate; others, like the Alhambra, are major works of poetry. The legacy of an architecture is then that language of constructional forms which most clearly expressed the needs and the dreams of a culture, whether or not it had a significant impact beyond itself. Like any heirloom, it can be useless, sentimentally valuable, or a uniquely meaningful contribution. In the case of Islam, however, special circumstances exist which pose a series of problems of much wider significance than the culture itself or any one of its monuments. In order to understand them we must try to define the meaning for architecture of the extraordinary decades of the seventh and eighth centuries A.D., when apparently almost *ex nihilo*, an Islamic civilization was created.

The central peculiarity of the Muslim world is, as has often been said, that it is a cultural moment in the development of many ethnically or geographically definable entities and not the expression of any one people or region. It is further agreed that Islam penetrated into and developed within a world which had already acquired an extraordinary formal complexity. Traditionally, art historians have divided that world into a Hellenistic *koiné* west of the Euphrates and an Iranian one east of it; but recent scholarship has shown that the problems are very much more complex and that the use and understanding of artistic forms in the pre-Islamic Mediterranean basin and Near East varied not only regionally, but also across regions, according to many social and intellectual levels. In general terms there were, before the appearance of Islam, several architectural traditions in which a wide variety of technical means ranging from very ancient and simple trabeated systems all the way to the most sophisticated vaults were used for purposes which spread from the open streets or public baths of a city to highly restricted and unique holy sanctuaries. Much uncertainty still exists as to how the formal wealth and the technical virtuosity of the Near East around A.D. 600 were actually translated into purposes and functions. Both the single cupola of Sasanian architecture and certain kinds of basilical halls with apses in Christian architecture could be interpreted equally easily as secular or religious buildings and the actual contemporary identification was probably made through such means as decoration as much as through architectural forms. What is essential, however, is to realize that Islamic architecture was formed out of a world of tremendous architectural wealth as far as forms and techniques are concerned, but apparently also a world of considerable fluidity in the meanings to be given to forms and techniques.

The other component in the making of Islamic architecture is

Islam itself. The remarkable point here is that in its formative moments Islam neither required nor desired an architectural identification. The eventual acceptance by the Prophet of the Kaʿba in Mecca as a holy sanctuary transformed it into a unique site, a symbolic *omphalos* and *qibla*, a centre and a direction. This uniqueness removed the Meccan sanctuary from becoming, as the Holy Sepulchre became in Christianity, a theoretically possible model for later Islamic architecture. There is only scattered later evidence—much of it quite unclear and uncertain—of an actual impact of the Kaʿba on other buildings and, while its sacred character was largely responsible for this lack of physical impact, it could also be argued that its formal primitiveness—an irregular cube set in an ovoid space identified by use and ideology rather than as an aesthetic conception—made it an unsuitable symbol of Islam to compete with the great sanctuaries of Christianity and even of Zoroastrianism. There is nothing strange about this formal primitiveness, since the Meccan sanctuary was—as a physical entity—a creation of the rather primitive world of pre-Islamic Arabia.

What is far more original is that the new faith itself—as it was revealed to the Prophet and as it grew under his first successors—did not seek or need a monumental expression. The word *masjid* (place of worship, whence mosque) in the Koran may have referred only once to a specifically Muslim building and even there the passage is not very clear: 'For had God not repelled some people by means of others, churches (? *ṣawāmiʿ*), synagogues (*biyaʿ*), oratories (*ṣalawāt*) and *masājid* would have been destroyed' (xxii. 40). Only because of the juxtaposition of the word *masjid* with more precise terms for churches and synagogues can we suggest that a specifically Muslim sanctuary was meant, but it is almost as probable that we have in this passage a typical rhetorical device of pairs of terms with the same meaning and that no precise type of building was meant. The place of worship of the early Muslim, his *masjid*, was, to paraphrase a celebrated tradition, wherever he was himself. It seems clear that there was no physical setting imposed or created by the faith and that no physically perceptible symbol was developed which could identify the new faith. The term *muṣallā*, literally 'a place for prayer', seems to have referred simply to a space outside the city where, on certain occasions, the Prophet met with his followers for prayer alone. No evidence is known to me which would suggest that the *muṣallā* had any sort of unique architectural feature. Without clergy and without building or symbol, early Islam was a uniquely pure system of faith. And it is interesting to note that as late as in the early fifteenth century, Ibn Khaldūn mentions in his chapter on *masājid*, only three sanctuaries, Mecca, Medina, and Jerusalem, while he discusses what we know as mosques in relation to cities or to the question of legitimate and illegitimate authority.[1]

Islam also involved a number of practices. There were set hours for prayer, individual or communal. There was a call to prayer and a direction for prayer. There was an obligation of ritual cleanliness, and Fridays were identified as days for the community as a whole to demonstrate its force and cohesion not only for itself but also for others to see. The Prophet used to sit on a *minbar* or chair on such occasions, and he would lean on a lance.[2] These practices may have taken place in the Prophet's own house but they rapidly acquired a ceremonial, if not yet liturgical, character. These were all activities which unified the community of the Muslims and which separated them from others. They were signs of identification and of restriction but they had no architectural connotation.

Further research and especially archaeological work in Arabia may some day modify the conclusion of an architectural *tabula rasa* in the peninsula just before the beginning of Islam and during its formative decades. Yet, for the time being, such is the premiss

[1] Ibn Khaldūn, *The Muqaddimah*, translated by F. Rosenthal (New York, 1958), ii. 249 ff.

[2] See C. H. Becker, 'Die Kanzel im Kultus des alten Islam', *Orientalische Studien Theodor Nöldeke gewidmet* (Giessen, 1906), i. 331–51, reprinted in *Islamstudien* (Leipzig, 1924–32), i. 450–71; S. D. Goitein, 'The Origin and Nature of the Muslim Friday Worship', *The Muslim World*, xlix (1959), 183–95, reprinted in *Studies in Islamic History and Institutions* (Leiden, 1966), pp. 111 ff.

with which we have to begin. It compels us to set the problem of Islamic architecture in terms of the relationship between a new faith and system of life without actual architectural setting and a highly complex and immensely developed architectural tradition in the Near and Middle East. The problem as such is not peculiar to Islam; it is also the problem of Christian art several centuries earlier. But, whereas in the latter instance it was only a very small number of new purposes which had to find a new architectural expression within an otherwise shared vocabulary of forms and needs—and yet the process took three centuries—in the case of Islamic architecture almost all aspects of life had to find architectural forms and the process took only a few decades. By the time of al-Walīd I (705–15), an Islamic architectural *koiné* seems to have been established, at least as far as religious architecture is concerned. The degree to which this official *koiné* was actually accepted is a debatable point and it is likely that all sorts of anomalies and oddities were cropping up, since in 778 the Caliph al-Mahdī ordered the destruction of all *maqṣūra*s and *minbar*s in congregational mosques and their replacement by new ones according to the standard of the Prophet's mosque in Medina.[1] The process by which a characteristically Islamic secular architecture was created is a far more complicated one, and in spite of the numerous examples of secular architecture which have been preserved from the first half of the eighth century, the *Islamic* quality of any part of this architecture is difficult to determine because of our considerable lack of comparative non-Islamic material evidence.

The reasons for the rapidity and success with which a definable Islamic architectural tradition was formed are to be sought primarily in the necessity—so amazingly seen by rulers like ʿUmar, ʿAbd al-Malik, al-Walīd, and by their provincial governors—to make visible the physical reality of Islam as something different from what surrounded it and yet understandable as Islamic.[2] The importance of this point is considerable in attempting to assess

[1] al-Ṭabarī, *Annales*, ed. M. J. de Goeje *et alii* (Leiden, 1879–1906), iii. 486.
[2] O. Grabar, 'Byzantium and the Arabs', *Dumbarton Oaks Papers*, xviii (1964).

the legacy of Islamic architecture, for to the historian of architecture the formation of Islamic architecture may be used to illustrate a rarely observable phenomenon, which is how a culturally definable architecture creates itself, whereas to the historian of Islam it illustrates what the culture chose and what it rejected and thus suggests something of its own image which the culture sought to project. But the very existence of an Islamic architecture—perhaps even of an Islamic culture—raises an even more fascinating and fundamental question. Since the forms and techniques of the architecture were all provided by a wide variety of non-Islamic cultures but since Islam itself was, at least at the beginning, a unified entity, was the architecture which was eventually created a sort of architectural Esperanto without roots and usable or meaningful only as a convenience? Or is it impossible to speak of an *Islamic* architecture and should one limit one's self to the consideration of a presumably definable number of separate regional or ethnic traditions of architecture which are only accidentally Islamic? Or, finally, did there indeed occur a 'structural'[1] modification in all the areas of Islamic civilization to the point where a fully meaningful and deeply rooted Islamic architecture would have been created out of definable mutations in a vast number of separate formal systems? These are, it seems to me, the crucial questions posed by a consideration of the legacy of Islamic architecture, and the appropriate parallels here are no longer those of early Christian architecture but those of Renaissance or Baroque times, where also certain kinds of change were imposed on a wide variety of traditions. Yet it must be admitted that answers to these questions can only be attempted, for the state of scholarship in the field of Islamic art has not reached the point where theories and general considerations can find a proper place between unproved intuitions and demonstrable nonsense. It is with some uncertainty

[1] In dealing with architecture, the term 'structural', so important and so fashionable in contemporary thought, is of course ambiguous. Whenever we use it to mean not construction but such internal characteristics, explicit or implicit, by which a building is understandable, we shall put it in quotation marks.

as to which of these two extremes best qualifies our essay that the following remarks are presented. We shall first attempt to define the architectural *koiné* created in the eighth century and refined over the ninth and tenth centuries which seems to have been the starting-point of most later developments. Then we shall take up some of the themes created by the *koiné* and illustrate their later evolution and meaning. In conclusion we will try to suggest a few answers to the questions posed here.

Since Sauvaget's work on the Umayyad mosque of Medina—and regardless of the modifications which may have to be added to it[1]—it can be agreed that it was during the first two decades of the eighth century that the new Islamic religious architecture acquired its most characteristic first forms. Best known through the well-preserved mosque of Damascus (Fig. 1), which has, however, too many unique features to be considered wholly typical, this first Islamic architecture was the dominant type for at least four centuries and its masterpieces are found all the way from Spain with the celebrated mosque of Cordova (Fig. 2) to Egypt (the mosques of Ibn Ṭūlūn, Fig. 3, al-Azhar, al-Ḥākim) and Iraq (the great Sāmarrā mosques). It is almost certain that the majority of early Iranian mosques belonged to the same type, although the remaining examples are known mostly through texts or through partial archaeological sources. The type may appropriately be called *hypostyle*, for its essential characteristic is that space is created by the skilful, if very simple, use of a single unit: the bay or open space between two supports (columns or piers). Numerous compositional variations are possible with this simple module, many of which were in fact used. Into this flexible system of composition a number of more or less fixed features were introduced: courts with or without trees, minarets, *miḥrāb*s (i.e. niches indicating the *qibla* or direction of prayer) often preceded by an honorific

[1] J. Sauvaget, *La Mosquée Omeyyade de Médine* (Paris, 1947); see also O. Grabar, 'La Mosquée de Damas et les origines de la mosquée', *Synthronon, Bibliothèque des Cahiers Archéologiques*, ii (Paris, 1968), pp. 107–14.

dome, axial naves, *maqṣūra*s or reserved spaces for princes usually combined with the *miḥrāb*, fountains or pools, and, somewhat later, formal doors and gates. In most early examples the place for ablutions was outside the mosque proper. Each of these elements has its own history and poses its own problems and few have been satisfactorily analysed so far. There is no need to do so in this essay, but it should be pointed out that only the *miḥrāb* seems to have become fairly rapidly a symbolically or liturgically required form. In varying ways all other features were optional.

Equally optional is the decoration of the mosque. Lavish in the mosque of Damascus, subordinate to architectural lines in the mosque of Ibn Ṭūlūn, it is limited to a few areas of the mosque of Cordova or of al-Azhar and almost absent from the mosques of Sāmarrā and from many small sanctuaries. Except in a few early instances—as in Damascus[1] and possibly Medina—this decoration had a limited direct iconographic meaning, in the sense that, so far as we can judge today, the identifiable decorative designs served to embellish or to emphasize certain parts of the building but did not, as designs, define functions, purposes, or other possible lessons of the faith, as decoration did in Christian, Buddhist, or pagan architecture. When it was felt necessary, iconographic meaning was introduced through inscriptions, and such meanings were limited to expressions of piety (mostly through appropriate quotations from the Koran) or to technical matters, primarily the recording of foundations, repairs, and additions. By being set in the precincts of the mosque such inscriptions exemplified for all times the piety of the men mentioned in them but they also served as decorative elements in the composition of the building.

Altogether, however, the large space of the hypostyle mosque is its most obvious characteristic and we must on the one hand explain it and on the other evaluate it as an achievement. Even though it can be related formally to ancient *apadana*s in Iran, to certain parts

[1] R. Ettinghausen, *Arab Painting* (Geneva, 1962), pp. 62 ff.; K. Otto-Dorn, *Kunst des Islam* (Baden-Baden, 1964), pp. 30 ff.

of ancient Egyptian temples, or to certain types of Roman forums, there is little doubt, it seems to me, that the hypostyle mosque was not influenced by any older architectural type but was an original Muslim creation. There are many reasons for this conclusion, in particular the fact that its first developments took place in the newly founded Muslim cities of Iraq where none of the possible parallels to the Muslim hypostyle can be found. But perhaps an even more important point is that the needs which led to the creation of the mosque were original needs which could not be met by existing architectural traditions. These were not primarily religious needs, in the sense that there was no obvious ceremonial or liturgical purpose to a Muslim building; several decades after the erection of the mosque of Kūfa, its ground was still unpaved and complaints were made that the dust which arose during the mass movements of the ceremony of prayer was a hazard to cleanliness and health. The mosque was the social centre for all sorts of public and private activities and early writers have preserved an amazing number of anecdotes illustrating the highly official or the ludicrously trivial and even vulgar events which took place in mosques. These were indeed civic centres with all the implications of the term. Yet, to the extent that the great Roman tradition of a monumental civic architecture was still in use—at least west of the Euphrates—its forms could not readily be used by the newly arrived Muslims, because on one essential point the activities which took place in the mosque were different from those which took place in the earlier forums or *agorai*: they were restricted to the Muslim *umma*, to the new Community of the Faithful. And especially in those older cities like Damascus and Jerusalem where the Muslims were in a minority, their own architecture had to be at the same time something which could unite all Muslims for their manifold common activities and something which would clearly and visibly separate them from non-Muslims. It is thus a combination of the need for a common space for the Muslim community alone and of the necessity to have a space which would distinguish itself from other, Christian, Zoroastrian, or Jewish spaces which created the Muslim mosque. The latter was not a necessary product of the faith of Islam revealed and elaborated in Medina but a direct result of the nature of the conquest which, initially at least, either put Muslims in a minority or segregated them in separate towns. In either case the mere utilization or imitation of older buildings was not possible and, while it is true that instances exist of the transformation of churches or other kinds of religious buildings into mosques, the amazing thing is how rarely this occurred. In such cases as Damascus and Jerusalem where a Hellenistic space was transformed into a Muslim sanctuary, the result of the transformation cannot be confused with a Roman or Hellenistic composition. Comparable instances are rare.

The conquered pre-Islamic world thus did not possess living architectural compositions which could have been used directly, or only with minor modifications, by the Muslims for their own restricted purposes. Few transformations occurred of complete pre-Islamic architectural units into Muslim ones. At the same time the structural details of the early mosque were entirely of pre-Islamic origin. The arch on pier or on column, the organization of naves, the systems of roofing, the towers, and the techniques of decoration were all earlier than Islam, often in fact taken from older buildings. Even such spectacular creations as the double tiers of polylobed arches in Cordova (Fig. 4) or the sturdy brick piers of Sāmarrā are but modifications—changes in accents—of earlier elements of construction. The architectural uniqueness of the Muslim hypostyle mosque does not lie in the minor technical improvements it may have brought into earlier building methods but in the fact that it succeeded in creating a new architectural expression by reshuffling and rearranging the constructional and 'structural' elements from older traditions. The process took only a few decades and its main centres were in Iraq and in Syria. In a way of course this achievement testifies to the remarkable possibilities of the architectural *koiné* which issued from Hellenistic and Roman times. But it also testifies to the extraordinary way in which the tightly knit early Muslim community was able to preserve its identity and to make it architecturally visible in the very terms of the previous cultures of the Near East.

In addition to its historical meaning the hypostyle mosque has yet another point to make. By having concentrated on the organization of internal space to suit the changing need of an expanding community, it became a remarkably flexible building which, thanks to its small module, could easily be expanded or contracted. In Cordova for instance three successive additions were made to an original unit. Similar additions are documented in Kūfa, Baṣra, Baghdad, and Cairo. The only instance of contraction which can clearly be proved, at least among major buildings, occurs at the Aqṣā mosque in Jerusalem.[1] From a theoretical point of view this possibility of modifying the shape of the building according to the needs of the community is a remarkably modern feature, completely unknown in earlier or contemporary architecture. From an aesthetic point of view it must probably be considered as less successful, for façades and the whole apparatus of external monumentalization and ordering which gave so much of their value to Roman temples or to Gothic cathedrals were impossible. Yet we must remember that the purpose of the hypostyle mosque as a whole was not aesthetic and it is only in exceptional buildings like the Great Mosque of Damascus that peculiar local circumstances led to the creation of a unified architectural ensemble. The severity and simplicity of the forms found in early Islamic mosques illustrate superbly the austerity of early Islam and its view of itself by which man can and must praise God directly, without the intermediary of a clergy or of a mystery. And in the more conservative areas of Islam, such as Morocco, the hypostyle remained for centuries the only type used, while quite often in newly conquered or converted areas, such as Anatolia or India, the hypostyle was the first type of mosque to be built, symbolizing no doubt the purest

[1] R. W. Hamilton, *The Structural History of the Aqsa Mosque* (Jerusalem, 1949); similar contractions may have occurred in smaller mosques, such as at Qaṣr al-Ḥayr al-Sharqī in the Syrian desert.

qualities of Islam, but also simple enough to be adapted to any architectural tradition.

Secular architecture was quite another matter. There was not much of an Arabian or early Islamic model to follow and, except in so far as a pious rejection of luxury and high living accompanied a partly admiring suspicion of alien ways and alien things, no religious or intellectual objection existed to any aspect of secular architecture. On the contrary, the very ideal of urban living which characterized early Islam automatically demanded the adoption of ways which had not been typical of pre-Islamic Arabia. What all of this meant architecturally is little known[1] and it is likely that the situation varied from region to region. On the simple level of the architectural infrastructure of Muslim life, therefore, it is not possible to define an 'Islamic' way as opposed to some pre-Islamic one nor can we suggest the creation of some new architectural type like that of the mosque.

A different picture emerges when we move away from the daily world of houses, streets, walls, baths, canals, and markets to that of princely constructions. A curious paradox occurs here. Whereas it is possible to identify nearly eighty sites of probable early Islamic palaces, not more than a dozen are known from texts as being unique in any way and we have no contemporary identification of the spectacular establishments discovered at Khirbat al-Mafjar, Quṣayr ʿAmra, Jabal Says, the two Qaṣr al-Ḥayr, or Ukhayḍir.[2] Either the literary sources are ill informed or these buildings were so typical that there was no need to mention them or else they were works of private art, not part of the official version of the history of early Islam as it was developed by the chroniclers. A discussion of the various hypotheses and explanations which can

[1] U. Monneret de Villard, *Introduzione allo Studio dell'archeologia Islamica* (Venice, 1966), is a partial attempt to gather documents on these problems.

[2] There is as yet no convenient list of early Islamic sites; I am helping to prepare one in conjunction with the work at Qaṣr al-Ḥayr and a comparable one is being put together by Dr. K. Brisch, of the Berlin Museum, in connection with his excavations at Jabal Says. For the time being the best introductions are in the notes and bibliographies attached to Monneret de Villard's posthumous book.

be woven around this rather extraordinary series of princely buildings need not concern us in this essay, except perhaps on one point. It is that, even though all these constructions are of related types, they are actually known through different kinds of sources. At one extreme are the Umayyad palaces, known only through archaeology; at the other extreme lies Baghdad, a unique entity known only through texts; and between the two are found such establishments as Sāmarrā in Iraq or Madīnat al-Zahrā' in Spain for which incomplete archaeological and textual material is available.[1] When we realize further that most archaeological sources have never been properly published while many texts are not very clear, it will become apparent that an exact typological definition of these palaces is difficult to achieve and that our conclusions have still to be very tentative.

In a general way three themes can be identified in the art of early Islamic palaces, none of which is a purely Muslim theme yet all three of which appear to have been accepted as parts of the fabric of secular princely life. The first theme is that of the clear-cut separation of the princely establishment from the surrounding world, a separation which may have found its origins in the *villa urbana* and *villa rustica* of ancient Rome.[2] At its most extreme in the sumptuous palaces of Umayyad princes hidden away in their domains all over the Syrian steppe, this separation occurs as well in Sāmarrā or in the heavily fortified city palace at Kūfa. Only Baghdad's original palace was less obviously remote, but then the whole of the original layout of the city had a unique palace-like quality and its central part, the palace proper, did not remain in use for very long. The consequences of this remoteness would be,

[1] Beyond the basic works in our bibliography, see various articles by J. Lassner, especially 'Massignon and Baghdad', *Journal of the Economic and Social History of the Orient*, ix (1966), and 'Municipal Entities and Mosques', ibid. x (1967). A more complete statement is in idem, *The Topography of Baghdad* (Detroit, 1970). For Madīnat al-Zahrā', see the bibliography in K. Brisch, *Kunst des Orients*, v (1968), 67 ff.

[2] A. Grabar and O. Grabar, 'L'Essor des Arts inspirés par les cours princières à la fin du premier millénaire', *L'Occidente e l'Islam nell'alto Medioevo* (Spoleto, 1965).

first of all, that the identifying feature of the palace on the outside is its walls adorned with towers and perhaps an impressive gateway (Figs. 5 and 7). A more important consequence would be that the interior of the palace tends to become a myth. Inaccessible to most and transforming itself quite often into a huge walled city within the city, the palace becomes the source of stories, adventures, and of all sorts of mysterious events in which fact and fancy are difficult to separate. Only the gateway remains as a physical tie between real and mythical lives.

A second theme is more specific. Like the mosques—and with the exception of Baghdad and of a small group of Umayyad constructions which are direct imitations of Roman castles—early Islamic palaces were not highly ordered and formally planned compositions. They consisted rather of a series of self-sufficient units which could be modified, increased, destroyed, or replaced, as needs or tastes changed. Among these units are found mosques or oratories, baths, audience-halls of varying degrees of formality, courts with fountains, gardens, gates, private kiosks, and a whole paraphernalia of living quarters and of service areas. Any one of these units can exist both alone as a separate architectural entity (like the single bath at Quṣayr ʿAmra) and as a cell in a larger composition. None of the units seems to have been a Muslim invention and their background may be either Roman or Iranian. The important point is that the palace was not an aesthetically conceived and aesthetically organized entity, but a series of separate elements related to each other by a small number of typical activities by which the life of the prince was identified. These included audiences, some of which reached extraordinary splendour, but also pleasure and pastime, drinking, bathing, singing, and so on.

Finally the palace was a far greater sponsor of decoration than the mosque. Mosaics, paintings, stone or stucco sculptures were media used for such an astounding variety of decorative or representational themes that the discoveries of Quṣayr ʿAmra, Mshatta, and even Khirbat al-Mafjar were greeted first with considerable doubt as to their Islamic origins. And yet what has remained is but a minor part of the decorative wealth of early Islamic palaces, for they must in fact be imagined with all the rich textiles and precious objects gathered in by the princes from all over the world. In the better-known Umayyad palaces there is at times something of a *nouveau riche* bric-à-brac (Fig. 6) in the accumulation of technical, stylistic, and iconographic features from many lands and from many periods, and the exact process by which this enormous vocabulary of forms was transformed into more coherent styles and programmes is still far from being well understood. That it was so transformed is likely indeed, for in the later fragments remaining from Sāmarrā, Madinat al-Zahrā', or Cairo a certain classicism of form can be detected. Yet this is a whole area of investigation in which more can be guessed than demonstrated.

These brief remarks on the earliest Islamic art may not yet have answered the fundamental questions raised earlier but they may provide us with a number of threads or 'modes' by following which we can usefully examine later monuments. One such thread is the extraordinary ease with which an Islamic architecture was created. One reason was no doubt that the architecture of previous centuries lent itself to the kind of transformations which were required by Islam. Another reason seems to have been the fact that the main concern of Islamic architecture did not lie in the maintenance or creation of certain forms but in the expression of certain activities. General needs of the faith—gathering of the faithful and separation from non-Muslims—rather than canonically or liturgically compelling forms created the mosque. The palace was identified in terms of activities, audiences, or pleasure, none of which had a necessary form attached to it. The corollary of this adaptability of Islamic architecture to a variety of forms should then be that what identifies it is not a set of forms, a style, but a way of transforming styles, an attribute or a group of attributes imposed on a variety of forms, which could be called a 'mode'.

A second conclusion is that, whereas religious art was limited both in its forms and its purposes, secular art, and especially the art of the palace, was not, and thus the conclusion may be drawn even for early Islamic architecture that secular inspiration tended to predominate and certainly offered a much greater field for development than religious architecture. It became most easily the crucible in which the infinite variety of themes offered to the new civilization by the past of the conquered territories could be moulded into something specifically Islamic. Finally, even though somewhat limited in mosques, architectural decoration clearly played an important part in the first monuments of Islamic architecture. Many techniques and many themes were involved in it. It is around these three threads of decoration, of secular inspiration, and of transformation of forms that I should like to discuss later developments of Islamic architecture.

It can indeed be argued that the vast majority of the more important and more original creations of Islamic architecture were inspired by needs and tastes other than those created by the faith of Islam. These needs and tastes which we shall call secular are of course less obviously Islamic than the needs of the faith and, in dealing with the secular arts, we should eventually learn to distinguish between the kinds of themes which are specifically Muslim and those which the Muslim world shared with many other living or dead cultures. This is unfortunately not possible within the space available and we have to limit ourselves to a consideration of a few buildings and to the conclusions which can be derived from them.

The most characteristic secular building was the royal or princely palace. After the ninth century, however, palaces are much less well preserved than those of the early centuries of Islamic civilization and it is through fragmentary ruins and through literary descriptions that we can best be made aware of the Cairene palaces of the eleventh century, of the Mongol extravaganzas rapidly erected in Azerbaijan or near Samarqand, or of the numerous residences in cities or in the country which are known in North Africa and Sicily, in the Euphrates valley, in thirteenth-century Anatolia, all over Iran, or in early Muslim India.[1] To this list of ruins and literary references there is one major exception, the extraordinary Alhambra in Granada,[2] and, even though there is some danger in using only one monument in the extreme west of the Muslim world for a whole culture, we shall attempt through the Alhambra to define some of the apparent characteristics of the Muslim palace in the later Middle Ages.

The Alhambra is located on a hill overlooking the city. It is surrounded by walls and has a fortified look, although in fact only the lowest part of the large enclosure could be and probably was used for any sort of military purpose. By its location and by its fortified aspect the Alhambra is characteristic of a tradition going back to the early Islamic period. It is of the city and yet not quite in the city. But it is not only part of what we have called the early fortified *villa* tradition. It has also been influenced by a later development, that of the *qalʿa* or urban citadel. The origins of the latter are far from being clear and in all likelihood several separate sources were involved in its formation: an eastern Iranian tradition of pre-Islamic origin, the growth of a military aristocracy of different ethnic stock from that of the city's inhabitants, and general insecurity going together with the growth in power of individual towns. Whatever the reasons, from the tenth century onward and

[1] A complete bibliography on this subject would be too long to include here, for it is a remarkably scattered one and for the most part difficult of access. One may suggest as beginnings for future investigations the monuments of Algeria, conveniently accessible through recent works by L. Golvin, such as *Le Maghreb central à l'époque des Zirides* (Paris, 1957); the descriptions of Cairo, primarily Maqrīzi's *Khiṭaṭ* (Būlāq, 1270/1854); and the Iranian monuments, for which information can be found in the numerous works of G. A. Pugachenkova, most recent *Istoriia Iskusstv Uzbekistana* (Moscow, 1965), or in excavation reports, French and Italian for Afghanistan, German for Iran.

[2] See F. P. Bargebuhr, *The Alhambra* (Berlin, 1968) for an exciting but controversial statement which does not entirely supersede the author's earlier 'The Alhambra Palace of the Eleventh Century', *Journal of the Warburg and Courtauld Institutes*, xix (1956), 192–258. The monument itself is still best described in various guide books such as L. Torres Balbás, *La Alhambra y el Generalife* (Madrid, 1953), or in *Ars Hispaniae*, iv (Madrid, 1949).

with considerable regional variations, the citadel appeared as a characteristic feature of almost every city. At times spectacularly located as in Aleppo (Fig. 8) or in Cairo, it was at other times, as in Damascus, barely visible above the rest of the city. The *qalʿa* never acquired the mythical qualities of the earlier royal palace, even though accounts and limited archaeological remains suggest that many citadels had considerable amenities of life. It did, however, emphasize anew the importance of military models in the development of architecture, and a number of technical novelties in vaulting and in the planning of gateways or of towers derived from the new architecture of citadels.

If the Alhambra's first characteristic is its fortified look relatable to two separate traditions of secular architecture, its second feature is that its vast area is not composed as one entity but is broken up into a series of separate units. Some of these are gardens with pavilions artfully set up on the slopes of the mountain, and such gardens are part of a Muslim tradition which extends to Iran and to India.[1] The most celebrated remaining units in the Alhambra are the two units of the Lions and of the Myrtles, where, around magnificent courts, more or less complex arrangements of square and rectangular rooms have been put together (Fig. 9). This additive principle of architectural composition appears to have been characteristic of all known Islamic royal constructions, except perhaps a number of late Iranian examples, and its sources are already to be found in the great palaces of Sāmarrā.

The most important point is that very few of the halls and courts of the Alhambra had an architecturally definable purpose. A curious dissociation seems to have occurred between building and function, as though individual forms which are definable in architectural terms as courts, porticoes, square or oblong halls, and so forth were merely generalized forms in which a variety of purposes, from traditional audiences to various pastimes, could be performed. On this point, just as in its fortified aspect, the Alhambra illustrates a phenomenon valid for Islam as a whole. Thus, for

[1] D. N. Wilber, *Persian Gardens and Garden Pavilions* (Rutland, Vermont, 1962).

instance, the masses of kiosks or pavilions known in Cairo, Istanbul, Konya, or Iṣfahān were also simple formal entities (generally a more or less developed domed unit) which do not in themselves suggest precise activities and in which many different events could take place. While at first glance quite different from what is known in most of Western architecture, this Muslim characteristic of the Middle Ages is remarkably similar in type to the 'multi-purpose' rooms of today's architecture. To be made secure, however, this point still demands further investigation, especially in the field of lexicography, for it would be essential to know as precisely as possible the terms which were used at any one time for different parts of the palace.

The third essential feature of the Alhambra is the extraordinary importance of its decoration. We shall return later to some technical aspects of this decoration, but the significant point is that the decoration provides the main effect of the building from the inside and, whether in Iran, in Central Asia, or in Turkey, the spectacular character of the themes and techniques of palace decoration is self-evident. The question we have to raise is whether this decoration had no further aim than to beautify, whether its aim was only luxuriously aesthetic. Thanks to F. Bargebuhr's work the Alhambra provides a clue, for it can be argued that much in it—from the Fountain of the Lions to the stupendous stalactite domes almost miraculously held on thin supports (Fig. 10)—can be related to the mythology which throughout the Middle Ages had developed around Solomon, the Prophet-King. The impression of an other-worldly and separate paradise, the gardens, the decorative tricks, and *tours de force* are perhaps attempts to translate into earthly terms the great and beautiful vision of what the jinns had made for Solomon and his Queen of Sheba. It cannot be within the purview of this chapter to recount the many instances all over the Muslim world which would tend to justify this interpretation, but what I should like to emphasize is that the Solomonic myth was not a Muslim invention but a generally medieval one which continued in the West as late as the Baroque period. In this sense the splendour of the palace architecture of Islam, like its textiles and objects, was a splendour meaningful far beyond the frontiers of Islam and its monuments may serve as major examples of medieval art in general.

Yet it would not be proper to illustrate Islamic secular architecture through palaces alone, for in a number of other areas the Islamic achievement, while less spectacular, was far more distinct. Most interesting is the monumentalization of common urban functions. Schools, shops, hostels, hospitals (Fig. 11), caravanserais, baths, street fountains, even warehouses acquired great façades and decoration and the latest and most sophisticated techniques of construction were used, as for instance in the spectacular caravanserais of Anatolia in the thirteenth century.[1] The reasons for this development are to be sought in a number of social and religious characteristics of the Muslim world: the importance of 'works' next to faith which gave particular stress to social activities, the power of an urban bourgeoisie with its own taste and needs,[2] the institution of the *waqf* which gave religious sanction and freedom from confiscation to many humanitarian and economic institutions, and the tendency of the medieval period to invest in construction and land rather than in trade or industry. The forms used in these various kinds of buildings tended to be alike, regardless of functions. Façades for instance, the first and most obviously visible part of a building, rarely if ever make it possible to distinguish a mosque from a hostel or from a school. For here again the activity of man—known to us today in disused buildings through inscriptions or through very minor variations in form—was the actual identifying feature of the building, and its visible forms, its plan, or its decoration were merely the contemporary signs of wealth and conspicuous consumption without necessary

[1] K. Erdmann, *Das Anatolische Karavanseray* (Berlin, 1961).

[2] O. Grabar, 'The Architecture of the Middle Eastern City: the Case of the Mosque', in *Middle Eastern Cities*, ed. I. Lapidus (Berkeley, 1969), and 'The illustrated Māqāmat of the Thirteenth Century', in *The Islamic City*, ed. A. H. Hourani and S. M. Stern (Oxford, 1970).

functional purpose or identification. Regardless of these uniquely Muslim characteristics, however, the significant point is that not since the Roman empire did there occur such a development of monumental architecture for a variety of secular purposes. Although there were a number of instances (Samarqand, Iṣfahān, Istanbul) of organized city planning for all these functions, in most cities the development tended to be more haphazard. In religious architecture itself the appearance and development of façades from the tenth century onward,[1] the growth of domes in front of *miḥrāb*s, the multiplication of highly decorated minarets, and the ubiquitous growth of mausoleums all served to publicize the building or the men who sponsored it in ways which are far more characteristic of secular than of religious art. It would not be an exaggeration to conclude that, in medieval art as a whole which is so often seen as centred on religion, Islamic architecture appears as a sort of conscious secular variant.

It has already been pointed out that decoration played from the very beginning an important part in Islamic architecture, especially in secular buildings. Interest in decoration continued over the centuries and it is indeed by the wealth of their ornamentation which at times hides the construction that Muslim buildings have been characterized from the time of the Dome of the Rock in 691 all the way to the great Iranian monuments of Ṣafavid times (Fig. 12). Whether in the development of stucco, in the extraordinary ways of laying bricks so as to make designs, or in the eventual discovery and development of coloured tiles,[2] there is much that is technically original in Islamic architectural decoration, just as many themes are unique and worthy of study. Yet what I should like to discuss here is a different and perhaps more original

[1] The earliest instances of monumental façades which seem clearly datable are the San Esteban gate in the mosque of Cordova in the ninth century and the mausoleum at Tīm in Central Asia of 976, for which see G. A. Pugachenkova, *Mavzolei Arab-ata* (Tashkent, 1963).

[2] D. Wilber, 'Development of Mosaic Faience in Islamic Architecture in Iran', *Ars Islamica*, vi (1939), 16–47; for more general remarks see D. Hill and O. Grabar, *Islamic Architecture and its Decoration* (London, 1965).

aspect of this decoration. It is the manner in which construction and ornament relate to each other, for in this way one of the most debated problems of Islamic architecture can be posed.

Already in the domes by the *miḥrāb* of the mosque of Cordova (Fig. 4) we can see a rather unusual combination of such features as ribs which appear to support the cupola and which yet have been shown to form a static mass with the cupola. The ribs are accompanied by squinches, a characteristic unit of domical support, which do not support anything in this instance, while below, the polylobed arches have been broken up into sections and recomposed. A century later in the north dome of Iṣfahān's great mosque (Fig. 13) a very unusual articulation of supports corresponding to every single part of the superstructure gives the impression of a type of structural grid or net which would then have been filled in with a highly decorative brick masonry. Yet here also it appears that from the point of view of statics a single mass was created and not a series of interplays and balances between separate parts.[1] Then, from its earliest known occurrence in the Tīm mausoleum to the spectacular compositions of Ṣafavid Iran or of Cairene façades and Andalusian domes, the *muqarnas*, a type of device which uses in many combinations a small number of three-dimensional shapes, appears no doubt as a decorative feature used in cornices and often without structural significance and yet also as something inspired by architectural forms (Fig. 14) and at times drawing attention to the principal parts of the building.

These three examples—two specific monuments and an architectural device—are all features which have an ambiguous value in that they are all meaningful in the construction of the building (or at least could be made to be meaningful) and yet none of them appears simply as a device for construction. In a unique fashion structural meaning and decorative value have been blended and

[1] We are still almost totally lacking in any sort of engineering study of Iranian monuments. The only usable work is found in M. B. Smith's exemplary publication of Barsiān, 'Material for a Corpus of Early Iranian Islamic Architecture', *Ars Islamica*, iv (1937), 7–41.

the respective importance of either can vary considerably. Several ways of interpreting this ubiquitous Muslim phenomenon (see Fig. 16 for the use of bricks) are open, and cogent arguments exist for each of these ways, although none is totally persuasive. It can be argued that these examples illustrate primarily solutions of constructional problems which, as in many instances elsewhere, moved from constructional to decorative. It can also be argued that the decorative impulse was the main one and that it is only exceptionally—in Spain in the tenth century, in Iran and in Egypt in the eleventh and twelfth centuries—that a constructional value was given to basically decorative forms. Or, perhaps in line with our earlier arguments about secular architecture, we could suggest that this particular development of Islamic architectural decoration is another instance of a sort of principle of formal ambiguity by which the visible forms of the architecture are not to be judged according to their variable relationship to a Vitruvian contrast between construction and decoration but rather according to the effect given to any one building or clear unit of a building. In the latter case, the opposition or the contrast between ornament and construction could become a false problem, like the misunderstanding of the phonetic structure of a word or the mistranslation of a sentence.

Much theoretical work and research are still necessary before this latter interpretation can be made secure. As a hypothesis it has several advantages. It sets the question of architectural decoration in its own cultural and temporal context rather than according to some external criterion. It explains the apparent contradiction of using architectonic themes without architectonic function or the transformation of walls and other means of support into tapestries or illuminations by means of colour and of decorative designs. It also compels us to look more closely at the total effect of an architecture rather than at its separate parts and to draw the conclusion that in a great masterpiece as opposed to 'typical' works the significance of the work of art is larger than the sum of its parts. It is in this fashion for instance that the *muqarnas* domes of the Alhambra (Fig. 10) can justifiably be interpreted as revolving heavens, for, as the source of external light moves around the base of the dome, the topologically complex surface of the cupola is constantly illuminated in a different manner and, like the heavens, never looks the same while remaining motionless. It is only the architectural context of the decorative designs which gives meaning to the ornament, but it is only by being decorated in a certain fashion that the static cupolas can be understood as revolving. In this particular instance, of course, additional epigraphic evidence exists to make the interpretation plausible.[1] Elsewhere we still have to learn to 'read' the monuments properly.

As far as architectural decoration is concerned, our central point would, therefore, be that, regardless of the aesthetic merits a foreign taste may see in the colourful decoration of Islamic architecture, this decoration when seen in its full context rather than as a series of themes was what gave meaning to the building. What that meaning was in each case is still problematic, for we are in effect in the presence of something like Minoan or Hittite, languages in which some words and some structures are clear but the language as a whole is not yet fully understood.

In dealing both with secular inspiration of architecture and with architectural decoration, we have tried to define the achievement of Islamic architecture less in terms of precise characteristics and motifs than as a series of attitudes such as the preponderance of activity over form, the monumentalization of an unusually large number of functions, and the partial replacement of the dichotomy of construction and decoration by a single morphemic entity whose exact meaning probably varied from century to century, region to region, and monument to monument in ways yet to be elucidated. These achievements appear to have been particularly original in the Muslim world and may serve as a convenient starting-point for a brief consideration of the last theme I should like to consider, the modal transformation of non-Islamic forms.

[1] G. Gómez, *Ibn Zamrak* (Madrid, 1943); D. Emilio Lafuente y Alcantara, *Inscripciones Arabes de Granada* (Madrid, 1859).

This theme, we may recall, derived from the fact that early Islamic architecture had to be created as a phenomenon *sui generis* out of a complex cluster of earlier or contemporary forms. It is a further remarkable feature of this architecture that the syntheses formed by the first two or three centuries were not the simple prime movers from which all later developments derived but that they were themselves but one example—admittedly the first and most influential one—of a unique power of transformation into something Islamic of many other formal or functional entities. This transformation occurred over the centuries on any number of different levels. The simplest one was that of transformation of non-Islamic forms into Islamic purposes. This is what happened probably in the eleventh century in Iran when a pre-Islamic *aywān* (a large vaulted hall opening directly on to an open space) was transformed into the axial feature of mosques (Fig. 15) and of a multitude of other buildings. A similar phenomenon occurred in Ottoman Turkey where a dome-centred type of edifice[1] was evolved, which, under the impact of Hagia Sophia, was to create the superb mosques of Istanbul. Things were somewhat different in India where several Near Eastern models were introduced and adapted to local media of construction, giving to the monuments a partly hybrid character which succeeded far better in highly thought-out compositions like the Taj Mahal than in the more common provincial monuments.

These instances merely illustrate the remarkable adaptability of forms from many different regions to the needs of Islam. Of even greater interest are functions which at a certain moment became Islamic. Such was the case of the mausoleum,[2] whose very existence went against the precepts of the faith. What made the mausoleum as an architectural form so characteristic of Islamic

[1] The subject of the formation of Ottoman architecture has been considerably modified in recent years by A. Kuran, *The Mosque in Early Ottoman Architecture* (Chicago, 1968), and R. Goodwin, *A History of Ottoman Architecture* (London and Baltimore, 1971).

[2] O. Grabar, 'The Earliest Islamic Commemorative Structures', *Ars Orientalis*, vi (1967), 7–46.

architecture is that, even though there are instances of very ancient cults transformed into Muslim ones and even though the forms used (Fig. 16) are relatable to pre-Islamic forms of mausoleums, it did not make its appearance as an influence from elsewhere but in response to the conscious need of the Muslim community, or certain sections of it. This ability to give a coherent Islamic meaning to a vast variety of styles is what we should like to call the Islamic mode. And it is in the existence of a history of an Islamic mode over and above the history of specific styles that Islamic architecture acquired one of its unique characteristics.

Any attempt at suggesting in a few pages the achievement of a thousand years of architecture over three continents is bound to leave out a great deal. There might have been a fuller discussion of aesthetic characteristics or of the particularly original decoration of Islamic architecture or even of such constructional features as may be considered peculiar to the Muslim world. But I think that these questions cannot be considered meaningfully until the nature and purpose of architecture within the culture have been determined, because the very occurrence and maintenance of an Islamic civilization over such diverse lands poses problems like that of its architecture in a unique fashion. Our most significant conclusions seem to be two. One is that what gave an Islamic quality to the architecture of the Muslims is less identifiable in terms of visually perceptible forms than in terms of human activities. Forms varied and there is almost nothing in common between the mosque of Cordova and the Süleymaniye in Istanbul or the mosque of Bībī Khānum in Samarqand. Yet the activities of men and the prayers uttered in these buildings have made all of them Islamic. An essential corollary of this point was that the forms themselves tended to be generalized ones, rarely acquiring a specific meaning and purpose. Only in this fashion was it possible to maintain Islamic needs in a vast variety of lands and of architectural traditions. More interesting perhaps is the point that Islamic architecture becomes in this way a remarkably modern architecture.

The second conclusion is a more obvious one, although it has a consequence which is less so. There seems to be little doubt that a variety of reasons—among which one of the most important was the lack of a Muslim ecclesiastical organization—led to the development of secular architecture of a far greater degree of originality than religious architecture. It is true, of course, that the faith is involved in such buildings as mausoleums and even in much of the urban architecture which we have discussed. Yet the primacy of the non-spiritual is made clear for instance by the lack in Islamic literature of statements about God and His buildings similar to those which Procopius or Suger wrote about churches, whereas the mythology of the palace is a commonplace subject in Arabic and Persian prose or poetry. It is in terms of this primacy of the secular that one has to understand, at least in part, the great Muslim achievements in architectural decoration. The consequence of this is a curious problem. Since much of palace architecture in particular was private architecture, not visible to most men and rarely built for more than passing enjoyment, should it not be considered like the miniatures as a secondary art in the culture as a whole, even though it was a particularly creative one? Should we conclude that its importance grew only by default, because the prime motive in the culture of Islam, the faith itself and all its social corollaries, could not be a major source of monumental and spiritually meaningful architecture? Or should we instead consider this architecture as a major historical document, an expression of the secular aspect of Islamic power? It is still much too early to answer these questions and many detailed investigations are needed before we can even attempt to do so. Yet in the final analysis, perhaps the most important achievement of Islamic architecture may be that, by providing a profile of a culture parallel to and different from the profiles suggested by literary sources, that culture is shown to have been far more complex and far more intricate than is generally believed.

It is, however, not sufficient to see Islamic architecture solely as a uniquely rich although poorly exploited source for an understanding of the culture. Its more profound achievement pertains to the history of architecture, for, issued from many of the same sources as Christian architecture of the Middle Ages, it utilized its inheritance in significantly different ways, and suggests a variety of new meanings for commonly known forms or provides old meanings for new formal inventions. While the precise explanation of each meaning and form lies within an understanding of Islamic culture, their actual occurrence can enrich our comprehension of architectural processes in general.

O. GRABAR

BIBLIOGRAPHY

Apart from the works quoted in the notes, the following may form a useful introduction to the field of Islamic architecture. The first group includes general works usually with good bibliographies, whereas the second group consists of more definitive publications.

(*a*) P. Brown, *Indian Architecture* (*Islamic Period*) (Bombay, 1942); D. Hill and O. Grabar, *Islamic Architecture and its Decoration* (London, 1967); J. D. Hoag, *Western Islamic Architecture* (New York, 1963); G. Marçais, *L'Architecture musulmane d'occident* (Paris, 1952); A. U. Pope, *Persian Architecture* (New York, 1965); G. A. Pugachenkova, *Iskurstvo Turkmenistana* (Moscow, 1967); B. Ünsal, *Turkish Islamic Architecture* (London, 1959); M. Useinov and others, *Istoriia Arhitektury Azerbaydjana* (Moscow, 1963).

(*b*) D. Brandenburg, *Islamische Baukunst in Ägypten* (Berlin, 1966); K. A. C. Creswell, *Early Muslim Architecture*, 2 vols. (new edn. Oxford, 1969); idem, *Muslim Architecture of Egypt*, 2 vols. (Oxford, 1952–9); A. Godard and M. B. Smith, various articles in *Athār-é Iran* (1936–49); L. Golombek, *The Timurid Shrine at Gazur Gah* (Toronto, 1969); O. Grabar, *The Formation of Islamic Art* (New Haven, 1973); M. E. Masson and others, *Mavzolei Ishrathana* (Tashkent, 1958); A. U. Pope (ed.), *A Survey of Persian Art*, 6 vols. (London, 1939–40); J. Sauvaget, *La Mosquée Ommeyyade de Médine* (Paris, 1947); D. Wilber, *The Architecture of Islamic Iran, the Ilkhanid Period* (Princeton, 1955).

(*B*) DECORATIVE ARTS AND PAINTING: THEIR CHARACTER AND SCOPE

Whenever we speak of the unique legacy which the Islamic civilization has bequeathed to the world in the form of its various arts, we postulate that, aesthetically speaking, they form an interconnected, all-embracing unit. We may be aware of the differences in the manifestations of the various regions of the immense area of the Islamic world, but nevertheless adhere basically to the belief that they are held together by some overriding and unifying characteristics. This assumption would have been axiomatic two generations ago and perhaps even more recently; it was demonstrated by various big exhibitions of Islamic art, which were organized for the first time in London in 1885 and as late as 1926 in Alexandria, the finest being held in Munich in 1910. By contrast the major exhibitions in recent decades have been dedicated to specific countries (such as Iran, Turkey, India, and Pakistan), presenting their arts from the earliest known periods. Thus the London exhibition of 1931 stressed primarily the Luristan bronzes and Achaemenid objects, and in 1935 the Leningrad exhibition excelled in its unique display of Sasanian art. Thirty years later, the Paris exhibition of 1961 called itself proudly 'Sept Mille Ans d'Art en Iran' although many diverse civilizations were involved, and it is even debatable whether we should rightly designate as 'Iranian' those of the early millennia of this period.

Today, therefore, the concept of Islamic art itself is sometimes seriously questioned, usually by implication and covertly, and then for one of two major reasons. On the one hand we are nowadays so much more aware of the specific character of the arts in the major geographical and cultural areas that at times their relative uniqueness may seem more striking than their interrelationship with other, particularly more distant, regions. Iranian, Turkish, and Indian painting of the sixteenth and seventeenth centuries is a case in point. This is so not only because a comparison of form and spirit within these schools seems to support the advocates of disparity, but even more so because at least two of them represent the period of major regional achievement in this medium and tend therefore to be looked at in isolation. The same restrictive attitude has resulted from the fact that in the various Muslim countries there is a new generation of scholars eagerly exploring their own artistic heritage. Having grown up in a secular and nationalistic period of history, most of them see their past primarily as a national achievement in which international religious and cultural factors played only a small part. Thus these scholars, and also a number of their Western colleagues influenced by them, speak exclusively of the art of their country, be it Turkey, India, Spain, or even Uzbekistan.

However, for various reasons the traditional point of view seems to be still fully warranted. In spite of 'dialectal' differences all the arts in the *Dār al-Islām* do speak the same basic language. For example, a comparison of ceramic production in centres as different as fourteenth-century Iran, Syria, Egypt, or the lower Volga lands of the Golden Horde makes this point quite obvious (Figs. 20–3). Indeed, after half a century of intensive international research, it is still often impossible to recognize regional differences. No one can name the country of origin of any of the many Koran illuminations up to the year 1000, or distinguish between Egyptian and Iraqi rock-crystal carvings of the tenth and eleventh centuries, or between Egyptian and Persian cut glass of the same period, or between the silks of those two countries dating from the late thirteenth and fourteenth centuries. Similarly—to give another example to underline this point—a number of illuminated Persian manuscripts of the first half of the fifteenth century are now attributed to Muslim India, not because there are any obviously Indian features to be found in them (there are few indications so far as we know), but because scholars have, so to speak, run out of possible Iranian places of origin.[1] This certainly indicates

[1] B. W. Robinson, *Persian Miniature Painting from Collections in the British Isles* (London, Victoria and Albert Museum, 1967), p. 85 and nos. 107, 111, and 113. Irma L. Fraad and Richard Ettinghausen, 'Sultanate Painting in Persian Style', *Chhavi: Golden Jubilee Volume of the Bharat Kala Bhavan*, Banares, 1972, pp. 48–66.

a uniformly inspired artisanry using similar methods of production which can be assumed to have existed in nearly every craft throughout the Muslim world. In other cases the attribution is not based on any stylistic clues, but is the result of epigraphic and, more recently, of technical considerations. Finally, it should be remarked that the 'Islamic' character in the arts and crafts is so pronounced that it is apparent even after a given region such as Spain or Sicily had been reconquered by Christianity and the main artistic trend become quite different. Thus it is clear that Islam exerted a very strong, even vital force, which was readily mirrored in the arts of the Muslim world.

This having been said, it should nevertheless be stressed again that divergences do of course exist under the umbrella of the universal Islamic civilization. We are not concerned at this moment with the stylistic changes from period to period, or with the different horizontal stratifications according to the various social classes, a feature which is only now slowly being recognized. There seem to have been distinct attitudes characteristic of certain major regions. Thus, in the middle of the twelfth century Egypt developed a compartmented geometric style, primarily of star configurations, which was readily taken up in North Africa, Spain, Anatolia, and later on in European Turkey (Figs. 24–5). There is comparatively little of this in Eastern Islam, especially not in Iran or India. By contrast Iran developed systems of free-flowing arabesques or floral *rinceaux* to cover such surfaces as the carpet, pages in manuscripts, doors, the sides of pulpits (*minbar*s), and so on. The reason for this East–West split is still rather obscure. We can only surmise with caution that the more rational mind of orthodox Islam apparently preferred a straight, more rigid, and calculated style, while a mystic orientation, as that of Iran, adopted an abstract, undulating approach which nevertheless seems in its orderly manner to represent the rationalization of an ineffable inner experience.

When we proceed to probe further into the various manifestations of Islamic art, a curious fact presents itself. The twelfth and thirteenth centuries are the great periods for pottery and metal production in Iran—well after the finest creations in glass had been achieved in the tenth and eleventh centuries—while the highest and most original accomplishments in painting were not to appear until between 1330 and 1550, and the best carpets still later on, in the course of the sixteenth and early seventeenth centuries. On the other hand, when we consider one medium such as pottery, we observe that the ninth century saw the flowering of the craft in Iraq, the tenth century in Eastern Iran and Transoxania, the eleventh and early twelfth centuries in Egypt, the late twelfth and thirteenth centuries in Iran and Syria, the fourteenth and fifteenth centuries in Spain, and the sixteenth century in Turkey. Rarer working materials made an even more sporadic appearance. Ivory was carved in Spain mainly in the second half of the tenth and the beginning of the eleventh century, and in Egypt in the twelfth century, and jade in the seventeenth and eighteenth centuries in India.

The conclusion to be drawn—and more could, of course, be said on this issue—is that we cannot speak of one great period in which all or most of the crafts flourished, nor is there a universal zenith for any one craft. In general, the development is related to political high points in time and space, reflecting peaceful conditions, an economic boom, and specific princely patronage; even in the great creative countries the phenomenon is not constant but occurs in waves resulting in variable creative foci. In practical terms this means, for instance, that there is not one great period of Iranian art, because the selection of one period as such would automatically exclude artistic creations, even masterpieces, of before or after that particular era. This also makes it difficult to compare the great creations of a country in different media, as they belong more likely than not to different centuries, thus reflecting a different spirit; or if objects of the same material are compared, they are from different areas and probably also date from different periods.

This situation has led to a fragmented approach to Islamic art, directed either to a narrow geographic segment of the Islamic world, with wide or limited historical boundaries, or to a specific subject with broad geographic limits. The result is that there are experts on Iranian, Egyptian, or Turkish Islamic art in general, or on architecture, miniatures, carpets, ceramics, or glass, usually of *all* Islamic countries, each scholar being outstanding in his speciality but in no other and thus missing the connecting links. Happily, however, we now have a series of general histories of Islamic art (although a few of them could well be avoided in spite of their fine pictures), and there are others in preparation. This being so, a chronological presentation of the material is unnecessary here.

Having said all this, it should be added that in the collective mind of persons interested in, although not professionally preoccupied with, Islamic art, there exists nevertheless a strongly entrenched notion of an all-pervading 'Islamic' *cachet* which goes well beyond the individual features developed by each country and period. They think specifically—and quite rightly so—of the vegetal arrangements, whether realistically rendered flowers or abstract arabesques, of geometric configurations which in the Islamic world were primarily conceived as fruits or objects,[1] and finally of calligraphically rendered inscriptions. These are indeed the main themes of Islamic art permeating both the sacred and the secular arts, and as such they demand further discussion.

But what is it that makes the floral, geometric, or epigraphic decorations so noteworthy and appealingly different and, indeed, memorable? And what makes them 'Islamic'? Starting with the latter issue, it is clear that it cannot be the rarity of human and animal figures, as these do occur, particularly on rugs, metalwork, and ceramics, and do not make these art objects any less 'Islamic' in appearance. Even when human figures appear in the decorative arts, they are usually not too obviously Near Eastern. They are more often than not of a non-specific appearance, as they represent crowned princes and not the common people clothed in kaftan and turban. Even the facial features do not help much, as a beard and bushy eyebrows are not sufficiently indicative. In many

[1] F. Sarre and E. Herzfeld, *Archäologische Reise im Euphrat- und Tigris-Gebiet* (Berlin, 1911–20), ii. 255–8.

instances the physical aspects are even misleading to the uninitiated, for the facial cast, especially the slanting eyes, appears to be Far Eastern, whereas it is actually characteristic of Tatars or Mongoloid Turks from Central Asia whose beauty, as sung by the poets, was proverbial.

Can it be said that an Islamic message is contained in the ubiquitous Arabic lettering? This element in the decoration certainly helps to establish the atmosphere, but it seems unlikely that its content is essentially Islamic. Many of these 'inscriptions' are only simulated writing, or they repeat stereotyped words of good wishes. Even when they contain a genuine message, it may not be Islamic, at least not in a religious sense. These inscriptions can be secular proverbs[1] or, as is very frequent, they may represent dedicatory eulogies to please royal or princely patrons (Fig. 26). Even more revealing is the fact that these inscriptions were not thought to be absolutely essential. They occur on Iranian prayer-carpets, but rather rarely on the many Turkish varieties of the genre, and not at all on those from India, the Caucasus, or Central Asia. Furthermore, there is a good deal of evidence that, when such inscriptions were most appropriately applied, they were not read even if they contained Koranic quotations.

Since this is an important issue, three examples may be quoted, one each from the earliest and latest periods of Islamic art and a third from an intermediate point in history. The oldest architectural monument of Islam, and one of its holiest, the Dome of the Rock, built in 691 in Jerusalem, has since the Caliphate of al-Walīd (705–15) been universally thought to represent a memorial to the Ascension of the Prophet, traditionally held to have taken place on this spot. However, its extensive inscriptions indicate that it is a victory monument commemorating triumph over the Jewish and Christian religions.[2] Five hundred years later a dedicatory

[1] L. Volov, 'Plaited Kufic on Samanid Epigraphic Pottery', *Ars Orientalis*, vi (1966), 133.

[2] O. Grabar, 'The Umayyad Dome of the Rock in Jerusalem', *Ars Orientalis*, iii (1959), 32–62.

inscription was applied to a silver-inlaid brass ewer made for the Lord of Mosul, Badr al-Dīn Lu'lu' (1231–59). Not only are there spelling mistakes, particularly in the name, but one is also of a near-defamatory nature, practically calling the ruler 'Father of Oppressions' (Abu'l-Maẓālim);[1] yet in spite of this implied insult the object was, as a graffito indicates, readily accepted for the royal stores. Finally, the large inscription on the façade of a splendid mosque recently built in a Western capital has a wrongly delineated letter which obviously changes the Koranic text; here again nobody—from the Azhar-educated imāms to the many cultural attachés of the various embassies—has read this spectacularly placed inscription and raised objections. There is, therefore, little doubt that the same attitude has prevailed throughout Muslim history and that, while verbal communications were sent out, they were seldom consciously received.

They contained, however, a non-verbal message which was understood by every Muslim, even though the writing was often in Kūfic characters which are difficult even for experts to read. An inscription in impressive Arabic letters, the vehicle of the Koran, had the most sacred and solemn connotations and made the viewer conscious of being a member of the *umma*, the community of Muslims. Thus, writing can have a symbolic meaning and it is only natural that it occurs as the only symbolic feature on coins and on the flag of at least one fundamentalist Islamic state, that of Saudi Arabia.

If there is no direct scriptural content, could we then perhaps assume a message through specifically Islamic symbols analogous to the use of Arabic writing? Several decades ago, in 1928, the British Orientalist Sir Thomas Arnold wrote an article on 'Symbolism and Islam'[2] and, while surveying only a limited amount of material, on the basis of his general experience he came to the conclusion that, unlike other religions, Islam did not develop

[1] See D. S. Rice, 'The Brasses of Badr al-Dīn Lu'lu', *Bulletin of the School of Oriental and African Studies*, xiii (1950), 633.

[2] *The Burlington Magazine*, liii (1928), 155–6.

a symbolic language. Professor Rudi Paret in his book *Symbolik des Islam* (1958) likewise does not impart an important role to symbolism in Islamic art. It seems, however, that the situation is not quite so negative as was assumed by these eminent scholars, although it remains ambivalent.

Let us first consider one typical example which is as Islamic as can be, a symbol of Allah, the Godhead Himself. Furthermore, it has all possible canonical sanction, as it is based on a Koranic passage in *Sūrat al-nūr*, the so-called 'Verse of Light' (xxiv. 35): 'Allah is the Light of the heavens and the earth. The likeness of His Light is as a niche in which there is a lamp. The lamp is in a glass. The glass is as it were a shining star . . .' Now in spite of the very unequivocal language, a symbol based on this image came into being only in the twelfth century, apparently instigated by the small tract *Mishkāt al-anwār* written by the eminent al-Ghazālī, which uses the same sacred verse. This symbol occurs mainly in Iran, Iraq, Syria, and Egypt (Figs. 27–8), but hardly in the regions to the east, west, and south. It is also found only in the thirteenth and fourteenth centuries, and not universally as it served almost exclusively for the decoration of *miḥrāb*s. That this symbol had such a limited application was not due to a theological reorientation or the rise of another symbol which might have replaced it; it was rather the diffident attitude towards such signs altogether (which made Arnold and Paret despair of their existence) which caused its eclipse, together with a built-in self-destruction factor which affected much of Islamic art (and, for that matter, Islamic literature as well). It was a general rule that when an artist tried to improve on a design he did so not by introducing new imaginative motifs and combining them ingeniously, but by elaborating on the concepts already available. In the case of the 'light symbol' this meant that its ground became more richly decorated with floral designs and the colour of the area between the suspension chains was changed, and in addition two candlesticks were placed below, at the sides of the lamp, in imitation of actual *miḥrāb* practice. This clouded the issue and the underlying meaning was gradually lost. This is shown best by the fact that the lamp soon turned into a flower vase (Fig. 29), if it was not replaced by an ornament or at times by a suspended ewer, suggested by the rite of cleansing before prayer (Fig. 30).

The conclusion is that, though at times symbolism existed, like the inscriptions it did not continue for long to express its message. The message becomes almost immediately purely 'decorative' and, therefore, devoid of a directly understandable meaning. It joins the flowers, arabesques, and starlike configurations which, it seems, never had a specific, explicit message to begin with. This is corroborated by the fact that when a symbol finally disappeared, its well-formed frame, that is, its 'carrier', nevertheless persisted.[1] In other words, the mere outer shape or the manner of presentation seems to have been more important than what is usually called the inner meaning or the message.

This being a significant aspect of Islamic art, it seems essential to demonstrate it by two other examples. Perhaps the most significant piece of evidence in an Iranian context is the wide application of the four-*aywān* system. This places a high, wide, and open hall half-way along each side of a rectangular courtyard. While this building scheme was well suited to the Iranian house and could also be properly adapted for the use of palaces and *madrasa*s, it was less appropriate for hospitals and caravanserais. It made no sense for the enclosure of burial grounds (such as that at Gazargāh near Herat[2]), and it was downright unfitted to its eventual major use for Friday mosques where the main *aywān* was combined with a large dome before the *miḥrāb*, a feature derived from Sasanian palace architecture. Thus the congregational and unitary aspect of the sanctuary part of the mosque was destroyed, as the heavy supports of the dome blocked off the centre section from the side wings, while beyond it a great deal of not really needed space was

[1] R. Ettinghausen, 'The "Wade Cup" in the Cleveland Museum of Art, its Origin and Decorations', *Ars Orientalis*, ii (1957), 355–6.

[2] L. Golombek, *The Timurid Shrine at Gazur Gah* (Toronto, 1969), *passim*.

built up to extend the lateral arcading to the depth of the side *aywān* (Fig. 33*a*). Here again, content or function is sacrificed for mere outer form, harmonious and impressive as it may be.

This phenomenon is further borne out by an equally convincing piece of evidence ultimately developed in Egypt: Muslim book-binding (Fig. 33*b*). This is characterized by a pentagonal flap attached to the lower cover which is tucked in under the upper cover when the book is not in use. It is commonly thought that in this way the manuscript is more tightly held together. Since there is no constricting pressure, this hardly seems to be the purpose. And it is worth noting that Europe never adopted the use of the flap, although it eventually accepted the paste-board foundation of Muslim bindings to replace the usual wooden core. The traditional explanation makes little sense. What happened was that in early Coptic bindings a long strap was attached to a flap of this shape, so that the book could be securely bound, for example while one was travelling. The gnostic manuscripts of Nag Hammadi of the fourth century are bound in this manner (Fig. 33*c*). The rather untidy-looking strap was later dispensed with, making the flap unnecessary. Neither of them, therefore, is to be found on the Coptic manuscripts of the Monastery of St. Michael of the Desert in the Fayyum of the ninth and tenth centuries, now in the Pierpont Morgan Library. But, as a result of the sacred aura which surrounded the early Koran manuscripts, the traditional flap was retained in Muslim binding, although without the strap which in urban libraries was unnecessary. Hence, we are here confronted with still another functionless form found everywhere in the Muslim world even today.

It seems reasonable to assume that the decisive Islamic element —the feature which has exerted such fascination on the viewer inside and outside the Muslim world—may well be a common denominator found in *all* the arts of the vast region. Since we are here concerned with decorative arts and painting, we have to isolate this factor primarily from them, although we are fully aware that it must equally be present in architecture.

With this aim in mind, certain features which have often been mentioned as representing the basic elements of Islamic art may be eliminated. For instance we may dispense with flat, two-dimensional design, as there is a good deal of plastically conceived carving in various media, with the Iranian stucco reliefs forming a particularly noteworthy group. Nor can infinite ornament be a feature, as there is a good deal of limited decoration, as for instance in those not infrequent medallion schemes whose corner designs differ from that of the central form, so that there is no suggestion of an endless repetition of the same pattern. There exist both richly moving kinetic ornamentation and perfectly static ornamentation.[1] And while there is an obvious preference for such simple materials as clay, glass, brass, bronze, wool, and cotton, yet precious metals as well as semi-precious stones, marble, ivory, and silk were also widely used. It is true that colour is very important, yet the dull tones of clay, wood, and ordinary metals also occur. Finally, we must eliminate the assumption that Islamic art is one dealing with abstract ornamentation; there are many designs representing figures, mainly in the paintings but also in the decorative arts, especially in princely themes and animal motifs.

While all these features are of primary significance, none of them is of a universal nature and none can, therefore, qualify as the decisive factor.[2] This leaves only one aspect for consideration: the general harmony, balance of parts, and perfection of the whole composition. This is, indeed, ubiquitously found and should, therefore, be regarded as the most important Islamic element. Its nature was well described about A.D. 1106 by al-Ghazālī in his *Kimīyā' al-saʿāda* ('Alchemy of Happiness'):

> The beauty of a thing lies in the appearance of that perfection which is realizable and in accord with its nature. When all possible traits of perfection appear in an object, it presents the highest degree of beauty. . . .

[1] L. Bronstein, 'Some Historical Problems Raised by a Group of Iranian Islamic Potteries', *Bulletin of the American Institute for Iranian Art and Archaeology*, v (June 1938), 225–35.

[2] M. Ağa-Oğlu, 'Remarks on the Character of Islamic Art', *The Art Bulletin*, xxxvi (1954), 175–202.

beautiful writing combines everything that is characteristic of writing, such as harmony of letters, their correct relation to each other, right sequence, and beautiful arrangement. There is a characteristic perfection for each thing, the opposite of which could under special circumstances be characteristic of something else.[1]

This finding must be underlined by two further considerations. First, harmony of design is only possible when there is design. Hence, it should be stressed that undecorated objects are rather rare in Islamic art. Even cheap unglazed pottery nearly always shows some form of decoration, at times a great deal of it made by stamping or mould imprints. Secondly, the categories of aesthetic judgement with regard to painters mentioned by Mīrzā Muḥammad Ḥaydar Dughlāt (*c.* 1500–51) are those of refinement and harmony, in which such values as delicacy, exquisiteness, finesse, agreeable effect, cleanliness, purity, finish, as well as firmness, are often mentioned, while terms of disparagement are 'unsymmetrical' and 'crude'.[2] Indeed, bizarre, caricature-like portraits occur in painting only relatively late, in seventeenth- and eighteenth-century Turkish miniatures, and to a lesser degree in contemporary Persian ones; and there are, with the exception of Chinoiserie designs, no freely moving, irregularly shaped compositions.

Is there any indication of how this basic element of inner harmony was experienced by a Muslim viewer? Although evidence to judge this is hard to come by, it seems that the approach was on several levels. On the first (which the metaphysician would call the lowest) there is the aesthetic appeal. Jalāl al-Dīn Rūmī says: 'Everything that is made beautiful and fair and lovely is made for

[1] *Das Elixier der Glückseligkeit, übertragen von H. Ritter* (Jena, 1923), p. 148. The subsequent quotations are on pp. 141–2, 158; see also R. Ettinghausen, 'Al-Ghazālī on Beauty', in *Art and Thought*, issued in honour of Ananda K. Coomaraswamy, ed. K. Bharatha Iyer (London, 1947), pp. 160–5; and Ananda K. Coomaraswamy, 'Notes on the Philosophy of Persian Art', *Ars Islamica*, xv–xvi (1951), 125–8.

[2] L. Binyon, J. V. S. Wilkinson, and B. Gray, *Persian Miniature Painting* (London, 1933), pp. 189–91; E. Schroeder was the first to recognize the importance of these critical terms: 'Persian Painting', *Parnassus*, xii (1940), 33.

the eye of him that sees' (*Mathnavī*, i. 2383),[1] because, as al-Ghazālī states: 'Everything the perception of which gives pleasure and satisfaction is loved by the one who perceives it.' It is this aspect of beauty and harmony which caused the work of art to be commissioned in the first place, or which made the object saleable after it had been fashioned. It is still the basis of today's appeal to the connoisseur.

On the second level the design satisfies a psychological need. It caters to human sensitiveness which is bewildered by the surrounding untamed, dangerous, and often phantasmagoric landscape, and displeased by the equally unappealing web of crooked and winding streets in villages and towns. The answer is a formal linear harmony which is rectilinear in the case of architecture and gardens. It is further enriched by colour which is the antidote to the all-pervading monotony of the ubiquitous sand or stone. How great was the need for colour is not only indicated by the wide range of richly glazed pottery but even more startlingly demonstrated by architectural wall coverings such as Iranian brick and faience mosaics, Central Asian carved terracottas, Egyptian and Syrian variegated marble inlays, and Spanish-North African tiled dados. While these are special efforts of communal and princely display, the same love of colour can just as easily be detected in works intended for private enjoyment. It appears even in such media as leather book bindings, for example those of the fourteenth, fifteenth, and sixteenth centuries in Egypt, Syria, Iran, and Turkey, or in objects of brass or bronze with their inlays of copper, silver, gold, and niello. The most revealing use of colour is, however, the most personal—clothing apparel. S. D. Goitein in his analysis of the colours and hues used for male and female clothing, in the Geniza documents of Old Cairo of the eleventh and twelfth centuries, has stressed this point, particularly when he speaks of 'the enormous variety of colours favoured in those times which

[1] This passage and those that follow are quoted after *The Mathnawí of Jalálu'ddín Rúmí*, ed. and translated by R. A. Nicholson (Gibb Memorial Series, London, 1925–60).

made the medieval man look like tropical singing birds with intricate nuances of glitter, gloss, iridescence, stripes, waves and patterns'.[1] At the same time this distinguished scholar pointed to the general harmony of attire which matched the richly coloured garments with suitable shoes and turbans.

While for the average person these two reactions to beauty and harmony may have been sufficient, others of a more reflective and religious nature may have derived inner satisfaction from viewing art in a more profound manner. Hence, another approach to art could be a moral one, viewing art as a reflection of virtue. 'Purity of writing proceeds from purity of heart', says Qāḍī Aḥmad, an Iranian writing about calligraphers and book illuminators at the beginning of the seventeenth century, and he bases this judgement on the highest authority: the goal of Murtaḍā ʿAlī (i.e. the Caliph ʿAlī) in writing was not the invention of letters and dots, but fundamentals: purity and virtue.[2] This opinion reflects an attitude already expressed five hundred years earlier by al-Ghazālī: 'The beautiful painting of a painter or the building of an architect reveals the inner beauty of these men.' Accordingly, in biographies of artists, painters, in spite of their theologically doubtful position, are often regarded as paragons of quiet piety, while their *confrères* who travelled widely or led violent lives were regarded with disfavour. The ideal Muslim artist or artisan had thus nothing in common with the Bohemian of the Romantic Age.

The highest level in contemplation of art is, however, the metaphysical approach, especially that undertaken by a Ṣūfī. It achieves a higher insight which goes well beyond the surface appearance of the object, as for instance that expressed by al-Ghazālī: 'The beauty of the outer form which is seen with the bodily eye can be experienced even by children and animals . . . while the beauty of

[1] S. D. Goitein, 'The Main Industries of the Mediterranean Area as Reflected in the Records of the Cairo Geniza', *Journal of Economic and Social History of the Orient*, iv (1961), 180–1.

[2] Qāḍī Aḥmad Son of Mīr-Munshī, *Calligraphers and Painters. A Treatise*, translated from the Persian by V. Minorsky, with an Introduction by B. N. Zakhoder, translated from the Russian by T. Minorsky (Washington, 1959), p. 51.

the inner form can only be perceived by the eye of the "heart" and the light of inner vision of man alone.' In this approach the art object becomes a clue to higher verities: 'The one saw in the mind only figured clay; while the others saw clay replete with knowledge and works' (*Mathnavī*, vi. 1144). The same idea is expressed in many other sayings of Jalāl al-Dīn Rūmī, as for instance in these verses:

Does any painter paint a beautiful picture for the sake of the picture itself, without hope of conferring benefit? . . .

Does any potter make a pot in haste for the sake of the pot itself and not in hope of water? . . .

Does any calligrapher write artistically for the sake of the writing itself and not for the sake of the reading? . . .

The external form is for the sake of an unseen form, and that took shape for the sake of another unseen (form) in proportion to your insight . . .

The first is for the sake of the second, like mounting on the steps of a ladder (*Mathnavī*, iv. 2881–92).

In this approach the parallel between the works of the human and the divine artificer becomes particularly illuminating as it is a means to comprehend great mysteries. Let us quote Rūmī again:

If you say that evils too are from Him (that is true), but how is it a defect in His grace?

(His) bestowing this evil is even His perfection. I will tell you a parable (in illustration), O respected one.

A painter made two kinds of pictures, beautiful pictures and pictures devoid of beauty . . .

Both kinds of pictures are (evidence of) his mastery; those (ugly ones) are not (evidence of) his ugliness; they are (evidence of) his bounty.

He makes ugly the extreme ugliness—it is invested with all (possible) ugliness.

In order that the perfection of His skill may be displayed (and that) he who denies His mastery may be put to shame.

And if He cannot make the ugly, He is deficient (in skill); hence He is the Creator of (both) infidel and faithful. (*Mathnavī*, ii. 2535–42.)

In further amplification of this idea artistic perfection becomes the extension and counterpart of 'the perfect man' (*al-insān al-kāmil*) who according to Ibn al-ʿArabī (1165–1240) '. . . united in himself both the form of God and the form of the universe. He alone manifests the divine Essence together with all its names and attributes (which include beauty). He is the mirror by which God is revealed to Himself and therefore the final cause of creation. Our existence is merely an objectification of His existence.'[1]

Whatever approach to the work of art was adopted, whether it was comprehended by way of a single experience or on several levels, whether it was a conscious encounter or one just vaguely felt, it was always the optically brilliant, harmonious, outer form which carried the message, especially so since symbolism or verbal communication played, as we have seen, only a minor role. It did not matter that arabesques, flowers, geometric configurations, inscriptions, and even the animals and human images suffered from a certain sameness of appearance which made them fall easily into specific types. The same characteristic may be seen in a good deal of the literature with its standard themes and general alignment of human beings to conform to the ideal types of king, vizier, scribe, littérateur, or sheikh. Actually the standardized harmony made Islamic art a *koiné* readily understood, enjoyed, and imitated everywhere within the world of Islam; it had an appeal which was wider than the Arabic language and even the Arabic alphabet, and was second only to religion; hence its pervasive influence in a mostly illiterate and publicly frugal but emotionally responsive community which was endeavouring to find salvation without the immediate intercession of a prophet or saints and without the help of a clergy.

Although Islamic art of the mature periods looks like itself and nothing else, it is actually of many origins incorporating even civilizations hostile to itself. When Islam developed its art, great

[1] Ibn al-ʿArabī, quoted by al-Ḥallāj, *Kitāb al-Ṭawāsīn*, ed. L. Massignon (Paris, 1913), p. 129, translation quoted by R. A. Nicholson, article 'Al-Insān al-Kāmil' in *Encyclopaedia of Islam*, 1st edn. (Leiden–London, 1913–34).

pain was, of course, taken to eliminate every vestige of the symbols of the preceding religions. There were ways and means to proclaim the victory of the new faith, but it could not be done by incorporating any overt symbols of the vanquished religions such as the cross or the fire altar. However, behind the older faiths stood still older ones, especially the age-old myths and magic concepts of a prehistoric past. Recent research has shown that, besides the usual placid-looking main themes of Islamic art, or the calligraphically rendered inscriptions, or the princely scenes, there are also ancient themes of cosmic lore and the power of natural and supernatural forces symbolically reflected in combat scenes, zoological configurations, and various other emblems.[1] Whatever the consciousness of their nature may have been—and it was probably very vague and non-specific—the fact remains that they continued to exist after hundreds of years of Islamic domination and were still thought to represent or to mollify powers to be reckoned with. But these old signs were successfully assimilated to the current Islamic idioms and as such they escaped detection. They appeared as merely some other harmless but aesthetically appealing designs which were ingeniously placed on some pottery vessel or metal object.

Naturally the imprint of the immediate region was the strongest. Royal themes of the Sasanian and Achaemenian period reappear in the twelfth and thirteenth centuries. Going even further back in the history of Iran there are prehistoric zoomorphic pottery containers which, after more than one or even two thousand years, show up again although their very shape contradicted Islamic concepts. Animal designs in the same silhouette style as was used

[1] W. Hartner, 'The Pseudo-planetary Nodes of the Moon's Orbit in Hindu and Islamic Iconographies', *Ars Islamica*, v (1938), 113–54; R. Ettinghausen, 'The "Wade Cup" in the Cleveland Museum of Art, its Origin and Decorations', *Ars Orientalis*, ii (1957), 327–66; S. Cammann, 'Ancient Symbols in Modern Afghanistan', *Ars Orientalis*, ii (1957), 5–34; W. Hartner and R. Ettinghausen, 'The Conquering Lion, the Life Cycle of a Symbol', *Oriens*, xvii (1964), 161–71; E. Baer, *Sphinxes and Harpies in Medieval Islamic Art* (The Israel Oriental Society. Oriental Notes and Studies No. 9, Jerusalem, 1965).

in prehistoric pottery are again used in the most developed period of the Middle Ages (Fig. 31), and even strange, ancient, representational problems and techniques have a way of being suddenly, and to all appearances inexplicably, re-employed (Fig. 32). What it amounts to is the existence of a subsurface stratum of former concepts which Islam was strong enough to face and to integrate into its art. In spite of its novel forms constituting a far-flung *koiné*, there is, therefore, a decidedly conservative streak in Islamic art, even though it is often overlooked owing to the neutralizing process, which is one of the ways of Islamization.

Islamic art emerges then as an art with many traditional roots in spite of many innovations in themes, their composition, and enrichment. In spite of its neutrality and blandness, it is not only primarily man-related but it has a definite task or message, although this is not a verbal one. What gives it additional greatness is that it transcends the complexities, frustrations, and miseries of human life in a manner which can only be called both serene and exhilarating. The motifs do not play the role of animals in fables which are nothing but masquerading human beings. They act and talk their own more rarefied, murmuring language. But still they were listened to, even in a hypnotized fashion, both inside and outside the *Dār al-Islām*. It is this which gives Islamic art its special, unique quality.

RICHARD ETTINGHAUSEN

BIBLIOGRAPHY

General presentations of major periods of Islamic art: R. Ettinghausen, *Arab Painting* (London, 1962); O. Grabar, *Persian Art before and after the Mongol Conquest* (Ann Arbor, the University of Michigan Museum of Art, 1959); idem, 'The Visual Arts, 1050–1350', in *The Cambridge History of Iran, v, The Saljuq and Mongol Periods*, ed. J. A. Boyle (Cambridge, 1968), pp. 626–59; D. Hill and O. Grabar, *Islamic Architecture and its Decoration A.D. 800–1500* (London, 1964); E. Kühnel, *Die Arabeske, Sinn und Wandlung eines Ornaments* (Wiesbaden, 1949); idem, *Islamic Art and Architecture*, translated by Katherine Watson (London, 1966); G. Marçais, *L'Art de l'Islam* (Arts, Styles and Techniques) (Paris, 1946); K. Otto-Dorn, *Kunst des Islam* (Kunst der Welt, ihre geschichtlichen, soziologischen und religiösen Grundlagen: Die aussereuropäischen Kulturen) (Baden-Baden, 1964); D. and J. Sourdel,

La Civilisation de l'Islam classique (Les Grandes Civilisations) (Paris, 1968); H. Terrasse, *Islam d'Espagne. Une rencontre de l'Occident* (Paris, 1958).

The problem of Islamic art: M. Ağa-Oğlu, 'Remarks on the Character of Islamic Art', *The Art Bulletin*, xxxvi (1954), 175–202; N. Brunov, 'Über einige allgemeine Probleme der Kunst des Islams', *Der Islam*, xvii (1928), 121–31; E. C. Dodd, 'The Image of the Word; Notes on the Religious Iconography of Islam', *Berytus*, xviii (1969), pp. 35–79; R. Ettinghausen, 'The Character of Islamic Art', in *The Arab Heritage*, ed. N. A. Faris (Princeton, 1944), pp. 251–67, E. Kühnel, 'Islamische Kunst', in *Der Orient und Wir* (*Sechs Vorträge des deutschen Orient-Vereins*) (Berlin–Leipzig, 1935), pp. 50–67; C. J. Lamm, 'The Spirit of Moslem Art', *Bulletin of the Faculty of Arts, Fuad I University, Cairo*, iii (May 1935), 1–7; L. Massignon, 'Les Methodes de realisation artistique des peuples de l'Islam', *Syria*, ii (1921), 47–53, 149–60.

(C) THE IMPACT OF MUSLIM DECORATIVE ARTS AND PAINTING ON THE ARTS OF EUROPE

FOR over 1,300 years the worlds of Islam and of Europe have been in more or less constant confrontation. It has been a dynamic relationship, and often a tense one. But in spite of violent Western denigration of the Muslim religion and its Prophet,[1] lasting practically until our own day, and of actual warfare, culminating in the Crusades and the Turkish campaigns, the West has had nothing but admiration for the arts of the Near East. This was something much more than mere passive acceptance. It manifested itself in the association of whatever was available of this art with its most revered institutions, whether sacred or mundane, and in artistic borrowings of one type or another by the West from the East.

This impact was not restricted to the regions where a wide and profound meeting of spirit was to be expected and indeed did occur. In border regions there are the Mozarabic paintings and South

[1] These polemics are described in N. Daniel, *Islam and the West, the Making of an Image* (Edinburgh, 1960); see also G. E. von Grunebaum, *Medieval Islam, a Study in Cultural Orientation* (Chicago, 1946), pp. 45, 47, and Chapter I, above.

Italian ivory carvings, as well as the bilingual coins of Spain, Amalfi, and Salerno.[1] The 52,000 complete or fragmentary Islamic coins found in northern European countries, some of them made into jewellery, dating from the early eighth until the early eleventh century, show that there were prolonged trade links of these regions with the Islamic world; more than 30,000 of these Islamic coins, minted by the Sāmānid dynasty of eastern Iran and Transoxiana, were discovered on the Island of Gotland alone (Fig. 34), and many others were found on other islands and along the shores of the Baltic.[2] The effect of the Near East on the Far North is further underlined by the fact that one of the oldest extant Oriental carpets which dates from the early fifteenth century (Fig. 35) was found in the village church of Marby in northern Sweden, and that there is a whole category of Scandinavian adaptations of Oriental textiles, some of them of Islamic derivation.[3] Even such fragile objects as Syrian enamelled glass of the thirteenth century have been found in Sweden. While noting that this influence covered the widest possible area, it is also necessary to stress that it encompassed many, if not all, of the media. On the other hand, the impact was usually sporadic and not as massive and noticeable as that of China in the eighteenth century. It is not by chance, therefore, that there is no generally accepted term in Western languages corresponding to 'Chinoiserie', although from the fifteenth to the eighteenth centuries there was in Europe enough

[1] G. C. Miles, 'Bonnom de Barcelone', *Études d'orientalisme dédiées à la mémoire de Lévi-Provençal* (Paris, 1962), ii. 683–93 (with complete bibliography). See also idem, *The Coinage of the Umayyads of Spain* (New York, 1950), pp. 539–40; *Corpus Nummorum Italicorum*, xviii. 2 ff., Pl. I (Amalfi), pp. 307 ff., Pls. XVIII–XIX (Salerno); D. Spinelli, *Monete Cufiche battute da principe Longobardi, Normanni e Suevi nel regno delle due Sicilie* (Naples, 1844); and B. M. Lagumina, *Catalogo delle monete esistente nella Biblioteca Comunale di Palermo* (Virzi, 1892), these last two works for the Normans of Sicily.

[2] M. Stenberger, *Die Schatzfunde Gotlands der Wikingerzeit* (Kungl. Vitterhets. Historie och Antikvitets Akademien, Stockholm, 1958), i. 247, 250–4, 351–2.

[3] A. Geijer, 'Oriental Textiles in Scandinavian Versions', in *Aus der Welt der islamischen Kunst. Festschrift für Ernst Kühnel zum 75. Geburtstag am 26. 10. 1957* (Berlin, 1959), pp. 323–35.

interest in and material from Turkey to have warranted the use of 'Turquerie'. Also, while many phenomena of this cultural impact have been observed and some have been described, it has hardly ever been systematically treated and evaluated as a whole.[1]

Before giving what at best can only be a brief and sketchy survey, we should first try to understand why the Eastern arts were so popular in the West. Here, the first point to be made is a negative one: there was no specifically Muslim iconography or overt religious symbolism, which would have been offensive to the Christian mind. The innocent blandness of the various quadrupeds and birds, arabesques, and occasional human beings made the objects on which they were portrayed fully acceptable, even for the wrapping of a sacred relic or the carpeting of the altar steps. No exception was even taken to the use of the Arabic script, which was widely used and can be found on the halo of the Madonna, along the edges of the garments worn by saints, on cathedral doors, and on every other possible surface.[2] Although Arabic writing had a symbolic meaning in the Muslim world, and certain formulas contain religious invocations including the name of Allah, the West apparently did not understand it as such. As this writing often occurred on Biblical figures, including the Jewish High Priest, it may have been interpreted as ancient Hebrew script or at least as that used by the New Testament figures and by Christian saints.

[1] The nearest approach to such a survey made in recent years is R. A. Jairazbhoy, *Oriental Influences in Western Art* (Bombay, Calcutta, etc., 1965).

[2] A. de Longperier, 'L'Emploi des caractères arabes dans l'ornamentation chez les peuples chrétiens de l'occident', *Revue archéologique*, ii (1845), 696–706; the recent literature is dealt with in K. Erdmann, 'Arabische Schriftzeichen als Ornaments in der abendländischen Kunst des Mittelalters', *Abhandlungen der geistes- und sozialwissenschaftlichen Klasse, Akademie der Wissenschaften und der Literatur in Mainz* (1953), no. 9, 467–513; G. C. Miles, 'Byzantium and the Arabs: Relations in Crete and the Aegean Area', *Dumbarton Oaks Papers*, xviii (1964), 20–32. Only very rarely is the writing not Kufesque, as Miles termed the meaningless simulation of ornamental Kufic (or Naskhesque), but renders an actual inscription; for a perfect fifteenth-century example see S. Reich, 'Une Inscription mamlouke sur un dessin italien du quinzième siècle', *Bulletin de l'Institut d'Egypte*, xxii (1940), 127.

As such, it would have differed from the Hebrew alphabet used by the little-esteemed Jewish contemporaries and so seemed innocuous enough to be used in a Christian context.

A more positive reason for the ready acceptance of Islamic objects was their obvious aesthetic quality—their harmony, opulence, and often the great richness of their colours. A further asset, especially in the early periods, was the high degree of technical skill evident in the execution, far surpassing anything possible in the West. To this was added their exotic quaintness and, what was particularly important, their true or assumed association with the Holy Land and specific saintly figures.

The reaction of the West took various forms. There was the outright acceptance of the object as it was, physically unchanged, with a readiness to adapt it to the West's own purposes. The very large numbers of imported Oriental carpets belong to this group, which was undoubtedly the most extensive. Culturally more significant, though numerically much rarer, are those objects which were not just passively taken over but adapted to specific functions, and modified according to the prevailing *Formgefühl*. Thus, a textile could be used as the lining of a luxurious manuscript's binding; then again it could be painted in place as if it were the original, and thus appear as a consciously envisaged *doublure*. In the same fashion carpets were employed for every possible purpose; yet they are also shown in paintings of interiors fulfilling their original function, at times with the designs changed. There is, for instance, in the Victoria and Albert Museum an English embroidered carpet of the seventeenth century which, though based on the motifs of the small-figured Holbein carpets, is different enough from the many known pieces of this Turkish group to be regarded as a new Western variant (Fig. 36).

The most creative and advanced adaptation appeared in those cases where the objects actually entered into the Western creative process and thus became catalysts. In *The Procuress* by Jan Vermeer in the Dresden Gallery, the richly coloured Ushaq carpet in the centre of the composition sets the keynote for the artist's palette and helps to determine the character of the entire painting.[1] An even more far-reaching effect is the rich colouristic range of Venetian painting, which is thought to have been due to the large number of Oriental carpets imported into Venice. This may be difficult to establish, but a more tangible and pervasive influence is evident in the works of two major artists. Rembrandt often used to try to establish a Near Eastern atmosphere when painting Biblical subjects, though it is difficult to point to specific features beyond the heavy Turkish turbans and cloaks; but the glittering silky textiles help to catch the Eastern atmosphere, as does the use of chiaroscuro. In any case, Rembrandt's interest in Mogul miniatures (of which more will be said later) indicates his real eagerness to acquaint himself with the elements of that exotic and alluring civilization. Much more direct, because based on real observation and study, is Delacroix's artistic involvement with Muslim civilizations, especially the Maghribī variety. His paintings, and more so his sketches (Fig. 37), have actual documentary value and here, for once, we have an *œuvre* in which the Muslim aspect forms an essential and fully integrated part of the imagery of a Western artist.

A different phenomenon is the appearance of Near Eastern human figures, with their characteristic turbans and patterned garments, which are to be seen in innumerable Renaissance, Baroque, and Rococo paintings, particularly as the Magi in the Adoration scenes, or as other Biblical figures such as King Saul, or Ahasuerus. The porcelain figurines of Turkish gentlemen and ladies are part of an eighteenth-century phenomenon (Fig. 38). The same century saw fit to place a Turkish mosque in a princely park, just as it enjoyed a Turkish type of martial music. The appearance of Oriental figures starts with the actual observations of Western artists in the Near East, a series which began with the sketches made by Gentile Bellini during his stay in Constantinople from September 1479 until November 1480, and later on was to include

[1] K. Erdmann, *Europa und der Orientteppich* (Berlin-Mainz, 1962), p. 57 and fig. 33.

other well-known artists such as Melchior Lorichs and Jean Baptiste Vanmour,[1] who, together with the designers of extensive costume books, preserved from extinction long-passed scenes and human types in Eastern cities. Such subjects were painted by official draughtsmen accompanying diplomatic missions, and they in turn were supplemented by the painters who observed the occasional Oriental types in Western cities.

In turning now to actual objects, the place of honour should be given to textiles which from the beginning were imported into Europe, and left an indelible mark. We have only to consider the many terms derived from Near Eastern words or place-names: cotton, divan, sofa, and mattress, as well as damask, muslin, and baldachin. Such imports must have started soon after the rise of Islam, if they did not actually pre-date it. This is indicated by the important group of silks of the seventh to the eighth century, made in Zandāneh near Bukhārā, which were brought to the West at an early date to be used, like so many other fabrics, as wrappings for holy relics in churches of France, Belgium, and Holland.[2] It should be pointed out that the comparatively large number of textiles brought to the West is not surprising as weaving was the foremost craft of the Muslim world, providing not only all the clothing but also essential home furnishings such as covers, bolsters, pillows, carpets, curtains, and tents. Being durable and easily folded, textiles were not difficult to transport. Once they reached the West, their use was usually an ancillary one: for instance, an early Muslim fabric with an Iranian bird design served as cover for the 'Veil of Our Lady' now in the Church of Chartres.[3] Occasionally, however, they were objects of veneration, occasionally being erroneously identified with persons of an earlier period of history. Such

[1] H. Harbeck, *Melchior Lorichs* (Hamburg, 1911); R. van Luttervelt, *De 'Turkse' Schilderijen van J. B. Vanmour en zijn School* (Istanbul, 1958).

[2] D. G. Shepherd and W. B. Henning, 'Zandanījī Identified?', in *Aus der Welt der islamischen Kunst. Festschrift für Ernst Kühnel*, pp. 15–40.

[3] Y. Delaporte, *Le Voile de Notre Dame* (Chartres, 1927), p. 13, Pls. VI and VII; R. Ettinghausen, 'Islamic Art and Archaeology', in *Near Eastern Culture and Society*, ed. T. Cuyler Young (Princeton, 1951), p. 18, fig. 4.

is the case of the 'Veil of Saint Anne' which is kept in a fifteenth-century Venetian bottle in the church of Apt, Vaucluse, France. Here the impossibility of the early date and of the alleged function is indicated by its Arabic inscription which contains not only the formula of the Muslim faith but also the names of the Fāṭimid Caliph, al-Mustaʿlī (reigned 1094–1101), and of his chief minister, al-Afḍal, as well as an indication that the textile was woven in Damietta, Egypt, in 1096 or 1097.[1] Since it was woven before the fall of Jerusalem and al-Afḍal's defeat at Ascalon, the fabric could very well have been brought back by the Lords of Apt or its Bishop, who took part in the First Crusade and who, like many other Crusaders, may have brought back precious objects to be presented to their church as a thanksgiving for a safe return.

The earliest Islamic figured silk with a datable historical name on it and which has had an ecclesiastical connection comes from eastern Iran. It must have been made before 961, when the Turkish general mentioned on it was put to death; it was once in the small church of Saint Josse-sur-Mer in the Pas de Calais and is now in the Musée du Louvre. On the other hand the first figured silk with the name of a town, part of the treasure of the Colegiata de San Isidoro in Leon, is of slightly later date, about the eleventh century.[2] It is indicated on it that it was made in Baghdad, but it may very well be a Spanish copy of an Iraqi model. Though many textiles reached Europe from distant regions, those found in Spanish churches were usually from a neighbouring Hispano-Islamic manufacturing centre. This was already the case when the 'Veil' of the Caliph Hishām II (976–1013), which is possibly part of a dress, was given as a battle trophy to the Church of San Estebán in San Estebán de Gormáz; the same applies to the great Almohad

[1] G. Marçais and G. Wiet, 'Le "Voile de Sainte Anne" d'Apt', *Monuments et Mémoires Fondation Piot*, xxxiv (1934), 177–94; H. A. Elsberg and R. Guest, 'The Veil of Saint Anne', *The Burlington Magazine*, lxviii (1936), 140–5.

[2] A. F. Kendrick and R. Guest, 'A Silk Fabric Woven at Baghdad', *The Burlington Magazine*, xlix (1926), 261–7; F. L. May, *Silk Textiles of Spain. Eighth to Fifteenth Century* (New York, 1957), pp. 24–5.

textiles of the twelfth century.[1] In contrast to these ecclesiastical uses, but no less significant and even more spectacular, was the secular history of the ceremonial cloak originally made for the Norman King Roger II in Palermo in 1133, and subsequently worn as the coronation robe of the Holy Roman Emperors until 1806. It is a large semi-circular garment with a twice-repeated, monumental scene of a lion destroying a camel, a deeply symbolic portrayal of the Norman conquest of the Arab land. Its origin as the creation of Muslim craftsmen in the service of their new Christian overlord is designated by a large Arabic inscription. In its new role, the garment appears in a drawing by Albrecht Dürer, showing Charlemagne somewhat incongruously clothed in this coronation robe.[2] From the twelfth to the sixteenth century a new use was made of Oriental textiles from Spain, Egypt, Persia, and Turkey which began to arrive in larger pieces which could be made into luxurious vestments for the Mass. The beauty of the pattern was more important than the design which was, at times, quite unsuited for the purpose. We thus find sacred vestments incorporating dedications to a Muslim ruler, or with episodes from a romantic poem, or even a drinking scene.[3]

In the twelfth and thirteenth centuries another important development took place. The Islamic textile patterns were taken over by European weavers who paraphrased them freely, albeit on a reduced scale. First, the Sasanian-type roundels with pairs of animals were copied in Lucca and Regensburg, then there followed ogival composition schemes and geometric tile patterns which

[1] May, op. cit., pp. 14–17; D. G. Shepherd, 'A Dated Hispano-Islamic Silk', *Ars Orientalis*, ii (1957), 373–82.

[2] H. Fillitz, *Die Insignien und Kleinodien des Heiligen Römischen Reiches* (Vienna–Munich, 1954), Pls. 23–4, and text illustration opp. p. 9.

[3] D. S. Rice, 'The Fermo Chasuble of St. Thomas-à-Becket', *The Illustrated London News*, ccxxxv (3 Oct. 1959), 356–8; M. Dreger, 'Die Stoffe', in F. Sarre and F. R. Martin, *Die Ausstellung von Meisterwerken muhammedanischer Kunst in München 1910*, iii (Munich, 1912), Pls. 182, 195, 201–2, 219; A. H. Christie, 'Islamic Minor Arts and their Influence upon European Work', in *The Legacy of Islam*, 1st edn., fig. 48.

were woven in Mudéjar patterns of Chinese derivation.[1] Later, Turkish and Italian artisans seem to have influenced each other when they created their large-scale designs with floral and artichoke patterns.[2] A special group of textiles consists of long silken scarves which in the eighteenth century formed part of the dress of Polish noblemen. The prototypes came from seventeenth-century Iran, but they were mostly brought from Istanbul by Polish-Armenian merchants, who in Poland's artistic history were important intermediaries between East and West. Soon the enormous demand had to be satisfied by the simpler but still exotic-looking Polish versions which supplied the market until the end of the century.[3] A belated influence of Near Eastern textiles appeared in the second half of the nineteenth century in the designs of William Morris.[4]

Carpets are considered here as a special category of the textile arts. The Oriental carpet as we know it is assumed to have been brought to the Near East by the Seljuq Turks when, in the middle of the eleventh century, they moved west from their Central Asian homes. The patterns of these early carpets are no longer known to us, but they were undoubtedly further developed in Anatolia in the twelfth and thirteenth centuries. At the end of this period we know that they had arrived in Italy because, at that time, they begin to be represented in ever-increasing number in Italian paintings, and then in others as well. They appear below the throne of the Madonna, on the floor of the interiors where the sacred rites take place, or they are seen hanging from windows as colourful decorations displayed on feast days. At first these carpets show one or two animals or birds in a series of octagons placed in squares; then

[1] O. von Falke, *Kunstgeschichte der Seidenweberei*, ii (Berlin, 1913), figs. 261–74, 293–6 (Italy), 308–16 (Regensburg), 371–9 (Spain), 351–2, 354–5 (Chinese influence).

[2] Ibid., compare figs. 501, 522, 528, 531, 549 with figs. 604, 605, 607.

[3] T. Mańkowski, 'Influence of Islamic Art in Poland', *Ars Islamica*, ii (1935), 105–13.

[4] L. F. Day, *William Morris and his Art* (London, 1899), figs. on pp. 20 and 25; R. Watkinson, *William Morris as Designer* (London, 1967), figs. 6, 53, 63, and 71.

from the middle of the fifteenth century purely abstract and geometric patterns begin to appear and these tend to become more elaborate. All the early carpets are Turkish; Egyptian carpets made in Cairo arrive in the second half of the fifteenth century, Persian ones in the sixteenth century, and finally come those from the Caucasus and India. As the paintings indicate, they now often fulfil a new function, serving as table covers, the 'tapedi da tavola' or 'tapedi da desco' of the Italian documents. These carpets reached Europe in large numbers. For instance, the Earl of Leicester, the favourite of Queen Elizabeth, left at the time of his death no less than forty-six 'Turquoy' carpets, some of them quite large, but, significantly, only one Persian piece. Earlier in the sixteenth century Venetian ambassadors had on Henry VIII's suggestion presented to Cardinal Wolsey first seven, then later sixty more, of the then fashionable Mamlūk carpets from Egypt, one of the first of such diplomatic gifts.[1] There is no doubt that carpets exerted a great fascination on would-be buyers and owners, whatever their social position—whether they were Hapsburgs or members of the royal house of Sweden, princes of the Church, the nobility, or were just well-to-do members of the bourgeoisie. Their esteem can be gauged by the fact that they served as the setting for coronations and other important festive occasions. They became what is now called a 'status symbol'.

The Near Eastern suppliers knew how to fan this passion for a luxury object and then to satisfy it. They not only sent the finest pieces to the European market; at times they even changed, probably on special request, the shape and size to satisfy specifically European needs, especially for the much-coveted table covers. For this reason the Egyptian carpet weavers of the Ottoman period made round, square, or cross-shaped carpets (Figs. 39–40).[2] In one instance a Persian knotter even went so far as to make a vestment by the usual carpet-making technique, in which the crucifixion

[1] K. Erdmann, *Europa und der Orientteppich*, pp. 11–17.

[2] Idem, *Siebenhundert Jahre Orientteppich. Zu seiner Geschichte und Erforschung* (Herford, 1966), pp. 220–1.

was placed in a typical carpet setting of floral motifs (Fig. 41). There is a group of carpets which carry European coats of arms, which were obviously made to specific order (Fig. 42), like those ordered in Kāshān in 1602 by King Sigismund III Vasa of Poland. In this case we actually know the prices, including the extra charge for the knotting of the blazons. In examples dating from the early seventeenth century a double coat of arms can be found indicating that these pieces commemorated a marriage between two noble families. Another such carpet was made by special order for a Latin archbishop of Lwow between 1614 and 1633, while yet another type of patron was the master of a guild, for instance the Girdlers' Company in London, who commissioned an emblazoned carpet in Lahore in 1634. Altogether there are still twenty such carpets with coats of arms in existence, of which ten were made in Ushaq, Turkey, six in Iran, and two each in Cairo and India.[1]

Because there was such a vast supply of beautiful Oriental carpets, it was practically impossible for European carpets modelled on these pieces to compete successfully with them. Some copies did indeed exist (Fig. 36), but more extensive efforts were not made until 1604 when a royal franchise and patent were given to a Monsieur Fortier, who became 'tapissier ordinaire de Sa Majesté en tapiz de Turquie et façon de Levant'.[2] The most notable of the Western competitive enterprises was the 'Savonnerie' founded in 1605 by Pierre du Pont, which quite naturally tried at first to copy Turkish patterns. Other European countries followed suit, but in view of the rich influx from the Near East of greatly varied and probably cheaper examples all these industrial endeavours were of little avail (Figs. 43–5); they either stopped after a short time, as did a factory in Westminster which existed between 1750 and 1755, or turned to Western themes.

A special case was in Poland. There, about 1643, the Hetman Stanislaw Koniecpolski started factories in Brody which produced both textiles and carpets. The original intention was to copy

[1] K. Erdmann, *Siebenhundert Jahre Orientteppich*, pp. 69, 227–32.

[2] Idem, *Europa und der Orientteppich*, pp. 63–4.

Italian models, but since material from Italy or Spain was not available the patterns used became Eastern, both Persian and Turkish. At the beginning the designs were fairly close to the originals, but in the course of the seventeenth and eighteenth centuries they became more simple and more rigid (Fig. 46), so that they eventually resembled folk art.[1] As such they are not unique, as in the eighteenth and nineteenth centuries peasants of Spain, Italy, and even East Prussia produced pieces which echo Near Eastern prototypes, at times quite faithfully.[2] Still later echoes are to be found in the productions of William Morris, although here the dependence is more deliberate and rather self-conscious.[3]

Important as the craft of the Muslim metalsmith was in the Middle Ages, it seems to have exerted only a minor influence on the arts of Europe, possibly because the individual objects were usually too heavy to be carried back by the weary pilgrim or crusader. Still there is some evidence of the existence of such pieces and of their eventual impact. The earliest and most famous is the bronze griffin of Pisa, one of the outstanding metal objects of the Fāṭimid period of Egypt. At a later period, possibly in the seventeenth century, another celebrated medieval piece entered a royal Western collection under now unknown circumstances. But whenever that was, the so-called 'Baptistère de Saint Louis' arrived too late for the all-too-different style of its decoration to make an impression on contemporary artists. It was and remained only a curio, although towards the end of the eighteenth century a legendary and sacred association with Saint Louis of crusading fame became attached to this large inlaid basin which had been made in Egypt or Syria around 1300.[4] Such a crusading connection actually exists in the case of another such imported object, a basin long owned by the Dukes of Arenberg, and now in the

[1] Mańkowski, 'Influence of Islamic Art in Poland', pp. 98–105.

[2] Erdmann, *Siebenhundert Jahre Orientteppich*, pp. 240–5.

[3] G. H. Crow, *William Morris, Designer* (London, 1934), fig. on p. 81; Watkinson, op. cit., fig. 58 (a carpet design executed as an embroidery).

[4] D. S. Rice, *Le Baptistère de Saint Louis* (Paris, 1953), p. 9.

Freer Gallery of Art.[1] It was made for the Muslim opponent of the Crusaders, the Sultan al-Malik al-Ṣāliḥ Najm al-Dīn Ayyūb, just before the middle of the thirteenth century, and at some stage entered the ducal collections at a now uncertain moment, although, to judge from the engraved blazon on the base, this must have happened not later than the seventeenth century.

Unlike these large, remarkable, but uninfluential pieces, some smaller objects had a specific impact. Often the precise prototype is not known and the model can be established only by means of related pieces. The earliest group are Romanesque animal-shaped vessels of the twelfth century, usually called aquamaniles, which were used for the pouring of water. As they existed in the Near East earlier than in Europe, had the same functional features such as inlet and outlet pipes and animal-shaped handles, reproduced the same, often fantastic creatures of Near Eastern derivation, and showed the same stylization, their descent from Oriental models can hardly be questioned (Figs. 47–8).[2] Also of medieval date are a group of French objects of the second half of the thirteenth century, the enamelled copper basins made in pairs in Limoges and called *gemellions*, whose compositional schemes and decorative motifs have such a pronounced Islamic character that they seem to have been inspired by related Muslim pieces.[3] Again, there are the astrolabes which were made in such profusion in the Near East and then closely copied in Europe.[4] Happily, these astro-

[1] M. van Berchem, 'Arabische Inschriften', in F. Sarre and F. R. Martin, *Die Ausstellung von Meisterwerken muhammedanischer Kunst*, i. 6–8.

[2] O. von Falke and E. Meyer, *Bronzegeräte des Mittelalters* (Berlin, 1935); K. Erdmann, 'Islamische Giessgefässe des 11. Jahrhunderts', *Pantheon*, xxii (1938), 251; E. Meyer, 'Romanische Bronzen und ihre islamischen Vorbilder', in *Aus der Welt der islamischen Kunst. Festschrift für Ernst Kühnel*, pp. 317–22.

[3] H. Buchthal, 'A Note on Islamic Enamelled Metalwork and its Influence in the Latin West', *Ars Islamica*, xi–xii (1946), 195–8.

[4] R. W. T. Gunther, *The Astrolabes of the World* (Oxford, 1932); D. J. Price, 'An International Checklist of Astrolabes', *Archives Internationales d'Histoire des Sciences*, xxxii–xxxiii (1955), 243–63, 363–81; L. A. Mayer, *Islamic Astrolabists and their Works* (Geneva, 1956); idem, 'Islamic Astrolabists: Some New Material', in *Aus der Welt der islamischen Kunst. Festschrift für Ernst Kühnel*, pp. 293–6.

nomical instruments are often signed and dated so that their diffusion can be easily followed.

The influence of Islamic metalwork became even more pervasive towards the end of the fifteenth century when, at the very end of the period in which the inlay technique was used in the Near East, a large number of basins, bowls, platters, pitchers, and candlesticks executed by this process appeared in Venice, and possibly in other Italian towns as well, and continued to do so during the first half of the next century.[1] They are all made of very shiny brass which is delicately chased and inlaid with silver, and at times signed by members of a small group of artists although the pieces are never dated. They are known as 'Azzimina work' (a designation derived from the Arabic term *ʿAjamī*, denoting non-Arabs, and especially the Persians), a fact corroborated by one of the masters who was a Kurd (Fig. 49). These pieces have long been reputed to be the work of Near Eastern craftsmen working in Venice, but this assumption has recently been challenged, particularly on the grounds that the stringent and restrictive Venetian guild rules would have made it impossible. They may thus be Muslim objects made for export, possibly in Iran, which might explain the bilingual signature on one of them, a unique occurrence on a Near Eastern piece.[2] However, there is no doubt that the group exerted a strong influence on north-Italian production, which often copied the technique on objects of the same general shape, but with more Western arabesques and linear patterns (Fig. 50). The Oriental designs were probably also the model or at least the source of inspiration of the six copper engravings with circular, white-on-black, graphic exercises consisting of interlaced cord patterns which are datable to about 1483 to 1499. They are of Milanese

[1] L. A. Mayer, *Islamic Metalworkers and their Works* (Geneva, 1959): s.v. ʿAlā al-Dīn al-Bīrjandī, Muḥammad Badr, Maḥmūd al-Kurdī, Muḥammad, Qāsim, ʿUmar, and Zayn al-Dīn. A new critical discussion of the problem in H. Huth, *Lacquer of the West* (Chicago, 1969); idem, '"Sarazenen" in Venedig', in *Festschrift für Heinz Ladendorf* (Cologne–Vienna, 1970), pp. 58–68.

[2] B. W. Robinson, 'Oriental Metalwork in the Gambier-Perry Collection', *The Burlington Magazine*, cix (1967), 170–1.

origin and most likely go back to a follower of Leonardo da Vinci, who may have worked after designs by the master.[1] About 1507 they in turn were copied as woodcuts by another great artist, Albrecht Dürer, who refers to them in the diary of his journey in the Netherlands as 'Knoten' (Fig. 51).[2] Ingenious as these compositions are, they nevertheless fall short of similar patterns on Azzemina work where the main motifs are made up of the same light, narrow, silver-inlaid lines of the same width throughout, which appear as the major theme and are set against a darker, more delicate, and denser secondary set of themes, which neither the Italian versions nor the German copies produced (Fig. 52). These designs together with those on the *Tükenbeute*, i.e. objects captured from the Turks, were the precursors of the widely spread fashion for *mauresques* which was started in 1530 by the woodcut book of Francesco Pellegrino, when working in Fontainebleau. They appear in a work entitled *La Fleur de la science de broderie*, *façon arabicque et ytalique*.[3] It contains black, flat arabesque and floral designs as well as interlacings set against a white background which, in their two-dimensionality, loose spacing, and spirited movement, are very close to their Islamic counterparts. From 1540 onwards, this idea was taken up by the printers of Paris and Lyons (Figs. 53–4), as well as by craftsmen designing for goldsmiths who worked in Italy, France, Switzerland, Germany, and Flanders.[4] However, the arabesques soon lose their sharp pristine outlines

[1] A. M. Hind, 'Two Unpublished Plates of the Series of Six "Knots" Engraved after Designs by Leonardo da Vinci', *The Burlington Magazine*, xii (1908), 41; R. Berliner, *Ornamentale Vorlageblätter des 15. bis 18. Jahrhunderts* (Leipzig, 1926), Pl. 23. 2 and text, p. 12.

[2] V. Scherer, *Dürer* (Klassiker der Kunst, iv), 2nd edn. (Stuttgart-Leipzig, 1906), Pls. 223–5; E. Panofsky, *Albrecht Dürer* (Princeton, 1943), i. 121, ii. 44, no. 360.

[3] P. Jessen, *Der Ornamentstich Geschichte der Vorlagen des Kunsthandwerke seit dem Mittelalter* (Berlin, 1920), p. 63; idem, *Meister des Ornamentstichs*, i (Berlin, n.d.), Pls. 134–5; R. Berliner, *Ornamentale Vorlageblätter*, i. 79–82, ii. 34.

[4] Jessen, *Ornamentstich*, pp. 63–6, 95, 103; idem, *Meister* . . ., i, Pls. 83–5, 91, 98, 136–7, 170–3; Berliner, op. cit., i, Pls. 83–99, iii, pp. 35–8.

and strict two-dimensionality, and become more complex, although they never belie their Near Eastern origin. Distinguished artists who worked in this manner were Peter Flötner, Manuel Deutsch, Jean de Gourmont, and the anonymous artist whose work was brought out by the Antwerp publisher, Gieronymus Cock. Even Hans Holbein the Younger belonged to this group, as he composed some arabesque designs in 1537. Limited in time as the style was, it was the closest approach to the adoption of a truly Islamic mode into the Western idion. It was much more than a mere exercise in design by some major or minor artists, for these *mauresques*, often closely resembling Near Eastern arabesques, appeared on many objects of daily use but of fashionable allure ranging from gaming boards and musical instruments to shields like those made in Venice for the Archbishop of Salzburg (Figs. 55–7).

Although pottery breaks easily and is consequently difficult to transport, medieval specimens reached Europe in limited numbers from the Near East. Proof of this is found in the so-called *bacini*, flat, round, glazed vessels which for colouristic effects are set into the fabric of some Italian churches, whether in the façade or the campanile.[1] As these are not easily accessible to investigators, they have never been systematically studied, but there is little doubt that wares from different Muslim countries, especially Egypt, are prominently displayed among them. That pottery was also put to more direct use is shown by a rare twelfth-century white, carved, semi-porcelain cup, a fragment of which is still preserved as the Chalice of Saint Girolamo, originally from S. Anastasia, now in the Museo Sacro of the Vatican (Fig. 58).[2] In the fourteenth century the Hispano-Islamic lustre pottery of Andalusia was valued very

[1] G. B(allardini), 'Pomposa e i suoi bacini', *Faenza*, xxiv (1936), 121–8 (mostly Egyptian); E. Biavati, 'Bacini di Pisa', ibid., xxxviii (1952), 92–4 (mostly Byzantine, at least one Persian).

[2] W. F. Volbach, 'Reliquie et reliquiari orientali in Roma', *Bolletino d'Arte* xxx, serie III (1937), 347–8. The Vatican owns a second ceramic object, once used as a reliquary, which is an Egyptian copy of the ninth or tenth century of a Chinese pottery type called 'splashed ware' (ibid., p. 348 and fig. 12).

highly, both in Europe and the Muslim East. Complete pieces have been found in the West as far apart as Sicily and Schleswig-Holstein, while fragments galore have been discovered in the rubbish heaps of Fusṭāṭ in Egypt. It is, therefore, not surprising that in the fifteenth and early sixteenth centuries the lustre platters, dishes, and vases of Valencia with appropriate coats of arms became the most coveted status symbols, owned not only by the great families of Spain but also by such leaders of European taste as the Dukes of Burgundy, the Medicis of Florence, the Kings of Naples, and even by a Pope, Leo X.[1] A more direct influence of Islamic pottery and particularly of its Hispanic-Muslim varieties with their tin glazes and *sgraffito*, or lustre decorations, can be seen in the nascent Italian pottery production, which was soon to enjoy such an extraordinary flowering.[2] Certain shapes, such as small bowls, vases, pots, and the drug jars called *albarelli*, as well as specific decorative motifs, were readily taken over, and the artistic effects of the techniques which had originated in the Near East and had been developed in Spain were still further refined in the different Italian centres. However, before long they turned to a figural imagery quite alien to the East and with it a specifically Western type of pottery came into being.

Islamic glass, being even more fragile than pottery, has been found in only a few medieval European sites, although the discovery of such glass objects in Sweden, southern Russia, and even in China, indicates that distance did not always prevent their being transported. As usual they found their ultimate resting place in cathedrals, churches, or abbeys, where they were thought at times to be crusader gifts, or to hail from Charlemagne himself.[3] The

[1] A. W. Frothingham, *Lustre Ware of Spain* (New York, 1951), figs. 58, 69, 82, 88, 109, 120, 123.

[2] B. Rackham, *Guide to Italian Maiolica* (London, 1933), pp. 1-2, 8, 82; idem, *Catalogue of Italian Maiolica* (London, 1940), compare with Frothingham, op. cit., *passim*, and José Martinez Ortiz-Jaime de Scals Aracil, *Colección cerámica del Museo Histórico Municipal de Valencia, Ciclo Paterna-Manises* (Valencia, 1962).

[3] C. J. Lamm, *Mittelalterliche Gläser* (Berlin, 1930), i. Pls. 274 (no. 1), 275 (no. 2), 329 (no. 1), ii, Pls. 96 (nos. 1 and 3) and 127 (no. 1).

most celebrated of these ecclesiastical treasures, now in St. Stephen's in Vienna, is an enamelled Syrian pilgrim bottle of about 1280, said to contain earth from Bethlehem which was saturated with the blood of the Innocents. The rich decoration of this piece, which was made for an unnamed sultan, is somewhat incongruous in a sacred setting, for it contains various secular subjects including a party of revellers and musicians seated at the water's edge.[1] Pieces in private collections exist also. Here the best-known piece (which according to a well-known legend should actually no longer exist) is a Syrian beaker of about 1240, the so-called 'Luck of Edenhall' whose alleged destruction, under dramatic circumstances, has been poetically described by Ludwig Uhland and, following him, by Longfellow (Fig. 59). Other objects are known to us from inventories.[2] For instance, those of Charles V, King of France (1379–80) list 'troys pots de voirre . . . à la façon de Damas', and in addition a basin, a lamp flacon, and other glasses from the same place. In the next century the inventory of Piero Cosimo de Medici is likewise full of such objects 'di vetro domaschini'.[3]

Some of these Syrian glass objects have been discovered in various places in the Holy Land, and it is, therefore, not surprising that fragments have also been unearthed in the Crusader Castle of Montfort which was destroyed in 1272. As far as one can tell, their decoration, consisting mostly of inscriptions, was completely in the Muslim idiom.[4] But there are five pieces, also apparently Syrian, which although executed in a traditional enamelling technique nevertheless show purely Western subjects. These include not only European coats of arms but also representations of the Holy Roman Emperor, an enthroned Madonna and Child, Latin invocations to the *Domina Mater*, and even the signature of an

[1] Ibid. i. Pl. 368 (no. 3), ii, Pl. 158 (no. 3); G. Schmoranz, *Altorientasische Glassgefässe* (Vienna, 1898), pp. 29–30, Pls. 4, 4A.

[2] Lamm, *Mittelalterliche Gläser*, i. Pl. 329 (no. 2), ii, Pl. 127 (no. 2).

[3] Ibid. ii. Pl. 494 (no. 68), 495 (no. 71).

[4] Ibid. i. Pl. 326 (no. 12), vol. ii, Pl. 126 (no. 12).

Italian Magister Aldrevandinus.[1] These pieces form a link with the later Venetian work. As is well known, the craftsmen there used the Near Eastern enamelling technique and they also copied certain forms of decoration, especially the ever-popular application of rows of pearls and of scale patterns.

Objects made of rock crystal and ivory might seem to be so rare as to be of little significance in this survey, yet they too contribute to our understanding of the underlying issue. They are almost exclusively known to us from the pieces preserved in the West, especially in ecclesiastical establishments. We know nothing about the use of ivory from Muslim sources. There is the case of the ivory hunting-horn, called *oliphant* in various Western languages, of which about thirty carved pieces with Islamic decorations have been preserved. These are the survivors of a much larger number, as according to early records there used to be nine such *cornea eburnea* in Winchester alone, and six in Speyer, while Salisbury and Limoges each had four, of which to judge from the still preserved examples, about half must have been Muslim.[2] The second point to be made is one which was made earlier: that although the ivory and rock crystal pieces were originally destined for secular use they were nearly always re-employed in a religious context. They usually became reliquaries (or were associated with them), as the magnificent bottles in the Treasury of Saint Marc, or of San Lorenzo in Florence testify, where one of them contains a relic as sacred as the Holy Blood. The rock crystals also became endowed with Christian didactic values. Owing to their hardness and penetrability by light, they came to symbolize the mystery of the Virgin birth. This was envisaged, for instance, by St. Bridget, according to whom Christ had said, 'I have assumed flesh without sin and lust, entering the womb of the Virgin just as the sun passes through a precious stone'.[3]

[1] Lamm, op. cit., i. 246, 278–9, vol. ii, Pl. 99.

[2] E. Kühnel, 'Die sarazenischen Olifanthörner', in *Jahrbuch der Berliner Museen*, i (1959), 33, n. 1; idem, *Die islamischen Elfenbeinskulpturen* (Berlin, 1971).

[3] M. Meiss, 'Light as Form and Symbol in some Fifteenth Century Paintings', *The Art Bulletin*, xxvii (1945), 177.

Even so ancillary an art as bookbinding showed the imprint of Islam. There were first the technical improvements which Europe learned from its Eastern neighbours. These were the substitution of cardboard for wood as the core material for the covers, and then the gilding of the leather, especially by means of a hot tool. In the latter case we have an actual gauge to establish the Muslim priority over Europe: the first mention of a gilding process occurs in a North African technical handbook pertaining to the arts of the book, written between 1062 and 1108, while the first gold-tooled binding for an Almohad sultan of Morocco dates from 1256. On the other hand the earliest known Western use of this technique is Italian and dates from 1459,[1] and the history of the craft in its most creative period, the second half of the sixteenth century, cannot be understood without taking Muslim bindings into special consideration. (Fig. 60).

Miniature painting is the last art to have made an impression on the West. Here it was primarily the art of the Great Moguls of India which exerted a noticeable influence. The reverse of a Milanese enamelled medallion showing a bust portrait of the Emperor Jahāngīr with a falcon on his right wrist is, so far, the earliest evidence of this cultural impact to come to light. We have internal evidence that the model painting must have dated from before 1605 when Jahāngīr ascended the throne.[2] It was then engraved on to the oval area, and the piece was undoubtedly intended as a diplomatic gift for the emperor who was an avid collector of Western *objets de vertu* and of miniatures as well. Of greater significance is the fact that Rembrandt had a collection of more than two dozen Mogul and even Deccani paintings which he copied in his inimitable style before he was forced to sell them about 1656.[3] They are portraits mostly of a courtly nature, and even

[1] R. Ettinghausen, 'Near Eastern Book Covers and their Influence on European Bindings', *Ars Orientalis*, iii (1959), 121–2; A. R. A. Hobson, 'Two Renaissance Bindings', *The Book Collector*, vii (1958), 265–6.

[2] T. Hackenbroch, 'A Royal Gift', *The Connoisseur*, clxxiv (1970), 152–7.

[3] F. Sarre, 'Rembrandts Zeichnungen nach indisch-islamischen Miniaturen', *Jahrbuch der Königl. Preussischen Kunstsammlungen*, xxv (1904), 143–58; idem, 'Ein

Rembrandt's chiaroscuro manner which was, of course, alien to the originals did not change their innate character and various subjects can still be identified. These hurried, though skilful, sketches were probably destined to serve as an iconographic repertory of Oriental themes to be used later on. What is, however, more important for us than this insight into Rembrandt's working methods is his fascination with these paintings which must have attracted him on account of their exotic flavour. It is significant that Delacroix too copied miniatures from the Muslim world. He copied figures not only from Indian but also from Persian paintings, apparently the first time that the latter actively charmed a great master of Western painting.[1] The pervasive influence of painting appears in still another totally different context, although the sources of transmission remain unknown. There are a number of Baroque automata, primarily clocks, which must ultimately derive from the book of automata by al-Jazarī, written about 1206 and illustrating the same kind of artfully complex machinery, full of startling surprises.[2] A clock of that type had long before been brought by an ambassador of Hārūn al-Rashīd to the Court of Charlemagne. Later on, however, the wheel clocks of Europe had in general replaced these earlier water-powered mechanisms which the Arabs had taken over from the Alexandrine physicists and further developed.

This survey may be likened to a searchlight which has illuminated a landscape and brought certain details into full view,

neues Blatt von Rembrandts indischen Zeichnungen', ibid. xxx (1909), 283–90; recently another of the missing seven copies of Indian miniatures has been found (*Sotheby's 217th Season, Oct., 1960–July, 1961* (London–New York, 1961), p. 138). It was there entitled 'Shah Jahan Talking to his Falconer', although the Emperor and the Falconer, apparently an Imperial Prince, are two individual sketches which were combined on the same sheet.

[1] R. Escholier, *Eugène Delacroix* (Paris, 1963), colour pl. opp. p. 192; J. Meier-Graefe, *Eugène Delacroix, Beiträge zu seiner Analyse* (Munich, n.d.), p. 162 (copies after Indian miniatures); R. Huyghe, *Delacroix* (New York–London, 1963), figs. 100–1 (copies after Persian miniatures).

[2] W. Born, 'Early European Automatons I', *The Connoisseur*, c (1937), 123–9.

while leaving others in a dim haze or even in darkness. However, it seems sufficient to provide certain insights into the nature of the meeting between Europe and the Near East. It has been shown that there were two major periods in which this encounter took place: the eleventh to the thirteenth century, and then again the years from the end of the fifteenth century and throughout the sixteenth. The first period, of course, is that of the Crusades, and although we do not have much information about how the objects were transported, there seems little doubt that those far-ranging events greatly aided a transfer of goods. The second period is that of the Renaissance when a new freedom of spirit and a new world-awareness overcame old prejudices. There were, of course, other times of cultural exchange even before the Crusades, but there was apparently never the same large and varied body of material involved.

A second conclusion to be drawn from this survey is that the regions of the Near East which were the primary sources of import and inspiration are located in the Mediterranean area, namely, Egypt, Syria, Spain, and North Africa, and later Turkey. Countries like Iran and India played a much less important role, and such marginal regions as the Caucasus and Central Asia were even less significant. It is indicative of these relationships that Caucasian carpets are very rarely represented in Western paintings, and that Central Asian rugs reached Europe only in the second half of the nineteenth century.

The third point concerns the aspects of the arts which served as models. It seems symptomatic that it was usually not the objects themselves, their shape and function, which were creatively taken over for further development, although this did happen—in the Azzimina type of metalwork, for instance. What the West appreciated and tried to imitate were the patterns. This applies particularly to the animal designs and their organizational schemes as found on medieval textiles, as well as to the arabesque and knot designs which fascinated the Renaissance artists. In other words, the West had from the beginning an instinctive awareness of what represented the most basic nature of Islamic art, namely its ability to decorate flat surfaces with appealing patterns.

The fourth point relates to the manner of incorporating Near Eastern art forms. It cannot be compared with the process which led to the appearance of certain words of Near Eastern origin in Western languages. These are like luggage acquired at a foreign port and carried along on an extensive journey. The nature of adoption is also different from the continuous challenge exerted by the arts of antiquity on those of the Renaissance. What we encounter is rather a sporadic digestive process in which certain patterns were assimilated into the general artistic complex, where they soon lost their identity.

What then was the value of this encounter? It must be admitted that, although our survey mentioned such illustrious names as Leonardo, Dürer, and Holbein, the impact of the Near East on the art of Europe has, on the whole, not been vital. It has enriched the fare and at times given it a special flavour. However, if it had never happened, the arts of the West would, with the possible exception of Rembrandt and Delacroix, have taken the same direction and come to the same conclusions. The encounter was probably too sporadic and limited in scope to have borne real fruit. Moreover the offered forms did not appeal to the deepest emotions, and as they were not akin to or identical with the major Western categories of painting and sculpture they were never readily appreciated. They remained largely curios tucked away in church treasuries rather than serving as inspiring models which touched the Western soul. The very blandness of the design, which first made it possible for Eastern art to be acceptable in Europe, militated against its making a deeper impression. A great deal of the production was also merely due to the manual dexterity of craftsmen who could not be observed in their workshops. Hence there were no great technical achievements involved which might have captivated the West.

The ultimate incompatibility is perhaps most clearly demonstrated by that group of art objects which probably made the longest and most pervasive impact on Europe, Oriental carpets.

Here the approach to the artefact is quite different in the East and West. In the East one sits and rests on the carpet, in closest physical and visual contact with it, so that its imagery can be readily studied, especially as it is unencumbered by massive furniture of a different material. In the West the carpet is not an object of similar scrutiny: one sits high up on a chair, in a room filled with tables, sofas, and *fauteuils* which obstruct the sight of the extensive floor-covering, while paintings, tapestries, or patterned wallpaper provide further distraction. It is true that the use of the Oriental carpet as a table cover provided the possibility of closer viewing, but here we are again confronted with a usage which was quite alien to Near Eastern custom. As a result of this disparity of spirit it was, therefore, natural that the West was never able to create an analogous product which could compete successfully with the Oriental carpet.[1]

The attitude of the West towards Eastern objects is brought into even sharper focus when we observe the impact of the political reality. Here we are referring to the Turkish Wars which, from the sixteenth century on, forced Europe to recognize and to come to terms with a formidable Eastern power. This resulted in a direct and often prolonged influence on the arts of the West. The impact of the Battle of Lepanto of 1571 lasted for well over 100 years and was made evident not only in paintings but also in sculptures, etchings, and broadsheets, as well as in church furniture and ecclesiastic implements (Fig. 61). When the power of the Turks waned in the eighteenth century, the Turks became less awe-inspiring and they could be rendered as dainty porcelain figures, or be admired in costume books. The presence of a Near Eastern political power remained, however, a conscious reality. No such long-lasting highly diversified response was exerted by the arts. Even so receptive a person as Delacroix was not primarily attracted by the arts when he visited Tangier, Morocco, and Algeria in 1832. What overwhelmed him were the human types and the whole *ambiance* with its teeming life of men and animals, 'the living,

[1] Erdmann, *Europa und der Orientteppich*, pp. 112–13, 117.

emphatic sublime' as he called it. The degenerative trend in Islamic art which had especially affected the Arab world may very well have contributed to this more ethnographic attitude. However, not only artists, but scholars too were equally blind. Four large albums with superb Persian paintings and drawings of the fourteenth and fifteenth centuries, which had belonged to the Prussian State Library since 1817, remained unknown until 1956 when they were discovered when a special exhibition was arranged in Tübingen. They had not been catalogued earlier because they contained no religious or literary texts! It was only in the opening years of the twentieth century that the development of research in the history of Islamic art created a new and deepening understanding of this field, and helped to educate the public by means of museum displays of outstanding objects and by the organization of many large and small exhibitions all over the Western world.

RICHARD ETTINGHAUSEN

BIBLIOGRAPHY

All the important books and articles published to 1st January 1960, are listed in K. A. C. Creswell, *A Bibliography of the Architecture, Arts, and Crafts of Islam to 1st January, 1960* (Cairo, 1961), columns 1297–1326. They are grouped there under the headings: Influence on the West; General; Architecture; Bookbinding; Ceramics; Metal; Painting; Textiles; Woodwork; Arabic Figures and Cufic Letters. The following presents a list of the more significant and more recent publications.

J. Alazard, *L'Orient et la peinture française au XIXe siècle, d'Eugène Delacroix à Auguste Renoir* (Paris, 1930); G. Amardel, 'Les Faïences à reflets métalliques fabriquées à Narbonne', in *Bulletin de la commission archéologique de Narbonne*, xii (1912), 421–35; Sir Thomas Arnold, 'Islamic Art and its Influence on Painting in Europe', in *The Legacy of Islam*, eds. Sir Thomas Arnold and Alfred Guillaume (Oxford, 1931), pp. 151–4; G. Ballardini, 'Alcuni cenni sull'influenza mongolo—persiana nelle faenze del secolo decimosesto', in *Faenza*, vii (1919), 49–59, and pls. III–VII; idem, 'Elementi orientali nella decorazione delle maioliche primitive', in *Faenza*, v (1917), 39–42 and pl. III; J. Baltrušaitis, *Le Moyen âge fantastique: antiquités et exotismes dans l'art gothique* (Paris, 1955); W. Bode, 'Die Anfänge der

Majolikakunst in Florenz unter dem Einfluss der hispanomoresken Majoliken', in *Jahrbuch der kgl. Preuszischen Kunstsammlungen*, xxix (1908), 276–98; L. Bréhier, 'Les Thémes décoratifs des tissus d'orient et leur imitation dans la sculpture romane', in *Études d'Art*, i (Alger, 1945), 25–63; B[ucher], 'Die Gürtelfabrik zu Sluck', in *Mitteilungen der k.k. Oesterreich. Museums für Kunst und Industrie*, N. F., x (1895), 481–2; H. Buchthal, 'A Note on Islamic Enamelled Metalwork and its Influence in the Latin West', in *Ars Islamica*, xi–xii (1946), 195–8; A. H. Christie, 'Islamic Minor Arts and their Influence upon European Works', in *The Legacy of Islam*, 1st edn., pp. 108–51; idem, 'The Development of Ornament from Arabic Script', in *Burlington Magazine*, xl (1922), 287–92; Mrs. R. L. Devonshire, *Quelques Influences islamiques sur les arts de l'Europe* (Cairo, 1935); C. Diehl, 'La Peinture orientaliste en italie au temps de la renaissance', in *Revue de l'art ancien et moderne*, xix (1906), 5–16 and 143–56; K. Erdmann, *Arabische Schriftzeichen als Ornamente in der abendländischen Kunst des Mittelalters*, Mainz Akademie der Wissenschaften und der Literatur, Geistes- und sozial Wissenschaftliche Klasse, Abhandlung, Nr. 9 (1953) (also vol. 1954, pp. 467–513); idem, *Europa und der Orientteppich* (Berlin-Mainz, 1962); idem, *Seven Hundred Years of Oriental Carpets*, ed. Hanna Erdmann, translated by M. H. Beattie and Hildegard Herzog (Berkeley and Los Angeles, 1970) (see in particular the chapters: Early Carpets in Western Paintings, Oriental Carpets in Paintings of the Renaissance and the Baroque, Carpets with European Blazons, Spanish Carpets, European Peasant Carpets); R. Ettinghausen, 'Foundation-Moulded Leatherwork—a Rare Egyptian Technique also used in Britain', in *Studies in Islamic Art and Architecture in Honour of Professor K. A. C. Creswell* (The American University in Cairo Press, 1965), pp. 63–71; idem, 'Near Eastern Book Covers and their Influence on European Bindings. A Report on the Exhibition "History of Bookbinding" at the Baltimore Museum of Art, 1957–58', *Ars Orientalis*, iii (1959), 113–31; A. Geijer, 'Oriental Textiles in Scandinavian Versions', in *Festschrift für Ernst Kühnel* (Berlin, 1959), pp. 323–35; Gerspach, 'Die alte Teppichfabrication in Paris', in *Orientalische Teppiche* (Vienna, 1892[–96]), 2 pp.; H. A. R. Gibb, 'The Influence of Islamic Culture on Medieval Europe', *Bulletin of the John Rylands Library*, xxxviii (1955–6), 82–98; H. Goetz, 'Oriental Types and Scenes in Renaissance and Baroque Painting', in the *Burlington Magazine*, lxxiii (1938), 50–62 and 105–15; idem, 'Persians and Persian Costumes in Dutch Painting of the Seventeenth Century', in *The Art Bulletin*, xx (1938), 280–90; T. Gottlieb, 'Venezianer Einbände des XV. Jahrhunderts nach persischen Mustern', *Kunst und Kunsthandwerk*, xvi (1913), 153–76; A. Graban, 'Elements sassanides et islamiques dans les enluminures des manuscrits espagnoles du haut moyen âge', in *L'Art de la fin de l'antiquité et du moyen âge* (Paris, 1968), ii. 663–8; idem, 'Le Succès des arts orentaux à la cour byzantine sous les Macédoniens', in ibid. i. 265–90; W. Hein, 'Islamische Gläser, Syrische emaillierte Gläser und ihre Rezeption vou der Gründer Zeit bis Gallé. Moscheeampeln und ihre Nachahmungen. Joseph Brocard. Ludwig Lobmeyr, Anonyme Gläser. Gläser aus Russland. Emile Gallé', in *Weltkulturen und Moderne Kunst* (for full title, see below, p. 320), pp. 80–8; G. F. Hill, 'On the Early Use of the Arabic Numerals in Europe', in *Archaeologia*, lxii (1910), 137–90; idem, *The Development of Arabic Numerals in Europe, exhibited in sixty-four tables* (Oxford, 1915), 125 pp.; W. L.

Hillburgh, '"Dinanderie" Ewers with Venetian-Saracenic Decoration', in *Burlington Magazine*, lxxix (1941), 17-22; H. L. (= H. Ludwig), 'Die Iznik-Kopien von Théodore Deck und seinen Zeitgenossen', in *Weltkulturen und Moderne Kunst*, pp. 66-8; idem, 'Graphik', in *Weltkulturen und Moderne Kunst*, pp. 134-8; idem, 'Odalisken', in *Weltkulturen und Moderne Kunst*, p. 122; idem, 'Paul Dresler', in *Weltkulturen und Moderne Kunst*, pp. 74-6 (followed by 'Persische-spanische Vorbilder und ihre Nachahmungen. Alhambra-Vasen. Metallarbeiten', pp. 76-80); 'Pfauenmotive', in *Weltkulturen und Moderne Kunst*, pp. 94-6; D. R. Howell, 'al Khadr and Christian Icons', in *Ars Orientalis*, vii (1968), 41-51; R. A. Jairazbhoy, *Oriental Influences in Western Art* (Bombay, 1965); idem, 'The Decorative Use of Arabic Lettering in the West', in *The Islamic Review*, xliv (November, 1956), 23-9; A. F. Kendrick, 'The Italian Silk Fabrics of the Fourteenth Century', in *Magazine of Fine Arts* (1906), pp. 202-11 and 415-23; E. Kühnel, 'Oriente y occidente en el arte medieval', *Archivo Español de Arte*, xv (1942), 92-6; idem, 'Persische Einflüsse in der Malerei des Abendlandes', in *Forschungen und Fortschrifte*, vii (1931), 250-1; S. Lane-Poole, 'A Venetian Azzimina of the Sixteenth Century', in *Magazine of Art*, ix (1886), 450-3; H. Lavoix, 'Les Arts musulmans: de l'ornamentation arabe dans les œuvres des maîtres italiens', *Gazette des Beaux-Arts*, 2e période, xvi (1877), 15-29; idem, 'Les Azziministes', in *Gazette des Beaux-Arts*, 1er période, xii (1862), 64-74; J. de Loewenstein, 'À propos d'un tableau de W. Schellinks s'inspirant des miniatures mongholes', in *Arts asiatiques*, v (1958), 293-8; A. de Longpérier, 'De l'emploi des caractères arabes dans l'ornamentation chez les peuples chrétiens de l'occident', in *Revue Archéologique*, 2e année (1845), 696-706; H. Ludwig, 'Aspekte zur Orientalischen Ornamentik und zur Kunst des 20. Jahrhunderts', in *Weltkulturen und Moderne Kunst*, pp. 123-33; 'Orientalische Motive in Buchpublikationen', in *Weltkulturen und Moderne Kunst*, pp. 138-43; L. Magne, *Le Palais de Justice de Poitiers: étude sur l'art française au XIVe et au XVe siècle*, Librairie centrale des Beaux-Arts (Paris, 1904), 172 pp., with 37 plates; É. Mâle, Études sur l'art à l'époque romane', in *Revue de Paris*, 28e année (1921), 491-513 and 711-32; T. Mańkowski, 'Influence of Islamic Art in Poland', *Ars Islamica*, ii (1935), 93-117; G. Marçais, 'Sur l'inscription arabe de la cathédrale du Puy', in *Comptes Rendus de l'Academie des Inscriptions et Belles-Lettres* (1938), 156-62; Marquet de Vasselot, 'Ornamentation inspirée des caractères coufiques dans les manuscrits de Citeaux', in *Bulletin de la Société Nationale des Antiquaires de France* (1925), 226-8; U. Martens, 'Orientalisierende Architektur in Berlin', in *Weltkulturen und Moderne Kunst*, pp. 59-65 (Einrichtungsgegenstände, pp. 63-5; Theaterdekorationen, p. 65); P. W. Meister, 'Orientalische Textilien und die europäische Mode', in *Weltkulturen und Moderne Kunst*, pp. 97-101; F. de Mély, 'Intaille avec caractères coufiques au reliquaire de la vraie Croix à Journai', in *Bulletin de la Société Nationale des Antiquaires de France* (1926), 187-9; E. Meyer, 'Romanische Bronzen und ihre islamischen Vorbilder', in *Festschrift für Ernst Kühnel* (Berlin, 1959), pp. 317-22; L. M. Michon, 'Influence de l'art oriental sur la reliure française au début du XVIe siècle', in *Bulletin de la Société Nationale des Antiquaires de France* (1938), 195; L. Olschki, 'Asiatic Exotism in Italian art of the Early Renaissance', in *The Arts Bulletin*, ii (1944), 95-106; R. Pinkham, 'William De Morgans islamische und östliche Quellen', in *Weltkulturen und Moderne Kunst*, pp. 69–74; P. Post, 'Orientalische Einflüsse auf die europäische Panzerung der Mittelalters', *Zeitschrift für historische Waffen- und Kostümkunde*, N.F., ii (1928), 239–40; A. Poulet, J. Mailey, V. K. Ostoia, M. Glaze, A. St. Clair, J. M. Dennis, J. Parker, E. Winternitz, and M. H. Heckscher, 'Turquerie', in *Bulletin*, *The Metropolitan Museum of Art*, xxvi (Jan., 1968), 225–39; S. Reich, 'Une inscription mamlouke sur un dessin italien du quinzième siècle', in *Bulletin de l'Institut d'Égypte*, xxii (1940), 123–31; A. Renan, 'La Peinture orientaliste', *Gazette des Beaux-Arts*, 3e période, xi (1894), 43–53; D. S. Rice, 'Arabic Inscriptions on a Brass Basin made for Hugh IV de Lusignan', *Studi Orientalistici in onore di Giorgio Levi della Vida* (Rome, 1956), ii. 390–402; A. Riegal, 'Die Beziehungen der orientalischen Teppichfabrication zu dem europäischen Abendlande', in *Mitteilungen des k.k. Oesterreich. Museums für Kunst und Industrie*, N.F., iii (1890), 210–11 and 234–41; Ét. Sabbe, 'L'Importation des tissus orientaux en Europe occidentale au haut moyen âge (IXe et Xe siècles), in *Revue Belge de Philologie et d'Histoire*, xiv (1935), 810–48 and 1261–88; F. Sarre, 'Der Import orientalischer Keramik nach Italien im Mittelalter und in der Renaissance', in *Forschungen und Fortschritte*, xi (1933), 423–4; idem, 'Ein neues Blatt von Rembrandts indischen Zeichnungen', in *Jahrbuch der kgl. Preuszischen Kunstsammlungen*, xxx (1909), 283–90; idem, 'Rembrandt Zeichnungen nach indischislamischen Miniaturen', in *Jahrbuch der kgl. Preuszichen Kunstsammlungen*, xxv (1904), 143–58; 'The Connexion between the Pottery of Miletus and the Florentine Maiolica of the Fifteenth Century', in *Transactions of the Oriental Ceramic Society* [*1931–1932*] (1933), 16–19 and pls. II–IV; F. Saxl, 'Probleme der Planetenkinderbilden', *Kunstchronik und Kunstmark*, N.F., xxx (1919), 1013–21; M. Shapiro, 'The Angel with the Ram in Abraham's Sacrifice: A Parallel in Western and Islamic Art', in *Ars Islamica*, x (1943), 134–47; H. Schmidt, 'Rembrandt der islamische Orient und die Antike, in *Festschrift für Ernst Kühnel*, pp. 336–49; J. H. Schmidt, 'Turkish Brocades and Italian Imitations', in *The Art Bulletin*, xv (1933), 374–83; T. Sehmer, *Das Geheimnis der Gabriels-Kapelle zu Salzburg. Ein einmaliges harmonisches Nebeneinander von Klassisch italienischer Renaissance und ebenso reiner islamischer Fliesen Kunst* (Innsbruck-Munich, 1972); D. G. Shepherd, 'A thirteenth-century textile', in *Bulletin of the Cleveland Museum of Art*, xxxv (1948), 111–12; D. E. Smith and L. C. Karpinski, *The Hindu-Arabic Numerals* (Boston, 1911), 160 pp.; M. L. Solon, 'The Lustred Tile Pavement of the Palais de Justice of Poitiers', in *Burlington Magazine*, xii (1907), 83–6; G. Soulier, 'Les caractères coufiques dans la peinture toscane', in *Gazette des Beaux-Arts*, 5e période, ix (1924), 347–58; *Les Influences orientales dans la peinture toscane* (Paris, 1924); K. M. Swoboda, 'Berührungen der christlich-abendländischen Kunst mit der des Islam', *Weiner Kunstwissenschaftliche Blätter*, *Alte und Neue Kunst*, i (1952), 7–33; J.-L. Vaudoyer, 'L'Orientalisme en Europe du XVIIIe siècle', *Gazette des Beaux-Arts*, 4e période, vi (1911), 89–102; Volbach, 'Über die Verwendung eines frühmittelalterlichen orientalischen motives in der romanischen kunst des Abendlandes', in *Amtliche Berichte aus den Königlichen Kunstsammlungen*, xlii (1919), col. 143–50 and Abb. 73–6; idem, *Weltkulturen und Moderne Kunst. Die Begegnung der europäischen Kunst und Musik im 19. und 20. Jahrhundert mit Asien*, *Afrika*, *Ozeanien*, *Afro- und Indo-Amerika*, ed. S. Wichmann (Ausstellung Veraustaltet vom Organisationskomitee für die Spiele der XX.

Olympiade) (München, 1972); S. Wichmann, 'Das Rosensprenggefäss in seiner Stellung zwischen Orient und Okzident um 1900', in ibid., pp. 91–3; idem, 'Lüstergläser des Art nouveau in der Begegnung mit dem Orient', in ***Weltkilturen und Moderne Kunst***, pp. 89–91.

VII

LITERATURE

AFTER the invention of writing, 'literature' was everything that was written for general communication. From the eighth century onwards, the spread of paper, a comparatively inexpensive and eventually ubiquitous writing material, made possible an unprecedented growth of literary production in the Muslim world. With it came an increasing compartmentalization of individual fields and scholarly disciplines. The border lines were, however, never drawn sharply. To some degree, it remained true throughout medieval Islam that every book or every pamphlet regardless of its contents was 'literature'. Our own restriction of the word to, primarily, non-utilitarian and entertaining writing was made possible only through another great step forward in technical efficiency, the invention of printing. It became fully accepted only during the eighteenth century.

The Muslim view of literature in a restricted sense can be deduced from the way in which Ibn al-Nadīm classified his material in his *Fihrist*, a comprehensive catalogue of books compiled around 987. The Koran and the Koranic sciences came first. For religious and historical reasons, this is as it should be. However, the Koran was also a linguistic document of incomparable importance. It was viewed as a source of grammatical and lexicographical information. Its stylistic inimitability notwithstanding, it even came to be treated as a standard for theories of literary criticism. The proper and elevated use of language was, in fact, the determining criterion for the *Fihrist*'s classification of literature. Following the Koranic sciences, Ibn al-Nadīm therefore logically lists the grammarians and lexicographers and their works. They provide the necessary foundation for all literary efforts. Philology is followed by historiography and poetry. These are the three major fields teaching and demanding the artistic use of language. The work done in these fields includes scholarly and didactic writings, but a large number of titles—of varying extent in the three fields—refers to works of literature in a narrow sense.

After the necessary linguistic and literary preparation has been acquired, the religious and secular sciences can and may be studied. Ibn al-Nadīm discusses them in the following chapters. But then, he has another chapter in which he lists a large number of titles on such subjects as military science, cookery, perfumes, erotica, oneirocritics, and various kinds of magic. This chapter also includes the titles of a variety of works of fiction, tales of Arab lovers, heroes, and humorists, mariners' tales (which already at an early date may have included the story of Sindibad the Sailor), and tales allegedly translated from Byzantine Greek and from Indian and Persian, such as the *Thousand Stories*, the forerunner of the *Arabian Nights*. The author of the *Fihrist* admits that these works were all famous in his time and much read, but in his few incidental comments on their contents and style, he leaves no doubt that he thought little of their literary quality and value.

The implications of Ibn al-Nadīm's view of literature are clear. There was a serious entertaining literature that was also eminently useful. It taught the fundamentals and the niceties of language and had the task of perpetuating and renewing all inherited cultural values beyond those of religion and science. There also was a sort of frivolous entertaining fictional literature, of a popular nature and hardly worth being called literature. Its flourishing existence had to be reluctantly admitted, but the truly educated, once they had outgrown the limited intellectual capacities of childhood and the great illiterate mass, could and as a rule did disregard it. This was the attitude of Ibn al-Nadīm and, it can be safely said, of all Muslim intellectuals with no known noteworthy exceptions.

The skilful and artistic handling of language, as the first requirement for all effective literary activity, tended to reinforce the pre-eminence of Arabic among the languages spoken by Muslim peoples. Grammar and lexicography[1] were particularly indebted to the genius of the Arabic language and the peculiar circumstances of its development in pre-Islamic as well as Islamic times. The early history of the systematic study of these sciences has been greatly embroidered by legend in Muslim scholarly tradition, but there can be little doubt that, even though the great creative philologists were mainly non-Arabs by descent, Arabic grammar and lexicography did not develop principally under the stimulus of interlingual contacts but from conditions existing within the Arabic linguistic situation itself, such as the great difference between the high poetical language and the language of the Koran on the one hand and the spoken dialect forms on the other. Foreign influences appear to have been mainly stimulatory in effect. Thus, the realization of the existence of Greco-Roman lexicography and of a grammatical literature in Syriac somewhat influenced by Greek logic appears to have spurred the efforts of Muslim scholars, and some knowledge of Indian phonetics is widely suspected of having shaped the phonetic views of al-Khalīl, the father of Arabic lexicography and prosody, whose lifetime spanned most of the eighth century. The elaboration of grammatical theory reached its peak already in the same century in the *Kitāb* or 'Book' of Sībawayh. Vast productivity, stimulated by practical need, remained characteristic of grammatical scholarship. Basically descriptive in its approach, Arabic grammar was a difficult but highly effective training ground for littérateurs no less than scholars. Lexicography also developed rapidly. Lexical monographs on particular topics were combined in multivolume collections to form dictionaries

[1] Only a very few bibliographical references are given in the notes, usually to recent publications providing ample information on all the earlier scholarly literature. For the history of Arabic lexicography, cf. J. A. Haywood, *Arabic Lexicography*, 2nd edn. (Leiden, 1965), and S. Wild, *Das Kitāb al ʿAin und die arabische Lexikographie* (Wiesbaden, 1965). For prosody, cf. G. Weil, *Grundriss und System der altarabischen Metren* (Wiesbaden, 1958), and the summary of it given in *Encyclopaedia of Islam*, 2nd edn., article 'ʿArūḍ'. I know of no recent comprehensive study on Arabic grammar, although introductions to such works as H. Fleisch, *Traité de philologie arabe*, i (Beirut, 1961), may be consulted with profit.

arranged according to topics. Dictionaries utilizing the root concept of Arabic words and arranged in rather free alphabetical order grew into vast compilations that adopted strict alphabetization, usually according to either the first or the last letter of the root. No discernible principle of organization was applied to the often vast and disparate semantic material falling under the same root. Definitions of meanings were frequently based on evidence from passages of the Koran and the traditions of the Prophet or relevant verses of poetry, thus providing a strong literary flavour. Etymological speculation centred around the idea of the free permutation of root consonants, and like all medieval etymology, was a mere exercise in ingenuity lacking any solid scientific basis. Foreign-language dictionaries were compiled even beyond the obvious choices of Arabic, Persian, and Turkish, but that only rarely.

The contribution of philology to literature included the compilation of large numbers of anecdotes, sometimes witty, sometimes dull, quite frequently far-fetched, concerning grammarians and lexicographers and the more arcane concerns of their science. It also included the collection and explanation of proverbs.[1] In the Muslim Near East, the proverb retained its pristine function to serve as the popular as well as literary embellishment of all verbal expression. The vitality of the genre showed itself in the constant development of new proverbs, so that the innumerable proverbs known from medieval literature have practically no correspondence in the equally large collections of proverbs made on the basis of modern usage. A counterpart of the proverb was the aphorism of popular philosophical content. Collections of wise sayings of ancient, preferably Greek, sages were a much studied and influential segment of entertaining, if at the same time educational and edifying, literature.

Adab[2] monographs and anthologies, while offering the cream

[1] Cf. R. Sellheim, *Die klassisch-arabischen Sprichwörtersammlungen* (The Hague, 1954); S. D. Goitein, 'The Origin and Historical Significance of the Present-Day Arabic Proverb', *Islamic Culture*, xxvi (1952), 169–79.

[2] Cf. for instance, F. Gabrieli, in *Encyclopaedia of Islam*, 2nd edn., article 'Adab'.

of what had been said in the form of verse, prose aphorism, and pithy anecdote on every conceivable subject which an educated man (*adīb*) was to know, paid much implicit and express attention to language and exemplary linguistic usage. These works were the very heart of prose belles-lettres in medieval Islam. They drew on the political literature of the 'Mirrors for Princes' type, on ethical theory and typology, on religious-inspirational thought, and, in the course of time, on many other fields of learning, always stressing the interesting, entertaining, and literary elements of the materials presented.

The archetypal representative of *adab* literature was al-Jāḥiẓ (*c*. 776–868 or 869). Born and raised in Baṣra, al-Jāḥiẓ spent much of his long life in the capital cities of Baghdad and Sāmarrā as a littérateur and as a publicist for Muʿtazilī dogmatics (for his role as a political and philosophical writer see below, Chapter IX (*B*), pp. 408–9). A sceptical, searching, critical spirit was abroad in his time more than seems to have existed before in medieval Islam and more than was ever to be found later on. It allowed for the wide curiosity and the free-ranging wit that inform all of al-Jāḥiẓ's writings, large and small, whether they are dealing with animal lore, Arabic rhetoric and poetry, supposed racial and national characteristics, ethical qualities, human sexual behaviour, the various professions and ways of making a living, or any of countless other matters. It also favoured the traditional dialectical device of the author's taking both sides of a question, seeing the good and the bad sides of a subject and defending or attacking two seemingly opposite phenomena or points of view. Loose association of anecdotes and verse was the inherited principle of literary organization. It dominates all Muslim *adab* literature, having had to give way only in scholarly and scientific writings under Hellenistic influence. It could lead to irrelevant digressions, but as handled by al-Jāḥiẓ it usually served to enlarge the reader's understanding of the manifold implications of the topic under discussion. Al-Jāḥiẓ achieved his greatest effect through stylistic means. Epithets that may be translated as 'sparkling', 'brilliant', or the like, are customarily employed to describe al-Jāḥiẓ's style, and, banal and meaningless as they are, it would be hard to find better words. His command of the Arabic vocabulary in all its richness appears to be perfect. The total impression is that of never-ending verbal fireworks and of a relentless display of intellectual agility, not for its own sake but out of deep concern with the moral and emotional strengths and weaknesses of man and his world.

Al-Jāḥiẓ's reputation remained unrivalled, although there were among later authors some who can well stand comparison with him. If any individual is to be singled out as the most accomplished Arabic man of letters, it would certainly have to be Abū Ḥayyān al-Tawḥīdī who died at an advanced age in the early years of the eleventh century, after the year 1009. He belonged to a different time. Philosophy and religion had almost but not yet fully hardened into their characteristic Muslim shape. The middle and high echelons of government officials, among whom al-Tawḥīdī moved, were no longer minor cogs in a big imperial administration but felt that they were themselves running things and making history. The unusual attraction exercised by al-Tawḥīdī's writings is the result of their stress on the personality of the author and of the nature of the particular problems discussed in them. In these respects, they are exceptional among the preserved works of medieval Islam. Their stylistic virtuosity is also remarkable but it should, perhaps, not be adjudged extraordinary for their time.

The preoccupation with language and style achieved another great triumph in the creation of a considerable literature of literary criticism. It was inspired to some degree by ancient precedents, but in the main was an original creation of Muslim littérateurs.[1] Like so much else that was important in Muslim civilization, it had its beginnings in the later ninth century and continued to be cultivated not only in Arabic, as its canons and methods were easily transferable to literatures in other languages. Concerned with the

[1] Cf. G. E. von Grunebaum, *A Tenth-Century Document of Arabic Literary Theory and Criticism* (Chicago, 1950), and S. A. Bonebakker, *Some Early Definitions of the Tawriya* (The Hague-Paris, 1966).

analysis of the figures of speech in both poetry and prose, it did much to heighten the understanding of the wonder of language and admiration for its artistic powers.

Historiography, so widely cultivated and highly esteemed throughout Islam, was, of course, much more than a mere function of language and literature. It served to instil in the students of historical works an awareness of the meaning of human and, in particular, Muslim existence. It was often presented in the form of collections of facts with a minimum of literary artistry. However, it was not without good reason classified among the branches of knowledge that were first and foremost linguistic and literary. History was indeed 'story'. The origin and central core of historical writing was the vividly reported episode, dramatized by the use of much direct speech and often building upon some piece of poetry. No matter how far away from this original concept of history later Muslim historiography moved, it continued to determine the view of what should constitute the literary form of historiographical presentation. Much—and the best—historical writing was guided by it.

Political history is replete with colourful descriptions of battles and the clashes of personalities. At certain periods, it also condescended to engage zestfully in the observation of the extraordinary occurrences of daily life, profiting from the literary effect of built-in drama. When writers of political history belonged themselves to the class of government officials, the great stylistic demands made on all government communications, with their elaborate rhymed prose and their self-conscious effort to hint at, rather than state, facts by means of the most artful and sophisticated rhetoric, added to the literary qualities of historical writing. A man such as Miskawayh (d. 1030) thus succeeded in transposing into vibrant prose the enormous tensions that beset political leadership in his time. The Kātib al-Iṣfahānī (d. 1201), who was in the service of Saladin, was rightly proud of the literary quality of his official documents which he incorporated in his works. Biography, on the other hand, was originally a handmaiden of the religious sciences. As such, it was expected to provide only a limited number of dry data. No matter how elaborate they were, biographies of scholars were inclined to renounce any literary ambition. While biographies of political figures as a rule shared the characteristics of political historiography, and, especially, the panegyrics of Persian court historiography relied on magnificent rhetoric, the artlessness of scholarly biography sometimes tended to affect them as well as to becloud in general the literary value of much of Muslim historical writing.

The work of the great Ibn Khaldūn (1332–1406) also shows clearly that the writing of effective history was considered to depend on literary skill.[1] The lasting fame of his *Muqaddima*, the first volume of a large world history, rests on the fundamental contribution it makes to knowledge, its discovery of the pivotal role of certain important factors in the formation and development of human society. Relying on earlier political and legal thought and fully aware of the trends and data basic to the understanding of the totality of Muslim intellectual life, Ibn Khaldūn succeeded in presenting a picture of his civilization that has remained authoritative and, in a way, definitive. The new ground he broke proved extremely fertile. He refused to brush aside human society as something ultimately irrelevant in the divinely determined unfolding of history. He saw it as founded upon the labour and co-operation of individuals, as held together by man's psychological need to form cohesive groupings ambitious of political domination, as achieving fruition in the material and intellectual culture made possible by urban life, and as constantly succumbing anew to inevitable internal decay, thereby making room for new blood while preserving traces of prior accomplishments and thus providing for some slight but steady linear progress in an otherwise circular movement. His overall view provided Ibn Khaldūn with the opportunity for a systematic study of such matters as the meaning of history, population growth and man's relationship to his

[1] The literature on Ibn Khaldūn to 1967 has been listed very comprehensively by W. J. Fischel, *Ibn Khaldūn in Egypt* (Berkeley–Los Angeles, 1967), pp. 171–212.

physical environment, economic theories explaining the functions of labour and commerce, the significance of science and non-material, spiritual and emotional factors in society—in short, all subjects that modern sociology has taken as its special province. Ibn Khaldūn's work attracted considerable attention among later Muslim historians. They were, of course, unable to appreciate the promise it held for future research undertaken in entirely different circumstances but they somehow sensed the depth of its insight into the forces of history and politics. Ibn Khaldūn's contemporaries praised above all the outstanding style of the *Muqaddima*, reminiscent of the classical style of al-Jāḥiẓ, 'more brilliant than well-strung pearls and finer than water fanned by the zephyr'. Whether or not such an exaggerated description is deserved, it confirms again that the historian's eloquence was adjudged as great a merit as, if not a greater one than, the contents of his work. Ibn Khaldūn's long *Autobiography*, though, naturally, conceived along the spare lines of scholarly biography, also pays respect to literary convention with the obvious quality of its writing and its ample quotations from poetry, artistic correspondence, and eloquent lectures. Ibn Khaldūn was exceptional in his approach to the study of history. However, his concern with language as the principal tool of the historian reflects a commonly held view.

A new literary form of great influence, albeit on a low level of artistry, thrived on themes derived from history and expanded into entertaining and inspiring fiction. This was the literature of historical romances. It had its greatest flowering from the twelfth to the fifteenth century. Contacts with the non-Muslim world gave point to the message of irresistible Muslim prowess these works were meant to convey. Taking as their starting-points events of the glorious early years of Islam or the figure of some later hero or ruler who caught the popular fancy, they are part prose epic and part romantic fairy tale, although with an almost complete repression of the erotic element. In their final written form, they were the product of continuous transmission and growth at the hands of storytellers. Muslim scholarly historians recognized them for what they were, and the educated as expected had a low opinion of them. They were nevertheless extremely effective in influencing the mind of the masses, and they served to store and preserve a large treasure of literary tradition and imagination.

Poetry represents most clearly the pre-Islamic Arabian heritage in Islam. Its basic form—quantitative metrics employing a number of set metres, two metrically equivalent half-verses constituting a verse, and, above all, a constant rhyme letter (or syllable) at the end of each verse continuing throughout the entire poem—is no doubt pre-Islamic, and so is its principal content. It can be classified as predominantly lyrical, expressing as it does the poet's personal feelings and aspirations, his experience of love and nature, and his relations, peaceful and warlike, with friend and foe, his own tribe, and outsiders. The language that was chosen as suitable for poetical expression is 'classical' Arabic with grammatical features preserved from very ancient times and largely discarded, it seems, already in pre-Islamic times from most forms of ordinary speech. The poetic vocabulary is rich and shows a noticeable predilection for the less common and often the far-fetched word. A poem may be long and elaborate, but the basic unit is the individual verse. The literary fortunes of the single verse made the poet or the poem. With the transition from the Arabian Bedouin environment to the Muslim city, greater attention was paid by poets to the conditions and customs of a bourgeois setting and the more varied experiences of a richer life and greater prosperity. Beginning with the golden age of the ʿAbbāsids, this produced a poetry closer to modern experience and taste than the descriptions of the heroic austerities of desert life. The inherited forms of poetry and the basic concept of what constitutes poetry have, however, shown themselves extraordinarily persistent and have remained little changed practically to this day. Reform movements aiming at introducing new forms are still facing a hard struggle for wider acceptance. Throughout the centuries, an enormous amount of beauty and emotional uplift was created in endless variations on eternal themes through the ingenious handling of the incomparable wealth of the Arabic language. The appreciation of poetry was universal and was not entirely restricted to those who possessed the considerable education needed for it. Much poetry in this mould was written also in languages other than Arabic. While there was, of course, a poetical heritage dating from their pre-Islamic past among all Muslim peoples, the Arabic forms and aesthetic preferences became widely preponderant, or, it may be safer to say, a give-and-take, the details of which are hard for us to pin down, resulted in a formally and aesthetically rather uniform type of poetry in Islam regardless of the language in which it was cast. A thorough acquaintance with Arabic poetry was the rule among the educated speakers of Persian, and with Arabic and Persian poetry among the educated speakers of Ottoman Turkish.

There were attempts to break through the classical norm. However, as compared with the incalculably large output of poetry in the traditional manner, all that is known of innovative types of poetry does not amount to more than a drop in the ocean. It is clear that the poets and those who considered themselves connoisseurs of poetry were averse to experimentation, since they were unwilling to risk their great investment of skill and craftsmanship, and the literary establishment was naturally reluctant to allow anything new and controversial to break into writing. Among the widely accepted innovations was the increasing use of an internal rhyme for the two half-verses (*muzdawij*, *mathnawī*) with simultaneous abandonment of the verse rhyme. This form of rhyme may have been Persian in origin. In Arabic, it was preferably used for didactic poetry in the *rajaz* metre (*urjūza*), involving the transposition of some scholarly subject into verse usually in a pedantic and essentially prosaic manner. Another more important innovation was the attempt to form stanzas. A popular development in this direction was the two-verse unit of two rhyming half-verses (commonly, either *aaaa*, or *aaba*), the *dū-bayt* (Persian for 'two verses') or *rubāʿī* ('quatrain'). Another step towards larger units beyond the individual verse consisted of stanzas of four verses in which the first three had different rhyme letters in each successive stanza, while the fourth line, called *simṭ* 'string', that concluded the stanza, retained the same rhyme letter throughout the entire composition (*aaab*, *cccb*, etc.). In the East where this form was sparingly used, it was called *musammaṭ* 'strung (poem)'. In Spain, a similar form came into being. It is very well possible that it was quite unrelated genetically to the *musammaṭ* of the East. Since it was held together by the concluding line as by a belt, and written down, the visual effect was that of a chain belt, it was called *muwashshaḥ* 'girdled (poem)'. Having been very successful in Spain, the *muwashshaḥ* was subsequently taken up also by poets of the Muslim East. The stanza started out with a couplet (*aa*), called *maṭlaʿ*, and then continued according to the scheme *bbbaa*, *cccaa*, that is, with, usually, a double concluding line, called *simṭ* or *qufl* 'lock'. More complicated variations were permissible. Remarkably enough, quite a few examples have been discovered of final concluding lines in the vulgar Arabic tongue or in a Romance dialect often interlaced with Arabic words. Called *kharja* or *markaz*, these verses were usually put into the mouth of a girl expressing her feelings towards her lover.

The use of spoken forms of Arabic in poetry was no doubt common all over the area where Arabic was spoken. Often, it was a case of the imperfect use of the proper classical language rather than the use of any pure dialect form. For the East, literary tradition has preserved a certain if limited amount of information on a variety of forms such as the popular quatrains called *mawālīyā*, the *kān-wa-kān*, and the *qūmā*.[1] From Spain, we have the famous *zajal*s composed in the vulgar tongue and less refined in their themes than the *muwashshaḥ*. With respect to metrical form, the *zajal* appears to differ from the *muwashshaḥ* by having only a single concluding line at the end of each stanza, which, moreover, is never in Romance. Much formal inventiveness and variation were possible and practised with all these and similar schemes divergent from the traditional forms.

[1] Cf. W. Hoenerbach's introduction to his edition: *Die vulgärarabische Poetik, al-Kitāb al-ʿāṭil . . . des Ṣafīyaddīn Ḥillī* (Wiesbaden, 1956).

Epic poetry in the form of long narrative poems was not cultivated in Arabic. Its place, as we have seen, was taken in part by the pseudo-historical romances which, however, inevitably lacked the strength and prestige of poetry. From north-west Africa, a few remnants of a poetical version of the conquest novel of the Banū Hilāl are preserved. In the Muslim orbit, Iran was the true home of the majestic verse epic. It is possible that secular poetry, lyrical or epic, was not much cultivated in pre-Islamic Iran where it might have had to contend with certain religious prejudices against it. It is therefore remarkable that even more than in Arabic-speaking countries, poetry in Muslim Persia came to be the most highly developed branch of Muslim literature nearly monopolizing all higher literary expression (apart from history). The beautiful lyric poetry in Persian was distinguished by its persistent efforts to probe into the significance of human life through an allusiveness that permitted the discerning of different levels of meaning. Persian epic poetry derived its power from a dramatic view of national history, evident already in the Behistun inscription of Darius. The transformation of this national tradition into the form of verse appears to have been a development that came about only in Islamic times. True to epic tradition, the size of the compositions was large. The *Shāhnāma* of Firdawsī (*c*. 940–1020) contains approximately 60,000 verses of the *mathnawī* type of rhyme. As the legendary heroic and passionate history of Persian kings from the beginning of the world it had some predecessors to build on. It was reserved, however, to the *Shāhnāma* to achieve unrivalled eminence as the great national epic *in* Islam, though it could hardly be said, *of* Islam. It served as a source of inspiration for numerous later works in Persian as well as in Turkish.[1] Romantic love, rather than history, often takes the centre of the stage. The earliest preserved representative of the Persian romantic epic is Gurgānī's *Vīs u Rāmīn*, dating from the middle of the eleventh century, which had considerable influence on later Persian works of the same genre.

[1] For differences between the Turkish epics and the Persian epics on which they are based, cf. I. Mélikoff, *La Geste de Melik Dāniṣmend* (Paris, 1960), pp. 42 f.

The term 'epic' is also the one most conveniently applied to the large number of poetical works in Persian using popular narrative material, sometimes within a 'frame' story and usually of a profoundly symbolic religious and mystic character, in order to express their authors' view of the world and to provide edification and guidance for the reader so as to enable him to cope with the perplexities of human existence.[1] A certain epic quality can also be claimed for the grandiose *Mathnavī* of the mystic of Konya, Jalāl-al-Dīn Rūmī (1207–73), which makes liberal use of the free association of ideas and topics in order to cover the entire realm of worldly experience as determined by metaphysical insights.

From the long line of Persian poets who wrote mainly lyrical poetry, the name of the great Ḥāfiẓ of the fourteenth century may be singled out as an example. His poetry can as a rule be understood on two levels, according to the external meaning of its words and as a parable of man's spiritual quest. Whichever aspect might have been uppermost in the poet's own mind has been hotly debated. It can often no longer be determined and is hardly important for the enjoyment and the historical significance and influence of his work. In comparison with Arabic poetry, it can well be said that Persian poetry, as well as the related Turkish poetry, as a whole stresses content and thought—ideological indoctrination, if you will—to a much greater degree. While aspiring to and often achieving perfection in the use of sublime language, it depends much less on it for its effectiveness than does Arabic.

Drama in the proper sense, or related forms of poetry acted out on a stage before an audience, were not cultivated in medieval Islam.[2] In a way, a substitute for them exists in the literary genre

[1] Cf. H. Ritter, *Das Meer der Seele, Mensch, Welt und Gott in den Geschichten des Farīduddīn ʿAṭṭār* (Leiden, 1955).

[2] Cf. J. M. Landau, *Studies in the Arab Theater and Cinema* (Philadelphia, 1958). Also, O. Spies, *Türkisches Puppentheater* (Emsdetten/West., 1959), and, for recent discoveries with regard to the *taʿziya*, E. Cerulli's reports, such as the one in *Rendiconti della Accademia Nazionale dei Lincei, Classe di scienze mor., stor. e. filol.*, viii–ix, 11–12 (1954), 507–15, or, more recently, 'Le Théâtre persan', in *Le Shîʿisme*

known as *maqāmāt*, whose most famous representative was al-Ḥarīrī (1054–1122). The *maqāmāt* literature exploits to the fullest the stylistic effects of rhymed prose and a vocabulary of a finesse quite incomprehensible to the ordinary, untutored speaker of Arabic. Scenes and problems of daily life are dramatically described by a protagonist often in interaction with some individual he is made to encounter. Current ideas and, in particular, the characteristics and foibles of the different population groups and professions are viewed preferably in a highly satirical way reminiscent of the ancient *mimus*. The *maqāmāt* were not acted out, but we have three librettos for shadow plays written in a combination of verse and artistic prose which are quite similar to the *maqāmāt* in spirit and form, if perhaps a little more inclined towards low farce. These librettos came from the pen of the Egyptian littérateur and wit, Ibn Dāniyāl (d. 1310). They were accepted as 'high' literature and as such are unique to our knowledge. However, they let us suspect the existence of some sort of stage performances based on written texts in older times, although oral transmission seems to have been the more common procedure. The Turkish Karagöz shadow plays are the best known surviving development.

A serious form of drama originated in Iran, possibly under Indian or Chinese influence. The *taʿziya*, 'consolation (through mourning)' as it is called, dramatizes the tragic events surrounding the death of al-Ḥusayn at Karbalā. *Taʿziya*s were performed around the time of the anniversary of this event. Their performances were, however, not entirely restricted to that particular time of the year. Other historical events were also dramatized and performed along similar lines. Numerous librettos for such *taʿziya* plays have been preserved.

With some of the aforementioned material, we have already entered the realm of what the author of the *Fihrist*, had he known about it, would have included in his omnibus chapter on diverse entertaining and rather sub-standard works of literature. It was

imâmite, 281–94 (1970, Travaux du Centre d'Études Supérieures spécialisé d'Histoire des Religions de Strasbourg).

something to be written down at times, but it greatly depended on memorization for its survival and practical usefulness. It was only rarely considered good literature and preserved as such in great libraries. Storytellers used written versions of entertaining fiction much as performers of plays used their librettos, but their fiction was much easier of access through reading for those who desired to acquaint themselves with it. Certain works of fiction did achieve a great measure of renown as literature, partly in consequence of their appealing contents but to no small degree also because they were introduced into Arabic literature early, just when it started to enter into its golden age, and by a littérateur of great skill and fame, Ibn al-Muqaffaʿ (d. 759), who is also important as a pioneer writer on political theory in Islam; for this activity of his see below, Chapter IX (*B*), pp. 407–8. Foremost among these works were the moralizing animal fables of *Kalīla wa-Dimna*, Ibn al-Muqaffaʿ's Arabic translation of a Middle-Persian version of the Indian *Panchatranta*, named after the two clever jackals, Karaṭaka and Damanaka, who dominate the first chapter. Like *Bilawhar wa-Būdāsaf* (corrupted to *Yūdāsaf*), the ascetic tale modelled on the life of Buddha, which exists in several versions, *Kalīla wa-Dimna* held sway over the minds of countless people within Islam and, through translation from the Arabic, outside Islam's borders. Nor was the *Tale of Sindibad* (*Syntipas*, or *The Seven Sages*) about the seven wazīrs who with their instructive stories kept the king from rashly killing his son upon the insistence of his wicked wife—likewise of Indian or, as has been suggested, Persian origin[1]—of less significance for world literature after having passed through that great communication centre that was the world of Islam. Most of the works whose titles were listed by Ibn al-Nadīm are not preserved. While Persian and Indian origin may often be correctly assumed for them, claims to Byzantine-Greek origin can as a rule not be verified with the limited information at our disposal. Some of the stories credited with independent existence in the tenth

[1] Cf. B. E. Perry, 'The Origin of the Book of Sindbad', *Fabula*, iii (1959–60), 1–94, also published separately (Berlin, 1960).

century are found later incorporated in the *Arabian Nights*, such as the *Tale of Shīmās and Jaliʿād*, or the just-mentioned *Tale of Sindibad*. The earlier independent versions certainly underwent many modifications before they reached the stage in which they are now known. All this popular material to which anybody could lay claim, as it were, as his own intellectual property, went through involved processes of change and evolution. In some cases, they can still be traced. The *Arabian Nights*[1] themselves offer a fertile field of speculation on the highways and byways of literary creation leading slowly to the final product or products. Originally they were the *Thousand Stories* whose one-time existence in Persian is not subject to doubt and which in all likelihood contained already the famous 'frame' story of ultimately, it seems, Indian provenance. Then, there were the Arabic *Thousand Nights*, as they are still called in the oldest fragment so far recovered dating from the ninth century, a title which was transformed at an uncertain date to *Thousand and One Nights* (our *Arabian Nights*), using, it seems, an idiomatic figure of speech making it clear that an indefinite but large number of nights is meant. The final form of the work includes Egyptian elements that can safely be dated as late as the fourteenth century, among the numerous contributions from different countries and times. However, no matter how wide the nets of literary recension were cast, a good deal of the material that might have been taken in remained outside. The *Arabian Nights*, *Kalīla wa-Dimna* and its peers, the Arabic stories of love and war incorporated in anthologies, the joke books and collections of facetious anecdotes, and the historical romances cover a vast ground and show the uniformly great demand for such entertaining literature all over the world of Islam. However, many more of the variations that were played upon the basic motifs probably never achieved literary permanence and are thus lost to us.

[1] Cf. N. Abbott, 'A Ninth-Century Fragment of the "Thousand Nights"', *Journal of Near Eastern Studies*, viii (1949), 129–64, and, for a literary analysis, M. I. Gerhardt, *The Art of Story-Telling* (Leiden, 1963). See also below, pp. 345–6.

The preceding, necessarily all too brief attempt to sketch the various components that together make up medieval Muslim literature has, I hope, provided us with a sense of the circumstances and limitations under which that literature was to meet Christian Europe and be met by it. Medieval Western Europe had sparse and comparatively late contacts with Persian and Turkish speaking peoples. Its natural and constant interaction was with the regions of the Muslim world in which Arabic was dominant. Arabic literature could be expected to have served as a source of inspiration to the West. Yet, as we have seen, Arabic literature was principally cultivated and esteemed as a complicated and involved function of the Arabic language in its most refined form. This made intellectual communication difficult, if not almost impossible. The classical poetry required intensive interpretation for even an elementary appreciation and thus was effectively barred from translation.[1] The vast historical literature was hardly ever tapped in medieval times; Ibn Khaldūn's work originated under circumstances that effectively prevented it from becoming known to the West before the nineteenth century. Europeans who for some reason or other lived for an extended period of time in Arabic-speaking countries observed much of interest to them but displayed a notable incomprehension of Arabic literature and, indeed, an unawareness of its very existence. Cervantes, for instance, it seems, never learned of the existence of any literary activity in Algeria where he was held prisoner,[2] and far beyond his times, visitors to the Muslim world much more favourably situated than Cervantes remained untouched by the literary life surrounding them, unless they made the most determined scholarly efforts to penetrate to it. However, the literature of the Orient had much to give to the West, and the gifts of both literary materials and new ideas were many. They were not always quite recognized for what

[1] On Hermannus Alemannus' late twelfth-century Latin translation of Arabic verses in Ibn Rushd's *Middle Commentary on Aristotle's Poetics*, see W. F. Bogges, *Journal of the American Oriental Society*, lxxxiii (1968), 657–70.

[2] Cf. W. Hoenerbach, *Cervantes und der Orient* (Bonn, n.d. [1953]).

they were, and let it be said already here that all the literary influences that can be traced did not extend as far as to affect what was considered by either the giver or the recipient to be the essential meaning of literature as art.

Three successive periods, of which the first two tend somewhat to overlap, may be distinguished, if only for the sake of convenience. The first period extends into the twelfth century. The possible contacts that can be detected during that time can be suspected to have been oral and, as it were, subterranean. With the twelfth century and the beginnings of an extensive translation literature from Arabic into European languages, we can expect to find literary influences as a result of the spread of written materials. The third period was ushered in with the first scholarly translations from Arabic literature in early seventeenth-century Holland and the simultaneous introduction of Persian literature in the form of translations of Saʿdī's *Gulistān*, first in an incomplete fashion by A. du Ryer (French) (1634), then by G. Gentius (Latin) (1651) and A. Olearius (German) (1654), translations that enjoyed a great vogue throughout Europe and were supplemented, towards the end of the seventeenth century, by translations of Saʿdī's equally famous *Bustān*. Arabic lexicography came into its own as the basis of Western Arabic dictionaries. Only during the latter half of the nineteenth century—R. Dozy's *Supplément aux dictionnaires arabes* appeared in 1881—did major lexicography try to find its way back to the texts themselves. Much of our lexical knowledge is to this day dependent on the accomplishments of medieval lexicographers. The highly individual Arabic grammar had to suffer much unnecessary adaptation to the categories of Latin grammar, a process that had started with Pedro de Alcalà's pioneering grammar of the Arabic dialect of Granada published in 1505.[1] However, its manifold and obvious advantages for the study of Semitic languages recommended its use for guidance on many points. This third period extends into the present and may in the future bring unsuspected surprises with respect to possible influences of medieval

[1] Cf. J. Fück, *Die arabischen Studien in Europa* (Leipzig, 1955).

Muslim literature upon modern intellectual life. It is, of course, the period about which we have the largest and most solid information. It is also one in which literary influences have come and gone in so many directions that the actual importance of any one of them is hard to assess.

Into the first period, we must place the controversial and much discussed relationship of Arabic poetry with Western European poetry, that is, the troubadour poetry of Provence.[1] The question is discussed in detail above in Chapter II, pp. 94 ff., in the evaluation of the cultural legacy of Islam in Spain. Clearly, the lines of communication were demonstrably wide open, and the appearance of an essentially new type of poetry such as that of the troubadours at the very time when Arabic poetry flourished with particular splendour in neighbouring Spain would seem to suggest something more than a mere coincidence. However, the relationship with respect to elements of aesthetic contents and poetic conceits has not been proved to be much closer than could be expected of love lyrics under generally similar cultural conditions.[2] Nor has the evidence of metrical forms, which has of late been much studied as the potentially most effective clue, led so far to any unambiguous conclusions. Although it does not seem very likely, the possibility, moreover, remains that the *muwashshaḥ* and the *zajal* were not original creations of Arab Muslim Spain but were influenced by native non-Muslim Spanish forms. As noted at p. 96 above, S. M. Stern, who stirred up the latest discussion of the problem by his discovery of *kharja*s in Spanish-Hebrew poetry, has taken an emphatically negative stand and rejected the assumption of any sort of dependence. As far as the concrete evidence produced up

[1] Cf. S. M. Stern, 'Esistono dei rapporti letterari tra il mondo Islamico e l'Europa occidentale nell'alto medio evo?', *Settimane di studio del Centro italiano di studi sull'alto medioevo*, xii (Spoleto, 1965), 639–66, 811–31; K. Heger, *Die bisher veröffentlichten Ḫarǧas und ihre Deutungen* (Beihefte zur Zeitschrift für romanische Philologie (Tübingen, 1960), p. 101; E. García Gómez, *Las jarchas romances* (Madrid, 1965).

[2] Cf. the material collected—mainly from classical poetry—by L. Ecker, *Provenzalischer und deutscher Minnesang* (Bern-Leipzig, 1934).

to now goes, this point of view would certainly seem to be well taken. But impressive surface similarities do exist. Now, as in the past, they appear to be indicative of some kind of exchange.

The situation is somewhat different, even if our conclusions are tainted by the same hue of indecision, with regard to Oriental influences on the great epic of *Tristram and Iseult*. The bare bones of the epic's plot bear a truly remarkable similarity to the bare bones of the plot of the Persian epic of *Vīs u Rāmīn* (where the title, in contrast to that commonly used for the Western epic, accords precedence to the female protagonist).[1] The Persian epic is stated by its author to go back to a Pahlavi original, and thus to have had its origin in the Sasanian period; it is even believed to have its roots as far back as Arsacid times. If, as seems likely, there exists some connection between the story of Vīs and Rāmīn and the proto-Tristram, the line of transmission is not at all clear. It may very well have been pre-Islamic and led through the Byzantine Empire or otherwise bypassed Islam. The additional theme of the two Iseults, Iseult the Beautiful and Iseult of the White Hand, has been traced in a story about Qays b. Dharīḥ and his two Lubnās, reported in the *Book of Songs* (*Kitāb al-aghānī*) of Abu'l-Faraj al-Iṣfahānī (897–967). Again, there are noteworthy similarities. In this case, transmission through Islam would seem more likely, although it certainly need not be assumed that the motif was of specifically Arab origin. The only sensible attitude to take at this time would seem to point out the existing similarities, and leave the matter at that, until, if ever, the connective threads become disentangled to our view. Any strictly literary contact on the part of the Western contributors to the Tristram epic with written Oriental sources in translation appears, at any rate, to be quite out of the question.

[1] Cf. F. R. Schröder, 'Die Tristansage und das persische Epos "Wīs und Rāmīn"', *Germanisch-Romanische Monatsschrift*, xlii (1961), 1–44, as well as the introduction of H. Massé's remarkable French translation of *Wīs and Rāmīn* (Paris, 1959), and *Encyclopaedia of Islam*, 2nd edn., article 'Gurgānī'. For further assumed connections of epics and chivalrous tales in East and West, cf. S. Singer, *Germanisch-romanisches Mittelalter* (Zürich-Leipzig, 1935).

The situation is different again with regard to another great Western epic, the *Parzival* of Wolfram von Eschenbach (*c.* 1170–1220) whose revelatory value for medieval Christian attitudes towards the Muslims is discussed above, Chapter I, pp. 24–5.[1] Fanciful parallels have been drawn between the Parzival and alleged Persian (Manichaean) concepts. These would in any case not have required Islamic mediation. However, it has also been contended that the central core of the mystical-philosophical legend of the Holy Grail—etymologized as derived from Greek *kratēr*—closely reflects ideas of Greek Hermetical writings and that the way these ideas took to reach the German author was through a Spanish source, indicated by him, which in turn relied upon translations of Arabic Hermetic literature. If this proves to be true or, at least, to contain a large kernel of truth, we would have here an early, if not the very first, instance of translations from Arabic playing an important role in the history of Western literature. Be it noted, however, that the Arabic Hermetic literature was no part of Arabic belles-lettres according to anybody's definition but belonged to the sphere of esoteric philosophical science. Most of the supposed Oriental material as it appears in Wolfram's definitive elaboration of the Parzival theme must indeed be classified not as in any way literary but as learned and scientific.

Written Arabic sources, it seems, are at least in part responsible for the Near Eastern story material that makes its appearance in the twelfth century in the works, particularly the *Disciplina Clericalis*, of a Spanish Jewish convert to Christianity, Pedro de Alfonso, who was born in 1062, converted in 1106, and died at a date still unknown (on his work see above, Chapter I, p. 15).[2]

[1] Cf. H. and R. Kahane (and A. Pietrangeli), *The Krater and the Grail: Hermetic Sources of the Parzival* (Urbana, Ill., 1965), and the instructive review by M. Plessner, 'Orientalistische Bemerkungen zu religionshistorischen Deutungen von Wolframs Parzival', *Medium Aevum*, xxxvi (1967), 253–66.

[2] Cf. H. Schwarzbaum, 'International Folklore Motifs in Petrus Alphonsi's "Disciplina Clericalis" ', *Sefarad*, xxi (1961), 267–99, xxii (1962), 17–59, xxiii (1963), 321–44, xxiv (1964), 54–73, and E. Hermes, *Die Kunst, vernünftig zu leben* (Zürich–

Folkloristic elements and narrative themes continued to show up repeatedly in Western literature, and in prominent places, as, for instance, in Boccaccio's *Decamerone* or Chaucer's *Squire's Tale*. In 1143, the daring enterprise of translating Muslim religious writings into Latin sponsored by Peter the Venerable, Abbot of Cluny, produced, among other works, a translation of the Koran.[1] Much as we are tempted to see in it a literary enterprise, this was far from being so. Even if, which is doubtful, the translators had any inkling of the artistic merits of the Koran, nothing was further from their minds than appreciating or showing any curiosity about them. Their only purpose was to gain an insight into Muslim theological thinking in the hope of thereby becoming better able to recognize and exploit its presumed weaknesses; the polemical aspect of Peter the Venerable's enterprise is discussed more fully above, Chapter I, pp. 15–17. The intensive translation activity which continued in the following century was predominantly utilitarian and stressed science and philosophy-theology. However, it also undertook translations into Hebrew, into Spanish, into Latin (which often in these cases was secondary to Spanish), and into other Western European vernaculars, directly or in adaptations, such works as *Kalīla wa-Dimna* and *Sindibad and the Seven Sages*. The sayings of the ancient philosophers collected by Ḥunayn b. Isḥāq (808–73) were translated into Hebrew, thereby gaining much currency all over Europe, and into Spanish (*El libro de los buenos proverbios*). Those collected by al-Mubashshir in Egypt in 1048–9 were translated into Spanish (*Los bocados d'oro*) by an unknown translator in 1257, and then into Latin, Provençal, French, and English. The great interest in this work was due to its instructive and edifying character and, perhaps, also to the steadily growing desire to learn more about the wisdom of Classical

Stuttgart, 1970). A lifetime from *c.* 1076 to *c.* 1140 has been suggested by A. Cutler in a communication at a recent meeting of the American Oriental Society.

[1] Cf. J. Kritzeck, *Peter the Venerable and Islam*, Princeton Oriental Studies, xxiii (Princeton, 1964). For the general subject of Christianity and Islam in the Middle Ages, see N. Daniel, *Islam and the West* (Edinburgh, 1960).

Antiquity. The existence of vernacular versions secured for it a wide distribution during the early years of printing. These versions contributed much to general edifying literature, a type of literature which until the time of Enlightenment enjoyed the lion's share of the publishers' market in Europe.

The religiously oriented translation activity was not interested in literature as such, but it may have made a significant contribution to one of the most celebrated monuments of Western medieval literature.[1] One of the works translated in the third quarter of the thirteenth century for Alfonso X of Spain was a rather lengthy and detailed account of the Prophet's journey through heaven under the guidance of the archangel Gabriel. To Christian eyes, this account appeared as a particularly authoritative sacred document of Islam written by the Prophet himself. M. Asín Palacios, who in 1919 aroused the learned world with his thesis that Dante's *Divina Commedia* was influenced by the rich store of Muslim legends connected with Muḥammad's heavenly ascent, the *miʿrāj*, had relied mainly on comparative evidence culled from the learned mystico-religious literature which even among Muslims was restricted to a comparatively limited circle of scholars and initiates and which was almost as unlikely to have become known to Dante as an original Persian epic was unlikely to have been known to the author of Tristram. Now, however, with the discovery of the treatise translated for King Alfonso, it was possible to show that the subject, treated on a popular level, was accessible to readers of Spanish as well as of Latin and French, the latter versions made from the Spanish having been preserved. Moreover, it has been possible to show that Italians were among those acquainted with the work in translation and that the text and related materials were indeed widely known throughout Western Europe. There can be no doubt that Dante *could* have read it. It could have inspired him with the thought of creating a profoundly Christian answer to the Muslim

[1] Cf. E. Cerulli, *Il 'Libro della Scala' e la questione delle fonti arabo-spagnole della Divina Commedia*, Studi e Testi cl (Vatican City, 1949), and J. Muñoz Sendino, *La Escala de Mahoma* (Madrid, 1949).

vision of the world beyond on the grand scale. Possible recollections of poetical conceits and imagery have been shown to exist in Dante's work. It is clear that even a lesser poet would have transformed all such borrowings in his mind to such a degree that in their final form they are no longer apt to furnish absolute proof of their origin. If we had documentary evidence to the effect that Dante did read a work on the *miʿrāj* in translation, and not merely that he might very well have read it, this greatest single instance of Muslim influence upon Western literature would advance from possibility to probability, and, perhaps, even certainty (also on this topic see above, Chapter II, p. 94).

Approaching modern times, we are confronted with the steadily widening historical curiosity of modern man to recover and know what there was in the past. The scholarly knowledge about Islam grew rather slowly. Its impact was at first overshadowed by that of Chinese civilization. However, the world of Islam soon worked its way into the consciousness of leading European intellectuals. The specimens of Muslim literature that became available through translation did not remain unnoticed. Interest in them may have been relatively greater when they were scarce, than it has been since they became part of the tremendous flood of material from all over the world that has engulfed us since the nineteenth century. Their influence was persistent, if usually minor. The exotic appeal of Muslim lore and of the many episodes from Muslim history considered as romantic was uniformly strong and inspired some famous works of European literature, even if the finished product would hardly show any real and tangible connection with matters Oriental, except, perhaps, in some romantic imagery or a name as in *Vathek*, the eighteenth-century Gothic tale of William Beckford.[1] There were some encounters that were of more than isolated significance. Three of them deserve mention here.

Antoine Galland's (1646–1715) French translation of the *Arabian Nights* transformed the grudgingly tolerated Cinderella

[1] On Islam in English literature, see the book of that title by B. P. Smith (Beirut, 1929) and S. C. Chew, *The Crescent and the Rose* (New York, 1937).

of Arabic literature into a beloved and bounteous fairy of Western popular and literary imagination.[1] The translation appeared in Paris between 1704 and 1717 and spread like wildfire all over Europe. Galland 'adapted his translation to the taste of his European readers, changing sometimes the wording of the Arabic text and paraphrasing things that were foreign to Europeans'. This kind of translation procedure helped to make the stories of the *Arabian Nights* more attractive to the reading public. It was, however, not the only reason for the success of Galland's work. Its appearance happened to coincide with a transition in European taste that turned from the adventurously superhuman, inhuman, and bizarre to the daintily over-sensitive and over-refined, and all of these qualities are found mingled in the *Arabian Nights* in gay profusion. And most important, the *Arabian Nights* made also possible an escape into a foreign world seemingly as free from the greyness of an oppressive traditionalism as the brilliant Eastern sky was thought to be from menacing clouds. The *Arabian Nights* opened up new horizons for the imagination and, although themselves a work of irrational fancy, helped to prepare the mind of the public for the enlightened rationalism of the times. Their pervasive intellectual influence spread far and wide. Thus it has been shown to have been constantly at work throughout the life and literary activity of Germany's greatest writer, Goethe (1749–1832).[2] Filtered through his poetical imagination, much of this influence is hardly recognizable any more in the form it appears to us. Here, however, in contrast to Dante and the *miʿrāj*, we have exact information concerning Goethe's reading of the *Arabian Nights* during various periods of his life. It is this sort of information that makes us predisposed to exclude mere coincidence and to accept the manifold if remote similarities as actual recollections of the *Arabian Nights*.

[1] Cf. E. Littmann, in the appendix to his German translation of the *Arabian Nights* (Wiesbaden, 1953), vi. 647–738, and condensed in the article 'Alf layla wa-layla' of the *Encyclopaedia of Islam*, 2nd edn., from which the following quotation is taken.

[2] Cf. K. Mommsen, *Goethe und 1001 Nacht* (Berlin, 1960).

Goethe, standing at the threshold of the new age of historicism, kept abreast of the scholarly progress of his age. Deeply impressed by the enthusiasm shown by Sir William Jones (1746–94) for Arabic and Persian poetry and helped along by the work of such scholars as H. F. Diez (1751–1817) and, especially, the translation of Ḥāfiẓ's *Dīwān* by J. von Hammer-Purgstall (1774–1856) published in 1812–13, he proved in his *West-östlicher Divan* that Persian lyric had eternal values that could be transmuted into great, modern, European poetry.[1] While thus confirming in his way that East and West were both in God's hands, partaking of the same divine inspiration, he showed in his notes and comments on the *West-östlicher Divan* that true understanding could result only from going into the poet's own country and learning about his history and the environment in which he lived. Able poets such as F. Rückert (1788–1866) and A. von Platen (1797–1835) followed the way Goethe had shown. It was one that classicists, romantics, and the rising breed of scholarly positivists could willingly take. While Goethe was not alone in making Near Eastern poetry unquestioningly acceptable in the West, he was by influence and personal genius the towering giant among them (further on his role in popularizing the exotic aspects of the East see above, Chapter I, pp. 43–4).

The fame that came to the English translation of the *Rubāʿīyāt* of the Persian scientist, ʿUmar al-Khayyām (d. 1123), is, in contrast, much harder to account for. The voice of Edward FitzGerald (1809–83) was not one of great authority, and his slight volume of verse first published in 1859 was not weighty enough by itself to make much of a splash in an ocean of publications. However, his sentimental reinterpretation of the Persian poet's words and ideas,

[1] Cf. H. H. Schaeder, *Goethes Erlebnis des Ostens* (Leipzig, 1938), and his appendix, entitled 'Der Osten im West-östlichen Divan', in E. Beutler's edition (Wiesbaden, 1948), pp. 787–839; also the studies by K. Mommsen on 'Goethe und Diez' and 'Goethe und die Moallakat', *Sitzungsberichte der Deutschen Akademie der Wissenschaften zu Berlin, Kl. für Sprachen, Literatur und Kunst.* (1960), no. 2, (1961), no. 4. A negative voice is that of G.-H. Bousquet, 'Goethe et l'Islam', *Studia Islamica*, xxxiii (1971), 151–64.

looking at life with resignation and at the same time with cheerful confidence and just a hint of libertinism, seemed to break through the dull and opaque walls of contemporary civilization and reveal glimpses into a freer, purer, more human world. As this kind of world is not likely ever to exist in the here and now, such glimpses will always be needed to provide spiritual refreshment. A measure of eternity beyond its first century of fame would thus seem to be assured to FitzGerald's creation. However this may be, it established once more an abiding awareness of the lasting and deeply human values of medieval Muslim poetry in the Western world.

H. A. R. Gibb has suggested that we should make a distinction between superficial 'borrowings' of literary elements and 'creative' influences affecting fundamental aesthetic sensibilities and cultural values. The borrowings are said to be fairly easily established, while possible creative influences are exceptionally hard to trace.[1] It would seem that the sum total of such borrowings, while large, remains a rather small percentage of what might have profitably been borrowed from the vast riches of Muslim literature. This is hardly surprising in view of the fact that the barriers to communications between Christendom and Islam were many in the Middle Ages. It is evident, too, that whatever the West learned about and from Muslim literature before the age of modern scholarship was usually not what Muslims themselves considered its truly great and important products. These, being the intimate property of Muslim culture, were simply not communicable. The more popular and lowly fringes of literary activity were. They were absorbed, and sometimes, it seems, were given greater weight than they originally were thought to possess, but again without altering the fundamental concerns of Western literature and its persistent efforts towards the literary expression of 'reality'. Yet, the influences coming from Muslim literature always provided a sense of differentness, a feeling of the existence of an alternative

[1] Cf. H. A. R. Gibb, 'The Influence of the Medieval Islamic Culture on Europe', *Bulletin of the John Rylands Library*, xxxviii (1955–6), 82–98.

to 'reality', in short, a broadened, more varied outlook on the world which no doubt immeasurably enriched Western literature and was one of the factors making possible its development towards a kind of universality new in human history.

FRANZ ROSENTHAL

BIBLIOGRAPHY

1. *Arabic literature*

(*a*) General surveys: R. Blachère, *Histoire de la littérature arabe*, 3 vols. (Paris, 1952–66). The part so far published deals with pre-Islamic and early Islamic poetry; F. Gabrieli, *Storia della letteratura araba*, 3rd edn. (Milan, 1962); H. A. R. Gibb, and J. M. Landau, *Arabische Literaturgeschichte* (Zürich–Stuttgart, 1968), contains a good list of literary works available in translation; R. A. Nicholson, *A Literary History of the Arabs*, 2nd edn. (Cambridge, 1930); G. Wiet, *Introduction à la littérature arabe* (Paris, 1966).

(*b*) Anthologies, texts, studies: A. J. Arberry, *The Koran Interpreted*, 2 vols. (London, 1955); G. E. von Grunebaum, *Kritik und Dichtkunst, Studien zur arabischen Literaturgeschichte* (Wiesbaden, 1955); A. Guillaume, *The Life of Muhammad. A Translation of [Ibn] Isḥāq's Sīrat Rasūl Allāh* (London, 1955); J. Kritzeck, *Anthology of Islamic Literature* (New York, 1964); C. Pellat, *The Life and Works of Jāḥiẓ. Translations of Selected Texts* (London, 1969). A highly informative introduction to Arabic prose literature.

2. *Persian and Turkish literature*

A. J. Arberry, *Classical Persian Literature* (London, 1958). This author has made numerous other translations from Persian and Arabic literature; A. Bombaci, *Histoire de la littérature turque* (Paris, 1968), E. G. Browne, *A History of Persian Literature*, 4 vols. (Cambridge, 1902–24); A. Pagliaro and A. Bausani, *Storia della letteratura persiana* (Milan, 1960).

3. *Cultural relations with the West*

U. Monneret de Villard, *Lo studio dell'Islam in Europa nel XII e nel XIII secolo*, Studi e Testi, cx (Vatican City, 1944); A. R. Nykl, *Hispano-Arabic Poetry and its Relations with the Old Provençal Troubadours* (Baltimore, 1946); R. W. Southern, *Western Views of Islam in the Middle Ages* (Cambridge, Mass., 1962).

VIII

PHILOSOPHY, THEOLOGY, AND MYSTICISM

EVERY religion is made up in essentials of a 'revelation', and of an interpretation of the revelation. The former is fixed, immutable, since it represents the actual expression of the divine will and embodies eternal truths. The interpretation is a reaction of the human spirit to this revelation, this spirit being involved in time and therefore conditioned by it. The revelation endures through the centuries without undergoing any alteration, whereas the interpretation is subjected over the ages to the pressures of internal and external forces, those pressures which, at every period in history, characterize a society.

For all three disciplines, philosophy, theology, and mysticism, there exist in the history of Muslim thought corresponding and well-defined terms, *falsafa*, *kalām*, and *taṣawwuf*. All these are the fruit of later, sometimes marginal, interpretation of the Koranic revelation and the commandments of the religious Law. All three are liable, at certain periods of history, to call down upon themselves the thunder of outraged orthodoxy and to be charged with intrusion upon a field which, it was thought, should remain jealously confined to pure religion. But they all ended, in varying degree, by becoming accepted, and they constitute a true title to fame for Muslim civilization. Furthermore, since they have come into contact, consciously or unconsciously, with similar labours in the West, they appear closer to Western scholasticism than the subtleties of Muslim jurisprudence or the chains of transmission of the traditions of the Prophet (the *ḥadīth*s). Clearly they belong to the universal legacy of humanity and, for this reason, are not alien to us.

In the first and longer part of this chapter we shall study the genesis of these disciplines, their characteristics, their reciprocal connections, and their place in the ensemble of Muslim civilization; in the second part we shall describe briefly the influence which they have been able to exert on the Christian West.

'In the beginning was the Koran': to some extent, this paraphrase of the well-known verse from the Gospel of St. John will help us to underline the fundamental place held by the Arabian sacred book all through Muslim religious sciences and civilization. Obviously, the Koran is not a work of philosophy and the Prophet of Islam has nothing, either in his conduct or in his teaching, in common with a Socrates or a Plato. He is a 'Messenger of God' who transmits a message, recalls the truths about God in his relation to man, about life in this world and in the next, quotes ancient stories, mixes promises with threats, and provides a religious Law which assures salvation. But the Koran contains, in addition to religious truths, philosophical elements or at least statements which offer material for reflection. Concerning God, the creation, the universe, man, destiny, the organization of the City, its indications are precise and guide the choice of the thinker in a clearly defined direction: *falsafa*, *kalām*, and *taṣawwuf* cannot contradict these essential data without one renouncing Islam.

They entail a theodicy, an anthropology, an eschatology, and, finally, a philosophy of nature.[1] The theodicy involves the fact that God is a 'personal' being, living, existing, eternal, all-powerful, unique, creator of heavens and of earth, merciful, omniscient. His will is creative. Even though He is transcendent ('Nothing resembles Him'), He is nevertheless near to man who implores Him. He is also a God of Justice who will demand an account from man.

The anthropology involves the fact that man is directly created by God, body and soul. Adam and Eve were disobedient, but this 'original sin' was not transmitted to their descendants. Each soul

[1] See G. Anawati, 'Philosophie religieuse de l'Islam', *Filosofia e Vita*, vii (1966), 257–66.

is responsible for its own actions. Man has been created to do homage to the unity of God, to adore his Creator, to praise Him and to serve Him. God has placed him in the centre of the universe so that he may have authority over it and be its king, or rather its administrator. The *homo islamicus* is essentially a man 'submissive' (*muslim*) to the will of God. What distinguishes him is just this total ascendancy of God over all his behaviour, this need to involve God in even the smallest detail of his life. The Muslim is a man living under the eye of God, and Muslim society is a theocentric society.

The eschatology involves the fact that man on this earth is a traveller. His destiny is in the world beyond. Death is in the hands of God and will come inexorably at the time assigned. The body will be destroyed but it will one day be restored to life and take part in the joys of paradise or suffer the torments of hell.

Lastly, there is a philosophy of nature, although this is obviously implicit only. It is theocentric, in that God, who is perfectly transcendent, is none the less at the heart of creation which must constantly be referred to Him. It is finalistic, in that nature has been created with wisdom; there is in it a uniformity of law which allows, however, full liberty for the divine will to intervene. Finally, it has an anthropocentric aspect: nature is at the service of man; and it makes use of a certain number of themes, in particular those of light, of water, and of the Original Covenant, which are apt to serve for the elaboration of a religious cosmology.

Alongside the Koran and the *ḥadīth* or body of traditions, which, where necessary, supplements its silences, Muslim thought first encountered Christian theological thinking at Damascus and Greek philosophy at Baghdad.[1] Damascus was a very old city of culture and Greek influence was strong there. Established from the very earliest times, Christianity had developed rapidly and, with some exceptions, the great names of Damascene Christianity date from the Arab period (St. Sophronius, St. Andrew of Crete,

[1] Cf. L. Gardet and M.-M. Anawati, *Introduction à la théologie musulmane* (Paris, 1948), pp. 21–93.

St. John of Damascus). Contacts between Christians and Muslims were not limited solely to trade and administration; there were also religious and intellectual exchanges. There were literary borrowings (theological and ascetic terms), structural analogies (meditations on hell and paradise, methods for the examination of conscience), fruitful graftings. Muslim mystics used to consult the Christian hermits on religious questions. From the eighth century onward there is positive evidence, in particular that of St. John of Damascus and his disciple Theodore Abū Qurra, pointing to polemical activity between Christian and Muslim intellectuals. Two problems above all were discussed, that of predestination and that of the created Koran. Likewise, it seems that it was through the intermediary of Christian apologetics that the problem of the divine attributes was discussed.

But the most important event for the formation of Muslim philosophic thought was undoubtedly its encounter with Greek philosophy at Baghdad, during the reign of al-Ma'mūn in the ninth century. It should be said from the start that the Greek philosophy received by the Arabs was not solely that of Plato and Aristotle, but what had been elaborated in the course of several centuries by their continuators and their commentators. Alongside Platonism and Aristotelianism there were Stoicism, Pythagorism, and, above all, the Neo-Platonism of Plotinus and Proclus. Philosophy appeared in the form of a unique wisdom, to whose formation all the great minds had contributed. The Muslim philosophers and even more the later intellectualist mystics were so deeply convinced of this that they made it the very foundation of their *Weltanschauung*. The Christians, especially perhaps the Syrians of Antioch, had already prepared the way by 'Christianizing' certain passages from the ancient writers or at least making them more religious. The adaptation was so discreet that it did not go beyond the stage of a 'natural theology', which corresponded exactly to what Muslim thinkers could accept.

Alongside these essential elements which contributed to the

formation of Muslim thought, a number of other factors must be noted which, though to a lesser degree, permitted this thought to take form.

First of all, the formation of the schools of grammarians, one at Kūfa and one at Baṣra. Discussions between philologists led to the elaboration of a certain number of categories with an exact vocabulary, of which philosophy did not fail to make use. Still more influential was the activity of the schools of religious law, especially when they tried to isolate the principles of jurisprudence (*uṣūl al-fiqh*); the former rector of al-Azhar, Shaykh Muṣṭafā ʿAbd al-Rāziq, went as far as seeing in them the real object of Muslim philosophy.[1] It is interesting to note the place taken by logic in these discussions, an 'ancient logic' centred entirely on reasoning by analogy (*qiyās*), but which was to free minds of their fetters and give them the habit of considering problems from all aspects. Finally, Iranian and perhaps also Hindu elements must not be overlooked, as well as Manichaean survivals.

Starting from the religious revelation which we have just described, and influenced by the various factors we have mentioned, Muslim thought tried out its wings. It did so in a movement of defence against the more or less aggressive ideas which threatened the Muslim faith. A number of Muslim thinkers, schooled in Greek philosophy, wished to place at the service of their faith the resources of reason and thereby take these weapons from their opponents and turn them against them. This belligerent intellectual tendency distinguishes those known in the history of ideas in Islam under the name of the Muʿtazila. Whatever may be the etymology of the word, they were made up of a certain number of intellectuals resident either at Baṣra or at Baghdad who boldly, at the risk of scandalizing the orthodox and incurring their wrath, tried to present the dogmas of Islam as acceptable to reason. They dealt with five main themes. Firstly, the oneness of God, upheld with all the vigour of a *via remotionis* utilized to the extreme, even

[1] For the different opinions on this subject see G. Anawati, 'Philosophie arabe ou philosophie musulmane?', in *Mélanges Chenu* (Paris, 1967), pp. 51–71.

at the cost of rejecting the real attributes of God. Secondly, the justice of God. They state that there is an objective good and an objective evil, prior to their determination by religious Law, and that God is obliged always to choose the good; and, since God does not desire evil, He does not ordain it. It is man who creates evil. The third thesis concerns the destiny of the believer, the sinner, and the infidel. The fourth concerns the 'intermediary state' between faith and disbelief. This is the state of the believer who is a sinner; condemned in after-life to eternal hell (less rigorous, however, than that of the infidel) he remains in this world a member of the Muslim community. Finally, there is the fifth thesis which regulates the practical attitude of the believer in Muslim society. When faced with evil, he is required to reject it in heart, word, and deed. If this does not suffice, then order must be restored by 'the sword'.

It would obviously be wrong to consider these first thinkers of Islam as 'liberals'. Liberal they were not, since, when masters of power, they displayed a fierce intransigence and forcibly insisted on having their own ideas accepted. But their power was only transient; in their turn they were persecuted and their books suppressed. However, their influence was to remain great upon those who desired a 'reasonable' religion. In particular, they paved the way for the philosophers who, like them, dreamed of reconciling Greek wisdom with Revelation.

PHILOSOPHY (*Falsafa*)

The preceding pages have sketched the background against which Muslim philosophical thought stands out, and in what follows we shall be content to present the characteristics of Muslim philosophy regarded as a whole, underlining on the way the role of this or that individual representative.

In the first place, this philosophy has an undeniable unity, despite the variety of the places where it arose and of its works; the same essential traits are to be found among the philosophers of the Muslim East as among those of the Muslim West. They have the same starting-point, viz. the Koranic truths and the everyday teaching of Islam. No one is rash enough to doubt them; at most, on certain points (creation in time, the resurrection of the body) there will be recourse to allegorical interpretation (*ta'wīl*). They also have the same rational basis, that of Hellenistic philosophy: Aristotelian logic, belief in reason, the supreme norm, God considered as a pure Being, the Prime Unmoved Mover, and, for the most part, the eternal and necessary creation of the world. They have the same scholastic structure derived from a common religious formation; the same conclusions on the essential points concerning God, creation, man, the organization of the City; and the same conditions of blossoming and development, i.e. medieval Muslim society.

Secondly, this philosophy is part of the trend of Greek thought. It continually appeals to the great sages of antiquity, believing firmly in the oneness of wisdom, a sort of inspiration among the ancient philosophers of which the Muslim revelation is only the continuation. The Muslim philosophers wish to remain faithful to this tradition of wisdom. This conviction of the unity of Greek philosophical thought is so strong that al-Fārābī devotes a special treatise to show how essentially Plato and Aristotle teach the same doctrine but in a different manner. He explains that they have the same conception of life, Plato carrying it out *in concreto* and Aristotle displaying it in his writings. The same is true for the manner of instruction: Plato makes use of myths, Aristotle of an obscure language, but both wish to compel their disciples to 'discover' truth by searching for it beyond superficial appearances. They have the same doctrine, says al-Fārābī; he explains that both hold the same theory concerning ideas, the problems of knowledge, customs, heredity, etc. Because of these links with the Greek tradition, Muslim philosophy comes very near to Western philosophy, at least up to the time of the Renaissance.

Thirdly, Muslim philosophy sets out to be a wisdom (*ḥikma*). Al-Fārābī (d. 950), Avicenna (d. 1037), and Averroes (d. 1198) were convinced of the oneness of knowledge, crowned by metaphysics or *Ilāhiyyāt*. In his *Iḥṣā' al-ʿulūm* ('Catalogue of Sciences'), al-Fārābī lists the various sciences, describes them, and finally names philosophy as their head, for it ensures the certainty of knowledge as obtained by apodeictic reasoning. And in his great philosophical 'Summa' entitled *al-Shifā'* ('The Cure', i.e. of ignorance), Avicenna embraces the totality of the sciences according to the following plan:

1. Logic; 2. Physics; 3. Mathematics; 4. Metaphysics.

Within the limits of metaphysics Avicenna includes all the 'revealed' data contained in the Koran. He establishes that God, the only necessity, is good, all-powerful, creator of all things, provident. He resolves the problem of evil by distinguishing causes *per se* and causes *per accidens*; he even treats the delicate problem of the resurrection of the flesh. This he does *more philosophico* and refers to the appropriate religious sciences for laying down the tenets of the faith on the matter. Further, and this shows the 'totalitarian' character of the metaphysical wisdom of the philosophers, Avicenna attempts to rediscover, by philosophic reasoning, even the positive social commands of the Koran: the Caliphate, the structure of the family, the justification of polygamy, repudiation, etc.

Averroes goes even further. For him there are three sorts of minds, corresponding to the three types of argument established by Aristotle. Firstly, demonstrative minds able to follow a rigorous argument and to reach necessary and evident conclusions. The concatenation of these demonstrations is what constitutes philosophy, but this is accessible only to a minority of minds sufficiently gifted to devote themselves to it. Secondly, logical minds satisfied by probable arguments. Thirdly, minds given to exhortation or oratorical argument unsuited to follow formal reasoning. These belong to all ordinary men, the great mass of humanity responsive only to imagination and passion. But, as Averroes states, one of the miraculous features of the Koran is that it is accessible to all three categories, each discerning in it the truth adapted to its intellectual capacity. For the verses which are clear and unmistakable there is no problem; they are apprehended and understood by all in the same obvious sense. Other texts are ambiguous; they make use of symbols and metaphors. They bear a literal and also a deeper, hidden meaning, and only the philosophers, the chosen spirits, are able to comprehend the strict sequence of reasoning and to understand the deeper meaning. As for the common people, they understand the texts in their literal sense, and one must beware of letting them catch a glimpse of the deep, hidden meaning which these texts conceal as they would not understand them and would be troubled in their faith. But what creates disorder and sows trouble is the intemperate work of the 'Theologians', the *mutakallimūn*, who, unable to appreciate an apodeictic demonstration, have recourse to dialectic reasonings which prove nothing. Averroes does not stint his sarcasm against these trouble-makers, and he would willingly appeal to the secular arm to prevent them pursuing their misdeeds.

This quality of wisdom which Muslim philosophy strives to adopt is none the less, at least in intention, religious. This is its fourth characteristic. It contains the religious elements taken from the Koran, but instead of borrowing them as religious elements, it sincerely seeks to 'reconcile' religion and reason with the intention of giving the former a scientific 'status'. It applies to religious principles the structure of Greek philosophy and thereby bestows on the latter a religious resonance which it did not have with the Greek masters. It was thus able to get a hearing from religious minds, or at least those desirous to harmonize their faith with reason and 'science'. This explains the success of the *Metaphysics* of Avicenna and of his *De Anima* in the Christian Middle Ages.

Finally, Muslim philosophy shows a predilection for the problem of knowledge, of θεωρία, and its psychological and ontological bases. In al-Kindī's and al-Fārābī's treatises *De Intellectu*, and above all in Avicenna, we have a delicate and detailed analysis of the various powers of the soul and the stages through which it must pass, including moral purification, to attain union with the source of all being. Greek Neo-Platonism thus finds itself reinforced by certain lights coming from the Koran.

Hence the philosophers tried to assimilate the data of revelation by fitting them into the framework of Greek philosophy. Their attempt did not fail to arouse the suspicion of traditional believers, and still more their reprobation. Even a mind as open as al-Ghazālī, and as closely in touch with philosophic doctrines, listed twenty erroneous theses drawn from their works: seventeen are considered blameworthy innovations (*bidaʿ*), the three remaining being plainly tainted with infidelity (*kufr*), namely, the eternity of the world, the non-knowledge by God of singulars, and the non-resurrection of the flesh. The marginal position of the philosophers did not fail to make their position uncomfortable and compelled them sometimes to take refuge in secrecy. So it would be wrong to compare their teaching with the philosophy of a St. Thomas Aquinas or a Duns Scotus. These two, it is true, were not properly speaking, philosophers but above all theologians. To find, at least to some extent, their equivalents in Islam, we must turn to the *mutakallimūn*, whom St. Thomas specifically calls the *Loquentes in Lege Maurorum*, and this we shall now do.

THEOLOGY (*Kalām*)

We can, for all practical purposes, refer to *kalām* as 'theology', but always with the proviso that this does not cover exactly what Christian scholasticism called by this name. The origin and the nature of this difference will become clear from an examination of the genesis of *kalām*.

When studying the sources of Muslim thought, we spoke of the Koran, of the *ḥadīth*, and of Greek philosophy. Obviously, they cannot all be placed on the same level. First comes the sacred text. It provides the 'matter' that is to be believed and interpreted. This is the basis on which exegesis builds. In various directions, however, we have seen it touch on philosophical speculation, and there has also been, always based on the text, Koranic exegesis (*tafsīr*) and jurisprudence (*fiqh*).

We may divide a historical outline into several stages. First of all, there is what we might call the period of 'creeds'.[1] This is not yet speculation in the full sense of the word, but attempts are made to concentrate in brief formulas the dogmas to be believed. Going beyond the basic formulas of the Profession of Faith, the *shahāda*, the *Fiqh akbar* summarizes in ten articles the entirety of the truths to be believed, not only in order to belong to the Muslim community (which is the function of the *shahāda*) but to take a position as regards aberrant sects. A specific profession, it makes no mention of the unity of God or of the mission of Muḥammad, which are not called in question.

With the *Waṣiyya*, attributed to Abu Ḥanīfa (d. 767), the major problems begin to emerge. They are not fully classified into homogeneous groups, but one already senses the work of collection getting under way. We can try to discern its main themes; the first of these groups together the articles concerning faith and its relation to works, whilst the second concerns predestination and its relation to human activity. The actions of man are, in fact, completely dependent on the divine will, and the relation of the two is the crucial problem of speculative moral theology. At the same time, a distinction is made between the three categories of works: the obligatory, the supererogatory, and the sinful. Then follow a dozen statements specifying eschatological beliefs.

With the *Fiqh akbar II* we are on completely different ground. The discussions forced the religious leaders to state their beliefs precisely, to reject everything which might reflect on the transcendence of God, to specify the role of the prophets, their value, and their message. The credo begins with a comprehensive exposition of the content of the faith: God, the angels, His messengers, resurrection, the decree (predestination)—the good and the evil

[1] For these credos see Wensinck, *The Muslim Creed* (Cambridge, 1932), Chapters VI, VII, and VIII, and Gardet-Anawati, *Introduction*, pp. 136–45.

thereof, the computation of sins, the balance, paradise and hell. Here we have an outline of the material which the *kalām* will be called upon to organize. The various clauses of the creed (about forty) summarize each point, developing it slightly, without, however, retaining the order of the subjects as set out at the beginning.

In the credo of al-Ashʿarī (d. 935),[1] founder of what one might call the traditional *kalām*, i.e. Ashʿarism, we have a thorough exposition of the beliefs of 'those who are faithful to the tradition of the Prophet' (*ahl al-sunna*). It is set out without logical order, just as the earlier ones. The author condenses in a general clause the totality of faith: belief in God, in the angels, in the Holy Books, in His Messenger. The clauses then follow one another without apparent order, and deal with 'the oneness of God' (*tawḥīd*), predestination and human actions, faith, the Koran, the Prophet, eschatology, the Caliphate, and worship.

An examination of these four creeds shows that if the *matter* of theology is already available, its organization has not yet been undertaken. In not one of them do we find the distinction between what is known by revelation and what is accessible to reason. It would, however, be unjust to demand that a formulary be presented as a compendium of theology, though one might expect from al-Ashʿarī a somewhat more rational organization of his profession of faith.

Another group of works which allows us to follow the formation of Muslim theology is that of the treatises on heresies and the polemics against them. It is a type which flourished quite early in Islam and which gave rise to works of great importance to the history of doctrine. Heresiology has to *classify* the doctrines which it has collected. It can do so in a material way, even according to the order of appearance of the heresies, but it must also try to reduce them to a certain number of types. It is therefore interesting to find out the method of classification. If the *Ibāna* and the *Maqālāt* of al-Ashʿarī and the *Farq bayn al-firaq* of al-Baghdādī

[1] Gardet-Anawati, *Introduction*, p. 146.

(d. 1037) are somewhat elusive on this particular point, the works of Ibn Ḥazm (d. 1065) and of al-Shahrastānī (d. 1153), do not fail to present a new viewpoint on the grouping of beliefs and by this shed much light on our subject. Let us look at the plans of these two treatises.

Ibn Ḥazm divides his treatise into two parts: the first concerns the non-Muslim sects, the second the Muslim schools and sects. We do not find here the distinction, which was to become classic, between the 'rational' and the 'traditional' data (*ʿaqliyyāt* and *samʿiyyāt*). Basically, we are still in the line of the earlier creeds, of which the general plan serves as framework. In the *Milal wa'l-niḥal* of al-Shahrastānī we have the most important work on Muslim heresiology. In contrast with Ibn Ḥazm, the author does not aim at refuting errors, but merely strives to state the doctrines as objectively as possible. The tone remains calm and sedate; it is a relaxation to read it after the tumultuous diatribes of the fiery Andalusian.

Muʿtazilī problems

We pointed out at the start the fundamental place held by the Muʿtazilīs in the birth and development of Muslim thought as a whole. We regarded them as philosophers, but we could equally well consider them as 'theologians' who tried to think out dogma in accord with the exigencies of reason and to defend reason against its detractors. They are the first who tried to give a systematic presentation of religious beliefs. In this way one of their first leaders, Abu'l-Hudhayl al-ʿAllāf (d. 849), adopted the following plan for the presentation of Muslim doctrine: firstly, predestination and (divine) attributes; secondly, divine unity and attributes; thirdly, eschatology (promises and threats); fourthly, legal terms and statutes; and fifthly, 'ordering the good and forbidding evil', the roles of prophecy and the Caliphate. The large encyclopedia, called *al-Mughnī*, of the Qāḍī ʿAbd al-Jabbār (d. 1025) which is now being printed in Cairo,[1] shows that the greater

[1] Cf. Anawati, Caspar, and Khodeiri, 'Une Somme inédite de théologie muʿtazilite:

number of these problems have subsequently been studied in detail.

From the via antiqua *to the* via moderna

In his famous *Prolegomena*, the Arab historian Ibn Khaldūn (d. 1406), describing the evolution of *kalām*, distinguishes a break in its development from al-Ghazālī onward. The *via antiqua*, marked by a dialectic inspired above all by the doctors of the law, is replaced by the *via moderna*, the foremost instrument of which is the Aristotelian syllogism. But it would be going too far to stress this break too heavily; the infiltrations, at least as regards the subjects discussed, must have taken place earlier through the Muʿtazilīs, some of whom had read Aristotle in translation. This is evident in al-Bāqillānī (d. 1013), their indefatigable opponent, and still more clearly in al-Juwaynī (d. 1085). The latter is still an ancient by his dialectic, but an ancient who foreshadows the triumph of the new method. This new method was finally to assert itself in the work of his disciple al-Ghazālī and to become, in the writings of the later theologians, ever more similar to that of the philosophers. A short comparison of three works will throw light on the evolution that was going on: the *Tamhīd* of al-Bāqillānī, the *Irshād* of al-Juwaynī, and the *Iqtiṣād* of al-Ghazālī. We will end with some treatises whose modern character is fully apparent.

In his *Tamhīd*, al-Bāqillānī has not yet freed himself from apologetic preoccupations and he mingles his statement of beliefs with long diatribes against the non-Muslim sects and against the dissidents.

Al-Juwaynī, also called Imām al-Ḥaramayn, mentions on several occasions the great classifications of the subject-matter; in one place he speaks of a division between what exists of necessity in God and what is possible, that is to say what God may or may not do, in another between things accessible to reason and things

le *Mughnī* du Qāḍī ʿAbd al-Jabbār', *Mélanges de l'Institut dominicaine d'études orientales du Caire*, iv (1957), 281–316.

reached only by the traditional path. But it is not easy to distinguish any of that in the *Irshād*.

Al-Ghazālī, of whom we shall speak of greater length in the section on mysticism, shows a certain reserve with regard to *kalām*; he wants to keep to essentials. He wrote a clear compendium which he called *al-Iqtiṣād fī'l-iʿtiqād* which may be translated as *The Golden Mean in Belief*. He aims at remaining faithful to the orthodox Ashʿarī doctrine, simplifying the dialectical debates to the utmost, suppressing the philosophical considerations that his master al-Juwaynī had inserted into his treatises.

Al-Ghazālī devotes four chapters to a general introduction to *kalām*. He first stresses the importance of this science; it allows us to know God, His attributes, the work of His Messengers. But, he hastens to add in the second chapter, this interests only a certain number of persons, for *kalām* should not normally be used save to dissipate the doubts of believers and to try to convince intelligent infidels. In the fourth chapter, he carefully analyses the sources used.

Al-Ghazālī then divides the questions envisaged into four main sections, closely linked. This is how the general plan of the work appears: after a preliminary section on the nature of *kalām*, its importance, and its methodology, he covers firstly, the divine essence; secondly, the attributes of God; thirdly, the actions of God; and fourthly, the messengers of God.

Development of the via moderna

As *kalām* widened its scope, it became invaded by philosophy to such an extent that problems properly theological were relegated to the end of a long analysis of the categories and problems of metaphysics or cosmology. To verify this one should consult the *Nihāyat al-aqdām* of al-Shahrastānī, the *Muḥaṣṣal* of Fakhr al-Dīn al-Rāzī (d. 1209), and the *Ṭawāliʿ al-anwār* of al-Bayḍāwī (d. 1286), or the last treatises of this line of evolution such as the *Mawāqif* of al-Ījī (d. 1355) with the commentary of al-Jurjānī (d. 1413). The combined work of al-Ījī and al-Jurjānī, together with the glosses of other commentators, is the largest (four volumes of more than 500 pages each) and the most systematic work of orthodox Moslem speculative thought. It is the basic work for the years of specialization at the Universities of al-Azhar (Cairo) and al-Zaytūna (Tunis). It must be acknowledged, above all when it is compared with the earlier works, that its fame is well deserved. If the sections which are properly traditional, and even theology properly speaking, are treated soberly, the philosophical section on the other hand with its long criteriological introduction receives ample development.

We have called *kalām* 'theology' while pointing out that the two notions do not cover the same ground in Islam and in Christianity. Let us, to conclude this section, make a few comments on the subject.

Compared with the contents of the books of Christian theology, those of the works of *kalām* are radically different. The few chapters which they have in common should not create any illusion; their only points in common are some sections of the treatise *De Deo Uno*, and even then only superficially. The subjects and the methods are different. The *kalām* is not presented as a scientifically organized whole, a total synthesis of all the data of revelation, but primarily as a defensive apologetic concentrated now on one point now on another, according to the attacks of its adversaries. Furthermore, given the 'legal' and positive character of Islamic morality, it is normal that *kalām*, a rational science, neither seeks to assure its foundations nor to integrate its conclusions, since these two have their sole justification in the data of revelation as established by the sciences concerned with 'tradition'. *Kalām* will undoubtedly have to defend the foundations of jurisprudence against its detractors, but it is not this which will give it its principles; these will come directly from the Koran. That is why the Muslim theologian will not feel the need of organizing, in a vast *summa*, all religious and human knowledge, speculative and practical.

MYSTICISM (*Taṣawwuf*)[1]

With *taṣawwuf* or Ṣūfism we come to one of the most arresting aspects of Muslim thought, even of Muslim civilization. The voices of its many authors move us and the brilliance of their descriptions arouses our admiration. Only by being familiar with the texts can we gain a true idea of the wealth of this field.

Numerous theories have been put forward about the origin of this movement in Islam: Syrian monasticism, Neo-Platonism, Persian Zoroastrianism, Indian Vedanta. It has, however, been shown that the hypothesis of more borrowings is untenable. From the very beginnings of Islam, the urge was felt by certain fervent believers to 'meditate' on the Koran by constant recitation and, so to speak, to 'interiorize' it. The sacred Book, as we have already pointed out, contains a certain number of ascetic and mystical elements. Some verses insistently recall the presence of God, the fear of judgement, the transience of all things human, the beauty of virtue, etc. Others offer the religious soul the opportunity of getting to the core of its faith. Thus we find a series of texts which remind man of his vocation, which insist on the need for building in his heart an edifice 'founded on piety towards God and not upon the brink of a crumbling, overhanging precipice'. The life of this world is like running water, like a scorched harvest. In the ritual sacrifice of the Pilgrimage, it is not the blood or the flesh of the victims, it is the piety which rises towards God. A word of affection that pardons is worth more than a word that wounds.

Many passages insist on the separation of the good from the evil. An abyss separates the fate of those who have sincere hearts and the fate of the hypocrites, of those who put their trust in God and those who rely upon themselves. The first are like the grain which sprouts, the ear which swells, the tree which grows; the second are like captives, dumb, deaf, like lost sheep which follow

[1] For the whole of this section see: Anawati-Gardet, *Mystique musulmane* (Paris, 1961); L. Massignon, article 'Taṣawwuf', in *Encyclopaedia of Islam*, 1st edn.

a mirage, like swimmers 'caught in a mysterious wave', like travellers carried away by an icy wind, their house as fragile as a spider's web. On the Day of Judgement, those souls devoid of good deeds will in vain pray to the others: 'Wait for us, that we may borrow of your light.'

The Koran incessantly reminds the believer of the dogma of resurrection: God who brings life to barren soil with water and produces fire from green wood will know well how to recall souls to their bodies like tamed birds.

Alongside these Koranic instances which insist above all on the ascetic aspect of life, there are others which set man on the path towards an inner life and which nourish, like so many living symbols, the meditation of the holy mystics. The cycles of the prophets provide abundant examples. Thus the Koran states that God plumbs the secret thoughts of Muḥammad; it describes the fall of Satan, the rivalry of the angels eager to serve Mary in the temple; it gives the words of the Annunciation, the arguments of Abraham and Noah with God, the discussion between Moses and his guide; it compares God's light with a mysterious luminary in which a lamp burns. It calls God 'light of lights' and declares in forceful terms that 'everything will perish except God's countenance'.

Finally, a certain number of typical allegories, which will frequently appear in the writings of the mystics, also have their source in the Koran: fire and the clarity of God; the veils of light and darkness placed upon the heart; the bird, symbol of resurrection (or rather of the immortality of the soul); the farther side of heaven; the tree representing the vocation and destiny of man; the cup, the wine, the greeting, which symbolize the special ceremony of the enthronement of the privileged in paradise, etc.

Let us add to these Koranic concepts those which come not only from traditions relating the words of the Prophet, inducing piety, but also those known as 'sacred Traditions' (*aḥādīth qudsiyya*) which are directly linked to God and whose evocatory power in the direction of interior meditation is much greater than that of the others. Let us recall only this one, with its striking Pauline touch: 'I have assumed this obligation with regard to a servant of Mine who loves Me and whose intentions I know, to become his ear by which he hears, his eye by which he sees, his tongue by which he speaks, his heart by which he perceives. While it is so, I will make detestable to him everything that prevents him from concerning himself with Me alone.'

Starting from these notions, we can distinguish, schematically, within the historic sweep of Muslim mysticism, three great periods: the first which covers the first three centuries of Islam (seventh to ninth centuries) can be called the struggle for existence; mysticism is searching for its right to exist and to overcome certain prejudices against it nourished by touchy and suspicious official authorities. The second period is marked by the attempt at reconciliation and the triumph of Ṣūfism, due, above all, to a man of genius, al-Ghazālī, in the eleventh century. Finally, the third period is marked by the spread of the great works of mysticism (twelfth to fifteenth centuries) and, from the sixteenth century onward, decadence. We shall outline these three periods very briefly.

The first period, as we have said, is a period of quest. Among the companions of Muḥammad, the ascetic element is predominant: fasting, spiritual retreat, meditation. In the seventh and eighth centuries asceticism becomes more vigorous and more complex. The ascetics still did not leave the community; they lived within it to fulfil the office of preachers or of 'censors'. At Baṣra especially there was a flourishing group of open-air preachers, the *quṣṣāṣ*, who spoke to the people and told them anecdotes in rhymed prose. Among these ascetics, who gave themselves up to devotion, some readers of the Koran made public exhortations to repentance; these were the 'weepers', while the preachers preached with vehemence, expatiating on the end of the world.

The most imposing figure of these first two centuries after the *hijra* is, undoubtedly, Ḥaṣan al-Baṣrī, the 'patriarch of Muslim mysticism', who died in 728. His mystical and ascetic doctrine is rooted in a feeling of contempt for the world. His rule of life is inspired not only by scrupulous abstention from all works questionable in the eyes of the religious Law (*waraʿ*), but also and above all by ascetic detachment towards everything that is transient. Face to face with God, he recommends over and above this *waraʿ*, awe of and attentive regard for the Word.

The influence of Ḥaṣan al-Baṣrī on Ṣūfism was very great, and Islamic religious confraternities consider him their founder. His disciples handed on his method. Without wearing any regular religious habit, they had reached some degree of unity by the second generation, and a coenobitic organization was formed at ʿAbbādān, near Baṣra, during the eighth century. To this group belonged an almost legendary figure who is considered, rightly, as a herald of divine love and whom Louis Massignon describes as 'the saint par excellence of Sunnī hagiography'. The medieval West also knew of her, through Joinville's *Life of St. Louis*. She was Rabīʿa al-ʿAdawiyya (d. 801), a freed slave and a former flute player who, remaining celibate, passed her long life (when she died she was past 80) in the search of the love of God.

Basing herself on a passage in the Koran where it is said: 'God will lead a people whom He will love and who will love Him,' she comments on it in this famous quatrain:

1. I love Thee with two loves, the (interested) love of my happiness and the (perfect) Love, the desire to give Thee what is worthy of Thee.
2. This love of my happiness means that I think only of Thee, alone, to the exclusion of all else.
3. As for that other love of which Thou art worthy, it is (my desire) that Thy veils fall and that I see Thee.
4. No glory for me, in the one or in the other (love). Ah, no! But praise to Thee, for this one as for that.

Contemporaneous with the school of Baṣra was the school of Kūfa, where there was also an Arab military colony. Contrary to the realist and critical tendencies of the former, this one was idealistic and traditionalist in temper. The Ṣūfis of this school swarmed to Baghdad, where they soon formed a group with many disciples at the beginning of the ninth century, and at that period many hermitages existed around the city.

One of the best-known members of this Baghdad school was al-Muḥāsibī (d. 857) whose nickname means 'he who strives to search his conscience'. His teaching was marked by a deep respect for tradition, an unrelenting search for inner perfection, and, finally, by a regard for exact philosophical definitions. What was fundamental in his eyes was a profound rectification of intent, the submission of individual or social activities to the imprescriptible rights of God. In his *Kitāb al-riʿāya* he describes the 'rule of life' to be observed, and shows how searching of the conscience dissipates illusions which one might have concerning one's devotions. The first knowledge required is to regard oneself as a servant submissive to a master. One must hold oneself ready to die, learn how to despise the world, struggle against the temptations of Satan, aim at acting only for God, without self-will, turn towards God in all activities; take account of the consequences of one's actions in so far as they concern others and guard against the risk of scandals, vainglory, and sadness at feeling oneself despised; in short, one must unify one's life with God, night and day. In one of his writings, he is not afraid to insist on the love of God for all true believers.

The influence of al-Muḥāsībī on men's consciences was profound and long-lasting despite the attacks he had to suffer from the traditionalists. Al-Junayd (d. 911), the most 'sedate' of the School and the master of al-Ḥallāj, was inspired by his teaching, and the Ashʿarī theologians hailed him as the forerunner of their reform. Baghdad became little by little a centre for many of the traditionalists and of literary men in sympathy with the mystics. It was at their meetings that the first miscellanies of anecdotes were drawn up, anthologies grouped around the virtues practised by the Ṣūfis.

One of al-Junayd's disciples, al-Ḥallāj, a native of Iran, was rejected by the school of Baghdad because of the audacity of his ideas. His conception of union with God whereby the soul is made perfect, consecrated, deified, becoming the free and living instrument of God, his ideas on the apostolate which, according to him, must apply to everyone, his 'miracles', which in the eyes of his disciples associated him with the prophets, caused him to be condemned by mystic, juridical, and political circles alike. He was imprisoned, tried, and, on 27 March 922, beheaded. Massignon devoted two monumental volumes to him, one of the finest works of comparative mysticism of the century.[1]

This cruel repression did not, however, suppress the mystical movement in the circles which devoted themselves to it. At the most, the more famous masters publicly rejected the 'excesses' of the 'great lover of God' and strove to show in their writings that the Ṣūfis were good Muslims, respectful of the traditions and the official teaching of the Community. This epoch saw a flourishing of classic accounts, such as the works of al-Sarrāj (d. 988), al-Kalābādhī (d. 990), al-Makkī (d. 990), al-Hujwīrī (d. 1072), and al-Qushayrī (d. 1074).

One of the characteristic features of this doctrine was the theory of 'stages' or stations and of 'states'. Sketched out by Dhu'l-Nūn al-Miṣrī in the ninth century in Egypt, perhaps under the influence of the ascetic and mystical spirituality of the Oriental monks (we think of the *Ladder to Paradise* by St. John Climacus), it assumed in the course of centuries of experience an almost stereotyped form.

The path is both ascetic and mystical. It requires purification which prepares the soul for union with the divine. He who takes this path passes through three fundamental stages: that of the novice, that of the graduate (*sālik*), and finally that of the adept. We find here the great divisions of Oriental Christian ascetism. The path is gone through step by step; one only advances to a superior degree after having passed through the degrees preceding it. The various stages of the ascetic path are called 'stations' or 'relays'. Al-Sarrāj listed seven of them: repentance, placed by

[1] *La Passion d'al-Ḥosayn ibn Mansoûr al-Ḥallâj*, 2 vols. (Paris, 1922).

most authors at the head of the list as the first relay; scrupulous delicacy of conscience, which must exceed that of the ordinary believer; absolute renunciation of the goods of this world, even if they are legitimate; poverty; acceptance of all adversity; trust in God; and acceptance of all that happens in actual conformity with the divine Will.

The task of becoming perfect is a struggle, an inner battle carried out under the indispensable guidance of a spiritual director. The novice must be in the hands of his director 'as a corpse in the hands of the washer of the dead'. It is the task of the director to take into account the dispositions of the novice, to mould him to humility, penitence, silence, fasts, and such-like practices. Meditation, vocal prayer, incessant repetition of the same ejaculatory supplications, searching of conscience, and other pious exercises take up the day of the Ṣūfī candidate.

Whereas the 'stations' are attained by personal effort, the 'states' are the effects of divine mercy. Al-Sarrāj names about a dozen: constant attention, proximity, love, fear, hope, desire, intimacy, tranquillity in peace, contemplation, certitude. But the classifications differ according to authors. Love is sometimes ranked among the 'stages acquired'; at other times it is considered the basis of 'unification'.

Al-Ghazālī, 'The Proof of Islam'

The man who was to contribute most to get mysticism accepted by official Islam and to break down the prejudices of an Islam too exclusively juridical was al-Ghazālī (d. 1111), the Algazel of the Western Middle Ages. The West, however, knew him only through certain of his philosophical works, especially his *Maqāṣid al-falāsifa* ('The Intentions of the Philosophers'), and could not, therefore, judge him at his real value, when, *mutatis mutandis*, he could be regarded as the St. Thomas Aquinas of Muslim thought.[1]

In a moving autobiography *al-Munqidh min al-ḍalāl* ('The

[1] For al-Ghazālī's significance as a political theorist, see below, Chapter IX(*B*), pp. 414–15.

Deliverance from Error'), certain features of which recall the *Confessions* of St. Augustine, al-Ghazālī describes his intellectual and spiritual itinerary, and states that he found peace only by following the 'way of the Ṣūfis'. Al-Ghazālī is certainly one of the greatest Muslim thinkers. Deeply versed in the Muslim religious sciences, he also assimilated all that the Arab world of his time knew of Greek philosophy, strongly influenced by Neo-Platonism. Furthermore, he had many opportunities of knowing Christianity. He studied in particular the Gospel of St. John, of which he wrote a refutation.

But these extra-Muslim influences would only have had the result of confusing his thought, had his mind not been nourished on the purest marrow of the Koran and the traditions and maintained an unshakeable faith in the truth of Islam. The doubts through which he passed did not concern his faith, but the power of reason to repulse the attacks against that faith. His religious certainty was an integral part of himself and it was in its light that he was to envisage all problems. But his most personal contribution was perhaps just to be himself; he wished to be a Ṣūfi not only in thought but in deed. That he was a 'spiritual' rather than a 'mystic' properly speaking did not prevent his knowledge being at the service of a sensitive and deeply religious soul that the majesty of God kept in suspense and that was drawn to His love.

At the same time he retained a profound sense of the Muslim Community, of its needs and of the diversity of the elements that composed it. He considered that certain exalted truths of a theological or mystical order could not with impunity be revealed to the ignorant masses, but that only so much truth should be given to each individual as he was able to 'bear'. Above all, he understood that Islam could not be satisfied with the juridical moralism of the canonists against whom he was passionately severe, but that a fervent inward attitude must illuminate the study of the Law. A disciple of al-Muḥāsibī, of al-Makkī, of al-Junayd, of the whole line of Ṣūfis of the past centuries, he understood that the essentials of their teaching could not remain the privilege of a small intellectual or spiritual aristocracy but that all life, the life of every day, must be filled with the presence of God and the desire to serve Him. Thus the essential contribution of al-Ghazālī is perhaps to have integrated and made acceptable to official teaching Ṣūfism and all the elements of an emotional order which gave it life. Henceforward one could love God without having to justify or hide oneself.

The Muslim world as a whole has been infinitely grateful to him. It considers him as one of its greatest glories, as the *Ḥujjat al-Islām*, 'The Proof of Islam', and up to our own day, in the great mosque-universities as in certain booths of humble and pious artisans in the bazaars of Cairo, Fez, or Damascus, men continue to bend fervently over the pages of his great work *Iḥyā' ʿulūm al-dīn* ('The Revitalization of the Sciences of Religion').

Intellectual Ṣūfism

The diversity of elements brought into play by al-Ghazālī resulted in his influence being directed along two distinct lines, one intellectual resulting in a mysticism which might be termed metaphysical or gnostic, the other in popular trends put into concrete form in the religious confraternities.

What characterizes the first of these was the conviction that it is possible to go beyond the tangible world, which is mere appearance, to attain the world of intelligible and spiritual realities; and this by means of an emotional intuition, the *maʿrifa* (gnosis). Using the metaphysical analyses of the great philosophers, in particular Avicenna, influenced by Neo-Platonic, Iranian, and Hermetic elements, these gnostic Ṣūfīs hold forth on the prophets and their mission, on the emanation of the many from the One, on the relation of creatures to their Creator, the structure of the world, the infusion of God in the soul of the mystic or the identification of the human Ego with the divine Ego, 'illumination', and the oneness of being. Their dissertations are in prose or in long poems, some of which are among the most beautiful in Arabic or Persian literature.

On the practical level, the methods employed varied and hardened more than once into techniques: scrupulous fidelity to the acts of worship, prolonged mortifications, *dhikr* (repetition of the Name of God) and *samāʿ* (listening to music). The search for union with God is coupled with the acquisition of mastery over nature, over the human nature of the Ṣūfi but also over external nature according to the gnostic interplay of the macrocosm and the microcosm.

Of this gnostic mysticism we shall set out two main themes: that of God considered as light, and that of 'The Perfect Man' in which are made manifest both the divinity and the riches of the cosmos.

The man who most profoundly orchestrated the first of these themes was a twelfth-century mystic born in Persia and put to death at Aleppo for his ideas which were regarded as heterodox. He was al-Suhrawardī (d. 1191), author of the *Hayākil al-nūr* ('The Temples of Light') and above all of the *Ḥikmat al-ishrāq* ('The Illuminative Wisdom') wherein he fully expounded his thought.

The point of departure of al-Suhrawardī's doctrine is the statement in the Koran that 'God is the light of the heavens and of the earth . . . Light upon light' (xxiv. 35). Starting from this essential statement, al-Suhrawardī, fusing and greatly adjusting the Neo-Platonic and Pythagorean trends transmitted via Avicenna, elaborates an explicit conception of the divine union which sometimes recalls that of al-Ḥallāj, but remains faithful to the favourite terms and myths of the Iranian tradition, especially its views on angels. At the base of this search for a living synthesis is the conviction that there is only one wisdom, a single mystical tradition, expressed in the course of centuries sometimes by Hermes, Plato, and Aristotle, sometimes by Agathodemon and Empedocles and the sages of India and Persia. This is what al-Suhrawardī wishes to rediscover and re-express in a Koranic framework.

In such a perspective, the synthesis of al-Suhrawardī can be summarized thus. Starting from God, considered as Light of light, irradiation engenders to infinity other sources of light which, in their mutual irradiations, enjoy the primal Light. There are various degrees of archangelic lights, which al-Suhrawardī links with Mazdean angelology, then the lights Regent of species and bodies, amongst which is the light Regent of every man. Each species, the celestial spheres, the simple elements and their combinations have a Lord of their own in the world of Light who is a distinct Intelligence, Regent of that species. Opposed to the sources of Light are the *barzakhs*, the dark repositories. The aim of spiritual life is to bear witness to the Unique, to produce in oneself the *tawḥīd*, which is realized in the last instance by the instantaneous dialectic of *fanā*ʾ (annihilation) and *baqā*ʾ (everlastingness).

As for the theme of 'The Perfect Man', it has above all been expressed by Ibn ʿArabī and by his disciple ʿAbd al-Qādir al-Jīlī (d. 1428) who wrote a book of that very name, *al-Insān al-kāmil* ('The Perfect Man'). Ibn ʿArabī was born at Murcia in Spain in 1165. At the age of eight he went to study at Seville where he learnt all the sciences then known: Koranic exegesis, *kalām*, Ṣūfism, etc. He studied there for twenty years and was acquainted with the great personalities of his time. In 1194 he undertook a long voyage to the East, lived for some time at Mecca, and visited Egypt, Syria, Iraq, and Anatolia. After having lived at Konya, he returned to Damascus where he died in 1240 at the age of seventy-five.

So long a life, coupled with an undeniable creative faculty, allowed Ibn ʿArabī to write a large number of books. The two main ones are *al-Futūḥāt al-Makkiyya* ('The Meccan Revelations'), a huge mystical treatise in twelve volumes, and *Fuṣūṣ al-ḥikam* ('The Gems of Wisdom'). The doctrine of Ibn ʿArabī is centred on his theory of the Logos. He uses no less than twenty-two terms in order to define this idea. This can be seen as a consequence of the variety of his sources and, more deeply, of his ontological monism, where all definitions tend to become equivalent. The Logos can, indeed, be envisaged in three ways: ontologically (and consequently as a conception of the Universe), mystically, and mythically (the myth of the Perfect Man). Ontologically, the eternal Logos is the Reality of realities, the rational creative principle of the cosmos. A hidden aspect of the Divinity, it is prior to the world only logically. It embraces all Ideas and all things, having absolute existence. It is multiplied with beings in actual existence but is not divided. It may be called God or Universe.

From it the Universe proceeds as the particular proceeds from the universal. It is the reservoir of intelligible ideas and of stable Archetypes of the world of becoming. It is God in so far as it manifests itself as universal conscience. Man alone (the Perfect Man, not animal man) manifests it synthetically, and the awareness that God has of himself reaches its climax in the Perfect Man. In him, therefore, is realized the object of creation, which is God's desire to know himself. In this *processus* of descent of God with regard to our knowledge, the Logos is the first epiphany of God.

Mystically, the Logos expresses the Reality of Muḥammad (and not his form). It is the First Intellect, the universal rational Principle. Each prophet is a logos, but Muḥammad is *the* Logos: all these *Verba Dei* made manifest in the prophets are united in a single universal Principle, which is the Spirit or the reality of Muḥammad and the active principle of all revelation or inspiration. Ibn ʿArabī professes the eternity of Muḥammad as the cosmic Principle. For the Logos in the form of Perfect Man is the most faithful of the manifestations of God. Does this show influence of Stoic philosophy? Like the Stoics, Ibn ʿArabī distinguishes between the 'inner Logos' and the 'uttered Logos'. He borrows from al-Ḥallāj his ideas of the 'world' of Humanity and the 'world' of Divinity, and lays stress upon them. He speculates at length on the essence of the Perfect Man, his body, his spirit, his knowledge, his spiritual faculties (which correspond to those of the angels), his part in the Universe. The Perfect Man is the Mirror which exactly reflects the perfections of God.

It is easy to note that many sources are interwoven in these speculations: Stoicism, Philonism, Neo-Platonism, Ismāʿīlī theories, the gnostic meditations of al-Ḥallāj, and others. The Christian influences certainly do not go very deep, or rather the Christian mysteries, the Incarnation and the Trinity, seem to present themselves to Ibn ʿArabī as so many myths which his 'sapiential gnosis' undertakes to integrate into a vision of the world predominantly Islamic. He thus tends towards a natural and universal love in which all distinctions and determinations are brushed aside and which heralds the deliberate 'existential monism' of his successors.

The religious confraternities

The second line of influence of al-Ghazālī was a response to the expectation of the mass of the people, more enamoured of 'God appealing to the heart' than gnostic speculation. The result was an extraordinary diffusion of 'orders' or confraternities throughout the whole Muslim world.

It was precisely non-esoteric Ṣūfism, that which held to the essential parts of Muslim dogma, which spread among the people, appealing to their religious feeling and their devotional impulses. What it sought was to touch men's hearts, to draw near to God in a heartfelt manner. Even before the time of al-Ghazālī the practices of *dhikr*, ejaculatory prayer incessantly repeated, and *samāʿ*, or listening to spiritual music, had been introduced. The defenders of the faith, not so long before, had protested in vain. In his *Iḥyāʾ*, al-Ghazāli was to devote whole treatises to *dhikr* and to *samāʿ*. After him, a wave of Ṣūfi practices was to spread to the most humble of the people. The 'wise men' tried their best to react but their teaching, only too often sapless, found no response in popular feeling.

It was thus that the 'confraternities', which had originally been groups made up of a master and his disciples, spread among the masses. This spread was aided by the facility which the Muslim 'missionaries' accepted new converts; all that they asked was the desire to join Islam, the sincere recitation of the Profession of Faith or 'testimony' (*shahāda*). They closed their eyes to ancient customs, if these were not too obviously polytheistic. The result of such liberalism was to change appreciably for some centuries the whole face of Islam. Until then, thanks to the acknowledged authority of the doctors, unity had been maintained. Once their unifying influence had disappeared, every newly converted Muslim area, and sometimes certain areas converted for a long time past, was coloured by its folklore and by the survival of ancestral customs. This regionalism of Islam coincided with the period when the religious sciences and all Arabo-Muslim culture itself began to become fossilized.[1]

This diversification was also to be found throughout the orders, or religious confraternities. Some spread mainly in the Muslim East, others in the Maghrib. Those which drew adherents in the towns remained in contact with the *madrasa*; many of their members were teachers in the mosques, and *kalām* itself absorbed Ṣūfī elements. The country orders, widespread in the villages, were more subject to local influences. There were also cases of a single family of confraternities having town branches which remained very close to official teaching, and country branches where animistic survivals appeared. Such was the great Shādhilī school of North Africa.

Persian mysticism

Religious literature in Persian would deserve a whole study to itself. The most famous of the mystical poets who wrote in Persian was undoubtedly the author of the *Mathnavī*, Mawlāna Jalāl al-Dīn Rūmī (d. 1273).

Rūmī placed all his poetic genius at the service of his mystical flame. His masterpiece was an immense poetical *summa* of 47,000 verses, the *Mathnavī*. The author wished, as he says in the preface which is written in Arabic, to give a commentary on the Koran and to redress morals. Using fables, pseudo-historical narratives, reflections, and allegories, Jalāl al-Dīn constantly takes up his

[1] Cf. the symposium *Classicisme et déclin culturel dans l'histoire de l'Islam*, ed. R. Brunschwig and G. E. von Grunebaum (Paris, 1957).

single motif: the love of God and the search for that love which alone avails. One must forget oneself to lose oneself in Him. The narratives follow one another and interlace, the most suggestive comparisons are given, symbols and descriptions are filled with poetic evocation, and the whole is immersed in that wisdom of the Orient which in Persia is often accompanied by a nostalgic note, sometimes bitter, sometimes full of humour, which seems to cast over men and things a light mist of scepticism. But the dominant note of the *Mathnavī* remains the search, sometimes painful, sometimes overwhelming, for the meeting with the Loved One. This can be verified by reading this immense work in Nicholson's admirable translation.

THE LEGACY TO THE WEST

It remains for us to consider what part of Muslim philosophy, theology, and mysticism has passed over into Western civilization.[1]

To begin with let us recall one important fact: the Arabs occupied Spain for almost seven centuries (see above, Chapter II, pp. 80–100). Cordova was the centre of an intense intellectual life, in which philosophy and theology obviously played their part. Contacts between Christians and Muslims were not limited to trade; Muslim culture had sufficient appeal to attract the finest spirits among the Christians. The bishops, furthermore, were anxious to become acquainted with the works of those whom it was their mission to convert and it was on their instructions that

[1] On the translators from Arabic into Western languages, see M. Steinschneider, *Die europäischen Übersetzungen aus dem Arabischen bis Mitte des 17. Jahrhunderts* (Berlin, 1904–5; reprinted Graz, 1956); C. H. Haskins, *Studies in Mediaeval Science*, 2nd edn. (Cambridge, Mass., 1927); M. de Wulf, *Histoire de la philosophie médiévale*, 6th edn. (Paris, 1936), ii. 25–51; U. Monneret de Villard, *Lo studio del Islam in Europa nel XII e nel XIII secolo* (Studi e Testi, cx, Vatican, 1944); G. Théry, *Tolède, ville de la renaissance mediévale, point de jonction entre la philosophie musulmane et la pensée chrétienne* (Oran, 1944); M.-Th. d'Alverny and G. Vajda, 'Marc de Tolède, traducteur d'Ibn Toumart', *Al-Andalus*, xvii (1952), 99–148; M.-Th. d'Alverny, 'Notes sur les traductions médiévales des œuvres philosophiques d'Avicenne', *Archives de l'histoire doctrinale et littéraire du moyen âge*, xix (1952), 337–58.

translations were made. When Toledo was recaptured from the Muslims in 1085, Bishop Raymond had translations made there; this was also done at Burgos, and in Sicily at the court of Frederick II (1215–50), where Michael Scotus (d. *c.* 1236) contributed actively to the 'Arab education' of his master.[1] The whole process of cultural interaction is considered in detail in Chapter II above, especially at pp. 80 ff.

What is remarkable about these translations is that they were selective; certain works were deliberately left aside, especially works of literature, in order to translate only scientific and philosophical works. Thus it was that the collections of *ḥadīth* and the problems that they posed, the basic works of jurisprudence, the whole of the great treatise of al-Ghazālī, the *Iḥyā'*, remained unknown. The Algazel of the Latin Middle Ages was to be almost exclusively the author of the *Maqāṣid*, a clear and simple résumé of the Oriental *falsafa*. From the *mutakallimūn* only a few themes (atomism, occasionalism) were known and disdainfully rejected by Thomas Aquinas. But to the extent that it had become the vehicle by which the scientific and philosophical wealth of ancient Greece was transmitted, the Arabo-Muslim contribution was warmly welcomed. This scientific contribution had been enriched by the personal labour of the Arabs. From the ninth century onward translations of Arabic works on astronomy, astrology, medicine, experimental science (and magic) were numerous. In the eleventh century, Hereford was a real English centre of Arabic studies.[2] A little later, it was perhaps just the translation of the Koran demanded by Peter the Venerable (d. 1155) which was to encourage, on the philosophical level, the continuation of the Toledan translations; but the preference was almost exclusively for *falsafa*.

For centuries past, only one or two texts of Aristotle saved after the collapse of the Roman Empire had been known. But from 1125

[1] On this 'astrologer' of Frederick II and his activity at the court of Sicily, see the excellent chapter in Haskins, op. cit., pp. 272–98.

[2] Cf. U. Monneret de Villard, op. cit., pp. 2 f. and references.

onward, translations by Boethius, lost until then, and other sources also, placed the complete *Organon* of Aristotle within the reach of Latin thought; and it was with this *logica nova* that a 'dialectic' revolution began. Some years later other works of Aristotle appeared in Latin. These comprised no longer only the logic but also the *Physics* (and a little later still the *Ethics* and the *Metaphysics*), and with these, more or less mixed up with them, the Neo-Platonic texts, the *Pseudo-Theology of Aristotle* (extracts from the *Enneads* of Plotinus), the *Liber de Causis* (extracts from the *Elementatio Theologica* of Proclus).

At the same time original works of Muslim writers also began to make their appearance: the *De Intellectu* of al-Kindī (d. 873), as also that of al-Fārābī, as well as his *De Scientiis* and his *De Ortu Scientiarum*; the *Shifā'* of Avicenna, in particular his *Metaphysics*, and his *De Anima*; the *Maqāṣid* of al-Ghazālī; and the *Fons Vitae* of Ibn Gabirol (Avicebron, d. 1058). From this Arab contribution two names above all emerge which had a considerable influence on medieval Christian thought, sc. those of Avicenna and Averroes.

The Neo-Platonic, even mystical and religious, tendencies of the former could not fail to attract the attention of the Christian theologians desirous of finding a philosophical basis for their Augustinism. Avicennan Augustinism was one of its fruits. The point of departure was the *De Anima* of Archbishop John of Toledo (twelfth century), at one time attributed to Gundisalvi, which is a personal work but completely inspired by Avicenna. The author comments on the Christian Neo-Platonism of St. Augustine in the light of the Arab Neo-Platonism of Avicenna and al-Fārābī.[1] As M. Gilson says: 'The *De Anima* attributed to Gundisalvi (XIIth century) marks the point of insertion of Avicenna-ism into the Christian tradition.' In the thirteenth century we shall again find the line more or less clearly in William of Auvergne (d. 1249), in the great Franciscan masters of the

[1] É. Gilson, 'Les Sources gréco-arabes de l'augustinisme avicennant', *Archives hist. doct. et litt. du m.-a.*, iv (1929–30), 101, and also his study 'Pourquoi saint Thomas a critiqué saint Augustin', ibid. i (1926–7), 5–127.

University of Paris, Alexander of Hales (d. 1245), Jean de la Rochelle (d. 1245), and St. Bonaventure (d. 1274), as well as in the English Franciscans, Robert Grosseteste (d. 1253) and John Peckham (d. 1292). This line coming from Avicenna was to expand and flourish to the extreme in the illuminism of Roger Bacon, so influenced by Avicenna (and by al-Fārābī) that his theory of the Sovereign Pontiff is in full agreement with the theories of the Caliphate put forth by Avicenna.

Let us add that the enormous influence exercised at that time by Avicenna's thought far exceeded the framework of the Avicennan Augustinism in its narrow sense. It is to be found extremely alive in Albertus Magnus's definition of the soul, and theory of prophetism. St. Thomas Aquinas was also to borrow from him many elements of his technical equipment, and Duns Scotus used Avicenna to some extent as a basis upon which to build his metaphysics.[1] Finally, some scholars have tried to find in Avicenna the antecedents of the Cartesian *Cogito*.[2]

With Averroes things did not go so well; for a certain period they were even frankly deplorable. The influence of Aristotle, as we have already said, had already crept in. His naturalism and determinism had put the religious authorities on the alert: the condemnation of 1210 forbade teaching his works at the University of Paris. Averroes arrived only later[3] and at first was received with sympathy, for no one was as yet aware of the inherent dangers of his teachings, indeed, his fame as a commentator on Aristotle earned him the title in the West of 'the Commentator' *par excellence*. But these dangers were soon to be revealed. We have already remarked on the position of the Cordova philosopher on the relation of philosophy to religion. In fact, it was religion which

[1] Cf. Gilson, 'Avicenne et le point de depart de Duns Scot', *Archives*, ii (1927), 89–149.

[2] G. Furlani, 'Avicenna e il 'Cogito ergo sum' di Cartesio', *Islamica*, iii (1927), 53–72; 'Avicenna, Barhebreo, Cartesio', in *Rivista degli Studi Orientali*, xiv (1934), 21–30.

[3] R. de Vaux, 'Première entrée d'Averroes chez les Latins', *Rev. des Sciences Philosophiques et Theologiques*, xxii (1933), 193–242.

was to pay the price of this 'agreement'.[1] It was philosophy which was to discount the apodeictic truth; religion did no more than 'clothe' the images to bring them to the level of the mass of the people. This accounts for the attempt of some Christian thinkers to interpret this attitude as the acceptance of a 'double truth' which the Commentator would have professed and which they would willingly have accepted as their position.[2] But in fact it meant destroying religion and theology, since it was estimated that on the essential points they could be in contradiction with reason.

But what was more serious was that Averroes in his psychology followed a materialist interpretation of his master Aristotle. For him man was, all told, only a superior animal, who was born and died like other animals. What distinguished him from them was the aptitude of his brain to get into contact with the separate intellects, active and passive, of the human species. A single intellect for the whole of humanity; such is the basis of Averroist 'monopsychism'. The active intellect is the last of the celestial intelligences which moves the sphere of the moon, and the passive or 'receptive' intellect receives from it the forms which it has 'abstracted'. The two Intellects are at the frontier of the spiritual world and have an abstractive activity with which they associate human beings by using their 'phantasms', whence they draw the intelligibles. It is precisely in as much as the passive intellect enters into activity that we have any awareness of thought. Consequently, nothing of us remains after death, save perhaps a memory in the passive and active Intellects; they alone are spiritual and immortal. Averroes' attitude here is thus one of a fairly radical materialism.

These ideas began to be introduced into the Faculty of Arts at Paris, and a certain Siger de Brabant (d. *c.* 1281) adopted them to

[1] It is clear why, in these conditions, it is inexact to speak of 'the theological Averroism of St. Thomas Aquinas'. Cf. Gardet-Anawati, *Introduction*, pp. 283 f.

[2] On the problem of the 'double truth' see Gilson, *Études de philosophie médiévale* (Strasbourg, 1921), pp. 59–69; *La Philosophie au moyen âge*, 3rd edn. (Paris, 1947), pp. 561–2; English translation, *History of Christian Philosophy in the Middle Ages* (New York, 1955), pp. 398–9 and 522–4.

a certain extent.[1] St. Thomas found himself forced to refute them in *De Unitate Intellectus Contra Averroistas.* The religious authorities had to react, and a vigorous touch of the helm was given. This was the condemnation of 1270 and even more that of 1277. The crisis calmed down for a time and 'Latin Averroism' which M. Vansteenberghen prefers to call 'heterodox Aristotelianism'.[2] for the moment seemed crushed. But it was to have a tenacious life and was soon to reappear and continue until the Renaissance.[3] In the fourteenth century, in fact, its presence at Paris called forth the repeated attacks of Raymond Lull (d. 1316) who wrote a number of pamphlets to refute it. The word Averroist soon became, in certain mouths, an insult; Averroes was branded as 'accursed', 'a furious barker', 'an impious Arab'. None the less, Parisian Averroism was revived under Jean de Jandun who in 1316 was Master of Arts at the College of Navarre. He attempted a peripatetic synthesis wherein the authorities were Averroes and Albertus Magnus.

From Paris, Averroism passed to Padua which had become, in Renan's phrase, the 'Latin quarter' of Venice. It was a doctor-astrologer, Pietro d'Abano (d. 1315), who brought it there at the beginning of the fourteenth century. Petrarch, who detested Averroism, has left us in his satire *De Sui Ipsius et Multorum Ignorantia* piquant details of the tumultuous triumph of this doctrine at Padua.[4]

In the fifteenth century it was Pomponazzi (d. 1525) who triumphed, while authors like Niphus (d. 1546) and Zimara (d. 1532) tried once again to reconcile Averroes with Christian theology.

[1] Cf. P. Mandonnet, *Siger de Brabant et l'averroisme latin au XIIIe siècle*, 2nd edn., 2 vols. (Louvain, 1908–10), and later the works of F. Van Steenberghen, *Siger de Brabant d'après ses œuvres inédites*, 2 vols. (Louvain, 1931–42); idem, *Les œuvres et la doctrine de Siger de Brabant* (Brussels, 1938).

[2] Cf. especially *Aristotle in the West. The origins of Latin Aristotelianism* (Louvain, 1955), Chapter VIII.

[3] Cf. M.-M. Gorce, *L'Essor de la pensée au moyen âge. Albert le Grand–Thomas d'Aquin* (Paris, 1933), a little too dependent on Renan (see following note) and Mandonnet.

[4] Cf. Renan, *Averroès et l'averroisme*, 2nd edn. (Paris, 1861), pp. 334–8.

The need to know the Commentator better led to fresh translations being made from the Hebrew and Arabic at Padua and at Paris; and the recently discovered craft of printing gave Averroes his last successes in Christian Europe. Whereas in the Islamic lands he had become almost unknown, he was published at Venice in 1481, 1482, 1484, 1489, 1497, and 1500. There were also complete editions in 1553 and 1557. Besides his many Venice editions, there were several others in the sixteenth century at Naples, Bologna, Paris, Lyons, and Strasbourg. After 1580, however, the number of readers of Averroes diminished. He was once more published at Geneva, in 1608. After that his folios slumbered in the dust of libraries. Averroism lasted as long as the Renaissance lasted. It is possible to see in this a certain savage affirmation of the autonomy of reason in relation to religious faith which drove some to make it a weapon against any religious idea. There is no doubt that if the Arab 'Commentator' had been able to participate in the destinies of his doctrine, he would vigorously have rejected those who called upon him to fight against religion.

Over and above the works of Avicenna and Averroes which had so great an influence, on the philosophical level, on the Middle Ages in the West, we must also mention the *Risālat Ḥayy ibn Yaqẓān* ('Story of Ḥayy b. Yaqẓān') of Ibn Ṭufayl (Abubacer), who died in 1185. In this sort of 'philosophical novel' which was entitled in its Latin translation *Philosophus autodidactus*, the author wished to show, in allegoric form, the concord of reason and faith. Ḥayy ibn Yaqẓān, a child without father or mother who has been left on an uninhabited island in the Indian Ocean, is brought up by a gazelle. Little by little, he becomes aware of life and discovers gradually the riches of the world and the laws of nature and ends by proving the existence of God, author of the world, and rediscovering all the truths of religion.

This work, a jewel of Arabic literature, had a great success in the non-Muslim Western world. It was translated into Hebrew in the fourteenth century and into Latin in the second half of the fifteenth century by Pico della Mirandola (d. 1494). In 1671 another Latin version was made from the Arabic by Edward Pocock the Younger (reprinted 1700), and then two translations into English from the Latin, one by the Quaker G. Keith (1674), who regarded the book as a work of edification. Anonymous Dutch translations (1672 and 1701) and the German translation of J. G. Pritius (1726) were made from the Latin. Simon Ockley made another translation from the Arabic (1708, 1731, 1905, and revised by A. S. Fulton, 1929). There was also a German translation by J. G. Eichhorn (1783), an abbreviated English one by P. Brönnle (1904), later translated into German (1907), a Spanish one by Pons Boigues (1900), another Spanish one by A. González Palencia (1934), and a French one by L. Gauthier (1900, 1936), who at the same time published a critical edition of the Arabic text, and one into Russian by J. Kuzmin (1920). It has been shown that Daniel Defoe's *Robinson Crusoe* owes its inspiration to the *Philosophus autodidactus*.[1]

Finally, we must say a few words on the influence of Muslim mysticism on the West. Two topics are relevant here. The first is that of the Muslim sources of the *Divina Commedia*, which has been posed by the great Spanish Islamic scholar Asín Palacios[2] and upon which definite light has been thrown by the publication of the *Liber de la Scala* by Cerulli.[3] The second is that of the theme of courtly love which may be linked to the Platonic love (*al-ḥubb al-ʿudhrī*) of the first centuries of Islam or to a little treatise by Avicenna on 'Love' (*Risāla fi'l-ʿishq*).[4] But these are really questions of comparative literary influences.

[1] A. R. Pastor, *The Idea of Robinson Crusoe*, i (Watford, 1930).

[2] Asín Palacios, *La Escatologia Musulmana en la Divina Comedia*, 2nd edn. (Madrid-Granada, 1943). There is an English translation, somewhat abridged, by Harold Sunderland, *Islam and the Divine Comedy* (London, 1926).

[3] E. Cerulli, *Il 'Libro della Scala' presunta fonte arabo-espagnola della 'Divina Commedia'* (Vatican, 1949). The question of oriental influences on Dante is considered at greater length in Chapter VII above, at pp. 344–5.

[4] A. J. Denomy, 'Fin Amors: The Pure Love of the Troubadours, its amorality and possible source', *Mediaeval Studies*, vii (1945), 139–207; idem, 'Concerning the accessibility of Arabic influences to the earliest Provençal Troubadours', ibid. xv (1947–58).

Let us, however, mention here briefly the work of Asín Palacios on the links between Muslim and Christian mysticism. Asín translated and commented upon a large number of texts by al-Ghāzālī and Ibn al-ʿArabī.[1] He also devoted a long study to a Spanish Muslim mystic, Ibn ʿAbbād of Ronda (d. 1390), in whom he sees a forerunner of St. John of the Cross[2] He came to that conclusion by basing himself primarily on an analysis of the vocabulary (e.g. *qabḍ* = constriction = *aprieto* and *basṭ* = détente = *anchura*) and by studying the Shādhilī doctrine of fighting shy of spiritual gifts. Asín Palacios's tendency to connect too readily parallel texts comes from his general basic view which he himself has expressed thus: 'It must not be forgotten that Muslim mysticism in general, and the Shādhilī form of it in particular, is the heir of oriental Christianity and at the same time of Neoplatonism.' Applying this principle to St. John of the Cross, he adds:

> If the hypothesis of literary transmission be confirmed, it would be a question of a normal case of cultural restitution; an evangelical and Pauline thought grafted on Islam in medieval times would have acquired, in these surroundings, so rich a development in new ideological nuances and such a wealth of unusual forms and expressions that, transferred to the soil of Spain, our sixteenth century mystics would not have disdained to draw on it for their works.[3]

In conclusion we shall make two remarks. On the one hand, Muslim philosophy marks an important stage in the development of human thought as a whole. The effort of the philosophers appears as a noble attempt to overstep man's destiny, a desire to become one with God and to organize the City in order to make man happy. As such, their spirit deserves to survive. On the other

[1] *La espiritualidad de Algazel y su sentido cristiano*, 3 vols. (Madrid, 1934–40); idem, *El Islam cristianizado* (Madrid, 1931).

[2] M. Asín Palacios, 'Un précurseur hispano-musulman de saint Jean de la Croix', *Études carmélitaines*, xvii (1932), 113–67; also 'Un precursor hispano-musulman de San Juan de la Cruz', *Al-Andalus*, i (1933), 7–79, reprinted in *Obras escogidas* (Madrid, 1946), i. 243–326.

[3] 'Un précurseur hispano-musulman de saint Juan de la Croix', p. 139.

hand, the masterpieces, both literary and religious, of the great mystics of Islam will continue to arouse the admiration of all those who are responsive to beauty and have a thirst for the absolute. In them they can find, when opportunity offers, nourishment for their own spiritual quest. Is this not the best sign of their everlastingness?

GEORGES C. ANAWATI

BIBLIOGRAPHY

Philosophy

R. Arnaldez, article 'Falsafa', in *Encyclopaedia of Islam*, 2nd edn.; S. van den Bergh, *Die Epitome der Metaphysik des Averroes* (Leiden, 1924) (= translation with introduction and notes); idem, *Averroes' Tahafut al-tahafut*, translated from the Arabic with Introduction and notes, 2 vols. (London, 1954); T. J. de Boer, *Geschichte der Philosophie im Islam* (Stuttgart, 1901), translated by E. R. Jones, *The History of Philosophy in Islam* (London, 1903, reprinted 1933); H. Corbin, *Histoire de la philosophie islamique*, i (Paris, 1964) (until the death of Averroes (with bibliography), an unusual approach, on which see G. C. Anawati, in *Mélanges Chenu* (Paris, 1967), pp. 51–71); M. Cruz Hernández, *Historia de la filosofía española*, *Filosofía hispano-musulmana*, 2 vols. (Madrid, 1957) (covers the whole of Muslim philosophy; extensive bibliographies); idem, *La filosofía árabe* (Madrid, 1963) (with bibliographies); L. Gardet, *La Pensée religieuse d'Avicenne* (Paris, 1951); L. Gauthier, *Ibn Rochd* (*Averroès*) (Paris, 1958); A.-M. Goichon, *La Philosophie d'Avicenne et son influence en Europe médiévale* (Paris, 1944, 2nd edn., 1951); idem, *Ibn Sīnā. Livres des directives et remarques*, traduction avec introduction et notes (Beirut-Paris, 1951); G. F. Hourani, *Averroes. On the Harmony of Religion and Philosophy. A translation* (London, 1961); J. P. de Menasce, *Arabische Philosophie* (Berne, 1948) (a critical bibliography); S. Munk, *Mélanges de philosophie juive et arabe* (Paris, 1859, reprinted 1927) (still excellent); F. Rahman, *Avicenna's Psychology. An English translation of Kitāb al-Najāt, Book II, Chapter VI* (London, 1952).

Theology

M. Allard, *Le Problème des attributs divins dans la doctrine d'Al-Ashʿari et de ses premiers grands disciples* (Beirut, 1965); J. van Ess, *Die Erkenntnislehre ʿAḍudaddīn al-Īcī* (Wiesbaden, 1966); R. M. Franck, 'The Structure of Created Causality According to al-Ašʿarī', *Studia Islamica*, xxv (1966), 13–76; L. Gardet, *Dieu et la destinée de l'homme* (Paris, 1967); idem and M.-M. Anawati, *Introduction à la théologie musulmane. Essai de théologie comparée* (Paris, 1948); M. Horten, *Die philosophischen Systeme der speculativen Theologen in Islam* (Bonn, 1912); H. Laoust, *Les Schismes dans l'Islam. Introduction à une étude de la religion musulmane* (Paris,

1965); D. B. Macdonald, *Development of Muslim Theology, Jurisprudence and Constitutional Theory* (New York, 1903) (the sections other than on theology to be used with caution); M. S. Seale, *Muslim Theology. A Study of Origins with References to the Church Fathers* (London, 1964); H. Stieglecker, *Die Glaubenslehren des Islam* (Paderborn, 1962) (a detailed descriptive account); J. W. Sweetman, *Islam and Christian Theology*: I. 1. *Preparatory Historical Survey of the Early Period* (London, 1945); I. 2. *The Theological Position at the Close of the Period of Christian Ascendancy in the Near East* (1947); II. 1. *Historical Survey of the Second Period* (1955); II. 2. *Medieval Scholastic Developments* (1967); A. S. Tritton, *Muslim Theology* (London, 1947); W. M. Watt, *Islamic Philosophy and Theology* (Edinburgh, 1963, Islamic Survey Series, 1); A. J. Wensinck, *The Muslim Creed* (Cambridge, 1932).

Mysticism

For a detailed bibliography, see G. C. Anawati, in *Angelicum*, xliii (1966), 153–66.

A. H. Abdel-Kader, *The Life, Personality, and Writings of al-Junayd* (London, 1962); A.-E. Afifi, *The Mystical Philosophy of Muh'yi l-Din Ibn al'Arabi* (Cambridge, 1938); G. C. Anawati and L. Gardet, *Mystique musulmane* (Paris, 1961); Italian translation, *Mistica islamica* (Turin, 1960); T. Andrae, *Die Person Muhammads in Lehre und Glauben seiner Gemeinde* (Uppsala, 1917); idem, *Islamische Mystiker* (Stuttgart, 1960); A. J. Arberry, *Sufism* (London, 1950); R. Arnaldez in R. Arnaldez *et alii*, *La Mystique et les mystiques* (Paris, 1964), at pp. 571–648; M. Asín Palacios, 'Šā̱diles y alumbrados', *Al-Andalus*, xiii–xvii (1945–9); J. K. Birge, *The Bektashi Order of Dervishes* (London, 1937); G.-H. Bousquet, *Vivification des sciences de la foi. Analyse et index* (Paris, 1955), a list of the chapters which have been translated into Western languages is found in *Die Welt des Islams*, N.S., x (1965), 100 f.; add.: *The Book of Almsgiving*, translated by Nabih Faris (Beirut, 1968); H. Corbin, *L'Imagination créatrice dans le soufisme d'Ibn 'Arabī* (Paris, 1958); idem, *Suhrawardi d'Alep (m. 1191), fondateur de la doctrine illuminative* (Paris, 1938) (with bibliography); É. Dermenghem, *Les plus beaux textes arabes* (Paris, 1951), Chapter IV, pp. 231–97, is concerned with the mystics; J. van Ess, *Die Gedankenwelt des Ḥāri̱t al-Muḥāsibī* (Bonn, 1961); R. Hartman, *Al-Kuschairis Darstellung des Sufismus* (Berlin, 1914) (study and part translation); F. Jabre, *La Délivrance de l'erreur (al-Munqidh min al-ḍalāl)*, translation (Beirut, 1959); L. Massignon, *La Passion d'al-Ḥosayn ibn Manṣoûr al-Ḥallâj, martyr mystique de l'Islam*, 2 vols. (Paris, 1922) (the work, entirely rewritten and augmented, is to be published posthumously in three volumes); idem, *Akhbār al-Ḥallāj, recueil d'oraison et d'exhortations*, ed. and translation (1st edn., Paris, 1914; 3rd edn., Paris, 1957); idem, *Essai sur les origines du lexique technique de la mystique musulmane* (Paris, 1954); M. Molé, *Les Mystiques musulmans* (Paris, 1965); M. M. Moreno, *Antologia della mistica arabo-persiana* (Bari, 1951); R. A. Nicholson, *Ibn 'Arabī, Tarjumān al-ashwāq*, ed. and translation (London, 1911); idem, *The Idea of Personality in Sufism* (Cambridge, 1923); idem, *Mathnawī-i Ma'nawī of Jalālu'ddīn Rūmī*, ed. and translation, i–vi (London, 1925–37) (and reprints); idem, *The Mystics of Islam* (London, 1914); idem, *Studies in Islamic Mysticism* (Cambridge 1921) (contains some translations);

P. Nwyia, *Ibn ʿAbbād de Ronda (1332–1390)* (Beirut, 1956); C. Rice, *The Persian Sufis* (London, 1964); H. Ritter, *Das Meer der Seele* (Leiden, 1955) (analysis of the writings of Farīd al-Dīn ʿAṭṭār, d. 1190, with bibliography); H. H. Schaeder, 'Die islamische Lehre vom Vollkommenen Menschen', *Zeitschrift der deutschen Morgenländischen Gesellschaft*, lxxix (1925), 197–288; M. Smith, *Rābiʿa the Mystic and her fellow saints in Islam* (Cambridge, 1928); W. M. Watt, *Muslim Intellectual: a study of Al-Ghazali* (Edinburgh, 1962).

IX

LAW AND THE STATE

(*A*) ISLAMIC RELIGIOUS LAW

ONE of the most important bequests which Islam has transmitted to the civilized world is its religious law, the *Sharīʿa*. It is a phenomenon so different from all other forms of law that its study is indispensable in order to appreciate adequately the full range of possible legal phenomena. I will not therefore attempt, within the limits of this section, to trace its history or to describe its salient institutions, but shall concentrate on showing those of its features which make it this unique phenomenon.

Islamic law is the totality of God's commands that regulate the life of every Muslim in all its aspects; it comprises on an equal footing ordinances regarding worship and ritual, as well as political and (in the narrow sense) legal rules, details of toilet, formulas of greeting, table-manners, and sick-room conversation.

Islamic law is the most typical manifestation of the Islamic way of life, the core and kernel of Islam itself. Theology has never been able to achieve a comparable importance in Islam; only mysticism was strong enough to challenge the ascendancy of the Law over the minds of the Muslims, and often proved victorious. But even at the present time the Law, including its (in the narrow sense) legal subject-matter, remains an important, if not the most important, element in the struggle which is being fought in Islam between traditionalism and modernism under the impact of Western ideas.

Islamic law is a particularly instructive example of a 'sacred law', but even the two other representatives of a 'sacred law' which are historically and geographically nearest to it, Jewish law and canon law, are sensibly different. Islamic law is much less uniform than both. It is the result of a scrutiny, from a religious angle, of legal subject-matter which was far from uniform, comprising as it did the various components of the laws of Arabia and numerous elements taken over from the peoples of the conquered territories. All this was unified by being subjected to the same kind of scrutiny, the impact of which varied greatly. This inner duality of legal subject-matter and religious norm is additional to the outward variety of legal, ethical, and ritual rules which is typical of a 'sacred law'. Jewish law was buttressed by the cohesion of the community, reinforced by pressure from outside. Canon and Islamic law, on the contrary, are dominated by the dualism of religion and state, where the state is not, in contrast with Judaism, an alien power but the political expression of the same religion. But their antagonism took on different forms; in Christianity it was the struggle for political power on the part of a tightly organized ecclesiastical hierarchy, and canon law was one of its political weapons. Islam, on the other hand, was never a 'Church', Islamic law was never supported by an organized power, consequently there never developed a real trial of strength; there merely existed a discordance between the sacred law and the reality of actual practice of which the regulations framed by the state formed part, a gap more or less wide according to place and time, now and then on the point of being closed but continually reasserting itself.

There were two important changes of direction within the history of Islamic law; one was the introduction at an early date of a legal theory which not only ignored but denied the existence in it of all elements which were not in the narrowest possible sense Islamic, and which reduced its material sources to the Koran and the example of the Prophet; the second, which began only in the present century, is modernist legislation on the part of contemporary Islamic governments, which does not merely restrict the field in which the sacred law is applied in practice but interferes with the traditional form of this law itself. Again this interference does not take the form of a struggle for power between competing organizations; it poses itself not in the terms of replacing the sacred by a modern secular law but of renovating its traditional form, and the postulate that Islam as a religion ought to regulate the sphere of law as well remains unchallenged.

Islamic law came into being and developed against a varied political and administrative background. The lifetime of the Prophet was unique in this respect; it was followed by the turbulent period of the Caliphs of Medina (632–61). The rule of the Umayyads, the first dynasty in Islam (661–750), represented, in many respects, the consummation of tendencies which were inherent in the nature of the community of Muslims under the Prophet. During their rule the framework of a new Arab Muslim society was created, and in this society a new administration of justice, an Islamic jurisprudence, and through it, Islamic law itself came into being. The Umayyads were overthrown by the ʿAbbāsids, and the early ʿAbbāsids attempted to make Islamic law, which was then still in its formative period, the only law of the state. They were successful in so far as the *qāḍī*s were henceforth bound to the sacred law, but they did not succeed in achieving a permanent fusion of theory and practice, of political power and sacred law. The result was that Islamic law became more and more removed from practice, but in the long run gained more power over the minds than it lost in control over the bodies of the Muslims.

There followed the gradual dismemberment of the Islamic Empire which was well on its way by about the year 900. Now Islamic law profited from its remoteness from political power; it preserved its stability and even provided the main unifying element in a divided world of Islam. Having until the early ʿAbbāsid period been adaptable and growing, Islamic law from then onwards became increasingly rigid and set in its final mould. This essential rigidity helped it to maintain its stability over the centuries which saw the decay of the political institutions of Islam. It was not altogether immutable, but the changes which did take place were concerned more with niceties of legal theory and the systematic superstructure than with positive law. Taken as a whole, Islamic law reflects the social and economic conditions of the early

ʿAbbāsid period, but has grown more and more out of touch with later developments of state and society.

The modern period, in the Western sense of the term, saw the rise of two great Islamic states on the ruins of the previous order, the Ottoman Empire in the Near East and the Mogul Empire in India; in both empires in their heydays (the sixteenth and the seventeenth century respectively) Islamic law enjoyed the highest degree of actual efficiency which it had ever possessed in a society of high material civilization since the early ʿAbbāsid period. The symbiosis, in the wake of Western political control, of Islamic law and of Western law in British India and in Algeria (starting in the eighteenth and in the nineteenth century respectively) gave birth to two autonomous legal systems, Anglo-Muhammadan law (on this see above, Chapter III (*C*), p. 139) and *Droit musulman algérien*. Finally, the reception of Western political ideas in the Near East has provoked, in the present century, an unprecedented movement of modernist legislation.

All this applies essentially not only to the law of the orthodox or Sunnī majority but to the laws of the Shīʿīs and of the Khārijīs as well. Particularly with regard to the Shīʿīs, it might be thought that their political doctrine should have led to the elaboration of an essentially different doctrine; but this was not the case, and their positive law, as that of the Khārijīs, developed in close contact with that of the Sunnīs, just as their respective communities for much of the time remained in close social and cultural contact with each other, and it underwent only some more or less external modifications which were made necessary by their particular religious doctrines. Only the law of inheritance of the Shīʿīs represents an independent systematization of the common principles found in the Koran. The Ṣafavid Shahs of Persia, whose empire for some time rivalled that of the Ottoman Sultans, were never willing or able to enforce Shīʿī religious law to the same degree as their western neighbours or the Mogul emperors with regard to Sunnī law.

The central feature which makes Islamic religious law what it is, which guarantees its unity in all its diversity, is the assessing of all human acts and relationships, including those which we call legal, from the point of view of the following concepts: obligatory, recommended, indifferent, reprehensible, forbidden. Law proper has been thoroughly incorporated in this system of religious duties; these fundamental concepts permeate the juridical subject-matter as well. It might therefore seem as if it were not correct to speak of an Islamic law at all, as if the concept of law did not exist in Islam. The term must indeed be used with the proviso that Islamic law is part of a system of religious duties, blended with non-legal elements. But though it was incorporated into that system, legal subject-matter was not completely assimilated, legal relationships were not completely reduced to and expressed in terms of religious and ethical duties; the sphere of law retained a technical character of its own, and juridical reasoning could develop along its own lines. That the concepts allowed/forbidden and valid/invalid were to a great extent coextensive made it possible for this last pair, together with the kindred concept of a legal effect, to be fitted into the system. There exists, thus, a clear distinction between the purely religious sphere and the sphere of law proper, and we are justified in using the term Islamic law of the legal subject-matter which, by being incorporated into the system of religious duties of Islam, was either materially or formally, but in any case considerably, modified. This legal subject-matter became Islamic law not merely by having considerations of a religious or moral kind introduced into it, but by the much subtler process of being organized and systematized as part of the religious duties of the Muslims. There remains a certain contrast between the legal subject-matter and the principles of its formal organization.

Although Islamic law is a sacred law, it is by no means essentially irrational; it was created not by an irrational process of continuous revelation (as Shīʿī law might have been but was not), but by a rational method of interpretation; in this way it acquired its intellectualist and scholastic exterior. But whereas Islamic law presents itself as a rational system on the basis of material considerations, its formal juridical character is little developed. Its aim is to provide concrete and material standards, and not to impose formal rules on the play of contending interests. This leads to the result that considerations of good faith, fairness, justice, truth, and so on play only a subordinate part in the system. It also follows that the rules of Islamic law are valid by virtue of their mere existence and not because of their rationality, and calls for the observation of the letter rather than of the spirit.

Islamic law is systematic, it represents a coherent body of doctrine. Its several institutions are well put into relation with one another; the greater part of the law of contracts and obligations, for instance, is construed by analogy with the contract of sale. Furthermore, the whole of the law is permeated by religious and ethical considerations, as we have seen, such as the prohibition of interest (or unjustified enrichment in general), the prohibition of uncertainty, the concern for the equality of the two contracting parties, and the concern for the just mean or average. That the several contracts envisaged by Islamic law resemble one another in their structure so much derives to a considerable degree from the fact that the same concern for the same religious and moral principles pervades them all.

There are two methods by which legal subject-matter can be brought into a system, the analytical and the analogical. The analytical method, the classical example of which is provided by Roman law, leads to the creation of logically organized legal norms in an ascending order. The analogical method leads to the organization of legal subject-matter by parataxis and association. Islamic law represents this latter type of systematizing in great purity, and this corresponds with the type of thinking expressed by the Arabic language. Closely connected with this way of thinking is the casuistical method, which is indeed one of the most striking features of traditional Islamic law. All these features are manifestations of a typical way of thought which pervades the whole of Islamic law and which has determined the organization of the legal subject-matter in all its aspects.

An important criterion of the sociology of law is the degree to which the legal subject-matters are distinguished and differentiated from one another. There is no such distinction in Islamic law. Even a systematic arrangement of the legal subject-matters is lacking. Public powers are, as a rule, reduced to private rights and duties, for instance the right to give a valid safe-conduct, the duty to pay the alms-tax, the rights and duties of the persons who appoint an individual as Imām or Caliph, and the rights and duties of this last. This is all the more significant as the Arabic language possessed an abstract term for 'authority, dominion, ruling power' in the word *sulṭān*, a word which came to be used as a title only from the tenth century onwards; but Islamic law did not develop the corresponding legal concept. For the same reason, the essential institutions of the Islamic state are construed not as functions of the community of believers as such, but as duties the fulfilment of which by a sufficient number of individuals excuses the other individuals from fulfilling them; in fact, the whole concept of an institution is missing. The idea of a juristic person was on the point of breaking through but not quite realized in Islamic law, and this did not happen at the point where we should expect it, with regard to the charitable foundation of *waqf*, but with regard to the separate property of a slave who is being sold not as an individual but together with his business as a running concern.

In the field of what, in modern terminology, is called penal law, Islamic law distinguishes between the rights of God and the rights of humans. Only the rights of God have the character of a penal law proper, of a law which imposes penal sanctions on the guilty. Even here, in the centre of penal law, the idea of a claim on the part of God predominates, just as if it were a claim on the part of a human plaintiff. This real penal law is derived exclusively from the Koran and the 'traditions', the alleged reports of the acts and sayings of the Prophet and of his Companions. The second great division of what we should call penal law belongs to the category of 'redress of torts', a category straddling civil and penal law which Islamic law has retained from the law of pre-Islamic Arabia where it was an archaic but by no means unique phenomenon. Whatever liability is incurred here, be it retaliation or blood-money or damages, is subject of a private claim, pertaining to the rights of humans. In this field, the idea of criminal guilt is practically non-existent, and where it exists it has been introduced by considerations of religious responsibility. So there is no fixed penalty for any infringement of the rights of a human to the inviolability of his person and property, only exact reparation of the damage caused. This leads to retaliation for homicide and wounds on one hand, and to the absence of fines on the other. There are a few isolated doctrines in some schools of Islamic law which show that the idea of a penal law properly speaking was on the point of emerging in the minds of some Islamic scholars at least, but again, as was the case of a juristic person, it did not succeed in doing so.

Extending equally to the two spheres, the sphere of the rights of God and the sphere of the rights of humans, is the discretionary punishment of *taʿzīr*. The *qāḍī* may punish at his discretion any act which in his opinion calls for punishment, whether it can be subsumed under offences against religion (or morals or good manners) or under torts committed against others. The *taʿzīr* belongs therefore to penal law proper, but even here Islamic law has never envisaged the imposition of fines. (Confiscation, which was frequently resorted to, particularly in early ʿAbbāsid times, was a political act and is ignored by the *Sharīʿa*.) *Taʿzir* belongs neither to ancient Arabian customary law which was ratified by Islam, nor to Islamic legislation which appeared in the Koran and in the 'traditions'. It was the first Muslim *qāḍī*s in the Umayyad period (towards the end of the seventh century) who found themselves called upon to punish, at their discretion, all kinds of acts which threatened the peaceful and orderly existence of the new Islamic society which was coming into being. But the needs of Islamic society did not stop there, and further extensions of penal law, and the creation of agencies which were to apply them, such as the office of the *muḥtasib*, an officer responsible for enforcing

Islamic morals and good behaviour, and the *naẓar fī'l-maẓālim* or 'investigation of complaints', a jurisdiction parallel to that of the *qāḍī*, became inevitable. At the time, however, when the functions of these organizations had been well defined and the specialists of Islamic law had to take notice of them, the outlines of the *Sharīʿa* had already been firmly laid down, and this is why strict theory could admit them, as it were, only on sufferance. Still later developments, such as the Ottoman codes or *kānūn-nāmes*, some of which treat in detail of penal law, were of necessity completely ignored by the theory. The sociological character of this portion of the reality of penal law in Islam has remained constant, although its place in the official theory of Islamic law is not uniform.

As regards the formal character of positive law, we can distinguish two extreme cases. One is that of an objective law which guarantees the subjective rights of individuals; such a law is, in the last resort, the sum total of the personal privileges of all individuals. The opposite case is that of a law which reduces itself to administration, which is the sum total of particular commands. Islamic law belongs to the first type, and this agrees with what the examination of the structure of Islamic 'public law' has shown. A typical feature which results from all this is the private and individualistic character of Islamic law. However prominent a place a programme of social reform and of improving the position of the socially and economically weak occupied in the Koran, Islamic law, in its technical structure, is thoroughly individualistic.

Islamic law represents an extreme case of a 'jurists' law'; it was created and developed by private pious specialists. Islamic jurisprudence or *fiqh* did not grow out of an existing law, it itself created the law; and the formation of Islamic law took place neither under the impetus of the needs of practice nor under that of juridical technique, but under that of religious and ethical ideas. At the very time that Islamic law came into existence, its perpetual problem, the contrast between theory and practice, was already posed. Because Islamic law is a jurists' law, legal science is amply documented, whereas the realities of legal life are much less well known and must be laboriously reconstructed from occasional evidence.

Islamic law provides the unique phenomenon of legal science and not the state playing the part of a legislator, of scholarly handbooks having the force of law. This depended on two conditions: that legal science guaranteed its own stability and continuity, and that the place of the state was taken by another authority, high enough to impose itself on both government and governed. The first was met by the doctrine of consensus, the highest authority among the 'roots' or principles of Islamic jurisprudence, and the second was met by the fact that Islamic law claimed to be based on divine authority.

The influences which Islamic law has exerted on other laws cannot compare in importance with the very fact of its existence. The most remarkable of these influences did not proceed from Islamic law proper but from the customary commercial law which developed under its auspices. Several of its institutions were transmitted across the Mediterranean to medieval Europe, and became incorporated in the law merchant, the customary law of international trade. This is attested by the terms *mohatra* (from Arabic *mukhāṭara*), the evasion of the prohibition of interest by means of a double sale, *aval* (French, from Arabic *ḥawāla*, transfer of debts), the endorsement on a bill of exchange, possibly *cheque* (from Arabic *ṣakk*, written document), and *sensalis*, *sensale*, Austrian-German *Sensal* (from Arabic *simsār*), broker; also the institution of *commenda* is most probably derived from the identical institution of *qirāḍ* in Islamic law. Another significant but purely formal influence occurred in Islamic Spain where the Christians who had become Arabicized, the Mozarabs (see above, Chapter II, p. 86), adopted the technical forms of Islamic written documents for their own contracts and maintained this custom in Toledo for about two centuries after the Christian reconquest in

1085. At the opposite end of the Mediterranean, Islamic law has exerted a deep influence on all branches of the law of Georgia, including the law of maritime commerce, during a period extending from the Seljuqs to the Ṣafavids (*c.* 1100 to 1500). There is finally the effect of Islamic law on the laws of the tolerated religions, the Jewish and the Christian, within the Islamic state. On the Jewish side, it seems that Maimonides (d. 1204) was influenced by some features of Islamic works in the arrangement of the subject-matter of his Code, the *Mishnah Torah*, which is unprecedented in Jewish literature; he also says in his Commentary on the Mishna which he wrote in Arabic (in the Introduction to the so-called Eight Chapters): 'Besides Talmud and Midrash, I have made use of the philosophers old and new, and many others, and one ought to accept truth from whoever expounds it.' But this whole matter has not been thoroughly investigated as yet.[1] On the other hand, it is certain that the two great branches of the Oriental Christian Church, the Monophysites and the Nestorians, did not hesitate to draw freely on the rules of Islamic law, not indeed in the law of family which was ruled by canon law, but in all those subjects which could conceivably come within the purview of the Islamic *qāḍī*, particularly the law of inheritance and the rules relating to pious foundations; for although the Muslims left to those communities, in principle, legal autonomy, it was open to every member who was dissatisfied with the decision of his ecclesiastical tribunal, to bring the case before the *qāḍī* who had, of course, to apply Islamic law. This is true in particular of the 'Codes' which were elaborated in those two churches between the eleventh and the thirteenth centuries but which remained literary exercises without legislative authority before the ecclesiastic tribunals. That the 'civil law' of the *sharīʿa* should have been incorporated in the laws of a number of contemporary states and become applicable not only to the Muslim but also to the non-Muslim parts of their populations, is really not a legacy of Islamic law but a consequence of the ideology of modern national

[1] I am indebted for this information to Professor S. D. Goitein.

states; the most important cases were those of the territories, and later states, which were detached from the Ottoman Empire after 1918, and of Cyprus; this condition has remained essentially unchanged in Cyprus, Israel, and Jordan.

JOSEPH SCHACHT

BIBLIOGRAPHY

For accounts of the general features of Islamic law, see:

G.-H. Bousquet, *Le Droit musulman* (Collection Armand Colin) (Paris, 1963); D. Santillana, *Istituzioni di diritto musulmano*, i (Rome, 1938); idem, chapter 'Law and Society' in *Legacy of Islam*, 1st edn. (Oxford, 1931); G.-H. Bousquet and J. Schacht (eds.), *Selected Works of C. Snouck Hurgronje* (Leiden, 1957).

On the history of Islamic law, see:

N. J. Coulson, *A History of Islamic Law* (Edinburgh, 1964); I. Goldziher, *Vorlesungen über den Islam*, 2nd edn. (Heidelberg, 1925); translation by F. Arin, *Le Dogme et la loi de l'Islam* (Paris, 1920); D. S. Margoliouth, *The Early Development of Mohammedanism* (London, 1914); J. Schacht, *The Origins of Muhammadan Jurisprudence* (Oxford, 1950); idem, *An Introduction to Islamic Law* (Oxford, 1964).

On the sociology of Islamic law, see:

J. Schacht, 'Notes sur la sociologie du droit musulman', *Revue Africaine*, xcvi (1952), 311–29; idem, *An Introduction to Islamic Law*, pp. 199 ff., and bibliography; *Max Weber on Law in Economy and Society*, translated by E. Shils and M. Rheinstein (Cambridge, Mass., 1954) (the ideas of Max Weber are fundamental, but the special section on Islamic law is highly unsatisfactory).

On influences of Islamic law abroad, see:

J. Schacht, 'Droit byzantin et droit musulman', in *XII Convegno 'Volta'* (Rome, 1957), pp. 197–218 (with bibliography); A. L. Udovitch, 'At the Origins of the Western Commenda', *Speculum*, xxxvii (1962), 198–207.

(*B*) ISLAMIC POLITICAL THOUGHT

ALL political theories in Islam start from the assumption that Islamic government existed by virtue of a divine contract based on the *Sharīʿa*. None, therefore, asks the question why the state exists. Political science was thus not an independent discipline aspiring to the utmost heights of intellectual speculation, but a department of theology. There was no distinction between state and society, or between Church and state; and no doctrine of the temporal end which alone belonged to the state and the eternal end which belonged to and was the prerogative of the Church. Religion was not separated from politics, or politics from morals; and since the speculative activity of the Muslim and his relation to the state had a metaphysical and religious basis, it follows that religious dissent amounted to political disaffection and even treason (further on this see above, Chapter IV, pp. 156 ff.).

With the expansion of the Muslim conquests from the year 657 onwards, peoples and communities of different races and varying cultural and social backgrounds were included within the Islamic empire. Gradually there evolved a body of Islamic political ideas, at the base of which lay pre-Islamic tribal tradition, and Hellenistic and Persian theories of state. Three main formulations can be distinguished. All set forth the divine nature of ultimate sovereignty and presupposed the existence of a state within which the earthly life of the community ran its course, and whose function was to guarantee the maintenance of Islam, the application of the *Sharīʿa*, and the defence of orthodoxy against heresy.[1] All tended to concentrate on the position of the ruler. Of the three the most truly Islamic is the formulation of the jurists, which is in some measure an expression of a religious ideal in opposition to practice.[2] The raw materials upon which it built were the

[1] Cf. E. I. J. Rosenthal, 'Some Aspects of Islamic Political Thought', *Islamic Culture*, xxii (1948), 1.

[2] Cf. J. Schacht, 'The Law', in *Unity and Variety in Muslim Civilization*, ed. G. E. von Grunebaum (Chicago, 1955), pp. 71–2.

scattered verses of the Koran dealing with political thought, the tradition of the prophet, the practice of the primitive Islamic community, and the interpretation of these sources in the light of later political developments, reinforced by the dogma of the divine guidance of the community and the infallibility of *ijmāʿ*.[1] The second is the formulation put forward by the administrators and writers of manuals of conduct for rulers and governors, the Mirrors for Princes. This formulation emphasizes the divine right of kings, and is concerned with the practice rather than the theory of government. It seeks, in some measure, to assimilate Islamic norms to Sasanian traditions of kingship. Its basis is justice rather than right religion. The third is the formulation of the philosophers, which owes much to Greek philosophy, and identifies the philosopher-king with the Imām. Its basis is righteousness and knowledge rather than right religion or justice. Not all theories of government found scattered through Islamic literature fit neatly into one or other of these categories. One, that of Ibn Khaldūn, is *sui generis*;[2] and many authors, notably various Ṣūfī writers and some historians, touch upon constitutional theory incidentally. Questions of space forbid discussion of all these in this chapter.

The basis of the political structure was the *umma*, the 'community', an assemblage of individuals bound to one another by ties of religion. Within the *umma* all were on an equal footing. There were no distinctions of rank, only of function. God alone was the head of the community, and His rule was direct and immediate. Its internal organization was defined and secured by a common acceptance of, and a common submission to, the divine law and the temporal head of the community. Obedience to rulers was laid down in the Koran in the phrase 'O true believer, obey God, and obey the Prophet and those who are in authority among you' (see also above, Chapter IV, p. 158).

[1] H. A. R. Gibb, 'Al-Māwardī's Theory of the Caliphate', in *Studies on the Civilization of Islam*, ed. Stanford J. Shaw and William R. Polk (London, 1962), pp. 154–5.

[2] See above, Chapter VII, pp. 328–9.

The main preoccupation of the constitutional theorists in the first and second centuries of Islam was over the question of the election and deposition of the Imām, and reflects the struggles between the Sunnīs, the Khārijīs, and the Shīʿīs, and the conflicts between the Muʿtazila and other schools. The civil war between ʿAlī and Muʿāwiya (see above, Chapter IV, pp. 164–5) inaugurated an era of revolt and disturbance (*fitna*). The schisms which emerged and threatened the purity of the faith were never fully healed. Some had a direct bearing on the conception of the ruler and the conduct of the state. Whereas the *ahl al-sunna wa'l-jamāʿa*, the proponents of the mainstream of Sunnī orthodoxy, taught that the nomination of a single Imām from the Quraysh was obligatory upon the community and obedience to him incumbent so long as his orders did not run counter to the Koran, the Khārijīs did not confine the Imām to the Quraysh, insist upon the duty of the community to elect an Imām, or lay down that there should be only one Imām. They maintained that all Muslims, including the Imām, became apostates upon the commission of mortal sin, and hence liable to death. This was in effect an invitation to civil war, and Khārijī doctrines, except in the more moderate form as professed by the Ibāḍiyya, proved unworkable. The Shīʿa, on the other hand, held that the only lawful successor of Muḥammad was his son-in-law ʿAlī, and that the Imāmate continued in his house after him. They took over the theory of divine light, which, however, became stationary with the disappearance of the last Imām, since when political authority, according to the main body of the Shīʿa, the Ithnā ʿAshariyya, had been in the hands of usurpers. They did not form a political organization until late in their history, and failed to develop a constitutional theory serving any functional purpose, although many Shīʿī thinkers made important contributions to the development of Islamic political thought.

Under the Umayyads, Hellenistic and Sasanian influences as well as Arab tradition began to shape the governing institutions of Islam, and gradually a semi-official interpretation emerged. No theory of constitutional government, however, was formulated, though the germs of a political theory can be discerned in the discussions of certain theological problems which had implications for the conduct of the state. For example, the short treatise addressed by Ḥasan al-Baṣrī (d. 728) to ʿAbd al-Malik, in which he seeks to demonstrate that divine predestination (*qadar*) did not extend beyond the metaphysical realm and denies its incompatibility with the moral and religious freedom of man, appears to have been written in part as a defence against those who attacked his doctrine of *qadar* as an innovation (and perhaps even represented it to the Caliph as undermining the authority of the state), and in part as a protest against the corruption and tyranny of officials who justified their acts by appealing to *qadar*.[1]

The rise of the ʿAbbāsids was followed by a transformation of the administration and society under the influence of Sasanian tradition. The supporters of the ʿAbbāsids in their secret propaganda apparently made use of extreme theories of the divine right of kings. Ibn al-Muqaffaʿ (d. 759), a convert to Islam, who had been first a secretary in the dīwān of the Umayyad governor of Iraq and the eastern provinces and later secretary to ʿĪsā b. ʿAlī, a cousin of the first two ʿAbbāsid Caliphs, saw the dangers of such extremism. Recognizing the crucial importance of right belief, he makes this the keystone of a political programme which he puts forward in the *Kitāb al-ṣaḥāba* ('Book of the Companions'), addressed about the year 757–8 to the Caliph al-Manṣūr. The ʿAbbāsids had come to power with the support of the Khurāsān army, and the main subject of the book is the army. Ibn al-Muqaffaʿ proposes that the Caliph should issue a short catechism defining the beliefs to be held by the army. He discusses the authority of the Caliph, and takes up a position between the Khārijī view that 'man owes no obedience to rulers who disobey God' and the view that the Caliph had the right to exact obedience even if his commands contravened the *Sharīʿa*. While accepting the doctrine that

[1] J. Obermann, 'Political Theology in Early Islam: Ḥasan al-Baṣrī's Treatise on *qadar*', in *Journal of the American Oriental Society*, lv (1935), 138–62.

there was no obedience in sin, he maintained that it was wrong to undermine the Imām's authority by giving licence to disobey him. In all matters concerning his governmental judgement and the administration, and in discretionary decisions based on the Koran and the Sunna in cases in which there was no precedent, the Imām had the exclusive right to obedience.[1] Ibn al-Muqaffaʿ held that *ra'y* was the domain of the ruler, and proposed to regulate this by the creation of a code based on (i) precedents and usage, (ii) tradition and analogy, and (iii) the Caliph's own decisions (which would be emended as necessary by succeeding Caliphs). This in effect was to propose a control by the state over religion and law. It is hardly surprising that orthodox Islam did not follow him.[2] Ibn al-Muqaffaʿ was moved, in part, by the need to achieve stability. None of the medieval writers on political theory could avoid the problem of security, any more than he could, and the achievement of stability was one of their primary preoccupations, though none of them made such radical proposals as Ibn al-Muqaffaʿ.

Al-Jāḥiẓ (d. 868), a man of letters from Baṣra with Muʿtazilī tendencies, was also concerned with stability from a somewhat different angle. In his political writings he covers much of the same ground as the jurists, and uses many of the same arguments. His purpose was to justify the assumption of power by the ʿAbbāsids. Taking the great struggles over the legitimacy of the early Caliphs as the basis for his discussion, he outlines a doctrine of the Imāmate. Having justified the designation of Abū Bakr and the nomination of ʿUthmān, he attacks Muʿāwiya's campaign against ʿAlī, declares the rule of the Umayyads to have been illegitimate, and asserts the right of the community to rebel against usurpers and tyrants.[3] He also attacks the Rāfiḍīs, and shows little sympathy

[1] B. Lewis, 'Islamic Concepts of Revolution', in *Revolution in the Middle East*, ed. P. J. Vatikiotis (London, 1972), pp. 34 ff.

[2] See further S. D. Goitein, 'A Turning Point in the History of the Muslim State', *Islamic Culture*, xxiii (1949), 120–35.

[3] C. Pellat, 'L'Imamat dans la doctrine de Ǧāḥiẓ', *Studia Islamica*, xv (1962), 23–52. In his essay against the Nābita, the supporters of the Umayyads, al-Jāḥiẓ rejects the doctrine of unconditional obedience, and asserts the duty of the believer

with their extreme Shīʿism. The Imāmate in his view was a necessary institution required by the public interest. It was the duty of the community to provide themselves with an Imām—and only one—in the event of power being vacated, and to dethrone tyrants and illegitimate Caliphs. Ideally the Imām ought to possess great intellectual and moral qualities, to be distinguished by the depth and extent of his religious knowledge, to practise virtue, and to resemble as far as possible the Prophet: in a word he ought to be the most perfect man of the community.[1]

While al-Jāḥiẓ was concerned at the disunity prevailing in the Islamic community and the bitter conflicts between Arabs and non-Arabs, Ibn al-Muqaffaʿ and Ibn Qutayba (d. 889) played an important part in the creation of a synthesis between Arab and Persian culture. The former discusses temporal government and the conduct of rulers in his *Adab al-kabīr* and *Adab al-ṣaghīr*, which are mirrors. In the *Adab al-kabīr* he states that kingship is based on (i) religion, (ii) the will to power, or (iii) personal desire. The first is the best kind of kingship; the second might give stability but is likely to meet with opposition; and the third is ephemeral. The ideal he holds up is to be found in the Sasanian monarchy. The purpose of rule is twofold: to achieve stability and to contribute to the splendour of the ruler. He shows little concern for the welfare of the people, and in contradistinction to later mirrors justice plays only a secondary role in his theory. In the *Adab al-ṣaghīr* he urges upon the ruler the need for care in the appointment of officials, and for his support of them.

Another important work belonging to this period which also attempts a synthesis of Persian and Arab traditions was the *Kitāb al-tāj* ('Book of the Crown'), written by an anonymous author

to denounce, and, if possible, to depose and remove the unrighteous ruler (see C. Pellat, 'La Nābita de Djāḥiẓ, un document important pour l'histoire politico-religieuse de l'Islam', *Annales de l'Institut des Études Orientales, Algers*, x (1952), 303–25).

[1] C. Pellat, 'L'Imamat dans la doctrine de Ǧāḥiẓ'.

probably between 847 and 861.[1] The writer identifies the state, which had its origin in divine ordinance, with the ruler, who is placed between God and the people. Obedience is due to him as it is to prophets; and the happiness of the people, who are entrusted by God to his government, lies in obedience. Justice consists in the king giving to each his proper status and to each class its due. Koranic sanction is sought for many of the precepts put forward, and it is categorically stated that the ruler should lead the prayers. The most important qualities required of the king are generosity and compassion. All his actions are good. As shepherd he is to have pity on his flock, as Imām compassion towards the faithful who follow him, and as master mercy towards his slaves.[2] The ruler was thus placed above the law: all was a matter of royal grace and compassion. This was very different from the position of the primitive Caliphate. The links between the ruler and his people had been severed.

While the ʿAbbāsid Caliphate was at the height of its power, although the introduction of foreign elements into the practice and theory of government aroused disquiet among the jurists—mainly on theological grounds—problems of constitutional theory do not appear to have attracted their attention. An exception to this is the introduction to the *Kitāb al-kharāj* ('Book of the Land-tax') of Abū Yūsuf, who was appointed *qāḍī* of Baghdād in 782. This is addressed to Hārūn al-Rashīd, and is an implicit protest against the current adaptation of the principles of Islamic ideology to Sasanian and other influences. Abū Yūsuf explicitly bases the principles of Islamic government exclusively upon the *sunna* of the orthodox Caliphs.[3] His protest, however, was unavailing.

As the Caliphate declined and the fragmentation of power took place, an imperative need was felt for the formulation of an ideal

[1] Professor Pellat rejects its attribution to al-Jāḥiẓ: *Le Livre de la couronne attribué à Ǧāḥiẓ* (Paris, 1954), pp. 13–15.

[2] Ibid., pp. 157, 160.

[3] H. A. R. Gibb, 'The Evolution of Government', in *Studies on the Civilization of Islam*, p. 45.

of Islamic government to which rulers could be appointed and which would enshrine the traditions of the community, threatened as it was on all sides. Islam knew no theory of an international society of states. The ideal was a universal society, between the members of which perpetual peace was assumed, and pending the establishment of this, relations with the outside world were governed by the theory of *jihād*. But there was a gap between theory and practice, and in fact there were a number of independent kingdoms and rebellious groups within the state.[1] A rationalization of the conflict between theory and practice was therefore required. This was provided by al-Māwardī (d. 1058), whose *Aḥkām al-sulṭāniyya* ('Principles of Government') is accepted by the Sunnīs as the classical exposition of ideal government. By the time al-Māwardī was writing the seizure of power by an unrighteous Imām and the deposition of usurpers had little relevance to existing circumstances: the Imām had become a puppet in the hands of the holders of power, and the question at issue was the continuance of his office and the justification of his position *vis-à-vis* the holders of power.

Al-Māwardī, taking up the Ashʿarī position as against the Muʿtazilī one, maintained that the Imāmate was obligatory by revelation and not by reason, and as against the Shīʿa held that the principle of election could not be dispensed with and that a duly elected Imām could not be displaced in favour of a worthier candidate. He strains the principle of election, however, by asserting that it is valid if there is only one elector, intending, no doubt, to cover thereby the Būyid practice of nominating the Caliph. Influenced by the dangers to the ʿAbbāsids of the rivalry of the Fāṭimids, he rejects the possibility of the co-existence of two or more Imāms, which some earlier jurists had permitted, as also did the Khārijīs. The qualifications he lays down for the office of

[1] The *Kitab al-farq bayn al-firaq* written by al-Baghdādī (d. 1038) is important as laying down the attitude to be taken towards schismatics and in legitimizing operations against extremists (see H. Laoust, 'La Classification des sectes dans le *farq* d'al-Baghdādī', *Revue d'Études Islamiques*, xxix (1961), 19–60).

Imām are membership of the Quraysh, male sex, full age, good character, freedom from physical or mental defects, competency in legal knowledge, administrative ability, and courage and energy in the defence of Islamic territory. The electors had to possess irreproachable character, the necessary knowledge to enable them to judge which persons possessed the necessary qualifications for the Imāmate, and the judgement and discernment to choose that person who under the given conditions was most worthy of the Imāmate.

Once the electors had made their choice and the person elected had agreed, the contract (which imposed duties on both parties but conferred no rights) was complete, although it required subsequent ratification by the formal giving of homage (*bayʿa*). The duties put upon the subjects by the contract of *bayʿa* included obedience to the Imām and the giving of assistance in every eventuality to the limit of human capacity. The duties incumbent upon the Imām were the defence and maintenance of religion, the decision of legal disputes, the protection of the territory of Islam, the punishment of wrongdoers, the provision of troops for guarding the frontiers, the waging of *jihād*, the organization of the tax administration and the collection of taxes, the payment of salaries, and the administration of public funds, the appointment of competent officials, and personal attention to the details of government. The authority of the Imām was thus simply a delegation of authority for the purpose of applying and defending the *Sharīʿa*. He inherited only the judicial and executive functions of the Prophet. He had no legislative function, and even his power of interpretation was limited since this was assumed to have been inherited by the community as a whole, though *ijmāʿ* tended to confine it to the *ulema*.

A termination of the *bayʿa* was permitted only if a change took place in the status or condition of the Imām, such as might cause prejudice to the rights of the community, or in the event of moral faults, as for example grossly heretical views—here perhaps al-Māwardī was guarding against the possibility of the instalment of a Shīʿī pretender in Baghdad by the Būyids—physical defects, or curtailment or loss of liberty. This last was a delicate matter, since it had been the situation of the ʿAbbāsid Caliphs for nearly a century. Al-Māwardī states that if control over the Caliph was seized by one of his auxiliaries, who arrogated to himself the executive authority, he could still be considered Imām provided the usurper acted conformably to the ordinances of the faith and the requirements of justice. If the Imām was taken captive by rebel Muslims, it was the duty of the whole community to seek his liberation, but if they were unable to do so, a substitute was to be appointed on his behalf—and here perhaps al-Māwardī was providing for the continuation of the ʿAbbāsid Caliphate in the event of a Fāṭimid capture of Baghdad.

Al-Māwardī discusses the relations of the Caliph with his governors under the office of *imāra*, primarily a military office giving the right to govern a region. The same obedience was due to the holder of the office of *imāra*, to whom the Caliph delegated his religious, legal, military, and administrative functions, as was due to the Imām, but should he act contrary to the *Sharīʿa*, the Caliph could depose him. Al-Māwardī introduces into his theory a second type of *imāra*, the *imārat al-istiqlāl* the emirate of seizure (which is what in fact most of the governments of his day were). After setting out the conditions required for this office, he then abolishes the need for their observance by stating that 'necessity dispenses with stipulations which are impossible to fulfil', and undermines all law by declaring that 'fear of injury to public interests justifies a relaxation of conditions'. On the basis of the concordat established between the Banu'l-Aghlab in Ifrīqiya and Hārūn al-Rashīd, by which the Caliph recognized the 'governor's sole control of policy and civil administration in return for recognition of his own dignity and right of administration in religious affairs', al-Māwardī admits the possibility of a contract between the Caliph and the governor, but permits it only if the concordat is a genuine agreement. Provided, however, the governor undertakes to govern according to the *Sharīʿa* and maintain the faith in word and deed, and if the two parties make a pact of friendship and mutual assistance, he states that the Caliph must grant the conqueror recognition in order to forestall the danger of driving him into rebellion.[1]

By the time of al-Ghazālī (d. 1111) the fictions put forward by al-Māwardī had become even more transparent, and it was even held by some that the Imāmate was dead because it lacked the required qualifications. Al-Ghazālī, rejecting this view, states categorically that the jurist is forced to acknowledge the existing power since the alternative is anarchy and the stoppage of social life for lack of a properly constituted authority.[2] And so, in order to preserve the religious life of the community, he accepts a diminution in the ideal qualifications of the Imām, and admits the possibility of his designation by the holders of power, which was, in effect, the only method followed in his day. He defines a new relationship between the Caliph and the Sultan. Constituent authority belongs to the Sultan, who designates the Caliph; but the validity of the Sultan's government is made dependent upon his oath of allegiance to the Caliph and the latter's appointment of him. The institutional authority of the Caliph, resting primarily on the Sunnī community, and his functional authority resting on the *Sharīʿa* were thus recognized. In this way al-Ghazālī also secured the recognition by the holder of power that the *Sharīʿa* was the organizing principle of the Sunnī community, and ensured that the Sultanate, by the maintenance of discipline, would provide a favourable field for the activity of the established Islamic institution. The Caliphate in al-Ghazālī's theory thus still stood for the whole of Islamic government, and contained three elements, the Caliph, the Sultan, and the *ulema*, who by their approval of the Sultan's choice of Caliph in the *bayʿa* and by their *fatwās* expressed the functional authority of the *Sharīʿa*.[3]

[1] See H. A. R. Gibb, 'Al-Māwardī's Theory of the Caliphate', in *Studies on the Civilization of Islam*, pp. 151–65, for a full discussion of al-Māwardī's theory.

[2] G. E. von Grunebaum, *Medieval Islam* (Chicago, 1946), p. 168.

[3] See L. Binder, 'Al-Ghazālī's Theory of Islamic Government', *The Muslim World*, xlv (1955), 229–41, for a full discussion of al-Ghazālī's theory.

Al-Ghazālī's theory was shortlived. The Caliphate before long ceased to have even institutional power. No authorization or validity was any longer sought for the government of the Sultan, who became the Shadow of God by whom he was directly appointed. Seizure of government itself gave authority, and it was held that a government, even if vicious, was to be obeyed because it was a lesser evil than anarchy. This change accompanied, if it did not contribute to, increased absolutism.

Already before the destruction of the Caliphate by the Mongols, the theory of the Sunnī jurists had largely reached an accommodation to fact. The position which was finally reached after the disappearance of the Caliphate was epitomized in the words of Ibn Jamāʿa, a *qāḍī* of Damascus (d. 1333), who states,

> The sovereign has a right to govern until another and stronger one shall oust him from power and rule in his stead. The latter will rule by the same title and will have to be acknowledged on the same grounds; for a government, however objectionable, is better than none at all; and between two evils we must choose the lesser.[1]

The theory of Ibn Taymiyya (d. 1328), who also lived in Damascus, rests on the thesis that God created the world to serve Him. He taught that if religion and power were separated, disorder would result in the state. He rejects the need for a single and universal Imām and for the possession by him of ideal qualities. He sees the real unity of the community—politically one at the time of the *salaf* or founding fathers of Islam—to consist not in a fictitious political unity but in the confessional solidarity which each autonomous state experienced by belonging to an organic whole. He stresses the importance of the *mubāyaʿa*, a double oath of allegiance joining the Imām and his subjects, which guarantees effective power to the former and social peace and prosperity to the latter, and gives a new basis to their relationship, namely co-operation (*taʿāwun*). The first duty of the Imām is to have recourse to consultation (*shūrā*), and that of the subjects obedience. This he interprets in a novel way as an obligation resting upon each

[1] Quoted by Von Grunebaum in *Medieval Islam*, p. 169.

individual to participate in the life of the community and to co-operate in the administration of the state. Justice is the basis on which the life of the community rested. Maintaining that public function is not bound up with the moral virtues of the holder, he introduces a distinction between the private conduct of the Imām and his execution of the law. Like al-Ghazālī he considers the authority of a leader to supervise the performance of canonical duties indispensable, and calls him the Shadow of God upon earth. An unjust or ignorant ruler is to be obeyed. Disobedience is only permissible in the event of the ruler's decisions being manifestly contrary to the Koran, the sunna, and the consensus of the *salaf*. No Muslim, he maintains, ought to draw his sword against a brother. A rupture of public peace (*fitna*) is one of the least forgivable of sins. Innovators are to be put down not because they are apostates but because they threaten public order.[1]

The constitutional theories found in administrative handbooks and mirrors for princes hold a position midway between the theory of the jurists on the one hand and that of the philosophers on the other. They go back beyond Ibn al-Muqaffaʿ, who played an important part in their development, to the epistles (*rasāʾil*) and political testaments (*waṣāyā*) attributed to various Caliphs. One such is the epistle of ʿAbd al-Ḥamīd, secretary of the last Umayyad Caliph, Marwān, written in 746–7 for the guidance of his son, who was to lead an expedition against a Khārijī rebellion in Iraq. After stressing the religious status of the Caliph, the epistle deals first with princely ethics and rules of conduct, in which it is influenced by both Sasanian tradition and Arab morality, and secondly with strategy and military administration. It takes the Aristotelian concept of the mean (*qaṣd*) to be the criterion of proper conduct.[2] Another example is the political testament of al-Manṣūr,

[1] See H. Laoust, *Essai sur les doctrines sociales et politiques de Ibn Taimīya* (Cairo, 1939) and *Le Traité de droit public d'Ibn Taimīya* (Beirut, 1948), for a full discussion of the theory of Ibn Taymiyya.

[2] See A. H. Dawood, 'A Comparative Study of Arabic and Persian Mirrors for Princes from the Second to the Sixth Century A.H.', unpublished Ph.D. thesis (London University, 1965).

the second ʿAbbāsid Caliph, composed for his son al-Mahdī,[1] which reflects the ʿAbbāsid pretension to the possession of hereditary wisdom, and identifies the authority of the Caliph with that of God. It recommends justice as the most effective means of preventing unrest, eliminating enemies, and modifying existing evils.[1]

The administrative handbooks and mirrors proper were intended primarily for the instruction of rulers and the official classes, and therefore represent the practical ethics of the ruling classes. They assume the God-founded power of the ruler, and discuss the exercise of that power. Some mirrors are, perhaps, in part political tracts: by holding up the ideal of justice they implicitly protest against contemporary evils. Although the concept of the Sultan in the mirrors owes much to the Sasanian theory, the purpose of the Sultan's government is still the formal establishment of the religion of Islam and conditions in which his subjects can fulfil their destiny. In the Sasanian theory the king ruled by divine right. The state was identified with the social order; and prosperity and virtue, summed up in the 'mean', were two facets of a unitary system.[2] This was largely taken over: the duty of the ruler was to preserve equipoise by keeping each in his proper place.

These trends can be seen in the *Siyāsat-nāma* of Niẓām al-Mulk (d. 1092), who was vizier first to Alp Arslān and then to Malikshāh. He assumes a close connection between righteousness and kingship, and between right religion and prosperity. The Sultan is directly chosen by and directly responsible to God; and his duties are a mixture of Sasanian ideals and Islamic theory. Niẓām al-Mulk's major concern was for stability. He implicitly denies the possibility of a state based on a contract between the ruler and the ruled. Rights are acquired and maintained by force, and the main function of the Sultan is coercive. Mistrust is the keynote of the system.

[1] Ibid.

[2] See R. C. Zaehner, *The Dawn and Twilight of Zoroastrianism* (London, 1961).

Ṭurṭūshī (d. 1126), who wrote at a time when Muslim power in Spain was on the decline, writes from a somewhat different angle. For him kingship existed primarily for the prevention of lawlessness. He regards the relationship of the Sultan to his subjects, the pivot around which the life of the community revolves, as that of the soul to the body. His right to rule was of divine origin and should, therefore, never be questioned. An eternal covenant between God and kings imposed on rulers the obligation to treat their subjects with justice, equity, and beneficence. The prime object of the last was the army. An unjust ruler was the punishment God meted out to His people for their disobedience, and therefore they were to endure his rule.

Mirrors were especially popular in the eastern part of the Islamic world. The earliest known Persian mirror is the *Qābūs-nāma*, written by Kay Kā'ūs, a Ziyārid princeling from northern Persia for his son in the year 1082–3. It treats constitutional theory superficially. Expediency is its basis, and justice is advocated on practical grounds. As in the *Siyāsat-nāma* the element of distrust is clearly apparent.

Another mirror, also composed in Persian, and one which had considerable influence on later works, is the *Naṣīḥat al-mulūk* ('Counsel for Kings') of al-Ghazālī, written in or shortly after 1109–10 for Sanjar, who was then governor of Khurāsān on behalf of his brother, the Seljuq Sultan Muḥammad. This sets out al-Ghazālī's conception of the Sultanate as distinct from the Caliphate. His theory is based on a metaphysical conception of the world, but the ideal community is no longer the primitive Islamic community of Medina, and its existence is no longer guaranteed by the *Sharīʿa* and the Imām. He interprets the phrase 'Obey God, obey the prophet and those in authority among you' to mean obedience to God, the prophets, and emirs, i.e. the temporal rulers. The Sultan is endowed with divine effulgence, and obedience to him as the chosen of God is incumbent upon the people, but only he who practises justice is the true Sultan. Religion is made strong by kingship, and kingship by the army, and the army by wealth;

wealth is assured by making the country populous and flourishing, and this result is achieved by justice. Al-Ghazālī lays considerable emphasis on the need for the Sultan to be strong. This must be seen against the background of contemporary circumstances, the often violent nature of Turkish rule, the disorders created by the Bāṭinīs or Ismāʿīlīs, and the prevailing intrigue. Al-Ghazālī divides the duties of the ruler into his duty towards God and his duty towards the people. The former includes the performance of canonical religious duties, the avoidance of innovation, and the suppression of heresy. The latter are comprehended in the practice of justice, by which al-Ghazālī means not legal justice but rather an inherent moral quality deriving from the perfection of the intellect, and consisting in the restraining of tyrannical instincts, passion, and anger.

Mirrors in the medieval tradition continued to be written down to modern times. Among them are the *Kitāb al-fakhrī* of Ibn Ṭiqṭaqā written for Fakhr al-Dīn ʿIsā b. Ibrāhīm, the governor of Mosul on behalf of the Mongol Il-Khān Arghūn (1284–91), which emphasizes the ruler's duty to preserve order and justice in return for which he is entitled to obedience, and the *Akhlāq al-salṭana* ('Ethics of Kingship') of Waṣṣāf written for the Il-Khānid ruler of Persia, Uljaytu (1304–16), which reflects a patriarchal conception of kingship modified by Islam. Another which achieved considerable popularity was the *Akhlāq-i muḥsinī* of Ḥusayn Wāʿiẓ Kāshifī (d. 1505), dedicated to Ḥusayn b. Bāyqarā, the Timurid ruler of Herat, which has some of the characteristics of the constitutional theory of the philosophers also. Kāshifī believed that men were impelled by nature to live together and that a law to regulate their affairs and prevent their aggression against each other was needed. This law was a divine law brought by the Prophet, but he does not relate it to the primitive Islamic community or the Caliphate. The Prophet having instituted the *Sharīʿa*, a king, endowed with the characteristics of the Prophet, is needed for its defence. This equation of kingship and prophethood had probably been current in Ṣūfī circles for some time, and is to be found in the writings of Najm al-Dīn Rāzī (d. 1256); it is also found in al-Fārābī's work (see below).

All, or nearly all, Islamic philosophers fall under the influence of Greek philosophy, which they tend to adapt either to Sunnī or Shīʿī theory. Central to their thought is the law, on which the state is founded and by which it is guided. Al-Fārābī (d. 950), known as the second teacher in contradistinction to Aristotle, the first teacher, is the first Islamic philosopher 'who sought to confront, to relate, and as far as possible to harmonize classical political philosophy with Islam' and to make it intelligible within the context of revealed religion.[1] His most famous work, *al-Madīna al-fāḍila* ('The Good City'), is concerned with the attainment of happiness through political life and the relation between the best regime as Plato understood it and the divine law of Islam.[1] Just as Plato's philosopher attains happiness only in the ideal Politeia, so al-Fārābī's 'adept of the speculative sciences gains ultimate perfection and happiness only in the perfectly led and administered ideal state which is ruled over by the philosopher who is identical with the Lawgiver and Imām.'[2] Al-Fārābī divides the citizens of the virtuous regime into three classes, (i) the wise and the philosophers, who knew the nature of things by means of demonstrable proofs and their own insights, (ii) the followers of the first class, who trusted their insight and accepted their judgement, and (iii) the rest of the citizens, who knew things only by means of similitudes. The ruler assigns to each their specialized duties, gives them laws, and commands them in war, and seeks by persuasion and compulsion to develop in everyone the virtues of which he is capable, and orders them hierarchically so that each class attains that perfection of which it is capable.[3]

The good city resembles a sound body in which all the members co-operate and of which the ruling member is the heart. The *ra'īs*,

[1] M. Mahdi, 'Alfarabi', in *History of Political Philosophy*, ed. L. Strauss and J. Cropsey (New York, 1963), pp. 160–1.

[2] E. I. J. Rosenthal, 'Some Aspects of Islamic Political Thought', p. 6.

[3] M. Mahdi, 'Alfarabi', pp. 164–5.

or leader, of the good city, whom he equates with the Imām, is the most perfect of its members, and is both philosopher and prophet. He communicates with the Active Intellect through his rational faculty as ruler-philosopher and through his imagination as ruler-prophet. In discussing the qualities required of the *ra'is* al-Fārābī does not refer to the Islamic community, but the impression he leaves on the reader is that he has this in mind and that his purpose is to show the wide area of harmony between Islamic theory and classical political philosophy.[1] As well as the good city al-Fārābī also describes several contrasting types of city: the ignorant city, whose people pursue the good in something in which it does not lie; the profligate city, whose people know in what the good lies but do not do it; the perverted city, which has fallen away from former virtue; and the injurious city, in which are false teachers and whose people pursue false knowledge.

Al-Fārābī profoundly influenced later writers. Among them, Ibn Sīnā (Avicenna, d. 1037) also links the ideal state of Islam with that of Plato's philosopher-king. Ibn Rushd (Averroes, d. 1198) similarly maintains the supremacy of the *Sharīʿa* as the ideal revealed law and the Islamic equivalent of the constitution of the ideal state of Plato.[2] Another, Fakhr al-Dīn al-Rāzī (d. 1209), who spent much of his life in Herat, attempts a reconcilation between philosophy and theology, and also adapts the theory of the philosopher-king to the Islamic ideal. Rather later, Naṣīr al-Dīn al-Ṭūsī (d. 1274), a Shīʿī, who at the end of his life was in the service of the Mongol ruler, Hulagu, in his well-known work, the *Akhlāq-i nāṣirī* ('Nasirean Ethics'), carries the theory still further.[3] After discussing the nature of man and his need for co-operation and association, he lays down the need for a divine institute, a governor, and a monetary currency for the maintenance of equity among the

[1] Ibid., pp. 162–3.

[2] E. I. J. Rosenthal, *Political Thought in Medieval Islam* (Cambridge, 1958), pp. 143 ff. and 175 ff.

[3] The *Akhlāq-i jalālī* of Jalāl al-Dīn Dawānī (d. 1502 or 1503), a *qāḍī*, who served the Black Sheep ruler, Yūsuf b. Jahānshāh, in southern Persia, is a popularization of the *Akhlāq-i nāṣirī*.

members of the community. The first he interprets as the *Sharīʿa*, which is the final arbiter to be obeyed by all; the third arbiter, money, is to be subject to the second, the governor. The proper regulation of affairs is secured by a law-giver, divinely inspired, who, Naṣīr al-Dīn states, is called by the 'moderns' the Imām and his work the Imāmate, by Plato the controller of the world, and by Aristotle civic man. A law-giver is not, however, always needed because a divine institute, once brought, suffices for many centuries. A controller to order the affairs of the community, on the other hand, is necessary in every age. Naṣīr al-Dīn adopts al-Fārābī's classification of civilizations but expands it and adapts it more narrowly to Islamic civilization.

The ideal in each of the three formulations examined in this essay was inspired by Islam. All assumed the ultimate source of power to be divine, and to come from God through the ruler, be he Caliph or king, which made the problem of the tyrannical ruler insoluble. All identified the state with religion, and disorders in religion with disturbances in the state. Power was not a central problem for any of them. It was its own justification, and its only vindication was the benefit its exercise conferred on the subjects. The keyword of all these formulations was justice, which medieval Islamic political thought understood to be the harmonious relationship of society in a divinely appointed system, the component parts of which were in perfect equilibrium. The Trojan horse from which abuses invaded the state was arbitrary power. Among its consequences were corruption which fed on insecurity, and the flattery expected and received by the ruler which destroyed the dignity of the citizen.

The mirrors, so far as they pointed to an ideal of justice, may, perhaps, have exercised a restraining influence. On the other hand, their emphasis on the ruler, directly appointed by God and directly responsible to Him, coupled with the 'concession' of power by the ruler to his subjects, denied responsibility to the citizen, and contributed to the abolition of personal liberty. The philosophers in their constitutional theory also placed the ruler above the law, and their assumption that wisdom and knowledge was the prerogative of a single class led to a contempt for the common man. Further, their emphasis on the hierarchical order of society reinforced its conservative tendencies. In the theory of the jurists on the other hand the ruler was subject to the *Sharīʿa*, though his accountability was, in practice, empty, since no means were devised to enforce it. Although the jurists attempted in some measure to rationalize the history of the community, there was at the same time a tendency for their political thought to become bound by tradition. In measure as this was the case the juristic theory exercised little influence on political activity, but its rigidity enabled it to survive as an ideal in spite of the political vicissitudes undergone by the community,[1] and it is the formulation of the jurists, not that of the mirrors or the philosophers, which lies at the base of the modern movements of Islamic constitutional reform.

A. K. S. LAMBTON

BIBLIOGRAPHY

Texts

Abū Yūsuf, *Kitāb al-kharāj*, French translation by E. Fagnan (Paris, 1921); Al-Fārābī, *Al-Madīna al-fāḍila*, German translation by F. Dieterici (Leiden, 1900); idem, *Alfarabi's Philosophy of Plato and Aristotle*, English translation by M. Mahdi (New York, 1962); Al-Ghazālī, *Naṣīḥat al-mulūk*, English translation by F. R. C. Bagley, *Ghazālī's Book of Counsel for Kings* (London, 1964); Imām al-Ḥaramayn, *Al-Irshād*, French translation by J.-D. Luciani (Paris, 1938); Ibn Jamāʿa, *Taḥrīr al-aḥkām*, German translation of Chapters 1 and 2 by H. Köfler in *Islamica*, vi–vii (1934–5); Jalāl al-Dīn Dawānī, *Akhlāq-i jalālī*, English translation by W. T. Thompson, *Practical Philosophy of the Muhammedan People* (London, 1839); Kay Kā'ūs, *Qābūs-nāma*, English translation by R. Levy, *A Mirror for Princes* (London, 1951); Al-Māwardī, *Al-Aḥkām al-sulṭāniyya*, French translation by E. Fagnan, *Les Statuts Gouvernementaux* (Algiers, 1915); Naṣīr al-Dīn, *Akhlāq-i nāṣirī*, English translation by G. M. Wickens, *The Nasirean Ethics* (London, 1964); Niẓām al-Mulk, *Siyāsat-nāma*, French translation by C. Schefer (Paris, 1891–7).

Studies

V. V. Barthold, 'Khalif i Sultan', English translation by N. S. Doniach in *Islamic Quarterly*, vii (1963), 117–35; L. Gardet, *La Cité musulmane* (Paris, 1954); M. H. Kerr, *Islamic Reform: the Political and Legal Theories of Muḥammad ʿAbdūh and*

[1] cf. J. Schacht, 'The Law', pp. 76–7.

Rashīd Riḍā (Berkeley–Los Angeles, 1966); A. K. S. Lambton, 'Justice in the Medieval Persian Theory of Kingship', *Studia Islamica*, xvii (1962), 91–119; idem, 'Quis Custodiet Custodes', *Studia Islamica*, v (1956), 125–48 and vi (1956), 125–46; idem, 'The Theory of Kingship in the *Naṣīḥat ul-mulūk* of Ghazālī, *Islamic Quarterly*, i (1954), 47–55; H. Laoust, *La Politique de Ġazālī* (Paris 1970); G. Lecomte, *Ibn Qutayba, l'homme, son œuvre, ses idées* (Damascus, 1965); D. B. Macdonald, *Development of Muslim Theology, Jurisprudence and Constitutional Theory* (New York, 1903); C. Pellat, *Le Milieu baṣrien et la formation d'al-Ǧāḥiẓ* (Paris, 1953).

X

SCIENCE

(*A*) THE NATURAL SCIENCES AND MEDICINE

OUR main purpose in this chapter is to show how far Islamic science and medicine is an element of the legacy bequeathed by medieval Islam to the West. This inevitably imposes a limitation on the selection of phenomena to be discussed, for we are not concerned with Islamic science for its own sake. But we hope no important achievement will remain unnoticed, for there was hardly anything that did not affect the West in one way or another.

1. *The historical background*

The influence of Islamic science on the West was primarily made possible by Arab conquests in the western Mediterranean. The presence of Arabs for almost 800 years on the Iberian peninsula has left indelible marks on the Spanish landscape and art, and the languages spoken there, Catalan, Castilian, and Portuguese. Arab rule in Sicily and parts of southern Italy was of shorter duration and the cultural impact less lasting, but it was hardly less intensive than in Spain, for the Arabs were not expelled by force during the Norman occupation (on these cultural influences see above, Chapter II). Even after the Moors had finally left the European areas of the western Mediterranean and become confined to North Africa, contact did not cease. At the same time the Muslims were reinvading Europe through the Balkans; by then, however, the nations of Europe had become strong intellectually and independent enough to emancipate themselves from their dependence on Islamic science.

Even today it is often thought that the Crusades played a significant part in Islamic–European cultural contacts, and that the influence of Islam came essentially from the East. In fact the decisive contacts had taken place earlier in the western Mediterranean;[1] even the ninety years of the Kingdom of Jerusalem (1096–1187) are of less than secondary importance from our point of view. The achievements of the Muslims of the Eastern Caliphate came to the knowledge of the West because the intensive interrelationship of Islamic countries enabled the works of Iraqi, Syrian, and Egyptian scholars to be studied either in the Maghrib or in the East by Maghribī Muslims who travelled thither.[2]

2. *The nature of Islamic science*

Islamic science was of course not the only factor that led to the revival of Western science; the classical scientific tradition had not entirely perished amid the upheavals of the migration era. It is true, however, that a new impetus was given to Western science by the Islamic scientists; above all it was materially enriched to an unprecedented degree both by the Arab translations from the Greek and by the independent work of the Muslims themselves. It is remarkable that despite an early acquaintance with the scientific achievements of other cultures, especially the Indian, it was the Greek tradition that was to be decisive for Islamic learning. One reason for this is the outstanding importance of the Hellenized Christians and the rather less Hellenized Persians, who made up the bulk of the indigenous population in the central lands of the Caliphate. Another reason is that Christian monotheism represented a perpetual challenge to that of Islam; Arab thinking was trained and matured in the polemic against a Christianity which already had a philosophically based theology. This meant that the Platonic, Neo-Platonic, and Aristotelian traditions supplied the categories by which Islamic thought came to under-

[1] Sir Ernest Barker's article 'The Crusades' in the first edition of *The Legacy of Islam* is still worth reading today.

[2] A convenient survey is W. Montgomery Watt, *Islamic Spain* (Edinburgh, 1965); see also *Encyclopaedia of Islam*, 2nd edn., article 'Arabiyya', appendix, 'Arabic Literature in Spain'.

stand and assimilate the achievements of Antiquity in the fields of medicine and science as well.

As Ibn Khaldūn emphasized, genuine Arabs played only a small part in the original development of Islamic science, and most of the credit must go to Persians, Christians, and Jews; even so, the Arabic language became the main vehicle of Islamic learning and played in the East the part played by Latin in the West. G. Bergsträsser has demonstrated briefly but convincingly that the Arabic language provided from the outset the possibility of scientifically exact expression.[1] But it was not that in itself that was to prove decisive, but rather the central position of Arabic as the language of Islamic religion and administration, that eventually led to its adaptation to scientific requirements. The success achieved in this process of adaptation was largely the result of deliberate effort, as shown by the fact that scientific works can be very well understood in Arabic without any deep knowledge of the old poetry or prose, let alone later artistic prose works, although syntax, morphology, and much of the vocabulary have changed little since the earliest times.

Islamic science did not remain exclusively in the hands of Muslims, even after its 'Arabization'. Christians and Jews continued to make so active a contribution that the *Fons vitae* of Ibn Gabirol (Avicebron) could pass for the work of a Muslim until the nineteenth century when S. Munk identified the author as Jewish.[2] The medical works of Isaac Israeli and Maimonides are in no way different from the works of Islamic authors; the same is true of the scientific writings of the Christian bishop Barhebraeus. The very fact that books of Islamic authors could be translated into Hebrew and Latin without significant changes demonstrates the 'inter-religiousness' no less than the internationality of Islamic science. Science was perhaps the one cultural area that was least

[1] *Einführung in die semitischen Sprachen* (Munich, 1928), pp. 146 ff.; G. Strohmaier, 'Arabisch als Sprache der Wissenschaft in den frühen medizinischen Übersetzungen', in *Mitteilungen des Institut für Orientforschung*, xv (1969), 77–85.

[2] *Mélanges de philosophie juive et arabe* (Paris, 1859).

accessible to 'Islamization'. Moreover, the continued and undiminished hostility of official orthodoxy against the ancient sciences[1] remained as characteristic of Islam as it was of Christianity until deep into the Middle Ages, and of orthodox Jewry to the very threshold of our present time. Knowledge not founded on revelation and tradition was deemed not only to be irrelevant but to be the first step on the path to heresy.

3. *The beginnings of Islamic science*

A concern for the ancient sciences in Islam began long before the period of translations; the constant dialogue with Christians and the newly converted bearers of Hellenic culture could not fail to stimulate an interest in science.[2] We exempt here philosophy and the exact sciences which are reserved for treatment in other chapters, and shall confine ourselves to medicine, the natural sciences, and geography.

There is no doubt that Khālid b. Yazīd, a grandson of the first Umayyad Caliph Muʿāwiya (661–80), showed scientific inclinations, and had a special interest in alchemy, though the true facts are lost in an impenetrable thicket of legends, and the alchemist texts handed down under Khālid's name are all pseudepigraphia.[3]

Alchemy is probably the first ancient science with which Islam became acquainted through external influences. The same does not, of course, apply to medicine, nor to a knowledge of the three realms of nature, nor to geography, for a preoccupation with these disciplines is a universal dictate of life itself. Islamic sources, it is true, point to the existence of scientific education only in the field of medicine. Al-Ḥārith b. Kalada, a contemporary of the

[1] I. Goldziher, 'Stellung der alten islamischen Orthodoxie zu den antiken Wissenschaften', *Abh. Preuss. Akad. Wiss.* (1916); M. Meyerhof and J. Schacht, *The 'Theologus Autodidactus' of Ibn al-Nafīs* (Oxford, 1968), pp. 6f.

[2] J. Schacht, 'Remarques sur la transmission de la pensée grecque aux Arabes', *Histoire de la médecine*, ii (1952). 11–19.

[3] J. Ruska, *Arabische Alchemisten, I. Ḫālid Ibn Jazīd ibn Muʿāwija* (Heidelberg, 1924).

Prophet, is supposed to have received his training at Gondēshāpūr, the famous academy and community of translators near the ancient Susa, which was the centre for the scholars who had left the Byzantine empire as heretics after the deposition of the Patriarch Nestorius by the Council of Ephesus in 431. After stopping at Edessa and Nisibis, they finally settled in Gondēshāpūr and, in free contact with Persian and Indian colleagues, laid the scientific and literary foundations for many Islamic fields of learning. Although the art of medicine was thus sanctioned by the Prophet, of whom tradition has it that he referred patients to al-Ḥārith, there were none the less doubts about its practice in religious circles: it was regarded as an interference with God's counsels. Even so late an author as Ibn al-Jawzī (d. 1200) deemed it his duty to open his book of recipes *Iltiqāṭ al-manāfiʿ* by quoting traditions in praise of medicine.[1]

We do not know anything of what the earliest alchemists actually thought and did. As with the writings of Khālid, we have to regard those of the sixth Shīʿī Imām Jaʿfar al-Ṣādiq (d. 765) as apocryphal, until proof is produced of their authenticity.[2] There are a few more definite references to medicine in the Koran and the Traditions attributed to the Prophet, but there is very little that rises above the level of popular medicine or superstitious practices.[3]

We may assume, though, that both medicine and alchemy were studied for pragmatic and rational reasons, on account of their actual or supposed practical usefulness. This cannot be said of descriptive natural science and geography, at least from what our literary sources would suggest. The early monographs on natural

[1] Cf. Griffini's description of Cod. Ambros. C.95, *Rivista degli Studi Orientali*, vii (1916), 568 f., as being in agreement with the MS. Bodl. Marsh 284 (The Bodleian Library is thanked for providing this writer with a microfilm.) See F. Rosenthal, 'The Defense of Medicine in the Medieval Muslim World', *Bulletin of the History of Medicine*, xliii (1969), 519–32.

[2] J. Ruska, *Arabische Alchemisten*, II. *Ǧaʿfar Al-Ṣādiq, der sechste Imam* (Heidelberg, 1924).

[3] K. Opitz, *Die Medizin im Koran* (Stuttgart, 1906); A. J. Wensinck, *Handbook of Early Muhammadan Tradition* (Leiden, 1927), s.vv. Incantation, Medicine, Sick, Sickness.

subjects betray a purely lexicological concern, being intended to elucidate a poem or provide stylistic training for the writer of artistic prose. The traditional knowledge of these subjects, too, was raised to the level of a science only by Islam's growing acquaintance with the Greek tradition.

4. *Translations into Arabic*

By far the most prolific and best translator from the Greek was the Christian Ḥunayn b. Isḥāq (809–74). In 1925 the original of an authentic report by him was discovered,[1] from which it is clear that Ḥunayn only named his predecessors when he had to deal with their works specifically, whether he improved upon their translations or replaced them completely, or else translated into Arabic a version only available in Syriac. So Ḥunayn's report is useful for the translations expressly mentioned by him, but it is not an exhaustive source for translations that had been done before his time, as we know from texts preserved.[2]

Apart from the wide range of his activity, Ḥunayn's merit lies in the philological method he used for establishing reliable Greek texts, in his excellent understanding of the originals, and in the scientific language which he evolved; his translations are far from being slavishly literal. In all of these fields he was unsurpassed by any of his colleagues.[3]

Max Meyerhof, in the first edition of this book, attributed to Ḥunayn's preference for Galen the unparalleled role that this medical author played in the Islam of the Middle Ages and consequently in the West. With all respect for Meyerhof's brilliant researches into Islamic medicine and its history, this seems a doubtful proposition. Meyerhof himself says that Ḥunayn also translated the works of other physicians whose subsequent importance in Islam was nothing like that of Galen. But can any develop-

[1] G. Bergsträsser, *Ḥunain Ibn Isḥāq. Über die syrischen und arabischen Galen-Übersetzungen* (Leipzig, 1925).

[2] Idem, *Ḥunain Ibn Isḥāḳ und seine Schule* (Leiden, 1913), pp. 26 f.

[3] G. Strohmaier, *Encyclopaedia of Islam*, 2nd edn., article 'Ḥunayn'.

ment at all, which takes place over centuries and continents, be regarded as the outcome of a single man's predilection, however important he may be? The appreciation of Galen was indeed already high in pre-Islamic days. The comprehensiveness of his work and the considerable philosophical interest of its author ensured that it would transcend medical boundaries, all the more so as its literary qualities would appeal to intellectuals of all kinds. To this must be added that the corpus of the 'Sixteen Books' (known by that name) or *Summaria Alexandrinorum*, which served as a basis for medical studies, seems to have been compiled as early as the Alexandrian period, so that Arab translators would have been familiar with it already. Ḥunayn specially mentions this corpus at the end of his discussion of the twentieth title of his bibliography of Galen.[1]

5. *Pseudepigraphia*

We have had occasion to refer to scientific or pseudo-scientific pseudepigraphy. Pseudepigraphy as a general literary phenomenon has hitherto received remarkably scant attention, however numerous the works recognized and individually assessed as such. Beginnings of a study of pseudepigraphy in Islam and medieval Judaism can be found in Steinschneider's preface to his book published in 1862, *Zur pseudepigraphischen Literatur insbesondere der geheimen Wissenschaften des Mittelalters*, yet the part of pseudepigraphy in the scientific writings of Islam is so substantial that it deserves a particular discussion here.

As pseudo-authors we find many writers who had already been credited by the ancients with spurious works, including Pythagoras, the president of an alleged assembly of alchemists, known as the *Turba philosophorum*,[2] as well as other Pythagoreans.[3] The late

---

[1] M. Meyerhof, 'Von Alexandrien nach Bagdad', *Sitzungsber der Preuss. Akad. der Wiss.* (1930), 394 ff.; see now H. Gätje, *Gött. Gelehrte Anzeigen* (1969), 92–103.

[2] J. Ruska, *Turba Philosophorum* (Berlin, 1931).

[3] E.g. M. Plessner, *Der ΟΙΚΟΝΟΜΙΚΟΣ des Neupythagoreers 'Bryson' und sein Einfluss auf die islamische Wissenschaft* (Heidelberg, 1928).

C. E. Dubler recently compiled a list of pseudepigraphic works attributed to Aristotle.[1] Ptolemy's apocryphal *Centiloquium* was translated into Arabic with a commentary by an important man of letters.[2] There was also Apollonius of Tyana, the assumed author of a lengthy *Book of Causes*, with the so-called *Tabula smaragdina* as its conclusion.[3] Under the name of Hermes Trismegistus a whole library of writings (not identical with the *Corpus Hermeticum*) was freshly compiled in Islam.[4] There were also the books of the *Corpus Hippocraticum*, the authenticity of part of which was guaranteed by Galen, and to name one non-Greek example, there were the Persians Zoroaster and Ostanes.[5]

In Islam there came also into being an extensive number of works to which famous Muslim names were attached. To mention only one example: two works on alchemy and magic composed in Spain in the eleventh century, the *Rutbat al-ḥakīm* ('The [High] Rank of the Philosopher') and the *Ghāyat al-ḥakīm* ('The Final Aim of the Philosopher'), the last one of which became known in its Latin version as *Picatrix*, were attributed to the mathematician and astronomer Maslama b. Aḥmad al-Majrīṭī who had lived almost a century earlier.[6] It is hardly ever possible to name the forger, i.e. the true author of these works. But in one case at least the reverse is true and the forger is known. He pretends to be a mere translator of works purported to have been written long before Islam. This is Ibn Waḥshiyya (*c.* 900),[7] renowned as a 'collector'

[1] 'Über arabische Pseudo-Aristotelica', *Asiatische Studien*, xiv (1961), 33–42.

[2] Aḥmad b. Yūsuf b. al-Dāya; cf. C. Brockelmann, *Geschichte der arabischen Literatur*, Supplement I, 229. A Latin translation by Johannes Hispanensis was repeatedly printed in the fifteenth and sixteenth centuries.

[3] J. Ruska, *Tabula smaragdina* (Heidelberg, 1926); P. Kraus, *Jābir ibn Ḥayyān* (Cairo, 1942), ii. 272–303; M. Plessner, *Encyclopaedia of Islam*, 2nd edn., article 'Bālīnūs'.

[4] M. Plessner, *Encyclopaedia of Islam*, 2nd edn., article 'Hirmis'.

[5] J. Bidez et F. Cumont, *Les Mages hellénisés, Zoroastre, Ostanès et Hystaspe d'après la tradition greque* (Paris, 1938) (containing also alchemical texts in Arabic).

[6] Thorndike, *History of Magic*, ii. 381 ff.; ed. H. Ritter (1933), translated by H. Ritter and M. Plessner (1962); an edition of the Latin version is in preparation.

[7] *Encyclopaedia of Islam*, 2nd edn., s.v. Ibn Waḥshiyya by Fahd; and on one aspect

and interpreter of ancient alphabets; as 'translator' of an astrological book by an author named Tankalūshā (Teucer); and as transmitter of supposedly old-Babylonian writings, the best known of which are the *Nabataean Agriculture*[1] and a *Book of Poisons*.[2] Under his name there are many more forgeries extant or mentioned in bibliographies. As is shown in this survey, it is by no means always a case of works of occult character, but also of writings of serious scientific value, even if they are not entirely free from superstitious material.

From the researches of the last 100 years we have been able to learn something about some of the social groups which had an interest in circulating such pseudepigrapha. Thus Ibn Waḥshiyya, who was close to the Shuʿūbiyya in Iraq, hoped by his supposedly ancient writings to prove the superiority of the Babylonians—the alleged ancestors of his own Nabataean nation—over the culturally inferior Arab conquerors, as von Gutschmid's brilliant analysis has proved.[3] He also was somehow related to the adherents of the old pagan religion who held out for two or three centuries after the appearance of Islam in Ḥarrān (Carrhae), maintaining that they were the Sabians who in the Koran were given the right of toleration as 'People of a Scripture'. The incentives for the forging of hermetic writings in Arabic can certainly be traced back to this group of Sabians,[4] and some of these writings are still extant.

The spirit of such books animated the extreme Shīʿīs, especially

of his later influence, G. O. S. Darby, 'Ibn Waḥshiyya in Mediaeval Spanish Literature', *Isis*, xxxiii (1941), 433–8.

[1] D. Chwolson, *Über die Überreste der altbabylonischen Literatur in arabischen Übersetzungen* (St. Petersburg, 1859); M. Plessner, 'Der Inhalt der Nabatäischen Landwirtschaft', *Zeitschrift für Semitistik*, vi (1928), 27–56.

[2] English translation in M. Levey, *Medieval Arabic Toxicology, The Book of Poisons of Ibn Waḥshīya*, Transactions of the American Philosophical Society, N.S., lvi. 7 (Philadelphia, 1966).

[3] 'Die nabatäische Landwirtschaft und ihre Geschwister', *Zeitschrift der Deutschen Morgenländischen Gesellschaft*, xv (1860) = *Kleine Schriften*, ii (Leipzig, 1890), 568–716.

[4] See D. Pingree, *The Thousands of Abu Maʿshar* (London, 1968).

the Ismāʿīlīs, who circulated a scientific literature which was sometimes of considerable merit. A close analysis of the texts reveals the extent to which it was also propaganda for their politico-religious heresy. The most important of these texts were the writings of the Ikhwān al-Ṣafā' or 'Faithful Friends', the true Ismāʿīlī character of which was long ago recognized by S. Guyard,[1] and the corpus of the writings attributed to Jābir.[2] A large number of all these works became known to the West either in their entirety or in excerpts found in other authors; they therefore belong to the legacy of Islam.

6. *Universal scholars*

One of the characteristics of medieval science and teaching, in Islam as in the West, was that many scholars excelled in more than one field. They did not even confine themselves to either the natural or humane sciences, but promoted research in both realms. Certain aspects of their scholarly activities therefore do not strictly fall within the framework of this chapter, but it would not do justice to them if we should confine ourselves to describing their achievements in medicine and science only, let alone subdividing their performance between separate disciplines. We will deal here with two of the most significant and prominent of these scholars.

One of the earliest of these universal scholars was the physician Abū Bakr Muḥammad b. Zakariyyā' al-Rāzī or Rhazes (865–925), whose fame in the West became immense and whose authority remained unquestioned till the seventeenth century. He was one of the pioneers of rationalism in Islamic science, like his contemporary al-Fārābī in the field of philosophy. Although he was familiar with the whole field of Greek science, as his great medical works *al-Ḥāwī* (*Continens* in Latin) and *al-Manṣūrī* (*Ad Alman-*

1 'Fragments relatifs à la doctrine des Ismaélis', *Notices et Extraits*, xxiii (Paris, 1874), 177–428; see also I. Goldziher, *Die Richtungen der islamischen Koranauslegung* (Leiden, 1920), pp. 190 ff.; Y. Marquet, *Encyclopaedia of Islam*, 2nd edn., article 'Ikhwān al-Ṣafā''.

2 P. Kraus and M. Plessner', 'Djābir b. Ḥayyān', in *Encyclopaedia of Islam*, 2nd edn.; M. Plessner, *Zeitschrift der Deutschen Morgenländischen Gesellschaft*, cxv (1965), 23–35.

sorem) prove, he challenged tradition in all fields, showing full awareness of what he was doing. In his book, *Dubitationes in Galenum*, he expressly quoted the criticisms which earlier scholars, including Galen himself, had made of their predecessors. This was 300 years before Maimonides, in the 25th Book of his *Aphorisms*, made his own criticisms of Galen, quoting al-Rāzī. The latter's independence can also be seen in his approach to Islamic theology, which provided his biographers with many opportunities for associating him with heresies of all kinds. He was in fact criticizing those very doctrines that others tried to pin on him, though at the same time he was also questioning orthodox theology. While not denying the existence of God, his attitude towards the positive religions was undoubtedly sceptical. He was, in this respect, not the only man in those centuries in which the tolerance of Islam made possible a confrontation with different religions to an extent that was unheard of elsewhere. Thus in metaphysical matters he was apt to adopt the Kantian attitude *sapere aude*, as he did too in the sciences he cultivated.[1] He recorded exact case histories which have become known partly through the researches of Meyerhof.[2] He wrote a famous and much-discussed book in which he, for the first time, correctly defined the difference between smallpox and measles.

In physiognomics, too, he went his own way,[3] and in the field of chemistry he was probably the first scholar whom it would be unjustified to describe as an alchemist. That he was familiar with the views of his predecessors is beyond doubt; but unlike them he provides a rational classification of the substances known to him, giving exact descriptions of the instruments and methods he used

[1] Cf. P. Kraus and S. Pines in *Encyclopaedia of Islam*, 1st edn., article 'al-Rāzī'.

[2] *Isis*, xxiii (1935), 321–72. A Latin version was published by O. Temkin, *Bulletin of the History of Medicine*, xii (1942), 102–17.

[3] The section concerned of the *Liber ad Almansorem* was separately printed under the title *Jumal aḥkām al-firāsa* (Aleppo, 1929). Cf. also M. Plessner, 'The Physiognomics of Rhazes and its Influence on Eastern and Western Authors', *Actes du XIe Congrès International d'Histoire des Sciences, Warsaw–Cracow, 1965*, ii (1967), 247–9.

in his experiments, and arriving at careful conclusions based upon his own observations.[1]

Only a few of his many writings, several of which were translated into Latin, survive. This is not the place to consider his philosophy, but it is not surprising that such an independent spirit created a deep impression upon the man who must be described as perhaps the greatest scholar of medieval Islam, Abu'l-Rayḥān al-Bīrūnī (b. 973, d. after 1050). He in fact wrote a biography and bibliography of al-Rāzī,[2] although he was at pains not to endorse his subject's religious and philosophical views. In doing so, he apologetically remarks that al-Rāzī had been more deceived than deceiver; so, without accepting the more unorthodox aspects of his work, he declared himself a follower of al-Rāzī in most other respects. The fact that he adds a bibliography of his own writings may be taken as proof that he regarded himself as a spiritual kinsman of the great doctor.

Al-Bīrūnī excelled even al-Rāzī in the universality of his interests. We cannot deal with his contributions to the exact sciences which form the bulk of his writings. But in his bibliography which extends to the year 1036—when, in his own words, he was sixty-five Islamic lunar years old—he not only mentions numerous works of descriptive natural science, history, and old poetry, but also a whole series of translations of scientific and non-scientific works from Indian and other languages.[3] His deep insight into

[1] J. Ruska, 'Al-Rāzī's Buch Geheimnis der Geheimnisse . . . in deutscher Übersetzung, *Quellen und Studien zur Geschichte der Naturwissenschaften und der Medizin*, vi, 1937. Cf. also G. Heim, 'Al-Rāzī and Alchemy', *Ambix*, i (1937–8), 184–91. The original was edited by M. T. Danechpajouh, *Al-Asrār et Sirr-al-asrār* (Tehran, 1964). On the Latin translations see J. Ruska, 'Übersetzung und Bearbeitungen von al-Rāzī's Buch Geheimnis der Geheimnisse' in *Quellen und Studien*, iv (1935), 153–239.

[2] *Epître de Bērūnī contenant le répertoire des ouvrages de Muḥammad b. Zakariyā ar-Rāzī*, ed. P. Kraus (Paris, 1936).

[3] See D. J. Boilot, *Encyclopaedia of Islam*, 2nd edn., article 'al-Bīrūnī'. His translation of the Patanjali was edited by H. Ritter, in *Oriens*, ix (1956). There is an English translation of the first chapter by S. Pines and T. Gelblum, in *Bulletin of the School of Oriental and African Studies*, xxix (1966).

linguistic problems is not immediately apparent from this list, but his notes on language, whenever the subject crops up, are sufficient evidence of his authority. He wrote a splendid account of India's spiritual and intellectual life. In his late seventies he wrote his *Book of Stones*, which is a radical departure from the conventional mineralogical literature of Islam in that it ignores completely any purported magical properties of stones. The author gives—apart from the explanations of the names—mining sites, specific weights, trading values, and other observations, partly of a medical and anecdotal nature. He also supplies the literary background[1] and critical glosses on his predecessors. He is indeed one of the very few Islamic scholars whose quotations amount to something more than a mere copying out of data; they are an organic part of his own treatment of the subject. At the same time he occasionally ridicules miracle stories, and the genuineness of the spurious *Book of Stones* attributed to Aristotle is, for instance, expressly denied.

Owing to insufficient manuscript evidence, Meyerhof found it impossible to edit more than the Introduction to al-Bīrūnī's *Pharmacology*, yet this is sufficient to show that the author, then 80, had still the same indomitable spirit and undiminished energy.[2]

Although we must leave aside his mathematical and astronomical writings, we cannot leave unmentioned his great chronological book, *Chronology of Ancient Nations*, which he wrote when he was about twenty-eight. This work, using and continuing Ptolemy's *Canons*, is not only a comparative study and description of the different eras of chronology, and as such the first work of its kind in world literature, but is also an invaluable source of material for the history of religions and folklore. His description of the festivals and other notable days of the various religions

[1] M. Y. Haschmi, 'Die griechischen Quellen des Steinbuches von al-Bērūnī', *Annales archéologiques de Syrie*, xv (1965), 21–56.

[2] M. Meyerhof, 'Das Vorwort zur Drogenkunde des Bērūnī', *Quellen und Studien*, iii (1934); the same in *Bulletin de l'Institut d'Égypte*, xxii (1940), 134–52.

whose calendars he reproduces is remarkable. He shows himself familiar with the sacred writings of these various faiths, and he quotes, for instance, from the Old Testament in Arabic transcriptions of the Hebrew original.

Important though al-Bīrūnī undoubtedly was in many spheres of knowledge, it must be confessed that, somewhat surprisingly, he does not form part of Islam's legacy in the sense in which we are using the word here. Perhaps the translators were afraid of the difficulty of language and treatment of the subjects in his works and preferred the more easily understandable writings of his predecessors and successors. Anyhow, it is a fact that the standard of scientific criticism established by al-Fārābī, al-Rāzī, and al-Bīrūnī, each in his own sphere, was not maintained in Islam itself. Not only did science, in spite of some splendid and even pioneering writings by individual scholars, degenerate in many cases into a kind of authority-bound syncretism, it also succumbed to the astrological and magical presuppositions that characterize medieval scholarly activity.[1] If we are to understand the spirit of Islamic science and appreciate its effect upon the West, we shall have to take account of these.

7. *The concept of causality: magic, astrology, alchemy*

Until relatively recent times the attempt to account for natural happenings on the basis of astrological or magical principles was considered as science. Any radical departure from those principles was quite beyond even those scholars who, whether on religious or rational grounds, rejected soothsaying founded on astrology and sorcery based on the concept, implied by magic, of the causal interconnection of all existing things. L. Thorndike showed this, as far as magic is concerned, in his first publication, *The Place of Magic in the Intellectual History of Europe*, published in 1905; it was based on an abundance of material and already revealed the

[1] A. Abel, 'La Place des sciences occultes dans le décadence', in *Classicisme et déclin culturel dans l'Histoire de l'Islam*, Symposium held at Bordeaux, 1956 (Paris, 1957), 291–318, offers rich material.

penetrating mind characteristic of this outstanding historian of Western civilization. It was this conviction that made him the great adversary of G. Sarton, who, as a mathematician, was at a loss to grasp this state of affairs, despite his own enormous historical knowledge and his familiarity with Oriental sources. It is obvious that it was mainly Sarton's opposition, some fifty years later, which inspired Thorndike's lecture on 'The True Place of Astrology in the History of Science'.[1] The following quotation may be taken from it:

> Ultimately Albert [the Great] reached the conclusion that, when God said, 'Producat terra' (Gen. 1: 24), He designated the earth merely as the material principle from which animals are formed, but that the active principle is the heavens. This rule of the heavens should be kept constantly in mind by every student of the history of science before Newton in evaluating any aspect of scientific or, for that matter, human activity. Most past critics of what they were pleased to call astrology never questioned this assumption, which was its very basis. They began to do so in the sixteenth and seventeenth centuries, as the distinction between earth and heavens was gradually obliterated, and this led on to Newton's new development. But to hold that natural or physical law was a concept then first inaugurated is to do astrology, . . . and also to the previous period, a grave injustice. . . . In previous periods astrology and astronomy had regarded themselves as far superior to physics and mechanics. Newton's *Principia* destroyed the age-long distinction between superiors and inferiors.

The same applies to magic as we understand the word here. All natural creations have specific properties which link them to the upper world, and these enable them to carry out their generally quite normal activities. To illustrate Thorndike's conclusions, which he drew from Western science, here are a few sentences from Jābir b. Ḥayyān's *Kitāb al-baḥth*, in the more concise form as given in the Arabic *Picatrix*:[2]

> You must . . . at the start of making a talisman concentrate your mind on the image and form of the 'receiving', so that the gift of the stars

[1] *Isis*, xlvi (1955), 273–8.

[2] Ps. Majrīṭī, *Ghāyat al-ḥakim*, ed. Ritter (Leipzig–Berlin, 1933), pp. 86 ff.; translated by Ritter and Plessner (see above, p. 432, n. 6), pp. 91 ff. with notes.

encounters a perfect receptivity, and so what is desired of the talisman comes about, its effect endures and its pneuma spreads widely. . . . For men will always make talismans without feeling aware thereof. For if you wish to fit together . . . or to produce . . . you will first attend to the parts . . . and assemble them . . . until your work on them is done. Nature and the Stars act upon it constantly and bring it to perfection. . . . The same is true when the wombs allow the different sorts of sperm to ripen till the final stages at which Nature and the Stars exert their influence upon it step by step.

The stars thus 'give' the talisman, through the irradiation from their particular astrological position, its power and efficacy, provided that it is constructed, charged with power, and used for its proper purpose, in the right way and at the right time. In the words of the source:[1] 'However, the total giving—and this is what one hopes to achieve with a talisman—is producing motion in the receiving object and transferring it from potentiality to actuality.' In alchemy, this concept of natural law had already, in a speculative way, foreshadowed the obliteration of the distinction between earth and heavens, which, as Thorndike points out in the words quoted previously, was only put on to a scientific footing by classical mechanics. This is understood from the Ninth Discourse of the *Turba philosophorum*[2]; the Islamic attributes of God and the angels were in a rational way integrated in a natural connection, and a parallel was drawn between the divine and the human artificer who delves into Alchemy.[3] It is obvious that the concept of causality which Thorndike expounded as the core of Western medieval science applies equally to Islamic astrology, magic, and alchemy, so much so that any understanding of Islamic science must depend very largely upon grasping this underlying principle. If the *Turba* seems to go further this is only apparent: the purpose of the *Discourse* is to make alchemy appear just as feasible as the Creation was to the Creator, for Creator and al-

[1] Ps. Majrīṭī, op. cit., pp. 95–100.

[2] J. Ruska, *Turba philosophorum* (1931), p. 117.

[3] An express statement to this effect by Jābir was discussed by Plessner, see *Ambix*, xvi (1969), 113–18.

chemist both work with the same materials and are governed by the same natural laws. Thus after all, there remains the dependence of the inferiors upon the superiors: without the Creation there would have been neither man nor matter on which the alchemist could practise.

8. *The astrologers*

The astrological literature of Islam was extensively translated into Latin, partly because of the indispensable astronomical tables attached to some of the works. In the present context we are only interested in those astrologers who have a more general cultural and intellectual significance. Though not the first of those whose works have come down to us, Abū Maʿshar Jaʿfar b. Muḥammad al-Balkhī (who was 100 years old when he died in 886), was by far the most respected and influential of the early astrologers.[1] His importance for the development of Western philosophy has recently been the subject of a thorough study.[2] Abū Maʿshar was well acquainted with ancient tradition, and the doctrine represented by him of the images rising in the sky together with the 36 'Decans' (thirds of the twelve signs of the Zodiac), the so-called *Parantellonta* described by Teucer the Babylonian,[3] had a considerable influence upon the painters of the Renaissance. This unsuspected facet of the legacy of Islam was shown by A. Warburg in a lecture that revolutionized research;[4] the pictures of the central band of the frescoes in the Palazzo Schifanoja at Ferrara[5] proved to be figures of the 'Decans' described by Abū Maʿshar in his so-called 'Persian', i.e. the Teucrian series as distinct from the Indian[6] and the Ptolemaic

1 J. M. Millás in *Encyclopaedia of Islam*, 2nd edn., article 'Abū Maʿshar'.

2 R. Lemay, *Abu Maʿshar and Latin Aristotelianism in the Twelfth Century. The Recovery of Aristotle's Natural Philosophy Through Arabic Astrology* (Beirut, 1962).

3 F. Boll, *Sphaera* (1903); W. Gundel, *Dekane und Dekansternbilder* (1936).

4 A. Warburg, in *Gesammelte Schriften*, ii (1932): '*Die Erneuerung der heidnischen Antike*', pp. 459–81, 627–44.

5 In colour reproduction in Paolo d'Ancona, *Les Mois de Schifanoia à Ferrara* (Milan, 1954). See Fig. 62.

6 On the Indian Decan tradition see now D. Pingree, 'The Indian Iconography

forms. In somewhat different form the 'Decan' images appear in the *Picatrix* (see below). They thus entered in at least two ways into Western astrology.

The most comprehensive textbook on astrology is that of ʿAlī b. Abī 'l-Rijāl of Qayrawān (Haly filius Abenragel in Latin).[1] His book *al-Bāriʿ fī aḥkām al-nujūm* ('The Most Excellent Book on Astrology') is one of the works which were translated into Spanish for Alfonso X el Sabio. The author lived to see the codification of the Toledan Tables by Azarquiel and his collaborators in 1040 and was therefore a contemporary of the unknown author of the *Picatrix*,[2] the Spanish translation of which, also done for Alfonso, has not so far been traced.[3]

The *Picatrix* deals not only with astrology as a subject in itself, but uses it as the foundation for a comprehensive philosophy of nature, covering the entire sublunar world and thus enabling us not only to understand the structure of the Universe, but also, like alchemy, endowing its practitioners with magical powers. Astrological magic and alchemy (also treated by the author in a separate work) are 'conclusions' or 'results' (*natīja*) of philosophy. Although the author goes so far as to include precise instructions for a planetary cult with sacrifices, ritual prostrations, and prayers prescribed literally and copied from a Ḥarrānian source, the book was translated into Spanish and Latin, and no less than three times into Hebrew. The influence of the work lasted even up to the time of the Reformation: Agrippa of Nettesheim, a contemporary of Luther, makes extensive use of it in his *Occulta philosophia* in spite of the express warnings against it uttered as early as 1456 by the personal physician of the Margrave Johann of Brandenburg.[4]

of the Decans and Horâs', *Journal of the Warburg and Courtauld Institutes*, xxvi (1963), 223–54.

[1] D. Pingree in *Encyclopaedia of Islam*, 2nd edn., article 'Ibn Abī 'l-Ridjāl'.

[2] See above, p. 432, n. 6.

[3] On the astronomical-astrological work at the court of Alfonso, see Evelyn S. Procter, *Alfonso X of Castile, Patron of Literature and Learning* (Oxford, 1951).

[4] *Johann Hartliebs Buch aller verbotenen Kunst*, ed. Dora Ulm (Halle, 1914), p. 24.

It is this *conclusio* of the medieval philosophy of nature which has survived, while the philosophy itself has long been superseded by the modern conception of the world which has gained acceptance since the Renaissance; astrology is still alive up to this very day.[1] This is the reason that modern science came to consider astrology and magic themselves as nothing but occult practices. Only in our time has their real significance for medieval *Weltanschauung* been understood.

9. *The alchemists*

The earliest work of Arab alchemy we can date is a pseudepigraph attributed to Apollonius of Tyana, the *Book of Causes* (or the *Secret of Creation*) already referred to. The first to draw our attention to it was Silvestre de Sacy (1799). After a long interval J. Ruska established (1926) that one of the most famous basic texts of all medieval alchemy, the *Tabula smaragdina*, consisting of a few lines in hymnic-style and dealing with the philosophy of nature, written on an emerald tablet and allegedly found by Apollonius in a subterranean vault in the hands of an old man, Hermes Trismegistus, comes from the *Book of Causes*. P. Kraus has shown firstly that the whole book, a comprehensive cosmography with a view to alchemy, is in fact nothing but an exposition of the doctrine esoterically summarized in the *Tabula*; secondly, he has shown that the book had already been dated by al-Rāzī as belonging to the time of the Caliph al-Ma'mūn (813–33). Translated into Latin by Hugh of Santalla in the middle of the twelfth century, the *Book of Causes* had its influence on the West less as a whole than through the text of the *Tabula*, which soon became independent of it, was quoted frequently in literature (e.g. in the

[1] Cf. Robert Eisler's vehement attack on modern astrologers, who amongst other things prove their complete ignorance of the genuine old astrology: *The Royal Art of Astrology* (London, 1946). Other points of view are stressed by Mark Graubard, 'Astrology's Demise and its Bearing on the Decline and Death of Beliefs', *Osiris*, xiii (1958), 210–57.

pseudo-Aristotelian *Secretum secretorum*),[1] and was the subject of many commentaries.

If the *Book of Causes* shows how Neo-Platonic philosophy and cosmology penetrated Islamic literature, a second pseudepigraph, the aforementioned *Turba philosophorum*, shows that the founders of science in Islam were also familiar with earlier philosophical doctrines, as preserved by the Greek doxographers. The author, whom we can assume to have been a contemporary of Ibn Waḥshiyya, makes use of the authentic tradition of the teachings of the pre-Socratic philosophers to provide alchemy with a basis at once philosophical and Islamic. Both works are therefore older than or contemporaneous with al-Rāzī and the corpus of the 'Jābir' writings.[2]

Indeed, 'Jābir' was concerned with practical alchemy, but at the same time he sought to explore and understand the structure of the universe. He therefore developed his science of the balance (*mīzān*), i.e. a system of numerical relationships by which substances were composed of elements. The *Turba*, on the other hand, uses philosophy in the same way as the Greek alchemists, namely to build up a reasonable theory of elements, and it also adheres to the Greeks in the alchemical part of the text, which is a collection of fantastic recipes in which the most abstruse and mystifying code names[3] are given to the ingredients and which are presented in the form of a sort of parliamentary debate with Pythagoras as chairman. Far from being a polemic against the Greek alchemists, as Ruska believed, it was precisely this book which made the fantastic and turgid style of the Greek texts the supreme influence on all subsequent alchemical writings.

[1] M. Plessner, 'Neue Materialien zur Geschichte der Tabula Smaragdina', *Der Islam*, xvi (1927), 77–113.

[2] See the author's forthcoming book, *Vorsokratische Philosophie und griechische Alchemie in arabisch-lateinischer Überlieferung*, as well as 'The Place of the Turba Philosophorum in the Development of Alchemy', *Isis*, xlv (1954), 331–8.

[3] A. Siggel, *Decknamen in der arabischen alchemistischen Literatur* (Berlin, 1951).

What appears to be the earliest work dependent upon the *Turba*, the book attributed to the philosopher Crates,[1] still concentrates for the most part on the practical aspects of the Greek texts, although it assumes a revelationary style on the lines of the *Corpus Hermeticum*. But Ibn Umayl al-Tamīmī, the Senior Zadith filius Hamuel of the Latins (d. in the second half of the tenth century), firmly established the trend of the chimerical lucubrations of the later alchemists initiated by the *Book of al-Ḥabīb*[1] in his *Epistola solis ad lunam crescentem* or 'Letter of the Sun to the New Moon', and the *Book of the Silvery Water and the Starry Earth*.[2] It was this development that led alchemy from one cul-de-sac into another and turned later scholars such as Avicenna into such determined adversaries of the art, however seriously they took its philosophical foundations.

10. *Medicine and pharmacology*

The connection between chemistry and medicine through the interlinking discipline of pharmacology, which of course still exists, found a strange expression in the Middle Ages when the absurd code-language of alchemy spread to dispensing. Goethe's Faust, on the Easter Day walk, describes the dispensary during the recently overcome pestilence by referring to his father's work:

> Who, with adepts their presence lending,
> Shut him in that black kitchen where he used,
> According to receipts unending,
> To get the contraries together fused.
> There was a lover bold, a lion red,
> Who to the lily in a tepid bath was wed.
> Both, tortured then with flames, a fiery tide,
> From one bride-chamber to another pass.
> Thereon appeared, with motley colours pied,
> The youthful queen within the glass.

[1] Ed. and translated by O. Houdas, in M. Berthelot, *La Chemie au Moyen Âge*, iii (Paris, 1893, reprinted 1967). Dating after the *Turba* is by Plessner.

[2] Ed. and translated by M. Turāb ʿAlī, H. E. Stapleton and H. Ḥusayn (*Mem. of the Asiat. Soc. of Bengal*, xii), 1933.

Here was the medicine, the patients died,
And no one questioned: who got well?

(G. Madison Priest's translation.)

In comparison with this, however, the pharmacological literature of Islam speaks remarkably to the point. This is true even for toxicology and the theory of antitoxics, although the dangerous nature of poison recipes and their usefulness for criminal purposes might lead one to expect a fairly cryptic terminology. Even in the *Picatrix*, toxicology is expounded in quite plain language, although the ingredients of the 'filth dispensary' play a considerable part.

No branch of Islamic medicine has been so thoroughly investigated as pharmacology.[1] Max Meyerhof, the author of the chapter on Science and Medicine in the first edition of this book, made accessible several of the most important texts and published a large number of monographs on the history of pharmacology in Islam.[2] He also explained the names of the drugs scientifically, and made an inventory of the drug bazaar of Cairo at the time of the First World War. Of the various works he edited, his edition of Maimonides (1135–1204) is the most important, for the book deals exclusively with the nomenclature of 'simple' drugs in different languages.

Although Islam became acquainted with other Greek pharmacologies,[3] the *Materia medica* of Dioscurides remained the greatest classic in the field. The name of the work served until the nineteenth century as the name for the subject of pharmacology in the teaching of medicine. The main translation into Arabic was done by Stephanus, son of Basilius. It was already known to Ḥunayn b. Isḥāq who corrected it. Only part of the names of the drugs were translated into Arabic, others merely transcribed. The impulse to complete the translation came from the splendid Greek codex which the Emperor Constantine VII sent to the Caliph ʿAbd al-Raḥmān III (912–61) in Cordova, and with the help of the illustra-

[1] B. Lewin, *Encyclopaedia of Islam*, 2nd edn., article 'Aḳrābādhīn'.
[2] His bibliography is given in *Osiris*, ix (1950), 20–6.
[3] B. Lewin, *Encyclopaedia of Islam*, 2nd edn., article 'Adwiya'.

tions in this manuscript it was possible to translate further names into Arabic. Manuscripts of this kind are still preserved; in many we find the Arabic, Latin, and other names entered by later users in the margins of the Greek text. C. E. Dubler, who in a monumental work studied the tradition of *Materia medica* down to the Castilian translation by Andrés de Laguna (1499–1560), was responsible for an *editio princeps* of the Arabic translation[1] prepared by Elia Terés.

As far as this chapter is concerned, the importance of medicine in the Islamic legacy is unparalleled.[2] But a brief summary of the achievements of Islamic medicine is even less possible today than it was fifty or a hundred years ago. Today we know too much to be satisfied by a few generalities, but not yet enough to replace the old by a new evaluation. However, the application of philological methods to medical history, thanks to men like E. G. Browne and Max Meyerhof, who were both doctors and philologists, has at least made a new approach possible. We omit doctors who recently have gained prominence only by the fortuitous progress of research and concentrate ourselves on individuals who made a significant contribution to the legacy.

As in many other disciplines, some of the prime achievements in medicine occurred during its earliest days; later on there are signs of decline or decadence. The oldest surviving Arabic encyclopedia of medicine, the *Firdaws al-ḥikma* or 'Paradise of Wisdom', is in some respects unsurpassed. Its author, ʿAlī b. Rabban al-Ṭabarī, wrote his work in the year 850 and was thus a contemporary of Ḥunayn b. Isḥāq. His importance consists firstly in the fact that he was acquainted with Ḥunayn's original work on ophthalmology and probably with his translation of the *Prognostics* of Hippocrates. Secondly, he devotes a special chapter to Indian medicine for the express purpose of comparing it with Greek medicine on which

[1] *La 'Materia Medica' de Dioscórides, transmisión medieval y renacentista*, 6 vols. (Barcelona, 1952–9).

[2] J. Chr. Bürgel, 'Die wissenschaftliche Medizin im Kräftefeld der islamischen Kultur', *Bustan*, viii (1967), 9–19.

the book is mostly based. Thirdly, in the book's extensive opening section on natural philosophy he has already adopted the terminology of Ḥunayn. The existing edition[1] badly needs revision on a proper philological basis.

Since we have already dealt with al-Rāzī, we can now pass on to ʿAlī b. al-ʿAbbās al-Majūsī.[2] His dates are only vaguely known but he was the personal physician of the Būyid Amīr ʿAḍud al-Dawla (949–82) in Baghdad. To this Amīr he dedicated his great medical work, which was translated into Latin as the *Liber regius* (*regalis*) of Haly filius Abbas. This has a special place in the history of medicine because it served as a model for the *Liber pantegni* (*pantechne*) which belongs to the corpus of works transmitted by Constantinus Africanus to the medical school of Salerno (see below). As it begins with a survey of the history of medicine, which was also included in the 1127 translation by Stephanus Antiochenus (printed in Venice in 1492), it provided the West with valuable material for the historiography of medicine.

Constantinus Africanus was a renegade Muslim whose original name is unknown, Constantinus being his baptismal name. He went from Africa to Italy and became a Benedictine monk in Monte Cassino. He also retired there after his working years at Salerno and died about 1087. The corpus of the writings collected and translated by him for the medical school at Salerno has recently been analysed by H. Schipperges;[3] to it belong the writings of the Qayrawān philosopher and doctor Isḥāq b. Sulaymān al-Isrā'īlī (Isaac Judaeus in Latin translations of his works).[4] Whilst in the first edition of this book Constantinus was still, in accordance with accepted opinion, described as an unashamed plagiarizer, Schipperges has proved that the attribution of translated works

[1] By M. Z. Siddiqi (Berlin, 1928).

[2] Cf. C. Elgood in *Encyclopaedia of Islam*, 2nd edn., article ʿAlī b. al-ʿAbbās.

[3] *Die Assimilation der arabischen Medizin durch das lateinische Mittelalter* (Wiesbaden, 1964), pp. 26 ff.; cf. also F. Gabrieli, 'La Medicina araba e la scuola di Salerno', *Salerno*, i. 3 (Mar.–Sept. 1967), 12–23.

[4] Bibliography in Saul Jarcho, 'Guide for Physicians by Isaac Judaeus, translated from the Hebrew', *Bull. Hist. of Medicine*, xv (1944), 180–8.

to Constantinus, which are found in later manuscripts, are interpolations which do not occur in the oldest manuscripts.

Although Ibn Sīnā (Avicenna) was a contemporary of Constantinus—he lived from 980 to 1037—his medical works do not figure among those translated by the African. His autobiography is preserved and has often been translated. His main medical work, the *Canon* (*Qānūn*) became a kind of bible of medieval medicine, replacing to a certain extent the works of al-Rāzī. It was printed in Rome in the original as early as 1593, shortly after the introduction of Arabic printing into Europe.[1] As far as his medical writings are concerned, however, it seems that he was less original than his popularity, resulting from his facile pen, would suggest. The pioneering studies of A. Z. Iskandar[2] have furnished incontrovertible proof that whole sections of his work are dependent upon al-Rāzī. Without wishing to diminish his significance as a teacher and doctor, it has to be admitted that his independence as a medical author is considerably less than was once believed.

Of the great medical authors we should mention Ibn Rushd (Averroes), whose well-known compendium, the *Kulliyyāt*, was translated into Latin with the title of *Colliget* by an otherwise unknown Bonacosa in Padua in 1255; its chapter on respiration contains a remarkable critique of Galen which was recently made the subject of a special study.[3] Of other critics of Galen we need only draw attention to the Christian physician and theologian Ibn Buṭlān (d. 1066) whose controversy with Ibn Riḍwān was concerned with some fundamentals of physiology,[4] and to the

[1] The Latin translator of the *Canon* is the first of his kind to form the subject of a special study: Francesca Lucchetta, *Il Medico e filosofo bellunese Andrea Alpago, traduttore di Avicenna* (Padua, 1964).

[2] *A Catalogue of Arabic Manuscripts on Medicine and Science in the Wellcome Historical Medical Library* (London, 1967), esp. pp. 29 ff.

[3] J. Chr. Bürgel, 'Averroes "Contra Galenum"', *Nachr. der Akad. der Wissenschaften in Göttingen*, 1. Klasse (1967), no. 9; he uses the translations of the second version of the *Colliget* by Jacobus Mantinus (Venice, 1552) and Jean Champier (Leiden, 1537).

[4] J. Schacht and M. Meyerhof, *The Medico-philosophical Controversy between*

discoverer by abstract reasoning, of the lesser circulation of the blood, Ibn al-Nafīs (d. 1288). It now seems likely that Michael Servetus was familiar with this last theory.[1]

Of the particular categories of medicine, ophthalmology deserves special mention, not only because more research has been done into it than into any other therapeutic sphere, but also on account of its achievements and its influence in the West. The special efforts of Islamic experts on ophthalmology can partly be accounted for by that prevalence of optical diseases in the East which is still noticeable today; but ophthalmology also owes its prominence to the great interest of Islamic scholars in optical problems (see the following section on exact sciences for a closer study of this point.

The best-known Arab oculist, ʿAlī b. ʿĪsā—a Christian, notwithstanding his name—refers to his own extensive practical studies, in addition to his book-learning which can be taken for granted. It does not detract from his importance that J. Hirschberg's statement to the effect that ʿAlī practised anaesthesia during operations was dismissed by A. Feigenbaum as a misunderstanding. His main work, the classical handbook of Arab ophthalmology, was translated once into Hebrew and twice into Latin, and was printed, with the title of *Tractatus de oculis Jesu ben Hali*, in Venice in 1497, 1499, and 1500.

Finally we must mention a unique example of the Islamic legacy to the West. The founder of modern anatomy, Andreas Vesalius, published in 1538 his six anatomical *Tables* as a study preparatory to his main work, the *Fabrica* of 1543. The Latin text of these tables gives a large number of Arab and Hebrew terms, some of which are even in Hebrew letters (Fig. 63). A thorough investigation of the *Tables* by Charles Singer and Chaim Rabin not only explained the texts thoroughly but showed how

Ibn Butlan of Baghdad and Ibn Ridwan of Cairo, The Egyptian University, Faculty of Arts, Publ. No. 13 (Cairo, 1937).

[1] J. Schacht 'Ibn al-Nafīs, Servetus and Colombo', *Al-Andalus*, xxii (1957), 317–36.

Vesalius came to know the terminology in Semitic languages which he did not himself command.[1] Thus the *Tables* carry the Arab tradition in medicine to the very threshold of modern times.

11. *Natural history*

The practical tendency of Islamic science, which has been apparent in all the fields so far considered, is most clearly manifested in those of botany, zoology, and mineralogy. In so far as books of plants were not intended for lexicological purposes they were of either a pharmacological or an agricultural character. There are remarkably few works on zoology proper, although a considerable number of books deal with hunting and other knightly arts, as well as veterinary medicine. The books on mineralogy are for the most part *Lapidaria*, mainly concerned with the magical powers of stones. Although it is true that 'in all these disciplines there were classical works translated into Arabic which could serve as models',[2] less use was made of these models in the genuinely Arabic literature than in other sciences.

The *Book of Plants*, that appears in our editions of Aristotle ($815^{a}10$–$830^{b}4$) and is known to be a forgery, represents a unique manifestation of the legacy of Islam, for it is a Greek retranslation of Alfred de Sareshel's Latin version of the *Book of Plants* of Nicholaus Damascenus (b. *c.* 64 B.C.), which he read in an abridged Arabic translation.[3] The Arabic text was edited by A. J. Arberry

[1] *A Prelude to Modern Science, being a Discussion of the History, Sources and Circumstances of the 'Tabulae Anatomicae Sex' of Vesalius*, Publications of the Wellcome Historical Medical Museum, N.S. 1 (Cambridge, 1946).

[2] F. Rosenthal, *Das Fortleben der Antike im Islam* (Zürich–Stuttgart, 1965), p. 223.

[3] M. Bouyges, 'Notes sur les philosophes arabes connus des Latins au Moyen Âge', viii, '*Mélanges de l'Université St. Joseph*, ix (1923–4), 71–89; B. Z. Wacholder, *Nicolaus of Damascus*, University of California Publications in History, 75 (Berkeley–Los Angeles, 1962); H. J. Drossaart Lulofs, *Nicolaus Damascenus on the Philosophy of Aristotle* (1965); idem, in *Journal of Hellenic Studies*, lxxvii (1957), 75 ff.

in 1933–4 and by ʿA. Badawī in 1954.[1] Not even the botany of Theophrastus, directly derived from Aristotle, was known to Islam. For the agricultural tradition Islam had at its disposal only a collection of older texts compiled by Cassianus Bassus Scholasticus for the above-mentioned Emperor Constantine VII and known under the name of *Geoponica*.[2]

It is not known whether Books of Plants proper, such as the work of Abū Ḥanīfa al-Dīnawarī,[3] exercised any influence upon the West. This is, however, partly true of the works on agriculture. Long extracts from the *Nabataean Agriculture* by Ibn Waḥshiyya, quoted in other works, were translated into Latin.[4] Also, the writings of two Andalusian agronomists, Ibn Wāfid (d. 1075) and Ibn Baṣṣāl (d. 1105), were translated into Castilian in the Middle Ages.

Most of the zoological works of Aristotle were known in Islam; the quotations attributed to him in zoological writings, such as the *Kitāb al-ḥayawān* or 'Book of Animals' by al-Jāḥiẓ, the *Manāfiʿ al-ḥayawān* or 'Usefulness of Animals' by ʿUbaid Allāh b. Jibrīl b. Bokhtīshūʿ, and the *Ḥayāt al-ḥayawān* or 'Life of Animals' by al-Damīrī, are only partly genuine, however.

Arabic literature on falconry survived in a curious form. The 'philosopher' Theodorus, who apparently came from Antioch and lived at the court of the Emperor Frederick II, probably took over the office of Court Astrologer from Michael Scotus, and translated for his master at least one book which is extant in two manuscripts. It served as the basis for Frederick's own work *De arte venandi cum avibus*, in which the Emperor not only referred to his sources but carried out his own research into the correctness of their data.[5]

1 Aristotelia *De anima etc. . . . de plantis*, ed. ʿAbdurraḥmān Badawī (Cairo, 1954), with bibliography.

2 J. Ruska in *Der Islam*, v (1914), 174–9, and *Archiv für geschichte der Naturwissenschaften und der Medizin*, vi (1913), 305–20.

3 B. Lewin in *Encyclopaedia of Islam*, 2nd edn., article 'Dīnawarī'.

4 See above, pp. 432–3.

5 C. H. Haskins, *Studies in the History of Medieval Science* (Cambridge, Mass.,

The mineralogical literature of Islam also attracted the curiosity of the West. The pseudo-Aristotelian *Book of Stones* was eagerly used by Islamic writers, and also exists in Hebrew and Latin versions (ed. J. Ruska in 1912). The Islamic mineralogical literature particularly engaged the interest of the other great ruler of the thirteenth century who was a scientist in his own right, Alfonso X el Sabio of Castile; his *Lapidario* is available in a colour facsimile reproduction.[1]

The study of these three disciplines in Islam produced not only specialist works, but the resultant material was incorporated in encyclopedias of all the sciences as well as in general cosmographies. Of the former the *ʿUyūn al-akhbār* or 'The Most Essential Information' by Ibn Qutayba should be mentioned; the zoological part of it is available in an English translation with commentary.[2] Among the cosmographies one is outstanding, that of Zakariyyā' al-Qazwīnī (d. 1283) which has also survived in illustrated manuscripts that have for long excited the curiosity of art historians. Al-Qazwīnī is the only Muslim who incorporated the fable about birds growing on trees (barnacle geese), widely spread throughout Islam, Jewry, and Christendom. As we now know, this fable is not originally Oriental, but comes from the British Isles where, according to al-Qazwīnī, the bird-bearing trees are located. The Emperor Frederick, who was ten years his senior, probably got knowledge of the story from a different source and in his book he reports that he sent an expedition to look into the matter and was able to prove that there was no truth in it. Al-Qazwīnī's book is also remarkable because he manages to fit the Islamic angelology and demonology into his scientifically orientated analysis of the world structure. His work served as a source for another Qazwīnī, Ḥamd Allāh Mustawfī, who was born some 80 years later and

1927), chap. XII, 'Science at the Court of the Emperor Frederick II'; F. Gabrieli, 'Frederico II e la cultura musulmana', *Rivista storica italiana*, lxiv (1952), 5–18.

[1] *Lapidario del rey D. Alfonso X*, ed. J. F. Monteña (Madrid, 1881).

[2] F. S. Bodenheimer and L. Kopf, *The Natural History Section from a Ninth Century 'Book of Useful Knowledge'* (Paris, 1949).

wrote his encyclopedia in Persian; the zoological section of this was edited and translated into English by J. Stephenson in 1928.

The Islamic encyclopedias and cosmographies have their parallels in the West. We will mention two works which quote Islamic authors most extensively. One is the book of Thomas of Cantimpré, written in the first half of the thirteenth century, which is available in a printed German adaptation by Konrad von Megenberg;[1] and the other is the four-part *Speculum* of the slightly younger Vincent of Beauvais which also contains a great number of quotations from the most varied works of Islamic literature.[2]

12. *Geography*

Mathematical geography will be considered in another section of this chapter, but we will say a word here about descriptive geography as it affects the Islamic legacy. The importance of the geographical literature of Islam is still considerable today, for the data contained in it add to our knowledge of the historical geography of the countries dealt with, and so indirectly to our knowledge of their history. The legacy in this respect is of a particularly positive nature. Among the authors we find private travellers and pilgrims to Mecca who later wrote books about their experiences, merchants organizing trade caravans, itinerant officials whose duties stimulated in them an impulse to learn more of the countries they visited, ambassadors to foreign courts, and politico-religious propagandists—not to mention those who travelled with a scholarly objective in mind or merely in search of adventure. In addition to serious geographical literature there are of course the literary fantasies about the picture of the world reflected in such works as the *Travels of Sindibad*, a part of the Arabian Nights literature. Similar features exist also in the knightly epics and adventures of the West, and the question of how far their partly genuine

[1] *Das Buch der Natur von Konrad von Megenberg*, ed. F. Pfeiffer (Stuttgart, 1861), reprinted 1962).

[2] *Bibliotheca Mundi*, Vincentii . . . episcopi Bellovacensis *Speculum Quadruplex*, 4 vols. (Douai, 1624, reprinted 1964).

and partly fantastic descriptions of the 'Orient' are to be traced back to Islamic influences is one that has not yet been systematically taken up.

From Sicily, that great meeting-point of Islamic and Western civilization right up to the end of the Hohenstaufen period, we have a huge geographical work in Arabic written at the request of a Norman ruler. This is the description of a large silver map of the earth made for Roger II, and in addition to seventy-one maps, it consists of a treatise of general geography by Muḥammad al-Sharīf al-Idrīsī[1] written some time before 1154. Al-Idrīsī also composed a work on geography for Roger's successor, William I.

Islamic maps and nautical works played a considerable part in the development of Western shipping.[2] Vasco da Gama's pilot was the Arab Ibn Mājid, who wrote a guidebook for seafarers in the Indian Ocean.[3] The Turkish seaman Pīrī Re'īs wrote in the sixteenth century a sailing handbook for the Mediterranean. It has been suggested that one of the maps included in his book was a copy of a map used by Columbus. Charles H. Hapgood has proved, however, that the map used by Pīrī Re'īs and drawn by him was based on ancient sources, and is not a *Portolano*, i.e. a map showing the route from harbour to harbour, but is based on mathematical principles.[4]

An extract from the book of al-Idrīsī in Arabic was printed in Rome in 1592 and in a Latin translation by two Maronites in 1619 under the false title *Geographia Nubiensis*. This is an example of how Arab geographical books helped to instruct the West at a time when Western geographical research into the Orient, let alone studies of the geographical literature of Islam, had not yet begun. Similarly in the seventeenth century the Paris professor

[1] G. Oman, *Encyclopaedia of Islam*, 2nd edn., article 'al-Idrīsī'.

[2] R. V. Tooley, *Maps and Map Makers*, 2nd edn. (New York, 1952, reprinted 1961), chap. II, 'The Arabs and Mediaeval Europe'.

[3] S. Maqbul Ahmad in *Encyclopaedia of Islam*, 2nd edn., article 'Ibn Mā<u>d</u>jid'.

[4] F. Babinger, *Encyclopaedia of Islam*, 1st edn., article 'Pīrī Re'īs; C. C. Hapgood, 'Ancient Knowledge of America and Antarctica', *Actes du Xe Congrès International d'histoire des sciences* (Ithaca, 1962), 479–88.

of Arabic, Pierre Vattier, translated from a manuscript in Cardinal Mazarin's library a description of Egypt which contained, apart from much geography, an often-transmitted account of the legendary history of ancient Egypt with special reference to its magical institutions.[1] Works such as these did much to form the Western image of the Orient during the period of the Enlightenment, which then found expression in art and literature and gave rise to prejudices that subsequent research has still not been able fully to dispel (see above, Chapter I, pp. 37 ff.).

13. *Historiography of medicine*

Islam evolved a biographical and bibliographical tradition that one could wish other nations and cultures had also adopted. True to the tradition of antiquity in which the treatment of a subject is preceded by a discussion of the achievements of the predecessors, eminent Islamic scholars like ʿAlī b. al-ʿAbbās al-Majūsī and al-Bīrūnī also inform us of earlier treatments of their subjects. At an early date Isḥāq, son of Ḥunayn b. Isḥāq, wrote a short independent history of medicine.[2] This was known to the author of the *Fihrist*, Ibn al-Nadīm, who lived at the end of the tenth century. Ibn al-Nadīm's work surveys all the scientific and other literature known at that time. He used highly authentic sources and reproduced them accurately, but their contents have so far been sufficiently exploited only as applied to Aristotle,[3] and not to Galen and other physicians and scientists. Other collections of biographies of scholars were written in the tenth century, like that of the Andalusian Ibn Juljul, and those of the Baghdad scholar Abū Sulaymān al-Manṭiqī (d. *c.* 985) who was head of a philosophers' circle which did much to spread scientific modes of thinking in Baghdad society. The discussions of his circle have

[1] Facsimile reproduction with Introduction and Commentary by G. Wiet, *L'Égypte de Murtadi fils du Gaphiphe* (Paris, 1953).

[2] Ed. F. Rosenthal in *Oriens*, vii (1954), 55–80; cf. *Journal of the American Oriental Society*, lxxxi (1961), 10 ff.

[3] I. Düring, *Aristotle in the Ancient Biographical Tradition* (Göteborg, 1957).

come down to us in several books written by one of its members, the mystic and man of letters Abū Ḥayyān al-Tawḥīdī (d. *c.* 1010).[1]

In the tenth century, too, the Toledan *qāḍī* and astronomer Ṣāʿid b. Aḥmad b. Ṣāʿid al-Andalusī wrote the first world history of science with the title *al-Taʿrīf bi-ṭabaqāt al-umam* ('Account of the Generations of Nations'), which gave separate treatment to the contributions of different nations.[2]

The medical historical work of the Damascene Ibn al-Maṭrān (d. 1198) is still to be edited. In the thirteenth century two works were written which sum up the whole preceding tradition and provide us with our fullest sources of information: these were the *Ta'rīkh al-ḥukamā'* ('History of Physicians') of the Vizier Ibn al-Qifṭī (d. 1248), which survives in a fairly extensive extract;[3] and the *ʿUyūn al-anbā' fī ṭabaqāt al-aṭibbā'* ('Important Information Concerning the Generations of Physicians') by the physician Ibn Abī Uṣaybiʿa (d. 1270). The latter, preserved in numerous manuscripts and edited by August Müller in 1884, is a lexicon divided according to countries and periods, and stretches from the legendary origins of medicine with Asclepius to the time when the author was writing.[4] At an early date it attracted the attention of Western scholars, among them physicians who were not satisfied with the Latin translations of Avicenna and wanted to study the *Canon* in the original. For instance, the Breslau physician and later professor at Uppsala, Peter Kirsten (1575–1640), printed a part of the *Canon* as well as an Arabic grammar for easier study of the text. The Holstein Orientalist and Biblical scholar Matthias

[1] See. S. M. Stern, *Encyclopaedia of Islam*, 2nd edn., articles 'Abū Sulaymān' and 'Abū Ḥayyān'.

[2] French translation by R. Blachère (Paris, 1935); M. Plessner in *Rivista degli studi orientali*, xxxi (1956), 235–57.

[3] J. Lippert's edition of 1903 which is now unchanged in its re-edition is full of errors and quite unusable without the still incomplete lists of amendments put forward by M. J. De Goeje in *Deutsche Literaturzeitung* (1903), C. F. Seybold in *Zeitschrift der deutschen morgenländischen Gesellschaft*, lvii (1904), H. Suter in *Bibliotheca Mathematica*, iii (1903), and A. L. Kapp in *Isis*, xii–xxiv (1934–6).

[4] Continued by Dr. Aḥmad ʿĪsā Bey, *Muʿjam al-aṭibbā'* (1942) in alphabetical order.

Wasmuth prefaced his *Grammatica Arabica*, printed at Amsterdam in 1654, with a long introduction in which he emphasized the importance of Arabic for the study of medicine, and expressly quoted Ibn Abī Uṣaybiʿa. At the beginning of the eighteenth century John Freind printed in his *History of Physick from the Time of Galen to the Beginning of the 16th Century* a single biography from a partial translation of Ibn Abī Uṣaybiʿa's work made by Sulaymān al-Aswad (Salomo Negri). Finally, the Leipzig Arabist Johann Jacob Reiske in 1745 copied some parts of the work for his doctoral dissertation, and this has found its way into the Copenhagen Library together with some of his other manuscripts.[1]

The interest in the transmission of Islamic science can be further seen from a study printed in 1664, by the Zürich Orientalist Johann Heinrich Hottinger, the *Bibliothecarius quadripartitus*. The third part, *De theologia patristica*, contains an appendix, *De scriptoribus arabicis*, a survey specially devoted to the history of scholarship by the Moroccan Leo Africanus (who came at the beginning of the sixteenth century to Rome as a prisoner), translated and commented upon by Hottinger. For a whole series of medical-historical details Leo is our sole source, although his reliability is not always above suspicion.

We can say, therefore, that the medical-historical writings of Islam form a considerable part of Islam's legacy to the West, the significance and impact of which has continued until the present day.

MARTIN PLESSNER

[1] See on all this, J. Fück, *Die arabischen Studien in Europa* (Leipzig, 1955), and Plessner, in *Medizingeschichte in unserer Zeit* (Stuttgart, 1971), 223–32.

BIBLIOGRAPHY

General accounts

R. Arnaldez and L. Massignon, in *Histoire général des sciences*, ed. René Taton, i (Paris, 1957), 430–71; D. M. Dunlop, *Arabic Science in the West* (Publ. of the Pakistan Historical Society, xxxv, Karachi, 1958); Ch. Pellat, 'Les Encyclopédies dans le monde arabe' in *Cahiers d'Histoire mondiale*, ix (1966), 631–58; M. Plessner, in *La Civiltà dell'Oriente*, ed. Giuseppe Tucci, iii (Rome, 1958), 447–92; L. Thorndike, *A History of Magic and Experimental Science*, 8 vols. (New York, 1923–58) (up to the seventeenth century).

(The book of Aldo Mieli, *La science arabe* (Paris, 1938, repr. 1966), is unsatisfactory.) For individual scientists and translators see G. Sarton, *Introduction to the History of Science* (Baltimore, 1927–48) (up to the fourteenth century).

Translations into Arabic

U. Monneret de Villard, *Lo studio dell'Islam in Europe nel XII e nel XIII secolo* (Studi e Testi, cx, Vatican, 1944); A. Müller, 'Arabischen Quellen zur Geschichte der indischen Medizin', *Zeitschrift der deutschen morgenländischen Gesellschaft*, xxxiv (1880); H. Ritter and R. Walzer, *Arabische Übersetzungen griechischer Ärzte in Stambuler Bibliotheken*, Sitzungsber. Preuss. Akad. Wiss. (1934); F. Rosenthal, *Das Fortleben der Antike im Islam* (Zürich-Stuttgart, 1965) (an excellent anthology); M. Steinschneider, 'Zur Geschichte der Übersetzungen aus dem Indischen in's Arabische', etc. *ZDMG*, xxiv–xxv (1870–1); idem, *Die arabischen Übersetzungen aus dem Griechischen* (Graz, 1960) (a reprint of a series of papers printed in various periodicals from 1889 onwards).

Translations from Arabic into Latin and vernacular languages

M.-Th. d'Alverny, 'Avicenna Latinus', *Archives d'histoire doctrinale et litteraire du Moyen Âge*, xxviii– (1961–); J. M. Millás Vallicrosa, *Las traducciones orientales en los manuscritos de la Biblioteca Catedral de Toledo* (Madrid, 1942); M. Steinschneider, *Die europäischen Übersetzungen aus dem Arabischen bis zur Mitte des 17. Jahrhunderts*, Sitzungsber. Akad. Wiss., Wien, cil, cli (1904–5, repr. Graz, 1956); F. Wüstenfeld, *Die Übersetzungen arabischer Werke in das Lateinische*, Abh. Ges. Wiss., Göttingen, xxi (1877).

Astrology

C. A. Nallino, *Raccolta di Scritti*, v (Rome, 1944).

Alchemy

M. Berthelot, *La Chimie au Moyen Âge*, i–iii (Paris, 1893, repr. 1967); A.-J. Festugière, *La Révélation d'Hermès Trismégiste*, i (2nd edn., Paris, 1950); J. W. Fück, 'The Arabic Literature on Alchemy according to An-Nadīm', *Ambix*, iv (1951),

81–144; E. J. Holmyard, *Alchemy* (Pelican Books, 1957); idem, 'Alchemical Equipment' (Ch. 21 in *A History of Technology*, ed. Ch. Singer *et al.*, ii (New York–London, 1956), 731–56); P. Kraus, *Jābir ibn Ḥayyān, contribution à l'histoire des idées scientifiques dans l'Islam*, 2 vols. (Cairo, 1942–3); E. Wiedemann, article 'Kīmiyā'' in *Encyclopaedia of Islam*, 1st edn. (dated but still useful).

Medicine

E. G. Browne, *Arabian Medicine* (Cambridge, 1921) (an authoritative account); D. Campbell, *Arabian Medicine*, 2 vols. (London, 1926) (concentrates on the Latin translations); *Current Work in the History of Medicine*, ed. by the Wellcome Historical Medical Library, London (four times a year); C. Elgood, *A Medical History of Persia and the Eastern Caliphate* (Cambridge, 1951); J. Hirschberg, *Die arabischen Lehrbücher der Augenheilkunde*, Abh. Preuss. Akad. Wiss. (Berlin, 1905); idem, *Die arabischen Augenärzte nach den Quellen bearbeitet* (Leipzig, 1904–5); L. Leclerc, *Histoire de la médecine arabe* (Paris, 1876, repr. New York, n.d.) (uncritical); M. Ullmann, *Die Medizin im Islam* (Leiden, 1970); On the writings of M. Meyerhof, see above, p. 446, n. 2; On the writings of A. Feigenbaum, see *Koroth*, a quarterly journal devoted to the history of medicine and science, iv (Jerusalem, 1968), lxxiii–lxxx.

Botany, Zoology, Mineralogy

J. Clément-Mullet, 'Essai sur la minéralogie arabe', *JA* (1868; also separately printed, Paris, 1869); Ernst H. F. Meyer, *Geschichte der Botanik*, iii (1856), 43–327 (still the best account); K. Mieleitner, *Geschichte der Mineralogie im Altertum und Mittelalter* (1922); D. Möller, *Studien zur mittelalterlichen arabischen Falknerei-Literatur* (Frankfurt, 1965); Ch. Pellat and others, article 'Ḥayawān', in *Encyclopaedia of Islam*, 2nd edn.; M. Plessner, article 'Bayṭār', in *Encyclopaedia of Islam*, 2nd edn.; idem, article 'Ḥadjar', in *Encyclopaedia of Islam*, 2nd edn.; H. Ritter, 'La Parure des chevaliers und die Literature über die ritterlichen Künste', *Der Islam*, xviii (1929), 116–54; idem, 'Orientalische Steinbücher', *Istanbuler Mitteilungen*, iii (1935), 1–15; J. de Somogyi, 'Index des sources de la Ḥayāt al-ḥayawān de ad-Damīrī', *JA*, 213 (1928), 1–128; M. Steinschneider, 'Arabische Lapidarien', in *ZDMG*, xlvii (1893), 244–78; Various authors, article 'Filāḥa'' in *Encyclopaedia of Islam*, 2nd edn.; F. Viré, articles 'Bayzara' and 'Faras', in *Encyclopaedia of Islam*, 2nd edn.

Geography

Articles, 'Djughrāfiyā', by J. H. Kramers in *Encyclopaedia of Islam*, 1st edn., Suppl.; ibid., by S. Maqbul Ahmad and Fr. Taeschner in *Encyclopaedia of Islam*, 2nd edn.; V.-V. Barthold, *La Découverte de l'Asie*, translation by B. Nikitine (1947) Chapter IV and Suppl. to the bibliography by B. Nikitine, 334–67; J. J. Krachkovski, *Istoria Arabskoi Geograficheskoi Literatury* (Moscow–Leningrad, 1957), Arabic translation: *Ta'rīkh al-adab al-jughrāfī al 'arabī*, 2 vols. (Cairo, 1963–5); J. Sauvaget, *Relation de la Chine et de l'Inde* (Paris, 1948), Introduction; idem, 'Les Merveilles de l'Inde', in *Memorial Jean Sauvaget*, i (Damascus, 1954), 189–309.

(*B*) MATHEMATICS, ASTRONOMY, OPTICS

IN their development in the world of Islam the exact sciences show three clearly defined stages. The first is the work, undertaken by numerous translators and adaptors, of quarrying the knowledge reached up till that time by the nations which had cultivated the sciences before the Arabs, and with whom they had come into contact during their rapid expansion throughout Asia and Africa. This period of assimilation is followed by the years of mature achievement—the stage in which new values are created—and finally by the years of decay, lasting for many centuries, a decay checked from time to time by a brilliant stroke of genius by one of the Islamicized peoples such as the Turks or the Persians.

The first stage not only instructed the Arabs in the scientific knowledge of neighbouring or conquered countries, but also gave them access, either directly (by written texts) or indirectly (by oral tradition), to the mathematical and astronomical discoveries made by the peoples of the Near East many centuries before. Therefore the syncretic character of the exact sciences among the Arabs, a character maintained throughout the whole of the Middle Ages, gives a special colouring to their contributions; side by side with the later doctrines, which are their own, we find other notions, sometimes out-of-date and incorrect, dating back to earlier times.

In the ninth century and before, this mixture is particularly noticeable. The use of fractions with the numerator 1, although not exclusive, points to an Egyptian origin of the system. The same may be thought of the allusions in the Koran in xl. 36–7 and xxxviii. 10 which must be related to the ceremony of stretching the cord cited by Clement of Alexandria (*c.* 150–214), which allowed the East–West line to be drawn by means of the attachment of the meridian of a triangle of string divided by knots in the proportion 3, 4, 5 ($3^2+4^2=5^2$).

Indian influence has traditionally been considered as the determining factor in the birth of Arab astronomy and trigonometry, and we have a specific initial date after which its influence grew greater and greater: literary texts tell us of the embassy of one Kanká (or Manká) to the Baghdad of al-Manṣūr in 770 and refer to his scientific contacts with the astronomers of the Caliph. The difficulty is that the documents are few and that the scientific embassies undertaken by learned men belong to legend. In any case, it must be remembered that scientific doctrines are rarely assimilated at once in a cultural climate different from their native one. So we must assume that the Indian influence was a constant force throughout several centuries, reaching its climax in the time of al-Bīrūnī (d. 1048), who had direct access to original Sanskrit sources. From the first contact, which is what interests us now, Islam retained elements of considerable importance, such as the great cosmological periods (to which, in general, little attention was paid) or the very rudimentary trigonometrical formulas which would later contribute, with the help of Greek geometry, to the flowering of Arab mathematics.

Yet this transmission, which at first sight seems pure enough, is far from being so since it was almost always effected through the medium of Persian culture. Unfortunately we lack Pahlavi books on these themes, and so it is difficult to separate the Persian remains—such as they are reflected, for example, in the *Zīj-i Shāh*—from other Indian and Greek elements which infiltrated into the Sasanian empire as a result of the immigration of Greek scholars persecuted in Byzantium for their religious beliefs. For certain subjects, the old Arabic astrological texts written by Islamicized Persians like Abū Maʿshar (d. 886) are a good guide.

The lion's share of the origins of Arab mathematics, astronomy, and optics falls, as one would expect, to Greece. Almost all the books by Greek scholars were translated at least once into Arabic; these translations were revised and corrected over the centuries, and even when their technical contributions had clearly been superseded, they went on being copied so that learned libraries—as happens today—might have the 'classics' of antiquity on their shelves. It is surprising to see how in the thirteenth century Naṣīr al-Dīn Ṭūsī re-edits the 'little astronomy'[1] which the Arabs called *Kitāb al-mutawassiṭāt bayn al-handasa wa'l-hay'a*, the first version of which was made by Qusṭā b. Lūqā (d. *c.* 912).

A quick but by no means exhaustive glance over the subjects we are interested in shows just how important these translations were. Thus, in mathematics we have translations into Arabic of Euclid: (1) *Elements*, translated later into Latin and Hebrew, (2) *Data*, (3) *Optics*, (4) *Appearances of the Celestial Sphere*; of Apollonius Pergaeus: (1) *Conics*, translated later into Latin and Hebrew, (2) *The Section of a Ratio*, (3) *The Determinate Section*, (4) *Construction of Hydraulic Machines*; of Theodosius of Tripoli: (1) *Spherics*, later translated into Latin, (2) *The Book of Places*, (3) *The Book of Days and Nights*; of Nichomachus of Gerasa: *Introduction to Arithmetic*; of Menelaus: (1) *Spherics*, (2) *The Determination of Adulterated Bodies*, (3) *Elements of Geometry*, (4) *The Book of Triangles*, etc. But among all these mathematicians Archimedes stands out. The body of his work now extant was known almost in its entirety by the Arabs: (1) *The Sphere and the Cylinder*, (2) *The Measurement of the Circle*, (3) *The Equilibrium of Planes*, (4) *Floating Bodies*, (5) *Stomachion*, and (6) *Lemmata*. Besides these, they attributed to him and transmitted the texts of some ten books, some of which are also known to us through old quotations. The difficulty in accepting these attributions stems in most cases from the fact that the same title (*The Book of Triangles*, *The Book of Tangential Circles*, etc.) is used over and over again by different authors, and from the fact that there are textual borrowings between these works, so that only by a detailed, theorem-by-theorem, analysis can one come to a relatively certain conclusion on the matter. None of this applies naturally, to those cases where the fragmentary Greek text is completed by the Arabic, or those other cases (such as *Lemmata*) in which the Arabic text is traditionally considered authentic.

[1] The title given to some works by Autolycus, Aristarchus, Euclid, Apollonius, Archimedes, Hypsicles, Menelaus, and Ptolemy which owed their survival to having been copied, one after the other, in the same manuscript.

We find a similarly large quantity of translations in the field of astronomy, where many of the ancient writers were known through being quoted in the *Almagest*. Either indirectly through quotation or directly, the Arabs knew of Meton and Euctemon, and others, and had access to texts such as those of Autolycus: (1) *The Sphere in Movement*, later translated into Latin, (2) *The Rising and Setting of the Stars*; of Aristarchus: *The Size and Distance from the Earth of the Sun and the Moon*; of Aratus; of Hypsicles: *The Ascensions of the Signs*; of Hipparchus; of Geminus of Rhodes: *Introduction to Astronomy*, later translated into Latin and Hebrew; of Theon of Alexandria, etc. But the most important astronomer studied by the Arabs was, as one might expect, Ptolemy, whose basic work, *Mathematical Syntax*, was called by them the *Almagest*, and of which two or three different translations were made, the one by Isḥāq b. Ḥunayn being translated into Latin by Gerard of Cremona. Other Arab astronomers summarized it, commented on it, simplified it, modified Ptolemy's theories by changing the numerical values of his tables, and even on occasion criticized him explicitly. As well as this basic work, they knew as Ptolemy's, or they attributed to him, the *Manual Tables*, the *Hypotheses*, the treatise on astrology known as the *Tetrabiblos*, the *Geography*, the *Optics*—which, with the Euclidian work on the same subject was the basis for the further development of that science among the Arabs—the treatise on stereographic projection which is known now only through Latin versions translated from the Arabic, with glosses by the Cordovan astronomer and Hellenist, Maslama of Madrid; and many other works whose authorship, as with the works of Archimedes, is more uncertain. To sum up, it can be seen that the Arabs had continuous and direct access to the best of the classical writings, that they knew thoroughly the works of Antiquity, and that in many cases—the most notable is that of the *Conics* of Apollonius—their translations, since the original Greek is lost, are our only source of information on certain authors and works.

On this basic material the critical minds of the Muslim scholars worked. From the autobiographies which some of them wrote (and these are more numerous than would at first appear), or from the prologues to or incidental phrases in their writings we can see just how hard they tried to understand their inheritance—although they did not always succeed. Thus, for example, Naṣīr al-Dīn Ṭūsī says in the preface to his revised version of *The Sphere and the Cylinder*:

> For a long time I tried to find the solution of various problems quoted in *The Sphere and the Cylinder* of Archimedes, since I needed them to solve various geometrical matters. Finally I found the famous copy of the book revised by Thābit b. Qurra, but several propositions were missing from it, since the Arab translator had been unable to understand them and consequently to translate them. Nevertheless I studied the book and realised that the whole book was spoiled by the ignorance of the transcriber. I corrected as much as was possible and strove to solve the problems mentioned in it until I got to the second book and reached the things omitted by Archimedes in the prologomena, in spite of the fact that several problems depended on them. I was puzzled and my desire to understand them grew. When I was at that stage I happened on an old notebook which contained the commentary of Eutochius of Ascalon on the problems in the book. It had been intelligently translated into Arabic by Isḥāq b. Ḥunayn and had the text of the book from the beginning to the end of the fourteenth theorem of the first book; the translation too was that of Isḥāq. Eutochius' commentary was found in that copy.[1]

In the works of other authors—such as Ibrāhīm b. Sinān—we find valuable autobiographies in which what counts is not anecdotal detail but the motives for the author's scientific work, the reasons why his attention was focused on certain mathematical subjects more than on others, and what he believed he had achieved, with his monographs analysed briefly, one after the other. We see that Muslim scientists were already, in the ninth century, sure that through their efforts they were advancing in all its aspects, and that their translations of the ancient texts were more correct, as a general rule, than the original manuscripts. And they were

[1] Archimedes, *Kitāb al-kūra wa'l-usṭuwāna*, revised by Naṣīr al-Dīn Ṭūsī (Hyderabad, 1359/1940), p. 2.

not often mistaken, just as the translators from Arabic to Latin would not have been mistaken, centuries later, in making similar assessments.

Mathematics

The original development of this science begins, to be precise, with the Koran itself, with its complex series of rules for the sharing-out of inheritances. But the first great mathematician is al-Khwārizmī (d. *c.* 846), to whom we owe the attempt to systematize in Arabic all scientific knowledge—geography, mathematics, astronomy, and calendar science—that came to his hands. We are indebted to him for the Spanish word *guarismo* (figure, digit, cipher) and the English *algorism* or *algorithm* which, in fact, comes from his patronymic in the Toledan translation: *Algoritmi de numero indorum*, of the book written by him under the title *al-Jamʿ wa'l-tafrīq bi-ḥisāb al-Hind*, whose original has been lost. In it he set out the rules necessary to work with Indian numbers (as opposed to the *ghubār* and the 'notaries' or 'Roman' figures) or, as we call them today, Arabic numerals, and the use of numeration by position. By the end of the ninth century, and at the latest by the middle of the tenth century, the Western world knew this system, as is proved by the miscellaneous manuscript from Oviedo in the library of the Escorial, restored by Saint Eulogius (d. 859) and brought to Oviedo in 884, and by the Albeldensian codex written by the monk Vigila and finished in 976. The form of the ten ciphers (the word comes etymologically from the Arabic *ṣifr*, an empty space, the place which zero was to occupy later) was then, as now, changeable, depending to a great extent on the handwriting of the scribe. Hence the fact that several medieval authors, e.g. Alvarus of Toledo, were to make tables of equivalences in order to understand each other, and in certain places (e.g. Florence, 1299) their use was forbidden because of the enormous variations incurred by a tiny alteration of the form. Although the origin of the idea of numeration by position originated in the Near East, the form of our ciphers cannot derive from those used there, which has given rise to the supposition that those used in the Western world came from the Visigothic letters in use in Spain in the second half of the tenth century.

The second field in which al-Khwārizmī worked was that of algebra, a branch of mathematics which, until that time, had not been the object of any serious, systematic study. Its origins are found in Greek and Indian texts and in those of Ancient Babylon, access to the latter probably being gained, indirectly, through the Hebrew work *Mishnat ha-Middōt*. Al-Khwārizmī's book has the title *al-Kitāb al-mukhtaṣar fī ḥisāb al-jabr wa'l-muqābala*, in which the last two words describe the auxiliary processes by which problems are reduced to six equations of the type:

$$\begin{aligned}
&(1)\ ax^2 = bx\\
&(2)\ ax^2 = c\\
&(3)\ ax = c\\
&(4)\ ax^2+bx = c\\
&(5)\ ax^2+c = bx\\
&(6)\ bx+c = ax^2
\end{aligned}$$

The definitions of the technical terms *jabr* and *muqābala* vary slightly from one writer to another. In general the meaning of the first word corresponds to the transposition, restoration, or reduction of a fracture (both meanings are retained in the Spanish word *algebrista*, an algebraist or a bone-setter). In this new branch of mathematics it came to mean the transposition of terms in order to make them all positive. Thus

$$6x^2-36x+60 = 2x^2-12$$

is transformed by *jabr* into

$$6x^2+60+12 = 2x^2+36x.$$

By *muqābala* is meant the reduction of similar terms, or

$$4x^2+72 = 36x$$

and consequently we find we have an equation of type 5 which can be simplified by dividing the two sides of the equation by 4 (*ḥaṭṭ*, *radd*) to

$$x^2+18 = 9x.$$

It must be noted that these first algebraists never took negative or irrational solutions into account.

An extraordinary series of developments followed these first hesitant steps. Abū Kāmil Shujāʿ (tenth century) resolved systems of equations of up to five unknowns and worked out indeterminate or diophantine problems. His contributions were partially known in the West through a medieval Spanish (not Latin) translation, but some details of his theories had previously reached the monastery of Reichenau, possibly around A.D. 1000. To this same stream belongs al-Māhānī (d. *c*. 874) whose study of a lemma of Archimedes (*The Sphere and the Cylinder*, ii. 4: 'To cut a sphere by a plane so that the two parts are in a given proportion to each other') led him to the correct posing of the problem

$$x^3+a = bx^2$$

which was solved years later by al-Khāzin (d. *c*. 971). Then al-Karajī (at times wrongly called al-Karkhī) wrote an algebra in which he developed the ideas of Diophantus, and finally ʿUmar Khayyām (d. 1123) classified by class and kind the algebraic equations up to the third degree, according to the number of terms and the distribution of coefficients, which he considered as always positive, and also of the roots, and he resolved the cubic equations which could not be reduced to quadratics by means of conic sections.

Another field in which the inquiring minds of the Arabs were concerned was that of the theory of numbers, in which their preoccupation with magic squares and amicable numbers led them to make some discoveries. Magic squares, which have talismanic value, are characterized by the fact that the sum of the numbers which they surround, whether read in columns, lines, or diagonals, is constant. For example:

20	22	3	2	18
25	12	17	10	1
5	11	13	15	21
7	16	9	14	19
8	4	23	24	6

The Brethren of Purity knew the squares of 9, 16, 25, and 36 components and the occultist al-Būnī (d. 1225) gave a general solution which allowed the creation of successively larger squares.

By amicable numbers they understood those which taken in pairs have the property that one of them is the sum of the divisors of the other, e.g. 220 and 284, since, as the Brethren of Purity point out in the *Epistles*

$$220 = 142+71+4+2+1$$
$$284 = 110+55+44+22+20+11+10+5+4+2+1.$$

But 142, etc., are the factors of 220, and 110, etc., are the factors of 284.

Thābit b. Qurra established a rule for finding amicable numbers: if the numbers

$$a = 3.2^n - 1$$
$$b = 3.2^{n-1} - 1$$
$$c = 3^2.2^{2n-1} - 1$$

are primes for $n > 1$, then the numbers

$$A = 2^n ab \quad \text{and} \quad B = 2^n c$$

are amicable.

It is interesting to remember that al-Khujandī (d. 1000) enunciated a particular case of the theorem of Fermat 'the sum of two cubes cannot be another cube', and that Naṣīr al-Dīn Ṭūsī established that 'the sum of two squares each of which is an odd number cannot be a square'. The study of these relationships led them to the analysis of arithmetical and geometrical progressions, and so al-Karajī (in his *Kitāb al-fakhri*) summed up:

$$1^3+2^3+3^3+\ldots+n^3=(1+2+3+\ldots+n)^2$$

At about the same time, al-Bīrūnī had given as a solution to the famous problem of the grains of wheat on the chessboard (that is, the sum of $1+2+4+8+\ldots$) the value:

$$18_3446,\ 744_2073{,}709_1551{,}615.$$

In the field of geometry the brothers of the Banū Mūsā b. Shākir (ninth century) stands out. Their principal work, the *Kitāb maʿrifat misāḥat al-ashkāl*, was one of the bridges by which Greek influence came to Baghdad, and original additions began to be made to it. This book, translated into Latin centuries later by Gerard of Cremona with the title *Verba filiorum Moysi filii Sekir*, introduced to the West (Fibonacci, Jordanus Nemorarius, Roger Bacon, Thomas Bradwardine) the first ideas of higher mathematics: the proof of the first proposition of *De mensura circuli*, somewhat different from that of Archimedes but also based on the method of exhaustion; the theorem of Hero on the area of the triangle as a function of the sides; formulae for the area and the volume of the cone and the sphere; solutions to the problem of finding two proportional means between two given quantities, which is resolved firstly according to the method attributed by the Banū Mūsā brothers to Menelaus and by Eutochius to Archytas, and secondly, according to the method which the Banū Mūsā brothers give as their own and which Eutochius attributes to Plato; the first Latin solution to the problem of the trisection of the angle, which recalls that which Archimedes gives in his *Lemmata* or *Liber assumptorum*; and a method for extracting cubic roots with whatever approximation may be required.

The most interesting aspect of the matter is that Thābit b.

Qurra (d. 901) collaborated with the Banū Mūsā. He must have gone on working on cubatures and quadratures according to the Archimedean directrices although he did not know—indeed, the Arabs did not know—three of the principal works of Archimedes on this subject: *The Quadrature of the Parabola*, the *Letter to Eratosthenes* or *Method*, and *On Conoids and Spheroids*. Therefore his method of exhaustion is partially independent of the Greek method and can be considered as a glimpse of modern integral calculus. In his work on the *Quadrature of the Parabola* he determines the area of the segment of the parabola by the method of integral sums; he carries out a calculation of the integral

$$\int_0^a \sqrt{x}\, dx$$

and applies the division of the segment of integration in unequal parts forming an arithmetical progression. In the *Cubature of the Paraboloid*, a more laborious work than that of Archimedes, he had, however, the advantage of generalizing even more the method which he used and which Ibrāhīm b. Sinān (d. 946) and al-Kūhī (*fl.* 988) later developed successfully. Ibn al-Haytham (d. 1038) for his part worked in the field of isoperimetry, and following on the suggestions found in the proposition 2, 9 of *The Sphere and the Cylinder* and in the work of Zenodorus, managed to demonstrate that 'of two regular polygons inscribed in the same circumference, that with the greater number of sides has the greater area and the greater perimeter'.

Another question which preoccupied Arab geometers was the fifth postulate of Euclid: 'If a straight line, cutting two other straight lines, forms internal angles on the same side less than two right angles, the two straight lines produced to infinity will meet on the side of the two angles less than two right angles.' Several of their most prominent thinkers tried—as Wallis, Playfair, etc., did after the Renaissance—to substitute an equivalent for it, to demonstrate it or to wrap it up in fallacious arguments. Ibn al-Haytham, ʿUmar Khayyām, al-Jawharī (*fl.* 829), Thābit b.

Qurra, Naṣīr al-Dīn Ṭūsī (d. 1274), and Shams al-Dīn al-Samarqandī (*fl.* 1276) were notable in this field of research.

Astronomy

This science had as heterogeneous an origin as mathematics. The pre-Islamic names of the stars were very quickly inserted into the great frame of Hellenic tradition, itself the inheritor of Mesopotamian tradition. So, when al-Ṣūfī (d. 986) wrote his uranography, it became the source of almost all later studies and, through the Spanish version of Alfonso X el Sabio, in the *Libros del saber de astronomía*, strongly influenced the stellar toponymy of our modern languages. The 'sphere' thus established, which from the scientific point of view was based on the Ptolemaic catalogue of the *Almagest*, was the object of corporeal representation in a series of celestial globes in which the constellations with their principal stars were depicted. These, in general, were considered to be fixed in the eighth sphere, and because of the difference in their magnitudes, it was held that they were of different sizes.

The oldest of all these representations is that of the zodiac of the Umayyad building of Quṣayr ʿAmra (*c.* 711–15) from which, it seems, we may deduce that the model which was used for its plan was made in accordance with a stereographic projection.

From the time of Ibn al-Haytham the Milky Way was pictured as a group of weak stars, very close to each other, smaller than the sixth magnitude, whose light reaches us in a confused and jumbled manner, and of whose position in the sphere of the fixed stars there is no doubt, since it lacks parallax, and the light of Saturn, the most distant planet, is unchanged when it passes through it. Some stars (nebulous or not) like the Pole Star, Suhayl (Canopus), and the Magellan clouds(?) were used as points of reference by navigators on the high seas, and there are frequent references to them in collections of navigational charts. The astrological texts, for their part, concentrate basically on the colour, so important for relating their nature to the benevolent or malevolent planets and so for drawing conclusions as to their influence on human affairs. There is evidence in folk legend which leads us to suspect that they knew of the variability of Algol, which fluctuates between magnitudes 2·3 and 3·5, and perhaps of the much slower variability of Mira Ceti.

The planetary system, the only universe conceivable at that time, never stopped increasing its dimensions. We are already far from the time when the shepherd Etana, on the back of the mythical eagle, was on the point of reaching the sky and, failing in the attempt, fell for two Babylonian hours (four hours of our time); far from the time when it took Vulcan a day to cover the distance between the sky and the earth (*Iliad*, i. 573–94). Greek scientific astronomy had considerably broadened the limits of the universe, the dimensions of which were, according to different scholars, expressed in terms of radii of the earth:

	Bīrūnī	Farghānī	Ibn Rusta
Moon	33·33	$33\frac{1}{2}+\frac{1}{20}$	
Mercury	64·20	$64\frac{1}{6}$	$64\frac{1}{6}$
Venus	169·46	167	166
Sun	1161·45	1120	1079
Mars	1260·15	1220	1260
Jupiter	9169·14	8876	8820
Saturn	14881·29	14405	14187
Stars	20774·39	20110	20000

These distances are all much less than their real value, but they are already commensurable.

On the edge of the system there remained, evidently, the comets which, like the Milky Way in the *Physics* of Aristotle, were assumed to belong to the corruptible or sublunar world. For this reason, the mention which Tycho Brahe in his *Progymnastica* makes of Albumasar as the first scientist to refute the opinion of Aristotle, saying that he had observed comets in the sphere of Venus, must be taken with some reservations since Albumasar may be referring to the astrological pseudo-planet Kayd, the final philological development of Ketu, the name given by Indian scholars to the descending node which showed itself at times in the form of a little cloud and to which was attributed a period of revolution of 144 years.

Another interesting feature related to uranography is that of the popular 'calendars' such as those we find represented by the most famous of them, the so-called 'Calendar of Cordova', a typical 'farmers' almanac' of the time. The genre appears to have come from the ancient East and through Greece (Hesiod, Conon of Samos, Aratus, etc.) and with infinite changes to have reached Islam. As we find it presented in the Andalusian work, it consists of a chronological account, month by month and day by day, according to the Julian calendar, of the agricultural tasks which must be done, of feast days, of the entry of the sun into the signs of the Zodiac, of the houses of the moon and of the acronyctous risings and settings of pairs of stars called *anwā'* which, according to popular lore, allowed one to predict the meteorological development throughout a week. These texts almost always show features of glaring archaism and of indecision in regard to the data selected (hence they give, indiscriminately, various dates for the same event), but from time to time they proceed to modernize their content: as, for example, the astronomical data of al-Battānī (d. 929) inserted into the 'Calendar of Cordova'. This tradition continues through Ibn al-Bannā' (d. 1321) almost to the present day.

Astrology appears side by side with astronomy. Some astronomers, indeed some great astronomers, like al-Bīrūnī, did not hesitate to write manuals on judicial astrology and to correspond with pure astrologers like ʿAlī b. Abī'l-Rijāl (d. after 1040). And almost all the manuals of astronomy dedicate some pages to the scientific part of astrology (spherical astrology): the means of determining the position of the planets, the phases, the nodes, the ascendant, etc., at the moment of birth of the subject; or else, in reverse, they try to determine the moment at which a celestial configuration will be produced which is favourable to the starting of a given act, to laying the foundations of a city, e.g. Baghdad, whose horoscope of foundation is still in existence. At other times it is a matter of verifying the position of the stars at the moment of the spring equinox in order to proceed to the yearly predictions of the future and to achieve a tendentious astrological interpretation of history. From this came the necessity of making extremely complex calculations, retrospective or otherwise, which required the perfection of mathematical resources, and which were at the root of the perfecting of the sets of instruments of observation, and also led to the actual creation of a new branch of mathematics: trigonometry.

The basic instrument used in astronomy is the astrolabe, that is, the stereographic projection of the celestial sphere on the plane of the equator taking the Pole as the viewpoint. The rules for this are already found in Ptolemy, and as the circles of declination and the azimuthal co-ordinates—almacantar and vertical—are represented on the plate of the apparatus while the asterisms appear on the net or spider, it is clear that one would need as many plates as the number of latitudes for which one wished to use the instrument, which thus became extremely heavy in spite of its small dimensions. In order to find an answer to this, the Andalusian ʿAlī b. Khalaf (eleventh century) invented the 'universal plate', the stereographic projection of the sphere on a plane perpendicular to the ecliptic which cuts it according to the solstitial line Cancer–Capricorn, and shortly afterwards Azarquiel (d. *c.* 1087) constructed a type of astrolabe, *ṣafīḥa*, which presented on the same surface the two stereographic projections of the circles of the equator and of the ecliptic; it was revived centuries later by Gemma of Frisia (1508–55) under the title *astrolabum* (sic) *catholicum*. The linear astrolabe or 'staff' of Muẓaffar al-Dīn Ṭūsī (d. 1213) can be considered as an ultimate simplification of these instruments.

But earlier attempts had been made to increase the accuracy of the astrolabe by disengaging one of its quadrants. This permitted the numerical values of its arc to be read with greater approximation. Abū Mansūr ʿAbd al-Malik al-Khwārizmī, the author of the *Mafātīḥ al-ʿulūm* (flourished in the tenth century; to be distinguished from the mathematician al-Khwārizmī), describes it to us. It consisted, as its name indicates, of a quadrant from which hung, on each of the extreme radii, perpendiculars which allowed the numerical values of the sines and cosines of the corresponding arc to be read off directly. Different variants gave rise to the types known as *vetustissimus*, *vetus*, and *novus*, while another series of quadrants was derived later from Azarquiel's *ṣafīḥa*, in its variant *shakkāzī*.

Another type of instrument, which today we should call 'mechanical', allowed the position of the planets and stars in the sky to be ascertained by means of a gearing mechanism. In fact they were, at first, modified astrolabes whose furthest antecedents are to be found in the Greek apparatus of Antikythera. Literary quotations (e.g. in Vitruvius) prove its existence in Antiquity, and already in the world of Islam the Cordovan polymath ʿAbbās b. Firnās (ninth century) was said to have prepared a room in his house in which the stars, the clouds, thunder, and lightning appeared, and finally, and much more convincingly, we have the drawing of an astrolabe with gears belonging to al-Bīrūnī. This mechanical contrivance, perfected by Ibn al-Samḥ into the 'plate of the seven planets', and then by Azarquiel, was finally to give rise to the equatorial instruments of the Dark Ages, which in their turn were the forerunners of the mechanical clock.

The instruments used in the practice of observation were generally small and were correct only within ten degrees of an arc. We know that large-diametered ones were sometimes used, for example by the Banū Mūsā brothers, but the discrepancies obtained in the readings—due to the lack of dividing engines which were only invented much later—brought them into discredit.

In general, the observations consisted of the determination of the horizontal co-ordinates of a star, azimuth and height, which were transformed into equatorials or ecliptics according to the type of problem being dealt with. In cases in which the required approximation was not too great, people could use one of the simple-to-operate instruments already described, which gave the answer quickly. But in general and for astronomical-astrological purposes or for the determining of the *qibla*, they resorted to trigonometrical calculations.

This branch of mathematics had its beginning in the most elementary Indian knowledge (primitive sine tables), and it may be considered as one of the greatest achievements of Arab scientists that they abandoned the theorem of Ptolemy with which the Greeks had approached those problems by means of cords. The astronomers rapidly discovered the fundamental formulae of spherical trigonometry; al-Battānī established

$$\cos a = \cos b \cos c + \sin b \sin c \cos A.$$

Abū'l-Wafā' (d. 998) introduced the theorems of the tangents

$$\frac{\tan b}{\tan B} = \frac{\sin c}{1}$$

for the spherical oblique-angled triangle, and introduced the secant and the cosecant. We owe to the same writer the formula for the addition of angles

$$\sin(a+b) = \sin a \cos b + \cos a \sin b$$

which Rheticus, a pupil of Copernicus, rediscovered in his *Opus palatinum de triangulis*.

Abū Naṣr (d. *c.* 1036), the teacher of al-Bīrūnī, may have been one of the discoverers of the theorem of sines

$$\frac{\sin A}{\sin a} = \frac{\sin B}{\sin b} = \frac{\sin C}{\sin c}.$$

Ibn Yūnus (d. 1009), for his part, gave the formula

$$\cos a \cos b = \tfrac{1}{2}[\cos(a+b) + \cos(a-b)]$$

and Ibn al-Haytham gave the theorem of the cotangent to determine the azimuth of the *qibla*

$$\cot \alpha = \sin \phi \cos(L_2 - L_1) - \frac{\cos \phi_1 \tan \phi_2}{\sin(L_2 - L_1)}.$$

These theorems and many others made possible a direct approach to the solution of general spherical triangles. Despite this, Arab astronomers showed a preference for more elementary and cumbersome methods—also discovered by them—like that of resorting to dividing general triangles into two right-angled ones (the inventor of the *sennero* quadrant used this method, for example, to transform celestial co-ordinates), or for other types of calculations, such as we find in Azarquiel and al-Bīrūnī, who prefer to try to use sines and cosines in preference, ignoring the remaining lines which were known to them and of which they have tables calculated for different values of the radius: 12, 60, 150, 120, and even 1, as we do today. And it is not out of place to note that the same writer uses different values according to the nature of the problem he has to solve.

Being able to find the position of the planets in their respective orbits with relative facility, they could move on to the analysis and development of the planetary theories handed down from Antiquity.

Thus, the mathematician al-Khwārizmī wrote tables of which he made two editions: the lesser, adapted by Maslama to the meridian of Cordova and translated into Latin by Adelard of Bath, and the greater, whose whereabouts are unknown, but whose existence is confirmed for us by the commentary made on it by Ibn al-Muthannā which has been preserved in a Hebrew version of Abraham ben Ezra and a Latin version of Hugh of Santalla. This work is of special interest because it tried to unite empirically Greek and Indian theories of astronomy. The compilation and assembling of material of such different origins complicated, sometimes needlessly, the methods of Arab astronomy: the theory of the moon came from circles in which the *Almagest* was unknown and the table of latitudes was calculated by the sine method alone; the procedures for determining the true longitude of the planets and their mean movement came from India while those for determining the stationary points and retrograde movements derived, directly or indirectly, from the manual tables of

Theon. These and the Persian *Zīj al-Shāh* must have been the principal sources of inspiration of al-Khwārizmī, who also had contact with people of every race and religion, provided that they could teach him something, as is proved by his *Treatise on the Jewish Calendar*, the first scientific work on that subject which is still extant.

In order to correct the information which appeared in the translated texts, a series of observations was undertaken, which almost always resulted in the compilation of astronomical tables which, since they were based on experiment, were given the name of *mumtaḥan* (the *probate* of the Latin writers). The best known of all were those compiled by a group of astronomers in the service of the Caliph al-Ma'mūn. The same group measured on the plains of Mesopotamia, in Sinjar, near Mosul (between 35° and 36° north), the value of a degree of a meridian, finding it to be equal to 111,814 metres (real value: 110,938 metres); a value similar to that obtained by Sanad b. ʿAlī who, by order of the same Caliph al-Ma'mūn, measured the depression of the horizon from the top of a mountain on the shore of the Mediterranean and from this was able to deduce the size of the circumference of the earth.

Al-Battānī stands out among all Arab astronomers. He was the author of *mumtaḥan* tables and of many observations of such precision that he was able to demonstrate the existence of annular eclipses of the sun and, many centuries later (1749), enabled Dunthorne to determine the secular acceleration of the movement of the moon. After al-Battānī came Ibn Yūnus (d. 1009), Azarquiel, by whose group of collaborators the 'Toledan Astronomical Tables were compiled, and many others.

The numerical values which appear in some tables do not correspond *exactly* to the Ptolemaic planetary model: they represent the introduction of corrections which in practice helped to reconcile the almanacs based on calculations with those based on observation, and which in fact was equivalent to admitting tacitly the existence of other planetary systems. The fact that they make Mercury and Venus satellites of the sun recalls the attempts of

Heraclides and Tycho Brahe; the fact that Azarquiel, in order to explain the movement of Mercury, thought of an ovaloid orbit shows a notable parallel with the evolution of Kepler's thought in the case of Mars; Jābir b. Aflaḥ (*fl. c.* 1150) believed that Mercury and Venus were beyond the sun. Even more, the kinematic schemes of some planets in Naṣīr al-Dīn Ṭūsī, Ibn al-Shāṭir, and other authors remind us of the Copernican theory. But they all agreed that the earth did not change its position.

The philosophers, particularly in Spain, were preoccupied by purely theoretical problems. Avempace, Ibn Ṭufayl, Averroes, and Maimonides were vexed because the Ptolemaic system, with its epicycles and eccentrics, went against the principle which placed the earth in the real centre of the universe, and finally one of their disciples, al-Bitrūjī (twelfth century) attempted a form of return to Eudoxus' system of homocentric spheres.

That the celestial position of the stars is affected by the precession of the equinoxes was possibly discovered by Hipparchus and incorporated, although its numerical value was modified, in the *Almagest*. But even in Hellenistic times this continuous movement of retrogression of the vernal degree was not unanimously accepted, and according to the testimony of Theon 'the ancient astrologers say, basing their statements on conjecture, that the solstitial points advance towards 8° east during a certain period and then they return to their original positions'. Theon and Proclus did not accept this fluctuation, or trepidation, but they, especially the former, expounded with great clarity the period of advance and retreat. This doctrine was known to the Indians and the Arabs. Some astronomers, those of the Western world in particular, accepted it (others continued to use the Ptolemaic precession, e.g. al-Farghānī, al-Battānī, Ibn Yūnus, etc.) and tried to adapt it to the needs of the time, contriving for it kinematic models which would make the theory correspond to the observed reality, as, with the passage of time, more and more discrepancies arose. Because of this, books entitled *Movement of the Eighth Sphere* or *Movement of the Sun* are relatively common, and very soon not only the movement of trepidation came to be considered, but also that of the solar perigee (or apogee, which is the same in this case). Thus Thābit b. Qurra and Azarquiel introduced movable circles in the most convenient places in the celestial sphere, which enabled them to explain the movements of trepidation and of oscillation of the plane of the ecliptic within certain limits. In order to build their models both writers were obliged to make use of the most remote observations they knew and to use to the full all their trigonometric knowledge, complicating unnecessarily the work of later astronomers—some of whom, like Alfonso X, came to form an idea of a hybridization of precession and trepidation.

Closely connected with astronomy are the problems of chronology. The Muslim calendar being lunar and the beginning of its months depending on the *real* and *testified* observation of the new moon, the interest which the scientists of the Golden Age took in fixing their constants can be understood. They applied themselves first to determining the sequence of the intercalary years (that is, those with 355 days instead of the 354 of the normal year) within a cycle of thirty Arab years, and among the various proposed solutions that of al-Battānī was finally imposed. The impossibility of making the agricultural cycle coincide with the lunar calendar led them to keep, at the same time as the latter, the Julian calendar in those countries which had belonged to the Roman Empire, and the ancient Persian calendar in the rest. This last was the object of a reform, the Jalālī calendar, ordered by the Seljuq Sultan Jalāl al-Dawla Malikshāh, which came into force on 16 March 1079, and in the preparation of which ʿUmar Khayyām is said to have intervened. It formed a first-class chronological instrument, capable of competing in exactness with the Gregorian reform.

They also determined, using methods which were Babylonian in their origins, the moment of the appearance of the new moon and they strove to simplify the tables, auxiliary or not, in which the elements necessary to fix the moment of the neomenia appeared. They discovered, possibly around the thirteenth century, the system for giving the ephemerids of the sun and the moon—later extended to the other planets—as a function of concrete annual dates. Such was the origin of the almanacs which were to be so widely used when transoceanic navigation began.

Optics

The Arabs faithfully observed the optical phenomena which the atmosphere offered them, and they described them in the most exact manner possible, trying to explain them scientifically to the best of their ability. The Brethren of Purity describe the rainbow and halos, noting in both cases the part played by the reflection of light and by humidity. For the first they note that the height of the sun must not be excessive and they determine that the lower the sun the greater the rainbow, and that the greatest value—180°—is reached at the moment when the sun is on the horizon, since its rays are tangential to the surface of the earth. The colours which are distinguished, from top to bottom in order, are red, yellow, blue, and green. Al-Qazwīnī (d. 1283) distinguishes eight separate colours, and mentions amongst them, and in the same order, red, yellow, purple, reddish-brown, and violet. He also quotes the case (which also appears in much more detail, and as a justification of the theory of the colour spectrum, in the *Tanqīḥ* of Kamāl al-Dīn al-Fārisī) of a rainbow which, observed from the top of a mountain, formed an almost complete circumference since only the part of the sky hidden by the mountain peak was missing from it.

The explanation of the rainbow was based on the supposition that the rays of light are reflected on the drops of rain which act like little flat mirrors whose behaviour is described in such a way that the authors sometimes seem to be speaking more of a prism than of a mirror; in them, we are assured, one does not see the shape of things but spots of colour of different shape. Quṭb al-Dīn al-Shīrāzī (d. 1311) and Kamāl al-Dīn al-Fārisī (d. *c.* 1320) supposed that the light, on crossing the transparent sphere which is the drop of water, is refracted twice and reflected once (or twice in the secondary rainbow) and they tried to determine the cause of the colours. Similar explanations were also given for mirages. They tried to explain some optical illusions such as, for example, that produced by a millstone the sections of which have been painted different colours, when it turned rapidly (a precedent for Newton's disc), noting that only one colour is seen, this being the result of the mixture of all.

Of greater interest are the observations or theories made or elaborated by the scientists who took as their starting-point the work done in Antiquity by Euclid and Ptolemy. This tradition gave them a choice of three theories of vision: (1) the eyes emit rays which, when they strike the object, enable it to be seen (Aristotle, following the Pythagoreans); (2) vision is a result of a double emission: that of the eye and that of the object (Empedocles); and (3) objects emit rays in all directions: some of them pass through the pupils and are the cause of vision (Epicurus). This last theory, approximately the correct one, was that accepted by Ibn al-Haytham, who is in agreement in this with Avicenna and al-Bīrūnī and opposed to Euclid, Ptolemy, and al-Kindī. Ibn al-Haytham is one of the greatest students of optics of all time and his theories flourished until the seventeenth century.

The great work which has immortalized him was the *Optics* (*Kitāb al-manāẓir*) translated into Latin and published at Basle in 1572 by Frederick Risner under the title *Thesaurus opticus*. As a result of his experiments he accepted that the perceptible image is formed on the crystalline, since if, in accordance with his experiments with the camera obscura—discovered by him simultaneously with and independently of the Chinese Shen Kua—he had accepted that it was formed on the retina, he would have been unable to explain the reversal of the image. Later he solved the problem which bears his name: there are two points A and B in the plane of a circle of centre O and radius r. To determine on the circle (idealized in a mirror) the point M on which the ray of light emitted by A must be reflected so that it passes through B. Ibn al-Haytham's very complicated proof leads to a fourth-degree equation which he solved by the intersection of an equilateral hyperbola with a circle. Centuries later Leonardo da Vinci would solve it by mechanical means and Christian Huyghens would give, finally, the most elegant and simple solution. In the latter part of the book Ibn al-Haytham dealt with refraction, observing that the relation between the angle of incidence and refraction is not constant, and that the line of incidence, the line of refraction, and the perpendicular to the surface of separation are on the same plane. Developing these theories his commentator Kamāl al-Dīn al-Fārisī gives a description of the refraction of light which implies the following knowledge about the velocity of light: (1) it is finite but very great, so great that at times it appears infinite (in this direction al-Bīrūnī, a contemporary of Ibn al-Haytham, had already established that it was immensely superior to that of sound); (2) in different media it is inversely proportional to the optical density.

He also examined the properties of lenses, whose burning power, as well as their power of magnification, had been pointed out by the classical writers (Aristophanes, Pliny, Seneca) but it is doubtful whether he knew the help they could give to the presbyopic; the only certain thing is that we have written testimony of their use from 1306, and that medieval iconography from 1352 onwards shows old men with spectacles (that is, long before G. B. della Porta spoke of them in *Magia naturalis*, 1598) and that the great Persian poet Jāmī (d. 1492) says:

> My hair is white like a tree in blossom; but this tree only gives me sorrow for fruit.
>
> My mirror has showed me, hair by hair, that defect known as white hair: I don't want to look at it any more.
>
> Before, at night, I could read by the light of the moon; now I can no longer even read in sunlight.
>
> Thanks to the lenses from Europe I have four eyes instead of two; but even that is not enough to read the Koran.
>
> Heaven, which is playing with me, deceives me with bits of glass, exactly as it does with children.

This is a fair proof that, for whatever reason, in the fifteenth century the centre of development of the new industry was Europe; the attempts of Roger Bacon to combine lenses had not led to the telescope nor the microscope because for medieval science—distant echo of the apostle Thomas—only the tangible had a real existence, while the visual was susceptible of being deformed by optical illusions.

We also owe to Ibn al-Haytham the correct explanation of the apparent increase of the diameter of the sun and of the moon in the vicinity of the horizon, the discovery of spherical aberration (although he did not take the caustic curve into account), and the proof—independently of Cleomedes—that atmospheric refraction makes the sun still visible when it is in fact already below the horizon.

The work of Ibn al-Haytham was completed, in part, by his commentator Kamāl al-Dīn al-Fārisī who, two centuries later, developing the theory of Ibn al-Haytham on the camera obscura, was able to prove firstly, that the images are clearer the smaller the aperture; secondly, that they are independent of the shape of the aperture; and thirdly, in the interior of the camera obscura the images appear inverted and the objects are arranged in the opposite sense to that which they have in reality. The Jew Levi ben Gerson of Bagnols (d. 1344) was to go one step further when he observed the eclipses of the moon in a camera obscura.

East and West

The scientific contribution of the Muslims passed to the West in two well-defined periods. The first, in the second half of the tenth century, was due to the translations undertaken by the Mozarabs in monasteries throughout the Iberian peninsula, although at present we can only document this translating industry seriously with reference to the Catalan monastery of Ripoll and to the city of Barcelona; we can suspect it with regard to the monastery of Albelda, and infer it for the rest of the peninsula. The astronomical and mathematical translations of Ripoll and Barcelona became quickly known in the centre of Europe thanks to the active commercial route which, following the Rhone and the Rhine, reaches the heart of Germany, and thanks also to the fact that the monk Gerbert, later Pope Sylvester II, studied in Catalonia. In some cases, such as that of Lupitus (Llobet), we know the name and nationality of these primitive translators; in others we can only guess at their origins by the characteristics of the vocabulary which they used.

The eleventh century marks a pause in this movement of cultural transmission, a pause which cannot have been complete at the moment towards the end of that century when Ibn ʿAbdūn says that books must not be sold to Christians because they translate them and attribute them to their bishops.[1] In the twelfth century this movement gathers extraordinary momentum: in Sicily, and particularly in Spain, the number of texts translated is impressive, classical science flows into European monasteries through Arab minds, and the discoveries made by Arabs are incorporated into the stockpile of Western culture. Many cities (Tarazona, Pamplona, Barcelona, Saragossa, Tortosa) which had bishops eager for knowledge, gave their names to the mathematical and astronomical codices of the time. Far above them all stood Toledo, where a great number of European scholars anxious to acquire Eastern scientific knowledge had come together. In spite of the fact that they did not work together as a 'school', their copious and intense work transformed Western society. Although they were able to assimilate easily the texts which they were handling, they failed to develop those texts any further. (For example, the Muslim series of problems about the fifth postulate of Euclid, from the ninth century onwards, has no Western parallel until after the Renaissance.) The thirteenth century, with the secularization of culture begun by Alfonso X replacing Latin by Spanish, marks a decisive turn in the transmission of scientific knowledge: on one hand the great period of translations ends, since those of the fourteenth century, except those into Hebrew,

[1] E. Lévi-Provençal and E. García Gómez, *Sevilla a comienzos del siglo XII* (Madrid, 1948), p. 173.

were for the most part based on texts written much earlier or, in the case of classical texts, were derived directly from the original language. European science, as shown in such personages as Grosseteste, Roger Bacon, Buridan, Oresme, etc., starts on its own way at the same time as the Mongol invasions opened the door to influences from China, so that some of the Chinese scientific and technical discoveries penetrated in surprising and rapid manner to the very heart of Europe.

Such a swift transmission is due above all to the patronage of the first Persian Il-Khānids, who let themselves be advised by Naṣīr al-Dīn Ṭūsī whom we have repeatedly mentioned and who constructed in Marāgha the first observatory in the Muslim world which carried out its operations in complete autonomy, independently of the state, and which kept in close contact with both Chinese and Andalusian astronomers. It is, indeed, a good example of the internationalization of science.

From this moment West and East take parallel but separate lines in this field; it seems that the astronomical observatory of Samarqand (founded by Ulugh Beg in 1420) had a decisive influence on the foundation of that of Istanbul (1577) which in its turn may have been the cause of the development of observatories in the Western world from the seventeenth century onwards. According to what evidence we have, its instruments were very like those used at the same time by Tycho Brahe. But this influence, if such it was, seems to have been the last. The Arab scientific texts which were printed in the fifteenth century were those already known before the thirteenth century. This means that, for example, the extension of the decimal system to fractions carried out by Ghiyāth al-Dīn Jamshīd al-Kāshī (d. 1429) was not known to Simon Stevin of Bruges (1548–1620).

Nevertheless there is evidence to show the existence of a faint current of cultural interchange between Islam and the West in the Renaissance period as a result of Spanish politics which, by throwing the non-indigenous minorities out of Spanish territory, turned them into a vehicle for the transmission of science in both directions: medical works, technical works, and even the *Almanach Perpetuum* of Zacutus, were translated into Arabic, and the orthographic projection of the astrolabe of Rojas was copied in Persia at the beginning of the eighteenth century. And, working the other way, the work of the Moroccan mathematician Ibn al-Bannā' and of his commentator al-Qalaṣādī (d. 1486) seem to have been known in sixteenth-century Christian Spain and would explain the mysterious method for extracting square roots used by Juan de Ortega (*fl.* 1567), which seems to be based upon continuous fractions. If it is so, it would lead us to conclude that this mathematical trick was used by the Arabs before Bombelli (d. 1572) used it.

These contacts are, in fact, the last important ones until the beginning of the twentieth century, when a new era of scientific translations begins which, like that in the eighth to the tenth centuries, brings the science of the Western world to Islam. We may hope that from these translations may arise an Arab scientific renaissance similar to that of the Middle Ages.

JUAN VERNET

BIBLIOGRAPHY

General Works

W. Hartner, *Oriens. Occidens* (Hildesheim, 1968); A. P. Juschkewitsch, *Geschichte der Mathematik im Mittelalter* (Basle, 1964); E. S. Kennedy, 'A Survey of Islamic Astronomical Tables', *Transactions of the American Philosophical Society*, N.S., xlvi (1959), 123-77; J. M. Millás, *Assaig d'història de les idees fisiques i matemàtiques a la Catalunya medieval* (Barcelona, 1931); C. A. Nallino, *Raccolta di Scritti editi e inediti*, V. *Astrologia, Astronomica, Geografia* (Rome, 1944); O. Neugebauer, *The Exact Sciences in Antiquity* (Oxford, 1951; repr. Providence, 1957); M. Plessner, 'Storia delle Scienze nell'Islam', in *La civiltà dell'Oriente*, iii (Rome, 1958), 449-92; G. Sarton, *Introduction to the History of Science*, 3 vols. (Baltimore, 1929-48); A. Sayili, *The Observatory in Islam and its Place in the General History of the Observatory* (Ankara, 1960); H. Suter, *Die Mathematiker und Astronomen der Araber und ihre Werke* (Leipzig, 1900; repr. 1963).

Special Monographs

C. E. Bosworth, 'A Pioneer Encyclopaedia of the Sciences: al-Khwārizmī's "Keys of the Sciences"', *Isis* liv (1963), 97-111; M. Clagett, *Archimedes in the Middle*

Ages. I. *The Arabo-Latin Tradition* (Madison, Wisc., 1964); B. R. Goldstein, 'On the Theory of Trepidation', *Centaurus*, x (1965), 234–47; J. M. Millás, *Estudios sobre Azarquiel* (Madrid-Granada, 1943–50); J. Samso, *Estudios sobre Abū Naṣr Manṣūr ʿAli b. ʿIrāq* (Barcelona, 1969); J. Vernet, *De Islam in Europa* (Bussum, 1973).

The Transmission of Science to Europe

M. Destombes, 'Un astrolabe carolingien et l'origine de nos chiffres arabes', *Archives Internationales d'Histoire des Sciences*, lviii–lix (1962); C. H. Haskins, *Studies in the History of Mediaeval Science* (Harvard, 1924; 2nd edn., 1927; repr. New York, 1960); P. Kunitzsch, *Arabische Sternnamen in Europa* (Wiesbaden, 1959); J. M. Millás, *Las traducciones orientales en los manuscritos della Biblioteca Catedral de Toledo* (Madrid, 1942); J. Vernet, 'La ciencia en el Islam y Occidente', in *Settimane di studio del Centro italiano di studi sull'alto Medioevo*, XII (Spoleto, 1965), pp. 537–76.

(*C*) MUSIC

FOR Muslim[1] theorists, as for their medieval counterparts in Europe, music belonged to the mathematical sciences. Consequently, although many of their treatises are of considerable interest for the way they treat technical matters such as the numerical analysis of intervals and tetrachord species, it is sometimes difficult to judge how far they represent contemporary practice as against an academic reworking or development of ideas inherited from Greek theory and pursued for their own sake. The difficulty is exacerbated by the fact that it is precisely such treatises which provide virtually the only source from which a reconstruction of the salient features of musical practice might be attempted. Furthermore, the earliest notated compositions to have survived date from the thirteenth century, so that throughout the period when Europe was most affected by the contact with Islamic civilization the musical system of the latter is known to us in rough outline only. It is primarily because of this that the scholarly debate on the subject of Islamic[1] musical influence

[1] In the present context 'Muslim' and 'Islamic' are to be understood as purely cultural, and not religious, terms.

in Europe has not been, and may never be, conclusively resolved.

Already in the ninth century we find a distinction made between *ghinā'*, singing (i.e. the practical art), and *mūsīqā*, theory. But unfortunately little of a descriptive or analytic nature is said about the former, although works of a general literary nature such as the tenth-century *Kitāb al-aghānī* and the *'Iqd al-farīd*, which are in addition invaluable sources for the early social history of the Arabs, provide a wealth of biographical material on prominent musicians and depict vividly their role in court life. They also contain a certain amount of technical information, but the terms used are frequently not defined, and hence can be elucidated only by a study of textbooks of theory.

The first major theorist whose writings have come down to us is the celebrated philosopher al-Kindī (d. *c.* 873). In their treatment of scale his works betray familiarity with Greek sources which were then becoming available in Arabic, although the presentation is in terms of frettings on the Arab lute (*'ūd*). Al-Kindī also accords importance to the cosmological implications of the doctrine of *ta'thīr*, ethos, thus foreshadowing a great many later writers, among whom the Ikhwān al-Ṣafā' (tenth century) are noteworthy on the scientific side for the theory of the spherical propagation of sound. The Peripatetic approach is represented above all by two other great philosophers, al-Fārābī (d. 950) and Ibn Sīnā (Avicenna, d. 1037). The most important of the latter's musical writings is the masterly section in the *Kitāb al-shifā'*, while the former's monumental *Kitāb al-mūsīqā al-kabīr* has been claimed to be 'the greatest work on music which had been written up to his time'.[1] It contains not only a comprehensive study of intervals and their combinations, but also a valuable account of the principal melody instruments then in use and the scales produced on them. In both works the treatment of rhythm is detailed and elaborate. The method of analysis employed com-

[1] H. G. Farmer, 'The Music of Islam', in *The New Oxford History of Music*, i (London, 1957), p. 460.

bines elements of Arabic prosody with the Greek concept of the *chronos protos* (*zamān aqall*, *zamān awwal*), the fundamental and indivisible time-unit from which cyclic patterns are compounded. An original and more succinct approach to the codification of the rhythmic cycles is to be found in the *Kitāb al-kāfī fī 'l-mūsīqā* of Ibn Zayla (d. 1048), one of Avicenna's pupils.

After Ibn Zayla the next theorist of importance whose works are extant is Ṣafī al-Dīn al-Urmawī (d. 1294), the founder of the Systematist school. His two treatises, the *Kitāb al-adwār* and the *Risāla al-sharafiyya*, are noteworthy above all for a sophisticated extension of the Pythagorean scale system (perhaps influenced by the theoretical values assigned by al-Fārābī to the fretting of the *ṭunbūr khurāsānī*, a long-necked lute) whereby the analysis of certain intervals found in practice, but not amenable to definition in terms of simple ratios,[1] is distorted in order to integrate them into a self-contained and symmetrical scheme. The symmetry (as well as the distortion) is demonstrated by transposing the modes through a cycle of fourths so as to begin on each of the seventeen notes of the octave, a procedure no practising musician would have adopted. His exposition of rhythm contains fewer novelties, but is clear and concise. During the fourteenth to sixteenth centuries Ṣafī al-Din's methods were propagated and commented on in several treatises in both Arabic and Persian, the most notable of which are the section on music in the *Durrat al-tāj*, an encyclopedia by Quṭb al-Dīn al-Shīrāzī (d. 1311); the *Sharḥ Mawlānā Mubārak-Shāh*, a detailed commentary on the *Kitāb al-adwār* attributed by Farmer to al-Jurjānī (d. 1413); and the works of ʿAbd al-Qādir al-Marāghī (d. 1435) and al-Lādhiqī (late fifteenth century). His approach was also to be adopted by Turkish theorists, and the *Kitāb al-adwār* translated into Turkish.

The respect for *auctoritas* displayed in these writings should not blind us to the considerable originality and critical acumen

[1] Specifically those of the form $x+1:x$, where x is an integer. Since the octave, fifth, fourth, etc., could be thus expressed, all smaller intervals of this ratio were considered consonant by definition.

many of them reveal. Definitions are tested, and often found wanting—especially in discussions on the physical nature of sound. But of perhaps even greater interest is the fact that in addition to preserving and expounding a traditional framework of theory some of these authors present a detailed account of the modes, rhythms, forms, and instruments used in the art-music of their own day, supplemented on occasion by rudimentary examples of notated compositions. As a result we are able to gain a somewhat clearer insight into the musical system obtaining in the eastern Arab world and Persia from the thirteenth to sixteenth centuries, and of the internal factors which determined the particular line of development taken by this subtle and complex art form.

The extent to which Islamic musical theories have influenced the West is difficult to evaluate, and has been a subject of some controversy. In related disciplines the number of works rendered into Latin provides an initial rough guide to the size of Europe's intellectual debt, but of Arabic texts dealing with music only two are known to have been translated: the *Iḥṣā' al-ʿulūm* (*De scientiis*), a compendium by al-Fārābī, and the *De ortu scientiarum*, a similar but slighter work which has been attributed to him also. Much of the musical material in these reappears in the relevant section of the *De divisione philosophiae* of Gundisalvi (*fl.* 1130–50), while a number of later treatises concerned specifically with music also contain borrowings from them. Virtually the whole section on music in the *De scientiis* is included by Jerome of Moravia (thirteenth century) in Chapter V (*De divisione musicae secundum Alpharabium*) of his *De musica*, and less extensive borrowings from the same source occur in the Pseudo-Aristotelian treatise *De Musica* (thirteenth century) and the *Quatuor principalia musicae* by Simon Tunstede (d. 1369). Passing references to both the *De scientiis* and the *De ortu scientiarum* are also to be found in the *Opus tertium* of Roger Bacon (d. 1280), but allusions to al-Fārābī in later philosophical works such as G. Reisch's *Margarita philosophica* tend, one suspects, to reflect his status as an authority rather than a knowledge of his theories. In effect, neither the *De scientiis* nor the *De ortu scientiarum* contains much of theoretical importance; it would hardly be an exaggeration to say that their main contribution resided in reintroducing a distinction between theory (*musica speculativa*) and practice (*musica activa*) that had been made in Graeco-Roman times.

The influence of Avicenna seems to have been even more circumscribed. In fact, he hardly appears to have been known except as the author of the dictum that 'inter omnia exercitia sanitatis cantare melius est', being thus cited in Roger Bacon's *Opus tertium* and in the *De speculatione musice* by Walter Odington (*c.* 1300). Apart from this unimportant reference one can only point to the *De musica* by Engelbert (d. 1331), which contains a definition of *musica humana* for which Avicenna is listed as an authority along with Aristotle, Galen, and al-Ghazālī.[1]

Faced with such evidence, it would seem reasonable to suppose that none of the more significant musical writings of al-Fārābī, Avicenna, and al-Kindī (who is hardly even mentioned) were ever transmitted to medieval Europe. Given the respect in which they were held, it can hardly be doubted that these works would have received careful study had they been known, and would have exerted considerable influence on the subsequent development of musical theory in the West.

There are, however, one or two further borrowings from other sources. Odo of Cluny (d. 942) gives the following names to the *chordae*: *buc*, *re*, *scembs*, *caemar*, *neth*, *u*(*c*)*iche*, *kaphe*, *asel*, *suggesse*, and *nar*. Some of these are clearly Arabic, and in all probability their origin (which has unfortunately not yet been traced) should be sought among the sets of associations arising out of speculation on the cosmological affinities of music. Another borrowing, itself probably of little significance, is worth mentioning because of the broader issues involved. The thirteenth-century treatise *De*

[1] The source is not, however, a text on music, but is stated to be 'among his medical books'.

mensuris et discantu (Anonymus IV) employs the terms *elmuarifa* and *elmuahym*, which are obviously of Arabic derivation, in its treatment of mensural notation, and this has been used to support the theory that measured music itself was taken over from the Arabs. The main argument adduced in favour of this theory, however, relates to the fact that Europe did not acquire a system of rhythmic modes until after coming into contact with those that already existed in Islamic art-music. Unfortunately there are considerable differences between the two sets of rhythmic modes.[1] The methods of mensural notation are also quite dissimilar, while the theoretical approaches to rhythm might be diametrically opposed: Arab writers, as we have seen, generally work upwards from a minimum value, whereas for Franco of Cologne 'the perfect long is called first and principal, for in it all the others are included'.[2] Even if Gregorian Chant was unmeasured, there is no reason to believe that European secular music was too—certainly not the dance-songs; and whether or not the rhythmic modes originated here it is clear that some method of mensural organization was rendered necessary by the development of part-music. It must be conceded that such considerations do not in themselves suffice to disprove the Arabian theory: but whatever validity this may possess, it is not generally strengthened by the presence of the terms *elmuarifa* and *elmuahym*, for these do not seem to occur as technical terms in Arabic texts on rhythm. The same difficulty arises with the proposed derivation of hocket from *al-qaṭʿ*.[3]

Borrowings from Islamic sources also appear in medieval Hebrew writings on music. Al-Fārābī is again the chief authority,

[1] Because of historical changes it is impossible to make a precise comparison. But of the rhythmic modes known to the Arabs in the tenth and eleventh centuries, for example, three can perhaps be equated with (somewhat later) European modes. Thus 5 of the 8 rhythmic modes of Islamic music and 3 of the 6 European ones find no place in the other system.

[2] O. Strunk, *Source Readings in Music History* (New York, 1950), p. 142.

[3] Despite the interesting parallel of *qaṭʿ* with *truncatio* (*vocis*). But even if the term hocket proves to have an Arabic source (*īqāʿāt* has also been suggested), there is no guarantee that the technique has.

his *Iḥṣā' al-ʿulūm* being known to Ibn ʿAqnīn (*fl.* 1160–1226), and to Kalonymus ben Kalonymus (d. *c.* 1328), who translated it. More interesting, perhaps, is the inclusion of material from al-Kindī's musical treatises in the *Kitāb al-amānāt* by Saʿadya Gaon (d. 942), especially in the passages on rhythm.

Despite the spread of Islam into South and South-East Asia, the impact of its musical theories in these areas has been negligible. It might be thought that the teachings of Ṣafī al-Dīn and his school, which dominated Islamic theory down to the sixteenth century, would have been introduced into India during the Mogul period. But the strictly mathematical analysis of scale, perhaps the most characteristic element in this corpus of theory, was alien to the native Sanskrit tradition, and later Persian works on Indian music are either concerned with practice—or at least with the classification of modes and the related doctrine of ethos—or are simply translations of Sanskrit texts.

Ancient Greek music, the theory of which was to prove of great importance for Muslim scholars, had ceased to exist long before Muḥammad's day. The major influences on musical practice were to stem from Byzantium and, especially, Persia, for it was with these that the Arabs first came into direct contact as a result of the vast conquests of the first century of the *hijra* (sc. the seventh century A.D.). Many of the great musicians of the Umayyad period (661–750) incorporated into their native tradition elements from the musical systems of both, which they became acquainted with through captives, or through their own extensive travels. The emergence of these virtuoso singers and instrumentalists (among the most important being Ibn Misjaḥ (d. *c.* 710?), Ibn Muḥriz (d. *c.* 715), Ibn Surayj (d. *c.* 726), and Maʿbad (d. 743)), whose performances took place at court or in the houses of the wealthy, probably marks the beginning of a separation between urban art-music and the folk idiom of the rural and nomadic populations, although the distinction at this stage was in all likelihood no more than one of relative technical proficiency and polish.

Another important development in the early years of Islam concerns the status of the musician, and the attitudes of society towards his art. The growing dominance of the male musician—accounts of pre-Islamic musical practice mention chiefly female performers—may be connected with the emergence of the *mukhannathūn*, a class of effeminates who indulged in various immoral, as well as artistic, activities. The violent disapproval they provoked among the pious may have contributed significantly to the strong anti-musical bias of the four orthodox law-schools which, if it could not hinder the efflorescence of court music, at least prevented the acceptance of music as a respectable activity in society at large. In such a situation there could be no parallel to the use of music in the Christian Church, and the importance it was later to acquire in Ṣūfī ceremonies depended upon its being interpreted symbolically.

The musical system elaborated under the Umayyads continued in force for another century, its last great exponent being the celebrated Isḥāq al-Mawṣilī (d. 850). According to Ibn al-Munajjim (d. 912), Isḥāq's 'practical theory', to use Farmer's expression, consisted of relating the melodic modes to a normative series of notes provided by the two upper strings of the *ʿūd*, which was fretted to produce a Pythagorean scale of whole-tones and limmas. It is clear from this that the eight melodic modes known at that time were diatonic in structure, although the precise nature of their melodic characteristics remains uncertain, especially as we know so little about the use of ornamentation, which was certainly of great importance. The earliest account of the corresponding rhythmic modes is that of al-Kindī. He lists eight, each consisting of a cycle made up of a certain number of time-units within which a particular accentual pattern must be adhered to. It is possible that variant forms also occurred in which—to judge by later texts—the cycle was extended, so that the existing pattern of beats was added to rather than altered internally.

The first century of the ʿAbbāsid Caliphate saw an increase of Persian influence on many aspects of court life. Music too was affected, and Isḥaq al-Mawṣilī found himself obliged to defend the traditional forms against the innovations of a rival school of musicians led by the formidable Ibrāhīm b. al-Mahdī (d. 839). According to the *Kitāb al-aghānī* it was Isḥāq who won the day, but his victory was short-lived; the testimony of al-Fārābī and Avicenna shows conclusively that the modal system was undergoing a process of rapid change during the ninth and tenth centuries, its diatonic basis being undermined by the introduction of new intervals. The most significant of these—not necessarily Persian in origin—was the (approximate) three-quarter-tone, which has remained down to the present a characteristic feature of the art-musics of the Middle East, differentiating their scale structure from those of the surrounding musical systems of Europe, Central Asia, and India. Persian influence also manifested itself in the instrumental sphere, the *ṭunbūr khurāsānī*, a long-necked lute, becoming especially popular.

The 'classical' system championed by Isḥāq al-Mawṣilī may have survived somewhat longer in Spain, however. Ziryāb, his most illustrious pupil, swiftly established himself at the court of ʿAbd al-Raḥmān II (d. 852), becoming an arbiter of taste as well as the most admired musician of his time. Lack of documentation unfortunately makes it impossible to trace subsequent developments, but it seems reasonable to suppose that his immense prestige as teacher as well as performer would have ensured the survival of much of the traditional repertoire at least until the overthrow of the Umayyad Caliphate in Spain (1031), especially when one takes into consideration the absence of the Persian (and later Turkish) influence that was so important in the East.

The weight of this influence is reflected in the fact that of the twenty modes listed by Ṣafī al-Dīn (d. 1294)—in an account which presumably relates to the art-music of Baghdad immediately prior to the Mongol conquest—less than half have Arabic names. The majority are presented in the form of octave scales, but this does not adequately reflect their modal structure: it would be more accurate to think of them as composite entities made up of smaller units consisting of tetrachord and pentachord species, most of them containing two three-quarter-tone intervals. The quasi-independent status of these units is confirmed by the fact that Ṣafī al-Dīn analyses them separately, and an examination of the modes formed from them shows that they could not be juxtaposed at random, but were combined according to principles of consonance requiring partial or total parallelism at the fourth or fifth. The evidence of later texts indicates that modes containing a less than average degree of parallelism tended to be altered or even discarded, and that new forms evolved from satisfactory structures when the pivotal fourth assumed such importance that it usurped the role of the tonic. The richness and flexibility of this system is shown even more clearly in the *Durrat al-tāj* (*c.* 1300), which also lists a number of what might be termed horizontal combinations where similar laws govern a succession of units having the same tonic. However the units might be combined, the performer would tend to exploit the melodic potential of one before passing on to the next. In some cases the order of progression would be fixed, so that, in addition to the overall intervallic organization, the modal (*maqām*) structure may be said to be determined by the position of initial, final, and medially prominent notes, and sometimes by the sequence of occurrence of the constituent units, a few of which were also characterized by certain obligatory features of melodic articulation. Although a composition would generally be based on just one mode, extraneous units could also be judiciously introduced, especially in improvisatory passages displaying to the full the performer's technical prowess.

It has sometimes been suggested that at a time when Europe was embarking on new paths leading to complex polyphonic and harmonic procedures, Islamic art-music tended to lose its creative impulse and become an ossified tradition. The available literature, however, indicates that it continued to progress on the less dramatic, but no less vital and creative course of further refining the modal principle which was being discarded in the West.

Comparable developments also took place in the rhythms and forms. The former were enriched by Persian and Turkish contributions, so that by the time of al-Lādhiqī (late fifteenth century) the number of rhythmic cycles in use had grown to nearly thirty, several of them containing an unusually large number of time-units (twenty and more). The rhythms of certain dances peculiar to Ṣūfī ceremonies were also adopted. For each cycle theorists give a characteristic pattern of beats, often producing an asymmetrical division (e.g. 3+3+4+2+4), and the example of notation in the *Durrat al-tāj* suggests further that within a particular pattern cross-rhythms and syncopations could be employed to add variety. Descriptions of the principal forms found in art-music from the fourteenth to the sixteenth centuries (that of ʿAbd al-Qādir being perhaps the most comprehensive) unfortunately tend to dwell more on the nature of the verse set than on the purely musical structure. The most extended form was the *nawba*, a suite consisting of four movements. (ʿAbd al-Qādir claims to have added a fifth, but it is not clear whether this innovation gained general acceptance.) The first movement (*qawl*) and the fourth (*furūdasht*) apparently resembled the *basīṭ*, a form in which an instrumental introduction prefaced a setting of Arabic verse in one of three rhythmic cycles. This restriction did not apply to the second movement (*ghazal*), which was sung to Persian poetry, although the cycle chosen for the first might run through the whole *nawba*. The remaining movement (*tarāna*) consisted of a setting of a *rubāʿī* in either Arabic or Persian. Another important vocal form was the *nashīd al-ʿarab*, made up of four couplets in Arabic, the first and third unmeasured, and with a vocalise separating the second and third. Several other forms are also mentioned, some in a lighter, more improvisatory style, some suggesting strict techniques of composition. In the *kull al-nagham*, for instance, a progression through different modes resulted in the inclusion of all the seventeen notes of the octave gamut, while in the *kull al-ḍurūb* several rhythmic cycles were successively introduced. The two forms, we are told, might even be combined—a feat of conscious virtuosity which could have been appreciated only by a highly sophisticated audience.

The examples of notation which survive from this period are with one important exception little more than skeleton outlines. It would seem that in many cases the actual 'composition' consisted of a melodic framework which the singer would fill out by a copious use of ornamentation (*zawā'id*), thereby demonstrating his technical dexterity. Although vocal music remained supreme, most forms of composition were prefaced by a purely instrumental introduction, a practice which is mentioned by al-Fārābī and may have begun even earlier. The instrumental side was thus by no means neglected; new types were constantly being added, and modifications and improvements made in already existing forms. The manufacture of instruments became a highly developed skill for which certain towns, notably Seville, were famous.

The most important of the instruments employed in art-music was the *ʿūd*, a short-necked lute, originally with a parchment belly, which had four strings tuned in fourths. A fifth string was added by Ziryāb. Various forms were known: the *ʿūd qadīm*, *ʿūd kāmil*, and the *ʿūd al-shabbūṭ* invented by Zalzal (d. 791), a lutenist who is also credited with the introduction of a fret (*wusṭā Zalzal*) producing a neutral third. Two long-necked lutes, with completely different frettings, are described by al-Fārābī: the *ṭunbūr baghdādī* and the *ṭunbūr khurāsānī*, the latter of Persian origin. The Persians and Turks later developed several other types, among them the *ṭunbūr shirwān*, the *chahārtār*, and the *ṭunbūr turkī*. The lute family was further represented by the *rabāb* and the *murabbaʿ*.

Al-Fārābī also provides the first description of a bowed instrument, the *rabāb*. This was later known in two forms, one without a separate neck, the other a spike-fiddle with a hemispherical sound-chest.[1] A larger bowed instrument was the Persian *ghizhak*, mentioned in later texts, which was equipped with sympathetic strings. Another important group of chordophones was constituted by instruments played on open strings. Of these the best

[1] The *rabāb* with a shallow rectangular sound-chest is a folk instrument.

known were the *qānūn*, a trapezoidal psaltery (a rectangular variant, the *nuzha*, was invented by Ṣafī al-Dīn), the *sanṭūr*, dulcimer, and the *chang* or *jank*, harp. Flutes and reeds (mostly double) were equally numerous, the former being represented by the *quṣṣāba* and the smaller *shabbāba*, the latter by the *zamr*, *surnāy*, and *ghayṭa*.

Among percussion instruments perhaps the most important in the art-music context was the tambourine (*lār*, *dā'ira*), while the *duff*, frame-drum, was common to most levels of society. The drum (*ṭabl*), kettledrums (*naqqāra* and the larger *qaṣ'a*), and cymbals (*kāsāt*) formed part of the military band (*nawba*, *ṭabl-khāna*), which contained in addition reed instruments, horn (*būq*), and trumpet (*nafīr*), and had apart from its purely military function an important role to play on ceremonial occasions. The band varied in size according to the rank of the person to whom it was allotted, becoming in effect a status symbol.

Disseminated along trade-routes, instruments are more readily exportable than the particular sound-structures the donor culture produces on them. It is thus hardly surprising to find that the musical legacy of Islam to the surrounding cultures, in Asia and Africa as well as in Europe, is most apparent in the instrumental sphere. The influence may be of different kinds: apart from the introduction of absolutely novel instruments it may suggest modifications of types already known, or their employment in fresh combinations or in different social contexts, so that it should not be automatically assumed that in all the cases mentioned here the instrument concerned was quite unknown to the recipients.

The dominance of Islam in western Africa and its extensive spread down the east coast have resulted in the introduction of, for example, the *ghayṭa*, shawm, the *ghūghā*, a one-string fiddle, and certain types of drum. Instruments of Islamic origin may even have penetrated well beyond the areas in which the religion itself took root: the Arabic terms *ṣanj*, cymbal, and *shabbāba*, flute, for example, are found as far south as Madagascar. But even within such areas the various indigenous musical systems do not seem to have been much affected by the contact with those of Arabia and North Africa. A similar situation may be observed in East Asia and Indonesia: several instruments of Middle Eastern provenance were adopted in China, and the *rabāb* has been assimilated into the traditional ensembles of Java (and has even reached non-Muslim Bali), but in neither case does this appear to have led to any change in idiom.

The case of India is somewhat more complicated. Muslim hegemony in the north undoubtedly hastened, even if it did not actually cause, the split between the musical systems of north and south, and many of the most eminent practitioners of the former have been Muslims—and still are today. But although Persian music was cultivated under the Moguls as well as under earlier dynasties it is difficult to judge how radically it affected the Indian tradition. Accounts of Amīr Khusraw's (d. 1325) innovations, for instance, are evidently exaggerated; but among the numerous modes, rhythms, and forms he is credited with introducing there are nevertheless several that can be traced to Persian and Arabic sources: the modes *ʿushshāq*, *nigār*, and *zangūla*; the rhythms *khamsa* and *sul-fakhta*; and the forms *qawl*, *basīṭ*, *furūdasht*, and *tarāna*, the latter two apparently much altered.[1] But whether we should regard these innovations as a significant influence on the development of Indian music, or as attractive exoticisms which were gradually assimilated, it is likely that the most important change was one of attitude—the introduction of the Islamic conception of music as an essentially secular activity.[2] A typical result of this attitude and the fresh impetus it gave to the art may be seen in the emergence of *khayāl*, a virtuoso, emotional style of singing, in opposition to the austere indigenous *dhrupad*. On the instrumental side one of the most striking importations was the

[1] *Furūdasht* is in fact listed as a rhythm.

[2] This attitude was not, however, shared by those Ṣūfī orders, which viewed music as a means towards religious (specifically mystical) ends, and contributed to Indian music the popular tradition of *qawwālī* singing.

military *nawba*, especially the kettledrums and shawms (*shahnay*). These were to be found until quite recently at princely courts, and were also employed to sound the hours at city gates. In the Hindu south they have been used to provide temple music, and are to be heard even further afield in the Muslim courts of Malaya.

The particular combination of instruments in the Islamic military band was also a novelty for the Crusaders. In practical terms the main effect was on the drum family, while the historian Joinville records the impact of the *cors sarrazinois*. At a much later date the Janissary band was to exert a similar and even stronger influence in Eastern and Central Europe, where the late eighteenth century saw a craze for the Turkish march resulting in the use of triangle and military drum in the classical orchestra. Turkish domination in the Balkans also led to the adoption in various provinces—at the folk-music level—of instruments such as the *zurna*, shawm, and the *baglama* and *saz*, long-necked lutes. For Western Europe the most significant and fruitful contact with Islamic musical culture took place in Spain, and among the many instrument names recorded in Spanish are the *guitarra morisca*, *adufe* (*al-duff*), *albogue* (*al-būq*)í *añafil* (*al-nafīr*), *atabal* (*al-ṭabl*), *laúd* (*al-ʿūd*), and *rabel* (*rabāb*).[1] Several of these, and others, spread to other parts of Western Europe, so that we find in England, for example, the canon (*qānūn*) and naker (*naqqāra*) as well as the lute and rebec. The reintroduction in the ninth century of the *hydraulis* may also have been due to this contact, or at least to Arabic texts on its construction, for the instrument itself was never wholeheartedly adopted by the Arabs.[2]

Unfortunately, it appears well-nigh impossible to tell how much of the music was adopted along with the instruments used to produce and accompany it. On the positive side one may mention

[1] See C. Sachs, *Reallexikon der Musikinstrumente*, for the ancestry of the instrument itself.

[2] A list of Arabic instrument names found in European languages may be consulted in H. Hickmann, 'Die Musik des arabisch-islamischen Bereichs', *Handbuch der Orientalistik*, Erste Abt. *Der Nahe und der Mittlere Osten*, Ergänzungsbard IV: *Orientalische Musik* (Leiden/Cologne, 1970), pp. 129–33.

the presence of Moorish musicians at Christian courts (as in Sicily under the Normans), which indicates at least that their music was appreciated and hence could have exerted some influence. But, as we have seen, Islamic music in Spain is poorly documented, and political separation, distance, and the lack of contact with the Persian and Turkish traditions combine to render it unlikely that the account of musical practice in the Middle East given above could be considered valid for Spain too. It is true that the old Arab system of diatonic modes, if it survived, would have borne a greater similarity to the European system than that which evolved in the East. But it cannot be claimed with any confidence that the predominance of the classical Arab school outlived the Umayyad Caliphate in Spain, especially when one considers the ethnic complexities of a country where significant contributions to culture were made by the Jews as well as by the Arabs, who were in any case greatly outnumbered by the Berbers, not to speak of the native Christian population, itself of mixed descent. Nevertheless, the Spanish vocabulary records borrowings outside the purely instrumental sphere in terms relating to singing and dancing such as *anejir* (*al-nashīd*), *leila*, and *zambra* (*zamr*), and the incorporation into Arabic of the words *gaita* and *pandero* points to an atmosphere of fruitful interchange. Arab practices no doubt influenced the minstrel class too, as well as the Morris dancers, and on a more technical plane the evidence of the anonymous *Ars de pulsatione lambuti* (1496–7) suggests an Arab origin for one form of instrumental tablature. But for all this modern scholarship is unwilling to entertain the notion of an Arab influence on the actual musical structures themselves, as represented for instance in the *Cantigas de Santa María*. On issues such as this, as on the cognate question of the relationship between Arabic poetry and the Provençal lyric (see above, Chapter II, pp. 94–7, and Chapter VII, pp. 340–1), critical opinion has swayed back and forth, and until further evidence is brought to light no final answer seems possible.

O. WRIGHT

BIBLIOGRAPHY

Translations of important Arabic texts on music by al-Fārābī, Avicenna, Ṣafī al-Dīn, and others may be consulted in:
R. d'Erlanger, *La Musique arabe* (Paris, 1930–59), vols. i–iv.

For general accounts of contemporary practice (some of which contain historical introductions) see:
M. Barkechli, *La Musique traditionnelle de l'Iran* (Tehran, 1963); A. Berner, *Studien zur arabischen Musik auf Grund der gegenwärtigen Theorie und Praxis in Ägypten* (Leipzig, 1937); N. Caron and D. Safvate, *Les Traditions musicales: Iran* (Paris, 1966); A. Chottin, *Tableau de la musique marocaine* (Paris, 1939); R. d'Erlanger, op. cit., vols. v and vi.

The history of Arabian music is dealt with in:
H. G. Farmer, *A History of Arabian Music to the XIIIth Century* (London, 1929; repr. 1967); idem, 'Islam', *Musikgeschichte in Bildern*, Bd. III. *Musik des Mittelalters und des Renaissance*, Lief. 2 (Leipzig, 1966); idem, 'The Music of Islam', *New Oxford History of Music*, i (London, 1957); H. Hickmann, 'Die Musik des arabisch-islamischen Bereichs', *Handbuch der Orientalistik, Erste Abt. Der Nahe und der Mittlere Osten, Ergänzungsband IV. Orientalische Musik* (Leiden/Cologne, 1970); J. Rouanet, 'La Musique arabe', *Encyclopédie de la musique* (Lavignac), 1re partie, v (Paris, 1922).
Works concerned with the question of Islamic musical influences are:
H. G. Farmer, *Historical Facts for the Arabian Musical Influence* (London, 1930); idem, *Saʿadya Gaon on the Influence of Music* (London, 1943); J. Ribera, *La Música de las cantigas* (Madrid, 1922); M. Schneider, 'A propósito del influjo árabe en España', *Anuario Musical*, i (1946); O. Ursprung, 'Um die Frage nach dem arabischen bzw. maurischen Einfluss auf die abendländische Musik des Mittelalters', *Zeitschrift für Musikwissenschaft*, xvi (1934).

INDEX

FIG. 1. Damascus, mosque, general view of courtyard

FIG. 2. Cordova, mosque, general view of interior

FIG. 3. Cairo, mosque of Ibn Ṭūlūn, general view

FIG. 4. Cordova, arches and dome in front of *miḥrāb*

FIG. 5. Qaṣr al-Ḥayr East, caravanserai, façade

FIG. 6. Khirbat al-Mafjar, reconstruction of a room in the bath

FIG. 7. Qaṣr al-Ḥayr West, palace, façade

FIG. 8. Aleppo, citadel

FIG. 9. Granada, Alhambra, Court of the Lions

FIG. 10. Granada, Alhambra, Hall of the Two Sisters, dome

FIG. 11. Damascus, hospital of Nūr al-Dīn, façade

FIG. 12. Iṣfahān, Masjid-i Shāh, façade

FIG. 13. Iṣfahān, Masjid-i Jumʿa north dome

FIG. 14. Cairo, mausoleum of Sultan Barqūq, interior dome

FIG. 15. Iṣfahān, Masjid-i Jumʿa, aywān in court

FIG. 16. Dashtī (near Iṣfahān) detail of masonry

17 18 19

FIG. 17. Obverse and reverse of a *dirham* of the Sāmānid Ismāʿīl b. Aḥmad (279/892–295/907)

FIG. 18. Obverse and reverse of a *dīnār* of the Almoravid ʿAlī b. Yūsuf (500/1106–537/1142)

FIG. 19. Obverse and reverse of the 'dinar' of Offa, king of Mercia (757–796)

Fig. 20. Glazed Pottery Bowl, so-called Sultanabad Type. Iran, Mongol period, early 14th century

Fig. 21. Glazed Pottery Bowl from Sarai Berke on the Volga. Empire of the Golden Horde, Mongol period, 14th century

FIG. 22. Glazed Pottery Bowl, said to be from Fusṭāṭ. Egypt, 14th century

FIG. 23. Glazed Pottery Bowl, said to be from Gurgān. Iran, Seljuq period, early 13th century

FIG. 25. Hispano-Moresque Wall Tiles. Spain, 14th century

FIG. 26. Glazed Pottery Plate. Egypt, Mamlūk period, 14th century

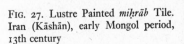

FIG. 27. Lustre Painted *miḥrāb* Tile. Iran (Kāshān), early Mongol period, 13th century

FIG. 24. (*left*). Pair of Doors. Egypt, Mamlūk period, late 13th or early 14th century

FIG. 28. Prayer Carpet from Gördes. Turkey, Anatolia, Ottoman period, 19th century

FIG. 29. Prayer Carpet from Mujur. Turkey, Anatolia, Ottoman period, 18th century

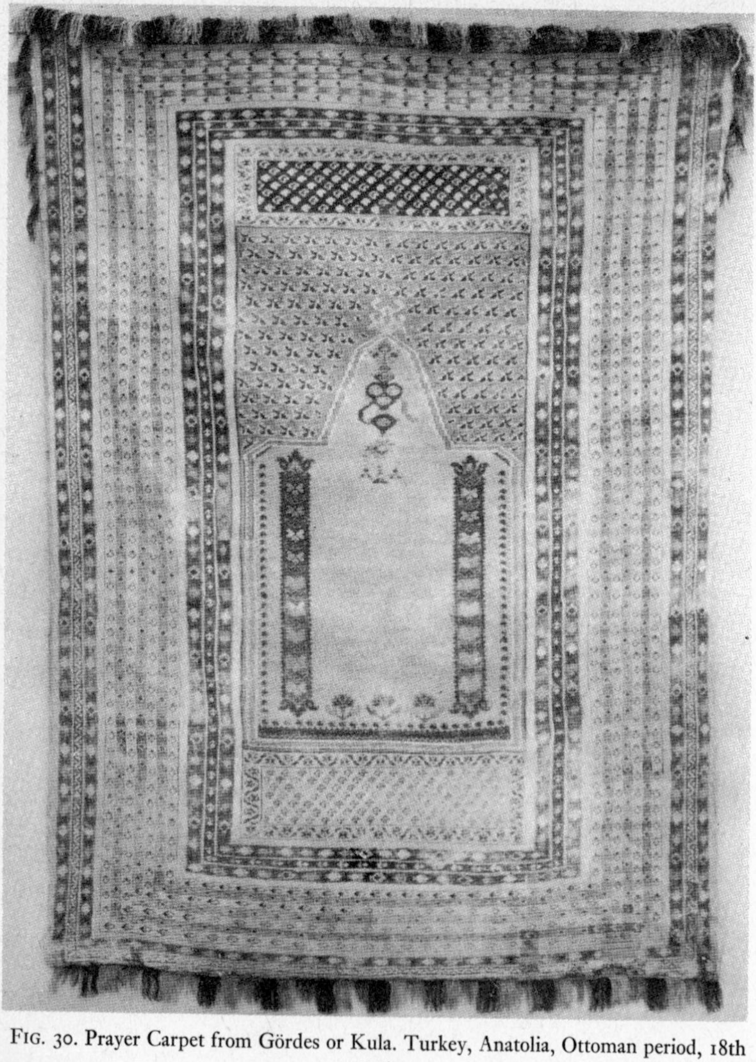

FIG. 30. Prayer Carpet from Gördes or Kula. Turkey, Anatolia, Ottoman period, 18th century

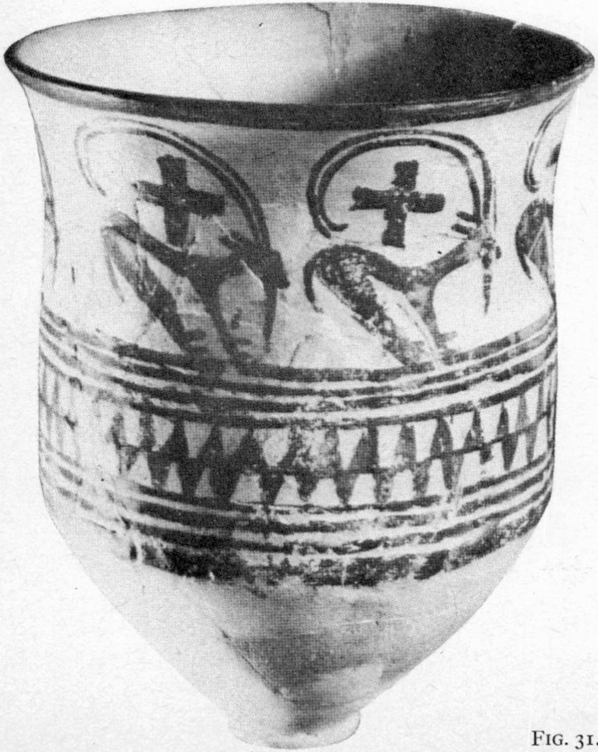

FIG. 32. Glazed Pottery Ewer. Iran (Rayy), Seljuq period, late 12th century

FIG. 31. Pottery Beaker from Sialk III

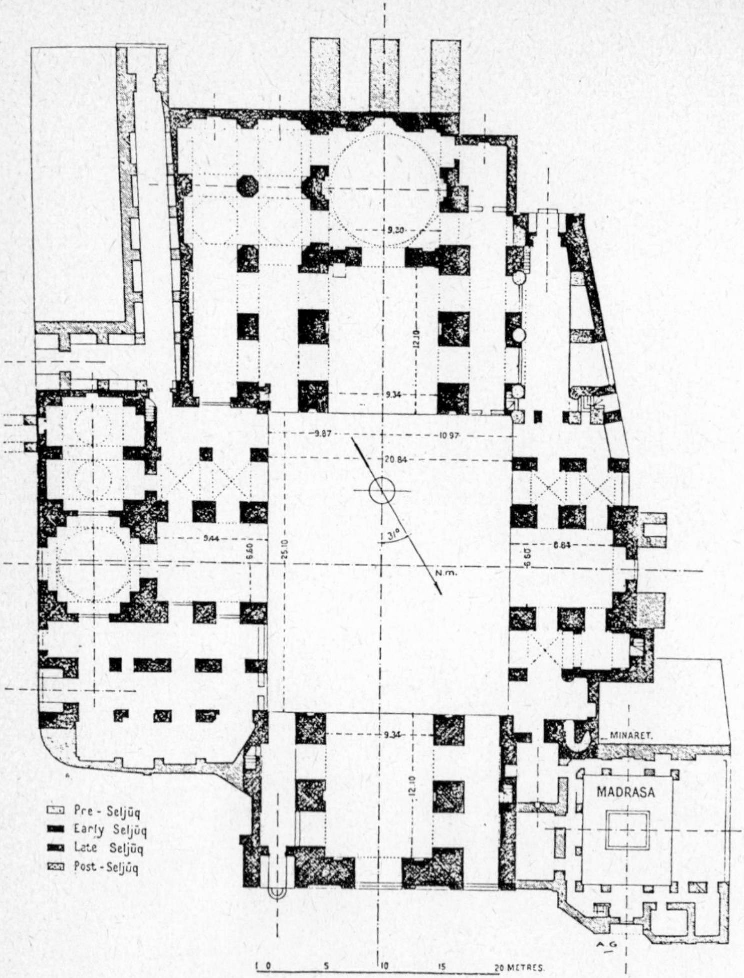

FIG. 33*a*. Four Ayvān Plan of Masjid-i Jāmiʿ in Ardistān. Iran, mostly Seljuq period, 12th century

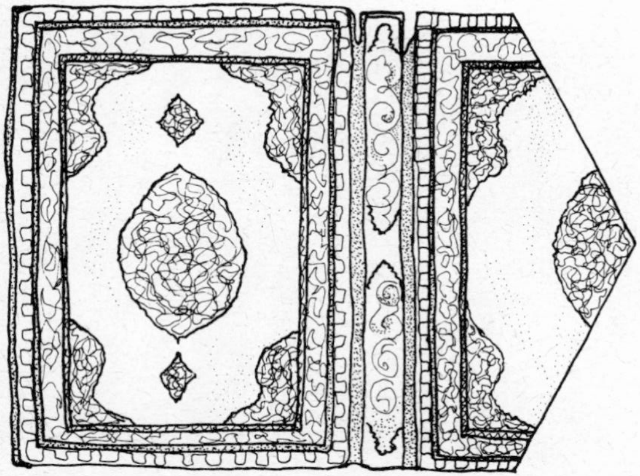

FIG. 33*b*. Scheme of Persian Bookbinding with Flap, 16th century

FIG. 33*c*. Gnostic Manuscript of Nag Hammadi. Egypt, Coptic period, 4th century

FIG. 34*a*. Dirham of the Sāmānid Aḥmad b. Ismāʿīl. Struck in al-Shāsh in 299/911–12. Loop of Nordic Type added later

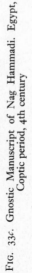

FIG. 34*b*. Dirham of the Sāmānid Manṣūr b. Nūḥ. Struck in Samarqand in 363/973–74. Found with 192 other Arabic coins in Mannegårda in the parish of Lye in Gotland

FIG. 35. Animal Carpet from the church of Marby in Jämtland, Sweden. Anatolia, *c.* 1400

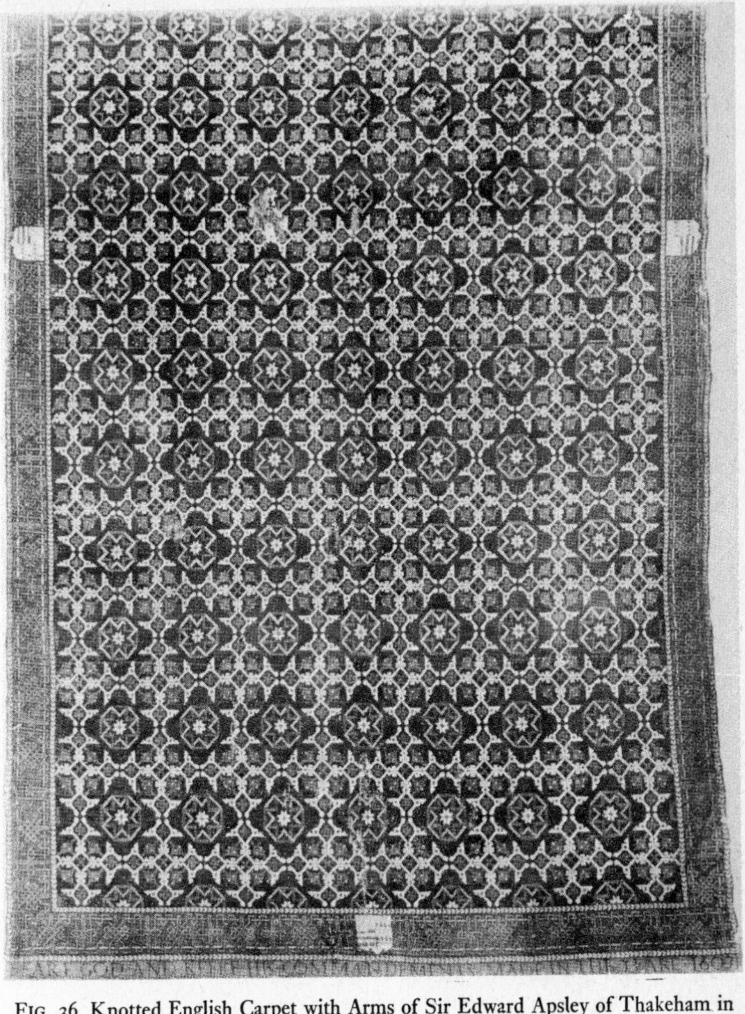

FIG. 36. Knotted English Carpet with Arms of Sir Edward Apsley of Thakeham in Sussex and his wife Elizabeth Elmers of Litford. Dated 1603

FIG. 37. Water-colour Sketch by E. Delacroix of a Moorish Interior, probably in Meknes, Morocco

FIG. 38. Salt-glazed Stoneware. Figure of a Turk (One of a Pair). English, Staffordshire, probably by the Enameller William Littler, *c.* 1760

FIG. 39. Round Mamlūk Carpet. Egypt (Cairo), first half of 16th century

FIG. 40. Cross-shaped Ottoman Carpet, to be used as a Table Cover. Egypt (Cairo), 16th century

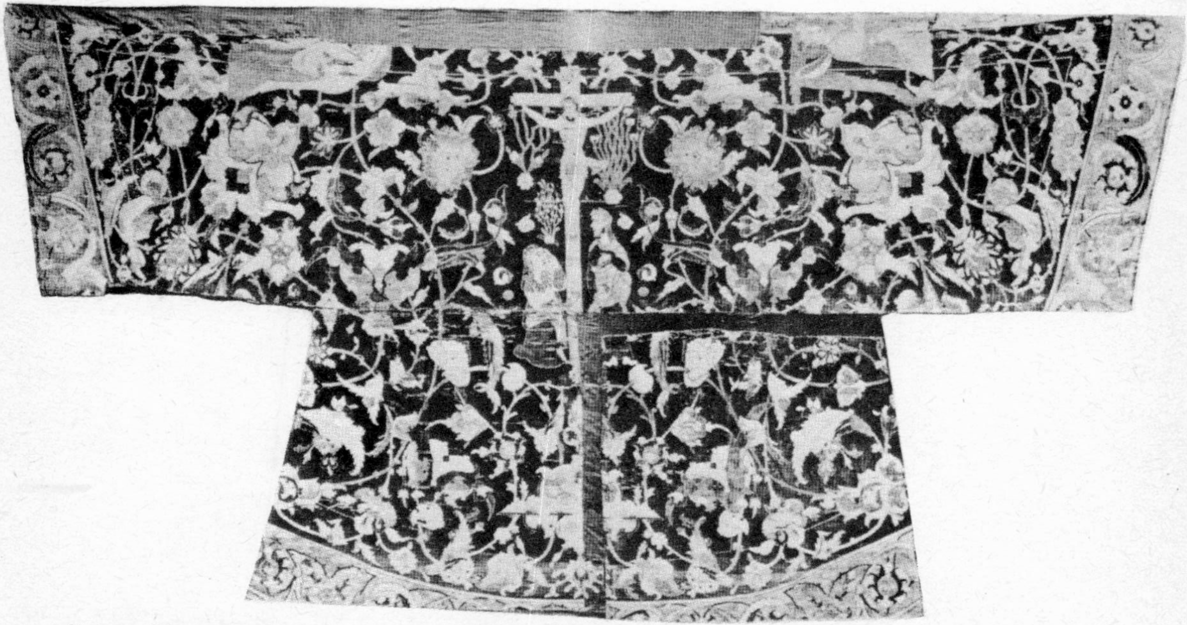

Fig. 41. Silk Carpet woven in the shape of a Chasuble with Crucifixion and Annunciation. Iran, early 17th century

FIG. 42. So-called Polonaise Silk Pile Carpet with Unidentified European Coat of Arms

FIG. 43. Embroidered Carpet with Iranian Motifs. Portugal (Arraiolos), second half of 17th century

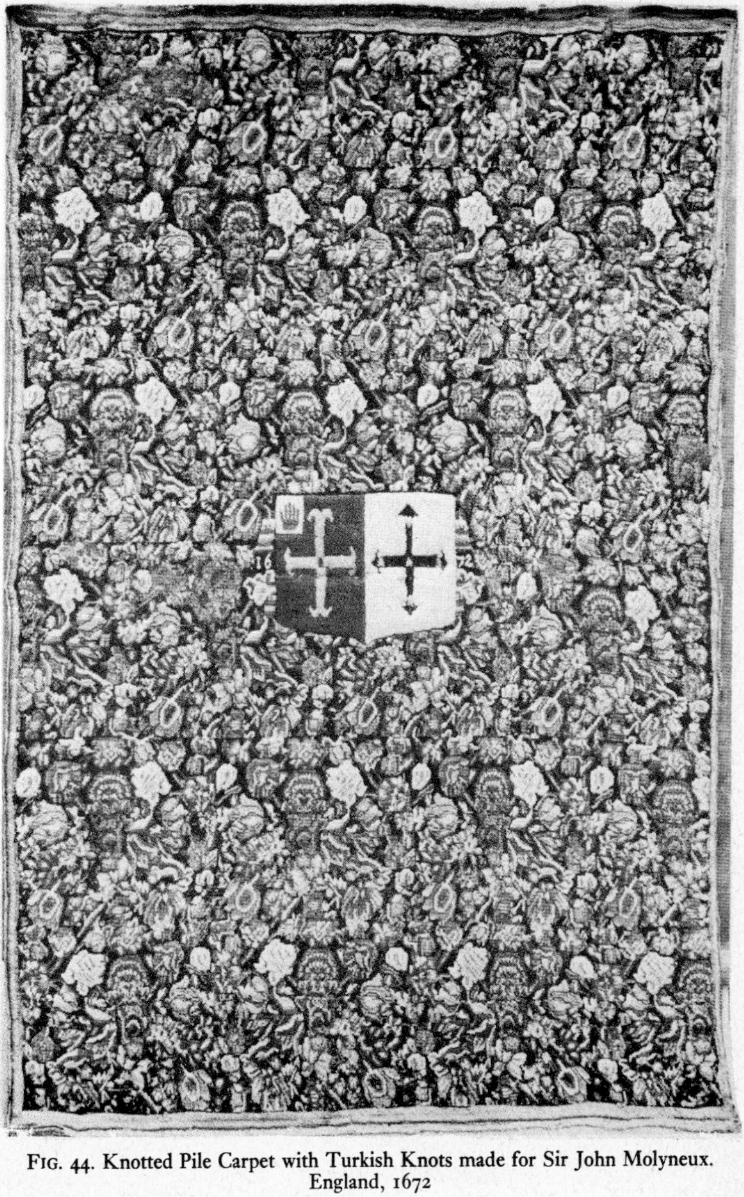

FIG. 44. Knotted Pile Carpet with Turkish Knots made for Sir John Molyneux. England, 1672

FIG. 45. Fragment of Knotted 'Turkey Work'. England, 17th century

FIG. 46. Carpet with Birds and Floral Design Executed with Turkish Knots. Poland, 18th century

FIG. 47. Aquamanile with Dog-headed Winged Animal with Feline Paws and Peacock Tail, Gilt Bronze with Silver Inlay and Niello. Mosan, mid-12th century

FIG. 48. Silk Textile with Dog-headed Winged Animal with Feline Paws and Peacock Tail. Iran, Sasanian period, 5th–7th century

FIG. 49. Silver Inlaid Brass Platter (Azzimina Work). Signed by Muʿallim Maḥmūd al-Kurdī. Iran(?), first half of 16th century

FIG. 50. Platter (Azzimina Work). Italy (Venice), mid-16th century

FIG. 51. 'The Sixth Knot'. Woodcut by Albrecht Dürer *c.* 1507

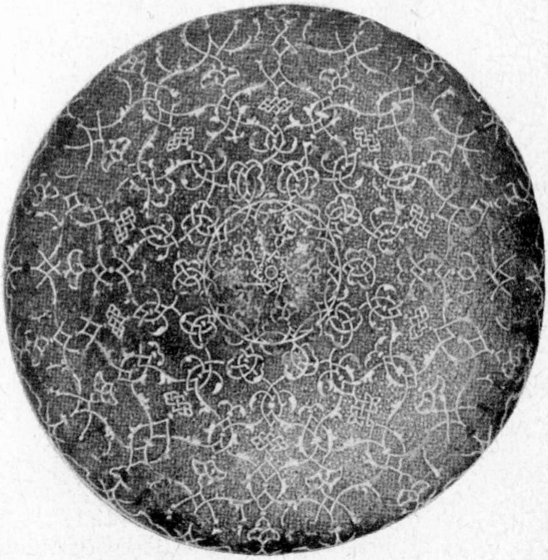

FIG. 52. Bottom of Silver Inlaid Brass Bucket (Azzimina Work). Iran (?), first half of 16th century

FIG. 53. Initial 'S' on Arabesque Ground in Columna, *Le Songe de Polyphile*. Paris, Kerver 1554, fol. a ii verso

FIG. 54. 'Evangelis Matthew' with Arabesque Side Panels from *Biblia Latina*. Lyons, J. de Tournes, 1556, 2nd edition, p. 530

FIG. 55. Backgammon or Tric-Trac Board with Arabesque Designs. Silver with Champlevé Enamel. Spanish, first quarter of 17th century

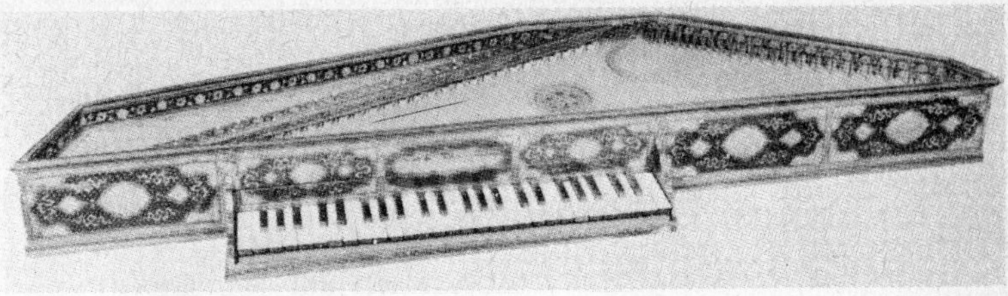

FIG. 56. Virginal with Panels Imitating Turkish Bookbindings with Arabesques and Cloudbands. Made by Benedetto Floriani. Venice, 1571

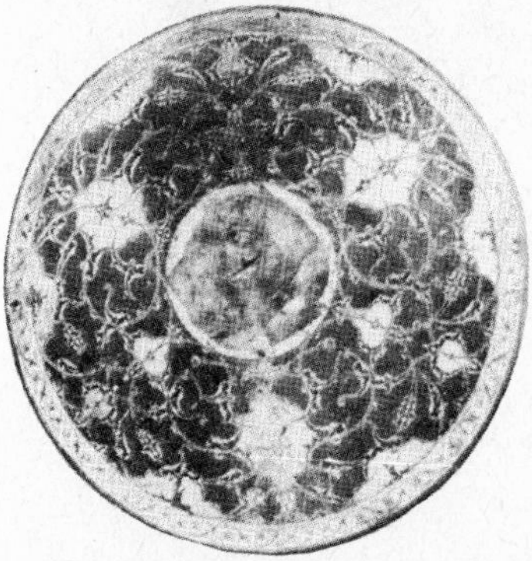

FIG. 57. Parchment Shield made for the Bishops of Salzburg. Venice, late 16th century

FIG. 58. Persian White Glazed Pottery Cup in the 'Chalice of Saint Girolamo', from S. Anastasia

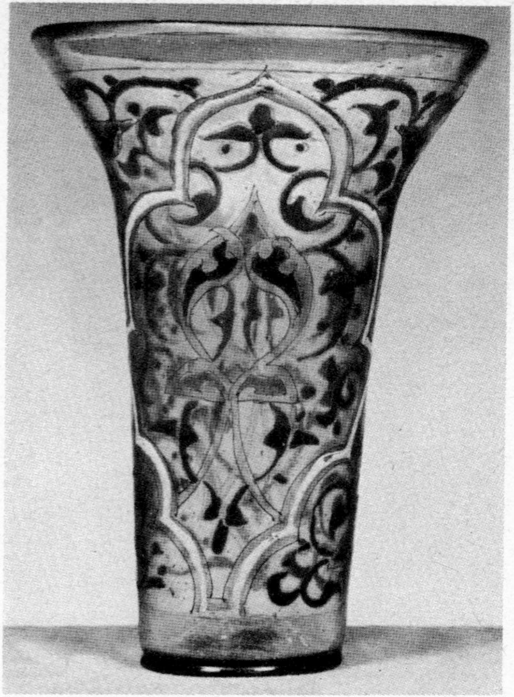

FIG. 59. Enamelled Glass Beaker called 'The Luck of Edenhall'. Syria, 13th century

FIG. 60. Venetian Binding in Persian Style, early 16th century, enclosing Leonardo Loredano, Ceremonial of His Accession as Doge. Venice, 1502, with later additions

FIG. 61. Fresco Showing the Battle of Lepanto of 1571, painted by an Unknown Artist in 1603

Fig. 62. Francesco del Cossa, The May fresco in the Palazzo Schifanoia at Ferrara. *Above*: Aurora driving Apollo's triumphal carriage, to the right the Nine Muses and Pegasus at the fountain. *Middle*: The Gemini touching the Sun, with their three Decans according to Arabic sources (cf. E. Jaffe in A. Warburg, *Gesammelte Schriften*, ii, p. 635). *Below*: This section destroyed

IECVR SANGVIFICATIONIS OFFICINA, PER VENAM PORTAM, QVAE GRAECIS ςελεχιαία, Arabibus vero [Hebrew] varidhascori appellatur, ex ventriculo & intestinis chylum trahens sumit, ac in lienem melancholicum succum expurgat.

FIG. 63. Detail (*see below*)

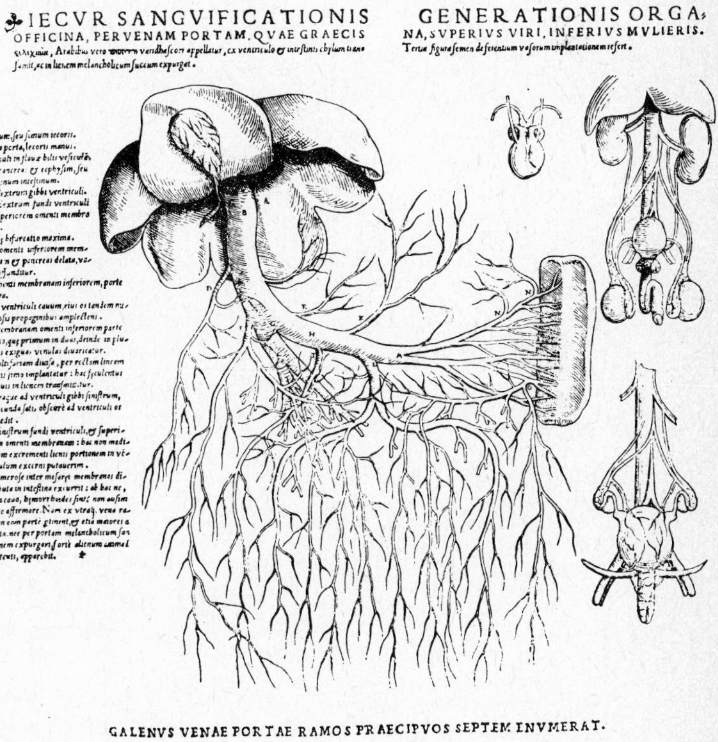

IECVR SANGVIFICATIONIS OFFICINA, PER VENAM PORTAM, QVAE GRAECIS
GENERATIONIS ORGANA, SVPERIVS VIRI, INFERIVS MVLIERIS.
GALENVS VENAE PORTAE RAMOS PRAECIPVOS SEPTEM ENVMERAT.

FIG. 63. Andreas Vesalius, tabula I (lower half) of his *Tabulae anatomicae sex* (1538) *Left*: The liver as a blood-producer. Note the 'Arabic' in fact Hebrew, name of the gate vein, translated from the Arabic and written in Hebrew and Latin characters (see line three of the detailed heading above.) *Right*: The genital organs (above: Male; below: female)